'Patrick Diamond's magisterial analysis of the last 40 years of Labour's history, comprising both government and opposition, provides the essential foundation upon which Labour has to construct its future path . . .'

Charles Clarke, *former Home Secretary and Labour Party MP, 1997–2010*

'. . . Patrick Diamond's book adds a new drive by putting new Labour firmly in its post-war historical context. His argument is nuanced, punchy, original and a compelling read.'

Andrew Hindmoor, *University of Sheffield, UK*

'At last, a well-informed book about Labour that neither idealises nor reviles its record. An essential primer for Keir Starmer and for Labour's new post-Corbyn generation.'

Martin Kettle, *Chief Leader Writer, the* Guardian, *UK*

'. . . compulsory reading for anyone interested in the Labour party.'

Eric Shaw, *University of Stirling, UK*

'As Labour stands yet again at a crossroads, considering whether to be a protest movement or a party of power, Patrick Diamond's book could not be more timely . . .'

Rachel Sylvester, *Chief Political Commentator at the* Times, *UK*

THE BRITISH LABOUR PARTY IN OPPOSITION AND POWER 1979–2019

This book provides a novel account of the Labour Party's years in opposition and power since 1979, examining how New Labour fought to reinvent post-war social democracy, reshaping its core political ideas. It charts Labour's sporadic recovery from political disaster in the 1980s, successfully making the arduous journey from opposition to power with the rise (and ultimately fall) of the governments of Tony Blair and Gordon Brown. Forty years on from the 1979 debacle, Labour has found itself on the edge of oblivion once again. Defeated in 2010, it entered a further cycle of degeneration and decline. Like social democratic parties across Europe, Labour failed to identify a fresh ideological rationale in the aftermath of the great financial crisis.

Drawing on a wealth of sources including interviews and unpublished papers, the book focuses on decisive points of transformational change in the party's development raising a perennial concern of present-day debate – namely whether Labour is a party capable of transforming the ideological weather, shaping a new paradigm in British politics, or whether it is a party that should be content to govern within parameters established by its Conservative opponents.

This text will be of interest to the general reader as well as scholars and students of British politics, British political history, and the history of the British Labour Party since 1918.

Patrick Diamond is Associate Professor of Public Policy at Queen Mary University of London, UK. He was Senior Policy Adviser to the Prime Minister (2001–05), and Head of Policy Planning in 10 Downing Street (2009–10).

THE BRITISH LABOUR PARTY IN OPPOSITION AND POWER 1979–2019

Forward March Halted?

Patrick Diamond

Routledge
Taylor & Francis Group

LONDON AND NEW YORK

First published 2021
by Routledge
2 Park Square, Milton Park, Abingdon, Oxon OX14 4RN

and by Routledge
52 Vanderbilt Avenue, New York, NY 10017

Routledge is an imprint of the Taylor & Francis Group, an informa business

British Library Cataloguing-in-Publication Data
A catalogue record for this book is available from the British Library

Library of Congress Cataloging-in-Publication Data
Names: Diamond, Patrick, author.
Title: The British Labour Party in opposition and power 1979–2019 :
    forward march halted? / Patrick Diamond.
Description: Abingdon, Oxon ; New York, NY : Routledge, 2021. |
    Includes bibliographical references and index.
Identifiers: LCCN 2020023451 (print) | LCCN 2020023452 (ebook) |
    ISBN 9781138817876 (hardback) | ISBN 9781138817890 (paperback) |
    ISBN 9781315745466 (ebook)
Subjects: LCSH: Labour Party (Great Britain) | Great Britain—
    Politics and government—1979–1997. | Great Britain—Politics
    and government—1997–2007. | Great Britain—Politics and
    government—2007–
Classification: LCC JN1129.L32 D526 2021 (print) | LCC JN1129.L32
    (ebook) | DDC 324.2410709/045—dc23 LC record available at
    https://lccn.loc.gov/2020023451
LC ebook record available at https://lccn.loc.gov/2020023452

ISBN: 978-1-138-81787-6 (hbk)
ISBN: 978-1-138-81789-0 (pbk)
ISBN: 978-1-315-74546-6 (ebk)

Typeset in Bembo
by Apex CoVantage, LLC

CONTENTS

FIGURES

TABLES

DRAMATIS PERSONAE

- Margaret Beckett, deputy Labour Party leader (1992–94) and acting leader (1994)
- Tony Blair, Labour Party leader (1994–2007) and prime minister (1997–2007)
- Gordon Brown, chancellor of the exchequer (1997–2007), leader of the Labour Party and prime minister (2007–10)
- Alastair Campbell, chief press spokesman to the leader of the Labour Party (1994–97) and No.10 director of communications and strategy (1997–2003)
- Charles Clarke, chief of staff to the leader of the Labour Party (1983–92)
- Jeremy Corbyn, Labour Party leader (2015–)
- Harriet Harman, deputy leader of the Labour Party (2007–15)
- Patricia Hewitt, chief press secretary, leader of the Opposition's office (1983–92)
- Neil Kinnock, Labour Party leader (1983–92), transport commissioner and vice president, European Commission (1995–2004)
- John McDonnell, shadow chancellor of the exchequer (2015–)
- Peter Mandelson, Labour's director of campaigns and communications (1985–90), member of parliament and cabinet minister (1997–2010)
- Ed Miliband, Labour Party leader (2010–15)
- John Prescott, Labour Party deputy leader (1994–2007)
- John Smith, shadow chancellor (1987–92) and Labour Party leader (1992–94)

ACKNOWLEDGEMENTS AND PREFACE

I would like to thank the following who were kind enough to grant me interviews that informed this study: Lord Andrew Adonis, Baroness Hilary Armstrong, Lord John Birt, Rt. Hon. Tony Blair, Rt. Hon. David Blunkett, Rt. Hon. Andy Burnham, Rt. Hon. Charles Clarke (twice), Paul Corrigan, Dan Corry (twice), Lord Bernard Donoughue, John Dunford, Naomi Eisenstadt CB, Lord Roy Hattersley, Sir Jeremy Heywood, Gavin Kelly, Martin Kettle, Peter Kyle MP, Professor Sir Julian Le Grand MBE, Dick Leonard, Lord Roger Liddle, Lord David Lipsey, James MacIntyre, Lord Peter Mandelson, Professor David Marquand, Will Marshall, Pat McFadden MP, Dr Tony McNulty, Rt. Hon. David Miliband, Rt. Hon. Estelle Morris, Geoff Mulgan CBE, Dr Martin O'Neill, Geoffrey Norris, Will Paxton, Nick Pearce, Lord Raymond Plant, Lord Giles Radice, Lord Bill Rodgers, Will Somerville, Matthew Taylor OBE, Anna Turley, Sam White and Lord Stewart Wood. I would also like to thank two anonymous reviewers for their insightful comments and feedback. I had a series of very fruitful conversations with several leading political commentators: Andrew Grice, Martin Kettle, Peter Riddell and Philip Stephens. In addition, I would like to thank my colleagues at Queen Mary University of London for beneficial discussions over the last seven years: Professor Michael Kenny, Professor Tim Bale, Dr Madeleine Davis, Dr Robert Saunders, Dr James Ellison, Dr Karl Pike and Colm Murphy. Andrew Taylor and Sophie Iddamalgoda at Routledge were a pleasure to work with, helpful and patient throughout.

In the book I have drawn on material from the following published articles: 'Breaking the Mould? Roy Jenkins' "Radical Centre" and British Social Democracy in the "New Hard Times", *Political Quarterly*, Volume 90 (1), pp. 134 142, 2019; and 'Introduction: The Progressive Dilemma in British Politics', *Political Quarterly*, Volume 88 (1), pp. 6–12, 2017 (with Professor Michael Kenny). I would also like to thank the librarians at the London School of Economics

(LSE); the Museum of Labour History in Manchester; the Bishopsgate Institute in London; and the Archives Centre, Churchill College, Cambridge. This account draws inevitably on numerous intellectual perspectives. The first is my training as an academic political scientist. The second outlook reflects the experience of serving as a special adviser in the Labour governments between 2000 and 2010 in the Northern Ireland Office, the Downing Street Policy Unit and the Cabinet Office. As a consequence, I have been able to draw on testimonies and documents not otherwise available to the scholarly community.

Patrick Diamond
June 2020

PROLOGUE

The recent history of the Labour Party and the mainstream Left in Britain is the subject of this book. Drawing on a wealth of sources including interviews and unpublished papers, it tells the story of how Labour overcame the succession of political disasters that befell it in the 1980s to make the arduous journey from opposition to power. By 1987 the party's forward march was firmly halted while British Labourism was in terminal decay. Labour's support was confined to its Welsh, Scottish and Northern English industrial heartlands. It had no coherent response to the free market counter-revolution inaugurated by Thatcherism. The party appeared shipwrecked, unable to break out of the impasse.

In the following decade, Labour embarked on the long march to power, sustaining a remarkable recovery. The task of intellectual revitalisation meant assimilating lessons from Labour's experience in government. British social democrats paid attention to the rejuvenation of centre-left movements across the world from Sweden to the United States. Eventually, the Labour Party won the largest parliamentary majority in its history. Far from being the heir of Thatcherism, the Labour governments after 1997 pursued reforms advancing constitutional innovation, liberal internationalism and social justice.

Yet after a decade in office, supporters had grown disillusioned; such was the breach between promise and performance. Many feared New Labour had a mission to change the party rather than the country. Having gained control of the levers of power, Labour's mind-set was distrustful and domineering. Committed to the centralised British state, the Blair/Brown administrations imposed policies from Whitehall and Westminster, and they remained wedded to the British model of capitalism where unregulated markets were an engine to generate wealth for material redistribution. Both assumptions proved defective. Iraq then destroyed the confidence of progressive opinion: New Labour, it appeared, had won power but was unable to win decisively the battle of ideas in British politics.

Defeated in 2010, Labour entered a further cycle of degeneration and decline. British politics appeared more divided and polarised. Like social democratic parties across Europe, the party failed to identify a fresh ideological rationale in the aftermath of the great financial crisis. In France and Germany, centre-left parties stood on the brink of electoral oblivion. Was the Labour Party in Britain about to join them?

1

INTRODUCTION

The Labour Party and the reinvention of social democracy in post-war Britain

I notice now that there are Thatcherites in every audience. She has armed a lot of bright young people with powerful right-wing arguments, and, although I enjoy discussing them, I realise I am no longer dealing with the old consensus but with a new breed of right-wing concepts. It confirms my belief that there will be a hard inheritance which will never be forgotten, even when all Thatcher's legislation has been replaced.

Tony Benn[1]

Introduction

This book provides a novel account of the Labour Party's years in opposition and power since 1979. The focus is Labour's sporadic recovery from political disaster, followed by the rise and fall of the governments led by Tony Blair and Gordon Brown. Marx's dictum that history repeats itself 'first as tragedy, then as farce', could scarcely be more apposite.[2] Forty years after the 1979 disaster, Labour was on the brink of political oblivion once again. The book's focus is the New Labour project, an undertaking that sought to reinvent post-war social democracy while reshaping its core political ideas. As an organising theme, New Labour was at the centre of the party's evolution and development over the last forty years. The world that Labour confronted in the 1980s and late 1990s was being fundamentally transformed, a stark contrast to the post-war era. In *The Age of Extremes*, Eric Hobsbawm remarked that 'the short twentieth century' that began in 1918 ended with Communism's demise in 1991.[3] The revolution in global capitalism, rapid deindustrialisation, alterations in Britain's class structure alongside the fall of the iron curtain necessitated sweeping reorientation of the Left's political thought.

Drawing on a wealth of sources, the book tells the tortuous story of how Labour overcame innumerable political setbacks and adversities. The party's onward march was halted abruptly in the wake of the 1979 defeat. British Labourism displayed the hallmarks of terminal degeneration. Labour's support was now confined to its Welsh, Scottish and Northern English industrial heartlands. It had no coherent response to the free market counter-revolution inaugurated by Thatcherism. Shipwrecked, the party was unable to break free of the impasse created by permanent Conservative rule.

Yet the ensuing post-mortem into Labour's political failure in the twentieth century, accompanied by sustained inquiry into the decay of Labourism, was the seedbed of eventual political and intellectual recovery. The revitalisation of the British Left from the mid-1980s absorbed the lessons of historical experience, drawing inspiration from the rejuvenation of social democratic parties across advanced capitalist countries from the United States to Sweden. Labour experienced an astonishing rebirth, undertaking the long march back to power and winning the largest parliamentary majority in its history. Far from being the heir of Thatcherism, optimists insist the post-1997 governments advanced constitutional radicalism, widely shared economic prosperity, liberal internationalism and social justice.

Even so, many commentators on contemporary British history and politics conclude that Blair and Brown's party was nothing other than an expedient adaptation to Thatcherism. The 1997 victory is portrayed not as a watershed in post-war Britain, but a point of continuity with the era of the New Right and the Thatcher administrations. It has become a cliché in what passes for scholarly debate that New Labour's ideas were the inheritance of neo-liberalism. Blair and Brown were 'sons of Thatcher'. Proceeding from where the neo-liberals left off, New Labour is said to have governed according to the ideological blueprint imposed by Conservative administrations.[4] New Labour was apparently determined to accommodate itself to the Thatcherite political order. As Blair and Brown came to office, class politics was abandoned. There was no reversal of anti-trade union legislation. Aggressively cut back, the public sector was stripped of democratic legitimacy. The 'workfare' state replaced the welfare state, coercing the destitute unemployed into jobs. The commitment to globalisation meant centre-left ministers reining in the state's interventionist and regulatory powers. The perceived risk of capital flight ensured the Labour administrations maintained competitive rates of income and wealth taxation. The emphasis on fiscal orthodoxy rejected the post-war Keynesian legacy. New Labour's vision of governance encouraged market forces to dominate state and society, culminating in the 2008 financial crash.

The programme of Blair and Brown's party was thought to be 'virtually indistinguishable from Thatcherism'.[5] Labour abandoned the main postulates of post-war social democracy: a belief in regulating the capitalist economy through state intervention to strengthen prosperity and welfare. Having internalised Thatcherism, New Labour was believed to have performed catastrophically in government. Blair and Brown, it seemed, did little to reverse the rising tide of inequality. The Blair administrations became embroiled in disastrous wars in Iraq and Afghanistan, leaving the British public vulnerable to the virulent strain of jihadi global terrorism. The New Labour project was intellectually discredited. It then failed electorally as the party *lost* 5 million votes between 1997 and 2010. Scholars lamented that Labour's policies merely entrenched the Thatcherite settlement.

Emphasising that New Labour represented a fundamental break with the party's dominant tradition, the unfavourable comparison with the governments of 1945–51 was encouraged. Since the 1960s, the predominant tone of discussion of the Attlee era verged on eulogy. The 1945 administration initiated a programme of socialist reform that transformed British society. The party came to power by forging the unique alliance between the manual and professional classes, brain workers and industrial workers, pursuing a vigorous plan of national reconstruction and egalitarian reform. Ministers and parliamentarians, alongside the trade union and Labour movement, were united in enacting Attlee's agenda. The Labour administrations overcame daunting constraints, notably the 'financial Dunkirk' of the war-torn economy. Despite those obstacles, Attlee's ministry instituted the National Health Service (NHS) while establishing the post-war welfare state supporting each citizen from the cradle to the grave. In the words of Attlee's press secretary, Francis Williams, the 1945 government, 'was the manifestation not simply of a transitory mood at one general election, but of a genuine and cumulative increase over many years of popular support for Socialist policies'.[6] Fifty years later, Blair and Brown's party was depicted as the stark point of departure. New Labour, beholden to neo-liberal ideology, apparently embraced the Thatcherite consensus. The Blair/Brown years were subsequently airbrushed from the party's history in the wake of the 2010 defeat.

This book advances a perspective on Labour's development that diverges from the scholarship of Left critics who so often shaped the dominant view of New Labour.[7] The account breaks with the historiographical consensus that these critics have advanced, questioning a number of prevailing myths. The first is the widely held belief that New Labour was merely an electoral machine concerned with winning power, accommodating the preferences of Middle England's voters. In fact, New Labour was primarily an intellectual organising framework rather than an electoral strategy. The second myth is that in so far as Labour had any ideas, they represented an accommodation with neo-liberalism. Yet New Labour came from within the Left. Its intellectual antecedents were pluralistic and heterogeneous. The third myth is of the irrevocable divide between Old Labour and New Labour, modernisers and traditionalists. Yet it is possible to identify important political and intellectual continuities with the parties of the past.

The chapters then consider New Labour's performance in office. The account differs from previous assessments in avoiding the temptation to reach a simplistic binary verdict of success or failure.[8] To consider the efficacy of the Blair/Brown administrations, a range of yardsticks are used: how far did New Labour ministers construct economic and social institutions that outlived them? To what extent was Labour successful in shaping secular trends from economic growth to inequality? How far did the governing party alter the beliefs, values, principles, norms and preferences of citizens? And finally, did New Labour succeed in initiating a lasting progressive settlement, shifting the axis of British politics towards the Left while refashioning the political landscape? The overarching judgement is that while Labour was certainly successful in gaining power, it was unable to win the recurrent battle of ideas in British politics. What New *Labour* stood for was obvious enough. But Blair and Brown's vision of the New *Britain* remained oblique and ambiguous. This introduction delineates the book's overarching themes. The chapter begins by more closely examining the prevailing orthodoxies on New Labour in contemporary historiography, political science and popular commentary.

Myth one: New Labour and the role of political ideas

New Labour was an intellectual undertaking. It was principally driven by ideas. Previous scholarship that addresses the relationship between institutions and ideas in the British polity provides a theoretically persuasive framework.[9] Samuel Beer was an American scholar of British politics. His intellectual approach is still of ground-breaking importance. Beer believed that ideas were decisive in the conduct of political activity in modern states. Not only were ideas effective instruments to acquire power. They enabled politicians to construct programmes and agendas, forging their practical ideal of the good society. Comparative scholarship emphasises the continuing importance of ideas in propelling institutional and policy change in advanced democracies.[10]

Nevertheless in the contemporary era, ideas had less purchase than might have been anticipated in the field of political analysis, particularly in the study of political parties. As one scholar attests, 'It is notoriously difficult to explain the activity of any political movement in the context of ideas'.[11] Examining ideas systematically is methodologically burdensome. Influential perspectives from Marxism to rational choice theory assumed interests were the dominant force.[12] Yet as J.N. Figgis has written:

> If ideas in politics more than elsewhere are the children of practical needs . . . the actual world is the result of men's thoughts. The existing arrangement of political forces is dependent at least as much upon ideas, as it is upon men's perception of their interests.[13]

Even scholars who took ideas seriously conceived New Labour as an electoral machine where intellectual concepts are expediently traded to win voters' support.[14] Less attention has been paid to the modern Labour Party's relationship to ideas and their influence on the British Left's political strategy and thought.[15] Of course, ideas were not all that mattered in the party, given the salience of electoral politics, the balance of power between institutions from the trade unions to the national executive (NEC), the influence of sectional interests, alongside the external impact of a transformed society and economy.[16] Individuals and leadership mattered too in mobilising electoral support and defining Labour's governing agenda.

Nonetheless, there has been comparatively little focus on how ideas shape the strategies of parties and policy-makers, defining conventional wisdom and determining the boundaries of legitimate political action, a concern foreseen by John Maynard Keynes: 'The ideas of economists and political philosophers, both when they are right and when they are wrong, are more powerful than is commonly understood. Indeed, the world is ruled by little else'.[17] Ideas reflect prevailing assumptions, defining what politicians consider to be politically viable and achievable in current circumstances.[18] It is ideas that provide the intellectual scaffolding for the visions and programmes of parties. Ideas operate at different levels, while the relationship between them is critically important. Table 1.1 illustrates that as overarching ideas about society and the economy are altered, so governance strategies and the symbolic policies of parties have to adjust.

After 1979, Labour's policy prospectus changed appreciably as a consequence of the development of ideas. The overhaul of the party's agenda was more than an expedient reaction to defeat. Nor were the changes wholly focused on overarching ideologies. If first-order ideas emerge as background concepts that capture how the world works, symbolic policies exemplify the party's vision and habits of mind. For instance, drawing on an example from the Conservative Party in the early 1980s, 'Right to Buy' policies in social housing reflected the ideological appeal of free market individualism. The implementation of symbolic policies in turn entailed the restructuring of governance, leading in the case of housing policy to the diminution of local government's role.

The influence of ideas is ever present in the Labour Party's evolving fortunes. It is striking that in the 1987 election, Labour struggled to define an intellectually appealing programme. A litany of unpopular policies were discarded. Yet few credible alternatives had emerged. The party had neither compelling 'grand ideas' nor politically salient symbolic policies while the governance of public policy was merely an afterthought. Five years on, there had been discernible progress. Labour began to shape a distinctive ideological vision that did not merely replicate the post-war social democratic settlement. Totemic initiatives such as the national minimum wage and 'family-friendly' childcare policies appeared. Yet the party was again soundly beaten at the election in 1992. The overwhelming focus was still on jettisoning unpopular commitments, particularly relating to Europe and defence. Labour gave precious little thought to delivery. The electoral defeat that followed in 1987 and 1992 appeared almost inevitable in retrospect.

TABLE 1.1 Ideas on the British Left

Level of analysis:	Core ideational elements:	Empirical examples from the post-war era to New Labour:
1) Grand ideas (First order)	The prevailing intellectual images that define British social democratic ideology that have shaped Labour's evolution. These concepts relate to fundamental questions about the role of the state alongside the relationship between government and markets. The ideas are 'big picture' narratives, 'background ideas about how the world works'.[19]	Grand ideas include post-war corporatism and national planning, egalitarianism, the concept of the 'post-class' society, social mobility and meritocracy, as well as globalisation. The response to globalisation that prioritised brain and knowledge workers was the social investment state, which replaced as Labour's goal the common ownership of the national economy.
2) Governance strategies (Second order)	These strategies comprise the party's dominant approach to governing. They explain how power is used to realise major policy objectives. Governance concerns the level at which power is exercised within the state, how to organise institutions and agencies to implement policies, and how to most effectively regulate markets in the public interest.	Governance relates to specific practices: for example, joined-up policy-making to co-ordinate Whitehall departments; setting targets and performance indicators in managing the public sector; creating 'quasi-markets' in public service delivery and 'light-touch' regulation of product, capital and labour markets. Devolved delivery, innovation, evidence-led policy-making and 'light-touch' regulation supplanted the post-war social democratic consensus focused on centralised command and statism.
3) Symbolic policies (Third order)	The symbolic policy epitomises the overarching ideas of social democracy. Such policies translate ideological commitments into politically appealing proposals. Party programmes and the rhetoric of politicians exemplify those policies. Policies are presented to maximise political salience: for example, New Labour's 1997-style 'pledge card'. If the totemic symbolic policies of Thatcherism were council house sales, for Blair's Labour party it was extending 'consumer' choice in the NHS and schools.	New Labour's policies after 1997 included reducing NHS waiting lists, cutting primary school class sizes, imposing a windfall tax on privatised utilities to help the young unemployed into work, deregulating the financial sector and introducing the national minimum wage (NMW). The shift after 1979 was to prioritise measures that emancipated the 'citizen-consumer' from widening school choice to increasing police numbers. The emphasis on incomes and wages policies that aided producer interests in Labour's programme was gradually replaced.

By the mid-1990s, for the first time since 1964 Labour was outlining a distinctive governing vision that acknowledged the passing of Keynesian social democracy, the emergence of globalisation and the rise of disruptive technological forces. The boundaries of what was considered achievable politically on the Left were being redrawn. New Labour emphasised symbolic measures from helping the low paid through tax credits to investment in human capital. Implementing these policies entailed models of governance that devolved power, created new institutions and redesigned market regulation. New Labour wove these ideas together with unusual lucidity and coherence. The post-1997 governments had all the hallmarks of intellectual credibility and ingenuity. There was vigorous debate about social democracy's strategic goals in the aftermath of the Cold War. Global economic integration required transnational co-operation. It was recognised that the electorate's aspirations were changing, as voters became more educated and prosperous. Public services had to be improved to preserve universalism. Labour's policies were underpinned by rigorous analysis, empirical evidence and understanding of international best practice.[20] As David Coates remarks, 'The New Labour government has been, to an unprecedented degree in modern UK politics, intellectually informed and academically sustained'.[21] The principles informing the Blair/Brown government's political and policy-making strategy were, in the main, substantive and intellectually robust.

The key assumption is that ideas have long been the driving force of British social democracy. Of course, it is important to recognise that ideas are not always articulated consistently. In the maelstrom of political life, ideas can be applied in an incremental, reactive, sometimes chaotic fashion. Ideas jostle alongside the political imperatives of tactical calculation and the struggle for power. It is difficult to ignore the partisan and even dogmatic mind-set of the practising politician. As Keynes recognised in 1936, 'When my new theory has been duly assimilated and mixed with politics and feelings and passion, I can't predict what the final upshot will be in its effect on action and affairs'.[22] Neither do ideas seamlessly reflect the transformations underway in the economy and society. While 'changes in the social realm necessarily form a large part of the raw material out of which different political languages and practices may be forged', it remains the case that such developments 'are not bearers of essential political meaning in themselves'.[23]

All that said, politicians interpret alterations in the economic and social fabric through the lens of ideas. In a tumultuous world, ideas project clarity of purpose. They enable parties to build coalitions of support beyond their natural constituency. At the same time, ideas can be politically damaging and even toxic. The 'wrong' ideas provoke accusations of heresy and betrayal. They bring careers to a premature end, nowhere more so than in the British Labour Party. Moreover, ideas constrain thought and action, defining the parameters of political common sense. Politics is the struggle to make certain ideas the prevailing orthodoxy. It is difficult to disagree with Nigel Lawson, the former chancellor of the exchequer: 'Never, never underestimate the importance or the power of the tide of ideas.

No British government has ever been defeated unless and until the tide of ideas has turned against it'.[24]

Palpably swimming against the tide of ideas, Labour in the 1980s was repeatedly defeated. New Labour arose as the crisis after 1979 compelled the reformulation of the Left's dominant ideas. While Left thinkers played a pivotal role, it is striking that throughout the twentieth century, intellectuals had expressed their lack of confidence in the British Labour Party. They found Labourism to be uncongenial, recoiling at its tendency to prioritise loyalty over effectiveness. Keynes railed against, 'sectarians of an outworn creed mumbling moss-grown demi-semi Fabian Marxism'.[25] Defined by the relationship between the party and trade unions, Labourism's mind-set remained insular, wedded to male industrial labour and collectivism. Yet by the mid-twentieth century, Labour had become the main left-of-centre movement in British politics. Progressives who sought influence in bringing an end to perpetual Conservative rule had little choice but to co-operate with the Labour Party.

Invented *within* the Left's distinctive ecosystem, New Labour's governing project was the result of vigorous intellectual debate over Labourism's long-term decline. The post-mortem into the party's historical failure was animated by overarching themes elaborated in subsequent chapters: the crisis of socialist ideology; structural changes in society and the economy of post-war Britain; the party's declining status as a credible competitor for power; the organisational atrophy of Labourism; the demise of institutions umbilically tied to the Left; and Labour's political vulnerability as a governing party. Such ideas proved more decisive than Thatcherism in reshaping the party under Blair and Brown. A multitude of ideas from diverse sources and intellectual traditions were crucial in revitalising the Labour Party. Ideas have remained the currency of political change on the British Left.

Myth two: New Labour as neo-liberalism?

Having emphasised the decisive role of ideas, the book takes issue with the conventional belief that New Labour represents a sanitised form of neo-liberalism: Thatcherism with a human face. The claim that New Labour and neo-liberalism are indistinguishable became received wisdom among numerous scholars of British politics, commentators and leading politicians. Time and again, the argument about New Labour and Thatcherism resurfaces. David Edgerton in his otherwise convincing account of twentieth-century British history disparages New Labour's neo-liberal tendencies. Edgerton maintains, 'what was striking about New Labour was not that it was a response to Thatcherism but its child'.[26] Among historians he is in distinguished company. Eric Hobsbawm chastised the Blair project as 'essentially framed and moving on terrain defined by Thatcherism'. Blair, Hobsbawm remarked was, 'Thatcher in trousers'.[27] Stuart Hall, a leading post-war theorist of the New Left, spoke of New Labour's 'Great Moving Right Show'. The political scientist Colin Hay insisted Labour under Blair surrendered its social democratic beliefs in response to Thatcherism, redefining the British political consensus.[28] More recently, Christine Berry and Joe Guinan asserted the Blair governments 'surrendered to the hegemony of the market'.[29] So why has the view that New Labour embraced neo-liberalism dominated the popular commentary and literature on British politics?

Certainly, internal critics were determined to discredit the 'new' party. Moreover, conceiving New Labour as the perpetuation of neo-liberalism fits with the prevailing view of British political history. The conventional interpretation divides the decades into discrete periods: the end of the Second World War to 1979 when welfare state social democracy was the dominant public policy framework; and 1980 to the present, an age of neo-liberalism that eschewed collectivism to push back the frontiers of the state. This demarcation is an orderly approach to understanding post-war politics in Western European societies. Yet its elegant simplicity is deceptive. The alleged continuities simplify a more nuanced picture. While its policies were inevitably marked by New Right ideas, the Blair/Brown agenda is wrongly depicted as unreservedly 'neo-liberal'. Given the extraordinary impact of neo-liberalism in winning the contest of ideas, it is hard to deny its long-term influence in UK politics. Yet there is an important distinction between particular social and economic policies containing traces of an ideology as fluid as neo-liberalism, and New Labour being interpreted as an unremittingly neo-liberal project. To explain this point, the concept of 'neo-liberalism' ought to be briefly elaborated.

Not surprisingly, the academic literature on neo-liberalism is voluminous.[30] As an ideology, neo-liberalism emerged in the aftermath of the First World War, developing as a critique of socialist state planning. It came to prominence in the 1970s against the backdrop of the perceived failure of post-war social democracy. Neo-liberal doctrine originated in the vigorous attack on statist command economies, evolving subsequently into an indiscriminate assault on Keynesian economics. At its core, neo-liberalism provided an alternative framework for structuring the political economy of advanced capitalism. In the British context, neo-liberalism meant shrinking the size of government, removing regulatory barriers and liberating market forces. Neo-liberalism necessitated the triumph of economic imperatives over the institutions of representative democratic politics.[31] The doctrine of monetarism as a plank of neo-liberalism was elaborated by professional economists, notably Milton Friedman, Robert Lucas and Phillip Cagan. The critique of state intervention derived from the Austrian intellectual, Friedrich Hayek, was their inspiration.[32] In the inter-war years, Hayek was an eloquent critic of central planning: government interference and intervention were considered detrimental to efficient economic performance.

Taking his cue from Hayek, the monetarism elaborated in Nigel Lawson's 1984 Mais Lecture involved, 'the conquest of inflation . . . not the pursuit of growth and employment . . . [as] the objective of macroeconomic policy'.[33] Lawson's outlook vehemently rejected post-war Keynesianism. The Thatcher governments pursued neo-liberalism prioritising the 'free economy and the strong state'.[34] The motive was allowing capital and product markets to flourish untamed, restoring profitability and growth after the perceived stagnation engendered by the post-war settlement. Late twentieth-century neo-liberalism reimposed the dominance of capital over labour that post-war Keynesianism temporarily shifted dramatically in favour of the working class. As such, neo-liberalism was as much 'a class project' as a 'theoretical argument'.[35]

Unleashing market forces necessitated the strong state. The liberalisation of markets acquired political legitimacy through democratic representation and the maintenance of 'elective dictatorship'.[36] Governments accumulated powers at the centre to protect national security and public order. Deindustrialisation inflicted painful restructuring of the economy. Stuart Hall wrote: 'Under this regime, the market is to be free; the people are to be disciplined'.[37] The redistributive function of the welfare state was deliberately weakened, shifting resources to 'policing the crisis' provoked by economic liberalisation. Public spending in Britain and the United States scarcely fell but was increasingly focused on the punitive politics of law and order. While Hayek wrote that Thatcher and Reagan were 'modest in their ambitions', the emphasis of fiscal policy shifted from direct to indirect taxation, cutting taxes on the wealthy leading to rising economic inequality.[38]

For all that, neo-liberalism is over-interpreted as an internally consistent ideology. Hall remarked that its ideas 'lump together too many things to merit a single identity. It is reductive, sacrificing attention to internal complexities and geo-historical specificity'.[39] Neo-liberalism in Britain entailed an inherent ambiguity: the emphasis on the 'free, possessive individual' combined with the centralising state. The politics of 'authoritarian populism' were uneasily conjoined to free market individualism. Neo-liberalism was an unstable amalgam of capitalist institutions, governing practices and political ideas.[40] More historically informed perspectives rightly emphasise that neo-liberal ideas were underpinned by 'profound contradictions': 'there was never a unified neo-liberal ideology' in Britain.[41] The government's economic and social policies cannot be read off from dominant ideologies since policy programmes inevitably reflect prevailing circumstances, governing traditions and political contingencies.[42]

Margaret Thatcher defined neo-liberalism as 'a man's right to work as he will, to spend what he earns, to own property, to have the State as servant not as master: these are the British inheritance. They are the essence of a free country and on that freedom all our other freedoms depend'.[43] Yet her government's agenda involved, 'huge new areas of intervention and institution-building', safeguarding the property rights of the market.[44] New Labour's relationship to authority, capitalism and class was very different to Thatcher's. Blair and Brown strove to end the class war. They put the ethic of community before class, rather than taking sides in the perpetual battle between labour and capital. Depicting public policy after 1997 as a capitulation to the New Right over-simplifies more complex realities.[45]

Other scholars view Labour's programme not as the retreat towards neo-liberalism but as a necessary adjustment to social change. The party was compelled to confront the altered character of Britain's economy and society.[46] The

New Labour project entailed the fundamental reappraisal of social democracy's governing orthodoxies. The party could no longer defer to the canon of Keynesian economic management. The power of organised labour had declined precipitously since the 1970s. Trade union membership had plummeted. Memories of the Winter of Discontent and the governments of Wilson and Callaghan were politically toxic. It is claimed Blair and Brown sustained the necessary work to modernise the party begun under Neil Kinnock.[47]

Myth three: Old Labour versus New Labour

The final historiographical myth is that *Old* Labour and *New* Labour were irrevocably divided. On the contrary, under Blair and Brown Labour stood in the line of descent with modernising and revisionist traditions in the party. New Labour's priorities echoed Attlee in the 1940s and Wilson in the 1960s.[48] Their overarching purpose was to achieve economic efficiency and prosperity within an egalitarian framework.[49] The rift between traditionalists and modernisers which Blair and Brown's rhetoric self-consciously encouraged overrides important continuities. The post-1987 *Policy Review* reacquainted the party with the measured and judicious programmes of twentieth-century Labour governments. The *Review* acknowledged the primary importance of the market economy yet advocated the regulation of capitalism, promoting security and tackling inequality.[50] This agenda emerged not merely to win over voters in marginal constituencies but to uphold Labour's historical purpose. At its core, Blair and Brown's vision of social democracy was familiar to all post-war Labour parties: the desire to reduce poverty, to combat inter-generational disadvantage and to advance fairer outcomes through government activism and intervention. Their generation did not reject the centre-left tradition. New Labour believed in redistributing wealth, ownership and power to working people.[51]

The identification of New Labour with neo-liberalism emphasised divergence. *New* Labour was believed to fundamentally differ from *Old* Labour. Blair himself encouraged the perception of freshness and novelty. The leadership's aim was to reconstruct the party's identity, having been the leading working-class force in British politics since the First World War. While it espoused the commitment to collectivism, the old Clause Four of the party's constitution was jettisoned at the Methodist Central Hall in 1995 where the original statement had been agreed in 1918. *The Red Flag* was no longer sung at party gatherings. Tony Benn despaired that 'Labour's heart is being cut out'.

The declining influence of organised labour transformed the internal balance of power in the party. The trade unions accepted the leadership's fervent desire to rewrite industrial and employment policies. Fewer workers now joined unions, especially in the private sector. The majority were employed in small- and medium-sized enterprises. Self-employment was mushrooming. The world of industrial labour was disappearing. Twenty years before, the writer Jeremy Seabrook observed: 'The kind of human being which the Labour party served is disappearing, and will never reappear in that form again. . . . The old working-class is an anachronism.[52]

Since the First World War, Labour's role was anchored in the party's representation of the British working class safeguarding its institutions, most importantly the trade unions.[53] Through involvement in the party, working-class representatives would enter Parliament in growing numbers. During the Attlee years, Labour forged its identity as the party of nationalisation, heavy industry and above all, the organised working class. Gaitskell's effort to rewrite Clause Four following the 1959 defeat was ultimately abandoned, since Clause Four espoused Labour's core identity centred on industrial labour. Rejecting those ideological shibboleths, particularly the emphasis on state ownership, posed a fundamental threat to Labour's character as a working-class party. The removal of nationalisation meant abandoning the culture of male-dominated industry and political organisation that shaped British working-class life in the twentieth century.

In stark contrast, the modernisers who made New Labour – an eclectic group that comprised Blair, Brown, Philip Gould, Alastair Campbell, Charles Clarke, Patricia Hewitt and Peter Mandelson, in due course extending much more widely in the party – believed Labour's traditional identity was now obsolete. The transformed nature of class undermined the centrality of organised labour. Merely capturing the state's commanding heights had done little to realise popular expectations of social reform. By the mid-1950s, the party's traditional ethos was alienating voters, especially women and non-industrial workers who had little instinctive empathy with Labour's proletarian culture. As a consequence, during the course of the twentieth century, Labour politicians grew disaffected with the apparently fickle electorate that rejected loyalties of class.[54] Labour's moderate Right Wing instinctively distrusted voters, maintaining that 'the gentleman in Whitehall' and bureaucrats in the Town Hall knew best. On the Left, there was acute frustration: apparently seduced by the pleasures of affluence, the working class preferred hedonistic consumerism, cinema, television, the pub, movies and fashion over participating in the socialist society.

As Britain's political sociology rapidly evolved in the twentieth century, Labour transformed itself into a 'catch-all party'. Rhetoric and ideas were adopted that transcended class identities, while downplaying the traditional ideological cleavage between Left and Right. Reformers insisted New Labour should distance itself from images of industrial decline. The political tradition of Labourism embedded in proletarian culture had to be sidelined: Labour must cease appealing to a better yesterday. New Labour was a celebration of the future – a *New Britain* – that unsentimentally renounced the past. The decline of organised labour and the projection of 'New' Labour led to further alterations in political ideas. The belief that national government should plan the economy was abandoned along with collective ownership. There would be no reversal of the privatisation programme undertaken by the Thatcher administrations. New Labour rejected post-war corporatism, transcending the Left/Right divide, while actively encouraging ideological ambiguity. New Labour was the by-product 'of the shift in power from politicians to voters and the decline of ideology'. This was an age where 'voters want to think for themselves', refusing to accept 'the pre-fabricated opinions of Left or Right'.[55] Ideas were devised for rejuvenating the economy and polity fifty years after the end of the Second World War that discarded 'old-style' social democracy.

Yet despite the impression Blair's entourage created, the dichotomy between Old and New Labour was always exaggerated, and even fictitious. In key respects, Labour in the 1990s remained the party of labour. The institutional link with the trade unions was still intact. The new model party had much in common with centre-left parties and governments of the post-war era. Labour's leaders even in the 1920s and 1930s acknowledged Labour would only succeed as a broad-based movement, an alliance bridging organised labour with the property-owning middle-class: the coalition of conscience and class in British politics. Indeed, New Labour advanced the age-old credo of revisionist social democracy throughout the twentieth century, striving to regulate capitalism and expand public services by managing a prosperous economy. The strategy of using government and welfare expenditure to ameliorate market forces appeared as relevant in the Blair/Brown era as for Attlee and Wilson's generation.

New Labour in power: a critique

This book demonstrates that New Labour's strategy and ideas were moulded by these political traditions alongside the rethinking taking place on the Left after Thatcher's rise to power. Neil Kinnock's former economic adviser, John Eatwell, believes the Conservatives' economic ideas were of 'virtually no significance' in shaping the revision of Labour's domestic policies in the 1980s.[56] New Labour's mission was to define a novel agenda for social democracy after the perceived failures of the Wilson/Callaghan era. The term 'modernisation', a central organising concept for reformers, implied inevitable forward movement and incremental advancement towards a desirable economic and social future. Labour modernisers in the 1950s and 1960s identified their vision of a dynamic society and polity with Kennedy's America.[57] By the late 1980s, modernisation was associated with Northern Europe. Germany provided the model of an efficient and cohesive political and economic order. Yet as this book shows, the modernisation ethic imposed innumerable contradictions and ambiguities on New Labour's project.

The inconsistencies became glaringly obvious in examining the governing performance of the Blair/Brown administrations. The conventional criticism of Labour's record focuses on the breach between promise and administrative achievement. The persistent theme in the literature is why all Labour governments appear destined to disappoint. It is evident that after four successive defeats, New Labour embraced a raft of cautious, safety-first assumptions about what the Left could achieve having won power. Blair and Brown adopted the rules of the constitutional game centred on the Westminster model, upholding indivisible parliamentary sovereignty and the doctrine of ministerial responsibility. The electorate was assumed to be instinctively hostile to higher taxes and public spending. Voters were judged to be antipathetic to the European Union (EU). Social democratic parties were electable only if they adopted robust positions on personal responsibility in welfare alongside a punitive criminal justice agenda.

Scarred by the experience of defeat, Blair and Brown struggled to realise the political potential of New Labour. Debilitated by their deference to current orthodoxies, Labour after 1997 struggled to alter the terms of political trade. All too often, New Labour was obsessed with refighting the ideological battles of the 1980s, rather than looking to the future. The critical question was how social democracy should prepare Britain's society and economy for the 2030s. Yet the Blair/Brown administrations failed to grasp emerging policy problems from millennials' struggle to enter the housing market and the catastrophic impact of climate change to the growth of low-waged employment. Blamed by commentators on the 2008 economic crash, the housing crisis and in-work poverty preceded the financial meltdown.[58] These issues were never substantively addressed by the post-1997 Labour governments. Moreover, the refusal to outline the future direction for the polity and economy of the UK proved immensely costly. To convincingly explain the mismatch between promise and performance, this book examines the critical failings that bedevilled the Labour administrations after 1997.

THE CHAPTERS

The literature on New Labour shaped by Left critics perpetuates the belief that the party was electorally motivated, crafted in Thatcherism's image and predicated on the irreparable division with Old Labour. Instead, throughout the book, Blair and Brown's Labour Party is revealed to be predominantly ideas driven, reflecting the protracted post-mortem into British Labourism's decomposition and decay after 1979.

Part I: Labourism in decay

Chapter 2: the crisis of Labourism

The first four chapters are structured thematically rather than chronologically. Chapter 2 deals with the inquiry into British Labourism's demise that was primarily focused on ideas. It demonstrates there was a gradual shedding of apparently obsolete assumptions after 1979 and a search for revised political strategies. Dismissed as hopelessly discredited, the Labour Right in the 1970s was believed to be attached to a controlling and bureaucratic mind-set, unable to confront the altered realities of British society. Having considered Labourism's atrophy, the chapter delineates New

Labour's main strategic assumptions. The nature of Blair and Brown's response to Labourism's decline subsequently defined their actions in government.

Chapter 3: historical roots

The New Labour project was shaped by the belief that the party chronically under-performed during the twentieth century. Blair and Brown's mission reflected the perceived lessons of history which are examined in Chapter 3.[59] New Labour was haunted by the ghosts of past failure, constructed in diametric opposition to Old Labour, its 'foundational myth'. As such, the past was subtly re-imagined to legitimise the contemporary modernisation agenda.

Chapter 4: New Labour and the global centre-left

The Blair/Brown project disparaged the blinkered mind-set of socialism in one country. It was believed British developments ought to reflect the ideology of European social democracy alongside the evolution of progressivism in the United States under Franklin Roosevelt, John F. Kennedy and Bill Clinton. Scholarship on the Labour Party itself was vulnerable to insularity and parochialism.[60] This chapter notes that the political and sociological forces shaping the party were certainly not unique to Britain.

Chapter 5: modernisation in hard times

Chapter 5 examines the political dynamics of Labour's protracted post-1979 rejuvenation. Initially, Neil Kinnock struggled to respond to the transformation wrought by Thatcherism, including the altered structure of the economy, women's growing presence in the workplace and the emergence of popular capitalism – all of which had a profound impact on the landscape of British politics. Nonetheless, Kinnock navigated formidable obstacles to organisational reform and intellectual renewal in the Labour party. Blair was the fortunate legatee of Kinnock's gruelling spadework. In 1997, defying those who feared Labour might never win again, the years of opposition were at long last over.

Part II: New Labour in power

Chapters 6–8: New Labour's impact in government

Part II of the book turns to the performance of the Blair/Brown administrations in office. What was New Labour's effect on the institutions and structure of Britain? The critical question relates to the *difference* Labour made in policy and politics. Did Labour bequeath a substantive institutional legacy? Had Blair and Brown's ministers decisively altered social and economic trends? Was the governing party able to transform popular attitudes? The fundamental question throughout concerns whether Labour entrenched a new progressive settlement in British politics.

Part III: New Labour's legacies in British politics

Part III then turns to the inheritance New Labour bequeathed to British politics. All political legacies are inevitably contested. The claim that Blair and Brown's Labour Party merely entrenched neo-liberalism in Britain is questionable. Yet UK politics certainly became more fragmented and polarised in New Labour's wake – a relative political failure given social democracy's aspiration to integrate classes and communities across Britain. Having been defeated in 2010, the party entered a further spiral of degeneration and decline. In this climate, Blair's promise of a 'new' politics in the UK appeared threadbare.

Chapter 9: New Labour's broken inheritance

New Labour's ambition was to end the historical conflict between labour and capital, to broker a truce in the class war inaugurated by Thatcherism, building a more cohesive and harmonious society. This chapter focuses on New Labour's long-term political legacy. The major themes include the condition of British representative democracy in the wake of the post-1997 constitutional reforms, the remaking of the Conservative Party under David Cameron, and subsequent developments under Ed Miliband and Jeremy Corbyn as the Labour Party swung sharply to the Left.

Chapter 10: conclusion

The final chapter provides a précis of the main arguments throughout the book while examining Labour's prospects as a continuing force on the British Left. The party was thrown out of office in 2010 against the backdrop of the pervasive crisis of global capitalism. It has suffered four successive general election defeats. Like social democratic parties across Europe, Labour has struggled to define a compelling ideological rationale in the aftermath of the great financial crash. In France and Germany, centre-left parties are staring into the electoral abyss. Will the British Labour Party now join them?

Notes

1 T. Benn, *The End of an Era: Diaries: 1980–90*, p. 257, London: Hutchinson, 1992.
2 K. Marx, *The Eighteenth Brumaire of Louis Bonaparte*, London: International Publishers, 1852.
3 E. Hobsbawm, *The Age of Extremes, 1914–1991*, London: Michael Joseph, 1994.
4 Among the best examples of this literature are C. Hay, 'Labour's Thatcherite Revisionism: Playing the "Politics of Catch-up"', *Political Studies*, Volume 17 (3), pp. 700–707, 1994; R. Heffernan, *New Labour and Thatcherism: Political Change in Britain*, p. 43, Basingstoke: Palgrave Macmillan, 1999; L. Panitch & C. Leys, *The End of Parliamentary Socialism: From New Left to New Labour*, London: Verso, 1997.

5 R. Heffernan, *New Labour and Thatcherism: Political Change in Britain*, p. 43.

6 F. Williams, *Fifty Years March: The Rise of the Labour Party*, p. 358, London: Odhams Press, 1950.

7 See, for example: R. Heffernan, *New Labour and Thatcherism: Political Change in Britain*; R. Heffernan & M. Marqusee, *Defeat from the Jaws of Victory*, London: Verso, 1993; C. Hay & M. Watson, 'Labour's Economic Policy: Studiously Courting Competence', in G. Taylor (ed.), *The Impact of New Labour*, Basingstoke: Macmillan, 1999.

8 Of course, the scholarship of other authors has unquestionably contributed towards the development of a more balanced view of New Labour – in particular, the work of Mark Bevir, John Callaghan, David Coates, Jim Cronin, Steven Fielding, Andrew Gamble, Eric Shaw, Florence Sutcliffe-Braithwaite and Andrew Thorpe.

9 Among the classic texts is S. Beer, *Modern British Politics: A Study of Parties and Pressure Groups*, London: Faber & Faber, 1965.

10 J. Kingdon, *Agendas, Alternatives and Public Policies*, Boston: Longman Press, 1984; P. Hall, 'Policy Paradigms, Social Learning and the State: The Case of Economic Policy-Making in Britain', *Comparative Politics*, Volume 25 (3), pp. 275–298, 1993.

11 A. Vincent, 'New Ideologies for Old', *The Political Quarterly*, Volume 70 (2), pp. 175–184, 1998.

12 S. Steinmo, 'Historical Institutionalism', in D. Della Porta & M. Keating (eds.), *Approaches and Methodologies in the Social Sciences: A Pluralist Perspective*, p. 130, Cambridge: Cambridge University Press, 2008.

13 J.N. Figgis, *Political Thought from Gerson to Grotius*, p. 1, Cambridge: Cambridge University Press: 1916.

14 C. Hay, 'Labour's Thatcherite Revisionism: Playing the "Politics of Catch-up"'; R. Heffernan, *New Labour and Thatcherism: Political Change in Britain*.

15 The work of Mark Bevir, in particular, offers something of a corrective to the dominant pre-occupation of the political science literature on New Labour: M. Bevir, *The Making of British Socialism*, Princeton: Princeton University Press, 2011; M. Bevir, *New Labour: A Critique*, London: Routledge, 2005; M. Bevir, *The Logic of the History of Ideas*, Cambridge: Cambridge University Press, 1999. In addition, see M. Freeden, 'The Ideology of New Labour', *The Political Quarterly*, Volume 70 (1), pp. 42–51, 1999. Richard Hill's work on Labour's economic strategy after 1979 similarly emphasises the pivotal role of ideas: R. Hill, *The Labour Party's Economic Strategy 1979–1997*, p. 39, Basingstoke: Palgrave MacMillan, 2001.

16 N. Randall, 'Understanding Labour's Ideological Trajectory', in J. Callaghan, S. Fielding & S. Ludlum (eds.), *Interpreting the Labour Party*, Manchester: Manchester University Press, 2003.

17 J.M. Keynes, *The General Theory of Employment, Interest and Money*, p. 383, London: Macmillan, 1936.

18 N. Randall, 'Understanding Labour's Ideological Trajectory', p. 19.

19 D. Kennedy, *A World of Struggle: How Power, Law, and Expertise Shape Global Political Economy*, p. 7, Princeton: Princeton University Press, 2016.

20 D. Coates, *Prolonged Labour: The Slow Birth of New Labour Britain*, p. 186, Basingstoke: Palgrave Macmillan, 2005.

21 D. Coates, *Prolonged Labour: The Slow Birth of New Labour Britain*, p. 186.

22 Cited in P. Clarke, *The Keynesian Revolution in the Making*, p. 309, Cambridge: Cambridge University Press, 1988.

23 G. Stedman-Jones, *Languages of Class: Studies in English Working-Class History 1832–1982*, p. 242, Cambridge: Cambridge University Press, 1984.

24 Cited in A. Wright, *British Politics: A Very Short Introduction*, p. 35, Oxford: Oxford University Press, 2013.

25 J.M. Keynes, cited in J. Crotty, *Keynes Against Capitalism: His Economic Case for Liberal Socialism*, p. 134, London: Routledge, 2019.

26 D. Edgerton, *The Rise and Fall of the British Nation: A Twentieth Century History*, p. 506, London: Allen Lane, 2018.

27 Cited in R.J. Evans, *Eric Hobsbawm: A Life in History*, p. 626, London: Little Brown, 2019.
28 C. Hay, 'Labour's Thatcherite Revisionism: Playing the "Politics of Catch-up"'.
29 C. Berry & J. Guinan, *People Get Ready!: Preparing for a Corbyn Government*, p. 4, London: Or Books, 2019.
30 For example, see: D. Harvey, *A Brief History of Neo-Liberalism*, Oxford: Oxford University Press, 2005; P. Mirowski, *Never Let a Serious Crisis Go to Waste: How Neo-Liberalism Survived the Financial Meltdown*, London: Verso, 2013; C. Crouch, *The Strange Non-Death of Neo-Liberalism*, Cambridge: Polity Press, 2013; D.M. Kotz, *The Rise and Fall of Neo-Liberal Capitalism*, Cambridge, MA: Harvard University Press, 2015.
31 W. Davies, *The Limits of Neo-Liberalism*, London: Verso, 2014.
32 A. Gamble, 'Neo-Liberalism', *Capital & Class*, Volume 25, p. 128, 2001.
33 N. Lawson, 'The Fifth Mais Lecture: The British Experiment', 18th June 1984. The lecture can be accessed at: https://839d6adc517f14a0ad6ab9527bc5dce0df4456f4c55 48db2e5c2.ssl.cf1.rackcdn.com/840618%20Lawson%20Mais%20Lecture%20MT%20 ANNOTATED%20THCR%201-17-112%20f3.pdf
34 A. Gamble, *The Free Economy and the Strong State*, Basingstoke: Palgrave Macmillan, 1994.
35 D. Coates, *Models of Capitalism*, p. 104, Cambridge: Polity Press, 2000.
36 A. Gamble, *The Free Economy and the Strong State*.
37 S. Hall, 'The Neo-Liberal Revolution', *Cultural Studies*, Volume 25 (6), p. 706, 2011.
38 Cited in N. Wapshott, *Keynes/Hayek: The Clash That Defined Modern Economics*, p. 134, New York: W.W. Norton, 2012.
39 S. Hall, 'The Neo-Liberal Revolution'.
40 D.M. Kotz, *The Rise and Fall of Neo-Liberal Capitalism*.
41 A. Davies, J. Freeman & H. Pemberton, '"Everyman a Capitalist?" or "Free to Choose?" Exploring the Tensions within Thatcherite Individualism', *Historical Journal*, Volume 61 (2), pp. 477–501, 2018.
42 D. King & S. Wood, 'The Political Economy of Neo-Liberalism: Britain and the United States in the 1980s', in H. Kitschelt et al. (eds.), *Continuity and Change in Contemporary Capitalism*, pp. 371–397, Cambridge: Cambridge University Press, 1999.
43 M. Thatcher, Speech to the Conservative Party Conference, 10th October, 1975.
44 M. Moran, *The Regulatory State*, pp. 6–8, Oxford: Oxford University Press, 2003.
45 B. Jackson, 'Currents of Neo-Liberalism: British Political Ideologies and the New Right, 1955–79', *The English Historical Review*, Volume 131 (1), p. 824, 2016.
46 S. Driver & L. Martell, *New Labour*, Cambridge: Polity, 2005.
47 S. Driver & L. Martell, *New Labour*.
48 S. Fielding, *The Labour Party: Continuity and Change in the Making of 'New' Labour*, Basingstoke: Palgrave Macmillan; M. Kenny & M. Smith, 'Discourses of Modernization: Gaitskell, Blair and the Reform of Clause Four', *British Elections and Parties Review*, Volume 1, pp. 110–126, 1997; A. Gamble & A. Wright 'The New Social Democracy', *Political Quarterly*, Volume 4 (1), pp. 1–4; D. Coates, 'Labour Governments: Old Constraints, New Parameters', *New Left Review*, Volume 1/219, September–October 1996; P. Anderson & N. Mann, *Safety First: The Making of New Labour*, London: Granta: 1997; G. Foote, *The Labour Party's Political Thought*; D. Rubinstein, 'A New Look at New Labour', *Politics*, Volume 20 (3), pp. 161–167, 2000.
49 D. Rubinstein, 'A New Look at New Labour'; S. Driver & L. Martell, 'From Old Labour to New Labour: A Comment on Rubenstein', *Politics*, Volume 21 (1), 2001.
50 M. Smith, 'Understanding the "Politics of Catch-up": The Politics of the Labour Party', Volume 17, pp. 710–718, 1994; S. Fielding, *The Labour Party: Continuity and Change in the Making of 'New' Labour*.
51 G. Mulgan, 'Special Issue: Wrong', *Marxism Today*, p. 15, 1998.
52 J. Seabrook, *What Went Wrong? Working People and the Ideals of the Labour Movement*, p. 243, London: Victor Gollancz, 1978.

53 J. Cronin, *New Labour's Pasts: The Labour Party and Its Discontents*, Harlow: Pearson Education, 2004.
54 L. Black, 'What Kind of People Are You?' Labour, the People and the New Political History', in J. Callaghan, S. Fielding & S. Ludlum (eds.), *Interpreting the Labour Party*, Manchester: Manchester University Press, 2003.
55 P. Mandelson, Institute for Public Policy Research (IPPR) fringe meeting, Bournemouth, 1999, personal archive.
56 Cited in R. Hill, *The Labour Party's Economic Strategy 1979–1997*, p. 15.
57 B. Brivati & D. Wincott, 'The Evolution of Social Democracy in Britain', *Contemporary Record*, Volume 7 (2), pp. 360–362, 1993.
58 This important point has been recently made by Paul Johnson, Director of the Institute for Fiscal Studies (IFS).
59 See J. Cronin, *New Labour's Pasts: The Labour Party and Its Discontents*.
60 For example, Jose Harris's otherwise lucid and compelling essay on the British Labour Party's political thought in the twentieth century omits to mention the European tradition of social democracy: J. Harris, 'Labour's Political and Social Thought', in P. Thane, N. Tiratsoo & D. Tanner (eds.), *Labour's First Century*, Cambridge: Cambridge University Press, 2000. I am grateful to Professor Colin Hay for drawing this point to my attention.

PART I

Labourism in decay

2

THE CRISIS OF LABOURISM

Britain in the New Times

New Times is a fraud, a counterfeit, a humbug. It palms off Thatcherite values as socialist, shores up the Thatcherite market with the pretended politics of choice, fits out the Thatcherite individual with progressive consumerism, makes consumption itself the stuff of politics. New Times is a mirror image of Thatcherism passing for socialism. New Times is Thatcherism in drag.

Ambalavaner Sivanandan[1]

Labour's own inured mentality – its continued acceptance of the destiny proclaimed for the party in the 1918 constitution, its stubborn rejection of the lessons of actual experience since 1918, stood in the way of actual adaptation.

Peter Clarke[2]

Since 1951 the electoral base of Labourism has been gradually contracting. . . . Labour's dominant image has become fixed by its role as the defender of the key institutions and gains of post-war social democracy.

Andrew Gamble[3]

Introduction

Following the Attlee government's defeat in 1951 which brought an abrupt end to the forward march of the British working-class, Labourism atrophied. By the late 1970s, it was in prolonged crisis. New Labour arose out of vigorous debate about the Left's degeneration in the radically altered economic and political environment of post-war Britain. This chapter examines the contours of the crisis leading to the development of New Labour's prospectus for modernisation in the 1990s. As rising stars on the Left during the Thatcher decade, Blair and Brown participated in the protracted inquiry into Labourism's decline. They did so alongside strategists and intellectuals who flooded into the Labour Party from the worlds of consulting, advertising, marketing and communications, alongside academic institutions and the universities. Irrespective of the performance of the Blair/Brown governments, thinkers and ideas that originated on the Left shaped New Labour's nascent programme by critically appraising the legacy of British Labourism.

This chapter considers the breakdown of Labourism in relation to six interwoven themes: the crisis of socialist ideology; structural change in post-war society; electoral vulnerability; organisational atrophy and fragmentation; the demise of social democratic institutions; and Labour's historical failings as an effective governing party. The central argument is that New Labour transcended the ambiguity of ideology and identity that bedevilled the post-war party, fashioning a more persuasive political and policy strategy. Even so, the influential 'New Times' analysis elaborated in *Marxism Today* reinforced New Labour's intellectual defensiveness and paranoia, eventually undermining its achievements in office. The chapter begins, however, by addressing the wider intellectual ecosystem of the British Left.

The backdrop to the discussion of Labourism's decay was the vexed relationship between the Labour Party and the British progressive intelligentsia. Noteworthy journals including *Marxism Today* assumed a renewed importance in the 1980s and 1990s, given that the association between the party and social democratic intellectuals that defined the post-war settlement was breaking down.[4] Revisionist social democracy appeared to have reached an impasse. In the aftermath of the Winter of Discontent, the post-war system of managed corporatism was discredited. Orthodox Keynesianism was undermined by the spectre of economic instability and stagflation. Moreover, the social democratic tradition struggled to address questions posed by the rise of relative affluence and the growth of post-materialism, particularly environmentalism; the recognition of personal identity as a major cleavage in democratic politics; the influence of feminism and the women's movement; alongside the politics of race and ethnicity. The launch of the Social Democratic Party (SDP) in 1981 underlined the breach between the Labour Party and the revisionist intellectuals of the Gaitskell/ Crosland era. During the 1980s, an alternative intellectual network emerged on the Left that supplanted the traditional ties between Labour and the progressive intelligentsia which blossomed in the post-war decades. As a consequence, there was a radical shift in thinking followed by a major reconfiguration of ideas.

The New Times and Marxism Today

The crisis of Labourism encouraged intellectuals to consider the impact of the 'New Times' on the shape of Left politics. Labourism remained an elusive identity primarily relating to the ethos and culture of the British Labour movement, its attributes of loyalty and defensiveness focused since the nineteenth century on safeguarding the material interests of the working class.[5] Even in the 1970s, the Labour Party was assumed to have a stable working-class support-base that provided moral legitimacy, and was best defended by maintaining the system of managed corporatism that institutionalised the power of the trade unions. As the focal point for debate about the manifest failings of Labourism, the importance of *Marxism Today*, a journal to which Blair, Brown and other leading figures contributed, has been emphasised repeatedly.[6] *Marxism Today* was the in-house magazine of the British Communist Party. In 1977, the University of Bristol academic and reforming Euro-Communist, Martin Jacques, was appointed editor. Euro-communism was the reformist tradition prevalent on the Left in Italy and Spain in the 1970s, emphasising the rejection of narrow class-orientated politics and embracing the tradition of liberal representative democracy. *Marxism Today's* editorial line remained vehemently anti-Soviet.

The journal became among the most influential on the post-war British Left. *Marxism Today* combined theoretical rigour, intellectual promiscuity and political ingenuity, attributes then in short supply in the British Labour Party. Pilloried in certain quarters as espousing metropolitan designer socialism, its writers were usually fearless, willing to attack age-old shibboleths that dominated British Labourism and post-war social democracy. As a consequence of its writing, socialism's vocabulary was extended into spheres of public and private life, 'which have, until recently, existed beyond the boundaries of Left politics'.[7] Stuart Hall wrote that the expressed aim of *Marxism Today* was 'to stimulate the Left to open a debate about how society is changing and to offer new prescriptions and analyses of the social conditions it seeks to transcend and transform'.[8] *Marxism Today* allowed Labour to be strategic rather than purely tactical, to consider openly how the world was changing and the implications for Left politics.

Marxism Today invented the label New Times to denote that structural changes in the economy and culture of late-twentieth-century Britain had major repercussions, altering the face of politics and demanding 'a complete reassessment of Left theory and practice'.[9] There was particular interest in analysing the phenomenon of Thatcherism, confronting the extent to which neo-liberal doctrine and the fracturing of the post-war Keynesian welfare state had restructured Britain's political and economic landscape. It was argued the post-1945 class compromise had been eroded by internationalisation and an open economy which invalidated national economic management. The persistence of chronic inflation and mass unemployment weakened the credibility of Keynesian economic theories. *Marxism Today's* contributors were particularly struck by the traumatic breakdown of the Social Contract under the Callaghan Government, and heretically questioned whether corporatism was a viable strategy for the Left. The deficiencies of central planning in Eastern Europe invalidated the political ideas of socialism.[10] According to *Marxism Today's* editorial line, Labour as the dominant Left force had to respond to recurrent electoral defeat alongside the breakdown of ideological orthodoxies in the context of a transformed capitalist society and new geopolitical realities. Jacques insisted that the most significant contribution of *Marxism Today* was to understand how the world was moving, especially 'the enormous shift in the centre of power from the developed to the developing world, in particular the rise of China'.[11]

Andrew Gamble wrote in the journal's pages in the early 1980s: 'Making sense of the new politics that emerged in Britain in the 1970s remains a crucial task for the Left'. It was striking that after 1979, politics was dominated by the Right in Western countries, particularly Britain, West Germany, Japan and the United States despite the deep recession, rising unemployment and cutbacks in the welfare state.[12] Throughout the 1980s, Labour appeared to have little immediate prospect of returning to office. The Left had reached a political and intellectual dead end. Following his election as leader in 1983, Neil Kinnock admitted, 'The Labour Party needs to modernise a lot of its attitudes because some of them are nothing more than sentimentality and mythology'.[13] In the climate of growing pessimism and uncertainty, *Marxism Today* offered, 'a tide of dissidence, an undercurrent of challenge to some of the guiding precepts of socialist and Marxist thought'.[14]

The inquiry into Labourism's predicament was not only concerned with new sociological and cultural forces. At issue was the historical failure of the twentieth-century Left, particularly Labour's inability to break the Conservative Party's hold on power to emerge as a more effective governing force. The intellectuals writing in *Marxism Today*, of whom the most distinguished was the historian Eric Hobsbawm, confronted the problematic legacy of the traditional Labour Right as much as Left sectarianism. Harold Wilson and Jim Callaghan's moderate Right-Wing Labourism imploded by the late 1970s. The party's historic claim to office centred on the belief that only Labour governments could manage the post-war settlement by harmonising the relationship between capital and labour appeared implausible. What was apparent was the breakdown of Keynesian economics following the eruption of industrial relations conflict.[15]

Marxism Today reacquainted the Left 'with the altered realities of British society'. The journal sought to 'challenge the mind-set and morality of the mainstream Left'.[16] In charting the demise of Labourism, the journal focused on 'post-Fordism' referring to the decline of mass industrial production and the emergence of a diversified and service-orientated economy. The nature of production was becoming globalised, fragmented and small-scale driven by highly disruptive general purpose technologies. In this context, Jacques explicitly acknowledged the decline of the Labour movement reinforced by the decaying institutions of the post-war settlement. In his landmark editorial, Jacques wrote that Labour was 'wedded to the past . . . backward-looking, conservative, bereft of new ideas and out of time'.[17] The young, urban Left was creating 'new alliances' in socialist politics.[18] *Marxism Today's* agenda emphasised post-material values. Movements that prioritised individual autonomy were supplanting traditional forms of political activism.[19] There was an emphasis on breaking with the post-war culture of queuing, rationing, controls and regulation to embrace post-collectivism and the new individualism. Jacques believed *Marxism Today* rapidly became the think-tank of Kinnock's Labour Party.

Yet although it provided British social democracy with vigorous theoretical analysis, *Marxism Today's* perspective proved controversial. As the historian Ross McKibbin pointed out, the claim that Britain's economic structure was post-Fordist and that the electorate felt disdain towards the bureaucratic state rested on the assumption that the British economy was once dominated by large-scale production. The UK economy was never obviously Fordist. Throughout the twentieth century British industry was centred on small firms, a major factor in post-war underperformance. Moreover, Thatcherism was less the product of the global movement towards neo-liberalism than a particularly English response to the threat of national decline.[20] *Marxism Today* implied that economic and social transformations were sweeping the world and negating historical contingency. Yet Thatcherism's triumph owed as much to the Labour Party's meltdown in the 1980s, alongside the boost to the prime minister's popularity provided by victory in the Falklands war. *Marxism Today* contributors were rarely well versed in matters of party politics. Their understanding of how formal governmental and parliamentary institutions worked was often perfunctory. Ralph Miliband also believed the journal provided the intellectual rationale for premature jettisoning of the Left's core ideological beliefs.[21] The writers who dominated *Marxism Today* were overwhelmingly male, underlining the troubled relationship between the magazine and the burgeoning women's movement.

Intriguing generational differences emerged by the end of the 1980s. Jacques and Hall believed the Left had to mount a 'counter-hegemonic' challenge to Thatcherism – in Gramscian terms seizing the ideological high ground by promoting a new popular common sense in British politics. Younger *Marxism Today* contributors, notably Charles Leadbeater and Geoff Mulgan, were now more empirical in their approach focusing on fine-grained adaptations in the fabric of the economy and society. Jacques and Hall became ardent critics of New Labour, whereas Mulgan and Leadbeater were eventually to play leading roles in the project.[22] Mulgan and Leadbeater believed rational, technocratic government had the potential to achieve far-reaching social reforms. Yet what was prescient given the eventual fate of New Labour was *Marxism Today's* disdain for Labourism's culture and institutions. Contemporary historians questioned the belief that society was being reconfigured by the ethic of liberal individualism and the decline of community.[23] In Raymond Williams's terms, *Marxism Today* had insufficient grasp of the 'structures of feeling' that shaped British working-class life deepening Labour's alienation from its proletarian heartlands, while encouraging the Left's intellectual defensiveness.

Nevertheless, *Marxism Today* unquestionably struck a chord with those in the Labour Party who acknowledged the need for far-reaching modernisation of the British polity and society. Tony Blair warned in his 1982 lecture at Murdoch University in Perth, Australia, that the Labour Right had run out of ideas. It courted favour with the press obsessively while remaining wedded to the complacent orthodoxies of the political establishment. Blair claimed subsequently that the seeds of the Right's obsolescence 'were sown in the Sixties and Seventies, when the leadership of the Labour Party was content to concentrate on stitching up the block vote, manipulating Party Conference . . . [while] at the grassroots the Party was withering'.[24]

Moreover, the Right of the Parliamentary Labour Party (PLP) was bitterly divided over British membership of the European Community, alongside industrial relations reform after the failure of the White Paper, *In Place of Strife*. The decomposition of the revisionist project during the 1970s implied that social democrats had little idea how to address the systemic weaknesses of the British political economy and the breakdown of the constitutional settlement.[25] Even more worryingly, after 1979 social democrats were at odds over the existential question of loyalty to the Labour Party itself. The Labour Right was perceived to be out of touch, unable to fully comprehend changes in personal identity, the rise of new forms of popular culture 'and the dissatisfaction at a corporatist state which people felt had become unaccountable and inefficient'.[26] In a letter to Michael Foot following his defeat in the 1982 Beaconsfield by-election, Blair lamented:

> T[ony] Benn is in one sense quite right in saying that the right wing of the Party is politically bankrupt. Socialism ultimately must appeal to the better minds of the people. You cannot do that if you are tainted overmuch with a pragmatic period in power.[27]

He then reiterated:

> The Left has generated an enormous amount of quite necessary re-thinking in the Party. We were in danger of drifting into being 'the natural party of government', but of a society that was unradicalised and unchanged. We had become managers of a conservative country.[28]

Such was the journal's sweeping influence, Stuart Hall quipped in 1994 that Blair was the '*Marxism Today* candidate' for the Labour leadership.

In the discussion of the New Times manifesto, it is striking that Gordon Brown, then Labour's Trade and Industry Spokesman, similarly embraced Hall and Jacques' view that the Left must confront the systemic failings of Labourism, addressing the structural alterations reshaping the British economy. In the new order of production:

> The economy is global, companies are transnational, capital flows are instantaneous, the mass production hierarchical factory is but one of the economy's commanding heights . . . the class structure has been modified, new political forces, not least the women's movement and green politics are in play.[29]

Even in the 1970s, Brown had insisted the Left must confront 'how working people . . . can increase the control they have over the decisions which shape their lives'. In *The Red Paper on Scotland*, he claimed traditional socialism had become 'little more than a scheme for compensating the least fortunate in an unequal society'.[30] Brown attacked core shibboleths of the Bennite Left warning, 'socialists must neither place their faith in an Armageddon of capitalist collapse nor in nationalisation alone'.[31] Renowned figures on the New Left, notably Antonio Gramsci, Eric Hobsbawm and E.P. Thompson greatly influenced Brown's thinking. As a consequence, he was highlighting very different intellectual themes to those preoccupying Crosland and Gaitskell thirty years before.

What made *Marxism Today* so influential in shaping the New Labour agenda? Martin Jacques points out he never subscribed to Blair and Brown's politics. Indeed, in 1998 *Marxism Today* published a highly critical review of the administration's first year in power.[32] Even so, it is clear that ideas and concepts generated within the pages of the magazine did influence leading modernisers. Charles Clarke, Neil Kinnock's chief of staff and minister in the Blair governments believed *Marxism Today* 'played an important role in the evolution of Left thinking throughout the 1980s'.[33] *Marxism Today* questioned the Left's traditional preoccupation with economic structure and class. It acknowledged the growing significance of the individual. *Marxism Today* acknowledged the increasing importance of diversity, pluralism and culture.

Marxism Today's impact on the New Labour project derived from the fact that its writers occupied similar territory in the intimate world of London metropolitan Left politics. There was a multitude of influential personal relationships and connections. Blair and Martin Jacques, for example, forged an unlikely political friendship. Geoff Mulgan became Gordon Brown's adviser on policy, subsequently head of the Number Ten Policy Unit. Charles Leadbeater worked closely with David Miliband, Blair's policy director. Questions were addressed in the pages of *Marxism Today* that were not on the agenda of post-war social democracy. As such, the journal filled the vacuum created by the breakdown of the close alliance between social democratic intellectuals and the Labour Party. Following the crisis of revisionist social democracy and the SDP's emergence in 1981, the progressive intelligentsia had become estranged from the party.

By the late 1970s, the synthesis of Beveridge, Keynes and post-war welfare state social democracy elaborated by Anthony Crosland in *The Future of Socialism* (1956) was manifestly exhausted. Revisionism exhibited numerous deficiencies associated with post-war British intellectual life, particularly its emphasis on empiricism over theory and its refusal to seriously address the emerging concerns of post-materialism – feminism, environmentalism, ethnicity, nationhood, and the politics of personal identity.[34] When younger revisionists such as John Mackintosh and David Marquand emphasised the importance of democratic popular representation, Crosland scorned the 'artificially contrived idea of equality of participation'.[35] He remained sceptical that the large majority of British citizens had any interest in deliberative decision-making. Most:

> preferred to lead a full family life and cultivate their gardens. And a good thing too. For if we believe in socialism as a means of increasing personal freedom and the range of choice, we do not necessarily want a busy

bustling society in which everyone is politically active . . . fussing around in an interfering and responsible manner, and herding us all into participating groups. The threat to privacy and freedom would be intolerable.[36]

As a consequence of Crosland's natural scepticism, revisionist social democracy initially refused to take seriously the atrophy of representative democracy alongside the breakdown of the governing machinery of the British state. There was no successor generation of Croslandites in the party. Giles Radice found Crosland personally arrogant and aloof. He gave younger MPs 'little encouragement in their own efforts to think out new strategies. . . . Crosland said at one point that he was "too bloody busy" to rethink his whole philosophy'.[37]

Marxism Today sought to fill the gaping void in the Left's intellectual armoury, while satisfying the thirst for new ideas among the rising generation of Labour politicians. The journal produced a compelling critique highlighting contradictions and ambiguities in the political identity of the post-war party subsequently elaborated by New Labour. *Marxism Today* highlighted the inadequacies of reformist social democracy, given its inability to address the paralysis of the English ancién regime that amplified post-war relative decline. Writers drew on the burgeoning 'declinist' literature that related the deterioration of the British economy to the inherent weaknesses of Britain's governing institutions and political culture. They argued Britain had neglected to create a more dynamic capitalism in contrast to post-war continental Europe.[38]

As a journal *Marxism Today* offered a very different account of Labour's historical failings to Crosland's generation. In the wake of the party's 1987 defeat, Stuart Hall wrote that:

> Electoral politics – in fact, every kind of politics – depends on political identities and identifications. People make identifications symbolically: through social imagery, in their political imaginations. They "see themselves" as one sort of person or another. They "imagine their future" within this scenario or that. They don't just think about voting in terms of how much they have, their so-called material interests. Material interests matter profoundly. But they are always ideologically defined.

Croslandite revisionism remained wedded to the politics of economic structures and material interests. During the 1970s, the Labour Party proved itself incapable of attuning to modernity and the politics of identity-based activism. Whereas the Labour Right believed that in Herbert Morrison's phrase, 'socialism is what a Labour government does', *Marxism Today* sought to elaborate, 'an intellectually articulated and justified strategy'.[39]

Of course, *Marxism Today* was not the only weighty journal of note on the Left. The prolonged inquiry into the decay of British Labourism involved periodicals including the *New Statesman and Society*, as well as *New Socialist*; the output of think-tanks, notably the Fabian Society, Demos, and the Institute for

Public Policy Research (IPPR); and liberal centre-left newspapers, particularly the *Guardian*, the *Observer*, and the *Independent*. The questions posed by the Left's degeneration informed an array of seminars, gatherings and conferences embracing the various tributaries of the British progressive tradition. In party meetings and debates throughout Great Britain, the ecosystem of the British Left, New Labour's political project gradually took shape.

During the 1980s, the predominant attitude towards the Labour Party was pessimistic. The party appeared incapable of thinking and acting strategically.[40] Labour seemingly had little effective capacity for sustained intellectual rejuvenation. In the crisis years of the 1970s, it began 'spurning new ideas at the point when it most needed them'.[41] The Wilson and Callaghan era was a huge disappointment. Then the party was unable to reflect constructively on its situation in the wake of the 1979 defeat. Thatcherism had become the dominant ideological force in Britain. The former cabinet minister, Peter Shore, remarked that Labour appeared to have 'lost the 1980s'. To assert that Labour was a party in crisis became an overworked cliché. Yet the party's electoral demise after 1979 was undeniably structural, stemming from the deep recesses of Britain's economy and culture. The Labour Party was shipwrecked, battered on the razor-sharp rocks of Thatcherism. Repeatedly, the Conservative Party defeated Labour in general elections. Meanwhile, social and political forces were undermining Labour as the dominant centre-left party. These defeats could not be explained away as the result of bad luck or unpopular leadership. It appeared the Labour Party had lost the ability to think and imagine for itself.

The New Labour project was a comprehensive response to the long-term collapse of Labourism in British politics. The thinking drew on the eclectic British progressive tradition, encompassing Labour and the Liberal parties; the trade unions; sections of the non-aligned Left including former Communists and nationalists in Wales, Scotland and Northern Ireland; and diverse organisations in civil society. The British progressive ethic emphasised personal liberty, social justice and economic equality achieved through the imperatives of national modernisation and democratic revitalisation. This progressivism was 'a kaleidoscope of political institutions, ideologies and mentalities that challenged laissez-faire capitalism and promoted . . . social justice on both a domestic and global level'.[42] Despite its failings and perceived limitations, the Labour Party continued to be viewed as the principal agent of social reform in Britain's majoritarian, First-Past-the-Post electoral system.

Of course, the doctrines of socialism and social democracy in Britain were never interchangeable, although the ideological linkages were obvious. Perry Anderson wrote that '[f]or all their mutual disclaimers, [western social democracy and eastern Communism] were joined as heirs of the ideals of nineteenth century socialism'.[43] Progressives on the Left perceived themselves to share a common heritage embracing the radical, dissenting tradition marked by the seventeenth century English revolution. Progressivism was a 'spectrum of thought' far broader than revisionist social democracy. Its ideas were elaborated by a diversity of 'organic' and 'traditional' intellectuals from across parties, genera-tions and political traditions who shared particular concerns and predispositions.[44] While sectarian conflict was gripping the Labour Party, those who inhabited the space of progressive thought continued to think hard about fashioning a cred-ible alternative to Thatcherism. The new generation of thinkers acknowledged, 'the mode of being of the new intellectual can no longer consist in eloquence, which is an exterior and momentary mover of feelings and passions, but in active participation in practical life'.[45]

Despite the prevailing mood of pessimism in the party, the culture of the British Left remained vibrant and inventive. The discussion of ideas was often energetic and animated, drawing on associated currents in British and continental European intellectual life. From the late 1970s, Britain's culture of publicly engaged scholar-ship was becoming more dynamic and vigorous in the light of the expansion of the universities, alongside the increasing numbers of graduates employed in the public sector, the law, the 'caring professions', charities and NGOs.[46] There was growing interest in post-structuralism, feminist social theory and post-colonialism. The disciplines of sociology, anthropology, psychology and psychoanalysis had become increasingly influential. As a consequence, there was a more lively Left-Wing fer-ment of ideas arising through journals, magazines and political conferences.[47] The relationship between intellectuals and social democracy remained vitally impor-tant. Intellectuals could both supply overarching theories and detailed policy programmes.[48]

Indeed, there was a striking parallel between the 1980s and the drive to for-mulate a Left programme in the aftermath of the 1931 collapse following the Labour government's implosion. From the aftershock of the financial meltdown until the outbreak of the Second World War, Labour experienced among its most fruitful periods of policy thinking in the twentieth century. The party was able to devise a credible governing agenda. Leading politicians, notably Hugh Dalton, Evan Durbin, Hugh Gaitskell and Douglas Jay, played a critical role in translating Keynesian theories and the associated 'deluge of ideas' into *Labour's Programme* (1937), the precursor of the 1945 manifesto, *Let Us Face the Future.*[49] The progressive intelligentsia 'could and did lay down the intellectual frame-work within which the battle for votes took place. They asked the questions which the politicians had to answer'.[50] Without these thinkers, the party 'would have been a kind of political dinosaur, all brawn and no brain'.[51]

One of those intellectuals, John Maynard Keynes, provided a masterful cri-tique of the limitations of unregulated capitalism which led to the catastrophic worldwide depression of the 1930s.[52] In *The General Theory of Employment, Interest and Money* (1936), Keynes insisted the spontaneous working of market forces was incapable of achieving the conditions for full employment. The Left focused on combining macro-economic policies of demand management with nationalisa-tion alongside economic and social planning. The New Fabian Research Bureau (NFRB) served as the influential vehicle for elaborating the party's programme translating Keynesian insights into practical policies. As the historian Elizabeth

Durbin suggests, on the basis of the work of the late 1930s, 'British democratic socialist thought has a rich tradition of designing realistic programmes'.[53]

In the early 1980s, Labour similarly appeared to be a party wandering in the intellectual and political wilderness. The 'sectarian neo-liberals' of Thatcherism were in the ascendency. Yet there was a determination to confront the deficiencies of ideology and strategy on the British Left as there had been in the 1930s, despite being crippled by the SDP's defection and the disintegration of revisionist social democracy. New political movements subsequently emerged focusing on constitutional and democratic revival. Among the most renowned was *Charter 88*, the broad-based movement for root and branch reform of the UK constitution. The upsurge of Scottish nationalism, the emergence of the European question, the inequity of the outcomes created by the electoral system, alongside the perceived abuse of the constitution by the Thatcher governments led to a wide-ranging coalition for change.[54] New journals and publications were subsequently launched. One noteworthy example is *Samizdat*, a magazine founded by Michael Young, the peer and author of Labour's 1945 manifesto. Institutions were created to unearth fresh ideas, notably think-tanks including Demos and the Institute for Public Policy Research (IPPR). These organisations were institutional pioneers and policy entrepreneurs that sought to fill the void created by the obsolescence of British Labourism.

The crisis of Labourism

Despite the remarkable spirit of shared endeavour, there were of course important divisions within British progressive thought. The major divergence since the 1930s remained whether to reform British capitalism to fulfil social democracy's egalitarian aspirations; or to replace capitalism with an alternative economic system no longer driven by private interest and greed. The age-old division on the Left between reformist and revolutionary politics persisted. Nonetheless, it is plausible to trace New Labour's ideas and programmes to the eclectic currents of the progressive tradition focused on the multitude of think-tanks and journals on the British Left. During the 1980s there was an intellectual reawakening that acknowledged the need to revise the party's strategy and ideology even more fundamentally than in the 1950s, despite the bitter doctrinal disputes of that period. The debate about the crisis of Labourism fashioned New Labour's agenda for national reform and modernisation, and was animated by overarching themes that are elaborated further below.

The ideological crisis: searching for the New Jerusalem

The first theme concerned the ideological crisis of the Left. Labour may have been a pragmatic party that owed more to Methodism than to Marx, the cliché beloved of Harold Wilson. Whether the Labour Party was ever a socialist party had long been a matter of controversy. Since the beginning of the twentieth century, Labour was a fractious and unstable coalition of ideologies from orthodox

Marxism to ethical socialism to the inheritors of the New Liberalism.[55] Antipathy to capitalism and the belief in planning brought about by nationalisation of the productive economy provided the ideological adhesive that bound the party uneasily together. Yet the paradox was that whenever the Labour Party entered government, ministers embraced the realities of markets. Their commitment to public ownership usually softened while private property rights were upheld. This division between principle and pragmatism has continued to structure conflict in the party.

The Labour Party's ideological agenda was definitively shaped by British ideas, as such largely untouched by the European Marxist tradition. The emphasis in the work of Tawney, Dalton, Durbin and Crosland – the party's dominant intellectuals – was on working through British political institutions to achieve 'legislative and administrative change'.[56] Durbin wrote that those 'who believe in democracy, have faith in moderation, and search for agreement in the field of politics, have behind us the long and splendid tradition of British political thought and practice'.[57]

In so far as Labour had any discernible ideological creed beyond its rhetorical adherence to socialism, it developed during the twentieth century by melding together distinctive traditions.[58] The first tradition was the ideology of corporate socialism centred on state ownership of the means of production. The second tradition was guild socialism, emphasising worker's control and participatory democracy. The third was the Fabian tradition that prioritised the expert-driven centralised state. The fourth tradition was social liberalism according primacy to personal liberty together with the freedoms afforded by government intervention. The fifth was the 'Tory-socialist' tradition affirming the communitarian values of the working-class in industrial Britain.[59] And there was the related tradition of non-statist 'socialism from below' emphasising co-operation, mutualism and neighbourliness forged through 'gas and water socialism' at the local municipal level. The status of local government in Labour's ideology remained tenuous, however, given the proclivity towards centralisation.[60]

The direction afforded by such ideological traditions was to prove important, given that Labour remained an idealistic party. The commitment to the ideal of the New Jerusalem evoked the utopian desire to create a better world – the belief in 'heaven on earth' – leading not only to material improvements in the lives of the working class but wider spiritual awakening: from selfish, acquisitive materialism to a community of fellowship and solidarity. Yet while the Labour Party had a 'diffuse ethical yearning for socialist utopia', it still required a practical governing programme.[61] The response to the ambiguities of ethical socialism was the drafting of Clause Four in 1918. Clause Four committed Labour governments to enact the socialised planned economy, although ironically the original statement never mentioned the word 'socialism'. According to the historian Tony Judt, Clause Four gave legitimacy on the British Left to 'transformational change: the displacement of capitalism with a successive regime based on an entirely different system of production and ownership'.[62]

Although Clause Four espoused the doctrinaire belief in nationalisation, it was intended to be a pragmatic commitment to the socialisation of industry, diluting the appeal of Marxism and class struggle in the aftermath of the First World War. Yet by the late 1980s, the party's official socialist ideology appeared profoundly discredited. It had been undermined by:

> The almost universal popular identification of socialism with an extension of central state ownership and control. Socialism is generally seen as the nationalisation of industry, rather than other forms of common ownership, and as central state control, rather than decentralisation and local autonomy.

The party was crippled given that socialism was 'widely and almost exclusively identified as the central state'.[63] In the wake of the 1983 election defeat, intellectuals began to ask what it meant to be on the Left when the goal of collective ownership was so widely demeaned? The faith in nationalisation among the working class had precipitously declined since the 1970s. How should Labour and the Left deal with the dissipation of long-standing ideological certainties? The party's failure to clarify a persuasive body of socialist doctrine in post-war Britain created persistent difficulties.

Even reformist social democracy, the politics of accommodation with capitalism centred on harmonising the labour/capital dynamic, was struggling following the decline of the post-war settlement. As Labour emerged from the wreckage of the Wilson–Callaghan years, the issue of what socialism meant was shrouded in confusion and ambiguity. The post-1945 social democratic consensus was decaying. Throughout the 1980s, the ideology of socialism slipped further into disrepute, culminating in the fall of the Berlin wall and the collapse of 'actual existing socialism'. This situation provoked a wide-ranging debate about the final demise of socialism. Crosland's landmark text, *The Future of Socialism* (1956), had sought to clarify the Labour Party's ideology in post-war Britain. Crosland insisted socialism meant the pursuit of equality through the welfare state rather than nationalisation and government control of the economy.

By the early 1980s, even Croslandite revisionism appeared exhausted reflecting the Labour Right's ideological fatigue. Blair believed the arguments of *The Future of Socialism* were relevant to post-war society rather than Britain after 1979.[64] Revisionism distinguished between ethical ideals, the guiding moral spirit of socialism, and means, the technocratic machinery required to take practical action and put policies into effect. While Blair talked of separating means and ends as a Christian socialist, he believed moral responsibility was necessary to achieve social justice. The philosopher A.J. Ayer promoted logical positivism which had won the allegiance of Gaitskell's generation in the 1950s, Blair was uncomfortable with Ayer's disregard for ethical principles. He was determined to restore the early-twentieth-century precept of moral obligation to the Left's values. Yet Blair turned to Christian socialism emphasising the reciprocal relationship between individual and society enunciated by his intellectual hero, the philosopher John MacMurray. MacMurray's idealism led him to espouse Quakerism and pacifism emphasising ideals of fellowship, mutual obligation and community.

Shortly after the downfall of Margaret Thatcher in 1990, Blair remarked that the task for socialism was 're-establishing the agenda for public action without the old failings of collectivism'.[65] Gordon Brown insisted, 'instead of Hayek's vision of selfish individuals endlessly competing against each other stands a socialist view of a community of citizens pursuing objectives they hold in common'.[66] Influential figures on the British Left from Neil Kinnock to the university academic Raymond Plant envisaged the return to ethical socialism, prioritising community-mindedness over selfishness and consumerism while ending the confrontation with market capitalism. Blair foresaw as 'social-ism's' goal a society of citizens shaped by 'an ethical and subjective judgement that individuals owe a duty to one another and to a broader society – a Left view of citizenship'.[67] In an edited collection of socialist writings, Brown concurred: 'The most distinctive feature of British socialism historically has been its insistence on the moral basis of politics'.[68] This communitarian view diverged from the liberal egalitarianism of John Rawls that emphasised individual rights as the cornerstone of a more equal society. The critique of Rawls was eloquently elaborated in Michael Sandel's book, *Liberalism and the Limits of Justice* (1982) on which Brown subsequently drew.

Even so, having become leader, Blair struggled to articulate a coherent concept of communitarianism as his guiding ideology. It proved fiendishly difficult to define what the Left meant by 'community'. For many, community remained a conservative idea. Michael Oakeshott believed that 'to be conservative . . . is to prefer the familiar to the unknown . . . the near to the distant'.[69] New Labour's communitarianism became prescriptive and moralistic in the eyes of scholars, emphasising a socially conservative ethical impulse.[70] Moreover, the communitarian belief in decentralising power to localities and communities contradicted Labour's dominant twentieth-century statecraft, prioritising uniformity and central direction in the name of equality. Having embraced the ethic of community, Blair diluted his commitment in government more conventionally relying on the institutions of the market and state. After discarding Clause Four in 1995, Blair was unable to devise a conception of socialism that went beyond the vague, abstract espousal of the communitarian ideal. New Labour's emphasis on technocratic governance in the face of globalisation and technological disruption undermined the enduring effort to revitalise the British socialist tradition.

Other thinkers confronted the crisis of British Labourism by emphasising the turn to 'post-ideological' politics.[71] The loss of faith in Marxism led to their shift away from ideology, emphasising the virtues of expert technocracy and techno-futurism, a world-view that grew in salience from the late 1950s. New Labour's ideology sought to reconcile the diverse streams of ethical, Christian and technocratic socialism. Yet for many scholars, any distinctive socialist ideology was all but abandoned. By the mid-1990s, the party was on the brink of power yet it palpably lacked an overarching theory: a governing idea that could propel Labour through the hard grind of achieving political and economic reform in a market society.

Structural change and political sociology in post-war Britain

The second theme in Labourism's decay related to the structural alterations in Britain's economy and society from the end of the Second World War. The transformation of capitalism and the fragmentation of the pre-1945 class structure were reshaping the landscape of British politics. A series of sociological investigations demonstrated that social change was eroding the class base of the Left's support. Scholars debated whether the decline of the industrial working class made Labour's defeat somehow inevitable. A prominent historian of modern Britain concluded, 'There are subterranean springs which cannot be dammed – changes in the political sociology of Britain which leave the Labour party's power base looking like an anachronistic anomaly'.[72] Yet the shifts in British society went beyond the class structure. Jacques and Hall claimed that society had changed, 'not just incrementally but qualitatively, that Britain and other advanced capitalist societies were increasingly characterised by diversity, differentiation and fragmentation, rather than homogeneity, standardisation and the economies and organisations of scale which characterised modern mass society'.[73]

According to Jacques and Hall, the system of industrial mass production once underpinning the Left's political ideas was rapidly decaying. In the twentieth century, Fordism gave bargaining power and a stable career structure to semi-skilled manual workers, integrating the classes and moderating industrial conflict. *Marxism Today* addressed the impact of technological adaptation on the industrial economy and the future of work. The concept of post-Fordism indicated the centralised industrial economy was being replaced by disaggregated small- and medium-sized enterprises. Paul Hirst believed that 'flexible specialisation' was the new technological paradigm: 'the manufacture of a range of specialised goods for particular and changing markets using flexible general purpose machinery and predominantly skilled labour'.[74] The economy was being altered through the application of computing technology.[75] The British economy had experienced relative decline despite the drive for industrial modernisation in the 1960s.[76] As a consequence, the stability that Fordism provided in the mid-twentieth century was dissipating.

Meanwhile, the growth of deindustrialisation eroded Labour's traditional strongholds in Northern and Celtic Britain. The long boom in the knowledge and service economy in the 1980s reinforced the structural dominance of London and the South of England. As Charles Leadbeater observed, the centre of gravity in the British economy was shifting from its 'manufacturing heartlands' where trade unionism had been influential to sectors that remained 'barren territory for the unions'. Another *Marxism Today* contributor remarked:

> [t]he new 'union-free', capital intensive small-scale industries of the Information Technology sector and the service sector, emerging alongside the

giant British multinationals, are creating a social and occupational pattern in many areas of the country which so far have remained outside traditional Labour politics.[77]

Of course, deindustrialisation did not begin in the 1980s. More coal mines closed when Harold Wilson was prime minister after 1964 than during the Thatcher premiership. The forces of deindustrialisation reshaped the British economy continuously after 1960.[78] Yet the long-run shift from industry to the service economy had stark implications. It led to the demise of Britain's 'proletarian culture', chiefly characterised by industrial employment, undermining the political vitality of the working class. The nature of work was transformed. Suburbanisation dispersed long-established working-class communities. The development of the consumer culture undermined traditional leisure pursuits, from dog racing to breeding pigeons. These adjustments inevitably sapped the political self-confidence of the Labour movement, which in 1945 was still at the height of its influence and prestige. One *Marxism Today* author acknowledged, 'there is plenty of evidence to suggest that trade unionism in general is not nearly as popular with its own members as a healthy movement ought to be'.[79] Technology then revolutionised the world of work. The labour market was expanding in service occupations employing women, often in part-time roles. In these sectors, trade unions had little history of effective organisation.[80] The privatisation of heavily unionised industries – water, gas, telecoms, aerospace – reduced the scope for collective wage bargaining.[81] The polarisation of the labour market then followed: relatively skilled workers were comparatively well remunerated. Yet the low-skilled segment of the labour force was increasingly exposed to low wages and insecurity.[82]

The structural transformation was not confined to the economy. The growing salience of personal identity radically reshaped British politics. There was the struggle for recognition of individuals through the feminist movement; anti-racism; disability rights activism and the expansion of ethical campaigns, especially environmentalism. These agendas were ill-served by conventional party politics and the 'traditional definitions of Left and Right'.[83] The theorists Ernesto Laclau and Chantal Mouffe reflected, 'Socialist political struggle takes place today on a terrain which has been profoundly transformed by the emergence of new contradictions'. It was necessary 'to modify the notion of *class* struggle in order to be able to deal with the new political subjects – women, national, racial and sexual minorities, anti-nuclear and anti-institutional movements . . . whose identity is not constructed around specific "class interests"'.[84] Beyond individual emancipation, there was the struggle for recognition by distinct communities. Nationalist sentiment was awakened in Scotland, Wales and Northern Ireland. There was anger in Northern English industrial areas marginalised by the structural shift in the economy.

The political implications by the 1980s proved decisive. Labour modernisers observed that:

Class identity has fragmented. Only about a third of the population now regard themselves as "working-class". It is possible to analyse Britain in terms of a strict Marxist definition of class: but it is not very helpful to our understanding of how the country thinks and votes.[85]

The Left failed to keep pace 'with the enormous cultural changes which have occurred since the 1950s'.[86] Alterations in the nature of capitalism and the market society meant for many individuals 'a life somewhat less constrained, less puritanically regulated, less strictly imposed than it had been three or four decades before'.

The debate on the Left concerned the clarity and coherence of Labour's response. Changes in housing provision and the nature of social class, the restructuring of the workforce and the growing consumption of goods and services had occurred across Western Europe. Yet of all the social democratic parties, the British Labour Party appeared most adversely affected. The 'world of labour' that shaped the trade union movement at the end of the nineteenth century was steadily disappearing. Figure 2.1 highlights the fundamental shift in Labour's political and social constituency:[87]

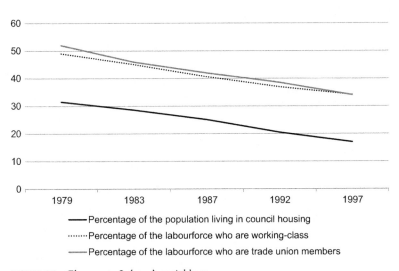

FIGURE 2.1 Changes to Labour's social base

Between 1979 and 1997 according to the Office for National Statistics (ONS), the proportion of the electorate residing in local authority-owned council housing declined from 31.5 to 17 per cent. Those classified by occupational status as working class fell from 49 to 34.1 per cent. The demise of union membership was similarly dramatic. Labour risked political annihilation since its heartlands were shrinking while the party had yet 'to find a role in the new times'.[88] *Marxism Today* concluded the Labour Party should abandon 'the old language of collectivism', embracing policies that 'tap those popular desires for choice and individuality but which also extend the repertoire for local democratic representation through citizenship'.[89] In the new world of personal autonomy and individualism, Labour could not simply reassert the old ideals of collectivism. 'The idea of a spontaneous class politics arising from a typical kind of labour', at the centre of the political thought of the British Left for decades, 'is much less convincing that it once was'.[90] Stuart Hall alongside the theorists of the New Left stressed the importance of social movements and civil society, breaking away from outworn conceptions of statism.[91] The Labour Party must understand the role of identity in shaping politics, as well as the long-term effect of structural change in Britain. New Labour emphasised the need to fully comprehend the transformed social and economic landscape.

Labour as an electoral force in British politics

Many on the Left believed if Labour was incapable of effectively responding to economic and social change, the party would inevitably perish. An additional facet of the crisis of Labourism related to the party's electoral viability. The debate concerned the fate of Labour as a credible competitor for power in the British polity. The party was not the only force on the Left in Britain. Since the First World War, Labour had sustained a monopoly of the centre-left vote. Yet it was apparent Labour's electoral base was fracturing. Dire results in 1979 and 1983 indicated the party's support was in long-term abeyance. During the 1950s, electoral sociologists warned of the effects of the decline of the traditional working class as a share of the electorate alongside the breakdown of the relationship between class and voting. Even among those classified officially as working class, loyalty to Labour was dissipating.

Yet the party's position proved relatively weak ever since the full democratic franchise was conceded in the 1920s. A third of the working class never voted Labour. Many commentators questioned why the party struggled to fashion a credible national appeal outside the traditional 'heartlands' in the industrial urban north of England, the Welsh valleys and the central belt of Scotland.[92] The Labour Party's experience in the second half of the twentieth century thwarted its confidence in the inevitability of socialist reform through parliamentary democratic institutions. The party was compelled to re-consider its adherence to socialist policies, given Labour's declining electoral fortunes. In 1983, the manifesto espoused the ideological commitment to nationalisation and the planned economy. The programme was decisively rejected by voters. By 1997, party policy appeared less conventionally 'socialist' than at any point since the Second World War, abandoning public ownership and 'tax and spend' measures. Labour then secured a landslide majority.

The implications of this chastening political experience were difficult to swallow.

Furthermore, debate on the Left focused on the degree to which alterations in the nature of the middle class eroded Labour's electoral position. The middle class was expanding in the decades after the Second World War. The divide between public and private sector employment became a crucial indicator of party support. Labour became the party of white-collar middle-class public-sector workers, eventually narrowing its electoral coalition. By the 1980s, the party's traditional emphasis on material living standards and the welfare state sat uneasily with the post-materialist concerns of the well-educated, focusing on civil liberties, the environment, identity and culture. According to Stuart Hall, Labour had been guilty of 'a vulgar economism' which wrongly assumed that 'pure class position guarantees voting behaviour'.[93]

In the wake of Labour's 1979 defeat, the electoral pendulum was swinging decisively against the party. One commentator warned, 'The old-style Labour coalition cannot probably now be revived'.[94] Many feared Britain was 'a Conservative country which occasionally votes Labour'. Certainly, the party fought a particularly weak campaign in 1979, outmanoeuvred by the Conservatives who hired the advertising agency *Saatchi and Saatchi* to produce the iconic billboard 'Labour Isn't Working'. As Hall wrote:

> In any long term electoral perspective, the underlying trends must be deeply worrying. Labour seems incapable of becoming a national popular political force, commanding the votes of the popular majority. . . . Labour is losing votes in exactly those class, strata and social categories required if it is to achieve that kind of electoral leadership. Its defeat in 1979 was, specifically, achieved by the penetration of the radical Right into the very heartland of its support and . . . a massive haemorrhage of working class votes.[95]

The party then experienced four successive defeats as the resurgent Conservative Party constructed a durable base of electoral support among the working class. In the mid-1990s, Blair reminded readers of the journal *Renewal*, another influential Left publication that:

> It is over twenty years since Labour won 40 per cent of the vote. It is more than 21 years since we won an election. By 1996 we will have been out of power for longer than any other mainstream party of the Left in the Western world. Our 1992 vote was actually lower than our 1979 vote. And the swing required at the next election is larger than any required since 1945. So the task is immense.[96]

The existential question was how Labour should recover its electoral strength when social and political forces were undermining the party? The long-term shift in electoral behaviour indicated support was becoming polarised geographically.[97] In the 1990s, the Labour MP Giles Radice wrote a series of pamphlets highlighting Labour's *Southern Discomfort* underlining the party's detachment from the prosperous constituencies of South-East England. The Labour Party risked confining its electoral support to the former industrial communities in Northern England and the Celtic periphery. In the wake of the 1992 defeat, political scientists speculated as to whether the party would recover.[98] The task for Labour was to discern 'how to win support for progressive politics amongst the new and growing sections of society'.[99]

Reformers were gloomy about Labour's prospects, despite the Major government's meltdown. Writing in the aftermath of the 1987 defeat, Blair observed that over the previous decade, Thatcher had been the beneficiary of 'a divided opposition . . . with Labour and the Alliance often competing for exactly the same political territory'.[100] Even before the 1997 election, Blair believed Labour might still be compelled to govern in a coalition, leading to his conscientious courting of Paddy Ashdown's Liberal Democrats and his commitment to a radical constitutional agenda.[101] So widespread was Labour's 'pessimism of the intellect' after the 1992 defeat, it was believed a pluralist common front of centre-left parties in an electoral pact might be necessary to finally defeat the British Conservative party.

Labour's organisational atrophy

The fourth theme of Labourism's decay related to ideology, structural alterations in society and electoral failure: the organisational crisis epitomised by the Labour movement's atrophy as a major force in British politics. Labour appeared to be facing terminal decline. The 'morbid symptoms' of the party's demise included the sharp drop in membership. Since the 1960s, Labour was losing 11,000 members every year. Trade union density reached its highest-ever level in the late 1970s, but declined thereafter. The party lacked basic political resources. It was out-spent and out-fought by the Conservatives, far removed from the cutting-edge techniques of political campaigning, marketing and opinion research that reshaped how parties in Western democracies fought elections. Harold Wilson in an internal report written in the mid-1950s concluded, 'compared to our opponents, we are still at the penny-farthing stage in a jet-propelled era, and our machine, at that, is getting rusty and deteriorating with age'.[102] By 1979, it appeared little had changed.

As momentous was the deterioration of traditional working-class institutions once the bedrock of Labourism: the co-operative movement, working-men's clubs, drinking houses, pubs, sporting pastimes, recreational pursuits and of course, mass membership of unions. The historian Eric Hobsbawm noted, 'Britain, the home of mass trade unionism, has clearly fallen behind some other countries'.[103] The cohesion of the working class, alongside the political self-confidence of the Labour movement, was imperilled. The 1984–85 Miner's

Strike proved pivotal. The miners, among the most well-organised sectors of industrial workers, were defeated. The attack on the mining industry and the debilitating experience of the strike provoked a debate about the long-term prospects for the Labour movement as an insurgent political force.

By the mid-1980s, the party's organisational structures appeared even more archaic. Labour was male dominated, obsessed with bureaucracy and administrative procedure, disconnected from communities it purported to represent. The parochial politics of 'heartland' industrial areas bred complacency and at worst, low-level corruption and clientelism at the municipal level. Stuart Hall was struck by 'the hierarchical nature of the movement: its reliance on formal organisational procedures, on hierarchies of command and communication, and on an exaggerated respect for office and position which is fundamentally at odds with its democratic character'. Above all, the mind-set of Labourism remained 'intrinsically statist – reforms will be brought from above by the state through experts for the working class'.[104]

In his influential essay on Labour's forward march, Eric Hobsbawm concluded, 'The development of the working class in the past generation has been such as to raise a number of very serious questions about its future and the future of its movement'.[105] The historian Ben Pimlott saw Hobsbawm as New Labour's 'founding father'.[106] Hobsbawm asked how the party should respond to the Labour movement's failure. Unions provided the Left with its political energy and moral purpose since the nineteenth century. As rising MPs, Blair and Brown participated in the post-mortem into the party's 1987 and 1992 defeats, although their views were presented in a cautious, carefully calibrated and often calculating fashion. Both were members of the *Tribune Group of MPs*, which elaborated plans for a mass membership party where trade union levy-payers became full members. The cause of party reform was advancing by the late 1980s. The power of the block vote was reduced. Members had greater say in parliamentary selections while policy-making procedures were less focused on conference motions and staid plebiscitary democracy. Labour was being reshaped by reformers under Neil Kinnock into a new model party. Yet its survival as a political movement in the twenty-first century was by no means guaranteed.

Declining post-war institutions

The further theme in Labourism's long-term degeneration was the acknowledgement that by the late-twentieth century, post-war social democratic institutions, including the British welfare state, were in abeyance. If organisations linked most closely to Labour were decaying, what did that say about the Left's future prospects? The criticism of the welfare state during the 1970s inevitably came from the radicalised New Right who believed that welfare expenditure bred a culture of dependency, undermining the productive capacity of the economy while 'crowding out' resources from the private sector. Anthony King referred to 'the overloaded state' as corporate socialism imposed ever-increasing burdens on government. King and

Crewe believed working-class voters were turning away from the totemic policies of nationalisation, high-welfare spending and central planning of the economy.

As a consequence, the attitude to the post-war Beveridge state from the *Left* grew more sceptical and questioning. By the late 1960s, criticisms of welfare-state social democracy began to emerge from the group of younger revisionist parliamentarians.[107] It was claimed that the Labour Party 'identifies itself too closely with the welfare state instituted in the immediate post-war period and has tended to adopt a relatively uncritical approach to it'. After 1945, the party embraced a position 'of trusting social service institutions and bureau professionals to create welfare. This would be very well if the institutions of the welfare state were worthy of staunch and unquestioning support. Unfortunately, they are not'.[108]

In the aftermath of the Second World War, social democrats believed continuous economic growth would permit painless redistribution. This optimism appeared increasingly questionable by the mid-1970s in the wake of the OPEC oil price shock, enforced IMF loan and public expenditure cuts. Meanwhile, Howard Glennerster and Julian Le Grand demonstrated welfare spending was being disproportionately allocated to middle-class households. The welfare state was not the engine of egalitarianism that British socialists had imagined. Courageously, Callaghan admitted in his 1976 lecture at Ruskin College, Oxford, that state education remained inadequate despite the comprehensive school revolution inaugurated by Crosland in the mid-1960s. Meanwhile, structural pressures on post-war institutions were growing. By the late 1970s, market capitalism across the Western world was in recession. Marxist scholars believed that Beveridge's model of social insurance was propping up the failing and dysfunctional system of western capitalism. Feminist writers highlighted the degree to which the welfare state prioritised male earners, reinforcing the dependence of women on the patriarchal family. Yet deindustrialisation ensured the labour market increasingly relied on the female workforce.

Intellectuals asked how the Left should respond to the decline of institutions at the heart of the post-war social democratic settlement? Was Labour's goal still to preserve the welfare state? Or should the Left overhaul the post-1945 social contract? As the 1980s unfolded, there was wide-ranging debate about the future of the welfare state. The Left began to reconsider its position on the relationship between government and markets. The emerging philosophy was known as 'market socialism'. In an influential collection of essays, *The Alternative: Politics for a Change* (1989), Le Grand suggested the traditional Beveridge model should be dismantled. Having acknowledged the limitations of post-war provision, government bureaucracies must offer voters 'wider choice wherever possible', adopting 'quasi-markets' in health and education where money follows the user.[109] It was striking that 'Labour's management of public housing', in particular, 'had developed within a framework of centralised bureaucracy and a tradition of Victorian paternalism' that was repellent to working-class voters.[110] Another shift in direction related to the feminisation of the welfare state. The welfare state was only productive and efficient if it met the needs of modern parents and families. It appeared the male breadwinner model was already in rapid decline.

At the forefront of this new thinking was the New Left in London which acquired control of the Greater London Council (GLC) in the early 1980s. Importantly, they advocated redefining the relationship between the individual citizen and the central state. John McDonnell, then GLC deputy leader, advocated the transformation of local government encouraging democratic participation rather than bureaucratic paternalism. Hilary Wainwright, a leading figure on the libertarian Left, believed policy-making must give a role to those 'directly affected', breaking with the 'objectifying positivism' of post-war administrative social policy.[111] The various streams of progressive thought that responded to the perceived crisis of social democratic institutions then had a decisive impact on New Labour.

Labour's historical failure as a governing party

The final theme of the debate about Labourism's predicament concerned the belief that Labour underperformed as a governing party in the twentieth century. While Labour enacted landmark reforms that enhanced working-class prosperity in the Attlee years, the general view was that it never evolved into a credible party of government. Labour's programme after 1945 altered fundamentally 'the framework of British social and economic institutions'. Yet Attlee's administration 'showed no interest in planning the economy . . . and lacked any long-term strategy for the future'.[112] The prevailing tone of discussion by the 1970s was disapproval towards those past administrations. Labour governments made significant errors, dashing the hopes of supporters and demoralising the Left. The 1964–70 administrations were the target of venomous criticism, as expectations that Wilson would lead a radical administration were confounded. The breach between Labour's promise and its perceived performance appeared vast.

The Marxist scholar Ralph Miliband insisted the disappointments of the period after 1945 were unsurprising. The party was operating within the framework of orthodox political institutions. Parliamentary democracy imposed insurmountable constraints on the achievement of socialism. Labour's accommodation with capitalism meant the party would end up frustrating the hopes of working-class socialists.[113] On the Right, the Oxford academic Philip Williams admitted that the post-war party became tactical and expedient under Wilson devoid of the ethical impulse that motivated the generation of Durbin, Dalton, Jay and Gaitskell.[114] Worst of all, Labour governments came to office unprepared, failing to appreciate 'the seriousness of the crisis of the British economy and the reality of Britain's decline as an international power'.[115]

It was the destruction of Labour's reputation for economic competence and its refusal to prioritise the goal of full employment that outraged the Left. Labour administrations all too often abandoned their principles in office, embroiled in unseemly compromises. New Labour's 'year zero' view of history, its tendency to disavow the past and its airbrushing of moderate leaders such as Wilson and

Callaghan were much lamented. Yet Blair and Brown's project reflected the historical awareness of Labour's past failures.[116] According to Matthew Taylor, a former Downing Street adviser, having experienced the 'gut-wrenching' defeat of 1992, the modernisers 'took it as read that Labour could not be elected unless they had completely eradicated any connection to the discredited party of the Winter of Discontent [of 1978–79] and the 1983 manifesto'.[117] The historical context for the decay of Labourism is fundamentally important, dealt with more expansively in the next chapter.

New Labour's response

So how effectively had the Labour Party by the mid-1990s addressed the protracted debate about Labourism's political atrophy? To what extent did the fundamental questions raised about the future of the Left help to forge New Labour's prospectus for power?

In addressing ideology, modernisers believed socialism's historic purpose centred on collective ownership of productive assets and the imperative of a planned economy was now obsolete. In redrafting Clause Four, it was emphasised that the primacy of nationalisation was outdated. Yet Blair and Brown still battled to define a compelling ideological rationale. Having swept aside the doctrines of twentieth-century socialism, New Labour was never entirely confident what to put in their place. Reformers made the claim that traditional socialism was withering and society was being transformed, making it discernibly harder for the Left to win. British society had been fundamentally altered since the 1940s. The sociologist Anthony Giddens wrote that in the aftermath of the Cold War, Britain was entering a 'brave new world'.[118]

As a consequence, modernisers acknowledged that the Labour Party was in crisis, doomed to defeat unless its political and electoral strategy was overhauled. The dominant images of Labour in the electorate's eyes were those of incompetence and failure. Even those who viewed it positively had a predominantly nostalgic view of the party. Future electoral viability meant coming to terms with Thatcherism. Furthermore, the status and esteem of manual industrial labour anchored in heartland industrial communities was eroding. Regardless of the incoming government's sympathy towards the legal rights of trade unions, this model of industrial organisation would not easily be rekindled. Nor would corporatism be reinstated following the economic management fiascos of the 1970s. New Labour did not sever its ties with the trade unions. Even so, the modernising leadership made clear that Labour governments would allow 'fairness' but 'not favours'.

In relation to declining post-war institutions, Labour sought to update its policies following the 1992 defeat by taking account of the perceived failure of 'tax and spend' policies. It is misleading to characterise New Labour's stance as replicating the ideology of Thatcherism. Even in the early 1970s, before Thatcher became Conservative leader, important figures on the Left began to reappraise the Beveridge settlement. By 1993, the Labour leader John Smith had established the Social Justice Commission (SJC) to reappraise the future direction of the welfare state and social security.

Finally, reformers insisted Labour must absorb lessons from its past performance as a governing party. In economic policy, Gordon Brown believed New Labour should learn from the errors of previous governments, while acknowledging the intellectual demise of the Keynesian settlement. The ideas that emerged from the prolonged debate about the atrophy of Labourism had a decisive impact in the framing of New Labour in the 1990s. Brown summarised the core postulates of the modernising prospectus to supplant corporatist social democracy:

- Tackling entrenched interests and unjust power that holds people back without instigating a war on capitalism.
- An enabling state offering new pathways out of poverty: 'the welfare state should not just be a safety net but a springboard'.
- A new constitutional settlement between individuals, communities and the state: 'to reinvent government we must first reconstruct the very idea of community'.
- A new economic egalitarianism that believes that citizen's potential, their human capital and their labour is the driving force of the modern economy.[119]

In Brown's account, there is barely any mention of restoring the power of organised labour. Nationalisation and public ownership were discarded. Brown ultimately appealed to the ethic of communitarian Christian socialism to underpin his ideological position: 'People do not live in isolation', he ventured. 'People do not live in markets. People live in communities. I think of Britain as a community of citizens with common needs, mutual interests, shared objectives, related goals, and most of all, linked destinies'.[120] *Marxism Today* supplied the sociological analysis to legitimise radically recasting British social democracy. Yet New Labour's political appeal simultaneously entailed reaching back to the tradition of Christian socialism. This was a potent yet perplexing synthesis that exacerbated Labour's intellectual incoherence and confusion, particularly over economic questions where revisionists, notably Gaitskell and Crosland, had been at their most audacious. Still, it is clear that influential strategies emerged from the inquiry into Labourism's long-term degeneration which then shaped and moulded New Labour's agenda.

Reinventing the Left: modernisation and reform

It is apparent that Labour's advance in the 1980s and early 1990s was not a straightforward path of accommodating Thatcherism. Neither was the party's evolution following an ineluctable, pre-determined trajectory. Having acknowledged Labourism's obsolescence, a series of strategic decisions led to institutional and policy change. Parliamentarians and party bureaucrats heralded new thinking responding to the transformation of British society. They were engaged in hard-headed and often penetrating reassessment of the Left's prospects. These actors set a new direction for the party, employing the tools of political discipline and the cult of strong leadership under Kinnock and Blair.[121] The party's activists became more supine and accommodating after initial defeats, influenced by important shifts in the intellectual climate and the currency of ideas. What emerged was a model of political thought and practice that marked a significant departure from traditional Labourism and the doctrine of post-war social democracy. The array of alternative strategies are elaborated in the final section of the chapter.

The progressive alliance from Lloyd George to Blair

The first strategy was to reassemble the progressive coalition that previously unified electoral support for the Left and centre-left in Britain. The concept of the progressive alliance originated in the late-nineteenth century. During the 1906 Liberal government, co-operation with Labour MPs led to its historic programme of social reform. Yet the pattern of British politics resulted in Labour replacing the Liberal Party as the dominant anti-Conservative force in the aftermath of the First World War. The breach between the parties created what the historian David Marquand labelled the 'progressive dilemma'.[122] The progressive dilemma had two components. The first was electoral. The Conservatives had won elections by default while dominating British politics as the Liberal and Left vote was divided. By the end of the First World War, the Edwardian progressive coalition was shattered. The Labour Party was ambitious, reflected in its more self-confident doctrinal commitment to socialism. The adoption of Clause Four imposed a 'clear dividing line', which meant 'liberals could not cross without becoming socialists, and renaming their liberalism'.[123] While leading Liberals joined Labour, many defected to Baldwin's Conservative Party, emphasising socialists and liberals were by no means natural allies. From the 1920s, Liberal politicians sided frequently with the Conservatives against the threat posed by socialism to the existing distribution of class privilege. While 'the governing assumptions of Edwardian progressivism lived on in Macdonald's Labour party', the 1931 crisis then widened the breach between socialism and liberalism. Labour opted for an uncompromising programme of state planning and nationalisation following the economic crash, while the stricken party was dominated by its industrial wing.[124] In these circumstances, it was at risk of becoming a Labourist trade union party 'rather than a broad people's party'.[125]

The second feature of the progressive dilemma was the deficit of ideas. The liberal intelligentsia rarely felt at ease in the Labour Party. Keynes disparaged the party's 'doctrinaire state socialism'. He concluded, 'The intellectual elements in the Labour party will never exercise adequate control'.[126] Keynes did not believe that 'class war or nationalisation is attractive or stimulating to modern minds'.[127] The party's intellectual outlook struggled to advance since its relationship with the intelligentsia was fractious, characterised by mutual distrust. Intellectuals dismissed its 'fanciful illusions', while the historical breach between Liberals and Labour persisted throughout the 1950s and 1960s. Labour was unable to bring 'middle-class minds' into its confidence, drawing on the thinking classes in devising a credible programme for government. There were exceptions, notably the accomplished translation of Keynesian theories into public policy during the late 1930s, alongside the party's adoption of the Beveridge report during the wartime coalition. In the mid-1960s, Thomas Balogh and Nicholas Kaldor had a decisive influence on the Wilson government's economic policy. Richard Titmuss, A.H. Halsey and Brian Abel-Smith shaped the new frontier of the British welfare state. Yet the ties between the party and intellectuals remained apprehensive and strained. The progressive dilemma was so acute that radical intellectuals outside the narrow milieu of revisionist social democracy were reluctant to work within the party. Labourism's intolerance of dissent and its insistence upon group loyalty were off-putting. Yet if they refused to assist Labour, the risk for progressives was perpetual Conservative rule.

Moreover, Labour's difficulty in converting socialism into a viable programme was illuminated by the pervasive contradiction illuminated by Peter Clarke's conception of mechanical and moral reform.[128] Clarke wrote that Labour's forebears in British liberalism were 'moral' reformers. They believed 'the engine of change . . . properly lay in the social purchase of ideas, as norms and motives, rather than in the expedient implementation of prescriptive programmes and policies'.[129] In the spirit of moral reform, citizens would shape politics through their deliberative engagement and participation in democratic life. The Fabian legacy, in contrast, emphasised the mechanical view of political and social change. The Webbs 'calculated how to get their hands on the right levers in order to give effect to their deeply-held convictions about policy'.[130] Labour governments were led by 'wirepullers' and 'technocrats' who believed that society resembled a giant machine manipulated by bureaucratic action from the centre.[131] The Fabians imagined 'major social problems could be solved by the attention of appointed experts acting at the Government's behest'.[132] This doctrine of high modernism was hardly unique to the Labour Party, permeating Britain's intellectual culture from the early-twentieth century.[133] Yet it had a particular purchase on the Left, and by the 1970s modernist ideas contributed to the perceived decay of Labourism and socialism.

For party reformers, the flow of new ideas into the party throughout the last century had been glaringly inadequate. Only at exceptional moments such as 1945 did the party succeed in designing a credible prospectus. The desire to socialise the economy through state nationalisation appeared to be a blind alley. Blair was convinced that Labour must create a progressive alliance uniting disparate strands of the Left and centre-left. His motives were both political and intellectual. Blair believed the decision to create an independent Labour Representation Committee (LRC) outside the Liberal Party in 1900 was 'a historic mistake. . . . By splitting Labour from other progressive forces, the decision ensured that the party was in office for a mere 23 years in the twentieth century, opening the way for Conservative domination'.[134] In the run up to 1997, Blair held talks with the leader of the Liberal Democrats, Paddy Ashdown. Even in the 1992 election, there was tacit endorsement of tactical voting between Labour and Liberal candidates. That informal arrangement reached its apotheosis in the historic defeat of the Conservatives five years later.

Meanwhile, in relation to ideas Labour advanced a constitutional reform agenda in co-operation with other progressive political forces. The programme was initially proposed under John Smith with contributions from leading public intellectuals including Raymond Plant and Paul Hirst. The leadership encouraged Liberals and non-aligned progressive thinkers to contribute to the embryonic debate about political and social reform. Perry Anderson, a leading Marxist intellectual, agreed that 'a condition of relative industrial revival in Britain is some political reorganisation, as the decline of the economy appears inseparable from the arrest of the state'.[135] A ferment of organisations emerged to promote pluralist socialism and the common progressive front in British politics. New Labour's strategy built on this two-pronged critique of Labourism that was elaborated by the progressive dilemma.

Winning a second term: the loyal and deferential party

The second of New Labour's strategies was relatively straightforward: securing re-election. New Labour's creed of 'national renewal' acknowledged the need for a governing agenda that prioritised the election of a second-term Labour administration. Labour's fundamental difficulty in the twentieth century had been its sporadic experience of power. It was never in office long enough to reset the public policy framework in Britain. Blair believed that the party failed to leave its mark on society and politics as it governed for only brief periods. For him, being re-elected meant the politics of 'safety first', refusing to offend Labour's fragile class coalition. During the late 1940s, Attlee's government rushed through a wave of reforms but ran out of steam, despite winning a landslide in 1945. There was a marked failure in the late 1940s to strengthen the party's political and institutional foundations. The prime minister's judgement about election timing had proved inadequate. Defeated in 1951, Labour spent the next decade in opposition. Wilson won a landslide majority in 1966, but within four years, the political advantage was squandered once again. As a result, the party lacked practical governing experience.

The principal goal of the Blair administration was to achieve re-election with a parliamentary majority large enough to govern for an entire second term. In a letter to party members in 1995, Blair wrote, 'We need more than one general election victory to achieve our mission. . . . We need an unprecedented second term in office'.[136] If Labour could hold office for at least a decade, it would disrupt the pattern of twentieth-century British politics, overcoming the debility of Labourism and the electoral dominance of the Conservative Party. And if the strategy succeeded, the Tories would be forced onto the defensive, compelled to rethink their own ideological direction.

To fulfil the aim of winning a second term, Labour had to resist an 'elaborate set of commitments' that was impossible to achieve within a single period of office.[137] It was essential that the party was not beholden to vested interests, as it was in the 1970s by its allies in the trade union movement. Corporatism, once the centrepiece of British Labourism, destroyed the party's reputation for economic competence. To win not just intermittently but often, New Labour believed it was vital to create a more loyal and deferential party.[138] This compliant Labour Party was maintained through managerialism and centralised control, enabling ministers to govern Britain efficiently. Furthermore, it was necessary for Blair's party to build a 'big tent' of supporters from across the class divide, an approach known among political strategists as 'triangulation'.

Triangulation: moral responsibility and social order

The most controversial of New Labour's strategies in response to the crisis of Labourism was the view that to win elections, the party must adopt the tactics of political triangulation. Triangulation is frequently understood as splitting the difference between Left and Right. Triangulation encourages the party's leader to pick fights with their own supporters on the Left, establishing an uncompromising position in the minds of centrist voters. Yet in practice, the Labour leadership believed triangulation meant invading political territory once held by its opponents on the Right. The Left was undermined and demoralised throughout the 1980s and 1990s. Labour fell into the trap of merely accepting the dominant paradigm of politics, where the Conservatives were ruthless but uncaring while Labour was portrayed as compassionate but incompetent. The leadership believed opponents could vilify them, depicting Labour as a soft-hearted tax-and-spend party weak on national security that lacked the resolve to take difficult decisions. Blair and Brown moved to shut down the vulnerable flanks in Labour's armoury.[139]

Obsessed with defending working-class institutions, the party in the 1960s and 1970s had vacated crucial political territory – particularly on crime, social disorder, moral responsibility and patriotism – then considered 'Tory' issues. The authoritarian populist tone of Thatcherism appealed to the aspirations and insecurities of British working-class voters. It was claimed that Britain was a country in which citizens did not feel 'safe on the streets'. Voters now demanded 'less tax and more law and order'.[140] The rise in lawlessness was blamed on a generation of feckless liberals. Among the most reviled by the authoritarian Right were the social workers who 'created a fog of excuses in which the muggers and burglars operate'.[141] In this climate, triangulation did not mean shallow compromise, repositioning issues as equidistant between Left and Right. Triangulation entailed the Left reclaiming agendas once monopolised by the Conservative

Party, shifting the axis of debate while redefining the terms of trade in British politics. As Labour leader, Blair explicitly acknowledged 'the immense strength of Conservative values . . . selectively appropriating both its rhetoric and its constituency'.[142] Even so, the price exacted by triangulation was the perception that Labour's ideals were being compromised.

The dilemmas of party modernisation: moral and mechanical reform

By the early 1990s, social democratic modernisation was taking shape in British politics, a consequence of the crisis of Labourism and the perceived failures of the Thatcher era. This conjuncture created the springboard for the New Labour project. However, the reform agenda in the party, a response to the manifest inadequacies of Labourism, was neither uncontested nor internally coherent leading to a number of contradictions and ambiguities that are examined further in subsequent chapters. The most glaring was the putative divide between 'mechanical' and 'moral' reform.[143] The rethinking instigated on the pages of *Marxism Today* and in other progressive outlets appeared to assume the Labour Party would serve as a convincing vehicle for moral reform.

Moral reformers believed in democratic participation and self-government. They were sceptical of the centralised state governance to which both the Left and revisionist social democrats adhered after 1945. Moral reformers advocated decentralisation to localities and provincial communities dispersed throughout Britain. Their view of human nature was optimistic, affirming the potential of citizens to transform society.[144] The moral reform tradition has its roots in the democratic republican strand of British socialism, linked to the political thought of Thomas Paine, John Stuart Mill and the Levellers. The moral reformer believes that social change stems 'from the free will, spontaneous endeavours and democratic efforts of citizens'.[145] The relevance of moral reform is captured in the striking turn towards constitutional and political change in the late 1980s. Scholars, including Hirst and Marquand, emphasised the importance of participatory and deliberative democracy, insisting economic revitalisation was only viable if power was decentralised and the state reorganised. It was vital to develop 'a stronger regional and territorial dimension to the politics of the Left'.[146] Moral reformers were less obviously focused on traditional egalitarianism, underlining the importance of fellowship, human dignity and community. Progressive change meant nurturing the consciousness of active citizens rather than imposing reform on a recalcitrant society.

Nevertheless, the principal tradition in the British Labour Party remained that of mechanical reform. Mechanical reformers were 'wirepullers' who believed political transformation meant harnessing the 'desiccated calculating machines' of centralised bureaucracy: technocratic institutions, the enlightened civil service, knowledge supplied by the social sciences. In gaining control of institutions, social democrats had acquired the instruments to build a fairer world.[147]

As Marquand puts it, 'The point of social democratic politics was to get back in the engine room and search for the levers'.[148] Yet mechanical reformers were pessimistic by temperament, believing citizens could not be trusted to achieve reform.[149] Wily politicians and experts wielding controls in Whitehall would enact social democracy, implementing policies to create a more efficient society. Mechanical reform was Fabian *etatisme* par excellence, characterising the social democracy advanced under Gaitskell and Wilson in the 1950s and 1960s.

The unbridgeable divide between moral and mechanical reform was the fault line running throughout the Labour Party's history. The Attlee governments epitomised the ethos of democratic collectivism. Yet there was continuity between the era of Attlee and Blair. New Labour's reforms implied 'both democracy and managerialism, the doctrine of individual rights and dirigisme, asymmetrical devolution and centralism'.[150] It was the ethic of mechanical reform that often prevailed, as discussion of Labour's record in subsequent chapters reveals. Another difficulty posed by co-operation with the Liberal Democrats, triangulation and 'big tent' politics was that Blair became increasingly estranged from his long-suffering party. He encouraged his portrayal as openly disparaging and dismissive of the Labour tradition. Blair's relationship with the Labour Party since initially being selected as a parliamentary candidate in 1982 remained ambivalent. As opposition leader, his approach entailed bursts of radicalism, particularly the audacious move to rewrite Clause Four. Yet the reform broke a long phase of prevarication and caution in New Labour's political management style. In contrast to the Gaitskell era, covert methods of manipulative managerialism were often preferred to direct confrontation. As a consequence, in government Blair appeared increasingly disconnected from trade union general secretaries and the Labour Party grassroots.[151]

Conclusion

This chapter showed that New Labour arose from the protracted inquiry into Labourism's degeneration three decades after the end of the Second World War. An extended post-mortem was carried out into the obsolescence of socialism and the party's political failure in the twentieth century. Labour's history cannot be understood by viewing New Labour myopically as the next instalment of Thatcherism. Ideas cultivated among progressively minded parliamentarians, journalists, intellectuals and scholars shaped the modernisation agenda throughout the 1980s and 1990s. This intellectual ecosystem emerged on the Left following revisionist social democracy's implosion during the Wilson/Callaghan era.

Labourism's demise meant modernisers had to rethink the party's approach to achieving power and governing in the post-industrial society. They outlined distinctive strategies – notably the progressive alliance, the focus on winning re-election through safety first and adopting triangulation to revise the party's programme while reclaiming territory from the Right. At the outset, New Labour professed to be radical. Yet it was perceived to become increasingly conservative.

Journals such as *Marxism Today* and *New Society* provided iconoclastic thinking. But as time went on, new ideas were often sidelined by the modernisers, particularly where they conflicted with the party's attachment to mechanical reform. It was claimed that there was only a single legitimate trajectory of modernisation. Moreover, critics on the Left believed the apocalyptic warnings of *Marxism Today* that Labourism was on its deathbed reinforced the party's intellectual paranoia and defensiveness, encouraging capitulation to the ideology and political economy of the New Right.

Even so, it is apparent that New Labour's rethinking went beyond tactical calculation in response to electoral pressures. The Blair and Brown leadership's efforts focused on political ideas. Their approach entailed re-imagining Labour's identity and political appeal in late-twentieth-century Britain. The British Left should no longer focus on the goal of state control but harness:

> The belief in the notion of action through the community, in the idea that individuals do not stand alone, and that it is not only morally right that we should think of ourselves in this way but that it is the most rational way to organise our lives.[152]

Labour's task was not to abandon the collective provision enshrined in the post-1945 welfare state 'but to refashion it so that real power is exercised by people and not by institutions or bureaucracies' – a prominent theme of the reformist Left.[153] The ultimate purpose was to apply that insight to radically recast Labour's programme distancing the party from the endemic failings of the traditionalists of 'Old' Labour, the central theme of the chapter that follows.

Notes

1 A. Sivanandan, 'All that Melts Into Air is Solid: The Hokum of New Times', *Race and Class*, Volume 31 (3), p. 1, 1989.
2 P. Clarke, *A Question of Leadership: From Gladstone to Thatcher*, p. 328, London: Penguin, 1991.
3 A. Gamble, 'Thatcher: The Second Coming', p. 18, *Marxism Today*, July 1983.
4 R. Desai, *Intellectuals and Socialism*, London: Lawrence & Wishart, 1991.
5 J. Cronin, *New Labour's Pasts: The Labour Party and Its Discontents*, pp. 7–8; H. Drucker, *Doctrine and Ethos in the Labour Party*, London: Harper Collins, 1979.
6 M. Kenny, *The First New Left: British Intellectuals After Stalin*, London: Lawrence and Wishart, 1995; M. Kenny, 'Habits of the Mind: *Marxism Today* and Today's Left', *Juncture*, Volume 18 (3), pp. 30–35, 2011.
7 A. McRobbie, 'Review: New Times: The Changing Face of Politics in the 1990s by S. Hall & M. Jacques', *Feminist Review*, Volume 36, Autumn 1990.
8 S. Hall, 'The Meaning of New Times', in S. Hall (ed.), *Selected Political Writings*, p. 248, Durham: Duke University Press, 2017.
9 A. McRobbie, 'Review: New Times: The Changing Face of Politics in the 1990s by S. Hall & M. Jacques'.
10 P. Allender, 'What's New About New Labour', *Politics*, Volume 21 (1), pp. 56–62, 2000.
11 See the interview with Martin Jacques: https://ippr.org/juncture/learning-the-lessons-of-marxism-today. Accessed 12th August 2019.

12 A. Gamble, 'The Great Divide', *Marxism Today*, 1981.
13 Cited in S. Aaronovitch, 'Interview with Neil Kinnock', p. 8, *Marxism Today*, June 1983.
14 A. McRobbie, 'Review: New Times: The Changing Face of Politics in the 1990s by S. Hall & M. Jacques'.
15 B. Schwartz, 'The Thatcher Years', *Socialist Register*, pp. 116–151, 1987.
16 M. Kenny, 'Habits of the Mind: *Marxism Today* and Today's Left', p. 130.
17 Cited in https://washingtonpost.com/archive/politics/1988/10/07/british-labor-searches-for-winning-formula/2d790156-ee53-4848-8691-9de5ad42d41d/?noredirect=on&utm_term=.5ee817d9871b. Accessed 14th December 2018.
18 A. Campsie, 'Socialism Will Never be the Same Again: Reimagining British Left-Wing Ideas for the "New Times"', Volume 31 (2), p. 169, 2017.
19 For instance, see S. Driver & L. Martell, *New Labour*; F. Faucher-King & P. Le Gales, *The New Labour Experiment*.
20 https://lrb.co.uk/v12/n01/ross-mckibbin/the-way-we-live-now. Accessed 11th November 2018.
21 R. Miliband, 'The New Revisionism in Britain', *New Left Review*, Volume 150, 1985.
22 M. Kenny, 'Habits of the Mind: *Marxism Today* and Today's Left', pp. 30–35.
23 J. Lawrence, *Me, Me, Me: The Search for Community in Post-War England*, Oxford: Oxford University Press, 2019.
24 T. Blair, 'Diary', *The London Review of Books*, Volume 9 (19), 29th October 1987.
25 S. Meredith, 'Labour Party Revisionism and Public Expenditure: Divisions of Social Democratic Political Economy in the 1970s', *Labour History Review*, Volume 70 (3), pp. 253–273, 2005.
26 T. Blair, 'Diary', *The London Review of Books*.
27 https://telegraph.co.uk/news/uknews/1521418/The-full-text-of-Tony-Blairs-letter-to-Michael-Foot-written-in-July-1982.html. Accessed 12th March 2018.
28 T. Blair, 'Lecture in Perth, Western Australia', p. 14.
29 G. Brown, 'Debate: Smaller Worlds', *Marxism Today*, pp. 37–38, November 1989.
30 G. Brown, 'Introduction: The Socialist Challenge', in G. Brown (ed.), *The Red Paper on Scotland*, Edinburgh: EUSPB, p. 8, 1975.
31 G. Brown (ed.), 'Introduction: The Socialist Challenge', p. 18.
32 *Marxism Today*, 'Special Issue: Wrong', November–December 1998.
33 https://ippr.org/juncture/learning-the-lessons-of-marxism-today. Accessed 12th September 2019.
34 R. Desai, *Intellectuals and Socialism*.
35 Interview with R. Plant, House of Lords, February 2015.
36 Cited in S. Fielding, *The Labour Governments 1964–70: The Labour Party and Cultural Change*, p. 195, Manchester: Manchester University Press, 2001.
37 K. Jeffreys, 'The Old Right', in R. Plant, M. Beech & K. Hickson (eds.), *The Struggle for Labour's Soul: Understanding Labour's Political Thought Since 1945*, p. 78, London: Routledge, 2004; Interview with G. Radice, House of Lords, 16th December 2014.
38 H. Pemberton, 'Relative Decline and British Economic Policy in the 1960s', *The Historical Journal*, Volume 47 (4), 2004.
39 S. Hall, 'The Meaning of New Times', in S. Hall (ed.), *Selected Political Writings*, Durham: Duke University Press, 2017.
40 R. Desai, *Intellectuals and Socialism*, p. 117.
41 D. Marquand, 'Inquest on a Movement', *Encounter*, p. 14, July 1979.
42 J. Davis & R. McWilliam (eds.), 'Introduction', *Labour and the Left in the 1980s*, p. 3, Manchester: Manchester University Press, 2018.
43 Cited in R. Desai, *Intellectuals and Socialism*, p. 2; P. Anderson, *English Questions*, p. 324, London: Verso, 1992.
44 R. Miliband, 'The New Revisionism in Britain'.
45 A. Gramsci, *Prison Notebooks*, p. 10, London: Lawrence & Wishart, 1971.
46 R. Desai, *Intellectuals and Socialism*.
47 R. Desai, *Intellectuals and Socialism*, p. 187.

48 R. Desai, *Intellectuals and Socialism*, p. 8.
49 E. Durbin, *New Jerusalem: The Labour Party and the Economics of Democratic Socialism*, p. 4, London: Routledge & Keegan Paul, 1985.
50 D. Marquand, 'Inquest on a Movement', *Encounter*, pp. 8–17, July 1979.
51 D. Marquand, 'Inquest on a Movement', p. 9.
52 J. Grahl, 'The Liberal Revolutionary', p. 18, *Marxism Today*, June 1983.
53 E. Durbin, *New Jerusalem: The Labour Party and the Economics of Democratic Socialism*, p. 7; B. Pimlott, *Labour and the Left in the 1930s*, Cambridge: Cambridge University Press, 1978.
54 R. Desai, *Intellectuals and Socialism*.
55 S. Fielding, *The Labour Party: Continuity and Change in the Making of 'New' Labour*.
56 B. Harrison, 'The Centrist Theme in Modern British Politics', in *Peaceable Kingdom: Stability and Change in Modern Britain*, Oxford: Oxford University Press, p. 374, 1982.
57 E. Durbin, *The Politics of Democratic Socialism*, p. 321, London: Routledge, 1940.
58 M. Francis, *Ideas and Policies Under Labour 1945–1951: Building a New Britain*, Manchester: Manchester University Press, 1997.
59 M. Pugh, *Speak for Britain! A New History of the Labour Party*, London: Vintage, 2015.
60 A. Reid, *A Short History of the Labour Party*, Basingstoke: Palgrave Macmillan, 2015.
61 R.H.S. Crossman, *New Fabian Essays*, London: Fabian Society, 1952.
62 T. Judt, *Socialism in Provenance 1871–1914: A Study in the Origins of the Modern French Left*, p. 236, Cambridge: Cambridge University Press, 1979.
63 G. Hodgson, 'Overstating the State', p. 19, *Marxism Today*, July 1984.
64 T. Blair, *A Journey*, London: Random House, 2010.
65 T. Blair, 'Forging a New Agenda', *Marxism Today*, 1991.
66 G. Brown, 'Debate: Smaller Worlds'.
67 T. Blair, 'Social-ism', Fabian Tract 565, p. 4, London: The Fabian Society, 1995.
68 G. Brown & T. Wright, *Values, Visions and Voices: An Anthology of Socialism*, Edinburgh: Mainstream Press, 1995.
69 M. Oakeshott, *Rationalism in Politics and Other Essays*, p. 347, New York: Liberty Fund, 2010.
70 S. Driver & L. Martell, 'New Labour's Communitarianisms', *Critical Social Policy*, Volume 17 (52), pp. 26–42, 1997; S. Hale, 'The Communitarian Philosophy of New Labour', in S. Hale, W. Leggett & L. Martell (eds.), *The Third Way and Beyond: Criticisms, Alternatives, Futures*, Manchester: Manchester University Press, 1998; W. Kymlicka, 'Liberalism and Communitarianism', *Canadian Journal of Philosophy*, pp. 181–203, Volume 18 (2), 1988; E. Frazer, *The Problems of Communitarian Politics: Unity and Conflict*, London: Routledge, 1999.
71 G. Mulgan (ed.), *Life After Politics*, London: Fontana Press, 1997.
72 P. Clarke, *A Question of Leadership: From Gladstone to Thatcher*, p. 279.
73 M. Jacques & S. Hall (eds.), *The Changing Face of Politics: New Times*, p. 11.
74 P. Hirst, *After Thatcher*, London: Harper Collins, 1989.
75 R. Murray, 'Benetton Britain: The New Economic Order', *Marxism Today*, p. 29, November 1985.
76 B. Rowthorn, 'The Past Strikes Back', *Marxism Today*, 6th January 1982.
77 A. Gamble, 'Thatcher: The Second Coming', p. 13.
78 J. Tomlinson, *Managing the Economy, Managing the People*, Oxford: Oxford University Press, 2015.
79 T. Lane, 'The Unions: Caught on the Ebb Tide', *Marxism Today*, p. 9, April 1982.
80 C. Leadbeater, 'The State of the Movement', *Marxism Today*, September 1986.
81 W. Brown, 'Industrial Relations in Britain under New Labour', 1997–2010: A Post-Mortem', *Journal of Industrial Relations*, 2011.
82 R. Murray, 'Benetton Britain: The New Economic Order'.
83 D. Miliband (ed.), 'Introduction', in *Reinventing the Left*, p. 1, Cambridge: Polity, 1994.
84 E. Laclau & C. Mouffe, 'Socialist Strategy: Where Next?', *Marxism Today*, p. 17, January 1981.

85   T. Blair, 'Diary', *The London Review of Books*.
86   S. Hall, 'The Culture Gap', *Marxism Today*, p. 18, January 1984.
87   Source: IFF Post-Election Survey, 19th November 1987, The Kinnock Archive, Churchill College, Cambridge.
88   M. Jacques & S. Hall (eds.), *The Changing Face of Politics: New Times*.
89   A. McRobbie, 'Review: New Times: The Changing Face of Politics in the 1990s by S. Hall & M. Jacques'.
90   G. McLennen, 'Class Conundrum', p. 30, *Marxism Today*, May 1984.
91   M. Kenny, 'After the Deluge: Politics and Civil Society in the Wake of the New Right', *Soundings*, Issue 4, pp. 13–26, 1996; M. Kenny, *The First New Left*.
92   M. Pugh, *Speak for Britain! A New History of the Labour Party*, p. 514.
93   S. Hall, 'A Long Hall', *Marxism Today*, p. 6, November 1982.
94   A. Gamble, 'The Rise and Rise of the SDP', *Marxism Today*, p. 9, January 1982.
95   Cited in S. Hall, 'A Long Hall', p. 6.
96   T. Blair, 'Power for a Purpose', *Renewal*, Volume 3 (4), pp. 11–16, 1995.
97   A. Gamble, 'The Great Divide'.
98   J. Curtice, R. Jowell & T. Heath, *Labour's Last Chance: The 1992 Election and Beyond*, London: Dartmouth, 1992.
99   D. Massey, 'The Contours of Victory: Dimensions of Defeat', p. 18, *Marxism Today*, July 1983.
100   T. Blair, 'Diary', *The London Review of Books*.
101   P. Ashdown, *The Ashdown Diaries 1988–1997*, London: Penguin, 2001.
102   'Interim Report of the Sub-Committee on Party Organisation', *Labour Party Annual Conference Report 1955*, p. 65, cited in S. Fielding, *The Labour Party: Socialism and Society Since 1951*, Manchester: Manchester University Press, 1997.
103   E. Hobsbawm, 'The Forward March of Labour Halted', *Marxism Today*, p. 285, October 1978.
104   S. Hall, 'A Long Hall', p. 10.
105   E. Hobsbawm, 'The Forward March of Labour Halted', p. 286.
106   Cited in R.J. Evans, *Eric Hobsbawm: A Life in History*, p. 522. According to Richard Evans, Hobsbawm was to be offered a knighthood by Tony Blair after the 1997 election, but Hobsbawm made clear he would refuse such preferment. Hobsbawm eventually accepted the Companion of Honour (CH).
107   D. Marquand, J. Mackintosh & D. Owen, 'Change Gear! Towards a Socialist Strategy', *Socialist Commentary*, 1967.
108   A. Walker, 'Why We Need a Social Strategy', *Marxism Today*, p. 29, September 1982.
109   B. Pimlott, A. Wright & T. Flower (eds.), *The Alternative: Politics for a Change*, p. 121, London: WH Allen, 1990.
110   D. Griffiths & C. Holmes, 'To Buy or Not to Buy? Is That the Question?', p. 9, *Marxism Today*, May 1984.
111   H. Wainwright, *Labour: A Tale of Two Parties*, p. 100, London: Hogarth Press, 1987; R. Desai, *The Intellectuals and Socialism*, p. 192.
112   E. Hobsbawm, 'Past Imperfect, Future Tense', *Marxism Today*, p. 15, October 1986.
113   R. Miliband, *Parliamentary Socialism: A Study in the Politics of Labour*, London: Merlin Press, 1969.
114   P. Williams, *Hugh Gaitskell: A Political Biography*, London: Jonathan Cape, 1979.
115   E. Hobsbawm, 'Past Imperfect, Future Tense'.
116   See J. Cronin, *New Labour's Pasts: The Labour Party and Its Discontents*.
117   Cited in E. Shaw, 'Retrieving or Re-Imagining the Past', in J. Davis & R. McWilliam (eds.), *Labour and the Left in the 1980s*, p. 27, Manchester: Manchester University Press, 2018.
118   In D. Miliband (ed.), *Reinventing the Left*.
119   G. Brown, 'The Politics of Potential', p. 114, in D. Miliband (ed.), *Reinventing the Left*.
120   Cited in G. Foote, *The Labour Party's Political Thought*, p. 343; G. Brown, *Constitutional Change and the Future of Britain*, pp. 6–7, London: Charter 88 Trust, 1992.

121 Interview, Rt. Hon. Charles Clarke, former Secretary of State for Education and Skills, November 2019.

122 D. Marquand, *The Progressive Dilemma*.

123 A. Thorpe, cited in P. Sloman, 'Partners in Progress? British Liberals and the Labour Party since 1918', *Political Studies Review*, Volume 12 (1), p. 43, 2014.

124 P. Sloman, 'Partners in Progress? British Liberals and the Labour Party Since 1918'.

125 A. Gamble, 'The Rise and Rise of the SDP', p. 7.

126 Cited in R. Desai, *Intellectuals and Socialism*, p. 5.

127 P. Clarke, *Keynes: The Twentieth Century's Most Influential Economist*, p. 68, London: Bloomsbury, 2009.

128 P. Clarke, *Liberals and Social Democrats*, Cambridge: Cambridge University Press, 1978.

129 P. Clarke, *Liberals and Social Democrats*, p. 8.

130 P. Clarke, *Liberals and Social Democrats*, p. 14.

131 D. Marquand, *The Progressive Dilemma*.

132 G. Hodgson, 'Overstating the State', p. 20.

133 R. Skidelsky, *John Maynard Keynes: Economist, Philosopher, Statesman*, London: Penguin, 2003.

134 P. Riddell, *The Unfulfilled Prime Minister*, p. 206.

135 P. Anderson, *English Questions*, p. 351.

136 Cited in T. Blair, *New Britain*, p. 56, London: Fourth Estate.

137 J. Cronin, *New Labour's Pasts: The Labour Party and Its Discontents*.

138 J. Cronin, *New Labour's Pasts: The Labour Party and Its Discontents*.

139 A. Gamble, 'New Labour and Political Change', *Parliamentary Affairs*, Volume 63 (4), pp. 639–651, 2010.

140 P. Riddell, *The Thatcher Government*, p. 193, London: Martin Robertson and Co, 1985.

141 P. Riddell, *The Thatcher Legacy*, p. 171, Oxford: Basil Blackwell, 1989.

142 P. Clarke, *A Question of Leadership: From Gladstone to Thatcher*, p. 330.

143 The concept of the fault line between 'moral' and 'mechanical' reform, between democratic republicanism and democratic collectivism, was initially examined in Peter Clarke's *Liberals and Social Democrats* and W.H. Greenleaf's *The British Political Tradition: The Rise of Collectivism Volume I*, London: Routledge, 1983. Greenleaf argued that the putative conflict between 'collectivism' and 'libertarianism' was the key division of ideas in British politics. The theme of collectivism and republicanism arises too in D. Marquand, *Britain Since 1918: The Strange Career of British Democracy*, London: Weidenfeld & Nicolson, 2009.

144 P. Clarke, *Liberals and Social Democrats*, pp. 5–6.

145 P. Clarke, *Liberals and Social Democrats*, p. 15.

146 M. Rustin, 'Power to the Provinces!', p. 31, *Marxism Today*, January 1983.

147 D. Marquand, *Britain Since 1918: The Strange Career of British Democracy*, p. 34.

148 D. Marquand, *The Unprincipled Society*, p. 9.

149 P. Clarke, *Liberals and Social Democrats*, p. 15.

150 K. Morgan, *Ages of Reform: Dawns and Downfalls of the British Left*, p. 76, London: IB Tauris, 2013.

151 P. Riddell, *The Unfulfilled Prime Minister*, p. 206.

152 T. Blair, 'Diary', *The London Review of Books*.

153 T. Blair, 'Diary', *The London Review of Books*.

3

HISTORICAL ROOTS

Conscience and class in British politics

The tradition of all dead generations weighs like a nightmare on the brain of the living.
                                                                    Karl Marx[1]

The Labour party has been peculiarly disabled . . . because so many of its own members have written off its history. Thatcherism was in practice distinctly vulnerable to attack – but not from a party that denied its own past. . . . If an ideological alternative to the Conservative Government is to be made acceptable to the electorate, both folk memory and the Labour party will have to change their minds about the 1964 and 1974 governments. . . . The Labour party has committed the cardinal rhetorical error of any political party, by apologising for its own past.
                                                                    Ross McKibbin[2]

Introduction

The Labour Party was acutely aware of its failings in office. Indeed New Labour felt compelled to apologise for its past. Although in the Attlee era, practical social-ism improved the relative prosperity and welfare of the working class, there was suspicion that even then Labour underperformed as a party of government. Over time, the prevailing tone of discussion on Left *and* Right was embarrassment over the party's egregious incompetence. Labour administrations confounded the hopes of supporters. They seemed doomed to disappoint. The alleged betray-als primarily lay in economic policy: drastic cuts in welfare expenditure accom-panied by the failure to prioritise full employment. What dismayed the Left was the suspicion that ministers abandoned their principles cynically for the pres-tige of holding office. This outlook allegedly degenerated into an unsavoury politics of accommodation and serial pragmatism. In the climate of discord after 1979, the Labour establishment was judged to be ineffectual and incompetent as well as expedient. The party became haunted by the images of political and governmental failure, decisively shaping New Labour's identity and strategy.[3]

This chapter aims to reconstruct the historical interpretation of 'Old' Labour that underpinned 'New' Labour as a political project, scrutinising relevant speeches, policy papers, memoirs, diaries and documents. It was the antagonism to Old Labour's perceived ideology and political culture rather than Thatcherism that provided the seedbed for New Labour. The importance of rhetoric in the political narratives of 'modernisation' is noted elsewhere.[4] This chapter examines the rhetorical framing of Old Labour by the modernisers alongside the historical understanding Blair's party derived from the past as it advanced political ideas.

Old Labour/New Labour and the lessons of history

The fundamental argument of the chapter is that New Labour was constructed in diametric opposition to Old Labour, premised on the irreparable divide between traditionalists and modernisers. Blair, Brown and their followers saw the party's inheritance of post-war Labourism as disastrous. They distanced Labour from everything that went before. Indeed, 'there were times when it seemed there was nothing in Labour's past from which New Labour did not want to disassociate itself'.[5] The portrayal of *Old* Labour in opposition to *New* Labour was far more than a superficial presentational tactic.[6] The modernisers believed Old Labour was synonymous with failure and defeat. Trade unions, Labour local government, the era of Wilson and Callaghan, and the Winter of Discontent symbolised the party's demise. Old Labour referred to beer and sandwiches with trade union barons in Downing Street, the cloth cap, old-style municipal local authorities, industrial militancy, faceless public bureaucrats and singing the red flag at annual conferences. New Labour's appeal to modernity, the future and the national interest supplanted the culture of proletarianism, union dominance and working-class sectarianism. New Labour was the party of national purpose rather than class struggle. Its identity meant 'the rejection of the past'.[7]

As such, Old Labour was everything that occurred before 1983, except the Attlee years. New Labour, the organising framework for Blair's modernisation of the party, was predicated on renouncing the errors of 'Old' Labour: not merely its programmes and policies, but its doctrine, its ethos, its rhetoric, its style of politics and its institutions. On the face of it, the party's structures and practice had remained largely unchanged since the 1930s.[8] Blair broke out 'in a rash at the thought of being lumped with the failures of Labour's past. . . . He hates losers, hates impotence, hates meaningless protest'.[9] New Labour carried out a virtual 'Kulturkampf', a 'cultural struggle' designed to eradicate the last vestiges of Old Labour from popular political memory.[10] Old Labour was a category manufactured for public consumption, 'the centrepiece of a past that was constructed and imagined for political purposes'.[11]

Their rejection of what went before applied to the Right of the party as much as the Left, given the perceived incompetence of *every* Labour government since

Attlee. Blair's repudiation of Wilson and Callaghan was as vehement as his dismissal of Michael Foot and Tony Benn. A former adviser insists that Blair 'put as much distance as possible between New Labour and its perceived failed past of economic mismanagement, of picking "winners", of incomes policies and of excessively powerful trade unions'.[12] Blair told the 2005 party conference:

> The seeds of 18 years of opposition were not sown in 1979, but in the 1960s . . . instead of understanding we were simply being tested by the forces of change, we lived out a sad episode of charges of betrayal, questioning integrity and motives.[13]

Comprehending the New Labour project meant 'understanding the psychological imprint [of Old Labour] on the minds of Tony and Gordon, of what they saw as their political inheritance'.[14] Paraphrasing the Irish novelist James Joyce, Blair and Brown came to view Labour's history in the twentieth century as a nightmare from which they were trying to awake.[15]

This negative portrayal meant Blair pointedly refused to associate his political strategy with the post-war revisionists who similarly battled to remake the party in an era of rapid economic and social transformation. This distancing was advanced despite obvious affinities with New Labour, particularly during Gaitskell's leadership. Published before the 1997 election, Peter Mandelson and Roger Liddle's *Blair Revolution* sought to elaborate New Labour's programme in government. Yet the book mentions Gaitskell once, giving little attention to revisionist ideas. Even the previous generation of modernisers were considered politically undesirable. Mandelson and Liddle believed Croslandite social democracy was moribund, declaring that to proffer 'yesterday's solutions to today's problems is not just negligent but facile'.[16] The breach between Old and New Labour meant modernisers neglected important traditions of economic and social thought, as revisionist social democracy was consigned to the historical scrapheap. As one observer concluded, 'The reinvention of the party during the 1990s was impatient of sentimental attachments to Labour's heritage, most particularly when these impinged on party structures, or approaches to policy'.[17]

As such, the New Labour agenda was a decisive response to the legacy of electoral and ideological decline. Mandelson's mission 'was about more than making New Labour electable. It has also been about learning the lessons of the past . . . to ensure that Labour succeeds in government next time'.[18] For Blair, 'a party that neglects the past is doomed to fail'.[19] The only exception in the grim depiction of past catastrophes was the legacy of 1945. Blair gave a noteworthy lecture about the Attlee governments' legacy, envisaging a line of progressive descent since the post-war era. He declared, 'In 1945, as now, we faced enormous changes in the global economy. . . . Then, as now, Labour spoke for the national interest and offered hope for the future'. Embracing the Attlee inheritance, Blair proclaimed, 'Britain needed rebuilding and the voters turned to Labour to take on that task'.[20] As such, New Labour 'sought to define and defend its novelty by constructing its own version of the history of the party'.[21] Blair insisted the post-1945 administration was 'the greatest peacetime government this century'. After the war, the party became 'the voice of the nation'. Attlee's administrations were portrayed as unashamedly heroic and patriotic. They embodied a conception of British national identity that resonated with the working-class electorate who experienced the adversities of a long war, while acknowledging the prevailing insecurities of the professional middle class. Similarly, Blair maintained that New Labour's purpose was to forge an enduring cross-class coalition in late-twentieth-century Britain.

In contrast, New Labour perceived the 1970s as a decade of unremitting political and economic deterioration. Even if recent accounts offer a more subtle perspective of advancing towards equality and social liberalisation, New Labour saw the 1970s as the nadir of the British Left's fortunes – the epitome of Old Labour's failed legacy.[22] Throughout the twentieth century, Old Labour policies were perceived as dogmatic and ill thought through. They reeked of incompetence and ineptitude. Nevertheless, while New Labour was resolute in expunging all traces of Old Labour from the modern party, there were unquestionably continuities with Attlee, Wilson, Callaghan and the party of Neil Kinnock and John Smith. Even Philip Gould, Blair's political strategist, believed that the revisionists of the 1950s 'were the first modernising tendency in the party. . . . The language used by Gaitskell in public and others in private is uncannily similar to that used by Tony Blair and other modernisers a generation later'.[23] Yet Gould's was a rare acknowledgement of the shared ideological heritage.

Labour's past legacies

The party's inheritance decisively shaped New Labour's programme, particularly the experience of defeat alongside the traumatic degeneration that followed losing office. If Labour was to recover electability, 'it needed to separate itself from the disastrously negative perceptions of the performance of previous Labour governments'.[24] For Blair and his entourage, there were a series of historical controversies that defined Old Labour's legacy. The first controversy was recurrent electoral failure. The second controversy was mismanagement of the economy. The third controversy was the centralised British state and constitutional conservatism. The final controversy was Labour's view of Britain's world role. The remainder of the chapter considers each controversy in turn.

Electoral failure

Blair's party was unusual in rejecting the optimistic assumptions that shaped the British Left's outlook since the First World War. Old Labour's belief in the forward march of the British working class was refuted. The British economy was no longer dominated by heavy industry. The solidarity of male manual labour was vanishing from the world of work. The self-confidence of the British working class dissipated following the brutal defeats of the 1970s and 1980s, culminating in the Miner's Strike in 1984–85 (Photo 3.1). Labour's electoral vulnerability was underlined by the fact that even in 1945, 'it took two world wars and the most serious economic crisis that industrial capitalism had ever experienced before a Labour government was elected with a workable majority'.[25] Blair's followers rejected Old Labour's 'complacent illusions'.[26] They believed that traditional political identities were being reshaped by the growing salience of immigration and ethnicity in British politics, divisions over national identity that threatened popular conceptions of Britishness, the gender gap in voting, alongside the party's tenuous geographical foothold in England outside its industrial heartlands.

For the modernisers, the 1992 election result was symptomatic of Labour's decline. The party was expected to emerge triumphant. Instead, Labour lost heavily, achieving a lower share of the popular vote than in 1979. The 1992 defeat was another reminder of the party's long-term electoral decomposition, beginning with the Attlee government's ejection from office in 1951. The defeat of the post-war administrations underlined the difficulties Labour faced since the 1920s, particularly its struggle to build an effective alliance embracing the progressively minded middle class with the industrial working-class 'heartlands'

PHOTO 3.1 The Miner's Strike in 1984–85

Source: Photo by Peter Skingley/Bride Lane Library/Popperfoto/Getty Images

in Northern England, the South Wales valleys and the central belt of Scotland. The party's reputation for governing ineptitude, internal division and sectarian discord inflicted inestimable damage on Labour's standing in the country.

The rejection of the Attlee years

Although Blair and Brown admired Attlee's achievements, they believed the post-war government committed serious political errors that epitomised Old Labour's weakness.[27] The critical lesson of the Attlee years was the party's inability to capitalise on its enormous majority in 1945.[28] The relapse into 'consolidation' of the nationalisation programme and insensitivity to voters' impatience with rationing and austerity paved the way for Conservative recovery. During the 1945 campaign, Attlee proclaimed, 'The Labour party is a Socialist Party, and proud of it'.[29] The government's aim was to overhaul the economic and social structure of Britain, converting the British people to democratic socialism. Yet within three years according to the *New Statesman*, 'The plain truth is that the Labour party is reaching the end of the road which it first set itself to traverse in 1918, and then mapped out in full detail in *Let Us Face the Future*'.[30] Exhaustion made Labour's defeat in 1951 appear, in retrospect, all but inevitable.

The cabinet minister, Richard Crossman, believed Attlee's government made fundamental mistakes that typified Old Labour's political vulnerabilities, ensuring it was out of power within six years. The party failed to adequately prepare for government while its 1945 programme heavily relied on the policies of the wartime coalition. The particular vulnerability was the struggle to determine how the Left should advance the planned economy. Labour lacked clear policies to improve industrial efficiency. It had no robust solution to the problem of controlling wages while preventing an inflationary spiral following trade union opposition to incomes policies. Nationalisation grew more unpopular with working-class voters during the late 1940s. Hugh Gaitskell declared Labour's 'doctrinaire belief in public ownership' to be a 'vote loser'.[31] By 1950, there was overt hostility to rationing and controls. The post-war governments created socialist institutions but failed to take 'the next step' of enabling citizens 'to run the old and new institutions of our society, participating at all levels as active members – workers, consumers, citizens – of an active democracy . . . full employment, a rising standard of life, social justice and equality of opportunity for individuals to fulfil all their great and as yet untapped capacities'.[32] As such, the roots of British socialism remained shallow.

Crossman believed that Attlee's party understood its role as brokering political consensus. The welfare state sought to dilute working-class grievances, bringing the trade unions closer to Whitehall.[33] As such:

> Attlee's socialism operated against the backdrop of a much more deferential society, preserving intact many hierarchies and inequalities that were, by the time of his death in 1967, already beginning to seem questionable,

whether in the family, schooling, the universities, the House of Lords, the civil service, the military, the management of industry, or come to that, the leadership of the trade unions.[34]

In these circumstances, did Labour have the appetite to become a party of radical reform? It was little wonder the *New Statesman* concluded Attlee's government 'contributed almost nothing new or imaginative to the pool of ideas with which men seek to illuminate human nature and its environment'.[35] Throughout the history of the British Left, 'there can seldom have been an administration so conservative in its solicitude for the stuffier constitutional conventions, so instinctively suspicious of all suggestions for popular political participation'.[36]

In 1951, a prominent Constituency Labour Party (CLP) newsletter naively predicted that the British electorate would be:

> glad to return to the Socialist planning now interrupted, which has saved and revived this country, and will turn again with relief to the policy of social justice which is implicit in Labour principles. . . . This Tory night can only be brief. With the first light of dawn, they and their misdeeds will vanish.[37]

Yet the Conservatives governed Britain for the next thirteen years. Attlee was judged to be an incompetent party manager. The government failed to maintain its constructive relationship with organised labour. The party's campaign machinery atrophied. As a consequence, Labour was ill prepared to fight the election in 1950 and 1951. Little consideration had been given to generating political ideas. The party lacked a credible forward programme. The mantra of 'consolidation' proved inadequate. While the loss of Labour's majority in 1951 stunned the party, defeat underlined the relatively narrow coalition which enabled Labour's landslide victory six years before. In the prosperous suburbs of the English cities and provincial towns, Old Labour's rhetoric of capitalist oppression and the demonology of cowards and traitors scarcely enthused the white-collar middle class. Labour never assembled the breadth of social and geographical support that elected the Liberal-led progressive alliance in 1906.

Since the 1920s, the party struggled to forge a viable electoral coalition which set the frame for Old Labour's subsequent defeats. The party's base was confined to the industrial regions, where coal, steel, textile production, the railways and shipbuilding dominated. Middle-class recruits were few. Those in the professional classes who joined Labour were either the remnants of the suffragette movement or World War One pacifists. Ramsay MacDonald sought to remake the party as a force for reformism rather than class struggle. Yet only in the late 1930s when the moderate unions began to assert their influence, led by the formidable personality of Ernest Bevin, did Labour's fortunes begin to improve.[38] Even Attlee's party had limited reach in non-Labour Britain, a verdict not lost on Blair's generation of modernisers.

While Old Labour insisted public ownership and statism had deep support across society, the playwright Dennis Potter remarked in the 1950s that social-ism spoke 'a language remote from almost everything except the memories of the thirties, meaningless as these might be to the post-war generations'.[39] As one revisionist noted, 'The youngest one-third of voters in 1959 had no recollection of the Conservatives' pre-war days. . . . Traditionalism in Britain is no monopoly of the right'. The party was becoming 'the most conservative and fundamen-talist in the world', a position from which it could not hope to win elections.[40] An editorial in *Socialist Commentary* in the aftermath of the 1951 defeat declared, 'Socialists must now devote at least part of their efforts to examining what is needed for creating not only an equal society, but a good and rich one'.[41]

Blair's party did not entirely reject Attlee's legacy in the 1990s. They wel-comed the fact that the post-war administration differed from the Old Labour governments of the 1960s and 1970s. Ministers were viewed as patriotic, com-fortable in espousing British national identity. The liberal intellectuals Keynes and Beveridge were skilfully co-opted by Labour, underlining the vitality of the progressive coalition. Yet Labour was defeated after only six years, having won a landslide in 1945. The appeal to the middle class was limited, failure to reform Whitehall's institutions had catastrophic consequences, while the party's elec-toral machine was allowed to implode. The modernisers still viewed the Attlee era as integral to Old Labour's inept inheritance.

Misinterpreting the affluent society

Yet it was the 1959 election that was among the party's most traumatic defeats, one of three consecutive losses that exemplified Old Labour's electoral vulner-ability. The result underlined the party's protracted struggle to come to terms with affluence and the social changes of the post-war decades. For New Labour, the pattern of politics in the late 1950s prefigured the troubling experience of the 1980s. Philip Gould referred to Labour's inability to deal with the material prosperity and affluence of the 1950s in his celebrated tract, *The Unfinished Revo-lution*.[42] Blair addressed Labour's struggle to understand the rise of consumerism in his memoir, *A Journey*.[43] For that reason, it is worth dwelling at some length on the experience of that decade.

The Tories fought the 1959 election adopting the slogan 'Life is better with the Conservatives, don't let Labour ruin it'. The British economy was enjoying the long phase of post-war expansion. Gaitskell fought to project Labour as a modern and dynamic party, focusing on the issue of pensions; the rising cost of living; the NHS; education, particularly the commitment to abolish the 11-plus exam; and housing, notably the case for rent controls.[44] The party's manifesto proclaimed only the wealthy in Britain had 'never had it so good'.[45] Labour promised 'a clear policy based on the ethical principles of socialism'. Yet the campaign misfired badly. Gaitskell promised not to raise income tax, despite the party's manifesto pledging to increase spending on pensions. On tax Labour recognised that 'politicians preaching pessimism about the long-term, amidst plenty in the short-term, don't succeed'.[46] As a result, it was easy to claim that Labour's figures did not add up. Gaitskell's tax commitments gave the Conservatives 'an opening to challenge not only the financial policy of the party but the integrity of the leadership'.[47] Labour was immediately thrown onto the defensive. More generally, as Lawrence Black remarked, 'Affluence had made quality and choice central issues, but Labour found the development of acquisitive materialism unsettling'.[48] The party felt compelled to increase welfare spending, but in the affluent society it was under pressure to cut taxes.

Meanwhile, during Gaitskell's leadership British society was being reshaped, throwing Old Labour's world-view into disarray. Rising incomes led to a sharp increase in personal consumption from 1951 to 1959. The growth in living standards was greater than throughout the inter-war years from 1918 to 1939. Working-class voters began to identify as middle class, exhibiting weaker attachment to Labour as the proletarian party. The rise of disruptive technologies and the expansion of the manufacturing and service sector at the expense of heavy industry undermined manual labour's status, alongside the associated symbols and class identities of Labourism.[49]

The 1959 result was a turning point in British politics, 'a political watershed' compelling each of the main parties to address the incipient rise of affluence.[50] Television played a major role for the first time: in 1959, 61 per cent of voters watched a party political broadcast compared to only 33 per cent in 1955.[51] The Conservative leader, Harold Macmillan, was an accomplished television performer. Newspapers remained influential. According to an editorial in the *Daily Mail*:

> Some general elections come and go, like a shower of rain, freshening things up a bit but not changing anything radically, not penetrating to the roots of our political soil. This is not likely to be said of the General Election of October 1959. It will be remembered as a major upheaval. Nothing in politics will ever be quite the same as it was before, either for the three parties, for the trade unions, or for any of us as individuals.[52]

The party's national executive (NEC) published its analysis of the 1959 defeat, much of which prefigured the moderniser's attack on Old Labour.[53] The first cause was judged to be growing prosperity: Labour suffered its strongest reversals in the most affluent parts of Britain, only performing well in industrial Scotland, the coal mining areas and the Lancashire cotton districts. New towns, such as Dagenham and Edmonton, populated by prosperous working-class electors swung heavily towards the Conservatives. The second reason for defeat according to the NEC was the refusal to explain how Gaitskell's administration could pay for its promises, given the pledge to increase the state pension while reducing income tax. Another factor that damaged Labour was 'the general unpopularity of nationalisation'. The issue for voters was not renationalising steel and road haulage but the general threat to bring the top 500 companies into public ownership. Meanwhile, the Tory campaign effectively portrayed Labour as 'anti-British' following Gaitskell's attack on British foreign policy in Suez and Cyprus. A fifth factor was Labour's internal divisions, particularly over nuclear weapons: many believed the party supported unilateralism. Overall, voters saw Labour 'as an exclusively class party, and a party of restrictions and controls'. The Conservatives portrayed the opposition 'as a party of bureaucrats, tied to political doctrines irrelevant today'.[54] Labour was judged to be 'feeble', lacking clear policy and overwhelmingly 'class-based'.[55]

At heart, the 1959 election underlined the class system was being remade to the structural disadvantage of the Labour Party. Tribal loyalties were fracturing. Established patterns of support were declining. Large-scale industrial production in factories as well as tight-knit working-class housing was disappearing, usually at the behest of Labour local authorities that sought to improve the decaying housing stock, but inadvertently loosened the traditional ties of community. Working-class households were acquiring consumer goods at a rapid rate. Many of these electors believed voting Labour was in conflict with the desire for self-betterment and national strength.[56] The Conservative MP Quintin Hogg declared in 1958:

> The fantastic growth of the economy, the spectacular rise in the standard of living, the substantial redistribution of wealth, the generous development of social welfare, and the admitted humanising of private industry have rendered obsolete the whole intellectual framework within which Socialist discussion used to be conducted.[57]

The Left struggled to convincingly refute Hogg's declaration. The Labour Party's identification with the working class 'was a clear political liability for the simple reason that the working-class is shrinking in size', while the electorate was characterised by 'a growing group of socially ambivalent, fluid, cross-pressured voters'.[58] The relative size of the professional, clerical and technical occupations increased by 55 per cent since the early 1930s, while manual employment grew by only 12 per cent. The importance of the manual working class, traditionally most loyal to the party, was declining while the association between class status and voting behaviour was weakening. Meanwhile, in the 1959 election Labour polled fewer votes among the middle class than four years previously as Figure 3.1 below illustrates.

It was clear that electoral dealignment was underway. Labour had never been able to rely on working-class support in its industrial heartlands to secure a parliamentary majority. Anthony Crosland wrote that Labour 'would be ill-advised to continue making a largely proletarian class appeal when a majority of the population is gradually attaining a middle-class standard of life, and distinct symptoms even of a middle-class psychology'.[59] The new society, so bewildering to the party's traditional wing, was depicted poignantly by J.P. Priestley as a world of:

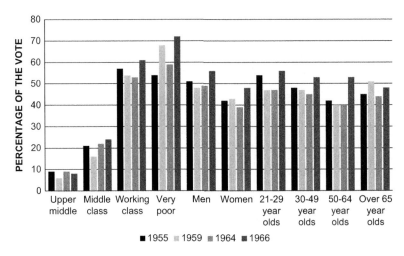

FIGURE 3.1 Labour's vote in general elections 1955–66 (British Election Study 1966)

> Arterial and by-pass roads, of filling stations and factories that look like exhibition buildings, of giant cinemas and dance halls and cafes, bungalows with tiny garages, cocktail bars, Woolworths, motor coaches, wireless, hiking, factory girls looking like actresses, greyhound racing and dirt tracks, swimming pools, and everything given away for cigarette coupons.[60]

As Stephen Brooke has noted, Old Labour's conception of modernity emphasised collective discipline and self-restraint in the service of a more rational economic and social order. Yet the politics of affluence in the 1950s brought to the fore consumer choice and self-actualisation, values that threatened Labour's established ideological outlook.[61]

Sociologists focused on adaptations in the working-class occupational structure to explain the party's electoral fragility.[62] Their findings are reflected in revisionist texts, particularly Crosland's landmark work *The Future of Socialism* (1956) and Douglas Jay's *Socialism in the New Society* (1963). Less well understood were changes within the middle class that had disturbing implications for Labour's ability to construct a viable electoral alliance. Whereas in the early-twentieth century, the educated professional classes lent their expertise and knowledge to advancing working-class social reform, by the 1950s and 1960s the situation had markedly altered. The tradition of Christian liberal philanthropy was dissipating in the face of secularisation. Middle-class occupations were fragmenting. Meanwhile, working-class prosperity and political organisation, driven by free collective-wage bargaining and the growth of trade unionism, shook the paternalistic mind-set of the middle class.[63] The dominance of labour interests and rising union militancy threatened Labour's historic role as an agent of social progress. One defeated MP told Gaitskell the party lost in 1959 because 'we are associated in the public mind too much with sectional interests and grievances'.[64] The revisionists believed Gaitskell should advance a credible appeal to the electorate across all classes – 'a radical protest against the terrible conservatism and complacency of British society'.[65]

Nonetheless, 1959 exposed Labour's shortcomings in appealing to the English middle class. The Conservatives were astute in focusing on the 'class hybrids', those working class in education and occupation but 'middle-class in income and material comforts'.[66] Party activists appeared stuck in the past, refusing to reappraise their political beliefs. A CLP newspaper implored in the late 1950s:

> We are striving to convince people of the innate decency of the Labour cause; we are demonstrating that to live and work for each other is to become truly civilised; we are arguing that to eliminate greed and the profit motive is not only good for our standard of living, but also good for our souls . . . those who have political ambitions must . . . *live* socialism, so that their words are backed up by the shining example of their deeds.[67]

Yet the determination to convert voters to socialism flew in the face of sociological adaptation. Socialism was a set of ideals, 'but events have proved the British people are not ready for it'.[68] The population of skilled workers was expanding. At the end of the 1950s, more than half the population owned their own home; 8 million had purchased a car; in 1951, 1 million households had a television; by 1958, the figure was 13 million.[69] The perceived character of the party dominated by 'the Red Flag boys, the unofficial strikers and the professional haters scared the living daylights out of people of moderate views'.[70]

Furthermore, the 1959 defeat underlined the alienation of women voters since the widening of the franchise. Labour's arcane policy-making procedures and its focus on the ownership of industry marginalised the preoccupations of working-class women.[71] Old Labour's inability to devise a persuasive concept of socialism underlined the difficulties the party faced in attracting women's support. The party's culture under Old Labour was shaped by predominantly masculine identities. The purpose was to achieve improvements in the living standards of industrial workers.[72] The ethos of male solidarity enforced by membership of unions, alongside cultural pursuits from gambling to pigeon breeding, still defined the movement. Even in 1945, the Labour tradition had less resonance with women struggling to overcome the privations of rationing and controls. Gaitskell acknowledged in 1959:

> Our failure this time was largely a failure to win support from the women. . . . It is no use dismissing the problem, as some do, by saying that women are too snobbish or too politically apathetic. They are voters and count just as much as men.[73]

The post-election analysis demonstrated that:

> Appeals to vote Labour in order to prevent a return to pre-war conditions of slumps and unemployment will cut little ice with the young housewife today. Her life is one in which a new house (Council or private), a family car, a television, an electric washer, cooker, and perhaps even a "frig", predominate.[74]

As the 1950s progressed, Labour became more out of touch with prolific alterations in women's lives. Working-class women were entering the world of work and becoming more independent within the family. They were having fewer children and marrying later. Women were embracing the choices afforded by the consumer society. The Labour Party displayed, at best, limited understanding of the recomposition of gender identities, despite the efforts of Ellen Wilkinson, Barbara Castle and even Michael Young, who claimed Labour needed policies that supported women while nurturing the extended family. By the 1980s, women's rights in the Labour Party were still being 'suppressed both because they represented a radical force in the party that couldn't be controlled, and a women's vote that couldn't be controlled by men'.[75] Labour suffered electorally as a consequence of its inability to speak to women 'as *women*'. The party's refusal to acknowledge gender's importance had adverse consequences. Successive defeats in the 1950s and 1980s were the result of women's drift towards the Conservative Party. This fact was uppermost in the minds of party modernisers.

Yet structural alterations in post-war Britain did not alone determine Labour's failings. New Labour saw the party as divided, sterile and irretrievably stuck in the past, the author of its own misfortune. Whether to continue with nationalisation was a point of bitter contention. The conflict was between those who wanted 'the Labour party to cling to its traditional sentiments and fundamentalist principles' and those 'who wished in some way or other to modernise'.[76] Aside from divisions over domestic policy, there was growing concern about the proliferation of nuclear weapons. The trade unions began to shift leftwards, epitomised by Frank Cousins's replacing the loyalist Arthur Deakin as general secretary of the Transport and General Workers' Union (TGWU). As disillusioned intellectuals abandoned the Communist Party over the Soviet invasion of Hungary in 1956, the New Left's emergence gave fresh impetus to Bevanism.[77]

As a consequence of the ensuing conflict on the Left, paranoia and mistrust became 'familiar features of Labour's psychological landscape'. The trading of 'juvenile insults' between delegates and MPs dominated the annual conference.[78] These images were not historical fictions invented by Blairite modernisers. Gaitskell's biographer, Philip Williams, presciently wrote that:

> Labour's crisis . . . was more than a struggle over a doctrinal point like Clause Four, or over a policy issue like nuclear disarmament, or over a personality clash about Gaitskell's leadership, or even over the location of power within the Party. It was a conflict about its character: whether the

party was to be a protest movement or a prospective government of the country.[79]

Such events in turn moulded New Labour's perception of Old Labour's failings.

Moreover, continuing discord meant the party had few 'creative ideas' to put before the British electorate.[80] In an infamous meeting at Gaitskell's home in Frognal Gardens, Hampstead, on the Sunday after the 1959 election, revisionists began diagnosing Labour's defeat. Douglas Jay insisted Labour must '(1) drop nationalisation (2) drop the trade unions (3) drop the name 'Labour party' (4) drop the principle of political independence, and . . . make agreements with the Liberal party', if it was to stand any chance of retaking power.[81] The instinctive loyalty of voters was dissipating. Too many viewed socialist doctrines with intrinsic suspicion. A party activist in Bury, Lancashire, wrote to Gaitskell in the aftermath of the election in terms that foresaw subsequent criticisms of Old Labour: 'We can recover again if we gear ourselves to the modern outlook and refuse to be hamstrung to policies and a constitution decided forty to fifty years ago'.[82] He believed Labour's association with 'the old days of class warfare' was damaging. It was out of touch with 'thousands of business men, shopkeepers, technicians, managers who could feel we belonged to a modern twentieth century party of progress and social conscience'.[83] The party should separate itself from the unions, he believed, even renaming itself 'the reform party', appealing to voters' conscience rather than their class background. Nevertheless, Labour found doctrinal adaptation almost impossible, underlined by Gaitskell's struggle to rewrite Clause Four. The modernisers in the Blair era were convinced Gaitskell made fundamental errors, failing to get the trade unions on board and striking at the wrong moment before the organised Left were marginalised. Yet in the circumstances of the 1950s, Gaitskell's task proved impossible.

New Labour learnt important lessons from Gaitskell's failure which it saw as emblematic of Old Labour's weakness. The leadership should refuse to allow traditionalists to influence the reform and modernisation process. Philip Williams's judgement that the party's crisis was 'a conflict about its character' shaped New Labour's strategy and appeal.[84] Gaitskell sought initially to placate the Bevanite Left. After the 1959 defeat, however, he adopted a confrontational stance, insisting that Labour's third consecutive loss resulted from the fact that it was too ideologically Left-Wing. Although Blair compromised with the party, he refused to accommodate the views of the 'doctrinaire' Left. He sought to dominate the party using the institutional levers of centralised managerial control. Above all, he believed Labour must be perceived as a credible governing party fit for office.

The second lesson of the age of affluence was that the party must be capable of projecting a cross-class appeal. Labour could only secure a parliamentary majority if it attracted support in regions of Britain that enjoyed rising prosperity, alongside industrial communities that suffered long-term decline at the sharp end of Thatcherism. Blair's party internalised Jay's message from four decades before: Labour must be 'up to date and recognise society to be what it is today, and not what it used to be thirty years ago'.[85] New Labour drew on the long-term rethinking and revision underway inside the party. Blair and Brown acknowledged Labour required an electoral strategy that appealed to new occupational groups in the emerging service-orientated economy. They had to devise a concept of social democracy tailored to the post–Cold War generation.

The degeneration of the Wilson/Callaghan years

The modernisers, notably Blair and Brown, came of age politically in the 1970s. Labour's underwhelming, even disastrous experience in government left an indelible mark. The Wilson/Callaghan era was typical of Old Labour's inadequate performance. For Wilson, it had all begun so optimistically. Victories in 1964 and 1966 signalled the party's rebirth promising the 'white heat' of industrial modernisation. The 1964 manifesto, *Let's Go with Labour for the New Britain*, promised Labour would mobilise:

> the resources of technology under a national plan . . . harnessing our national wealth in brains, our genius for scientific invention and medical discovery; reversing the decline of the thirteen wasted years; affording a new opportunity to equal, and if possible surpass, the roaring progress of other western powers.[86]

The Labour administration came to power with plans to revitalise central government as the powerhouse of reform, reversing the relative decline of Britain as an industrial economy. Two years later, the party won a landslide majority.

Wilson was hailed as the British President Kennedy, able to uniquely fuse together 'the disparate strands of post-war radical thinking into a cohesive and inspiring new doctrine'.[87] While Gaitskell was derided for his establishment Keynesianism, Wilson was eulogised by the New Left for his commitment to rejuvenating Britain through modernising state intervention in the economy.[88] Launched in 1965, the National Plan promised to shake up ossified private sector industries. The Department of Economic Affairs (DEA) was established under George Brown to promote firm-level technological investment and training. Wilson enunciated a compelling national story, building on 1950s' revisionism to achieve successive election victories. He emphasised appealing to the middle class, those concerned with an efficiently run economy and rising living standards, rather than the indiscriminate 'application of egalitarian principles'.[89] Wilson sought to position Labour as the natural party of government. Given the despair after 1959, it was a major turnaround in the party's fortunes. The leadership supplanted the party's emphasis on welfarism and income redistribution with a novel strategy focused on increasing the economy's productive capacity. In keeping with the prospectus outlined by Crosland in 1956, the manifesto guaranteed 'that a sufficient part of the new wealth created goes to meet urgent and now neglected human needs'. In 1966, Labour achieved its decisive victory, winning 48 per cent of the vote. UK growth averaged 2.6 per cent despite the pattern of 'stop-go' macro-economic policies. Wilson had resurrected the alliance between the working class and the professional middle class that eluded Labour since the Second World War.

Given these notable successes, why were Blair and his followers intent on depicting Wilson's party as irrevocably Old Labour? Within four years, Labour's electoral recovery under Wilson came to a staggering halt. The government was buffeted by the prolonged economic crisis, hastened by ministers' inability to resolve a credible strategy for dealing with sterling's weakness and the deteriorating trade balance. Under Wilson, Labour sold itself as the party of growth that could enlarge the economy. Yet George Brown admitted his own department, the DEA which 'recast the machinery of government . . . to counter the financial orthodoxy of the Treasury' was 'a social revolution that failed'.[90] The party then proved itself incapable of achieving industrial relations reform that removed the obstacles to growth, the result of endemic conflict with the unions.

The Wilson government's White Paper, *In Place of Strife*, published in 1969 was intended to tackle the underlying causes of industrial disputes. Yet the plans had to be abandoned as a consequence of opposition within Wilson's own cabinet. Ministers believed their loyalties still lay with organised labour. The Wilson governments then struggled to make the choices required to modernise Britain: ministers initially refused to devalue sterling; they were unable to devise a coherent economic strategy and slow to withdraw British troops East of Suez; and they demonstrated weak leadership over Europe.[91] In 1967, three backbenchers, John Mackintosh, David Owen and David Marquand, published a pamphlet titled *Changing Gear*, a response to the perceived drift of the Wilson years.[92] They advocated the devaluation of sterling and an immediate increase in spending alongside constitutional reform, including devolution to Wales and Scotland. Yet the proposals were dismissed by the Labour leadership who had little interest in new thinking.

The party's claim to government rested on its ability to make corporatism function, both to ensure industrial peace and to arrest the relative decline of the British economy. Yet by the 1960s the trade unions, still umbilically attached to the party, grew hostile to reform. After all, full employment gave them the industrial power to bargain over wages. The perceived obduracy of the union leadership led to growing disquiet, not least among working-class voters. By 1970, the Labour movement was degenerating due to the escalation of industrial militancy, leading to almost inevitable defeat. Following the decay of Labour's reputation as the natural governing party during the Wilson/Callaghan years, New Labour believed the party could win only by adopting a strategy of 'fairness, not favours'. In government, Blair's party gave priority to the 'national interest' over the 'sectional interest' of dominant producer groups including the trade unions.

Another element in the political disintegration of the Wilson years was the growing fault line between working-class populism and liberal social reform. It was alleged that Wilson's government was so focused on introducing permissive legislation on abortion, gay rights, the death penalty and racial discrimination that it spent less time improving the material living conditions of its 'core' electorate.[93] On immigration, Old Labour was apparently slow to acknowledge ill feeling in traditional working-class communities. Legislation introduced in the late 1960s outlawed racial discrimination in housing while stemming the inward flow of migrants. The public response to Enoch Powell's infamous 'Rivers of Blood' speech in 1968 had troubling implications for the Left. Dockers in the East End of London marching vigorously in Powell's support underlined doubts about the progressive nature of working-class politics.[94] In a discussion of race relations at Bedford CLP:

> A member said that we might just as well give the whole damn country to the Blacks as they would get it in the end anyway. Before long we would have a black king on the throne and then it would be God help us! The poor old white man might just as well emigrate and leave the place to them.[95]

In the inner-London constituency of Bermondsey, two-thirds of General Management Committee (GMC) delegates supported immigration controls. The situation led Callaghan to introduce restrictive legislation, imposing a quota on the number of Kenyan Asians entering Britain.[96] Richard Crossman declared:

> A few years ago everyone there would have regarded the denial of entry to British nationals with British passports as the most appalling violation of our deepest principles. Now they are quite happy . . . doing just that. Mainly because I am an MP for a constituency in the Midlands where racialism is a powerful force, I was on the side of Callaghan.[97]

On European Community (EC) membership, the party put the objective of faster economic growth ahead of voters' unease about the perceived loss of national sovereignty. By the 1960s, 'British national identity was assailed by forces more powerful than any it had undergone before: Americanisation, decolonialisation, black and Asian immigration, Scottish and Welsh nationalism, and a drive towards European integration'.[98] Support for the Scottish National Party and Plaid Cymru began to advance, particularly in Labour's 'heartland' constituencies. *British* democratic socialism and its associated narrative of working-class solidarity across the four nations of the UK was under growing threat. Blair and Brown believed Old Labour had failed to respond effectively to the growing atrophy of the UK polity, hastening the party's electoral decline in the 1970s.

PHOTO 3.2 Jim Callaghan in a rare public appearance with Prime Minister Tony Blair

Source: Photo by Andy Paradise/*The Independent*/Shutterstock

The triumph of Thatcherism

The lesson New Labour drew from the 1979 defeat centred on the crippling effect of the Winter of Discontent, which, driven by the power of organised labour, destroyed the government's reputation. The industrial relations crisis shaped folk memories of the party for generations. During the 1979 campaign, Anthony King wrote that according to opinion surveys, 'the British people deeply resent trade union power'. Nor were they enthusiastic about the indiscriminate growth of public expenditure three decades after the Second World War. Indeed, voters became 'profoundly suspicious of nationalisation and government intervention in the economy'.[99] There was little evidence that the working class was crying out for further public ownership, 'nationalising Marks & Spencer's'.[100] Old Labour's doctrine became politically discredited.

At the 1979 election, Labour suffered a heavy swing among skilled workers in the Midlands and the South of England. The safest seats were still in the depressed industrial areas in the Northern and Celtic periphery. The 1979 defeat confirmed the decline of the traditional labour interest, underlined the previous year in Eric Hobsbawm's lecture on 'The Forward March of Labour Halted'. Hobsbawm noted the number of manual workers as a proportion of the workforce in Britain was shrinking. This thesis was endorsed by the French sociologist Andre Gorz in his classic study, *Farewell to the Working-Class*.[101] Across the advanced economies, the share of skilled industrial workers was rapidly falling. In the meantime, the white-collar middle class was expanding, hastening a period of crisis for the British Left. Hobsbawm acknowledged that union membership was at its peak in the late 1970s. The issue for the Labour Party, however, was that the fastest-growing unions were in the white-collar public sector. These workers, Hobsbawm observed, were noticeably less solidaristic, focused on the preservation of wage differentials and privileges. Voters resented growing militancy and overmighty union power. Hobsbawm concluded that not only were the manual working class no longer the numerical majority in Britain's occupational structure. They no longer cohered around a single body of political ideas (if they ever had).[102] Although Hobsbawm's analysis indicated long-term structural changes were eroding Labour's electoral position, he believed the crisis was fundamentally of the party's making: 'If we are to explain the stagnation or crisis, we have to look at the Labour Party and the labour movement itself. The workers . . . were looking to it for a lead and a policy. They did not get it. They got the Wilson years'. Instead, centre-left parties should become 'people's parties with which the majority of their nation interested in progressive change and reform could identify'.[103]

Hobsbawm's contribution represented a major attack on Old Labour's world-view. Disastrously by the late 1970s, sections of the British working class 'regarded Conservative policies and objectives as being more in line with their own interests and values'.[104] Political identities were mutating. Solidaristic class struggle ignored, or refused to recognise, the new identities. It was particularly noticeable that unions were reluctant to mobilise collective bargaining power in the fight for equal pay. Throughout the post-war period, 'male and female politicians alike remained disinterested in, or even hostile to, issues specifically relating to women'.[105] Marxism was being scrutinised for allegedly reducing human experience exclusively to class struggle rather than acknowledging the dimensions of oppression that related to gender and race.[106] The iconography of the British Labour movement was still dominated by the imagery of the industrial worker. Even the New Left in the 1960s 'romanticised the working-class male hero as the hope for the future'.[107] Hobsbawm's invigorating critique provided the intellectual stimulus for the modernising project of the 1980s and 1990s.[108] New Labour concluded that the party should never again be perceived as the instrument of narrow class-based interests.

Old Labour and electoral failure

The principal understanding New Labour derived from the legacy of post-war defeat was that unlike Old Labour, the party should secure a broad electoral alliance to win power in British politics. Labour must understand why the party alienated key constituencies, especially women, alongside the property-owning middle class. The party proved itself incapable of making the transition from its role as an opposition force in the early-twentieth century to becoming a permanent party of power. In 2018, the Trade Union Congress (TUC) celebrated its 150th anniversary. It was a salutary fact that in the 150 years of the TUC's existence, Labour was in power for only 39 years. The party needed to confront why in the era of full-franchise mass democracy, Labour still failed to emerge as an effective contender for office. Only in five elections since the First World War had Labour secured a workable parliamentary majority.

Another lesson was that to displace the Conservatives as the de facto governing party, Labour should remain a united, tightly disciplined force. Party reformers in the 1980s consolidated Gaitskell's effort to restore the institutional authority of the PLP. Rules changes to make MPs accountable to CLPs and the annual conference were reversed. While intra-party democracy emphasised the supremacy of conference in formulating policy, New Labour undermined that authority by creating the National Policy Forum (NPF). The NPF instituted a 'rolling programme' of policy deliberation in close consultation with the leadership. By the mid-1990s, there was less scope for resolutions at the conference to undermine the leadership's position. As Lewis Minkin writes, New Labour sought to end the party's 'dangerous proclivity to public exhibitions of internal conflict'.[109] While the NPF's role was to promote dialogue and inclusive political debate, the covert aim was control of the party's internal agenda and institutions using the instruments of manipulative managerialism. To remain electable, Labour had to behave as a disciplined political force while projecting its respectability.

For Blair and Brown, the party's repeated defeats, its sporadic experience of governing and the infrequency with which its leaders became prime minister were 'morbid symptoms' of a failed inheritance. The leadership battled to distance the party from its legacy of electoral vulnerability, learning lessons from Old Labour's strategic mistakes. New Labour's approach in the 1990s consciously sought to confront the party's endemic historical weaknesses. Blair's party aimed to reconstruct the political alliance that the party managed only at brief moments in its past. As such, by castigating Old Labour, the party's inheritance was 're-imagined and reconstructed in a very particular way'.[110]

Economic mismanagement

Similarly, New Labour disassociated itself from Old Labour's legacy in economic management. Neil Kinnock's former chief of staff, Charles Clarke believed, 'Throughout the twentieth century, economic policy and taxation were the electoral millstone which prevented Labour holding power other than intermittently'.[111] Labour governments failed to develop a credible economic strategy. After 1918, the dilemma that shaped the party's approach was whether to manage capitalism more efficiently than the Conservatives or to construct an alternative economic system conducive to 'socialism'.[112] Nowhere was Old Labour's apparent failure more acute than in economic policy. Its post-war doctrine emphasised nationalisation; state planning; higher taxation and public spending; regulation of the private sector; and insistence upon a close, organic relationship with trade unions.[113]

As shadow chancellor, Gordon Brown sought to grasp the historical weaknesses of post-war economic policy.[114] He believed Labour governments habitually resorted to ineffectual policy levers of state intervention, public ownership and indicative planning. Ministers were unable to devise efficient industrial policies that raised the economy's productive potential and the long-term rate of growth. Brown told the 2002 party conference that New Labour was governing the economy quite differently to previous administrations:

> Let us remember that while all past Labour governments were forced to retrench, cut back, and were overwhelmed by world conditions in 1924, 1931, 1951 and 1967, it is because we painstakingly built the foundations in economic management that we are the first Labour government with the strength to be able to plan for the long term on the basis of stability, not stop-go.[115]

Old Labour governments adopted traditional Keynesian measures that led eventually to economic instability and fiscal incontinence. Indeed, Brown believed Old Labour's strategy implied high public spending, big government, an anti-business ethos, hitting the rich – the politics of envy. Brown told the *Guardian* commentator Hugo Young that Labour kept losing because it was a party battling to redistribute wealth, rather than generating growth.[116] What disturbed the modernisers was the government's inept handling of the economic management problems of the 1960s and 1970s with painful echoes of the 1930s, destroying the party's reputation for economic and financial competence. Even in the aftermath of the 1992 defeat, voters said they still could not support Labour despite their disillusionment with the politically hapless Major administration. Painful memories of the Winter of Discontent remained alive, continuing to define Old Labour's inheritance. Despite criticising his government's policies, Brown agreed with Harold Wilson: 'All political history shows that the standing of a government and its ability to hold the confidence of the electorate at a general election depend on the success of its economic policy'.[117]

The 1931 financial crisis

New Labour believed that Old Labour's failure in economic management began not in the 1960s and 1970s, but in the aftermath of the great depression in the 1930s. The absence of robust economic and financial policies in 1929–31 ensured that Ramsay MacDonald's administration was damaged incontrovertibly. The impact of the financial collapse was felt across Britain. Ill prepared for office, the Labour government was plunged rapidly into a sterling crisis. The administration then all but collapsed following its decision to cut unemployment benefit, dividing the cabinet and inflicting inestimable hardship on industrial communities. During the 1920s, the party had assembled 'an unimaginative and prescriptively infertile mix' of policies. Labour's economic programme was disparaged as 'a hopeless mess'.[118] The chancellor, Philip Snowdon, was an exponent of fiscal and monetary orthodoxy, which undermined the search for a viable solution to the government's most pressing problem, the growth of mass unemployment.[119] From the outset, MacDonald's ministers were obsessed with appearing fit to govern. In the wake of the crisis, the administration became 'a pathetic spectacle of indecision and intellectual emptiness'. Following the government's implosion and MacDonald's decision to lead a cabinet with Conservative and Liberal support, Labour's first prime minister was a pariah airbrushed from the party's history.

Not surprisingly, the traumatic events of 1929–31 reverberated throughout the twentieth century:

> Labour was structurally disadvantaged by the fear of a currency run. . . . New Labour's repudiation of the past was directed, as much as anything, at the financial markets reassuring them that a chastened Labour leadership now understood the constraints markets created.[120]

New Labour drew two lessons from the ignominious 1930–31 collapse. The first was that in contrast to Old Labour, the modernisers must assert the party's commitment to sound economic stewardship and fiscal responsibility. Moreover, Labour in office must avoid policy action that risked splitting the movement. The experience of 1931 emphasised that in a liberal democracy, the internal cohesion of the governing party was fundamental. It is striking that eighty years later following the 2008 crash, Gordon Brown was reluctant to permit radical spending cuts. Brown lived in perpetual fear of dividing his party, ending up as 'another Philip Snowdon'. Whereas in 1930–31 the alarming evaporation of political and economic confidence broke the resolve of Labour ministers, it is striking that the Brown government remained measured and purposeful in the wake of the financial crisis. Macro-economic policy became expansionary and activist. Despite the recession, unemployment in Britain remained lower than forecasts predicted. Labour appeared to have vanquished the ghosts of 1931, even if the Conservatives sought to resurrect the old fear of the bond markets that the UK was on the brink of defaulting on its debt.

The devaluation catastrophe

The inept management of sterling in the 1960s and Old Labour's continuing reputation as the party of devaluation meant it was further discredited in Blair and Brown's eyes. The party was haunted by the spectre of currency crises that erupted even in the Attlee years. After delaying decisive action following Wilson's victory in 1964, the government was forced to devalue in the face of plummeting confidence in the British economy, as the National Plan failed to stimulate an export-led recovery raising the growth rate to 4 per cent per annum. The National Plan emphasised the importance of establishing new industries, encouraging collaboration between the public and private sectors. There was a focus on state-led investment in science, technology and skills to enhance British productivity. Wilson was determined to avoid devaluation as the solution to stagnation, fearing the impact on UK living standards. In the run up to the 1966 election, he attacked the Conservative's record, telling voters, 'It is housewives, chancellors of the exchequer of Britain's households, who have to contend with the rising cost of living'.[121] As a consequence, Labour governments put the management of the exchange rate and the defence of sterling before the expansionary aims of growth and full employment.[122]

By the mid-1960s, Britain had the largest balance-of-payments deficit since the Second World War, 'The years from 1964 to 1967 witnessed essentially a continuous sterling crisis'.[123] Under unbearable pressure, the pound was devalued in 1967 after speculative selling in the foreign exchange markets. Sterling plummeted from parity of $2.80 to $2.40. Steps were then taken to deflate the economy by cutting public spending, offsetting the effect of rising import prices. The government's economic modernisation agenda, elaborated in the 1964 manifesto, promptly collapsed. Wilson and his chancellor, James Callaghan, had prevaricated over whether to devalue sterling, undermining market confidence. Repeated battles with the unions over pay restraint and the collapse of *In Place of Strife* at the end of the 1960s further undermined British social democracy's professed credibility.[124]

Wilson's antipathy to devaluation was itself a reaction against the economic vulnerability of MacDonald's and Attlee's governments. Forced by external events to devalue in 1949, Labour risked being depicted by the Right and the financial establishment as the party of habitual devaluation. Ministers were aware of the political dangers of the quick fix: 'An important element in the powerful resistance to an exchange rate cut was the perception that devaluation would involve a significant and politically damaging increase in the cost of living'.[125] Yet the problems in handling sterling meant the Wilson governments were forever portrayed as 'the paradigm of economic failure . . . a major reference point in charting the inadequacies of British democratic socialism as a programme for power'.[126] New Labour could not emphasise enough that it had absorbed the lessons of the post-war devaluation debacle.

The IMF crisis

The International Monetary Fund (IMF) crisis in 1975–76 further underlined Old Labour's chaotic reputation in economic management. After protracted instability in the mid-1970s following yet another balance-of-payments crisis, ministers had to negotiate an IMF loan to repay the credit from the G10 central banks to support sterling.[127] The government then suffered a gilt strike where financial markets refused to finance the UK's debt. The IMF bailout compelled the government to make radical cuts in public expenditure, condemned as a bitter betrayal within the Labour Party. Since the Second World War, the promise of rising public expenditure and expanding welfare had been the bedrock of

British social democracy. R.H. Tawney wrote: 'We must spend, not less, but more on education, health, housing, and the establishment of security against the contingencies of life'.[128] Between the end of the First World War and the 1970s, public spending as a share of national income grew from 10 to 40 per cent.[129]

Even so, under Wilson and Callaghan, it was a Labour government that made cuts. The party had returned to office in February 1974 with no clear governing strategy, offering voters little more than a 'ragged series of compromises'.[130] Within two years, it was plain that the government's economic programme was collapsing. The claim that Labour could manage the trade unions under the terms of the Social Contract was in tatters as the number of working days lost to industrial action rocketed, while the union leadership were portrayed as 'holding the country to ransom'.

Moreover, the Keynesian approach to economic management became discredited intellectually as unemployment and inflation soared, a crisis known as stagflation. In a desperate predicament, ministers battled to rewrite the government's economic programme. Prime Minister Callaghan's address to the 1976 party conference recognised that full employment could no longer be secured 'by a stroke of the Chancellor's pen'. The 'cosy world' of 'deficit spending' was gone. No government could spend its way out of recession, printing 'confetti money'.[131] According to his son-in-law, Peter Jay, Callaghan's speech (which Jay helped to draft) was 'the most breathtakingly frank public pronouncement since St Paul's First Epistle to the Corinthians'.[132] In the wake of the 1949 and 1966–67 financial crises, Labour was compelled to acknowledge the external constraints on expansionary policies, alongside the realisation that Britain's economic problems concerned the efficiency of production as much as insufficient aggregate demand. In the post-war era, it was believed the UK economy was simply not dynamic enough.

The Callaghan government's tough policy action improved the economic outlook by the spring of 1978. The balance of payments and the value of sterling had stabilised, 'a portent of happier tidings ahead'; affluence and the availability of consumer goods continued to improve.[133] Yet ministers failed to devise a sustainable incomes policy, leading to a further crisis in the winter of 1978–79 when public sector pay claims rocketed and the Social Contract collapsed. The proclamation in Labour's 1974 manifesto that 'the trade unions *voluntarily* will co-operate to make the [income's] policy successful' proved over-optimistic;[134] 29 million days were lost to strikes that winter. Resisting all efforts to restrict the right to pursue pay claims, the unions were radicalised. As the wave of strikes took hold, powerful images appeared of rubbish piling up in the streets and the dead lying in hospital morgues unburied. The former cabinet minister, Shirley Williams, recalled the months in which 'all hell broke loose . . . decent men and women outdid one another in their callousness towards the public'.[135] Unquestionably, it was a decisive turning point in post-war Britain. The government was gripped by an overwhelming feeling of impotence and powerlessness. As Bernard Donoughue, Callaghan's senior policy adviser, recollects: 'There was a deathly calm in Number Ten, a sort of quiet despair. . . . It was like being on the sinking *Titanic,* although without the music'.[136] The crises of the 1970s underlined the party's failure to acquire the reputation for successful economic management.

For Blair's party, the Wilson/Callaghan era underlined Old Labour's obsolescence. The crisis of the 1970s affirmed the importance of international institutions, notably bondholders and financial investors, in shaping national economic policy.[137] The lesson derived by New Labour, articulated in Brown's speeches as shadow chancellor, was that without a credible strategy to ensure fiscal discipline, Labour governments would soon acquire a reputation for economic chaos. Ministers should establish credibility with financial markets. Brown told his party conference in 1997, 'You cannot build the new Jerusalem on a mountain of debts'. He went on:

> We have learned from past mistakes. Just as you cannot spend your way through a recession, you cannot in a global economy simply spend your way through a recovery either. We will not make the mistake of 1964, when our government then failed to take the tough, long-term decisions for change early on. . . . We will not make the mistake of 1974, spending hopefully for the first two years, telling the people the party was over but acting as if it had barely begun, and then having to cut back on spending miserably in the next three years. It is only by being prudent and disciplined now, building a platform for long-term stability, that we will be able to deliver the people's priorities.[138]

Conventional post-war Keynesian doctrine was no longer a sensible guide to economic policy.

In September 1994 shortly after becoming leader, Blair gave a lecture on Labour's economic policy, depicted as abandoning 'Old Labour's Keynesianism'. The headline in the *Independent* was 'Blair ditches Keynes'.[139] Blair claimed deficit financing by governments was no longer tenable and that an incoming administration 'will not spend what we cannot afford to spend'. Rather than depending on counter-cyclical demand management, ministers should use supply-side reforms to improve access to the labour market and increase the supply of jobs.[140] It was the radicalisation of supply-side policy and micro-economics that marked the point of departure between New Labour and the pre-1979 orthodoxy.[141] This position led commentators to argue, 'New Labour . . . felt compelled to junk Keynes wholesale and accept the new right consensus that budget deficit manipulation only disturbs the natural rhythms of the economy'.[142] It was often forgotten that British governments, including Labour governments, actually ran surpluses throughout the 1950s and 1960s.

Despite these striking headlines, Blair was anxious not to repudiate Keynes' inheritance, acknowledging that his prudent vision of social justice in the capitalist market economy remained relevant to the British centre-left. Keynes was never a narrow-minded advocate of deficit financing, and he cannot be pigeon-holed as somehow Old Labour. The great twentieth century econo-mist was flexible and pragmatic in recommending policies, adapting theories to reflect political circumstances and what was considered necessary to alleviate economic hardship. Keynes believed the chief task of politics remained 'to dis-tinguish afresh the *Agenda* of government from the *Non-Agenda,* and the com-panion task . . . is to devise forms of government within a democracy which shall be capable of accomplishing the *Agenda*'.[143] Keynes and New Labour rejected the classical liberal doctrine of laissez-faire. They were both preoccupied by the fun-damental question of political economy that relates to the appropriate role of the state under capitalism. Both accepted that governments should take responsibil-ity for the total level of growth and employment. Accusations that New Labour discarded Keynes in favour of neo-liberalism during the 1990s are wide of the mark. Yet the direction of travel away from the inheritance of the 1970s could hardly have been starker.

Old Labour and economic crisis

New Labour viewed Old Labour's performance in economic management dur-ing the twentieth century as calamitous. The party had to take a different path, prioritising stability and demonstrating it would not take risks with the economy by deviating from the established policy-making consensus. Blair and Brown's followers were 'acutely conscious of the fear [their party] created on the money markets'. They were haunted by the folk memories of failure symbolised by:

> Ramsay MacDonald, Philip Snowdon, and the Great Slump, Stafford Cripps and devaluation, austere rationing, Harold Wilson and devaluation, British Leyland and "industrial disease", Jim Callaghan and the Winter of Discontent, Denis Healey and the IMF and 98 per cent rates of marginal taxation.[144]

New Labour's leaders put considerable effort into tackling the perception that 'a Labour victory would mean a financial panic'.[145] Social democrats in Western Europe and the United States accepted the limitations of what government inter-vention can achieve in integrated open economies. Blair and Brown believed macro-economic policies must recognise the central importance of global capital flows and the worldwide market in money. Labour had to accept the economy was incorporated within 'a highly efficient international market in short-term money', which made investor confidence decisively important.[146] The party should come to terms with the problems of post-war economic management in which 'the Butskellite mixture of macro-economic management and relatively ineffectual micro-economic industrial intervention' was replaced by 'a new mix-ture of monetarist macro-economic neglect and micro-economic neglect', both of which hastened Britain's industrial decline.[147]

The *Economist's* editorial in 1997 emphasised that unlike Old Labour, 'a left-of-centre government must establish credibility with the international financial markets before embarking on redistribution' while 'supporting free trade and globalisation was compatible with pursuing social justice at home'.[148] For New Labour politicians, the concept of the 'national economy' was an anachronism. The leadership never wanted to experience the acute feeling of powerlessness that plagued the administrations of the 1960s and 1970s. In Brown's opinion, 'Too many Labour Chancellors lurched from profligate post-election boom to fatal pre-election bust. Stability, rules, discipline, prudence and transparency: the mantras were more than election slogans. They were the means by which the New Labour government would exorcise the past'.[149] Moreover, where Old Labour was circumspect about the private sector, the modernisers would be unreservedly 'pro-business'.

New Labour's construction of Old Labour's incompetence hardly reflected the balanced assessment of economic history. The Wilson and Callaghan governments inherited serious structural problems from their predecessors. Labour ministers invariably pursued sensible policies. There was no easy route to economic growth in the post-war decades, while the tone of criticism has been excessively condemnatory.[150] And there is a persistent danger of overstating the discontinuities in economic policy: 'In the economic field, New Labour appears less of a departure [from previous Labour governments] than its rhetoric suggests'.[151] In government, Brown was more than prepared to use budgetary instruments to maintain aggregate demand, not least in the wake of the 'dot.com' bubble bursting at the end of the 1990s. What mattered, nevertheless, was the *perception* that New Labour politicians formed of the party's experience after 1964 and their overall opinion of Old Labour's policy-making as inept.

The inference New Labour drew from the experience of the 1960s and 1970s was that the party must win voters' trust on the economy. Labour's appeal should be to 'safety first' and fiscal rectitude, tackling the pattern of post-war 'boom and bust' and endemic 'stop-go' cycles. Blair's consigliere, Peter Mandelson, proclaimed in 1996: 'There is a rock-hard commitment on our part to the maintenance of macro-economic stability'.[152] Labour emphasised its conversion to 'constrained discretion', transferring policy-making responsibilities to independent 'arm's-length' bodies and experts over setting interest rates. The economic 'realities' of globalisation and the constraints it imposed on domestic policy were widely recognised. Globalisation was the centrepiece of New Labour's economic narrative.[153] New Labour's motive was less to assimilate the Thatcherite consensus than to recast the party's policies and identity away from demand management, high taxes, trade union militancy and above all, the economic ineptitude of Old Labour.

The centralised state and constitutional conservatism

From Blair and Brown's perspective, Old Labour in the post-war era was naive about the machinery of government as well as complacent and conservative about constitutional reform. The Attlee government believed in the virtues of

Britain's unwritten constitution. British socialists were convinced that parliamentary sovereignty would permit immediate implementation of the 1945 manifesto. The British state would enable the rapid growth of collectivism. Yet as the postwar decades unfolded, Labour was continually undermined 'by its reputation as the party of high taxes, controls, and bureaucracy'.[154] Old Labour's faith in the constitution accorded with its role as the patriotic party.[155] Labour politicians happily deferred to dominant institutions: the monarchy, the Church of England, the peerage, the armed forces, the English public schools. Attlee's ministers remained complacent about the civil service which they assumed would compliantly pursue socialism. They seemed unaware that Whitehall was ill suited to building the socialist planned economy. The cabinet's mind-set was old fashioned and traditionalist. Attlee insisted on retaining hereditary peerages in the House of Lords. The government refused to abolish the death penalty. It ignored the plight of persecuted Catholics in Northern Ireland. Local government was largely sidelined in the creation of the National Health Service (NHS), reinforcing the pattern of blanket centralisation. The party did little to reform the anachronistic British constitution, 'the secret operations of government, which are concealed by the thick masses of foliage which we call "the myth of democracy"'.[156] As Ross McKibbin noted, 'The ideological character of the war, the apparent democratic solidarity, the seeming success of 'fair shares', and, of course, victory further legitimated the state and the constitution in the eyes of the labour movement'.[157]

In the 1970s, concerns arose about the effectiveness of state intervention, the centralised nature of public administration and the internal cohesion of the UK following the growth of nationalism in Wales, Northern Ireland and Scotland. The commanding heights of Whitehall were being used to suppress local democracy. The new generation of revisionists insisted Labour could no longer view the British constitution as beyond reproach. Yet Blair and his followers believed Old Labour was slow to respond to declining faith in the machinery of state bureaucracy. In the post-war decades, 'Social democrats behaved, all too often, less like liberators, trying to give ordinary people more control over their lives, than like nannies determined to scrub recalcitrant humanity behind the ears'.[158] It was typical that Wilson's efforts to reform the House of Lords, reducing the voting powers of hereditary peers, were soon abandoned while efforts to create elected assemblies in Wales and Scotland were defeated.

By the late 1980s, the Left was compelled to take questions of political reform more seriously. In contrast to Old Labour, importance was now ascribed to decentralisation, making bureaucracies accountable, enabling citizens to take greater control of their lives, while promoting the virtues of participatory democracy. On becoming Labour leader, Blair declared that the party must abandon Old Labour's old-style bureaucratic collectivism. The Left's purpose was to make government 'subject to the public interest'. Blair claimed the state was effective as the guarantor of welfare provision – particularly housing, education and free healthcare after the Second World War. Yet in the intervening decades, public bureaucracies became another vested interest: '1960's social democracy created structures of Government and social organisation that attempted, in so far as possible, to equalise outcomes leading often to conformity'.[159] Taxpayers wanted to know their money was being efficiently spent. Citizens saw themselves increasingly as consumers rather than as producers. They demanded choice.[160] Meanwhile, there was dissatisfaction with the constitutional settlement, leading to the emergence of reform movements, notably *Charter 88* and the Scottish Constitutional Convention. This new thinking about the machinery of government, the constitution and state was perceptibly the very antithesis of Old Labour.

Post-war conflict over nationalisation

Labour's confusion about the role and purpose of government had its origins in the party's prolonged and damaging internal disagreements over nationalisation. Between 1945 and 1964, Labour was wracked by disagreement over how much of the economy should be under state ownership. Nationalisation was perceived to be the key achievement of post-war democratic socialism. The wartime economy legitimised state control. Moreover, the apparent strengths of the planned economy in the Soviet Union affirmed a positive role for the state in the economy. In the burst of legislative activity that characterised the Attlee governments after 1945, industries nationalised included the Bank of England, Cable and Wireless, civil aviation, coal, haulage, gas and electricity.[161]

Yet Labour's programme quickly ran into difficulties. The nationalised industries operated under Morrison's concept of the 'public corporation'. From the outset, there was little clarity about who the nationalised industries were accountable to: ministers or Parliament? The trade unions bemoaned the absence of industrial democracy. The Webbs claimed industrial democracy was 'a necessary element in the democratic state'.[162] Attlee's ministers were sceptical and refused to legislate. Meanwhile, voters became dissatisfied with the performance of the utilities and industries in the state's hands. The Soviet Union's central planning, which so impressed the Webbs and the previous generation of Fabians, appeared less successful by the late 1950s. As a consequence, nationalisation became more and more unpopular, particularly among working-class voters. Publicly owned industries were viewed as inefficient, loss-making enterprises that led to inflated prices for consumers. The defeats of the 1950s compelled Labour to accept the enthusiasm for nationalisation was waning. The 1964 manifesto adopted an unusually pragmatic stance. Harold Wilson affirmed his commitment to nationalisation in speeches to the party faithful, while intending to do as little as possible in government.

Blair and Brown believed their party's stance on public ownership was a critical factor in Old Labour's demise. By the 1990s, there was little support for reversing the privatisations undertaken by the Thatcher and Major governments. Brown imposed a windfall tax on the excess profits of the privatised utilities. That approach meant using regulatory instruments to curb corporate misbehaviour, avoiding fundamental change in the structure of ownership. The case for wide-ranging collective ownership of the means of production elaborated by Marx in the nineteenth century seduced party traditionalists. But it was less relevant to the service-orientated economy in which human capital and knowledge were the critical factors of production. The debate about nationalisation and government control of the economy was held by New Labour to be largely redundant.

Managing public services

The generation of New Labour politicians drew lessons from the party's experience of organising Britain's public services after 1945. The conflict over NHS charges that erupted between Gaitskell and Aneurin Bevan in 1951 epitomised Labour's difficulties in managing the public sector. The NHS was the jewel in the crown of Attlee's administration. The purpose of the NHS was to ensure, 'money must no longer be the passport to the best treatment'. Its principles were that planning should replace markets, provision was available on the basis of need, citizens were treated equally regardless of where they lived and resources were redistributed between classes and households.[163] The NHS would provide 'the best that medical science can offer', notably investment in medical research spurring the treatment of chronic diseases. Yet in 1951, Gaitskell imposed charges on patients for spectacles and dentistry, a reversal that Bevan regarded as the great betrayal of British socialism.

Gaitskell was concerned that public expectations and spending pressures were rising inexorably, even in the early 1950s. There were limits to how far governments could increase spending and raise income taxes. The question that arose in the decade after establishing the service was how far NHS care should be rationed? Other thorny issues arose: how far could the service be universal and state funded, free at the point of use? Was the model of the NHS centred on 'curative' treatment in hospitals rather than preventive remedies in the community effective in ensuring a healthier population? Should the power of professional vested interests in the NHS be confronted to uphold the public interest? By the 1990s, New Labour accepted the case for pragmatism. Unlike Old Labour, Blair's party turned to 'quasi-markets' and competition to improve the quality of public services. New Labour sought to discard outdated ideological shibboleths, insisting that in the management of the public sector 'what matters is what works'. The language used by ministers spoke of breaking away from monolithic bureaucracies which they perceived to be the damaging legacy of Old Labour from the post-war decades.

The failure of planning

New Labour was adamant that the party's post-war experience pointed to the dangers of untrammelled intervention in the economy. The collapse of the National Plan in the 1960s highlighted the deficiencies of indicative state planning. Government intervention had been central to Old Labour's post-war agenda, particularly during Dalton's tenure at the Treasury until 1947. Yet while Labour brought industries into public ownership, there was no coherent strategy to modernise the private sector. The concern about relative economic decline compelled Wilson to pursue an interventionist strategy, drawing on French and German experience in forging a new industrial policy. Tripartism – where government, unions and employers co-operated to achieve industrial modernisation – emerged in the 1960s as a remedy for the vacuum in Labour's ideas about economic policy.[164]

However, the limitations of the Wilson government's stance were quickly exposed. External constraints and the soaring trade deficit pushed the 1964–70 governments towards deflation rather than planning for growth. The civil service, whose alleged inefficiency led Wilson to commission the Fulton Report in the late 1960s, was no longer thought capable of planning and co-ordination.[165] As a result, New Labour was reticent about using national government to intervene in markets. Gordon Brown rejected 'the old centralisation that characterised industrial policy', Old Labour's legacy of 'picking winners', 'promoting national champions' and subsidising 'loss-making enterprises'.[166] He insisted public action should focus on investment in skills, science and infrastructure, with selective measures to eradicate regional inequalities. Even in the aftermath of the 2008 financial crisis, Brown remained sceptical that state intervention could restore growth and competitiveness. His unease reflected memories of the Alternative Economic Strategy (AES) and the advocacy of wide-ranging public intervention in the 1970s.

The collapse of the Alternative Economic Strategy (AES)

For Blair and Brown's entourage, the Alternative Economic Strategy (AES) first proposed in 1973 was the nadir of Old Labour in the post-war era. The strategy's aim was to modernise capitalism while eradicating class conflict by enabling rapid wage growth. The AES advocated wide-ranging state control of the economy.[167] Whereas the Attlee governments focused on nationalisation, the AES dictated that firm-level planning agreements should restructure private sector enterprise. Among the AES's most influential advocates was Stuart Holland, a former Whitehall official and adviser to Harold Wilson. Holland's work focused on the growing significance of multinational corporations that evaded regulations imposed by national governments.[168] Holland demanded 'a transformation of the prevailing class structures which concentrate economic and social power in the hands of a largely self-perpetuating oligarchy'.[169] The internationalisation of capital served to render less efficient the regimes of national economic management spawned in the Attlee era.[170] The AES stressed the importance of limiting foreign trade to protect the national economy, reversing deindustrialisation. The discretionary power of the nation-state would be used to insulate the economy, allowing British industry to be reorganised along socialist lines. The vulnerability of sterling to speculative attacks on the foreign exchange markets would be dealt with using capital controls.[171]

As the crisis engulfed the British economy in the 1970s, radical policies were considered, even in the orthodox bastion of the Treasury. Economics departments in British universities debated alternative ideas. Of particular significance was the work of the Keynesian New Cambridge School, an eclectic band of economists that included Nicky Kaldor, Robert Neild, Wynne Godley, Ken Coutts and Francis Cripps. Economists made the case for import controls to achieve a medium-term net balance of trade in manufacturing as an alternative to deflation or devaluation.[172] While the AES provided a rationale for state ownership, the strategy was preoccupied with protecting established industries, cultivating support among the trade unions. The difficulty was that by the 1970s, nationalisation was even more unpopular with British voters, particularly the skilled working class. There was little clamour for the extension of public ownership. The authors of the AES did not regard the overweening concentration of economic power, the pursuit of 'reform from on high' and 'centralised administration by the state bureaucracy' as troubling.[173] As such, the AES epitomised Old Labour's failings. It made 'a fetish of nationalisation' and planning in an age when voters 'were losing faith in the curative powers of the central state'.[174] Less attention was paid by the AES to establishing workers' democracy, increasing participation in the governance of the economy.

Old Labour and the machinery of government

The AES critique influenced the modernisers' conception of the state. In contrast to Old Labour, their reappraisal emphasised the limits of central government intervention. The experience of the Mitterrand administration in France in the early 1980s was held to be instructive. Francois Mitterrand's presidency was committed to advancing central planning and redistribution. Yet the French Socialists were forced to abandon their programme as confidence in the franc evaporated on the financial markets. The experience of Mitterrand's government brought home the futility of socialism in one country, a perceived weakness of Old Labour. In *Marxism Today,* Robin Murray insisted the Left should recognise the limits of Keynesian policy. He wrote, 'The power of any government to control the national economy through macro measures has been seriously eroded by the growth of multinationals and the openness of the British economy'.[175] As John Callaghan remarked, 'Rare was the analysis of the Mitterrand experiment which did not stress the international context of its defeat'.[176] Blair and Brown's party wholeheartedly rejected the alternative strategies of the 1970s.

More generally, New Labour believed the party must shed Old Labour's association with centralised post-war bureaucracy. The legacy of collectivism should be discarded. It was claimed that socialists must 'recognize the force of the antipathy that now exists towards "big government": the multiplication of bureaucracy, the increase in cost, the feeling that government already has too large an influence over people's individual lives'.[177] In this climate, Labour should champion the rights of citizens and consumers creating a responsive system of government, where necessary tackling public sector vested interests. Moreover, the party should advance constitutional reform, while overhauling institutions to promote account-able government. At the outset, New Labour was determined to modernise the British state through radical innovation: joining-up Whitehall departments, inventing new agencies and public bodies, rewiring the civil service to rational-ise policy-making, reforming the constitution while dispersing political authority across the UK.

Old Labour focused on shifting the balance of power away from capital towards labour. By the 1990s, however, the constitution and machinery of gov-ernment had moved centre-stage in British social democratic ideas. The British political system marked by the absence of a written constitution and the cen-tralisation of the executive was viewed as less conducive to the achievement of Labour's goals, a key factor in the gulf between promise and performance that characterised the Attlee and Wilson eras.

Britain's role in the world

Finally, Old Labour's inheritance in foreign affairs decisively influenced the world-view of the modernisers. Blair believed Old Labour's conception of Brit-ain's role in the world and its faith in socialist foreign policy was misconceived. New Labour identified critical vulnerabilities in socialist iterations of foreign policy. The first difficulty was the perception of the party among voters as 'weak' on defence and national security, the legacy of Labour's turn to unilateralism in the late 1950s. The second weakness was the party's identification as a protest movement, ensuring its attitude to world affairs was utopian rather than realist. That world-view was manifested as 'anti-Americanism', the desire for Britain to be a neutral force that rejected militarism and imperialism. The third perceived weakness in Old Labour's socialist foreign policy was Euroscepticism and oppo-sition to Britain joining the European Economic Community (EEC), defending national sovereignty and a socialist planned economy against the capitalist club of Europe.

The Labour Party was committed to reversing such policies by the mid-1990s, although the process of revision began under Kinnock. Blair's claim in foreign policy was that 'the government has moved beyond the traditional positions of old Left and new Right'.[178] New Labour emphasised responsibil-ity and realism in the conduct of British foreign affairs. The epitome of Old Labour's failings was the 1983 election manifesto. Labour's 'longest suicide note in history' committed the party to unilateral nuclear disarmament, rejection of the American alliance and withdrawal from NATO alongside departure from the EEC. The party's Right Wing implicated these policies in the severity of its defeat, underlining Labour's perceived unfitness for office. Over the next decade, the party's foreign policy was overhauled by Kinnock and John Smith. Yet the leadership's unease with Labour's foreign policy legacy went back much further than 1983.

Remaining apart from Europe

The Attlee governments advanced a confident, outward-looking post-war foreign policy. Britain was understandably treated as a pivotal power in the aftermath of World War Two. Ernest Bevin was the most influential foreign secretary since Palmerston. He fought to ensure the United States remained diplomatically and militarily engaged in continental Europe. Bevin helped construct the Marshall Plan of economic aid for Europe, as well as contributing towards the formation of NATO. The Americans were reassured that British foreign policy retained the guiding principles advanced by Winston Churchill and Anthony Eden. Labour ministers depicted the international arena as a struggle between 'democracy' and 'totalitarianism'. The rhetoric of a socialist foreign policy was muted.[179] The party's foreign policy after 1945 'appeared the ultimate sign of a movement of protest that had adjusted itself to the realities and torments of power'.[180]

Yet in the late 1940s, Attlee and Bevin decided to remain apart from Europe, rejecting membership of the European Coal and Steel Community (ECSC). They feared the ECSC would prevent the Labour Government from nationalising coal and steel. The very idea of putting steel and coal under joint management with Germany was unconscionable. Morrison told his colleagues, 'The Durham miners won't wear it'.[181] The post-war governments 'wanted nothing to do with a customs union that would compromise the UK's imperial role'. As Bevin implored, Britain was 'not just another European country'.[182] Even the Left perceived Britain to have a unique status, given the UK had led resistance to Nazism. As a consequence, the government acquired the reputation for standing aside from Europe while remaining wary of integration. When the Schuman Plan for the European Iron and Steel Community was launched, Attlee's ministers were 'solidly opposed'. The prime minister and his foreign secretary exhibited 'emotional xenophobia' towards Europe, attenuated by the fear of Germany. They believed that entering a customs union would weaken the UK's imperial role.[183] Attlee expressed concerns about a United States of Europe, reasserting the importance of parliamentary sovereignty in the advancement of British socialism. Gaitskell warned in his speech to the 1962 party conference that Europe threatened to sweep away 'a thousand years of British history'. Europe might bring an end to Britain's role as an independent nation. Meanwhile, Wilson described the EC as an 'arid, sterile and tight trading bloc'. Discussing the prospects for a second British application in 1967, Wilson's cabinet was bitterly divided. Ministers were concerned that membership would 'seriously damage our commonwealth interests', 'make us politically dependent on the six [other EC members]', which meant Britain would lose 'our power to control imports'.[184] What is more, the EC would weaken Britain's relationship with the United States at a time when Europe was 'wholly divided on issues of foreign policy'.

As leader fifty years later, Blair highlighted Attlee and Bevin's perceived errors over Europe following the Second World War. Peter Mandelson believed:

> Old Labour had an instinctive dislike of what was felt to be a continental
> cartel of capitalist-orientated Christian Democrats. . . . [In contrast] New
> Labour has the self-confidence in Britain's values not to fear loss of national
> identity in this process of European co-operation.[185]

In missing the opportunity of joining Europe, Blair claimed the Labour government surrendered the chance for Britain to lead from within. The New Labour leader insisted Attlee's administration failed to understand the realities of the new world order.[186] Historians have certainly questioned Blair's argument. Attlee and Bevin's decision to retain 'spheres of influence' in the Commonwealth and former colonies was more rational than it was portrayed.[187] Still, it is striking how hard Blair fought to keep the option of Britain joining the European single currency alive in the late 1990s. He believed that after the Second World War, Britain should have become the political leader of Europe. By the early 1990s, Labour was a conventional pro-European party.[188] The leadership's strategy sought to project influence within the European Union (EU) over defence and security, economic reform and the management of globalisation. Yet the Labour government's aim was ultimately to make the EU more akin to Anglo-America underlining the British Left's ambiguity about the European project.

Spending on defence and national security

Certain elements of Old Labour's legacy in foreign policy were less off-putting to the modernisers. The Attlee governments supported rearmament in the early 1950s. As a consequence, domestic reforms were sacrificed, allowing increased military spending to fight the war in Korea. Attlee declared, 'We'll have to support the yanks', emphasising Britain's continuing dependence on American power.[189] The British ambassador in Washington, Oliver Franks, warned that any failure to support the Americans in Korea would inflict irreparable damage on the special relationship. In Labour Britain, despite the rhetoric about building the New Jerusalem, the 'warfare' state was prioritised over the welfare state.[190] The dispute with Bevan over Gaitskell's 1951 budget underlined the potential for discord over the financing of rearmament. Gaitskell had imposed NHS charges while raising the basic rate of income tax to 47.5 per cent. Bevan (alongside Harold Wilson and John Freeman) subsequently resigned from the Government. In January 1951, Attlee announced a £4.7 billion defence expenditure package equivalent to 10 per cent of GDP.[191] Rearmament opened up the division between Left and Right, provoking clashes over defence and foreign policy that plagued the party in subsequent decades.[192] The ineffectual policies on defence and security epitomised the frailties of Old Labour.

The modernisers sought to radically rethink the party's position. The post-1997 governments undertook the *Strategic Defence Review* (SDR), aligning Britain's capabilities with threats faced after the Cold War. There was an effort to link Britain's defence assets with adjustments in the geopolitical landscape. The foreword to the defence review stated:

> The British are by instinct an internationalist people. We believe that as well as defending our rights we should discharge our responsibilities in the world. We do not want to stand idly by and watch humanitarian disasters as the aggression of dictators goes unchecked. We want to give a lead. We want to be a force for good.[193]

Given its openness to reappraising the UK's defence options, including the potential for more joint operations with European allies, the SDR was widely praised on the Left. An unprecedented effort at European defence co-operation was launched at St Malo in December 1998, leading to the momentous bilateral agreement between the French and British governments.

Unilateral nuclear disarmament

The Labour Party since the Second World War was haunted by conflict over unilateral disarmament. The 1960 conference voted for unilateralism against the wishes of the leadership, backed by major unions including the Transport and General Workers Union (TGWU). The policy was reversed in 1962 after the leadership abandoned the commitment to an independent deterrent while agreeing to the 'no first use principle'.[194] The British scientific community influenced the creation of the Campaign for Nuclear Disarmament (CND) in 1958 led by the socialist historian, E.P. Thompson. CND's launch had an enormous cultural and political effect on the Labour Party. The growth in support within the party centred on the immoral nature of nuclear weapons, alongside Labour's tradition of pacifist commitment since 1914. CND represented more than 'a protest against nuclear weapons; it embraced a social and cultural critique of the whole of technological civilisation'.[195] The antipathy to nuclear weapons reflected hostility to the United States. The increase in CND's support, 'had an explosive impact on the party'.[196]

By the early 1980s, Labour's policy shifted back to a 'non-nuclear position'. The party's 1983 manifesto proclaimed:

> The logic of the case for the nuclear deterrent, presented by British Conservative Ministers, is that all peace-loving countries should equip themselves with the same protection. It is a logic which would intensify the race and destroy the universe. The first task of a new Labour government will be to restore a sense of sanity in dealing with these supreme questions. . . . We are the only party that offers a non-nuclear defence policy. Multitudes of people in many other lands, on both sides of the Atlantic, in Asia and Africa and Europe too, are ready to join us in the campaign for a nuclear freeze, for fresh exertions to stop the proliferation of these weapons, to stop the whole monstrous nuclear race to destruction.[197]

Old Labour preached the virtues of neutralism and unilateral disarmament, envisaging a Britain no longer in thrall to the American special relationship outside the capitalist club of Europe.

The unilateralist position was reversed again during the 1980s, but the shift proved arduous for the leadership, epitomised by the fact that both Kinnock and Blair were members of CND. It was said that Kinnock's wife, Glenys, who took part in anti-nuclear protests at the Greenham Common military base in Berkshire, threatened to divorce him if he allowed the policy of unilateralism to be ditched. Labour's defence debate proved to be rancorous. In 1988, Kinnock sought to shift position in the aftermath of Labour's third election defeat. On the BBC Sunday politics programme, *This Week, Next Week*, he told an interviewer: 'There is no need now for a something-for-nothing unilateralism. The idea that there is a something-for-nothing thrust that can be made is redundant'. The intervention was a major alteration in Labour's defence policy. It provoked fury among the Soft Left in the shadow cabinet led by David Blunkett and Robin Cook, who broke with Tony Benn and the Campaign Group in the early 1980s. The Soft Left supported Kinnock's leadership but opposed the dilution of Labour's anti-nuclear defence policy. One party member described Kinnock's interview as, 'the most serious and most far-reaching blunder of his political life. . . . Labour's new policy means a continuation of the arms race'.[198]

The leadership then issued a hasty climb-down. Thereafter, Kinnock acted cautiously.[199] At the 1988 Blackpool conference, the motion promising to remove nuclear weapons by 'unilateral, bilateral or multilateral negotiations' was defeated. The general secretary of the Transport and General Workers' Union (TGWU), Ron Todd, implored, 'We will not allow . . . our non-nuclear defence policy . . . to be downgraded or discarded'. The former secretary of state for defence, Denis Healey, dissented telling delegates that they would, 'only win power if we can convince the people of this country that we take their security seriously'.[200] To Blair and Brown's followers, Kinnock ultimately failed because he refused to separate the modernised party from Old Labour's inheritance in defence policy.

According to an influential adviser, 'The Old Labour Party . . . was very suspect on defence, unilateral disarmament and so on, and one of the successes of New Labour was to construct itself as more trustworthy'.[201] By the early 1990s, Blair was adamant that unilateralism was untenable electorally. In the aftermath of the Cold War, the steady disappearance of non-nuclear policies among social democratic parties in Western Europe, amid the growth of support for multilateralism, aided the Labour leadership. The United States and Russia were now committed to an extensive programme of nuclear deproliferation. Modernisation was propelled by the shifting external context of Britain's world role.

Divisions over Britain's role in Europe

During the 1970s, Labour became split once again over British membership of the EEC. Harold Wilson conceded a referendum in a move to hold his fractious party together. In 1971, Roy Jenkins and a cabal of rebels joined the Conservative government in voting for membership on terms negotiated by Heath. Meanwhile, other senior figures on the Labour Right including Healey, Crosland

and Callaghan sounded a more sceptical note on membership in the immediate aftermath of the 1970 defeat.

The divisions over Britain's role in Europe went to the heart of Labour's purpose as a national party – to install a socialist economic strategy in one country or to be part of the burgeoning European common market that reversed national decline? Blair and Brown were adamant that Britain would only succeed on the basis of committed political and economic co-operation with Europe.

Old Labour's foreign policy

New Labour was constructed in diametric opposition to the foreign policy stance that the party under Old Labour adopted. Blair's infamous 1999 speech in Chicago promulgated a doctrine of liberal internationalism, widely criticised but still the most coherent statement intellectually on foreign affairs and Britain's role in the world produced by Labour since 1951. For the party to have a global strategy related to foreign affairs informed by a recognisable doctrine was unusual. The leadership's rethinking was aided by developments in global geopolitics and domestic affairs. The fall of the Berlin Wall and the end of the Cold War required a new strategy for British national defence. The impact of Thatcherism meant the Left looked increasingly to Europe to consolidate the gains of the post-war settlement. Yet there had long been enduring support for both the US alliance and European co-operation in the British Labour movement, particularly on the Right. The early leaders of the party, including Keir Hardie and Ramsay MacDonald, remained avowed internationalists.

The modernisers learnt from the party's experience in foreign policy, dismissive of Old Labour's drift to utopianism in the 1950s. Yet even in the late 1990s, ambiguities remained. New Labour combined support for Atlanticism, which saw Britain dragged into wars in Afghanistan and Iraq that caused unprecedented domestic unpopularity, with commitment to development aid and EU membership. The humanitarian 'responsibility to protect' missions to Kosovo, Sierra Leone and Rwanda gave Blair's strategy added moral legitimacy. Blair was aware of the damage done to Old Labour in being perceived as unreliable on defence. Yet that mind-set meant New Labour's strategy was often cautious and circumspect. There was a refusal to think more radically about Britain's strategic capabilities and its role in the world. The 'bridge' between Europe and the United States – the centrepiece of New Labour's approach – looked unstable as Blair departed from office in the aftermath of two major foreign wars. Blair's premiership exposed fundamental weaknesses in Britain's post-Suez national strategy of acting as the bridge between Europe and the United States.[202] New Labour refused to learn the central lesson of post-war policy: the UK was drawn closer to Europe after 1945 due to the economic realities of trade and the geopolitical realities of security, yet its political class was attached to America while many British voters wished to remain apart from both.[203] Despite ditching Old Labour, Blair's party struggled to identify a coherent response to that inescapable dilemma.

Conclusion

New Labour reflected the leadership's desire to separate the party from the legacies of defeat. Blair and Brown sought to disavow the past while learning from Labour's complex inheritance. New Labour politicians absorbed lessons from the dismal incompetence and failure of Old Labour, recasting the party's identity for the emerging global economy and society. Peter Mandelson recounts that the party's experience 'had a strong impact on New Labour in every sense. We ran a reassurance strategy to get elected and once in power didn't do anything like previous Labour governments had done'.[204] As a consequence, Labour's past 'was re-imagined and reconstructed in a very particular way'.[205]

Party reformers maintained the identity of Old Labour forged in the post-war era and centred on industry and state ownership was obsolete given the demise of the class-based society. As one of the party's rising political stars insisted, 'The Tories . . . were helped by the emergence, post-war, of a new social grouping proud of having come up 'the hard way' who saw Labour as part of the past they had escaped'.[206] This interpretation of historical experience shaped New Labour's strategic assumptions. The party constructed its programme in direct opposition to the rhetoric and image of Old Labour following the crisis of Labourism, an experience which proved far more compelling than the rise of Thatcherism. There was the constant desire among modernisers to project economic and social policies as fresh and novel. In so doing, New Labour was more than willing to deploy misleading stereotypes, dismissing the entire post-war era as derailed by 'old-fashioned Keynesianism'.

New Labour's distance from the past was important, even if fundamentally disingenuous. The category of 'Old' Labour concealed enormous diversity in the institutions and practices of the party, conflating the Wilson/Callaghan era with the chaos of Militant in local government during the 1980s. The breach between New Labour and previous governments was in fact, 'largely rhetorical if one recalls what Labour has done in office rather than promised in opposition. One does not have to buy into the far-left critique of Labourism to suggest that the Labour Party under Tony Blair is not so much *sui generis* as reverting perhaps to type'.[207] Modernisation and reform were integral to the party's dominant tradition: 'The constant striving for modernity, the stress on the future, and continual attempts to redefine Labour and its policies, have always been at the heart of the party's history'.[208] The 'Old' Labour of 1983, 'a party that lost elections, that had a series of unpalatable, extreme, often suicidal policies', was utterly different to the 'Old' Labour of Attlee, Wilson and Callaghan as their track record in defence and foreign policy underlines.[209] The construct of Old Labour versus New Labour, of 'traditionalists' versus 'modernisers', 'had only a tangential resemblance to reality'.[210]

Moreover, New Labour's negative portrayal of Old Labour as 'a graveyard of failed policies' ultimately proved costly.[211] Blair's relationship with the traditional Right deteriorated even prior to the 1997 victory. The Labour Right believed they saved the party in the early 1980s and grew embittered at Blair's perceived betrayal. Roy Hattersley claimed, 'The Blair project is not a continuation of Neil Kinnock's reforms. . . . Blair believes he has found an alternative [to socialism]'.[212] Many activists, trade unionists and parliamentarians felt the modernisers ignored their role in wrestling back control of the NEC and CLPs.[213] New Labour's desire to discard the party's 'tax and spend' image meant diluting the commitment to the Croslandite goal of equality. Blair insisted, 'I think one of the tragedies of the Left was that it allowed the term 'equality' to really become a term of abuse about levelling down'.[214] Hattersley found New Labour's equivocation about egalitarianism and progressive taxation contemptible, contributing to its loss of ideological purpose.

While Blair and Brown demonstrated intellectual dynamism and reforming zeal, they arguably lost impetus after taking office. As subsequent chapters will demonstrate, no compelling ideological prospectus emerged. The category of Old Labour obscured elements of prior thought that the modernisers and their followers might have found beneficial. Moreover, Labour's chequered performance after the First World War made the leadership too pessimistic about the post-1997 administrations' ability to govern competently. New Labour believed it was too risky to fundamentally overhaul the political system. They thought voters were implacably wedded to lower taxes. Blair's entourage was terrified of the Murdoch press and its attitude to Europe. The approach to law and order was unashamedly populist.

To paraphrase Marx, in their intellectual defensiveness the modernisers risked forgetting that while people do not 'make [history] as they please', political movements and parties have the capacity to 'make their own history' – as Attlee and Thatcher clearly demonstrated. The Labour Party in the twenty-first century could still be the agent of change, not simply the inheritor of a pre-existing settlement in a conservative society.

Notes

1 K. Marx, *The Eighteenth Brumaire of Louis Bonaparte*.
2 R. McKibbin, 'Homage to Wilson and Callaghan', *The London Review of Books*, Volume 13 (2), 1991.
3 D. Coates, *Prolonged Labour: The Slow Birth of New Labour Britain*.
4 A. Finlayson, *Making Sense of New Labour*, London: Lawrence & Wishart, 2003.
5 A. Gamble, *Between Europe and America: The Future of British Politics*, p. 192, Basingstoke: Palgrave Macmillan, 2003.
6 F. Faucher-King, 'The Party Is Over: The Modernisation of the British Labour Party', in T. Casey (ed.), *The Blair Legacy: Politics, Policy, Governance and Foreign Affairs*, Basingstoke: Palgrave Macmillan, 2009.
7 J. Cronin, *New Labour's Pasts: The Labour Party and Its Discontents*.
8 D. Howell, *British Social Democracy: A Study in Development and Decay*, London: Croom Helm, 1976.
9 P. Hyman, *One Out of Ten: From Downing Street Vision to Classroom Reality'*, p. 11, London: Vintage, 2005.
10 J. Cronin, *New Labour's Pasts: The Labour Party and Its Discontents*.

11 E. Shaw, *Losing Labour's Soul*, p. 150, London: Routledge, 2008.
12 G. Norris in O. Daddow, 'New Labour: A Witness History', *Contemporary British History*, Volume 29 (1), p. 111, 2014.
13 https://independent.co.uk/news/uk/politics/tony-blairs-speech-in-full-5348100.html. Accessed 17th December 2018.
14 P. Hyman, *One in Ten*, p. 53.
15 J. Joyce, *Ulysses*, p. 158, London: Wordsworth Classics, 2010.
16 Cited in C.V.J. Griffiths, 'History and the Labour Party', in J. Nott et al. (eds.), *Classes, Cultures and Politics: Essays on British History for Ross McKibbin*, p. 283, Oxford: Oxford University Press, 2011.
17 C.V.J. Griffiths, 'History and the Labour Party'.
18 P. Mandelson, 'Can New Labour Deliver', Speech, 1996, personal archive.
19 Cited in C.V.J. Griffiths, 'History and the Labour Party', p. 297.
20 T. Blair, 'Let Us Face the Future: 1945 Anniversary Lecture', *The Fabian Society*, 1995.
21 J. Tomlinson, *The Labour Governments 1964–70: Economic Policy*, p. 1, Manchester: Manchester University Press, 2004.
22 Pemberton, H., Black, L. & Thane, P. (eds.), *Reassessing 1970s Britain*, Manchester: Manchester University Press, 2013.
23 P. Gould, *The Unfinished Revolution: How the Modernisers Saved the Labour Party*, p. 33, London: Abacus, 2011.
24 J. Cronin, *New Labour's Pasts: The Labour Party and Its Discontents*, p. 7.
25 J. Saville, 'Labourism and the Labour Government', *The Socialist* Register, p. 44, 1967.
26 P. Clarke, *A Question of Leadership: From Gladstone to Thatcher*.
27 R.H.S. Crossman, 'The Lessons of 1945', in P. Anderson & R. Blackburn (eds.), *Towards Socialism*, p. 153, London: Verso, 1965.
28 D. Marquand, *The Progressive Dilemma*.
29 The Labour Party, *Let Us Face the Future*, p. 6, London: The Labour Party, 1945.
30 Cited in S. Brooke, 'The Party and the 1945 General Election', *Contemporary Record*, Volume 9 (1), p. 21, 1995.
31 *Report of the Fifty Eighth Annual Conference of the Labour Party*, London: The Labour Party, 1959 cited in S. Fielding, *The Labour Party: Socialism and Society Since 1951*, p. 54.
32 Michael Young, cited in S. Brooke, p. 23, 'The Labour Party and the 1945 General Election'.
33 B. Harrison, *Seeking a Role? Britain 1951–70*, p. 69, Oxford: Oxford University Press, 2009.
34 B. Jackson, 'Review: Citizen and Subject: Clement Attlee's Socialism', *History Workshop Journal*, forthcoming, 2018.
35 *New Statesman*, 'Clement Attlee: Editorial', London: The New Statesman, 12th October, 1954.
36 R. Crossman, 'The Lessons of 1945', p. 156.
37 Cited in S. Fielding, *The Labour Governments 1964–70: The Labour Party and Cultural Change*, pp. 260–261.
38 G. Stedman-Jones, *Languages of Class: Studies in English Working Class History 1832–1982*, p. 24.
39 D. Potter, 'Letter', *The Times*, 27th April 1959.
40 A. Crosland, *The Conservative Enemy*, p. 120, London: Jonathan Cape, 1956.
41 Editorial, *Socialist Commentary*, p. 247, Volume 11, 1951.
42 P. Gould, *The Unfinished Revolution: How the Modernisers Saved the Labour Party*, London: Abacus, 2011.
43 T. Blair, *A Journey*.
44 'Report on General Election Issues by the Labour Party NEC Election Sub-Committee: 19th September 1959', Gaitskell Archive, C192/1, University College, London.
45 The Labour Party Manifesto, 'Britain Belongs to You', London: The Labour Party, 1959.

46 T. Blair, Correspondence, 25th March 1985, LP/Policy Committees and Study Groups of the NEC Research Department (PCSG)/69/11 (Labour Party archives).

47 'Report on the 1959 General Election by the Labour Party NEC Election Sub-Committee: 22nd October 1959', Gaitskell Archive, C192/1, University College, London.

48 L. Black, *The Political Culture of the Left in Affluent Britain 1951–64*, p. 106, Basingstoke: Palgrave Macmillan, 2002.

49 V. Bogdanor, 'Labour in Opposition 1951–64', in V. Bogdanor & R. Skidelsky (eds.), *The Age of Affluence*, London: Penguin, 1970.

50 *Daily Mail Editorial*, cited in V. Bogdanor, 'The General Election 1959', Lecture at Gresham College, 11th November 2014.

51 Report on General Election Issues by the Labour Party NEC Election Sub-Committee: 19th September 1959', Gaitskell Archive, C192/1, University College, London.

52 *Daily Mail Editorial*, cited in V. Bogdanor, 'The General Election 1959'.

53 'Report on the 1959 General Election by the Labour Party NEC Election Sub-Committee: 22nd October 1959', Gaitskell Archive, C192/1, University College, London.

54 'Findings from the General Election Study by the University of Leeds Television Research Unit: 8th March 1960', Gaitskell Archive, C192/1, University College, London.

55 Report on General Election Issues by the Labour Party NEC Election Sub-Committee: 19th September 1959', Gaitskell Archive, C192/1, University College, London.

56 'Mark Abrams: A Report on the New Roots of Working-Class Conservatism', Gaitskell Archive, C192/1, University College, London.

57 Cited in A. Gamble, *The Conservative Nation*, p. 65, London: Routledge, 1975.

58 A. Crosland, 'Can Labour Win?', Fabian Tract 278, p. 10, London: The Fabian Society, 1960.

59 A. Crosland, 'Can Labour Win?', p. 11.

60 Cited in D. Howell, *British Social Democracy*, p. 80. The data in Figure 3.1 is taken from the British Election Study (1966).

61 M. Francis, 'The Labour Party: Modernisation and the Politics of Restraint', pp. 154–155, in B. Conekin, F. Mort & C. Waters (eds.), *Moments of Modernity: Reconstructing Britain 1945–64*, London: Verso, 1997.

62 For a summary of these accounts, see: J. Goldthorpe & D. Lockwood, 'Affluence and the British Class Structure', *The Sociological Review*, Volume 11 (2), pp. 133–163, 1963.

63 G. Stedman-Jones, 'Why Is the Labour Party in a Mess?'

64 Letter to Hugh Gaitskell from Arthur Palmer: 10th November 1959, Gaitskell Archive, C192/2, University College, London.

65 A. Crosland, Note to Hugh Gaitskell, November 1960, Crosland Archive, 6/1 (13), London School of Economics.

66 D. Butler & R. Rose, cited in S. Brooke, 'Gender and Working-Class Identity in Britain During the 1950s', *Journal of Social History*, Volume 34 (4), p. 773, 2001.

67 Cited in S. Fielding, 'Activists Against "Affluence": Labour Party Culture During the "Golden Age", circa 1950–70', *Journal of British Studies*, Volume 40, p. 258, April 2001.

68 Letter to Hugh Gaitskell from Donald Saunby: 27th October 1959, Gaitskell Archive, C192/3, University College, London.

69 V. Bogdanor, 'Labour in Opposition 1951–64'.

70 Letter to Hugh Gaitskell from Donald Saunby: 27th October 1959, Gaitskell Archive, C192/3, University College, London.

71 P. Graves, *Labour Women: British Women in Working-Class Politics*, Cambridge: Cambridge University Press, 1994.

72 M. Francis, *Ideas and Policies Under Labour 1945–1951: Building a New Britain*.

73 *Report of the Fifty Eighth Annual Conference of the Labour Party*, London: The Labour Party, 1959, cited in S. Fielding, *The Labour Party: Socialism and Society Since 1951*, p. 54.

74   'Report on Women's Organisation for consideration at special meetings of Women's Advisory Councils', January 1960 cited in S. Fielding, *The Labour Party: Socialism and Society Since 1951*, pp. 62–63.

75   B. Campbell, 'How the Other Half Lives', p. 19, *Marxism Today*, April 1984.

76   B. Donoughue & G. Jones, *Herbert Morrison*, p. 455.

77   D. Howell, *British Social Democracy*, pp. 203–204.

78   D. Howell, *British Social Democracy*, p. 185.

79   P. Williams, Hugh *Gaitskell*, p. 574.

80   P. Clarke, *A Question of Leadership: From Gladstone to Thatcher*, p. 256.

81   H. Dalton, *The Political Diary 1918–40*, p. 695, London: Jonathan Cape, 1987.

82   Letter to Hugh Gaitskell from R.T. Hodson: 16th October 1959, Gaitskell Archive, C192/3, University College, London.

83   Letter to Hugh Gaitskell from R.T. Hodson: 16th October 1959, Gaitskell Archive, C192/3, University College, London.

84   P. Williams, *Hugh Gaitskell*, p. 574.

85   D. Jay, *Socialism in the New Society*, p. 398, London: Longman Green, 1962.

86   Labour Party Manifesto, 'Let's Go with Labour for the New Britain', London: The Labour Party, 1964.

87   B. Pimlott, *Harold Wilson*, p. 305, London: William Collins, 1993.

88   P. Anderson, 'Components of the National Culture', *New Left Review*, Volume 1/50, 1968.

89   P. Ziegler, *Wilson: The Authorised Life*, p. 157, London: Weidenfeld & Nicolson, 1993.

90   G. Brown, *In My Way*, p. 88, London: Harmondsworth, 1972.

91   G. O'Hara & H. Parr, 'Conclusions: Harold Wilson's 1964–70 Governments and the Heritage of "New" Labour', *Contemporary British History*, Volume 20 (3), pp. 477–489, 2006.

92   D, Marquand, J. Mackintosh & D. Owen, *Changing Gear*.

93   J. Gyford & S. Haseler, 'The Labour Party: Beyond Revisionism', Fabian Tract 302, London: The Fabian Society, 1971.

94   A. Campsie, 'Socialism Will Never be the Same Again: Reimagining British Left-Wing Ideas for the "New Times"', pp. 166–188.

95   'General Management Committee Minutes', Bedford CLP, 12th October 1967 cited in S. Fielding, *The Labour Party: Socialism and Society Since 1951*, p. 83.

96   S. Fielding, *The Labour Party*.

97   Cited in Z. Layton-Henry, *The Politics of Immigration*, p. 52, Oxford: Blackwells, 1992.

98   R. Weight, *Patriots: National Identity in Britain 1940–2000*, Basingstoke: Macmillan, 2002.

99   A. King, cited in J. Shepherd, *Crisis? What Crisis? The Callaghan Government and the British 'Winter of Discontent'*, p. 162, Manchester: Manchester University Press, 2015.

100   Interview, D. Lipsey, House of Lords, 2nd March 2015.

101   A. Gorz, *Farewell to the Working-Class: An Essay on Post-Industrial Socialism*, London: Pluto, 1982.

102   A. Ware, *Inequality in Britain*, London: Routledge, 2019.

103   E. Hobsbawm, 'The Forward March of Labour Halted'.

104   D. Kavanagh, *The Politics of the Labour Party*, p. 11, London: Routledge, 1982.

105   M. Francis, *Ideas and Policies Under Labour 1945–1951: Building a New Britain*, p. 201.

106   G. Stedman-Jones, *Languages of Class*, p. 62.

107   Cited in S. Brooke, 'Gender and Working-Class Identity in Britain During the 1950s', p. 789.

108   F. Sutcliffe-Braithwaite, *Class, Politics and the Decline of Deference in England 1968–2000*, Oxford: Oxford University Press, 2013.

109   L. Minkin, *The Blair Supremacy: A Study in the Politics of Labour's Party Management*, p. 131, Manchester: Manchester University Press, 2014.

110   E. Shaw, 'New Labour's Faustian Pact', *British Politics*, Volume 7 (3), p. 228, 2007.

111   C. Clarke, 'Economic Policy and Taxation After Blair', *Life After Blair Lecture Series*, London School of Economics, 7th February 2007.

112 R. Skidelsky, *Politicians and the Slump: The Labour Government of 1929–31*, London: Penguin, 1970.

113 E. Shaw, 'Retrieving or Reimagining the Past?' in J. Davis & R. McWilliam (eds.), *Labour and the Left in the 1980s*, p. 29, Manchester: Manchester University Press, 2018.

114 P. Hall, 'Policy Paradigms, Social Learning and the State: The Case of Economic Policy-Making in Britain', pp. 275–298.

115 Cited in G. O'Hara & H. Parr, 'Conclusions: Harold Wilson's 1964–70 Governments and the Heritage of "New" Labour', p. 480.

116 H. Young, *The Hugo Young Papers: A Journalist's Notes from the Heart of Politics*, London: Penguin, 2009.

117 Cited in J. Tomlinson, 'It's the Economy, Stupid! Labour and the Economy, *circa* 1964', *Contemporary British History*, Volume 21 (3), p. 337, 2007.

118 A. Booth, cited in J. Tomlinson, 'The Limits of Tawney's Ethical Socialism: A Historical Perspective on the Labour Party and the Market', *Contemporary British History*, Volume 16 (4), pp. 1–16, 2002.

119 R. McKibbin, *Parties and People 1914–1951*, Oxford: Oxford University Press, 2008; R. Skidelsky, *Politicians and the Slump: The Labour Government 1929–31*, pp. 84–89, London: Macmillan, 1967; P. Clarke, *A Question of Leadership: From Gladstone to Thatcher*; J. Callaghan, 'Social Democracy and Globalisation: The Limits of Social Democracy in Historical Perspective', *British Journal of Politics and International Relations*, Volume 4 (3), pp. 421–450, 2009; J. Cronin, *Labour and Society in Britain 1917–89*, London: Harper Collins, 1984.

120 https://newstatesman.com/politics/economy/2019/11/old-monetary-world-markets-created-constraints-now-there-no-sense-where. Accessed 18th November 2019.

121 J. Tomlinson, 'It's the Economy, Stupid! Labour and the Economy, *circa* 1964', *Contemporary British History*, p. 343.

122 J. Bulpitt, 'The Discipline of the New Democracy: Mrs Thatcher's Domestic Statecraft', *Political Studies*, Volume 34 (1), pp. 19–39, 1986.

123 R. Roberts, *When Britain Went Bust*, p. 63, London: OMFIF Press, 2017.

124 D. Howell, *British Social Democracy*.

125 J. Tomlinson, 'It's the Economy, Stupid!', p. 343.

126 K. Morgan, *Labour in Power 1945–51*, p. 347, Oxford: Clarendon Press, 1984.

127 R. Roberts, *When Britain Went Bust*.

128 Cited in L. Goldman, *The Life of R.H. Tawney: Socialism and History*, p. 267, London: Bloomsbury.

129 A. Offer, 'The Market Turn: From Social Democracy to Market Liberalism', *University of Oxford Discussion Papers in Economic and Social History*, No. 149, December 2016.

130 B. Pimlott, *Harold Wilson*, p. 617.

131 http://britishpoliticalspeech.org/speech-archive.htm?speech=174. Accessed 14th February 2018.

132 Cited in J. Tomlinson, *Managing the Economy, Managing the People*, p. 174.

133 K.O. Morgan, 'Britain in the Seventies – Our Unfinest Hour?', *Revue Francaise de Civilisation Britannique*, p. 11, 2017.

134 'Let Us Work Together: Labour's Way Out of the Crisis', *The Labour Party Manifesto*, p. 9, 1974.

135 S. Williams, cited in J. Shepherd, *Crisis? What Crisis?* p. 149.

136 B. Donoughue, *Prime Minister: The Conduct of Policy under Harold Wilson & James Callaghan*, pp. 189–193, London: Jonathan Cape, 1987.

137 J. Tomlinson, *Managing the Economy, Managing the People*, p. 97.

138 Chancellor's speech to the Labour Party conference, 'A Stakeholder Economy', Brighton, September 1997.

139 https://independent.co.uk/news/uk/home0000000-news/blair-ditches-keynes-1450959.html. Accessed 24th June 2018.

140 R. Toye, 'The Forgotten Revisionist: Douglas Jay and Britain's Transition to Affluence 1951–1964', in L. Black & H. Pemberton (eds.), *An Affluent Society? Britain's Post-War 'Golden age' Revisited*, p. 468, London: Ashgate, 2004.

141 R. Skidelsky, *Money and Government: A Challenge to Mainstream Economics*, London: Allen Lane, 2018.

142 C. Hay & M. Watson, 'Labour's Economic Policy: Studiously Courting Competence', p. 116.

143 Cited in P. Clarke, *A Question of Leadership: From Gladstone to Thatcher*, p. 151.

144 C. Clarke, 'Economic Policy and Taxation After Blair', *Life After Blair Lecture Series*, London School of Economics, 7th February 2007.

145 B. Pimlott, cited in J. Tomlinson, *Managing the Economy, Managing the People*, p. 105.

146 S. Newton, 'The Sterling Devaluation of 1967, The International Economy, and Post-War Social Democracy', *The English Historical Review*, Volume 125 (515), pp. 912–945, 2010.

147 J. Eatwell & A. Hughes, 'Discussion Paper on Macro-Economic Policies and the Supply-Side', March 1985, LP/Policy Committees and Study Groups of the NEC Research Department (PCSG)/69/11 (Labour Party archives).

148 Cited in S. Mudge, *Leftism Reinvented*, p. 348.

149 P. Stephens, cited in E. Shaw, *Losing Labour's Soul*, p. 152.

150 J. Tomlinson, *The Labour Governments 1964–70: Economy Policy*.

151 Cited in G. O'Hara & H. Parr, 'Conclusions: Harold Wilson's 1964–70 Governments and the Heritage of "New" Labour', p. 486.

152 P. Mandelson, 'Can New Labour Deliver', Speech, 1996.

153 J. Tomlinson, *Managing the Economy, Managing the People*, p. 96.

154 A. Gamble, 'Thatcher: The Second Coming', p. 18.

155 G. Loewenberg, 'The Transformation of British Labour Party Policy Since 1945', *Journal of Politics*, Volume 21, pp. 234–254, 1965.

156 R.H.S. Crossman, *The Diaries of a Cabinet Minister Volume I*, London: Mandarin, 1991.

157 R. McKibbin, *Parties and People*, p. 146.

158 D. Marquand, 'Inquest on a Movement: Labour's Defeat and Its Consequences', *Encounter*, p. 10, July 1979.

159 The Prime Minister, Personal Note, 21st April 2001.

160 T. Blair, 'Forging a New Agenda'.

161 The Labour Party Manifesto, p. 6, London: The Labour Party, 1945.

162 S. Webb & B. Webb, *Industrial Democracy*, London: Longmans Green, 1893.

163 The Labour Party Manifesto, 'Let Us Face The Future', p. 6, London: The Labour Party, 1945; M. Francis, *Ideas and Policies Under Labour 1945–1951: Building a New Britain*.

164 J. Tomlinson, *Democratic Socialism and Economic Policy: The Attlee Years 1945–51*, p. 305, Cambridge: Cambridge University Press, 1997.

165 The Fulton report, an inquiry into the civil service, was instigated by Harold Wilson, who had become increasingly dissatisfied with the machinery of government.

166 http://smf.co.uk/wp-content/uploads/2004/05/Publication-A-Modern-Agenda-for-Prosperity-and-Social-Reform-Gordon-Brown.pdf. Accessed 23rd May 2018.

167 J. Tomlinson, *Managing the Economy, Managing the People*; L. Panitch & C. Leys, *The End of Parliamentary Socialism*; A. Glyn, *The British Economic Disaster*, London: Pluto, 1980.

168 S. Holland, *The Socialist Challenge*, London: Quartet Books, 1975.

169 S. Holland, *The Socialist Challenge*, p. 36.

170 J. Tomlinson, 'Can Governments Manage the Economy?', Fabian Tract 524, London: Fabian Society, 1988.

171 A. Gamble, *Britain in Decline*, pp. 185–187, Basingstoke: Macmillan, 1981.

172 K. Coutts & J. Eatwell, 'Trade Policy: The Case for Import Controls', March 1985, LP/Policy Committees and Study Groups of the NEC Research Department (PCSG)/69/11 (Labour Party archives).

173 B. Rowthorn, *Capitalism, Conflict and Inflation*, p. 8, London: Lawrence & Wishart, 1981.

174 J. Callaghan, 'Rise and Fall of the Alternative Economic Strategy: From Internationalization of Capital to "Globalization"', *Contemporary British History*, Volume 14 (3), p. 124, 2000.

175 R. Murray, 'Benetton Britain: The New Economic Order', p. 28, November 1985; H. Radice, 'The National Economy: A Keynesian Myth?', *Capital & Class*, Volume 8 (1), pp. 111–140, 1984.
176 J. Callaghan, 'Rise and Fall of the Alternative Economic Strategy', p. 124.
177 S. Williams, *Politics Is for People*, p. 28, London: Harmondsworth, 1981, cited in S. Fielding, *The Labour Party: Socialism and Society Since 1951*, p. 120.
178 T. Blair, 'The Left Should Not Weep If Saddam Is Toppled', *The Guardian*, p. 18, 10th February 2003.
179 D. Howell, *British Social Democracy*, pp. 148–149.
180 K. Morgan, *Labour in Power*, p. 284.
181 Cited in H. Parr, 'European Integration', in M. Beech, K. Hickson & R. Plant, *The Struggle for Labour's Soul: Understanding Labour's Political Thought Since 1945*, London: Routledge, 2018.
182 J. Callaghan, *The Labour Party and Foreign Policy*, p. 172, London: Routledge, 2007.
183 K. Morgan, *Labour in Power*, p. 421; J. Callaghan, 'Globalisation', pp. 172–173.
184 'Cabinet Minutes: 30th April 1967', CAB 128/42 Original Reference CC 1 (67)-74 (67), 1967 12 Jan–21 Dec.
185 Cited in R. Weight, *Patriots: National Identity in Britain 1940–2000*, p. 673.
186 T. Blair, 'Let Us Face the Future: 1945 Anniversary Lecture', *The Fabian Society*, 1995.
187 A. Milward, *The European Rescue of the Nation State*, London: Routledge, 1999.
188 A. Gamble & G. Kelly, 'The British Labour Party and Monetary Union', *Western European Politics*, Volume 23 (1), pp. 1–25, 2000.
189 K. Harris, *Attlee*, p. 459, London: Wiedenfeld & Nicholson, 1982.
190 D. Edgerton, *The Rise and Fall of the British Nation: A Twentieth Century History*.
191 P. Clarke, *A Question of Leadership: From Gladstone to Thatcher*, p. 238.
192 K. Morgan, *Labour in Power*.
193 Her Majesty's Government, 'Strategic Defence Review', p. 4, 1998.
194 P. Williams, *Hugh Gaitskell*.
195 M. Veldman, *Fantasy, the Bomb and the Greening of Britain*, p. 115, Cambridge: Cambridge University Press, 1994.
196 P. Williams, *Hugh Gaitskell*, p. 575.
197 The Labour Party Manifesto, London: The Labour Party, 1983.
198 Letter to the Labour Party General Secretary, 5th June 1988, LP/Policy Committees and Study Groups of the NEC Research Department (PCSG)/69/11 (Labour Party archives).
199 P. Kellner (ed.), *Thorns and Roses: The Speeches of Neil Kinnock 1983–91*, London: Radius, 1990.
200 Cited in https://www.washingtonpost.com/archive/politics/1988/10/07/british-labor-searches-for-winning-formula/2d790156-ee53-4848-8691-9de5ad42d41d/?noredirect=on&utm_term=.3329ce01b962. Accessed 4th November 2018.
201 R. Liddle in O. Daddow, 'New Labour: A Witness History'.
202 P. Riddell, *The Unfulfilled Prime Minister*, p. 158.
203 A. Gamble, *Between Europe and America*.
204 Interview, Rt. Hon. Peter Mandelson, former Secretary of State, Department of Business, Innovation and Skills, October 2011.
205 E. Shaw, *Losing Labour's Soul*, p. 153.
206 T. Blair, Correspondence, 25th March 1985, LP/Policy Committees and Study Groups of the NEC Research Department (PCSG)/69/11 (Labour Party archives).
207 T. Bale, *Sacred Cows and Common Sense: The Symbolic Statecraft and Political Culture of the British Labour Party*, p. viii, Aldershot: Ashgate, 1999.
208 G. O'Hara & H. Parr, 'Conclusions: Harold Wilson's 1964–70 Governments and the Heritage of "New" Labour', p. 487.
209 P. Hyman, *One in Ten*, p. 53.
210 E. Shaw, *Losing Labour's Soul*, p. 153.

211 J. Cronin, *New Labour's Pasts: The Labour Party and Its Discontents*, p. 14.
212 Cited in R. McKibbin, 'The Luck of the Tories: The Debt to Kinnock', *The London Review of Books*, p. 8, 7th March 2002.
213 D. Hayter, *Fightback! Labour's Traditional Right in the 1970s and 1980s*, Manchester: Manchester University Press, 2005.
214 T. Blair, interview on *The World This Weekend*, BBC Radio 2, 14th December 1995.

4

NEW LABOUR AND THE GLOBAL CENTRE-LEFT

There is no Right and Left in economic policy any longer, only Right and Wrong.

Tony Blair[1]

The old working-class ethos is being eroded by prosperity and the increasing fluidity of our society. People now know that they can improve their lot by their own efforts. And as they succeed, they change their values and cease to identify themselves with the class from which they sprang.

Mark Abrams, Richard Rose and
Rita Hinden[2]

Introduction

The political and intellectual strategy of the modernisers arose from the landmark debate about British Labourism's degeneration during the twentieth century. Blair depicted his rejuvenated party as a ground-breaking 'project' to transform the British social and political landscape. New Labour was more than the expedient reaction to electoral defeat. It followed from the prolonged inquiry into Labour's purpose, and the question of how national revival and modernisation would be achieved in the aftermath of Thatcherism. Yet during the 1980s, the Left's future was questioned throughout the major industrialised democracies, not only Britain. Social democratic parties appeared to be declining in almost every post-industrial society. The parties of the Left in Western Europe and the United States were shedding electoral support. Their memberships were shrinking. Organised labour was fast retreating. Even where these parties entered government, notably Mitterrand's administration in France, they soon abandoned their radical programme assailed by hostile forces in the international economy.

Having examined Labourism's long-term failure in Britain, this chapter considers how the ideological and strategic advance of centre-left politics across the major capitalist economies reshaped Blair and Brown's party. There are three interlocking themes that give structure to the discussion. The chapter begins by outlining the major debates that influenced Labour's narrative of modernisation. It then addresses the ideas, programmes and ideologies from continental Europe and America that shaped the New Labour project. Finally, the chapter examines the diffusion of ideas through the conveyor belt of diverse political networks and think-tanks across Europe and the Anglosphere. The chapter's core argument is that the progressive tradition in Europe and America proved significantly more influential in shaping Blair and Brown's agenda than Thatcherite neo-liberalism in UK domestic politics.

Socialism in one country?

Numerous accounts speculate that Blair and Brown's party was wholly influenced by British developments, reinforcing acquiescence to the Thatcherite agenda of policy and politics. The Labour Party was insular, parochial, narrow minded and nationally orientated. This view of 'socialism in one country' is comprehensible but fundamentally misleading. The constellation of ideas emerging from continental Europe, the United States and the Anglosphere reconfigured Labour's identity in the Blair/Brown era. This chapter examines the impact of Europeanisation and Americanisation on the formation of New Labour's strategy and identity. The leadership were obsessed with the structural crisis afflicting the Left globally. Bob Jessop's claim that Blair's agenda 'deliberately, persistently, and wilfully [drove] forward the neo-liberal transformation of Britain' is wide of the mark.[3] Since the late 1950s, the major social democratic parties across Europe were reframing their doctrines and electoral strategies in the light of alterations in society and the class structure. At the outset, modernisers sought to position British Labour as a *European* social democratic force.

New Labour distanced itself from the past by acknowledging the critical importance of European ideas. Since the early-twentieth century, 'Old' Labour's relationship with the continental parties was aloof and distant. There was sporadic contact with Social Democrats in Sweden and Germany, while early leaders of the party remained committed internationalists. Keir Hardie wanted the Second International to prevent the outbreak of war in 1914. Labour's first prime minister, Ramsay MacDonald, was well known to Eduard Bernstein, the founder of European revisionism who advocated the parliamentary road to socialism. Ernest Bevin, Labour's most influential trade unionist in the inter-war years, was close to German unions threatened by Nazism. Yet, by and large, the party remained detached from its counterparts in continental Europe. Victory in the Second World War encouraged Labour to stand aside from European co-operation.

The early advocates of modernisation, among them Patricia Hewitt and Charles Clarke, Neil Kinnock's aides who became ministers in 1997, believed the political identity of the party ought to reflect core tenets of European social democracy. British Labour should embrace the disciplines of the market capitalist economy while committing itself to the pluralist institutions of European representative democracy that flourished in the second half of the twentieth century. The Scandinavian and German parties were ideological models for New Labour to emulate. In the late 1980s, Blair observed, 'By comparison with its sister socialist parties in Europe, the Labour Party still has a very small number of members. The socialist party in Sweden has a million members . . . in West Germany 900,000'.[4]

The growing influence of Europe reflected political success. By 2000, thirteen out of fifteen EU member-states had Left governments, ushering in a period of social democratic dominance. Most parties pursued an approach consistent with the British 'third way' championed by Blair and Brown, although there was national divergence. The Swedish Social Democrats forged a revitalised welfare state that responded to the dilemmas posed by globalisation. The French *Parti Socialiste* (PS) opposed compromise with the demands of global capitalism. The PS viewed the nation-state as the guarantor of social protection.[5] Yet despite variance across countries, Blair believed Labour was well placed to lead the revitalisation of European social democratic politics.

Even so, it is hard to ignore American progressivism's enduring influence on New Labour. The electoral revitalisation of the Democratic Party in the United States had a decisive impact on Labour in the 1980s and 1990s. Bill Clinton's New Democrats pioneered the strategy of triangulation and the third way approach to governance. The New Democrats offered a blueprint from which British Labour could overcome the legacy of electoral and governing failure, breaking the Thatcher/Reagan domination of the political landscape. The Labour leadership, particularly Blair, were also influenced by the Australian Labor Party (ALP) under the leadership of Bob Hawke and Paul Keating. The ALP found its own unique formula for electoral success in the globalising market economy.

The key moment for New Labour was nonetheless the 1992 election where Clinton won the US presidency triumphantly. Victory was the product of pragmatism and the 'what works' philosophy. Clinton's party offered 'a third choice that rejects the Left's reflexive defence of the bureaucratic status quo, and counters the right's destructive bid to simply dismantle government'.[6] The governing agenda of the third way proved hugely persuasive to the modernisers in Britain. Blair and Brown visited the United States as parliamentarians, along with their polling strategist, Philip Gould. The Democrats were a pivotal influence on Labour's political and policy agenda. Blair insisted Clinton's third way was:

> Not an attempt to split the difference between left and right. It is about traditional values in a changed world. It draws vitality from uniting the two great streams of left-of-centre thought – democratic socialism and liberalism – whose divorce this century did so much to weaken progressive politics across the West.[7]

The reshaping of Labour's doctrine and appeal was profoundly affected by the Democrats.

The international context and strategic forces that moulded Labour's development were evident before the 1990s, however, even if they were marginalised in the post-war party. The chapter begins by addressing the importance of America and Europe in Anthony Crosland's revisionism during the 1950s and 1960s. The revisionist analysis had a lasting impact on New Labour, even if it was unfairly compartmentalised by Blair as part of Old Labour's failed inheritance.

Staging posts in the development of British and European social democracy

Crosland's seminal work, *The Future of Socialism* (1956), was an unusual treatise. Despite having been written by a leading figure on the British Left, the text subtly reflected international experience. Crosland examined doctrinal rethinking underway among Swedish and German social democrats in the 1950s. He admired centre-left parties throughout Europe for updating their appeal in the face of social change, discarding the outdated remnants of Marxist thought. Kenneth Morgan attests: 'There has been no significant statement of socialist doctrine in this country – perhaps in any country – since Crosland in the mid-1950s'.[8] Crosland believed that in the light of progressive reforms, Sweden and the United States were countries suitable for emulation by British socialists. Sweden was the country that offered a template for British social democracy: 'Sweden . . . comes much nearer to a socialist's view of the "good" society', Crosland wrote; it gave, 'a higher priority to social welfare and the social services'.[9] Sweden was cohesive, sustained by an ethic of egalitarianism. Since the Swedish party no longer prioritised collective ownership, the Social Democrats (SAP) focused on advancing social justice through welfare expenditure. The SAP were so successful, their leadership feared they would be taken for granted by voters. One figure lamented, 'We have had so many victories that we are in a difficult position. A people with political liberty, full employment and social security has lost its dreams'.[10]

The Swedish strategy mirrored Crosland's vision of how social democracy ought to mature in Britain. The revisionists believed their ideas were in harmony with the rethinking sweeping Europe. Crosland declared, 'A spectre is haunting Europe – the spectre of revisionism'. He noted:

> Among the European socialist parties, the British Labour Party is unique in the doctrinal energy which it still devotes to the issue of public ownership. In the comprehensive new draft Programme of the Swedish SAP, precisely two brief mentions are made of the extension of collective ownership. In Germany, the SPD abandoned ownership as a major goal as early as 1959 in the famous Bad Godesberg programme. . . . The Austrian party made no mention of nationalisation in its 13-point programme for their recent – and brilliantly successful – election campaign.[11]

The Dutch Labour Party was another beacon of reformism, adopting a programme in which socialism was defined as an ethical and moral endeavour, jettisoning the historical emphasis on state ownership. All the continental European Left parties had Marxist origins. The process of revision was more fundamental and deep rooted than in Britain, where socialism was a pragmatic doctrine owing more to Methodism than to Marx. Yet Crosland's colleague, Denis Healey, believed, 'The continental parties have adjusted much better to social and political change than the Labour party'.[12] Healey was instrumental in bringing Labour closer to them. For Crosland, revitalising social democracy meant synthesising post-war Scandinavian experience with the progressivism of Roosevelt's New Deal and Kennedy's activist presidency. By the 1990s, New Labour's world-view in harmonising European and US influence was remarkably similar.

Bad Godesberg

Another moment watched intently by reformists in the Labour Party was the restatement of SPD aims at Bad Godesberg in 1959. The German *Social Democratic Party Deutschland* (SPD) was the leading European party of the twentieth century, combining ideological vitality with electoral resilience.[13] The Social Democrats abandoned their concern with state ownership of the productive economy, embracing the social market underpinned by a vibrant and dynamic private sector. Bad Godesberg signalled the SPD would pursue ameliorative reform rather than class struggle, no longer waging war against capitalism. Private ownership was acceptable, even desirable, 'where it does not hinder the establishment of social justice'.[14] The SPD leader Willy Brandt insisted the purpose of social democracy was 'as much market as possible, as much state as necessary'.

In the late 1980s, Labour's deputy leader, Roy Hattersley, compared the drafting of the party's statement of *Aims and Values* to Bad Godesberg. Nevertheless, *Aims and Values* had astonishingly little political currency in the Labour Party. New Labour subsequently repositioned the party to reflect changes that occurred several decades before in the major European countries, jettisoning the commitment to public ownership. The party drew, 'from the experience of European social democratic parties', committed to social justice alongside economic efficiency.[15] These disparate influences proved far more enduring than Thatcherism.

The Mitterrand experiment

Inevitably, Labour's modernisation took account of the setbacks the Left endured in the post-war era. Mitterrand's victory in 1981 initially generated excitement: 'For the first time since 1947 a major capitalist country has a clearly left-wing government, committed, however moderately, to reducing the extent of capitalist rule'.[16] Yet within months, Mitterrand's experiment was close to ignominious collapse. Mitterrand united disparate strands of the French Left, securing a mandate to implement socialist policies analogous to the Alternative Economic

Strategy (AES). The aim was to use the power of government to insulate the national economy, reorganising the economy along socialist lines. However, the administration quickly ran into difficulties. Mitterrand abandoned his interventionist strategy under pressure from international financial markets in the adverse circumstances prompted by rising oil prices. The Socialist government devalued the franc repeatedly. Economic confidence soon evaporated. The Labour MP Bryan Gould believed Mitterrand 'allowed real economy objectives to be subordinated to the monetary measures invented by the financial establishment'.[17] Yet the French experience was invoked 'to show the folly of unilateral action in an increasingly interdependent world'.[18]

The defeat of Mitterrand's economic policy was not altogether surprising. At Labour conference in 1976, Callaghan rebuked the 'cosy world' of Keynesian demand management which relied on national governments to print money, relieving a shortfall in aggregate demand. A year later, the German chancellor, the SPD's Helmut Schmidt, also rejected such policies arguing, 'The time for Keynesian economics is past because the problem of the world today is inflation'.[19] Schmidt believed social democrats must eschew counter-cyclical deficit spending. By the 1970s, even the Swedish economic and welfare model had run into serious problems. Growing union militancy, rising wage inflation and soaring public expenditure threatened the long-term viability of Scandinavian social democracy.[20]

Mitterrand's difficulties ricocheted across the Left in Europe, laying the ground for the third way. The Mitterrand programme centred on pursuing the national economic strategy was a heroic failure. The perceived capacity of governments 'to control the national economy' was eroding.[21] Global integration and the importance of capital flows challenged the feasibility of 'socialism in one country'. Mitterrand's difficulties affirmed the obsolescence of traditional socialism. Governments had to operate economic policies so as not to undermine the confidence of international markets. Otherwise, they risked triggering gilt strikes, capital flight and balance-of-payments crises. This insight came not from the Thatcher governments, but the Socialist administration in France. A decade later, Blair told the National Assembly of France: 'There is no Left and Right in economic policy any longer, only Right and Wrong'.

Social Europe

Another key milestone was the British Labour Party's hesitant conversion to European integration. As the 1980s progressed, support for Europe on the Left began to strengthen. In 1988, the president of the European Commission, the French Socialist Jacques Delors launched a momentous plan for Social Europe (although Delors was widely criticised on the French Left for being too sympathetic to pro-market reforms). Social Europe would augment the single market launched at Thatcher's behest in 1985, creating legal rights to social and employment protection. Kinnock's party and the unions welcomed the initiative, a means of safeguarding the rights of British workers under threat from the Thatcher administrations. The Labour movement embraced social Europe, affording a bulwark against the free market Thatcherite experiment. Delors invited Britain's trade unions to become the 'architects of Europe'.[22] The social security and employment rights agenda outlined by the commission president was, 'the most elaborate proposal for a new left-of-centre vision we have yet seen', a response 'to the dramatic devaluation of national policy tools by globalisation'.[23] Labour moved towards enthusiastically supporting EC membership, renouncing the policies of the 1983 manifesto and taking seriously the 1984 European elections. Shortly after becoming leader, Kinnock published an article in *Socialist Review* with Stuart Holland, then a Labour MP, insisting Labour should embrace membership and campaign for socialist reform within the community.[24] Delors's vision cemented the British Left's commitment to Europe.

Labour began regular contact with major European centre-left parties. Officials travelled to Germany and the Scandinavian countries. At a 1988 Friedrich Ebert Stiftung (FES) Conference in Bonn, the Labour delegation discovered that 'parties were involved in major reviews of their policy programmes. There was a general feeling that many of their established positions were no longer relevant or adequate'. The SPD was losing support to the Greens and Christian Democrats. The party was unclear how to respond to demographic alterations in the German electorate, as well as the emergence of serious industrial and economic policy problems. The choice the SPD faced was whether to address ecological issues while eschewing higher growth and public spending or to focus on intervention in industry reducing mass unemployment. The extent to which governments should pursue industrial policies, directing private sector investment, divided the European socialist parties. The secretary of the Spanish Socialist Party (PSOE) reminded the Bonn gathering that socialism's purpose was not to destroy capitalism. Socialists were opposed neither to markets or competition. Their aim was to redistribute political rights, 'increasing the power of individual people, starting with those who have least'.[25]

Having undertaken a study visit to Sweden that year, the Labour Party's international officer, Mike Gapes, produced a memorandum listing the perceived virtues of the Swedish model:

> Strong party and trade union organisation at all levels. . . . Cohesive and close co-operation with the trade unions. . . . High taxation (55 per cent). . . . Very low unemployment and high living standards based on active labour market policies . . . concentration on forward looking, high technology industrial planning . . . high levels of local government autonomy. . . . A proportional electoral system with all elections on the same day every three years. . . . A commitment to an internationalist foreign policy.[26]

These themes were subsequently reflected in Labour's post-1987 *Policy Review*. As in the 1950s, Sweden continued to provide strategic and ethical inspiration for British Labour.

The fall of the Berlin Wall

After 1989, the European continent experienced a succession of peaceful revolutions that transformed the totalitarian states of Eastern Europe into democratic regimes. The entire geopolitical system was in flux. At Tiananmen Square in Beijing, thousands of protestors who took to the streets in support of human rights against the Communist-led Chinese government were shot dead by the military. The following year on 11th February 1990, Nelson Mandela was released from prison in South Africa after 27 years behind bars, sparking the collapse of apartheid. The disintegration of state socialism and the remaking of the world order had a major influence on Labour in Britain. The Berlin Wall's collapse epitomised socialism's obsolescence. The aspiration of the planned economy where the instruments of production are owned collectively appeared archaic. *Marxism Today* debated the implications of the iron curtain's fall. The collapse of the Soviet economy shattered the historical self-confidence once existing on the Left, compelling social democratic parties to reconsider whether central planning was the most efficient instrument for the allocation of goods and services.[27] 'What ha[d] been deleted from the human future' by the demise of Communism, wrote the political theorist John Dunn was 'any form of reasonable and relatively concrete social and political hope'.[28]

The second effect of Communism's disintegration was giving confidence to social democrats outside the Marxist tradition, who no longer felt any need to justify their faith in collective action or reassert the Left's commitment to human rights and parliamentary democracy. The Soviet Union's demise altered the geopolitical context. Perestroika, the Soviet Communist Party's movement for reform, entailed multilateral talks on nuclear disarmament between President Mikhail Gorbachev and Ronald Reagan, transforming the terms of debate about defence and NATO membership. The Cold War's end led to a shift in the centre of gravity on defence policy that gave Labour strategic advantages it hitherto lacked. The potency of the arguments against it as the party of unilateral surrender and weak defence receded.

Yet the Berlin Wall's collapse was not entirely good news. As long as Soviet Communism persisted, the controllers of capital in Western economies understood the necessity of integrating the working class through reforms of capitalism, alongside the preservation of the welfare state. The disappearance of the external threat to Western economies undermined the legitimacy of the post-war social democratic consensus.[29] As a consequence, capitalism across the Western world confronted fewer constraints thereafter. The full-throated global free market was unleashed in the 1990s, culminating in the triumph of globalisation and the so-called end of history with far-reaching implications for the efficacy of centre-left politics.

Left modernisation across the Anglosphere

While change was sweeping Europe, the Labour Party keenly observed developments on the Australian Left. Australia was important for several reasons. Many

British politicians had close personal ties to Australian society and politics. Tony Blair lived in Adelaide for two years as a child. He attended Oxford University with Geoff Gallop, who became Labor Party state premier in Western Australia. Moreover, Australia and Britain both had Westminster-style political systems, reinforcing common ties. In the 1992 election campaign, for instance, the British Labour Party adopted the ALP's slogan 'It's Time for Change'.

In advancing his modernisation strategy, Blair met the ALP leaders Bob Hawke and Paul Keating regularly during visits in the 1990s. Keating advised Blair how to handle the media mogul, Rupert Murdoch, warning him not to run on a platform of raising taxes for the middle class.[30] The Australian prime minister told Blair, 'Don't ever put up income tax, mate. Take it off them anyhow you please, but do that and they'll rip your fucking guts out'.[31] The ALP was a centre-left party that made peace with markets and capitalism well in advance of British Labour. The Hawke/Keating reforms paved the way for New Labour. The ALP believed that by the mid-1980s, Australia's industrial economy was becoming uncompetitive. They had little choice but to embark on a programme of liberalising reforms.[32] The shift in economic policy had little to do with Thatcherism. Keating claimed that Australia was 'in the vanguard of social and democratic progress'. In Blair's view, 'The positions adopted by the ALP are very good modern left-of-centre positions. . . . They are pro-business, pro-enterprise, but also have a strong commitment to social justice'.[33] Australia provided a reform blueprint for Labour's modernisers in Britain.

The rise of the New Democrats

Although Blair and Brown repositioned Labour as the party of European social democracy, American ideas became decisive following the emergence of Clinton's *New* Democrats. The Labour leadership adopted its triangulation strategy after two decades in which the New Right was in the ascendency in Britain and the United States. In 1989, Clinton became chairman of the Democratic Leadership Council (DLC), an influential network of moderate Democratic officeholders and state officials from across the nation. The New Democrat agenda sought to counter the dominance of Reaganism. Clinton believed territory once dominated by the Right notably law and order, taxation, defence and security must now be aggressively contested by the centre-left.

The DLC's aim was to reconstruct American liberalism. The DLC's origins lay in the failed 1972 presidential campaign of Maine senator, Edmund Muskie. Muskie claimed: 'Our challenge this decade is to restore the faith of Americans in the basic competence and purposes of government'.[34] In the aftermath of successive presidential defeats, Clinton confronted the caricature of the Left as 'caring but incompetent' and the Right as 'cruel but efficient'. Controversially, Clinton championed support for tougher sentencing laws. In 1992, he ensured a mentally ill prisoner, Ricky Ray Rector, convicted of multiple murders in Arkansas was given the death penalty. The presidential candidate insisted, 'Democrats should no longer feel guilty about protecting the innocent'. E.J. Dionne wrote that Clinton's Democrats sought to revise the view of moral and personal responsibility adopted by the 'Sixties Left' as well as the economic liberalism of the 'Eighties Right'.[35]

In symbolising that commitment, the US Democrats and New Labour demonstrated they were willing to confront producer interests in their parties, particularly 'old-fashioned' unions and public sector bureaucracies.[36] The New Democrats believed the Left in America identified with the 'have-nots', minority groups and special interests. Clinton insisted that to win power, the Democrats should appeal to aspirational working-class and suburban middle-class voters. His polling strategist, Stan Greenberg, conducted research with blue-collar workers who voted Republican in the 1980s, so-called Reagan Democrats who believed their former party lost touch with working men and women.[37] As Kenneth Baer explained in *Reinventing Democrats,* the New Democrats fought to move their party beyond the 'rainbow coalition' liberalism popularised by George McGovern in the 1972 election, considered repellent to skilled working-class voters. The Democrats were believed to have abandoned material interests at the heart of New Deal liberalism.[38] In their tough and uncompromising assessment of the party's situation, the public policy scholars Bill Galston and Elaine Kamarck averred the Democrats relied on 'faulty data' and 'false assumptions' to avoid painful questions about why they kept losing national elections.[39] The Democrats mislaid voters' trust on crucial issues: the fundamentals of defence, foreign policy, economic competence, the social agenda relating to family stability, the rise of violent crime. The party was perceived as weak and indecisive. Working Americans did not trust Democrats with their money. They feared that taxes would be redistributed to welfare claimants. The Republicans were far ahead on security, foreign affairs, defence and patriotism.[40]

The intellectual leadership of the New Democrats came from the DLC and the Progressive Policy Institute (PPI), a think-tank formed after the 1984 presidential election defeat.[41] PPI had close ties to the Institute for Public Policy Research (IPPR) in Britain.[42] The New Democrats were a caucus of political entrepreneurs who fought to transform their party, adapting to socio-economic forces altering American politics. They believed:

> A winning coalition must be built around ideas, not constituency groups. The only way for Democrats to reverse the Republican trend is to develop a message that has broad appeal to the American people. We cannot afford to become a Liberal party. We must attract moderates and conservatives as well.[43]

This strategic repositioning had a crucial impact on New Labour.[44]

Yet the Blair generation were not the first Labour politicians influenced by the US progressive tradition. In reading the works of American writers such as Edward Bellamy and Upton Sinclair, Attlee 'was impressed by a strong sense of the American progressive spirit, which translated into admiration for Franklin

Roosevelt's "New Deal'".[45] Reformers in the 1950s, including Crosland and Roy Jenkins, admired the United States deeply. Crosland was influenced by American sociologists who charted the declining influence of class:

> Crosland had been greatly influenced by American sociological writing. . . . He was right that class was nowhere near as prevalent in the United States. Social egalitarianism, equality of regard, did seem to be alive and well. Capitalism had changed; this wasn't the capitalism Roosevelt had fought against in the 1930s. America was the future and we could be like that if we tried hard enough.[46]

Throughout the post-war era, the Labour Party was impressed by American progressivism, particularly Roosevelt's New Deal, the muscular liberalism of John F. Kennedy and the Great Society championed by Lyndon Johnson. Evan Durbin depicted America as among 'the great capitalist democracies . . . founded upon the union of the political system of representative democracy with the economic system of capitalism'.[47] Crosland and Jenkins revered Democrats such as Kennedy and Adlai Stevenson who epitomised the meritocratic, classless America they prized so ardently.[48] For revisionists, America was the 'cultural reference point' for social democracy. Jenkins and Crosland saw the United States as affording moral and ethical inspiration for British socialism, a disposition embraced by New Labour.

There was inevitably suspicion on the Left. America was, after all, the world's leading capitalist democracy. During the 1970s and 1980s, few in the ranks of 'Old' Labour were willing to encourage contact with US Democratic politics. Yet by the 1990s, Labour witnessed directly the successful efforts of Clinton's team to win back Reagan Democrats, socially conservative voters disillusioned by the perceived legacy of high spending and taxes. Like British Labour, the Democrats were slow to shed the disastrous image they acquired for fiscal profligacy and vulnerability on national security during Carter's presidency in the late 1970s. The party was taken over by factions who believed the route to election victory lay in mobilising the 'rainbow coalition' of oppressed groups.

Clinton's advisers insisted Democrats would only win if they gained the support of the blue-collar working- and middle-class in 'rust belt' America. New Democrats had to take the core tenets of American conservatism seriously. The hedonistic individualism of the 1960s and 1970s eroded the social fabric, weakening the family and contributing towards crime and inner-city violence. Clinton went out of his way to praise the work of the neo-conservative sociologist Charles Murray, insisting the ethic of duty and self-discipline should be restored to American society. Blair believed similarly that in the 1960s, the Left developed a damaging 'disregard for moral structures'. Even though by 1997, 40 per cent of children were born outside marriage, Blair claimed:

> The family is the essential unit of social stability and should, therefore, be supported and not harmed, insofar as possible, by Government policy. . . .

Two parents, stable together offer the best prospects for children; and that is usually easiest found within marriage.[49]

In Britain and the United States, social democratic parties began to take seriously conservative political ideas.

The American democrats and New Labour in power

As such, unquestionably the most important influence on the New Labour leadership in preparing for government was the Clinton administration. Blair's party was the legatee of the Clinton era far more than Thatcherism. As Al From, the DLC's founder remarked, both British Labour and the US Democrats:

> Were born out of political defeat: consecutive losses in national elections resulting from the two parties veering far to the Left and losing touch with ordinary voters. Both had the same political goal: to build a majority coalition of those in the middle class and struggling to stay there with those aspiring to get there.[50]

Clinton and Blair faced a similar quandary. Both of their parties were in the political doldrums for a generation, losing national elections repeatedly.[51]

Gordon Brown and his chief economic adviser, Ed Balls, forged close ties with US policy-makers – in particular, Robert Rubin and Larry Summers who served in the President's Council of Economic Advisers and the US Treasury. Brown was an ardent Atlanticist who felt at ease on the liberal East Coast. He took holidays in Cape Cod, devouring historical works on American literature and politics. Bob Shrum, who advised a succession of Democratic politicians, including Robert Kennedy, was later employed as Brown's speechwriter. Brown 'felt much more affinity with the United States than with continental Europe. And he felt more affinity with the US Democrats – its key figures, its history, its language and politics – than with any centre-left party in the EU. . . . When Blair and Brown looked to develop progressive policies for transitioning people from welfare into work in the 1990s, it wasn't Copenhagen or Stockholm that they visited, but Wisconsin. . . . His love of the US Democrats was emotional, but it was also an affinity with a party who like Labour were trying to achieve progressive change in a liberal market economy that made it difficult to tack Left'.[52]

Like Crosland four decades before, Brown observed in America much he found admirable, 'its spirit of enterprise, its work ethic, its meritocratic outlook, its social egalitarianism'.[53] As a consequence, Labour made common cause with the Democratic administration in Washington that ended twelve years of Republican dominance. The genius of Clinton's Democrats was to identify a strategy that married the electorate's desire to transcend the divisions created by 'Reaganomics', while refusing to increase the tax liabilities of the middle class. Voters could support a presidential candidate committed to addressing the frayed social fabric after a decade of New Right governance, without fearing economic losses.

Clinton's team advised the British Labour leadership that macro-economic stability should be the lynchpin of their strategy, rather than resorting to demand-side interventionism and old-fashioned industrial policy. Central bank independence was fundamental, as it helped secure low inflation and interest rates. Governments could influence the growth rate of the economy not through short-term manipulation of aggregate demand but micro-economic supply-side reform. The Clinton administration took the decision in 1993 to focus on paying down the deficit rather than fulfilling the commitment to invest in education and training under the slogan 'Putting People First'. Robert Reich, Clinton's Labour secretary in the White House complained bitterly that 'deficit reduction is the only game in town'.[54]

The Rubin/Summers intellectual synthesis was christened wonkishly as 'post neo-endogenous growth theory', a term that led the then deputy prime minister, Michael Heseltine, to ridicule Labour's policy as 'not Brown but Balls'. The purpose was to raise the employment rate while ensuring price stability, bringing down the non-accelerating inflation rate of unemployment (NAIRU) by restructuring the labour market.[55] The economist James Tobin invented the term 'NAIRU', offering an explanation in economic theory for the stagflation that occurred in the early 1970s when inflation and unemployment simultaneously rose in defiance of the Phillips curve.[56] The emphasis on Keynesian demand management began to subside among policy-makers.

While the disposition of Blair and Brown was pro-European, by 1997 they emphasised reforming the European Union (EU) in the image of the flexible and deregulated regime of American capitalism well disposed to the globalisation era. It was the Clinton administration that signed the North Atlantic Free Trade Agreement (NAFTA) in the face of bitter opposition from organised labour. The economic dynamism and global competitiveness of America mesmerised and fascinated New Labour. To curry favour with the Murdoch press, Blair on occasion praised Reagan and Thatcher whose policies in the 1980s 'got certain things right. A greater emphasis on enterprise. Rewarding, not penalising success. Breaking up vested interests'.[57] As a consequence, there was growing scepticism even in Labour circles about the viability of European economic and social policy. The UK eventually ruled out membership of the single currency. Blair signed up to the social chapter of employment and workers' rights. Yet the Labour governments opposed the dilution of labour market flexibility, remaining wary of French initiatives such as the 35-hour-maximum working week. Blair's ministers had no intention of reversing industrial relations reforms introduced in the 1980s.

Across the landscape of social reform, the Clinton presidency was hugely important in shaping Labour's thinking. The future president proclaimed in a speech at New Orleans in 1989: 'There are too many problems, given the dramatic change in the relationship of children and child-rearing in this country, that cannot be solved by unilateral attempts by governments to help people without either empowerment or demanding responsibility'.[58] Clinton's philosophy echoed Blair's criticisms of past social democratic governments, which gave priority to the rights of the individual without acknowledging the importance of personal responsibility. Blair claimed that:

> During the 1960s and 1970s the Left developed almost in substitution for economic prescriptions – which by then were failing – a type of social individualism that sometimes confused liberation from prejudice with a disregard for moral structures. . . . It appeared indifferent to the family and individual responsibility.[59]

Welfare reform, employability programmes, Sure Start, tax credits, 'zero tolerance' policing, school discipline alongside measures to enforce parental responsibility were policy ideas directly taken from the United States.

For Blair, the aim was to entrench citizen's responsibilities and moral obligations. To claim benefits, the unemployed should actively seek work. A tough stance on law and order not only meant longer jail sentences for those committing

PHOTO 4.1 US President Bill Clinton (L) greets British Prime Minister Tony Blair (R), 1997.

Source: Photo by Doug Collier/AFP/Getty Images.

serious offences but renewed efforts to tackle anti-social behaviour. After 1997 hundreds of criminal offences were added to the statute book. Police numbers rocketed, officers had more powers to stop and search suspects, while sentencing policies became harsher, sending a 'tough' message to potential miscreants. Unashamedly New Labour followed the direction on law and order established by the Clinton administration. What drove change was not policy primarily, but politics. Blair, like the Democrats, was determined that never again should his party be caricatured as 'soft' on public order, criminality and lawlessness. The Labour leader declared that:

> Both the modernisers in the Labour Party and in the Democrats reached the same conclusions. First, that our political party has to have a broad, mainstream base, not to be the Amalgamated Union of Pressure Groups, with every interest group under the sun demanding policies. And second, we have to reconnect our parties with aspirational voters, those that were doing OK but wanted to do better, and those that were doing well but who wanted to do better still, as well as those left behind.[60]

The leadership were relentless in digesting the lessons of US experience. After 1997, Blair, Brown and their advisers continued to travel across the Atlantic. In the 2001 election, Brown sought to base Labour's campaign on the effort by Al Gore to succeed Clinton as president, standing for 'the people' against 'the powerful'. In a strategy document written before the election, Brown drew on the Gore playbook to insist on positioning Labour as, 'the people's government . . . working hard for hard-working families'. Brown believed the government needed a populist critique of what was wrong with Britain 'that speaks to the material and social concerns of everyday working families'. Labour's leaders looked across the Atlantic for political inspiration far more than the English Channel.[61]

New Labour and the third way

As a consequence, New Labour arose from sustained contact with political forces beyond the shores of Britain. By absorbing centre-left ideas from across the globe, the party's political identity was reshaped. The debate about Labour's modernisation reflected prolonged discussion of the decline of Keynesian economics, the potential for a third way in Left politics and the reinvigoration of liberal social democracy across Western Europe and the United States.[62] Certainly, New Labour cannot be said to have ignored Europe. Left parties in Western Europe were similarly compelled to confront their track record of electoral underperformance. Perry Anderson wrote that the Left was assailed by powerful historical forces:

> The end of the Soviet experience; the contraction or disintegration of the traditional working-class; the weakening of the welfare state; the expansion

of the video sphere; the decline of parties – have borne hard on the left everywhere in Europe, leaving none in particularly good shape.[63]

It was argued social democrats had to come to terms intellectually with the decline of the Keynesian post-war compromise, accompanied by the exhaustion of state bureaucracy as the solution to economic and social problems. The so-called third way was the product of ideological atrophy and the rise of technocracy from the 1970s, epitomised by the belief that 'what matters is what works' in public policy.

New Labour's evocation of the third way underlined the importance it attached to ideas. Blair and Brown insisted social democrats must think beyond conventional ideological categories of Left and Right. The third way was portrayed as revitalising social democracy in the wake of the Cold War, centred on rejecting Old Labour and the New Right. By the late 1990s, there was a wave of enthusiasm about the revival of progressive politics across the United States and Europe, propelled by electoral success alongside the governing strategy of Clinton and Blair. The third way became 'a metaphor for centre-left parties . . . to forge political settlements that combined a recognition of the increasing importance of the global economy with attention to the importance of social cohesion'.[64] The third way's 'easy mix of soft economics, common sense sociology, and a readiness to engage in policy-making played very well among academics and journalists'.[65]

Several ideas were emphasised repeatedly. The first was the primacy of strong economic performance. Investment in social justice entailed a high and sustainable level of economic growth. The second third way idea was the need for 'prudence' in public spending combined with fiscal discipline. In the aftermath of the 1970s, social democrats had to be wise spenders rather than big spenders. The third theme stressed achieving equality of opportunity through 'social investment', principally in education. There was less emphasis on equality of outcome through fiscal redistribution. The fourth idea concerned the importance of the active welfare state, encouraging citizens to move off benefits and into work.[66] Yet while third way rhetoric emphasised the radical implications of post-modernity, it is quite possible, 'to detect significant continuities with a number of Labour traditions'.

For those exhausted by electoral defeat, the third way was a persuasive response to the decay of post-1945 social democracy. It was a concerted effort to confront the structural crises undermining the post-war settlement. Third way ideas had currency, allowing New Labour to make sense of a changing world rather than serving as an expedient reaction to electoral demands.[67] Dramatic shifts were underway in the global economy, particularly the internationalisation of capital markets, the expansion of world trade, the impact of information and communications technologies, the rise of the knowledge-driven economy and the shift from manufacturing to services that heralded the 'post-industrial' landscape.[68] Furthermore, sociological changes were altering the fabric of British society: the fragmentation of traditional class structures, developments in the social status of women reflected in labour force participation, demographic changes such as population ageing and the acceleration of labour migration, the breakdown of the traditional family as well as the alarming decline of trust in governments and democratic institutions.[69] It is striking that the third way's analysis was derived principally from sociology rather than political theory or economics.

Third way social democracy confronted the abiding paradox of contemporary political life. On the one hand, economic and social transformation generated relentless demands for government intervention. The aim was to address the intractable problems of post-industrial societies, from rising crime to intergenerational structural disadvantage. Yet citizen's trust in government was receding, demonstrated by disillusionment with the representative political process and falling electoral turnouts. The third way fought to address dwindling faith in politics, re-establishing the activist state following the ascendency of neo-liberal ideas in advanced capitalist countries. The purpose was to 'restore public confidence in government . . . moving from a government that controls to one that enables'.[70]

The belief was that centre-left politics would be revitalised in the wake of Thatcher and Reagan's ascendency. The political philosopher Amitai Etzioni claimed the third way:

> Takes for granted that the state is neither the problem nor the solution, that unfettered markets can cause much havoc and suffering, and that carefully contained markets can be powerful engines of economic growth and employment. . . . It maintains that a society best relies on three pillars: a strong but lean government; a well-developed but encapsulated market; and a vibrant community.[71]

Blair's followers regularly cited Francis Fukuyama's book, *Trust,* which affirmed the belief that economic growth must be underpinned by institutions that protect social cohesion.[72]

Many commentators insist that rather than providing a political alternative, the third way epitomised the internalisation of neo-liberalism by social democrats.[73] The third way meant an 'uncritical embrace of market capitalism and its acceptance of inequality'.[74] The historian Tony Judt dismissed it as 'opportunism with a human face'.[75] Giles Radice worried 'the third way idea implies . . . [Blair's] project is equidistant between Thatcherism and old-style social democracy'.[76] Yet many of the third way's antecedents are traced back to ideas that precede market liberalism's dominance. Keynes argued in the 1920s that 'the true socialism of the future will emerge from an endless variety of experiments directed towards discovering the respective appropriate sphere of the individual and the social, and the terms of a fruitful alliance between these sister instincts'.[77] He outlined the definitive third way philosophy where public policy is a pragmatic partnership between the state and citizen. Keynes's views echoed early-twentieth-century New Liberalism, another precursor of the third way. In contrast to classical liberalism, New Liberalism emphasised the role of an activist state in enhancing the liberty of the oppressed: 'The New Liberalism professed to be a means of adjusting the apparently competing claims of collectivism and individualism, democracy and knowledge, social forces and rational progress'.[78] Liberals such as L.T. Hobhouse advocated 'the realisation of individual liberty contained in the provision of equal opportunities for self-development'.[79] The New Liberalism was a distinctive ideology in which government intervened to shape unfettered market forces, reconciling social justice with economic efficiency.[80] Hobhouse's aim was to chart an ideological course between 'laissez-faire liberalism on the one hand, and doctrinaire, economically deterministic socialism on the other. . . . He sought to justify in theory that which was largely achieved in substance half a century later: the rudiments of the liberal welfare state'.[81] In a pamphlet on the third way published in the late 1990s, Blair explicitly refers to Hobhouse's writings.[82]

Third way ideas were articulated by left-leaning intellectuals, notably Anthony Giddens, former director of the London School of Economics (LSE). Two concepts were central to Giddens's analysis.[83] The first was the theme of 'post-industrialism'. The American sociologist Daniel Bell coined the term 'post-industrialism' in the early 1970s. Bell insisted that Western societies were passing from an 'industrial' to a 'post-industrial' age where the most important asset was neither capital nor natural resources, but the production of knowledge. The problem of economic exploitation was no longer defined by the structural division between labour and capital, but inequalities in access to information. Bell's work pointed towards nurturing human capital through rejuvenation of education and training, an exemplary idea of the third way.[84]

The second concept that emerged in advance of neo-liberalism was the idea of 'post-materialism' elaborated by Ronald Inglehart, a political scientist. Inglehart believed voters were shifting from prioritising material goods and enhancing economic and physical security to the pursuit of self-actualisation and quality of life. As a consequence, traditional class-based issues notably income redistribution and collective ownership were declining relative to the concern with environmentalism, women's rights, gay liberation and lifestyle movements. Moral questions relating to abortion and same-sex marriage led to 'values-based polarisation', more significant as a source of division within the electorate than social class. Inglehart optimistically concluded that post-materialism was 'conducive to the spread and flourishing of democratic institutions'.[85] Shortly before launching his influential book on the third way, Giddens published among his most important works, *The Transformation of Intimacy*.[86] The book predicted 'a radical democratisation of the personal sphere', leading to new forms of politics beyond the twentieth-century categories of Left and Right.

During the 1990s, scholars whose work is scarcely read as an affirmation of neo-liberalism and Thatcherism contributed to the third way debate. Gosta Esping-Anderson, a Danish sociologist at the University of Pompeu Fabra in Barcelona highlighted the failings of the traditional welfare system across 'three worlds of welfare capitalism'.[87] Esping-Anderson's study averred that structural alterations in Western societies were undermining the male breadwinner model. The post-1945 social contract was 'the child of post-World War II recon-struction'.[88] Secure industrial employment was gone. Ageing and demographic change were testing the welfare state's viability. Meanwhile, gender equality was an imperative negated by orthodox welfare policies. The welfare state had to address new risks and needs, from family fragmentation and breakdown to mental health and lack of job-ready skills in a labour market characterised by growing economic insecurity.[89] The German sociologist Ralph Dahrendorf remarked that the preoccupations of the third way were similar to the com-mission he chaired in 1995–96 on *Wealth Creation and Social Cohesion in a Free Society*. The Dahrendorf committee sought to address how global economic expansion and personal prosperity should be combined with solidarity and the preservation of liberty.[90]

Moreover, the third way acknowledged growing pessimism about the efficacy of large-scale public bureaucracies. The New Deal in the 1930s and then the Great Society in the 1960s overestimated the putative impact of public policy intervention. Even the Left began to suspect social and economic problems may be less amenable to action by national governments. Many policy-makers sur-veying the accumulation of social pathologies in industrialised societies from ris-ing crime to relative poverty worried that 'nothing worked'. A notable example was the stubborn persistence of long-term unemployment. Reducing the unem-ployment rate through macro-economic instruments that boosted aggregate demand had proved spectacularly unsuccessful. Another instance was the rising level of violent and acquisitive crime. Throughout the 1980s, growing public disorder ravaged many Western societies. Innovative approaches were required to overcome the long-term legacy of policy failure. In Britain similarly, efforts to combat relative poverty and the geographical distribution of disadvantage in the 1960s and 1970s proved fruitless. The third way was a sustained effort not only to acknowledge the gravity of social change, but to confront the weakness of traditional bureaucratic institutions.

To deal with such problems, centre-left parties had to be in power. By the early 1980s, they were bereft electorally. Economic transformation made it harder to build the stable, cross-class coalition that matched the power of organ-ised labour in the 1950s and 1960s, the halcyon days of the post-war settle-ment.[91] The constraints imposed by globalisation alongside declining faith in government undermined national social democracy. More dynamic and volatile 'issues-based politics' supplanted the traditional preoccupation with class. Gov-ernmental performance proved decisive. Political parties were operating in a more febrile climate.[92]

Yet the claim that alterations in the class composition of the industrial societ-ies inevitably undermined social democracy proved to be exaggerated. Com-mentary on the fate of parties veered towards sociological determinism.[93] By the end of the 1980s, centre-left parties were in difficulty because they lacked a com-pelling governing prospectus. The vacuum in ideas had to be confronted. The widely held conviction that social democratic parties were doomed to defeat due to irreversible changes in the class structure was mistaken. Indeed, the changing status of class stimulated an unfinished feminisation process that raised the prominence of gender equality, increasing long-run support for centre-left parties among women. The third way countered the Left's ingrained pessimism.

Social democracy lived through two major intellectual cycles during the twentieth century. In the aftermath of the First World War and great depression, the Left focused on indicative economic planning, designed to humanize capitalism and strengthen the efficiency of the private sector economy. Then, after World War Two, socialist parties built the institutions of welfare state social democracy, deftly combining the ideas of Beveridge and Keynes. The purpose was to provide social services to each citizen from the cradle to the grave. The welfare state sought to reduce insecurity at each stage of life. Keynesianism would end slumps, ensuring full employment and growth. Economic expansion would permit painless redistribution. The system would be upheld by tripartite co-operation between workers, employers and government. Social democratic parties were aligned with the working class, given 'the industrial proletariat was numerically the largest component of the electorate, structurally the best organized, morally the most authoritative'.[94] Full employment was achieved through manipulating monetary and fiscal policy, an approach known as Keynesian 'fine-tuning'. As the 1950s and 1960s progressed, state intervention became less central to the agenda of social democratic parties, as problems relating to nationalisation and public ownership emerged. At Bad Godesburg in 1959, the SPD revised its programme to embrace the market economy. The welfare state enshrined a strategy of 'embedded liberalism', where governments provided a powerful counterweight to market forces. By the mid-1970s, the worldwide economic crisis undermined both the animating themes of social democracy – public control of the economy and the extended welfare state. Meanwhile, 'the centrality of the working-class' to Left politics was eroding.[95]

During the 1990s, social democracy entered a third cycle, advancing an ideological agenda that fought to reconcile economic efficiency with social inclusion. European centre-left parties were now following their own distinctive trajectories. The British Labour Party accepted globalisation accompanied by capital and labour market flexibility in return for investment in public services. The German party embraced liberalisation under Gerhard Schroder, but the tripartite 'Rhineland' model of co-determination between employers, workers and the state was retained. The Nordic social democrats were amenable to globalisation and free trade, yet maintained traditional pillars of the Scandinavian system, particularly collective wage bargaining and trade union membership. The French Socialists under Lionel Jospin were committed to social protection through national regulation, while accepting the need to reform government's role in the economy. Jospin explained in a pamphlet on the Left's future: 'We say yes to modernisation, but a collectively constructed modernisation, one that fits with our nation's character, and is acceptable to all our citizens'.[96] What emerged were many third ways for the Left.

The third way in crisis?

Yet although centre-left parties achieved electoral success in the 1990s, the third way scarcely emerged as a coherent governing blueprint. Social democracy's ideological rebirth in the 1990s was greatly exaggerated. The third way involved the tacit alignment between technocratic governance and the social democratic tradition. Following the New Right's exhaustion, centre-left parties in Britain, Germany and the United States governed for long periods. Yet according to critics, they seldom arrived in office with a compelling governing programme. Parties found themselves in power but without a coherent vision of social democratic governance to sustain them in the tough times ahead. They could win elections, but such parties were rarely equipped to win the battle of ideas and dominate the political landscape.

The Clinton Democrats' third way was dismissed as ideologically expedient. Within two years of Clinton's 1992 triumph, E.J. Dionne wrote that the Democrats suffered a huge defeat in the mid-term elections due to their failure to appeal to voters in the 'Anxious Middle'. They were no longer in control of the Senate or Congress.[97] Under the influence of the Machiavellian political strategist Dick Morris, Clinton defended his presidency successfully two years later. Yet Clinton won by flagrantly shifting to the centre-right, co-operating with the Republicans on key legislative issues. The radical potential of the pre-1992 third way appeared to be lost. Opponents of the third way feared social democracy was being shorn of its authentic ideological beliefs, a concern reawakened by the 2008 financial crisis. Centre-left parties were electorally successful. But did they have the strategy to achieve transformative political and social change?[98] Instead of furthering the commitment to egalitarianism, social justice, political liberty, environmental sustainability and democratic governance, centre-left administrations allegedly tinkered with the settlement initiated by Reagan and Thatcher.[99]

The Clinton Democrats confounded the aspirations of progressive liberals by pandering to conservative ideas.[100] In Britain and Germany, Blair and Schroder were depicted as agents of pro-market reform. Schroder and Blair published a joint declaration espousing their commitment to the 'Neue Mitte' or 'New Centre'. The French Socialists embarked on what Jospin termed 'Left Realism', embracing deregulation and liberalisation. The Socialist leader was adamant: 'We accept the market economy. It is the most effective means – provided it is regulated and managed – of allocating resources, stimulating initiative, and recompensing work and effort'.[101] The British, French and German social democratic traditions were converging. There was greater emphasis on fiscal discipline and prudent management of public expenditure, dictated by participation in European Monetary Union (EMU). EMU placed a fiscal straitjacket on member-states of the Eurozone, making it harder to put in place social democratic measures.

The sociologist Chris Pierson averred the third way overstated the impact of economic and social change, particularly the transformation associated with 'hyper-globalisation'.[102] Ashley Lavelle contended social democracy and the third way accommodated neo-liberalism too easily. The post-war political economy centred on government intervention that tamed unfettered market forces was jettisoned prematurely. In Britain, New Labour's social democracy entailed a 'Faustian pact' with financial capitalism.[103] As a consequence, income inequality soared even in countries with centre-left administrations. Financialisation destabilised the global economy. Although the third way emphasised investing in citizens' human capital, policies transferred risk from the private sector to workers.[104] Human capital itself was a concept originating in the neo-liberal philosophy of the rational economic individual. Moreover, third way ideas reflected the preoccupations of American politics which had a long tradition of constraining federal government, veering towards the Right. The third way exported dangerous free market concepts into British and continental European debate.

Criticisms of the third way provoked searching discussion. Yet they were not always well founded. It is questionable whether centre-left rethinking led to the abandonment of post-war Keynesian social democracy. Previous Labour governments during the 1940s and 1960s did not only practice Keynesian policies.[105] Ministers were committed to nationalisation and central planning in 1945, whereas Keynesian theories emphasised the superiority of the market mechanism. Meanwhile, the Blair and Brown governments retained the Keynesian goal of full employment. The rhetoric of 'credibility' created space for fiscal activism. Under Labour, public spending as a share of national income grew dramatically.[106] The Labour Party's 2001 manifesto acknowledged: 'We know the power and value of markets, but we also know their limits'.[107] The third way's adherents overstated the divergence between their approach and that of the programmes traditionally favoured by social democrats. Even Clinton and Blair's espousal of social conservatism was not a dramatic departure, an unequivocal shift to the Right. Such positions reacquainted the Left with early-twentieth century postulates – particularly the emphasis in ethical socialism and the New Liberalism on individual moral obligation and community. Still, economic policy was a weak spot in New Labour's intellectual armoury that the third way certainly failed to rectify.

Brokering ideas: making policy through networks

Social democratic parties were traversing a political landscape during the 1980s and 1990s in which the familiar landmarks of economy and class stratification were uprooted. Their parties' past legacies and reputations had been tarnished. The centre-left had to find a new formula to survive. Fluid networks and connections linking together politicians, intellectuals, policy entrepreneurs and research institutions across countries animated this wave of rethinking. The leading players were think-tanks and policy advisory bodies, creating the conditions for a sustained period of social democratic governance across the industrialised world. The process of building an intellectual movement mirrored the New Right in the 1970s and 1980s, countering the ascendency of neo-liberalism.

Marxism Today's editor Martin Jacques opined that 'right-wing think-tanks had been very successful as intellectual outriders for Thatcherism, bringing together different groups of people'.[108] A new breed of policy professionals populated the centre-left think-tanks, the policy 'wonks' who sought to navigate this world of growing scepticism towards expertise by embracing the ethic of technocracy. These players resembled 'a priesthood who had lost their faith and kept their jobs'.[109] Most researchers were generalist university graduates rather than trained academic specialists in particular disciplines. These 'experts' were more concerned with political and strategic positioning than the detailed substance of public policy. It is striking that the contribution of academic economics to government policy-making began to recede in the late 1970s, as professional economists entered the lucrative worlds of finance and consulting.[110] More generally, Labour was moving away from its reliance in policy-making on experts in the academy.

As Stephanie Mudge notes, the status of Anthony Giddens, Cambridge sociologist and third way guru, was unusual since Labour was supplanting academics with the new breed of ideas brokers in think-tanks, major sites of intellectual production. Gordon Brown's special advisers, Ed Balls and Charlie Whelan, saw their role as reassuring the financial markets and the media about Labour's fiscal prudence. In contrast a previous generation of advisers under Harold Wilson, notably Nicholas Kaldor and Thomas Balogh, focused on adapting the machinery of government and policy-making to enable the implementation of Keynesian ideas.[111] That said, Blair's team believed 'traditional' and 'organic' intellectuals could still assist Labour in forging the concept of governance and the ideological framework for reinventing social democracy. According to one commentator: 'Blair has shown an openness to intellectuals that marks a departure from the conservative, cautious, at times hostile, approach of traditional labourism'.[112] New Labour acquired a reputation for being 'serious . . . willing to rethink established orthodoxies and to try new solutions'.[113]

Geoff Mulgan, the former director of the think-tank Demos, was symptomatic of the new breed of centre-left ideas brokers. Mulgan graduated from Balliol College, Oxford, taking a first-class degree in politics, philosophy and economics (PPE). He initially worked as an adviser in the Greater London Council (GLC) while lecturing in cultural studies at the Central London Polytechnic where he focused on the growth of communications technologies. Mulgan subsequently served as policy adviser to the shadow chancellor, Gordon Brown. Mulgan went on to found Demos in 1993, a think-tank striving to question prevailing orthodoxies on Left and Right. Demos' aim was to be 'a catalyst for a different, less ideological politics', moving away from traditional structures and debates.[114]

Demos drew upon 'the most advanced thinking from throughout society and across the world'.[115] Research focused on themes from changing gender relations to what policy-makers should learn from evolutionary psychology, drawing on Marxist cultural theory. Demos was characterised by the restless urge to transfer ideas from around the globe. Mulgan was captivated by the experience of countries – particularly Singapore – that invested heavily in education and human capital. Western states, Demos believed, had much to learn from the rising Asian powers. Another theme was the importance of 'holistic government', getting away from addressing problems through traditional silos of centralised bureaucracy.[116] Mulgan believed that by the early 1990s 'there was little sign of imagination in any of the parties. . . . Above all we wanted to articulate an alternative to the hoarding habits of closed elites and share power'.[117]

The radical thinking advanced by Demos did not pass without criticism. Commentators noted the tendency, shared with New Labour's leadership, to use grand rhetoric about epochal change while advocating small-scale, incremental reforms. Demos claimed that education policy boosting human capital was the pivotal imperative facing all future governments. The remedy was piecemeal 'home-school' contracts ensuring pupils handed in their homework on time. The analytical originality of Demos' research was admirable, but its concerns were a long way from the practical reality of government. Demos publications had the reputation for being wonkish and jargon heavy. The role of think-tanks, critics claimed, was not just to think but to proselytise.[118]

Nevertheless, there is little doubt Demos was fundamentally important in sustaining international networks that provided the conveyor belt for ideas. Alongside Mulgan were a clutch of public intellectuals who penetrated international progressive circles: Anthony Giddens advanced the idea of the contemporary third way for social democracy; Manuel Castells, a Spanish social scientist, developed the concept of the 'network society'; Gosta Esping-Anderson framed the new rationale for the active welfare state; Ulrich Beck, a German sociologist and Giddens's collaborator, wrote tracts on the implications of modernity, globalisation and the risk society for Western countries. The new cadre of public intellectuals, think-tanks such as Demos alongside the Institute for Public Policy Research (IPPR), and the US Progressive Policy Institute (PPI) reflected the centre-left's dissatisfaction with established government and party bureaucracies. IPPR had the aim 'of feeding policies into the modernisation of the Labour party'.[119] Leaders like Blair and Clinton grew impatient with the timidity of the traditional civil service. They believed government policy-making structures were incapable of generating innovative ideas, still in the grip of producer interests. Mulgan insisted the most compelling ideas in the future would come not from government or bureaucracies but 'a management consultancy, or a multinational, a laboratory, a small inner-city project, a green campaigning group; anywhere but politicians'.[120] He wrote that politics would be shaped by 'designers, researchers and inventors', those who hammered out futuristic concepts 'by meeting and arguing in cafes, pubs and restaurants'.[121] The civil service was anachronistic as it made policy divorced from the real world and service users, whereas think-tanks sought to interact with citizens at 'street-level', the point at which policy ideas have greatest impact. The third way Left mirrored the New Right in expressing frustration with the traditional state. In creating think-tanks, Labour reformers set out to 'build the scaffolding, the institutions, the media enterprises, the academic institutions, the professional guilds' that promoted their project, ensuring more people saw the world as they did.[122]

Attlee and Wilson viewed the machinery of Whitehall and Westminster as fundamentally congenial to the fulfilment of social democratic aspirations. By the 1990s, the mood was shifting, another reason for centre-left parties to invest in think-tanks and networks, generating fresh ideas for the era of global modernity. This disillusionment with the existing institutions of public administration explains the growth in the appointment of outside advisers, helping to break open the civil service monopoly over policy advice. After 1997, New Labour altered the structure of governance at the centre. To oversee delivery and strategy, new units were created bringing the 'finest minds' from management consultancy and academia into Whitehall. The Left long cultivated the approval of experts.

It was clear the institutional structures for providing policy analysis and advice were adapting. A spider's web of policy networks and think-tanks were emerging. The European social democratic parties established their own research institutes in the early-twentieth century – the Friedrich Ebert Stiftung (FES) in Germany, the Renner Institute in Austria and the Wiardi Beckman Foundation in the Netherlands. These bodies were focused nationally and immersed in the bureaucratic structures of their respective parties. They were perceived to lack the agility and flexibility of the rising generation of think-tanks in Europe and the United States. The emergence of diverse policy networks underlined the point that New Labour took ideas seriously. Blair and Brown believed the political process was a contest of ideas. They fought to establish dominance over the intellectual agenda, as Thatcher and Reagan had done when social democracy disintegrated in the 1970s. Labour acknowledged the advancement of ideas was transnational rather than solely focused on domestic politics. The circulation of ideas and policies across the world mirrored economic globalisation: solutions for pressing problems could no longer 'be found within the boundaries of sovereign polities'.[123]

Moreover, policies were now devised within the 'new political spaces' of civil society and the private sector. Blair, Clinton and Schroder established the *Progressive Governance Network* to debate common problems confronting centre-left administrations. During the prime minister's first year in office, Blair met Clinton twice to discuss the third way. In September 1998, a meeting took place in the margins of the United Nations General Assembly at New York University involving Clinton, Blair, the Italian prime minister Romano Prodi and the Bulgarian prime minister Petar Stoyanov to discuss the third way in the global economy.[124] Clinton appointed the political commentator Sidney Blumenthal as his third way 'point man' in the White House. Yet the progressive network scarcely rivalled the New Right 'archipelago' that emerged in the 1970s. The third way ultimately was a technocratic philosophy. It lacked an overarching theoretical doctrine. The governing rationale of Thatcherism and Reaganism was relatively easy to espouse. The New Right think-tank ideologues believed in replacing the state and the public sector with market forces and competition. The progressive ideas of Blair and Clinton lacked the same intellectual clarity and lucidity. New Labour and the Democrats were accused of narrow electoralism in the absence of a compelling ideological vision, a false charge but one they struggled repeatedly to refute.

Conclusion

Blair's party materialised from the process of intellectual revitalisation that absorbed lessons from political history while drawing on global centre-left experience. This chapter made distinctive claims about the political and intellectual origins of New Labour. Ideas originating in the European social democratic and American progressive tradition proved extremely influential. The previous generation of party reformers analysed the salient currents in revisionist socialism across Europe to recast the British Labour Party's doctrine. Eduard Bernstein had sought to reformulate the relationship between capitalism and social democracy in the early-twentieth century. In the 1980s, the party learnt from the failures of Europe's Left, particularly the collapse of Mitterrand's socialism and the decline of Scandinavian social democracy. Devising policy ideas became a transnational activity. The growth of think-tanks staffed by the new breed of ideas brokers disrupted the traditional reliance on state bureaucracy. These networks across the centre-left were pivotal in exchanging and promoting key ideas. New Labour not only transformed the substance of public policy, but the mechanics that forged political and policy agendas in British politics.

The synthesis of third way social democracy emerged after successive defeats at the hands of Reagan and Thatcher. The third way compelled politicians and intellectuals to address new questions arising from structural change and deindustrialisation, particularly the shifting role of markets, the growth of information and communications technologies and the emergence of new forms of personal identity. Yet the third way was never a compelling governing agenda capable of decisively winning the battle of ideas in British politics. Above all, it lacked a serious analysis of the British political economy, a major lacuna which then impeded New Labour's achievements in government. There was a tendency among insurgent centre-left think-tanks to believe that somehow the major economic questions in Britain had been solved. Like Crosland, they merely assumed the well-oiled engine of economic growth would continue. Too little concerted thinking was done to address 'the appropriate role of government in the market economy, and the related question of how best to control the monetary system, the level of investment and employment, and what principles should be adopted in economic management'.[125]

In many scholarly accounts, it is merely assumed that Blair and Brown's party was moulded solely by the trajectory of British politics, explaining the acquiescence to Thatcherism. This perspective casts the Labour Party as insular, inward-looking and parochial. In contrast, the flow of political ideas from continental Europe, America and the Anglosphere irrevocably shaped Labour's doctrinal identity. The chapter affirmed the impact of Europeanisation and Americanisation on New Labour's strategy. The structural crisis afflicting the Left globally continually preoccupied Blair and Brown. Modernisation meant rejecting the mind-set of social democracy in one country.

Notes

1 Cited in Interview, R. Liddle, February 2011.
2 P. Abrams, R. Rose & R. Hinden, *Must Labour Lose?* p. 106, London: Harmondsworth, 1960.
3 B. Jessop, 'New Labour or The Normalisation of Neo-Liberalism', *British Politics*, Volume 2 (2), p. 282, 2007.
4 T. Blair, 'Diary', *The London Review of Books*.
5 B. Clift, *French Socialism in a Global Era: The Political Economy of the New Social Democracy in France*, London: Continuum, 2005.
6 W. Marshall et al., *The New Progressive Declaration: A Political Philosophy for the Information Age*, Washington DC: Progressive Policy Institute, 1996.
7 T. Blair, 'The Third Way', London: The Fabian Society, 1998.
8 K. Morgan, *Ages of Reform: Dawns and Downfalls of the British Left*, p. 145.
9 Dick Leonard notes that Crosland referred to Sweden and Scandinavia 38 times in *The Future of Socialism*. D. Leonard 'Introduction' in *Crosland and New Labour*, A. Crosland, *The Future of Socialism*, p. 179, 1956.
10 Cited in A. Crosland, *The Future of Socialism*, p. 64.
11 A. Crosland, 'Social Democracy in Europe', London: The Fabian Society, 1971.
12 D. Healey, *The Time of My Life*, London: Methuen, 2015.
13 D. Sassoon, *One Hundred Years of Socialism*, New York: The New Press, 1996.
14 A. Crosland, 'The Future of the Left', *Encounter*, March 1960.
15 M. Wickham-Jones, *Economic Strategy and the Labour Party*, pp. 220–221.
16 G. Therborn, 'Prospects for the European Left', *Marxism Today*, p. 21, November 1981.
17 Cited in J. Tomlinson, 'Can Governments Manage the Economy?', Fabian Tract 524, p. 2.
18 J. Callaghan, 'Rise and Fall of the Alternative Economic Strategy', p. 128.
19 Cited in B. Bartlett, 'Keynes and Keynesianism', *The New York Times*, 14th May 2013.
20 S. Steinmo, 'The Political Economy of Swedish Success' in A. Schafer & W. Streek, *The Politics of Austerity*, Cambridge: Polity, 2013.
21 R. Murray, 'Benetton Britain: The New Economic Order', p. 28.
22 Cited in P. Kellner (ed.), *Thorns and Roses*, p. 145.
23 J. Callaghan, 'Rise and Fall of the Alternative Economic Strategy', p. 125.
24 H. Parr, 'European Integration'.
25 'International Committee/Home Policy Committee: Perspectives for the 1990s', February 1988, LP/Policy Committees and Study Groups of the NEC Research Department (PCSG)/93/5 (Labour Party archives).
26 M. Gapes, 'Listening to the Labour Movement in Sweden', February 1988, LP/Policy Committees and Study Groups of the NEC Research Department (PCSG)/93/4 (Labour Party archives).
27 G. Foote, *The Labour Party's Political Thought: A History*.
28 J. Dunn, *Western Political Theory in the Face of the Future*, p. 122, Cambridge: Cambridge University Press, 1993.
29 D. Marquand, *The Progressive Dilemma*.
30 https://theaustralian.com.au/national-affairs/foreign-affairs/paul-keatings-secret-advice-to-britain/news-story/2f66f1a54ddd3a833a0642060c966867. Accessed 8th October 2018.
31 Cited in T. Blair, *A Journey*, p. 97.
32 C. Johnson & F. Tonkiss, 'The Third Influence: The Blair Government and Australian Labour', *Policy and Politics*, Volume 30 (1), pp. 5–18, 2002.
33 T. Blair, *The Australian*, 13th July 1995, cited in C. Johnson & F. Tonkiss, 'The Third Influence: The Blair Government and Australian Labour', p. 7.

34 Cited in A. From, *The New Democrats and the Return to Power*, p. 22, Basingstoke: Palgrave Macmillan, 2013.

35 E.J. Dionne, *Why Americans Hate Politics*, New York: Simon & Shuster, 1991.

36 A. Gamble, 'New Labour and Political Change', *Parliamentary Affairs*, pp. 632–654.

37 S. Greenberg, *Dispatches From the War Room: In the Trenches with Five Extraordinary Leaders*, New York: Thomas Dunne Books, 2009.

38 J. Bloodworth, *The Decline of American Liberalism 1968–1992*, University of Kentucky Press, 2015.

39 B. Galston & E. Kamarck, 'The Politics of Evasion', Washington, DC: Progressive Policy Institute, 1989.

40 Interview, Will Marshall, President of the Progressive Policy Institute, December 2019.

41 K. Baer, *Reinventing Democrats: The Politics of Liberalism from Reagan to Liberalism*, Lawrence: University of Kansas Press, 2000.

42 Interview, Will Marshall, President of the Progressive Policy Institute, December 2019.

43 'Al From Memorandum to Senator Gillis Long: November 1979', Cited in A. From, *The New Democrats and the Return to Power*, p. 50, Basingstoke: Palgrave Macmillan, 2013.

44 S. Bashevkin, 'From Tough Times to Better Times: Feminism, Public Policy, and New Labour Politics in Britain', *International Political Science Review*, Volume 21 (4), pp. 407–421, 2000.

45 J. Bew, *Citizen Clem: A Biography of Attlee*, p. 98, London: Riverun, 2016.

46 Interview, D. Marquand, *Renewal*, 24th July 2015.

47 E. Durbin, *The Politics of Democratic Socialism*, p. 77.

48 D. Riesman, *Anthony Crosland and the Mixed Economy*.

49 The Prime Minister, Confidential Memorandum, 'Family Policy', 27th December 1997.

50 A. From, *The New Democrats and the Return to Power*, p. 241, Basingstoke: Palgrave Macmillan, 2013.

51 Interview, Will Marshall, President of the Progressive Policy Institute, December 2019.

52 Stewart Wood, 'Gordon Brown', Series of Lectures at Hertford College, Oxford on 'Europe and Prime Ministers Since Thatcher', 3rd November 2018.

53 R. Skidelsky, *Britain Since 1918: A Success Story?*, p. 193.

54 R. Reich, *Locked in the Cabinet*, p. 157, New York: Knopf, 1995.

55 G. Brown, *Where There Is Greed*, Edinburgh: Mainstream Press, 1989.

56 https://scholar.harvard.edu/files/mankiw/files/jep.ballmankiw.pdf. Accessed 12th November 2018.

57 T. Blair, cited in M. Foley, *The British Presidency*, Manchester: Manchester University Press, 1998.

58 Cited in A. From, *The New Democrats and the Return to Power*, p. 125, Basingstoke: Palgrave Macmillan, 2013.

59 T. Blair, 'Power for a Purpose', p. 12.

60 Cited in A. Marr, 'Vanity Blair: Interview', *The Atlantic*, 18th December 1995.

61 G. Brown, Confidential Memorandum, Strategy Document, March 2000.

62 A. Giddens, *The Third Way and Its Critics*, Cambridge: Polity, 2000; A. Giddens, *The Third Way: The Renewal of Social Democracy*, Cambridge: Polity Press, 1998.

63 P. Anderson, 'An Invertebrate Left', *The London Review of Books*, Volume 31 (5), 12th March 2009.

64 J. Newman, *Modernising Governance: New Labour, Policy and Society*, p. 2, London: Sage.

65 J. Cronin, *New Labour's Pasts: The Labour Party and Its Discontents*, p. 393.

66 J. Sloam, 'The Language of Social Democracy', 2007.

67 A. Finlayson, *Making Sense of New Labour*, p. 10.

68 J. Callaghan, 'Social Democracy and Globalisation'.

69 G. Esping-Anderson, *The Three Worlds of Welfare Capitalism*, Cambridge: Polity Press, 1999.

70 W. Marshall et al., *The New Progressive Declaration: A Political Philosophy for the Information Age*.

71 A. Etzioni, 'The Road to the Good Society', *The New Statesman*, p. 25, 15th May 2000.
72 F. Fukuyama, *Trust: The Social Virtues and the Creation of Prosperity*, New York: The Free Press, 1996.
73 S. Mudge, *Leftism Reinvented*, Harvard: Harvard University Press, 2018.
74 E. Goes, *The Labour Party Under Ed Miliband: Trying but Failing to Renew Social Democracy*, p. 12, Manchester: Manchester University Press, 2016.
75 T. Judt, 'The Third Way Is No Route to Paradise', *The New York Times*, 27th October 1998.
76 G. Radice. *Diaries 1980–2001: From Political Disaster to Triumph*, p. 416.
77 Cited in P. Clarke, *Keynes: The Twentieth Century's Most Influential Economist*, p. 68.
78 P. Clarke, 'The Progressive Movement in England', *Transactions of the Royal Historical Society*, Volume 24, p. 170, 1974.
79 J.A. Hobson, *The Crisis of Liberalism: New Issues of Democracy*, p. xii, London: P.S. King, 1920. The link between the third way and the New Liberalism is traced in A. Holmes, *The Third Way: Globalisation's Legacy*, Leicester: Matador, 2009.
80 S. Berman, *The Primacy of Politics*, p. 7.
81 A. Grimes, 'Introduction', in L.T. Hobhouse, *Liberalism*, p. 6, Oxford/New York: Oxford University Press, 1964.
82 T. Blair, 'The Third Way', London: The Fabian Society, 1999.
83 I am grateful to Colm Murphy, my PhD student at Queen Mary, University of London, for highlighting the significance of post-industrialism and post-materialism as concepts in the political thought that shaped the third way of the 1990s.
84 D. Bell, 'Welcome to the Post-Industrial Society', *Physics Today*, Volume 29 (2), pp. 48–49, 1976.
85 R. Inglehart, 'The Silent Revolution in Europe: Intergenerational Change in Post-Industrial Societies', *American Political Science Review*, Volume 65 (4), pp. 991–1017, 1971.
86 A. Giddens, *The Transformation of Intimacy*, Cambridge: Polity Press, 1992.
87 G. Esping-Anderson, *The Three Worlds of Welfare Capitalism*.
88 G. Esping-Anderson, 'Equality and Work in the Post-Industrial Life-Cycle' in D. Miliband (ed.), *Reinventing the Left*, p. 167, Cambridge: Polity, 1994.
89 G. Esping-Anderson, *The Incomplete Revolution*, Cambridge: Polity Press, 2002.
90 R. Dahrendorf, *Report on Wealth Creation and Social Cohesion in a Free Society*, 1996.
91 J. Cronin, G. Ross & J. Schoch (eds.), *What's Left of the Left*, Durham: Duke Press, 2010.
92 G. Stoker, *Why Politics Matters: Making Democracy Work*, Basingstoke: Palgrave Macmillan, 2006.
93 B. Clift, *French Socialism in a Global Era: The Political Economy of the New Social Democracy in France*.
94 P. Anderson, 'Introduction', in P. Anderson & P. Camiller (eds.), *Mapping the West European Left*, London: Verso, 1994.
95 P. Anderson, 'Introduction'.
96 L. Jospin, 'Modern Socialism', London: The Fabian Society, 1999.
97 E.J. Dionne, *They Only Look Dead: Why Progressives Will Dominate the Next Political Era*, New York: Simon & Schuster, 1996.
98 S. White (ed.), *New Labour: The Progressive Future*, Basingstoke: Palgrave Macmillan, 1999.
99 A. Gamble, 'New Labour and Political Change'.
100 M. Weir, 'The Collapse of Bill Clinton's Third Way', in S. White (ed.), *New Labour: The Progressive Future*, Basingstoke: Palgrave Macmillan, 1999.
101 L. Jospin, 'Modern Socialism', London: The Fabian Society, 1999.
102 C. Pierson, 'Globalisation and the End of Social Democracy', *Australian Journal of Politics and History*, Volume 47 (4), pp. 459–474, 2001.

103 M. Ryner 'An Obituary for the Third way: The Financial Crisis and Social Democracy in Europe', *The Political Quarterly*, Volume 81 (4), pp. 554–563, 2010.

104 J. Andersson, *The Library and the Workshop: Social Democracy and Capitalism in the Age of Knowledge*, Stanford: Stanford University Press, 2009.

105 B. Clift & J. Tomlinson, 'Tale of a Death Exaggerated: How Keynesian Policies Survived the 1970s', *Contemporary British History*, Volume 21 (4), pp. 429–443, 2007'.

106 B. Clift & J. Tomlinson, 'Tale of a Death Exaggerated'.

107 Labour Party Manifesto, *A Lot Done, A Lot to Do*, p. 5, London: Labour Party, 2001.

108 Cited in https://independent.co.uk/arts-entertainment/geoff-and-martins-big-idea-these-men-think-theyll-change-how-we-think-one-is-a-former-communist-and-14 80495.html. Accessed 10th October 2018.

109 R. Unger, *The Critical Legal Studies Movement*, p. 119, Cambridge, MA: Harvard University Press, 1986.

110 S. Mudge, *Leftism Reinvented*.

111 S. Mudge, *Leftism Reinvented*, pp. 346–347.

112 G. Andrews, 'Shifting to the Bright – In Search of the Intellectual Left', in A. Coddington & M. Perryman (eds.), *The Moderniser's Dilemma: Radical Politics in the Age of Blair*, p. 47, London: Lawrence & Wishart, 1998.

113 J. Cronin, *New Labour's Pasts: The Labour Party and Its Discontents*, p. 393.

114 Interview, Ben Jupp, former Deputy Director, Demos, November 2011.

115 Cited in https://independent.co.uk/arts-entertainment/geoff-and-martins-big-idea-these-men-think-theyll-change-how-we-think-one-is-a-former-communist-and-1480495.html. Accessed 10th October 2018.

116 Interview, Ben Jupp, former Deputy Director, Demos, November 2011.

117 Cited in S. Mudge, *Leftism Reinvented*, p. 345.

118 https://independent.co.uk/arts-entertainment/geoff-and-martins-big-idea-these-men-think-theyll-change-how-we-think-one-is-a-former-communist-and-1480495.html. Accessed 10th October 2018.

119 J. Bentham, 'The IPPR and Demos: Think-Tanks of the New Social Democracy', *The Political Quarterly*, Volume 77 (2), pp. 166–187, 2006.

120 Cited in https://independent.co.uk/arts-entertainment/geoff-and-martins-big-idea-these-men-think-theyll-change-how-we-think-one-is-a-former-communist-and-1480495.html. Accessed 10th October 2018.

121 Cited in A. Campsie, 'Socialism Will Never Be the Same Again: Re-imagining British Left-wing Ideas for the 'New Times'', *Contemporary British History*, Volume 31 (2), pp. 178, 2017.

122 D. Kennedy, *A World of Struggle: How Power, Law, and Expertise Shape Global Political Economy*, p. 25.

123 M. Hajer, 'Policy without Polity? Policy Analysis and the Institutional Void', *Policy Sciences*, Volume 36 (1), pp. 175–195, 2003.

124 K. Baer, *Reinventing Democrats*, pp. 258–259.

125 E. Durbin, *New Jerusalem: The Labour Party and the Economics of Democratic Socialism*, p. 4.

5

MODERNISATION IN HARD TIMES

What do you say to a docker who earns £400 a week, owns his house, a new car, a micro-wave and video, as well as a small place near Marbella? You do not say, 'Let me take you out of your misery, brother'.

Neil Kinnock[1]

It is not an alliance with the Liberals that Labour needs, but the working-class vote. . . . If it concentrates on getting that it will not need to flounce around seeking new political allies.

Eric Heffer[2]

We will never regain power unless we win the support of the Basildon housewife, the Ste-venage technician working for British Aerospace, the Portsmouth Naval base or Austin Rover Longbridge skilled worker, the Cadbury-Schweppes middle manager, the North-West Regional Health Authority administrator.

Jack Dromey[3]

Introduction

In the wake of the humiliating 1979 and 1983 election defeats, the Labour Party transformed its political strategy while revising core precepts of the ideological agenda. The ideas that emerged in the 1980s and 1990s were not merely an expe-dient reaction to electoral failure and the perceived irreversibility of Thatch-erism. The embryonic approach to modernisation was integral to resolving long-standing dilemmas in the socialist tradition while responding to structural alterations in the economy and society of contemporary Britain. As previous chapters have demonstrated, the vigorous debate on the Left about Labourism's obsolescence and the decomposition of post-war social democracy led to New Labour's emergence. The process of rethinking did not begin when Blair became leader, nor when the party won the 1997 election triumphantly after eighteen years in the political wilderness. The venture hesitantly took shape after Labour lost office in 1979. Initially, it was Neil Kinnock who became the tough and uncompromising agent of the party's modernisation.

The claim that New Labour amounted to neo-liberalism with a human face presumed that a narrow elite captivated by power imposed internal reforms, epitomising the rise of the cartel party depicted by the political scientist, Peter Mair. In this account, co-opting Thatcherite ideas required the restructuring of the party and its institutions, weakening internal opposition and enabling leadership dominance. That perspective unquestionably had currency in the academic literature but was disingenuous. The New Labour project reflected grassroots movements and alliances, shaped by disparate forces across the pluralist British Left. Chapter 2 reiterated that it was the diverse community of centre-left scholarship and political activism that initiated New Labour. The grassroots Labour Co-ordinating Committee (LCC) was to play a particularly decisive role. The LCC was the key exponent of 'pluralist socialism' at the party's grassroots. The LCC encouraged the Soft Left to break with Tony Benn's political faction, subsequently endorsing New Labour's emerging agenda. It is striking that Matthew Taylor, once a prominent Bennite and LCC activist became director of the Institute for Public Policy Research (IPPR), and later advised Blair in Downing Street. Blair himself joined the LCC 'to break the hegemony of the Stalinist Left' within the party.[4] New Labour was conceived as traditional elite politics coinciding with the new movement of ideas and political energy, a dual response to prescient concerns about Labourism's post-war decay.

This chapter considers the dynamic of reform and modernisation within the Labour Party from 1979 to 1997. The focus is the promulgation of ideas and strategies during Kinnock's leadership. The reform of party institutions and the ruthless pursuit of electoral success were no doubt important. Even so, the weight attached to ideas by Kinnock, Blair and other leading modernisers has been understated in the literature. The emergence of New Labour reflected several decades of prolonged rethinking on the Left. While suffering a series of devastating general election defeats, the formative experience for the next generation of reformers was confronting the existential threat posed by the insurgent Social Democratic Party (SDP). The inescapable backdrop to these events was the long-term political and intellectual implosion of British social democracy.

Modernising Labour in hard times

In 1983, Labour suffered what was then its worst electoral loss since 1935, reduced to a rump of 209 seats. The party's survival owed much to the structural inequities of First-Past-the-Post (FPTP), which stymied the burgeoning SDP/Liberal alliance. In the wake of defeat, Kinnock immediately replaced Michael Foot as leader. A former member of the Left-Wing *Tribune Group*, Kinnock acknowledged the party must radically adapt to survive as a serious force in British politics. This account maps the unfolding events beginning with the founding of the SDP, and concluding with New Labour's victory in 1997.

Illiberal Labourism and the rise of the SDP

Given the depths of unpopularity to which the Callaghan government sunk, Labour's loss of office in 1979 was not unexpected. Even so, defeat was a traumatic experience. In the aftermath, momentum within the party lay with the Bennite Left following the discrediting of social democratic corporatism. After 1974, Labour governments were unable to reduce unemployment, contain wage inflation, resolve the balance-of-payments crisis or restore the post-war rate of growth. Moreover, Labour's aspirations for egalitarian redistribution lay in tatters. The Left-Wing journal *Tribune* attacked Callaghan's administration as a 'conservative monetarist government'.[5] Emboldened, the Left battled not only to alter the party's policies but to seize control of Labour's institutions, imposing rule changes to reduce the influence of the Parliamentary Labour Party (PLP) then dominated by the Right.

Wilson and Callaghan's perceived failure together with the impregnability of the Conservatives' electoral majority led to demands on the Left for 'extra-parliamentary action'.[6] The strategy emphasised mass industrial unrest, seizing control of local authorities creating the fortress from which to confront Thatcherism. In Lambeth and Liverpool, the Trotskyite *Militant Tendency* dominated local parties. More intelligible was the demand of activists 'to participate in a meaningful way in Labour party decision-making. Members wanted their elected representatives to be accountable'.[7] The party membership was increasingly well educated, reflecting momentous changes in education and the class structure. The white-collar middle class supplanted the blue-collar working class, marking the decline of loyalty and deference. The new breed of activists fought to transform Labour into a democratic participatory party. Benn 'articulated a vision of a new Labour party as a constituency of different social struggles, drawing on the energy of the women's and black movements'.[8]

Against this backdrop, the SDP's launch was a seismic event threatening to replace Labour as the dominant centre-left party. An alternative non-Conservative force spelt electoral and political disaster. The so-called Gang of Four, Bill Rodgers, David Owen, Shirley Williams and Roy Jenkins, who had all been Labour MPs, resigned from the party in 1981 in a state of despair; Jenkins had left British politics in 1976 to become Britain's commissioner in Brussels.[9] Denis Healey was then beaten decisively for the leadership by Michael Foot following Callaghan's resignation. The Wembley Special Conference in 1981 endorsed constitutional procedures that made MPs directly accountable to CLPs. The PLP was haunted by the spectre of mandatory deselection. What is more, Labour became a Eurosceptic party that favoured leaving the European Economic Community (EEC) and the North Atlantic Treaty Organisation (NATO). In a climate where Labour was abandoning its post-war role as a force for moderation, the SDP's ambition was 'to break the mould of contemporary politics . . . to create a new radical centre, push the Labour party into third place, change the electoral system and usher in a period of multi-party democracy'.[10]

The SDP's arrival on the political scene can be traced to Jenkins' resignation as deputy leader in 1972 following the decision of the shadow cabinet to support a referendum on EEC membership. Along with sixty-eight rebels, Jenkins voted in favour of the Conservative prime minister, Edward Heath's, legislation to enter the European Economic Community (EEC). The battles over Europe revived the spectre 'of the savage internal strife that kept Labour out office from 1951 to 1964'.[11] Following Wilson's resignation in 1976, Jenkins was beaten once again, the outcome sealing his fate in the party and cementing the growing divide.[12] Yet what encouraged the SDP's formation was less the attack on the PLP's sovereignty than the reality of British socialism's abject decline. The party was gripped by the intolerant culture of 'illiberal Labourism'. This was a unique moment to construct a new centre-ground position.[13] In his 1979 Dimbleby Lecture, Jenkins advocated cultivating the radical centre to 'break the mould' of British politics, overturning the traditional party system. In recognising the scale of the governing crisis, Jenkins warned that Britain required not merely 'more change', but 'greater stability of direction'. Continuity in institutions was previously thought advantageous, reinforcing civility and tolerance in British political life. In contrast, Jenkins believed the First-Past-the-Post (FPTP) system was a 'straightjacket'. The electoral system meant 'freezing the current pattern of politics'. The SDP emphasised political reform: fully committed EEC membership, decentralisation of public administration, alongside protection of civil liberties in the face of an 'elective dictatorship'.[14]

Jenkins' vision of the radical centre sought 'to bring into political commitment the energies of many people of talent and goodwill who . . . are at present alienated from the business of government by the sterility and formalism of the political game'. Jenkins's lecture called for a decisive shift. The SDP's purpose was not to win power at Westminster through single-party rule. The aim was to realign the political system, breaking with the sterile 'winner takes all' mind-set. Governments should no longer be judged 'by how many trees [they] pull up from the roots'. Jenkins repudiated the culture of 'excessive political partisanship' and pointless legislative upheaval, urging the consensual politics of adaptation. The progressive middle class and the 'great and the good' flocked to the new party in considerable numbers. Founder members included Keynes's biographer, Professor Robert Skidelsky, alongside the author of Labour's 1945 manifesto, Michael Young; the economists Sir Alec Cairncross and Professor James Meade; as well as former Labour politicians, including the former deputy leader, George Brown, alongside Dick Taverne, ousted from his Lincoln constituency by the hard Left.

The year before the Dimbleby lecture, Eric Hobsbawm declared the end of Labour's forward march. He repudiated the assumption that a political movement dominated by the working class would inevitably seize power, ruling through gradualist parliamentary reform. In a climate where class politics was supplanted by fluid and volatile voting patterns, the centre-left had to rethink its approach to electoral politics. Realignment meant breaking with FPTP, implementing a model of Proportional Representation (PR) normal elsewhere in Western Europe. Hobsbawm was inspired by the electoral success of Mitterrand's Left coalition in France, alongside the plural alliance of Felipe Gonzalez's Spanish

Socialist Party. He agreed with Jenkins that governments must be coalitions working to enact social reform in the national interest.

The vitality of the SDP starkly contrasted with the archaic statism of the Labour Right. The SDP's launch posed a fundamental question not merely about Labour's electoral viability, but its central political ideas. Political realignment was achievable by marrying the Edwardian liberalism of Asquith and Lloyd George with the social democracy of Keynes and Beveridge. There was considerable interest in the New Liberalism of J.A. Hobson, Hobhouse and Masterman, who established the 'Rainbow Circle' among the progressive intelligentsia in the 1890s.[15] From political ideas flowed electoral alliances. The SDP sought to resurrect the coalition that had been of considerable advantage to Labour in the aftermath of the Second World War. The English middle class was integral to progressivism's advance, motivated by the ethic of expertise, service and duty. As Paul Addison recounts, 'in every area of [Labour's] policy-making the main principles had been defined before 1939 by non-party experts'.[16] While Gaitskell told his followers they must show 'humility' to the working-class leadership of the unions, he believed the proletariat lacked the capacity for effective political action. For middle-class social democrats, the working class ought to be the object of compassion and pity. The SDP leadership were adamant that social reform was viable only if the working class submitted themselves to the intellectual discipline supplied by the enlightened professional classes. Beatrice Webb once said of William Beveridge: 'As of old, Beveridge is obstinately convinced that he and his class have to do the job, and the Trade Unionists have to be ignored'. The post-war social revolution was to be achieved 'by persons with training and knowledge'.[17] The SDP's outlook was redolent of Beveridge. Reform at the behest of the Social Democrats would improve the welfare of the working class rather than transferring political and economic power to citizens. The SDP stood for the resurrection of Victorian liberal philanthropy in 1980s' Britain.

The altered electoral landscape marked by the 'growing salaried class of managers and administrators, professionals and semi-professionals' underlined the political threat to Labour. The burgeoning middle class was 'politically footloose . . . attracted by the non-ideological mixture of economic and social policies offered by the Alliance'.[18] In 1964, Wilson appealed to the strata of technical and scientific professionals who comprised the meritocratic society. Similarly, the SDP sought to exploit new patterns of class and occupational stratification. The party's founding statement spoke reassuringly of 'reconciling the nation . . . healing the divisions between classes'. Pockets of support were to be found among the progressively minded middle class and 'caring' professionals. The cadre of managers and academics employed predominantly in the public sector dramatically expanded in the 1960s. By appealing to them directly, the SDP threatened Labour's ability to forge an effective alliance between the working class and the sympathetic, enlightened middle class.

Yet while its formation was unquestionably damaging for Labour, the SDP was less dynamic intellectually than is commonly assumed. Ralf Dahrendorf accused the Gang of Four of vainly searching for 'a better yesterday'. Jenkins identified the SDP with the non-doctrinaire Left, the legatee of the moderate social democratic post-war tradition exemplified by Dalton, Gaitskell, Durbin and Crosland. Yet Gaitskell's civil service Keynesianism had invested excessive faith in the legitimacy of the British system of government. The SDP leadership were too concerned to re-establish the Attlee settlement rather than confronting the decline of British class structures and institutions, the emergence of new forms of individualism in the face of resurgent capitalism and the shift of power from the West to developing countries. Edmund Dell wrote that 'the quality of its economic thinking was not the SDP's finest achievement'.[19]

Other than advocacy of PR at Westminster, Jenkins lacked a vision for the democratisation of the British polity. Even Bill Rodgers felt that in Dimbleby 'proportional representation loomed too large as a solution to all contemporary problems'.[20] Despite its rhetoric of moral reform the SDP was an elite-orientated party, a movement of mechanical change *par excellence*. When Dahrendorf criticised the SDP's vision, he alluded to the party's desire to restore the residual status and esteem of the British liberal elite. Within Jenkins's faction, it was not difficult to detect the 'continuity of assumptions from the days of pre-1914 progressive liberal imperialism'.[21]

Growing schisms exposed the SDP's weaknesses, personified by the divide between Owen and Jenkins. Unlike Jenkins, Owen advocated the social market economy, speaking approvingly of the structural transformations unleashed by the Thatcher governments. Owen admired the political energy and spirit of Thatcherism. He had little regard for working-class deference. On the other hand, Jenkins was determined to resurrect the post-war progressive alliance with the liberal middle class. Jenkins detested Thatcherism on moral grounds: the avaricious individualism, the encouragement of the flagrant 'get rich quick culture'. Yet the SDP soon confronted a crisis of purpose and conviction. As a leading political commentator remarked, 'What were they offering? What exactly was their alternative? What was the nature of their project? Why were they there?'[22]

The SDP was enveloped by nostalgia despite its advocacy of the new politics, hankering after a world shaped by patterns of class consciousness that hardly existed now. The historical literature paid attention to adaptations in the British working class as traditional allegiances and ties to the union movement broke down. Just as significant, however, was the re-composition of the professional middle class. Throughout the twentieth century, the Christian philanthropic tradition was dissipating in the face of secularisation. By the end of the Second World War, the English middle class had grown anxious, given declining differentials in living standards – a situation exploited by the Conservatives who promised immediate relief by cutting taxes. The middle class was reconstructed subsequently by economic change: new professions were expanding as the public sector, education, welfare services and social work grew in importance; women entered the professions in large numbers; the Campaign for Nuclear Disarmament (CND), protests against the Vietnam War, the student movement, and the New Left insurgency radicalised professional 'brain' workers.[23] The emerging middle class, as well as Labour's traditional working-class supporters were less receptive to the blandishments of Jenkins's 'establishment' party.

While divided over its purpose, the SDP failed to cultivate a productive relationship with organised labour. As such, it was unable to mount an effective challenge in the majoritarian two-party system. In 1983, the Alliance won 23 seats in the House of Commons on 26 per cent of the popular vote while Labour won 209 seats on 28 per cent. The concentration of support in its Northern and Celtic heartlands aided Labour enormously. The structural characteristics of the political system enabled the party to survive the most traumatic period in its history. The SDP ultimately failed since it was a new party trying to break into a political system where the two main parties still represented the dominant interests in society – the Conservative Party, organised business, and Labour, the organised working class. Moreover, the paucity of the SDP's ideas ultimately derailed the Gang of Four. Even so, the SDP had a decisive long-term impact in moulding New Labour's thinking. The SDP's presence emphasised to Kinnock's party that it could no longer take for granted Labour's monopoly over the centre-left vote. As a consequence, the SDP dragged Labour back towards the 'moderate centre' to become an effective competitor for votes. As important, whatever its intellectual deficiencies, the SDP offered the dose of doctrinal innovation absent from the Labour Party of the early 1980s. The SDP ultimately proved more influential in shaping Blair and Brown's party than Thatcherite neo-liberalism.

The 1983 defeat: 'the longest suicide note in history'?

Although it survived the threat posed by the SDP, Labour's political reputation continued to deteriorate throughout the early 1980s. The 1983 election in particular marked a disturbing decline in its share of the vote. Giles Radice remarked that the campaign 'has exposed our weaknesses – the incredibility of Michael Foot, the unpopularity of our defence policy, and the distrust which three years of infighting has built up for us'.[24] The result confirmed the party's problems were not merely to do with its poor campaign and unpopular leadership, but the refusal to come to terms with a changing society in the face of British Labourism's degeneration.[25] As the journalist Peter Jenkins remarked, the party was losing because it was Labour. An influential report by the LCC after the 1983 defeat concluded: 'Labour's old coalition and conceptions of the working-class are no longer adequate'.[26]

The collapse of support was most dramatic among skilled and semi-skilled working-class voters living in Southern England and the Midlands. These occupational groups were increasingly sceptical of government intervention, high taxes, trade unions and corporatism.[27] Labour's policies of withdrawing from the EEC and NATO aroused antagonism from working-class electors. Over a third of trade union members now voted Conservative. The Tory party secured more working-class support than at any time since the 1930s. In its total share of the vote, Labour was almost squeezed into third place despite the structural advantages afforded by FPTP.

The 1983 manifesto represented the most decisive shift to the Left since the establishment of the party. The programme *New Hope for Britain* was long and turgid, encompassing every major party conference resolution since 1970. Tony Benn claimed subsequently the 1983 election was a triumph since 8 million citizens voted for socialism. Eric Hobsbawm disagreed, insisting 'there is not a glimmer of comfort in the results of this election'.[28] Labour was losing support across all classes, age cohorts and genders, 'while only 39 per cent of trade unionists supported the party they had founded'. South of the line from the Wash to the River Severn, Labour won just three seats outside London. Not even Hobsbawm anticipated the scale of Labour's collapse. External factors were emphasised in explaining the defeat, including changes in the class structure disadvantageous for social democratic parties. Less scrutinised were the inept decisions of the shadow cabinet, particularly the collective failure to develop a credible economic policy following the breakdown of the Social Contract in the 1970s.[29] An internal review of the 1983 campaign demonstrated that 'many older supporters see Labour's anti-nuclear policy as "soft"'. Moreover, 'there [was] a general lack of belief that Labour can actually do the things that it is promising'.[30] Labour was perceived as a party of protest rather than government.

In the wake of defeat, Foot, a bookish and rather unworldly literary intellectual, resigned from the leadership. The 'dream ticket' of Kinnock, a former Left-Winger and Bevanite, and Roy Hattersley, stalwart of the traditional Right and protégé of Anthony Crosland, replaced the team of Foot and Healey. Kinnock convincingly won the leadership contest, securing a majority of the Electoral College with solid support in the CLPs.[31] It was a remarkable victory. Yet it is important to recall that Kinnock won because Benn was disqualified from the contest after losing his seat at Bristol South-East in the 1983 rout. Events could have played out differently had Benn been eligible to run.

So what kind of politician was Neil Kinnock? His political philosophy were rooted in the socialist ethos of Nye Bevan and the South Wales valleys. On the Left originally, Kinnock hated Thatcherism's 'smug and selective Victorian homilies. . . . The Tory party uses the hidden boot of unemployment as well as the invisible hand of Adam Smith'.[32] He not only objected to the Thatcher governments' economic and social policies. Kinnock believed the values of compassion, caring and solidarity in which he was steeped in his community of Tredegar, the birthplace of Bevan, was anathema to Thatcherism. Elected to the House of Commons for Bedwellty in 1970 at the age of twenty-eight, Kinnock served his apprenticeship in the Workers' Educational Association (WEA), a body providing education to working-class trade unionists. His heroes inevitably were Nye Bevan, alongside the English social historian R.H. Tawney. Kinnock's speeches often referred to Tawney's most important work, *Equality*.[33] At the start of the 1987 campaign in a rousing address at Llandudno in North Wales, Kinnock asked famously: 'Why am I the first Kinnock in a thousand generations to get to university?' When he spoke of the community 'translat[ing] its desires for those individuals into provision for those individuals', the essence of the post-war welfare state, it was an ethical impulse that derived from Tawney's writings. Tawney was Kinnock's lodestar.

In what circumstances, then, did Kinnock become the crusader for reform inside the Labour Party? During the 1970s, Kinnock had been a firebrand figure on the parliamentary Left, physically confronting Michael Heseltine after brandishing the mace at the opposition benches following a dispute over 'pairing' of votes. In his maiden speech, Kinnock defied convention by attacking the opposition as Bevan had done, condemning the Conservatives as 'a party whose very existence is an illustration of rapacity and selfishness'. Kinnock was echoing self-consciously Bevan's infamous speech at Belle Vue in 1948:

> No attempt at ethical or social seduction can eradicate from my heart a deep burning hatred for the Tory party. . . . So far as I am concerned, they are lower than vermin. They condemned millions of first-class people to semi-starvation.[34]

Yet as an ardent Left-Winger, Kinnock loathed Harold Wilson as much as the Conservative Party. He held the governments of the 1960s and 1970s in particularly low regard. In Kinnock's view, Labour ministers had traded political principle for the glamour of high office and access to the political establishment. He was an inveterate opponent of devolution to Wales, believing devolution threatened the unity of the British working class. Kinnock was an advocate of Benn's leadership throughout the 1970s. Yet having voted for Foot in the leadership ballot in 1980, Kinnock dramatically switched sides, despairing at the internecine battles threatening to destroy Labour in the aftermath of the 1979 defeat. In the deputy leadership contest in 1981, he shocked *Tribune Group* allies by abstaining rather than supporting Benn. Thereafter, Kinnock advocated the party's doctrinal and organisational rejuvenation.

The hard Left saw Kinnock's actions as cynical treachery, setting out to destroy Benn while securing the leadership for himself.[35] The MP Margaret Beckett (who ousted Dick Taverne in Lincoln) condemned Kinnock as Judas. Yet, in hindsight, destroying Benn's career was an improbable explanation of his motives. It is more plausible that Kinnock concluded modernisation was the only viable route to a Labour government in the face of recurrent electoral defeats. The rock-solid seat he represented in South Wales was manifestly suffering as a consequence of the policies of the Thatcher governments. It would never see a Labour administration again unless the party won outside its industrial heartlands. Moreover, the antics of the Left repulsed him. Kinnock grew to despise:

> The group of people in the Labour Party who are not motivated by any desire for amicable resolution of disputes. They do not care whether we win the next General Election – in fact they would rather like us to lose it so they can have what they call the Great Clear Out. Then the organisation would become entirely a repository for the assorted sectarians.[36]

As a consequence, Kinnock subsequently aligned himself with the party's factions on the Centre and Right. In the autumn of 1983, he was elected leader by an overwhelming margin on the 'dream ticket' with Hattersley. Even so, an underlying ambiguity remained in Kinnock's politics. He became a committed reformer, laying the foundations for Blair's transformation of the party in the 1990s. Kinnock sought to build his reputation as an engaging television personality, projecting himself as a modern family man at ease with middle-class Britain. Yet Kinnock never shed his ties to the South Wales valleys, to the socialism of Bevan, to the culture of solidarity that prevailed in the pit village communities of Tredegar. After Ed Miliband defeated his brother, David, in the 2010 leadership contest, Kinnock boasted to friends: 'We've got our party back!' He was almost literally 'the life and soul of the party', throughout his political career maintaining an intuitive empathy with the Labour movement. Kinnock grasped the party's ethos, fomented throughout a century of industrial and political struggle, better than almost any Labour politician. He cherished the symbols, ethics and practices that made it the party of labour, that made its membership 'Labour people'. Kinnock told the party conference in 1985: 'There is no need to compromise values, there is no need in this task to surrender our socialism, there is no need to abandon or even try to hide any of our principle'. Nevertheless, the reformulation of the party's identity and strategy was to prove a tortuous process in which fundamental principles were allegedly betrayed. Kinnock never entirely escaped the accusation that he was the modern-day Judas of the British Left.

1984–87: centralising power, routing militant

As the new leader, Kinnock nonetheless pursued a vigorous strategy to arrest Labour's decline.[37] The first plank of the strategy was to strengthen the capacity of his office, centralising authority around his team of advisers. Charles Clarke, ebullient son of the treasury mandarin Richard 'Otto' Clarke and leading personality in the Hackney Labour Party, was recruited as chief of staff. Patricia Hewitt, a Cambridge University graduate and former official at the National Council for Civil Liberties (NCCL), was appointed press secretary. Shortly afterwards, the party hired Peter Mandelson, a current affairs producer at London Weekend Television (LWT), as the party's director of campaigns and communications. Mandelson was

PHOTO 5.1 AND PHOTO 5.2 Early modernisers, Charles Clarke and Patricia Hewitt

Source: Photos by ullstein bild/Getty Images (L) and Jeff Overs/BBC News & Current Affairs/ Getty Images (R).

regarded as 'the most remarkable political strategist of his generation'. He became an unlikely continuity figure, bridging Kinnock's efforts at modernisation in the early 1980s with Labour's return to power under Blair and Brown.

Mandelson's grandfather was Herbert Morrison who dominated London Labour politics in the 1920s, organised the Home Front in the wartime coalition and was the architect of the Attlee government's domestic policy. Mandelson idolised him. In the inter-war years, Morrison insisted Labour should reach out to the English middle class, becoming a credible party of power. He believed that 'Labour must attract the black-coated (i.e. white-collar) worker', a strategy Morrison pursued in switching his constituency from Hackney South to the middle-class seat of Lewisham East in 1945. He proclaimed: 'Our appeal is to the community as a whole . . . for there is no cleavage of interest between the hand worker and the brain worker'.[38] Although they hardly knew one another, Mandelson and Morrison were remarkably similar political personalities. Both joined the Young Communists in their teenage years. Both were brilliant organisers who courted the company of journalists. Both desperately wanted to be foreign secretary, an objective Mandelson has yet to attain. Both were allegedly vain and manipulative, attracting the enmity of colleagues. Bevin's contempt for Morrison was matched by John Prescott's disdain for Mandelson, whom he saw as one of the 'beautiful people' promoting New Labour's glitzy image. Among the apocryphal stories about Mandelson was ordering mushy peas from a Fish and Chip shop during the Brecon and Radnor by-election which he allegedly mistook for guacamole.

Labour's new model army of communications professionals recruited by Mandelson had no hesitation in casting aside unhelpful precedents and formal procedures; principles were subordinated to ensure strategic clarity and presentation.[39] The party rule book was ignored or overridden. Mandelson's team were influential operators who through personal networks brought Labour closer to the new generation of knowledge workers revolutionising the media, marketing, advertising and management consultancy.[40] Their purpose was to create a 'new strategic paradigm' selling the party to footloose political consumers.[41] As the party was shedding its ties to the manual working class, so it was forming vital connections to Britain's burgeoning service and knowledge industries. By the early 1990s, as Eric Shaw has written, the traditional Labour Party that lacked any coherent centralised hierarchy was replaced 'by a powerful central authority exercising tight control over all aspects of organisational life'.[42]

The next plank of Kinnock's strategy was to restore the pre-eminence of the Parliamentary Labour Party (PLP) reversing the process of returning policy-making power to the constituencies at the behest of the organised Left in the 1970s.[43] Kinnock enabled the PLP, which had been routed in the early 1980s, to reassert its authority over activists. Thereafter, the PLP was involved much more closely in policy-making, while feeding into the party's electoral strategy.[44] Kinnock assembled a majority on the national executive (NEC) to drive through his reforms, winning the tacit support of well-known figures on the Soft Left – notably Michael Meacher, David Blunkett and Clare Short – all of them demoralised by never-ending electoral defeats. By the mid-1980s, Labour's economic and social policies were once again under the direct control of the moderate shadow cabinet and their advisers.[45]

The third dimension of Kinnock's strategy to regain control of the party meant enacting institutional reforms that weakened the power of the trade unions and sought to dilute the block vote. The influence of the unions at the party conference and in the Electoral College was reduced. The proportion of union votes to decide resolutions at the party conference was cut from 90 to 70 per cent. The balance of power shifted away from CLP activists and trade unions towards individual members, the PLP and the party bureaucracy in Walworth Road.[46] Despite their power base being under threat, union leaders were compelled to accept modernising policies, even the leadership's commitment not to reverse anti-union reforms initiated by the Thatcher governments.[47] There was a widespread belief that Labour had got its act together.

The Labour Party had been gripped by bitter discord since the convulsions and industrial crises of the 1970s. In responding to the takeover by the Trotskyite Left, there was a wave of expulsions and suspension of constituency parties controlled by the Militant Tendency and other far Left factions. Prominent figures including Derek Hatton and Tony Mulhern in Liverpool were ejected. At the 1985 Bournemouth conference, Kinnock memorably rebuked Militant's activities in running Liverpool City Council. For political commentators, the Bournemouth speech marked the beginning of the party's long road to electoral recovery. The leadership sought to assert Labour's moderate identity in the face of years of perceived extremism. Kinnock insisted the 'real' Labour Party was the upholder of the post-1945 settlement slaying the 'five giant evils' of ignorance, want, squalor, disease, and idleness – rather than an obscure Marxist sect. Experienced figures bolstered Kinnock's efforts including Denis Healey, a popular politician among Labour voters who remained shadow foreign secretary until the 1987 election, alongside younger rising stars, notably Blair and Brown.

Nonetheless, Kinnock was compelled to acknowledge that despite organisational reforms, the party remained sterile in its doctrine and ideas. At the leader's behest, Tony Blair, then a newly elected MP, established an advisory committee to re-examine Labour's economic and industrial policy in 1984. Blair observed:

> Debate within the labour movement is still very fragmented and does not have the priority it should. People are happy enough talking about how bad unemployment is and its social effects, but not about how we obtain growth in the economy and the future direction of industry.[48]

There was a concerted drive to involve leading experts from the City of London. The committee's agenda encompassed fundamental questions about Britain's political economy:

> What sort of economy do we want to achieve; how do we finance it; what is the impact of new technology; how is Labour to establish itself as the

party of production; what have we learned from socialist economics . . . and what should our economic priorities be after the election?

The discussion papers commissioned by Blair's team sought to dissect the party's economic prospectus. The initiative was a tentative signal that organisational reform on its own was likely to be insufficient. Once again, Labour must rethink its central political ideas.

The 1987 general election

Within four years, the totemic policies in the party's 'suicide note' manifesto on defence, public ownership and the EEC were discarded. Labour's reflationary economic programme was quietly jettisoned. It was acknowledged that the goal of full employment was unattainable within a single parliament.[49] Further changes meant the aim of public ownership was downgraded and a rules-based approach to macro-economic management was embraced; the party's rhetoric became ardently pro-European.[50] It was emphasised that a Labour government should protect the incentives for private sector investment, modernising capitalism instead of undermining the market economy.

The party made a concerted effort to sharpen its presentation to voters under the influence of the campaign co-ordinator, Bryan Gould. There were strenuous efforts to professionalise and overhaul Labour's communications. The party learned to effectively sell its policies to footloose, instrumentalist voters who were believed to have shed the ties of class loyalty.[51] Hopes among Kinnock's entourage were raised after the party won the Fulham by-election in 1986, defeating the Conservatives and polling 43 per cent of the vote, deploying the memorable slogan 'Nick Raynsford Lives Here'. Labour's campaign emphasised the local credentials of its candidate rather than ideology. The party was battling to overhaul its image. The filmmaker and producer of *Chariots of Fire*, Hugh Hudson, commissioned a series of dazzling party political broadcasts that focused attention on Kinnock's meritocratic rise from the Welsh valleys. In 1987, the party's general secretary, Larry Whitty, praised Labour's 'impressive and at times brilliant media campaign. The organisation in the constituencies and at national level was far better than most of us can remember for several elections'.[52] At the behest of Philip Gould who created the Labour-supporting Shadow Communications Agency (SCA), marketing techniques were being adopted to better understand the British electorate.

During the 1987 campaign, Kinnock relied heavily on his personal court overseen by Charles Clarke and Patricia Hewitt alongside his economic adviser, John Eatwell, a Cambridge economics don, and Peter Mandelson. The goal, above all, was to maintain discipline by centralising political control through the leader's office.[53] The Left had been marginalised. When Tony Benn and Eric Heffer ran against Hattersley and Kinnock for the leadership in protest against the modernising shift Rightwards, they were humiliated in the press by the new generation of 'spin doctors' condemned as 'figures who live in the dark'. For all the Left's complaints, by 1987 Labour had succeeded in re-establishing itself as the main opposition party: 'Labour – and particularly the Leader – came out of the election campaign far stronger than we went in', claimed an internal party memorandum. 'Neil Kinnock is now seen as strong and popular; Labour is a real contender, a party with a future'.[54]

Even so, despite these strenuous efforts to transform the party, in 1987 Labour suffered another major defeat. Although it was an improvement on the 1983 result, the party's vote share was 30.8 per cent, indicating Labour's support had plummeted to a level not seen since the 1930s. Labour's vote had declined in every election since the war, apart from 1966; 47 per cent of C1 (clerical) and 42 per cent of C2 (skilled manual) voters now supported the Conservatives. Women were more likely to vote Tory, although the gender gap was beginning to narrow. Just one skilled worker in three voted Labour. The only social constituencies among whom Labour had a decisive lead were the unemployed and the unskilled (DE) working class. Those voting Labour were still concentrated geographically in the depressed areas of Northern England and the central industrial belt of Wales and Scotland, as they had been in 1935. Even here, as Eric Hobsbawm noted, 'the position of Labour in its own heartlands is far weaker than the Tories in theirs'.[55] A *Guardian* editorial encapsulated the party's predicament:

> There is no Rainbow Coalition of minorities that will bring Labour back to power. . . . The growing underclass of have-nots, large and desperate though it is, can only in the end come to power through policies that assist, and are seen to assist, the not-so-poor and not-so-powerless.[56]

The political heartland of Thatcherism was the economic powerhouse of London and the South-East of England, beneficiaries of the long boom.[57] The Thatcher governments projected the appeal of popular capitalism, privatising industries, incentivising share ownership, selling council houses and limiting the power of the unions.[58] Unemployment sharply rose in the former industrialised regions, as the Thatcher administration instigated the monetarist experiment. The parties' regional share of the vote is highlighted in Figure 5.1.

Despite the updating of the party's programme and its younger, more dynamic leadership, the unpopular commitments in the 1983 manifesto were not yet fully reversed. Voters still feared 'the party's intention to leave Britain defenceless'.[59] An internal review found that popular folk memories of the party impaired 'perceptions of Labour's ability to govern': 'the Winter of Discontent', 'the miners' strike/ three-day week', 'soaring inflation', 'incompetent/extremist councils', 'inexperience of government'.[60] Diagnoses of the defeat indicated Labour's strategy continued to emphasise mobilising its heartland supporters. Larry Whitty told the party conference that Labour lost 'because we failed to deliver, to get out and turn out, the potential vote of the deprived, the youth, the old, the low paid, the ethnic minorities, those who suffer from the wreck of Thatcherism'.[61] Yet the party was unlikely to triumph by appealing to a 'rainbow coalition' of the dispossessed.

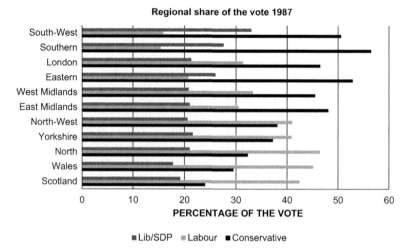

FIGURE 5.1 Regional share of the vote 1987 (British Election Study 1987)

Thatcherism was self-evidently in the political ascendency. Kinnock sought to supplant the Bennite Left's critique of capitalism with the moral politics of solidarity, attacking the selfish materialism of the Thatcher years. Labour's leader fought to revive the politics of compassion. Depressingly, his message fell largely on deaf ears.[62] Early in the 1987 campaign, there was panic in Conservative headquarters, given the party's hesitant tone and apparently inept appeal. One poll had the parties neck and neck. A terrified Thatcher contemplated firing Norman Tebbit, the Conservatives' campaign chairman. Yet as Labour's programme for the economy and taxation was vilified by the press, support crumbled: 'The Tories scored a runaway victory by frightening voters over Labour's threat to their pockets'.[63] According to its own polling strategists, the party's 'caring emphasis neglected self-interest/economic achievement'. Labour failed to understand that 'social/caring [issues are] not key voting influences'.[64] The party was unable to win back the moderately prosperous C2 voters lost in 1979 and 1983. Many questioned whether Kinnock's party offered a credible governing alternative to Thatcherism. As one observer commentated: 'Labour's original aim of improving the quality of life for the masses seems to have got lost. Labour needs to offer hope – not just harassment through higher taxes and more bureaucracy'.[65]

Coming to terms with Thatcherism

In the wake of the 1987 defeat, an official at the Transport and General Workers' Union (TGWU) acknowledged that while defence, tax and 'the image of extremism' cost the party votes, 'the main reasons for Labour's defeat . . . lie in the fundamental changes that have taken place in Britain under Mrs Thatcher'.[66]

The affluence spreading through Southern England following the expansion of the British economy enabled an impressive sweep of Conservative victories. Thatcher astutely played the politics of two nations, aligning the party with the South where living standards were rising sharply. Hobsbawm recognised, 'The workers in the ruins of Merseyside do not respond to the same appeals that strike home among the workers in Harlow and Basildon'.[67] Thatcherism understood blue-collar working-class instrumentalism, where voters supported parties that promoted material improvement.[68] As such, 'Mrs Thatcher's appeal to individualism and her "popular capitalism" may have bitten deep. . . . Too many believe that their aspirations and prosperity is better assured under the Tories'.[69]

The 1984–85 Miner's Strike further weakened Labour, not least in reinforcing the belief the party represented Britain's declining regions and industries. The eventual defeat of the National Union of Mineworkers (NUM) symbolised the fading status and prestige of industrial labour. The dispute inflicted incalculable damage on the party's standing. The graphic images of violent industrial unrest and unruly picketing were broadcast on television, an unpleasant reminder of the Winter of Discontent in the late 1970s. Kinnock, the son of a miner from the South Wales valleys, naturally identified with colliery communities. Kinnock once said that had he been a miner, he felt he would have had little choice but to join the strike. As the dispute unfolded, Labour's leader felt trapped. The NUM's mishandling of the situation, particularly its refusal to hold a strike ballot, the timing of industrial action – the strike began in March when coal stocks were high – and the debilitating militancy of the NUM's leadership personified by Arthur Scargill inestimably damaged the Labour Party's reputation.

Although it was confronted by a Britain that was becoming palpably post-industrial, the heroic tales of political struggle continued to captivate the Labour movement. The dignity of labour was the central theme in the growth of the trade union movement in the late-nineteenth century: workers arbitrarily sacked for talking or alleged incompetence, horrific injuries caused by poorly maintained machinery, the sheer tedium of monotonous manual work, returning at the end of the working day to housing conditions unimaginably grim with little access to essential welfare services. Yet the difficulty, as the writer Jeremy Seabrook acknowledged, was that in the light of the post-war settlement, 'that world is remote from the way we live now'.[70]

The Labour Party's vulnerability in the 1980s was the consequence of its inability to address Thatcherism's insurgency. In 1983, there was little effort to understand why the Thatcher governments captured the allegiance of voters. Following the 1979 defeat, the Left struggled to discern Thatcherism's appeal. Activists and MPs initially believed Thatcher's dominance was a temporary aberration. They were confident Britain would revert to the economic and social agenda of the Attlee settlement, particularly the commitment to full employment. What the Left underestimated was Thatcherism's 'strategic sense of the long-term' and its unrivalled capacity to seize the 'circumstances and opportunities encountered by government'.[71] The Thatcher administrations skilfully exploited antipathy among the skilled working class to nationalisation, public ownership, municipal planning and unfettered union power. The 1987 British Social Attitudes Survey demonstrated that only 14 per cent of voters supported a return to nationalisation.

Labour's response was muted, not least because Thatcherism was an ambiguous project at the outset, and the party was unsure how to respond. There were no Thatcherite 'policy blueprints' ready for implementation in 1979; Thatcherite policies were 'improvised according to particular circumstances'.[72] As the rate of unemployment soared and the government plumbed the depths of unpopularity, ministers were pragmatic enough to dilute the monetarist policies of high interest rates and public expenditure cuts. Thatcherism began from a position of historic weakness for the Right in British politics. When Thatcher became leader in 1975, the Conservatives had achieved their lowest share of the vote in the twentieth century, as their electoral support narrowed after the ignominious collapse of the Heath government.[73] In that light, many on the Left sought to discern the nature of Thatcherism more clearly: was it a coherent ideology? A political style? A grassroots movement? A neo-liberal governing project?[74] The confusion about the ideological purpose of Thatcherism arises throughout the academic literature. For particular scholars, Thatcherism was an ideological mission, the resumption of a war against the British working class that the Conservatives began to wage in the 1920s.[75] For others, Thatcherism was the belief in taking politics out of economic policy, governing through technocratic expertise rather than class confrontation.[76]

For all the apparent contradictions, Thatcherism's ideas had the potential to reshape British politics. Above all, the Thatcher governments sought to weld together 'the traditional Conservative emphasis on the need to uphold the political authority of the state with the New Right emphasis on the need to free the economy from the obstacles to competitive markets'.[77] During the 1950s, the Conservatives under Macmillan and Butler had emphasised conciliation between classes, upholding the welfare state and the post-war consensus. By 1979, that strategy was jettisoned. Thatcherism was reviving an older Conservative tradition of 'Gladstonian fiscal rectitude' centred on low taxes, free trade, market liberalism and the small state.[78] Thatcherism reshaped the role of government in managing the economy through liberalisation of markets; privatisation of assets in energy, transport and telecommunications; cuts in public expenditure and the scaling back of industrial policy.[79]

The aspirations of those who benefited from Beveridge's welfare state were rising after decades of relative prosperity. The politics of Thatcherism appealed to them. Ultimately, too many expected to be worse off under a Labour government.[80] Conservative ministers promised to spread the gains of resurgent capitalism through tax cuts and share ownership. The Thatcher administration was 'providing the only programme on offer with the object of changing the British economy'.[81] Britain then established comparative advantage in the knowledge-based service industries, particularly finance, as the Conservatives delivered faster growth.[82] By the late 1980s, GDP was expanding faster than the post-war average, almost 5 per cent per annum. The economy was now high-tech, powered by the microchip rather than the muscle of the industrial worker. The Labour Party seemed to be a movement, 'rooted in the past at a time when changes in the economy and social structure were creating values and forces which its old ideology simply did not recognise'.[83]

The 1987 defeat and the crisis of Labourism

The gravity of its third defeat encouraged Labour to undertake the fundamental reappraisal of strategy and ideology that it had hitherto avoided. The party could not merely tinker with its policies at the edges, but had to develop 'a perspective on what is happening to society now, a vision of the future, a capacity to articulate those vividly through a few clearly enunciated themes or principles, a new conception of politics'.[84] Labourism was vulnerable to structural collapse, given the decline of working-class support, alongside the weakening of class identification.[85] The Scottish MP Robin Cook believed that in 1987 Labour 'did not come across as a party with an economic programme tailored to making the economy stronger and its workers more prosperous'. Its agenda amounted 'to a programme of redistribution . . . presenting a series of discrete social policies without any underlying economic analysis to give them coherence'.[86] David Blunkett insisted that Labour must 'respond to and represent those who wish to see their own hard work provide them with well-earned comforts'.[87] The party had to offer a vision of economic revival that was 'human and responsible', emphasising market regulation, rebuilding the country's infrastructure, while securing a more highly educated and skilled labour force.[88] For too long, Labour had appeared determined to reverse the structural changes of the 1980s, returning Britain to the policies of the post-war settlement – an outlook that was increasingly irrelevant to younger voters.

Research presented to the shadow cabinet in November 1987 analysed why voters still rejected the party. The project 'Labour and Britain in the 1990s' was led by Patricia Hewitt, Philip Gould, Deborah Mattinson and polling experts Roger Jowell and John Curtice.[89] The findings are summarised in Table 5.1. The most important explanation for Labour's rejection at the ballot box was the fear the 'loony Left' might regain influence, that the party was dominated by the unions and that a Labour government would not defend the UK from foreign attack. It was believed the party's mismanagement of the economy would lead to rising prices. In 1987, Labour sought to focus debate on the health service and education. Even here, the Tories gained the political advantage, promising 'freedom of choice' for citizens. Gould, later Blair's polling strategist, believed that for millions of voters, 'Labour became a shiver of fear in the night, something unsafe, buried deep in the psyche. . . . Labour's negative identity became locked in time'.[90] The party was 'outdated, identified with an old agenda. Its policies no longer matched people's personal and family aspirations. . . . [It was] intent on telling people how they should run their lives, rather than enabling them as individuals to make their own choices'.[91] When Deborah Mattinson asked a Roehampton focus group in 1986 what characteristics epitomised the average Labour

TABLE 5.1 'Labour's Bad Points' 1987[92]

	'Non-Labour' voters	'Ex-Labour' voters
'Loony Left' would gain too much influence	36	42
'Labour too dominated by trade unions'	27	29
'Labour wouldn't defend Britain properly'	27	28
'Labour would undo good things done over last few years'	22	12
'Neil Kinnock wouldn't make a good PM'	19	15
'Soft on minorities'	15	16
'My standard of living would fall'	13	10
'Would restrict freedom to buy council houses/shares/ education/healthcare'	12	9
'Don't know how to run the economy'	11	10

voter, the respondents replied: 'Working-class, factory worker, drinks pale ale, smokes a pipe, holidays in Blackpool, takes the bus, lives in a council house'.[93]

The voters who continued to support Labour did so out of loyalty and habit in an era where the traditional ties of class were dissipating. A survey conducted after the 1987 defeat found that 27 per cent voted Labour because it was the 'party of the working-class', while 20 per cent did so because they had 'always voted Labour'.[94] Yet a report in the newspaper *Labour Weekly* acknowledged that it was the working class that 'had done well under Thatcherism. . . . They have had more money in their pockets at work and enjoyed real improvements in their disposable pay. Many have bought council houses and a quarter have become shareholders'.[95]

Another *Labour Weekly* columnist concluded:

> Economic arguments were by far the most important for the majority of voters. . . . The most inescapable conclusion is that no matter how well we do in Scotland, Wales and most of the north, Labour will never form another government unless the Tories can be defeated in crucial seats in the midlands and the south.[96]

Those voting Labour predominantly felt insecure and badly off. One supporter in the North-West commented, 'I just don't feel my job is safe nowadays'. Conservative voters felt more prosperous:

> If you're self-employed like me you're a lot better off by tax concessions. You get loans to start businesses. . . . She [Thatcher] must have bought massive amounts of money into the country. I mean, the confidence the world seems to have in her. The stock market's going through the roof.

Many feared Labour would mismanage the economy, drive out foreign investment, allow the country to be run by the unions and give help to the undeserving. The survey revealed that voters who bought shares or used private medicine, credible aspirations for C1s and C2s, were much less likely to vote Labour. The complaint of an Alliance supporter in the South-East of England that 'we're no longer a manufacturing country . . . the fiscal and monetary policies of this government are transient' was a minority view that fell on deaf ears among voters.[97]

In the wake of Labour's defeat, the modernisers' diagnosis not surprisingly gained traction within the shell-shocked party. Bryan Gould told the post-election conference of the Labour Co-ordinating Committee (LCC):

> If Labour is to win the next general election, we have to attract votes and win seats in those parts of the country – noticeably the south – where we did badly in 1987. The popular appeal of policy must be a prime consideration not an afterthought. . . . We must consciously think of ourselves as the party of the future, as the party to prepare Britain for the year 2000. We need to develop our own radical policies which . . . appeal to the self-interest of . . . those whose votes we need.[98]

The general secretary of the Amalgamated Engineering and Electrical Union (AEEU), Gavin Laird, told the *New Statesman*:

> What's wrong with people wanting cars? What's wrong with people wanting their own house? If in the States you speak to a guy who assembles cars, he sees no difference between himself and a doctor or a lawyer except in earning power. There's none of this class differentiation. It seems to me that we are heading in the same direction . . . what's wrong with that?[99]

The new revisionism shocked and dismayed the Left, who complained the 1987 defeat was being exploited to legitimise the jettisoning of socialist values, transforming the party's identity. Richard Heffernan and Mike Marqusee believed that 'responses to Labour's defeat bore a striking resemblance to responses to Labour's 1959 defeat . . . academics, pollsters and psephologists cited the gradual disappearance of the industrial working-class and the shrinking of Labour's industrial base'.[100] Heffernan and Marquesee believed reformers were drawing all the wrong lessons. Labour lost because its leader 'was seen as a man who would do anything or say anything, repudiate any conviction or embrace any prejudice for the sake of a handful of votes'.[101] Yet Heffernan and Marquesee's contribution was emblematic of the Left's quandary: vitriolic about Kinnock's attempt to rejuvenate the party, the authors struggled to provide a constructive account of late-twentieth-century socialism.[102] It was as if electing Tony Benn to the leadership was sufficient to energise the British Left and return Labour to power. Yet the essential ideas of socialism were subject to 'widespread discrediting'.[103] In the wake of recurrent defeats, it was less obvious other currents on the

Left offered a viable and persuasive alternative to Kinnock's neo-revisionism. Socialism, as the political theorist Alex Callinicos emphasised, always operated across two registers: an intellectual tradition and a political movement. Both of them appeared vulnerable to imminent collapse.

Eric Hobsbawm had demonstrated in 1978 that the class base that provided the political dynamic for socialist movements was weakening. The working class was shrinking as a proportion of the eligible voting population. Electoral de-alignment detached the remaining industrial workers from the party of labour. Socialist political economy was now in poor health. The planned economies of Eastern Europe and Soviet Russia, exemplars of 'actually existing socialism', were perceived as heroic failures at best. During the 1970s, Keynesian social democracy was discredited. Socialist political thought struggled to counter the rise of neo-liberal globalisation under Reagan and Thatcher, with its emphasis on the free economy and the strong state.[104] As an intellectual tradition, Marxism was in crisis, confronted by the wave of ideas rooted in post-structuralism. Whereas Marxism was once pre-eminent, post-structuralism was now 'the dominant radical voice in the Anglophone academy'.[105] Rather than the politics of industrial production and egalitarianism, the dominant theme in the 1980s was the rise of personal autonomy. Culture and identity replaced class stratification as the animating concern of the Left, rendering traditional conceptions of socialist politics redundant.[106]

Hobsbawm was a major intellectual influence during Kinnock's leadership. Indeed, Kinnock once remarked that Hobsbawm was 'his favourite Marxist'. The leader told the party conference in 1987: 'Democratic socialism has to be as attractive, as beckoning and as useful to the relatively affluent and the relatively secure as it is to the less fortunate in our society'. He reminded delegates: 'If this movement pretends . . . that a few million people owning a few shares each will not make any difference to their perception of their economic welfare, then this movement will be fooling itself'. Kinnock insisted the party must appeal to those who 'did not vote Labour last time or the time before'. Socialism 'was about ordinary people getting on: ordinary people having a better life, ordinary people being able to consume more and choose more, and gain greater comfort and opportunity and security'. Socialism's historic emphasis on collective ownership of productive assets was inevitably reappraised.

Yet Labour's inability to respond to Thatcherism had also underlined the bankruptcy of the British social democratic tradition. In his 1982 lecture in Perth, Australia, Tony Blair, then an up-and-coming parliamentary candidate, acknowledged that Labour was in difficulty because 'growing numbers of young often socially upward-moving people' were no longer willing 'to accept our basic ideology just because their forefathers did'. Meanwhile, those on the Right of the party offered only 'tired excuses of pragmatism'. Blair believed the Left had to understand the agenda of the professional middle class and skilled workers for whom nationalisation and redistribution were 'not a great priority'. White-collar voters were concerned increasingly with social issues: 'nuclear disarmament, ecology, race relations, feminism'. The stirring of fundamental rethinking in the party began to emerge.

The fundamental review of party policy

After 1987, Kinnock's party was compelled to come to terms with recurrent electoral losses, the apparent irreversibility of Thatcherism and the Left's decisive
defeat in the battle of ideas. The leadership's main response was to initiate the
Policy Review, the most far-reaching examination of Labour's policies undertaken
since the Second World War. The exercise was intended to be a 'fundamental and
radical review' of the party's programme.[107] Its overarching aim was to 're-establish
the economic case for socialism . . . on the grounds of its superior economic *efficiency*, rather than its commitment to economic *equity*'. The party had to overcome
the perception that, 'Labour's heart is in the right place but they don't know how
to run the economy, they are incapable of taking the hard decisions'.[108] The review
was intended to, 'convey a clear message of hope and optimism: that Labour is
in the process of developing imaginative modern policies'.[109] The authors of the
review sought to echo a number of pre-eminent themes throughout:

- *The party of the consumer*: 'especially the consumer of public services . . .
  services that enable people to have real choice . . . in a servant state, an
  enabling state'.
- *The party of competence, responsibility and good management*: 'to provide
  the conditions for competitive industry'.
- *The party of investment for the future*: 'Labour is the party best placed to
  manage change'.
- *The party of fair play*: 'a fair deal in taxation and social security to end
  dependence and poverty'.
- *The party of liberty and democracy*: 'the party that will sustain local
  democracy, provide for devolution of power from Whitehall'.
- *The party that believes in working together with people*: 'rather than
  encouraging conflict and divisions'.
- *The party of the environment and better quality of life*: 'in all its aspects from
  decent housing through to well planned, clean towns and cities'.[110]

The *Policy Review* overhauled Labour's strategy and ideology, entrenching the
modernisation effort within the party. The review epitomised Labour's determination to embrace the engine of the capitalist market economy. It represented 'a
major shift away from policies espoused earlier in the decade, and formed a platform on which New Labour could later build'.[111] The review was the brainchild
of the National Union of Public Employees' (NUPE) official, Tom Sawyer, a
close ally of Kinnock who chaired the party's Home Policy Committee. Having
suffered three defeats, Sawyer believed that Labour's policies must be fundamentally altered. It was no longer enough for the Labour leadership 'to announce
new policies and bully the membership into line'. According to Sawyer, 'better

and more acceptable policies would emerge from a lengthy period of open debate and widespread consultation'.[112]

Inevitably, ditching electorally disastrous policies proved to be easier than advancing a convincing formula for how the Left ought to manage markets in a capitalist society. The officials in Labour headquarters admitted: 'One of the most difficult tasks will be to define the desirable scale and composition of state intervention in the operation of markets'.[113] The language used in the review was upbeat in comparison to the 1983 manifesto: 'The market can be a powerful creative force, providing a competitive stimulus to innovation'.[114] The critique of Thatcherism was of its short-term 'get rich quick', 'anti-production, rentier philosophy'.[115] Even so, there was a reluctance to confront party members with the truth that 'the inevitable terminus of this process would be the death of some of the Left's most cherished projects – on defence, Europe, public spending and public ownership'.[116] The final report set out to chart a novel philosophical direction for Labour concluding:

> We have . . . been caricatured as the party that seeks to deny power and choice to the individual and gather all authority to the state. The reality has always been different. To us the state is an instrument, no more, no less: a means, not an end. Collective action has always been designed to create opportunities and advance the freedom of the individual and, cumulatively, of the whole community.[117]

Hattersley told the 1988 conference: 'The truth about markets is that sometimes they are right and sometimes they are wrong. If Mikhail Gorbachev can believe that, then I hope the Labour Party can, too'.[118] Bryan Gould echoed these remarks insisting markets remained, 'a more efficient and acceptable allocator and distributor of scarce resources, and a more sensitive means of meeting consumer preferences, than any system of planning'.[119]

The *Policy Review* sought to address Labourism's demise, taking account of the dominant nature of Thatcherism. The review reinforced the message that 'the party had changed the way it thinks and acts'.[120] The aim was to develop symbolic policies offering 'clear, immediate benefits' to individual voters . . . [that] illustrated Labour's competence in managing the economy, were not dictated by interest groups, and were new, exciting and modern'.[121] Party reformers acknowledged the Thatcher governments waged an effective war of ideas against the Left, consigning the post-1945 settlement to history. If the party was to remain a viable competitor for power, Labour required not only policies but an inspiring world-view that reconnected social democracy with modernity and the forces of transformation energising Thatcherism. Revisionists maintained that Labour must re-examine its 'strategy, policy and values' in the light of economic and social change.[122] Giles Radice wanted the *Policy Review* to provide a distinctive ideological direction. Above all, Labour should develop 'a radical cast of mind'. The Left must accept that the market economy was the most efficient allocator of goods and services in a liberal democracy. Voters were no longer motivated by the appeal to class and public ownership. At the 1987 conference,

Gould advocated the theme of 'popular socialism', a mass capitalist democracy where ordinary people would buy shares in companies and own their homes.[123]

The modernisers fought to recapture Thatcherism's appeal to material prosperity while attacking its vulnerabilities, particularly the belief there was 'no such thing as society'. Polling in the late 1980s demonstrated that 'Thatcherite values do not have majority support'.[124] Voters still cared about the social fabric and the condition of public services. Yet parents and patients yearned for greater power and control in their lives. The *Policy Review* reiterated that citizen's rights should be at the centre of the new settlement reconciling politics with markets. Modernisers believed that quality of life and community were becoming more important to the electorate than class identity and the politics of production.[125] In 1989, Labour published *Meet the Challenge, Make the Change*, the culmination of the review process. The document was full of admiring references to market forces and the private sector. As Patrick Seyd has written: 'It affirmed that a Labour government's task would be to stimulate a successful market economy and that it would intervene only where that stimulation was not coming from market forces'.[126] The review declared: 'The single most important objective of economic policy is to make Britain internationally competitive'. Kinnock's overriding aim was to position Labour as a mainstream social democratic party. To underscore this, he announced a flurry of symbolic policies from the review:

- *Productive and Competitive Economy:* Cabling of Britain to provide modern communications infrastructure; regional banks to ensure companies get investment; creating major institutions in the regions such as world-class technical universities and a national airport.
- *People at Work:* The national training and skills programme; flexible working including three months' parental leave for each child matching European standards; an employment charter of basic rights; improved childcare for working parents.
- *Economic Equality:* A more progressive tax system 'so the rich pay more'; helping people off benefit and into work; statutory minimum hourly wage; a modern social insurance system; National Personal Pension Scheme.
- *Consumers and the Community:* A Consumers' Charter; every local authority to set standards and targets for service provision; home-school 'contracts' in education; tailor-made health and social services to meet the needs of the individual.
- *The Physical and Social Environment:* An Environmental Protection Agency; European standards notably cleaner beaches and drinking water; tougher standards on food.
- *Democracy:* Replace the House of Lords with an elected second chamber with representation from the regions; a regional assembly for Scotland with powers to pass legislation and decide Scottish taxes; regional assemblies in Wales and England; protection of human rights.[127]

The policies in *Meet the Challenge, Make the Change* formed the bedrock of Labour's programme. The role of state ownership and planning was comprehensively downgraded. As a consequence, the 1992 Nuffield Election study concluded that Labour:

> increasingly resembled a social democratic party on Swedish or German lines. . . . The party had become sympathetic to the market as a means of creating wealth. . . . Labour was now perhaps divided less on traditional Left/Right lines than between old Labour and new Labour. "Old" Labour was identified with the values and interests of the past, with high taxes, public ownership, trade unions, council housing, heavy industry, and Northern England. "New" Labour sought to identify the party with skills and human capital, new forms of business organisation, improved public services, additional rights for women and families, alongside protection of the environment.[128]

In 1990, the party published a statement on economic policy, *Looking to the Future*, insisting that Britain should join the European Exchange Rate Mechanism (ERM) 'to provide long-term exchange rate and interest rate stability'. Supporting ERM membership bolstered Labour's claim to economic competence while underlining Tory disunity.

The political scientists Patrick Seyd and Paul Whiteley come to the striking conclusion that 'there was widespread support for the modernisation strategy in the party'.[129] Newspapers such as *Tribune* aligned themselves with Kinnock's leadership platform, despite supporting the Bevanites thirty years previously. Influential broadsheet newspapers including the *Guardian, Independent* and *The Observer* adopted an editorial position sympathetic to the modernisation agenda.[130] An in-depth survey found that Labour members endorsed a mass party with its leadership elected by one member, one vote.[131] There was considerable support for shifting Labour's defence policy to multilateralism. Nationalisation was no longer considered a major priority for party policy. The majority of members wanted to maintain the link with the unions but abolish the block vote at party conference.

On the face of it, Kinnock sought to return the party to the mainstream Labour tradition epitomised by the governments of Attlee and Wilson. Yet the emergence of Thatcherism made it implausible to turn back the clock to the heyday of British social democracy in the 1940s and 1960s. The Labour movement was gravely weakened by the Miner's Strike. By and large, working-class voters believed the Thatcher governments were correct in taming the industrial power of the unions, labelled by the prime minister 'the enemy within'. National government had been rolled back. Deregulation had 'removed many of the tools which the government might wish to use to attempt to restructure the economy'.[132] Popular attitudes to collectivism and personal prosperity were moving Rightwards.

For all it clarified about Labour's direction, the *Policy Review* was still dogged by fundamental confusion: was the main purpose to return Labour to the moderate revisionism of the post-war era or to find a new appeal suitable for the changed circumstances of Britain in the 1990s? The party's director of communications, Peter Mandelson, complained that the document contained too many 'generalised, regurgitated, unoriginal statements' and refused 'to take account of the country's mood of economic optimism'. It was necessary, he believed, 'to concede some economic gains and progress to the Government'.[133] Moreover, the review lacked an overarching analysis, a central organising theme, despite the efforts of Kinnock and Hattersley to inject doctrinal coherence. The LCC claimed that absent from the review was, 'a core of analysis, and a coherent strategy for social change, which could explain and inform the policies of a Labour government'.[134] Labour launched a plethora of symbolic policy initiatives. Yet the overarching vision remained opaque. Moreover, little consideration was given to governance and the institutional implementation of public policy. Labour's general secretary feared the review suffered from an absence of 'substance and intellectual rigour in the way which might impress the pundits and leader writers whose opinion we seriously need'.[135] To sympathetic observers, Kinnock had fought to transform Labour into a Gaitskellite party by routing Labourism. Yet perhaps unlike Gaitskell, the leadership struggled to posit an alternative doctrinal identity in the perplexing political world of Thatcherite Britain.[136]

Modernisation and its discontents

Rocked by successive defeats, tensions over Labour's modernisation agenda inevitably resurfaced. Reformers beyond the leadership were not convinced the party was advancing quickly enough. Kinnock's team had attacked the role of nationalisation in the party's programme but had not yet acknowledged the near universal exhaustion of post-war social democratic institutions. By the late 1980s, the prescriptions of orthodox Keynesianism appeared inadequate in responding to Britain's economic vulnerabilities. Keynesian social democracy was perceived to be centralising and dirigiste, relying on macro-economic levers in the Treasury wielded by enlightened experts.[137] Yet Britain was now a very different kind of society. The economy was fragmenting. Britain was more fissiparous and diverse. Deference was waning. The old ruling elites were under attack. In these circumstances, the Left's doctrine and strategy had to be fundamentally reappraised.

The Labour Left's objection was that leadership efforts to win the support of financiers and the business community were futile. Once an ardent reformer, by 1990 Bryan Gould feared the party was losing its radical edge, embracing the Thatcherite vision of political economy. Ken Livingstone complained Labour had failed to develop a programme to regenerate British industry, providing the resources for its social spending priorities.[138] Gould's arguments presaged Will Hutton's book *The State We're In*, insisting the centre-left should take the

European path to modernisation, embracing the developmental state that sought to rebuild manufacturing industry while prioritising the real economy over financial markets and the City of London.[139] Lurking beneath Gould and Hutton's ideas of 'stakeholding' was the indefatigable belief in national approaches to social democracy, although Hutton was vehemently pro-European. Gould, in particular, objected to Kinnock's embrace of Europe. Gould believed in the continuation of the national economy, convinced there were British industries, sectors and companies worth protecting.[140] Yet the *Policy Review* signalled the emergence of a different outlook, where the British Left embraced what were perceived to be the realities of global economic interdependence.

By the beginning of the 1990s, the Labour Party was feared to have been 'lobotomised'. It was a like a patient 'in search of nervous convalescence following a breakdown'.[141] Having jettisoned public ownership, Labour was plagued by lack of confidence about intervening in markets.[142] The party was no longer capable of thinking for itself, having discarded socialist doctrine. In particular, by acceding to the government's decision to join the ERM in 1990, Labour was now wearing a self-imposed 'macro-economic straight-jacket'. Gould lamented the leadership's position was one of 'surrender', 'an acknowledgment that really we had lost the argument, that a Thatcherite agenda had been established to which we could only accommodate'.[143]

David Blunkett, together with Professor Bernard Crick, attacked the capitulation to free market individualism. Crick was professor of politics at Birkbeck College, University of London, and Blunkett's former politics tutor. He made his name as George Orwell's biographer, publishing a landmark treatise, *In Defence of Politics* (1962). Detesting the authoritarianism of the hard Left, Crick believed the Labour Party should advance a communitarian philosophy in response to Thatcherism. In his submission to the party's *Policy Review*, Crick set out a distinctive formula:

> We believe in fostering that fellowship and sense of community that comes from working together for common purposes. But we also believe deeply in leisure and privacy. Just as individuals want to be helped by the state so they also want to be protected from abuse of public power. . . . The state should be the servant of the people not its master.[144]

Meanwhile, Ken Livingstone, Eric Heffer and Michael Meacher insisted the revised conception of socialism meant the betrayal of the working class and organised labour.

Yet taken as a whole, the Left's assault on the *Policy Review* had markedly little influence. Surveys of the membership demonstrated growing, if tentative, support for modernisation.[145] Many of those advocating change – feminists, environmental campaigners, constitutional reformers, civil society movements – came to believe the party's rejuvenation merited support, even if there were disagreements over the specifics of the revised economic and social policy. They concurred it was necessary for old-style Labourism to be renounced in order for Labour to emerge as a party once more in the progressive tradition. As the primacy of class was downgraded, Labour must embrace the revisionist politics of conscience and reform.

By the 1992 election, Labour moved decisively towards the centre-ground of British politics affirmed by countless election surveys.[146] The party was now pro-European, committed to NATO membership. Labour had been converted to market liberalism. The party promised not to indiscriminately raise taxes on the middle-class. Labour's political thought historically reflected the tension between ethical and efficiency socialism.[147] *The Policy Review* emphasised efficient management of the economy, combining macro-economic stability, higher productivity and rising living standards. Gone was the language of public ownership of industry and state intervention. Labour was the party of the supply side, of a talent-based economy, of investment in skills and technology, training and infrastructure.[148] In a confidential memorandum, John Eatwell opined: 'Macro-economics is not enough. Long-term efficiency requires both the organisation of strategic investment in research and in skills, a structured industrial policy'.[149] Dan Corry, a former Labour economic adviser, commented: 'By 1992, the policy had shifted markedly. A macro dimension seemed to have been given up as Labour went overboard on supply-side issues'.[150]

The historian David Marquand criticised Kinnock's prospectus as a series of 'modest and ill-thought out steps'. Yet Marquand conceded, 'the Labour party of the 1990s has become the social democratic party which Hugh Gaitskell tried and failed to create in the 1960s'.[151] The 1992 manifesto, *It's Time To Get Britain Working Again*, spoke of Britain's 'inventive genius', pledging to put Britain at the cutting-edge of science while echoing Wilson's talk of 'the white heat of technology'.[152] The newspaper in Britain closest to business interests, the *Financial Times*, came out in support of Labour in its final editorial of the campaign. Forty industrialists wrote to the *Times* backing Labour's proposals. The party had become a well-organised force at Kinnock's behest. Socialism was ostensibly sanitised by embracing material prosperity and the market.

The trauma of the 1992 defeat

Despite the monumental effort at organisational and ideological revival in 1992 Labour experienced its fourth consecutive loss. The defeat was a hammer blow to Kinnock's party. On hearing the first constituency result, a swing to Labour of only 2 per cent in Sunderland South, Kinnock remarked to his wife, Glenys, 'That's it. I have just wasted eight years of my life'. Labour was expected to win by the Tory press, but the party was trounced by Thatcher's heir, the uncharismatic but politically astute John Major. Major traded on his persona as 'the working-class boy made good'. He rose from the working-class streets of Brixton in south London, through a public relations job in a large bank in the City, to become a commanding figure in the post-1979 governments. Major looked every inch the provincial bank manager. In 1992, after a long and painful recession, that was exactly what the voters of Middle England required.

Major's allies acknowledged that to survive, the Conservatives must jettison the divisive aspects of Thatcher's legacy. The prime minister believed the welfare state was 'part of the instinct of the British people'. Major developed an agenda for the public services; Labour's lead on health and education shrank alarmingly.[153] An opinion poll in the *Observer* in January 1991 asked who was responsible for rising unemployment: 43 per cent said Margaret Thatcher, 28 per cent named the world recession while 9 per cent blamed the new prime minister.[154] Major escaped responsibility for the dire state of the economy. The Conservatives were even attracting defectors from the now moribund SDP, including David Owen (the former member of the Gang of Four), Daniel Finklestein, Rick Nye and the pollster Andrew Cooper. On the Right, thoughtful discussion was underway about the limits of free markets in eroding the institutions of family and community.[155] Major's shift towards the centre posed a decisive challenge to Kinnock's party.

Still, the 1992 defeat was shocking since the incumbent government was in office for thirteen years and appeared deeply unpopular. The Community Charge or 'poll tax', a flat rate form of local taxation levied irrespective of household income was despised, particularly in Scotland. The Conservatives presided over a deep recession felt in the prosperous South as well as the declining North of England. The Tories were losing the advantage in their claim to economic competence. What is more, Major's party was bitterly divided over Europe. Joining the ERM had destroyed the relationship between Thatcher and Nigel Lawson. The Maastricht Treaty then split the Conservative parliamentary party, appearing to imperil British national sovereignty and encouraging vocal opposition to European integration. The pragmatic belief of the Conservatives in membership as a response to national decline was eroding. Furthermore, by 1992, the mood in Britain indicated heightened concern about the impact of the Thatcher inheritance: the decline of manufacturing industry, the growth of inequality, the emergence of divisions in the inner-cities, the disturbing feeling that large sections of the country were being left behind.[156] Moreover, many believed that Labour had got its act together by now: 'Labour throughout the 1980s had been widely seen as extremist, irresponsible and disunited. *The Policy Review* and Kinnock's style of leadership generally reversed these perceptions'.[157] An internal report claimed that by 1989, 'incredible policies, disunity, poor leadership have been almost entirely eradicated'.[158]

Throughout the 1980s, the Conservatives won elections with a narrow base of electoral support. The electorate were never converted to Thatcherism unequivocally. They often voted for the Tories reluctantly: Labour was frequently perceived to be unelectable.[159] In the 1989 European elections, fighting on a joint manifesto with the Party of European Socialists (PES), the Labour Party finished ahead of the Conservatives for the first time in any national contest since 1974. Enormous swings were achieved in by-elections at Mid-Staffordshire and Monmouth. During the 1992 campaign, the leader of the Liberal Democrats, Paddy Ashdown, was struck that Tory ministers appeared 'wobbly and uncertain'.[160]

Labour insisted it was now the party of productive enterprise that could restore stable growth to the economy: 'It is time to rebuild Britain's industrial strength. For lasting recovery, Britain needs a modern industrial policy designed to build skills, upgrade technology, encourage industry in every region and expand exports'. The manifesto declared in a self-confident echo of 1964: 'Britain's industrial future depends on transforming our inventive genius into manufacturing strength. We will encourage the development of the most modern telecommunications networks. Labour's Minister for Science will develop a national strategy to promote high-quality science and technology'.[161]

Given it was so unexpected, the 1992 defeat was among the worst psychological traumas the party experienced: 271 Labour MPs were elected to the House of Commons. Gains were achieved by targeting marginal seats, including the southern constituencies of Southampton Itchen, Cambridge and Thurrock. Yet Labour's share of the vote was 34.4 per cent, more than seven points adrift of the Conservatives. The party still required a larger swing than it achieved in 1945 if it was to return to government. The class politics emerging in Britain in the twentieth century was replaced by a new geographical cleavage: electorally, there were 'two Englands' – the affluent South that supported the Tory party loyally, where population and wealth were growing; and the deindustrialised North that had voted Labour since the 1930s but where support was insufficient to win a parliamentary majority. Ultimately, the party was 'perceived as not comfortable with suburban England and new town England, and they are not comfortable with Labour'.[162] Labour performed particularly poorly in the English new towns, notably Corby, Swindon, Slough and Basildon. Kinnock's party was unable to reconstruct the alliance between its working-class heartlands and the professional classes that was pivotal to the election victories of 1945 and 1964.

In the aftermath of defeat, a lengthy post-mortem ensued. Kinnock's negative leadership ratings were a prominent factor. As David Sanders reports, 'It seems likely that Kinnock's weak image was in part responsible for the consolidation of Conservative support that appeared to take place at the very end of the campaign'.[163] Kinnock was a brittle performer in the House of Commons, a verbose debater at Prime Minister's Questions. Yet perceptions of Kinnock's leadership capacities could scarcely explain the erosion of the Labour vote since 1979. Modernisers believed it was 'traditional' socialism that was being rejected. Worse, 'the centre-left [still] had no clear and electorally attractive political message'.[164] Charles Clarke believed Labour lost because the task of revising its policies was not yet completed.[165] Kinnock had not gone far enough in overhauling party structures, insisting on the introduction of one member, one vote (OMOV) to aid the process of revising the party's core ideas. Everything Labour stood for – its ideology, its image, its institutions, its ethos – was being rejected by the electorate. The bankruptcy of Labour's political ideas was thought to be of particular importance. Party reformers sought to promote their own diagnosis of the 1992 defeat. Gordon Brown and Tony Blair were loyal members of Kinnock's shadow cabinet.

Yet they believed Kinnock proved himself incapable of equipping Labour with a credible programme. An internal review before the election admitted:

> We have not yet developed a compelling central message which has caught the spirit of the 1990s. . . . We have to demonstrate the connection between people's chance to better themselves and Labour's programme. We must establish the link between people's financial well-being/personal opportunity/national success and Britain's capacity to respond to the challenges of the new century.[166]

Modernisers acknowledged Labour's effort to reassure voters about its suitability for office, ditching unpopular positions on defence and EC membership. Yet the party failed to rebuild trust on the economy. The electorate were unnerved by Labour's plans for the national minimum wage, which even union leaders feared might cost 250,000 jobs. The party had many sensible economic and industrial policies, but they were 'too readily dismissed as the policies of the sixties which failed'.[167] John Smith's shadow budget was packaged adeptly: 'a pre-emptive move [by Labour] to try and present itself as a sober and reliable party with whom you can trust your money'.[168] Smith was portrayed as a dependable Scottish bank manager, chancellor of the exchequer in waiting. Yet the commitment to a modest rise in national insurance contributions to fund increases in child benefit and the state pension proved electorally damaging.[169] A headline in the *Daily Mail* read: 'Warning. Mr Smith's budget would at a stroke turn recession to slump. If you make it, they'll take it'. It was claimed middle-income voters would be forced to pay an extra £1,250 a year. The shadow budget emphasised raising taxes, ignoring voters' aspirations.[170] A report into the defeat found that 'the C1s and C2s do not trust Labour and think the party is against people "getting on"'.[171] One reformist MP wrote in the aftermath of the defeat: 'We have to understand that our nation has been part-Thatcherised, and that old appeals to altruism and sacrifice cut little ice in Basildon'.[172] Charles Clarke believes Labour's strategy on taxation and public expenditure in 1992 was naive.[173]

Smith was a traditional social democrat perfectly at ease with the Croslandite politics of the 1950s and 1960s. He was unmoved by the alleged disaffection of the British working class with rising taxes on incomes. One of his colleagues in the PLP opined: 'John was proud of the intellectual honesty of [the 1992 Shadow Budget]. . . . He had this naïve belief in the attitudes of the man on the street'.[174] A decent society with plentiful jobs, well-funded schools and a world-class NHS must be paid for: 'To pretend otherwise was an affront to his morality'. Smith's defence of Labour's position was that voters should trust him with their money.[175] Yet the Conservative's advertising campaign deployed provocative images of Labour's 'tax bombshell'. Kinnock agreed Labour appealed too much to the 'have nots' rather than the 'haves' or 'have enoughs'. Months before the election, the Labour leader contradicted his shadow chancellor, telling a gathering of journalists at *Luigi's Restaurant* that the increase in NI would be 'phased in' slowly. Kinnock feared the impact of Smith's tax plans, but the intervention merely sowed seeds of confusion in the minds of the electorate.[176]

The modernisers believed the party's election campaign was ineptly executed. Peter Mandelson was fighting the Hartlepool constituency and remained detached from the operation in Walworth Road. An election broadcast about the delays children experienced in gaining access to the cash-starved NHS backfired; the 'real-life' cases in the film were apparently riddled with factual inaccuracies.[177] The Sheffield rally eight days before polling day was interpreted 'not as the stirrings of movement [towards Labour] but as cynical manipulation and triumphalism'.[178] In fact, Kinnock had received polling before the rally showing that Labour's position was deteriorating alarmingly. What the media interpreted as triumphalism was actually an effort to enthuse party workers. Unfortunately, Kinnock lost his cool completely, bellowing 'well alright!' to the serried ranks of activists. Then, in the final week, the leader appealed to wavering Liberal voters by advocating Proportional Representation (PR) for Westminster elections. There was total confusion in high command. The shadow cabinet was not briefed on the shift of policy. As a consequence, 'the minutiae of electoral reform and Labour's previous divisions ran for a few days'.[179]

The NEC's report on the election concluded that for all the tactical errors, 'the electorate [in 1992] was just too apprehensive about Labour. . . . The general unease about economic competence or general distrust of the party and its leadership all took their toll'.[180] Labour was suffering from the catastrophic loss of trust it experienced during the 1970s and 1980s following years of division and extremism. The polling expert Paul Whiteley insisted: 'The tax bombshell is an urban myth. It has no substantial evidence'. What damaged Labour was 'lack of faith in the party's ability to improve services such as health and education'. Voters saw the party as divided.[181] Following the painful recession that damaged the living standards of middle-class families, voters were not prepared to risk a Labour government.[182] Blair felt the party's reaction to past defeats had been complacent. Labour got a real shock when it lost in 1983 and 1987, like 'a bucket of cold water thrown over it'. But within months of defeat, 'the sun comes out, and it says, "Oh, this isn't so bad. It's happened at every single election".[183]

Reformers concurred with Peter Jenkins that the party lost in 1992 because it was Labour. Still tied to the unions, Labour was perceived as the party of decaying and deindustrialising Britain. Kinnock sought to confront strategic problems courageously. The depiction of his leadership as empty-headed, determined to win at any price, is unfair. Kinnock sought to come to terms with the intellectual impasse that British socialism confronted, absorbing a multitude of ideas and new thinking on the Left.[184] Yet Kinnock was naturally immersed in the ethos of Labourism and the political culture of the South Wales coalfields. The politician who influenced him most was Aneurin Bevan. Francis Williams wrote in the 1950s: 'One can trace in many of Bevan's speeches an emotional fidelity to a concept of the exploited poor which takes hardly any practical account of the alteration in the class structure of British society'. British society and the economy had been transformed since the 1970s. Labour still appeared to be a political movement belonging in the past.

Even so, the Left's determination to discredit modernisation in the wake of the 1992 defeat had remarkably little currency. Kinnock's obsession with image was disparaged. A return to the party's core beliefs was necessary. But many now wondered: what were those beliefs? Was it feasible for Labour to return to the programme on which it won power in 1945? Did the Attlee governments offer a convincing blueprint given their 'small-c' conservatism in domestic policy? Were there other successful models of socialism to which Labour could turn in the wake of the Berlin Wall's collapse and the fall of Communism? The Left's inability to provide compelling answers meant political advantage passed to Blair and Brown's generation of reformers. The modernising wing sensed an opportunity. Blair recalled that:

> As the morning of another defeat dawned, the party was in despair. I wasn't. I felt energised. . . . I explained with the clarity of a man released from political and intellectual prison that the party had lost because we failed to modernise sufficiently.[185]

Brown agreed the *Policy Review* reacquainted Labour with 1950s' revisionism. This repositioning was an advance on the anachronistic statism of the Wilson/Callaghan era. Yet the *Policy Review* still reflected 'the reality of life in the 1950s', not the Britain of the 1990s. Brown believed if Labour was to return to government it should, 'cease to be seen as a tax and spend party. It must place skills and training at the very centre of its policy'. In an interview with the *Guardian* commentator Hugo Young, Brown urged Labour to shed its image 'as the party of state solutions over individual self-improvement, the party that will take your money away, the party that sees production as an afterthought'.[186] Labour should expunge its reputation as 'compensat[ing] people for the failure of capitalism'.

How far was the subsequent rejuvenation driven by modernisers at the party's centre? That grouping owed its allegiance to Kinnock. They believed fundamental transformation in Labour's strategy was necessary to stimulate electoral recovery. Even so, the impetus for modernisation was distributed widely across the party. London-based networks including the LCC pursued the argument for political renewal at the grassroots and in CLPs. In the unions, leaders including John Monks, Gavin Laird and Bill Jordan of the Amalgamated Engineering and Electrical Union (AEEU), alongside Margaret Prosser of the Transport and General Workers Union (TGWU), maintained the drive for reform. As Chapter 2 discussed, centre-left intellectuals sought to fundamentally revise social democracy.[187] David Miliband, then research fellow at the Institute for Public Policy Research (IPPR), claimed: 'There is as yet no clear response from the Left to the crisis of the free market. . . . The political style and substance of a second counter-market revolution remain to be forged'.[188] By the early 1990s, a comprehensive survey found that on public ownership, industrial relations, nuclear defence and public expenditure, 'one in three of the [Labour] members were modernisers, and only one in five were traditionalists'. Seyd concludes: 'Opponents of the modernisation strategy were a small minority of the membership closely associated with the party's Hard Left'. When Benn stood for the leadership in 1988, Kinnock won 88.6 per cent of the vote. In the constituencies, the leader's margin of victory was more than four to one.[189] It appeared unlikely that in the aftermath of the 1992 result, the party would revert to the Bennite Left orthodoxies of the early 1980s.

Within a few days of the defeat, Kinnock resigned. He subsequently served with distinction as Britain's European commissioner in Brussels. The principal author of Labour's economic programme, John Smith, took the helm, having overwhelmingly defeated his shadow cabinet colleague, Bryan Gould, in the leadership election. Gould fought the campaign on opposition to British membership of the ERM. Yet the issue of Europe and monetary union had little salience. Labour was by now an instinctively pro-European party. Gould, a highly talented and articulate politician, remarkably won less than 10 per cent of the Electoral College vote. Months later, Britain was forced out of the ERM, raising questions about the stance adopted by Brown and Smith. The Socialist *Campaign Group* declared, 'The ERM has failed', since it neither protected individual currencies nor ensured lower interest rates.[190] Yet doubts about the ERM came too late to assist Gould who tragically left British politics, taking up an academic post in New Zealand.

Labour's new leader, John Smith, was born in Argyll, Scotland, in 1938. Educated at Glasgow University, Smith was a stalwart of the Scottish legal and political establishment. He represented North Lanarkshire, which later became Monklands East, winning the seat at the 1970 election. Soon a rising star, he served as secretary of state for trade in the final year of the Callaghan government. Smith was on the traditional Right of the party, a close ally of Denis Healey. He then served as campaign manager to Roy Hattersley in the 1983 Deputy Leadership contest. In paying tribute after his death, Blair declared that Smith 'epitomised the decency of the Scottish Presbyterian tradition'.[191] His biographer, Mark Stuart, contends that Smith's major contribution was to 'heal the wounds' created by Kinnock's abrasive leadership style.

As a consequence, Smith quickly acquired the reputation for being cautious, a 'small-c' conservative politician. He strongly believed in retaining the institutional link with the trade unions. Smith was accused of turning a blind eye to endemic corruption on Labour-dominated Monklands Council in the early 1990s. As shadow chancellor, he was wary and distrusting of Neil Kinnock. Kinnock believed that committing to raise the NI threshold for workers on modest incomes set a trap for Labour on tax policy. Allies of Smith never respected Kinnock, who they saw as a lightweight opportunist. In a letter published in the *Guardian* following the 1992 defeat, the party's chief press officer, Colin Byrne, accused Smith 'of brushing aside his leader's views and three years of policy review', which 'cost the party dear'.[192] Byrne asked:

> What did the Right ever do about Militant during the bitter years up
> to Neil Kinnock taking over? What did they do about Europe? What is

Smith's view on trade union reform? After years of intense debate in the party, ask yourself, why we don't know these things?

One more heave?

From the autumn of 1992, Smith's canny long game rested on his belief that Labour's return to power was all but inevitable. He grew irritated by the modernisers, telling one young MP who expressed his frustration: 'That's all very interesting but I think you'll find that it will be our turn next time'.[193] The leader presented his party as a government in waiting. Smith 'inherited a party structure in 1992 in which the authority of the leader was once again paramount'.[194] Moreover, the Conservative government's luck was running out after its extraordinary victory in 1992. In September, sterling was forced out of the ERM. The chancellor of the exchequer, Norman Lamont, had to raise interest rates temporarily to 15 per cent, crippling mortgage-holders. Black Wednesday forced Lamont's successor, Kenneth Clarke, to increase taxes and cut spending. John Major then launched an ill-fated 'back to basics' campaign. Promising to restore moral decency to British society, high-profile 'sleaze' scandals besieged the Major government. One Tory MP was discovered having an extra-marital affair with a teenager.[195] Lamont rented his basement flat to a sadomasochistic sex worker. The Conservatives were portrayed as hypocrites and charlatans.

The surge of Tory unpopularity meant Smith felt confident enough to keep the tax and spend agenda at the heart of the 1992 Shadow Budget. Reformers, particularly Brown and Blair, privately complained that Smith was complacent. The leader was convinced Labour was certain to win the next election due to the growing unpopularity of the Conservative government, divided over Europe and the Thatcherite legacy. Major's administration was showing all the signs of being in power too long. Yet there was a strong underlying feeling the Labour opposition was failing to capitalise. Modernisers in the shadow cabinet were nervous. Stories briefed by anonymous sources believed to be Peter Mandelson appeared in the press decrying Smith's laidback attitude. Even grassroots organisations such as the LCC sought to put pressure on the leadership to accelerate modernisation. They feared Smith was a pendulum politician who believed Labour's time would inevitably come.[196]

For all that, there is little doubt Smith's leadership prepared the ground for the New Labour project. The reforms of the party constitution and the introduction of one member, one vote (OMOV) in 1993 reduced the power of the unions. The introduction of OMOV abolished the block vote – 'the most important single reform in Labour's history'.[197] Smith's launch of the Commission on Social Justice (CSJ) at the Institute for Public Policy Research (IPPR) stimulated fresh thinking about Labour's policies on the welfare state. The commission signalled not only the Left's rejection of Tory 'deregulation' but 'Old' Labour's legacy of 'levelling down' and redistribution. Labour sought to champion long-term investment in infrastructure and skills. There was substantive progress in devising an outline programme for constitutional reform in co-operation with the Liberal Democrats.

Yet there was less evidence the leadership was willing to undertake the fundamental reappraisal of doctrine and strategy necessitated by Labourism's long-term demise. Modernisation had reached a hiatus. Stuart Hall complained Smith was 'an able technician' but had 'little feel for how strategy and the construction of social constituencies of support match up'. He was unwilling to probe the decrepit 'culture of labourism'. As a consequence, his reforms lacked 'depth and substance'.[198] Smith was an ostensibly old-fashioned politician from the party's establishment Right, a figure steeped in the culture of the Scottish political elite. He achieved high office during Callaghan's premiership. Smith believed Labour must recreate its image as a safe, respectable party, as it was under Wilson, Gaitskell and Attlee. Smith was convinced voters unnerved by the divisiveness of Thatcherism were already moving in Labour's direction by the mid-1990s.[199] However, modernisers like Brown believed there was a refusal to confront awkward questions – in public or private. Labour was still perceived to be the party of 'high, incentive-killing, job-destroying taxation'.[200] Philip Gould felt that Smith, 'wanted to heal the party, not reform it. His instinct was for consolidation, not modernisation'. Mandelson derided the 'one more heave mentality' that dominated the leadership's outlook.[201] Yet before his strategy could be tested in the intense heat of electoral battle, Smith tragically died of a heart attack in May 1994 prompting an outpouring of public emotion.

Blair's mission

In July 1994, at the age of forty-one, Tony Blair was elected to replace Smith as Labour leader. During his political ascent, Blair cultivated an assiduous image in the metropolitan media as the modern family man, the product of the English aspirational middle classes, a lawyer educated at public school and St John's College, Oxford – in conscience a Christian socialist rather than a traditional figure of the Left. Born on 6th May 1953 in Edinburgh, Blair was raised in a professional middle-class family, his father a barrister and university law lecturer. His mother, Hazel Corscaden, was descended from the protestant farming community in County Donegal, Ireland. The future prime minister, one of the few Labour leaders to have attended public school, showed little interest in organised politics at Oxford, although he was intrigued by the teachings of the Scottish Christian philosopher, John McMurray who emphasised the essentially relational nature of the individual human being. A close university friend acerbically described Blair as 'part lawyer, part parson, part actor'.

Blair's interest in politics was encouraged by his wife, Cherie, herself a barrister and activist in the Hackney Labour Party in North London. His early forays into Labour politics were depressingly unproductive. Blair failed to gain selection for a Hackney council seat, while his proposal to author a Fabian Society pamphlet on Europe was rejected. Even so, Blair was a pupil in the chambers of an influential barrister, Derry Irvine, who had connections across the Labour movement. Irvine's chambers provided legal advice to Labour's Walworth Road headquarters in expelling members of the Militant Tendency. In 1982, Blair fought a by-election in the safe Conservative constituency of Beaconsfield. He was defeated but still shone as a charismatic and youthful candidate, tipped for the top by none other than Michael Foot. In a stroke of extraordinary good fortune, at the last moment Blair was then chosen to fight the traditional mining seat of Sedgefield, County Durham, at the 1983 election. He won the selection by one vote against more experienced machine candidates, including the former MP Les Huckfield. It was a remarkable ascent propelling him to the top of the Labour Party.

What made Blair so unusual was that he appeared to owe no personal allegiance or debt to the party's past. He once told *The Observer* newspaper, 'I never felt myself very anchored in a particular setting or class'.[202] Traditional Labourism was clearly obsolete, while he believed democratic socialism had to be fundamentally rethought. Blair was 'a problem solver who hates outdated attitudes whether they come from the reactionary or the progressive side of politics'.[203] He was the 'accidental leader' who seized the crown following John Smith's unexpected death at the comparatively young age of fifty-six. Blair then became the party's leading 'missionary of modernisation'. Yet New Labour's emergence owed a considerable debt to Blair's close political ally, the Scottish politician Gordon Brown. Brown did much of New Labour's intellectual heavy-lifting. Born in 1951, he was two years older than Blair and certainly better versed in organisational Labour politics. Brown soon became the senior figure in the relationship. The Blair/Brown partnership was solidified by sharing a tiny 'broom cupboard' office in the House of Commons, described memorably as 'cramped' and 'insanitary'. Brown's father, John, was a minister in the Church of Scotland. Biographies focused on his religious upbringing as 'a son of the manse'. A prodigious academic achiever, Brown attended Edinburgh University from the age of sixteen despite almost losing his sight following a rugby accident.

Brown rapidly rose through the ranks of the Scottish Labour Party, establishing himself as a leading intellectual on the New Left. His close friend, the Edinburgh University academic Henry Drucker recounts, 'All the older people [in Scottish Labour] hated him. Those over fifty, old Labour, just couldn't stand him. He was too fast for them, too clever, too popular, too good with the press. But he was the future'.[204] Brown authored the official biography of the radical Labour parliamentarian, James Maxton, while editing *The Red Paper on Scotland*, establishing the radical case for devolution. In 1979, Brown fought the marginal constituency of Edinburgh South where he was defeated narrowly. In 1983, he stood in the safe seat of Dunfermline East, entering the House of Commons in the same year as Blair.

Brown was soon tipped as a future leader. Yet despite rising quickly through the shadow cabinet, by the early 1990s his popularity was waning, especially in the PLP. Brown was perceived as an overbearing disciplinarian who mistakenly supported the Thatcher government's policy of entering the ERM. In contrast,

Blair's reputation steadily grew as a consequence of his subtle handling of industrial relations reform as Labour's employment spokesman. He was praised in the media for removing the party's commitment to the closed shop – where workers in a plant had been compelled to join the union – as well as his emotionally sensitive response to the horrific murder of the Liverpool toddler, James Bulger, as shadow home secretary. In the agonising days following Smith's death, Brown was persuaded that Blair was the most credible modernising candidate, standing aside following their meeting at the *Granita* restaurant in Islington, which began the longest-running soap opera in British political history. Brown extracted concessions in return for standing aside – in particular, the right to determine the party's key economic policies on employment, welfare and skills, 'the centre piece of Labour's programme'.[205] Allies of Brown let it be known they believed Blair agreed to give up the leadership after two terms as prime minister.

The contrast in style between Blair and Brown was striking. As metaphorical political animals, Brown was the tortoise, Blair the hare. Brown was an instinctively cautious, highly disciplined politician who sought to carefully formulate his views. He wanted to gather as much factual evidence as possible, choosing to consult favoured experts. Brown was a conscientious student of Scottish and English history. His overhaul of Labour's macro-economic strategy in the 1990s rested on forensic analysis of the shortcomings of Keynesian and monetarist policies in postwar economic history. Confronted by the looming financial crisis in 2008, Brown studied the response of American policy-makers to the great depression of the 1930s. Throughout his career, Brown rationed his broadcast appearances, never entirely at ease on television. Moreover, there was an abiding determination to prove he remained an authentic social democrat unlike Blair and Peter Mandelson:

> Having become Chancellor, Gordon Brown rather liked the idea that he was Crosland Mark II. He gave the impression the Blairites were emphasising equality of opportunity without remembering the Crosland argument that equality of opportunity was not enough. It was politically useful for Brown because it gave the impression he was more radical and more to the Left than Blair.[206]

Yet to his critics, Brown was indecisive by temperament – a paralysing, cautious politician who saw problems around every corner.[207]

On the other hand, the exuberant Blair was an adept politician who loved nothing more than being in the public eye. He was, without doubt, the most effective broadcast performer of the age, invariably fluent and eloquent, a compulsive communicator. Even when the prime minister grew unpopular in the wake of the Iraq War, he embarked on a 'masochism strategy', determined to win over sceptical voters. Blair rarely focused on one matter at a time. His strategy notes in Number Ten would refer to at least twenty-five separate priorities. Blair was never happier than keeping half a dozen balls in the air. Getting him to concentrate on a single issue proved all but impossible. When Blair sought to

shift position or advance a controversial argument, he moved swiftly by throwing caution to the wind. Blair rarely sought the approval of intellectuals. He saw
himself as a nimble risk taker, attuned to the perplexing mood of the times.

Blair's rise to power consolidated the centralised operation around the leader,
bolstering organisational structures fashioned during the Kinnock era. Having
observed Clinton's rise, Blair believed political life was becoming 'presiden-
tialised', shaped by the individual leader's personality. He engaged in strenuous
efforts to build up his political entourage. Jonathan Powell, the former foreign
office official who served in the British Embassy in Washington, DC, was
appointed chief of staff. Blair welcomed the fact that Powell had no previous
relationship with the Labour movement. Powell matched intimate knowledge of
Whitehall (his brother was Charles Powell, Margaret Thatcher's foreign office
adviser) with an absence of sentimental attachment to the Labour Party. He admitted 'putting his foot in it' regularly with party insiders. To enhance the leader's
profile, Alastair Campbell became Blair's chief press spokesman. Campbell was a
surprising choice, having predominantly worked in tabloid newspapers – notably
the *Daily Mirror*. He was an aggressive, even brutal, operator in dealing with the
print and broadcast media, a reaction to Kinnock's treatment by the Murdoch
newspapers in the 1980s. Campbell's efforts were bolstered by the advertising
executive Philip Gould, who represented the views of Middle England through
focus groups and quantitative opinion surveys.

Blair's team was perceived by outsiders, unfairly or not, to lack intellectual
substance. David Miliband from the Institute for Public Policy Research (IPPR)
was appointed head of policy. The IPPR played a formative role in devising
Labour's programme, including the Child Trust Fund (CTF) that gave an asset
stake to poorer children, alongside lifelong education initiatives such as Learn
Direct. Miliband convened regular meetings between Blair and a select cadre
of public intellectuals. An informal network emerged including Geoff Mulgan, director of Demos; Charles Leadbeater, former journalist at LWT; and the
academic sociologist Anthony Giddens. Mulgan soon gained the reputation as
Labour's favourite policy wonk, even if Demos was belittled for its outlandish
ideas, including time-limited marriages and public stocks for petty criminals.
These intellectual connections indulged Blair's appetite for big ideas. Yet the
party's relationship with the intelligentsia remained apprehensive, as it was for
much of the twentieth century. Blair and Brown's party remained intolerant of
dissent. Its authoritarian and managerial style was unlikely to be congenial to the
thinking classes. The refusal to put the party's relationship with intellectuals on a
constructive footing meant New Labour ultimately failed to resolve the progressive dilemma discussed in Chapter 2. The long-term breach between the party
and the intelligentsia was never satisfactorily healed. New Labour then paid the
price in government.

Despite the work on the *Policy Review*, when Blair became leader he felt
Labour's ideas were still shallow and intellectually under-developed. The party
patently lacked 'an alternative way of governing the economy'. There was the

palpable absence of compelling organising principles, a doctrinal framework for economic management and public policy akin to the synthesis of Beveridge and Keynes that emerged in the aftermath of the Second World War. Yet Blair's 1994 leadership statement was hardly a blueprint for fundamental reform. The language was undeniably evasive. The talk was of political 'renewal', yet specific policies were few. The future leader told his party during the 1994 leadership contest:

> Socialism is not a set of rigid economic prescriptions, but a set of values based around a belief in society and community: that individuals prosper best within a strong and cohesive society. We have to renew Britain as a strong society – one nation socialism – but do it for the modern world.[208]

Moreover, despite his self-projection as the politician of conviction, Blair's instincts were cautious. The leader had little desire to immediately confront the party's traditionalist wing, chiefly the trade unions. There was no mention of the intention to rewrite Clause Four, although the idea was tentatively proposed in a Fabian pamphlet authored by Jack Straw. There was less appetite to embark on reform of the party's institutional machinery, breaking up the tripartite structure of the rank-and-file membership, the PLP and trade unions. Blair still believed the unions could bolster the leadership in crushing dissent, a function they performed loyally under Attlee and Gaitskell. Many policies were inherited from the Smith era. New Labour's modernisation strategy was forged under Kinnock, with Blair at the heart of the shadow cabinet. As such, Blair was 'the residuary legatee of the spadework of his predecessors'.[209] What separated Kinnock from Blair was emotional attachment to the party's ethos, forged in the industrial heartland of South Wales. Blair, in contrast, refused to show deference to the Labour tradition. Above all, he was a vociferous opponent of 'the complacent illusions sustained . . . by the conventional Left'.[210] The dynamic provided by class conflict, the belief in the supremacy of the British working class, deep-seated faith in the agency of organised labour, the view that capitalism would one day be superseded by something called 'socialism' – these were 'the myths Labour lived by'. They were dismissed unsentimentally as delusions by Blair.

Reformers insisted the electoral supremacy of the Conservative Party and the death of traditional class politics killed Labour's onward march stone dead. Even in 1994, Blair dismissed the claim that the Conservatives were on the brink of political collapse. He shared the view of a *Guardian* editorial published in the mid-1990s that the Tories, for all they might have run out of ideas, were 'sitting on top of a remarkable economic recovery that is creating increasingly rich economic and political opportunities. . . . The twin appeal of the Union Jack and income tax at 20p has a special potency in our conservative society'.[211] Blair believed Labour must continue its reforms to have any realistic hope of victory. Despite the *Policy Review*, the party had not resolved fundamental contradictions in its ideology and doctrine that were a hangover from the post-war era. Even in 1994, socialism was identified with the commitment to nationalisation. Labour was slow to recognise the fundamental shift in which the British economy was increasingly dominated by consumers rather than producers, the service sector over manufacturing industry.[212]

Having won the leadership and strengthened his power base, Blair launched his effort to rewrite Clause Four of the party constitution as a symbol of change. Like Gaitskell forty years before, Blair believed the goal of indiscriminate nationalisation repelled voters. Bringing productive industries into public ownership made Labour appear backward looking and archaic. What the existing Clause Four symbolised was 'a refusal to confront reality, to embrace the modern world wholeheartedly'.[213] The new version stressed Labour, 'believes that by the strength of our common endeavour we achieve more than we achieve alone'. Blair's success was demonstration of the declining faith in traditional orthodoxies prevalent throughout the party. In ditching the original formulation of Clause Four and weakening the role of the unions, the leader positioned New Labour in antagonism to Old Labour. The Road to the Manifesto was then launched in 1996 to consolidate the overhaul of Labour's programme, requiring the membership to endorse the party's five symbolic pre-election pledges through the one member, one vote (OMOV) ballot.

As such, Blair's zeal for reform built on the previous decade of institutional reinvention. All-women shortlists for parliamentary selections were initiated, demonstrating the continuing impact of women's organisations. By 1988, every constituency had to include at least one woman on its shortlist where a woman was nominated; the general committee and executive committee of each CLP should consist of at least 40 per cent women; CLPs could voluntarily adopt all-women shortlists, while there was targeted use of shortlists in each region.[214] As a consequence, the party was more effective at shaping policies that appealed to women. The 1992 manifesto committed to the expansion of childcare, with measures to increase equality of opportunity in the workplace. The move away from the primacy of class identity was matched by acknowledgement of gender and women's issues. Feminists welcomed the fact Labourism's decline meant the abeyance of the masculine 'beer and sandwiches' culture. From their perspective, 'the Blairite modernisers appeared to be younger, more approachable, and more accustomed to working with women than their predecessors'.[215]

As Chapter 4 outlined, Labour was obsessed with learning the lessons of Clinton's electoral success. Blair's victory confirmed the long-term shift in decision-making authority within the party. There was a move away from formal institutions and procedures controlled by the NEC and the resolutions of annual conference. The emphasis was on informal processes, circumventing Old Labour by mobilising the plethora of think-tanks, opinion pollsters and strategy consultants. These approaches were enabled by Labour's willingness to accept donations from business entrepreneurs. Corporate money traditionally flowed into the coffers of the Conservative Party. Not any longer. Blair's party attracted support from the TV executive Greg Dyke and the boss of Formula One, Bernie Eccelstone, as well as companies from Granada TV to Somerfield. As a consequence, New Labour broke the party's historic reliance on the unions. To do so, Blair courted controversy. Within a year of Eccelstone donating £1 million to the party, it was revealed that Formula One was to be exempt from the ban prohibiting tobacco sponsorship in sport.

By the 1997 election, New Labour's project became more perceptible, assimilating the lessons of the party's inheritance while absorbing experience from centre-left parties across Western countries. Blair's party rejected the dominant paradigm of 'Left-wing compassion' versus 'Right-wing economy', 'heart versus head', Labour's belief in redistribution and public services versus the Tory mantle of tough on crime, low taxes, welfare reform and fiscal responsibility. New Labour jettisoned traditional agendas ruthlessly.[216] Modernisation was in the ascendency, not least because the alternatives, either a sharp turn to the Left or rekindling the revisionism of the 1950s and 1960s, no longer appeared viable.[217] The collapse of the Berlin Wall undermined residual faith in quasi-Marxist state socialism.

New Labour's analysis had growing purchase in the world of progressive thought and ideas. Sociologically, British society was transformed since the end of the Second World War. The new materialism and the growth of individualism replaced the old forms of collective organisation and identity. Large factories and tight-knit urban working-class housing were gradually disappearing. The 'proletarian mode of production' significantly declined since the 1960s and 1970s. The proportion of the workforce employed in manual and clerical jobs fell from three-quarters in 1945 to less than a third by the early 1990s. The pre-eminence of industrial production, coal, steel, shipbuilding and textiles passed its peak. The long-term shift away from industry to services prophesised by Keynes in the inter-war years was underway.[218] Voters ceased to identify themselves as producers, while 'citizens' and 'consumers' were less amenable to collective agency.[219]

Alterations in Britain's class structure over decades were accompanied by the transformation of gender roles and identities. Back-to-back terraced houses had been replaced by suburban estates, reshaping the physical organisation of working-class life. At the same time, 'the sexual landscape of working-class life was changing'.[220] Four decades previously, changes in gender politics stimulated by the absorption of women into the realm of paid work and the redefinition of popular conceptions of 'mothering' led to 'confusion and anger' among men depicted graphically in the working-class novels of the period, including Alan Sillitoe's *Saturday Night and Sunday Morning* (1958) and Stan Barstow's *A Kind of Loving* (1960). Labour was only beginning to catch up with such changes when Blair became leader. The party enjoyed a lead among women in only two post-war elections: 1945 and 1970. Labour struggled to understand the fabric of women's lives, perceiving women largely as 'non-working wives and mothers'.[221] New Labour signalled the intention to catch up.

By the 1990s, there was a revolution in the take-up of education in Britain. The proportion of men with no formal qualifications fell to less than a fifth.[222] As a consequence, less status was accorded to manual workers who once dominated the politics of industrial production. New identities replaced the established categories of class and occupational stratification. As Beatrice Campbell observed, 'the politics of new times challenges tradition'. The Left should understand voters 'in all their dimensions and identities – as sexes, races, workers, consumers, parents, and pensioners'.[223] These structural alterations meant the Labour movement's traditional assumptions appeared anachronistic. Voters no longer behaved according to settled patterns of habit and loyalty. They were non-committed political consumers with few fixed ties and allegiances.[224] As a consequence, Blair rarely referred to the 'working-class'. He believed the term was associated with being male, white, a manual worker from the North of England.[225] Blair urged his party to break out of the enclave of Labourism, re-connecting with voters 'at the cultural level'. He acknowledged initiatives like the *Red Wedge* concerts helped to re-acquaint Labour with modernity and youth in the mid-1980s. Yet Blair realised, 'we [also] needed to reach the people listening to Duran Duran and Madonna'.[226]

Even so, although Blair underlined the limits of class politics, New Labour was still committed to alleviating economic and social disadvantage. Blair told the 1999 party conference that while the class war was over in Britain, Labour's mission remained to liberate Britain from 'old class divisions, old structures, old prejudices, old ways of working and doing things'. He decried 'old elites, the establishment that have run our country for too long'.[227] Blair believed the UK suffered from a 'progressive deficit': an unproductive economy; rundown public services with insufficient investment; 'the crumbling fabric of society – poverty, crime, social division, inequality' – an isolationist country with a 'little Englander mentality' ruled by a political system that was 'centralised, secretive, out of touch'.[228]

The solutions Blair's party advanced to address Britain's economic and social problems in the aftermath of Thatcherism were perceived as credible in opinion-forming circles. Labour's analysis of traditional socialism's failings was broadly accepted among the progressive intelligentsia. The collapse of Fordist production led to the diversification of economic and social life across the industrialised nations.[229] The fall of Communism in Eastern Europe indicated long-standing assumptions about the role of bureaucracy and central planning were redundant. Doctrines of Keynesian economic management were discredited. More to the point, economic and social life were being transformed by globalisation. 'Statist and class-centred modes of thinking' were unlikely to produce electoral success.[230] As a consequence, *New* Labour was defined in opposition to *Old* Labour – a symbolic moment of renouncing and breaking with the past as Chapter 3 demonstrated.[231]

Blair's advisers believed Labour should confront the Thatcherite legacy. In a presentation to business leaders in 1996, Peter Mandelson and Roger Liddle claimed that since the Thatcher administrations came to power:

> the business environment has markedly improved: manufacturing productivity has risen. The productivity gap with our European partners has substantially narrowed. Greater efficiency has led to increased returns on capital. Leading British companies stand comparison with the best in the world. And there can be no doubt that government policies made some contribution to this success.[232]

Labour's argument was that in the 1980s and early 1990s, 'economic efficiency and a strong society were in competition. If you wanted economic success you had to pay a social price'.[233] Thatcher's advertising guru, Maurice Saatchi proclaimed: 'The Conservatives were cruel and efficient, Labour incompetent and caring'. New Labour's belief was that 'community and society are essential, not just to build social cohesion and fairness, but to enhance economic efficiency'. It was hoped the formula of aligning a productive economy with social justice provided the centrepiece of the new governing consensus.

The historic 1997 election victory: revitalising the progressive alliance?

In 1997, Blair's Labour Party swept to power. The composer Andrew Lloyd Webber's threat to leave the country if Labour won failed to dissuade the British electorate. Blair's party secured 13,518,167 votes (43.2 per cent of the total), an unprecedented majority in the House of Commons of 179 seats. Labour's performance broke all records, although the party's share of the vote was lower than it achieved in 1945 and 1950–51. The class composition of Labour's support demonstrated that it had re-emerged as a national party: 47 per cent of white-collar workers voted Labour, an increase of 19 per cent since 1992; 54 per cent of skilled workers supported it, as did overwhelming numbers of homeowners and the young. The gender gap was eliminated.[234] The BBC's exit poll found that 87 per cent of voters thought Labour would be 'good for all classes', while 71 per cent believed the Conservatives were for only 'one class'.

The seats won by the party stood out because they were so 'redolent of Tory England' with its 'shady oaks, mock Tudor villas, well-watered lawns, and a Jaguar (or at least one of the larger Fords) in every drive'.[235] New Labour forged an alliance across the English middle class encompassing those described by polling strategists as 'comfortable greens' and 'urban networkers' with 'Daily Mail disciplinarians' and 'squeezed strugglers' hurt by the recession of the early 1990s. It was the unexpected loss of the cabinet minister, Michael Portillo, at suburban Enfield Southgate that symbolised the scale of the government's rejection by Tory England. Blair's reforms made obsolete the central historical purpose of Conservatism in Britain – to contain the threat posed by socialism. New Labour was not a party middle England feared. It no longer posed any discernible threat to the prosperity or property rights of the middle class.

Of course, the scale of Labour's victory was exaggerated by the electoral system. Labour won only 43 per cent of the vote, yet the party secured 419 out of 650 seats in the House of Commons, the consequence of tactical voting and differential turnout. Tacit co-operation between Labour and the Liberal Democrats helped both parties increase their share of seats. The Labour Party was assisted by James Goldsmith's Referendum Party, a precursor to UKIP that won 3 per cent of the vote where it stood a candidate, disadvantaging the Conservatives. In the meantime, the Tory share of the vote fell to its lowest level since 1832. Of greater concern to observers was the dramatic decline in turnout, which sank to 72 per cent. Turnout decreased most in Labour-held seats. Some commentators claimed the party's traditional supporters and the 'urban poor' were less enthused by New Labour's agenda.[236]

Nevertheless, the magnitude of Labour's electoral triumph proved to be significant in judging the party's subsequent performance in office. Blair and Brown fought to manage expectations of what could be achieved in government. The leadership claimed that in the past, the party indulged in idle rhetoric about the possibility of radical transformation which inflated expectations that could not plausibly be met. Yet the sheer scale of Blair's victory completely redefined Labour's prospects, making talk of piecemeal and incremental reform appear delusional. With its overwhelming parliamentary majority, Labour acquired the mandate to undertake far-reaching reform of the polity and economy. In a moment of unguarded optimism, David Marquand enthused that after an eighty-year detour, the Left should now pick up 'where Asquith and Lloyd George left off'.[237]

David Miliband believed that when New Labour came to office, it was effective tactically, but strategically unprepared. The party's anthem was 'things can only get better', positioning Labour vaguely in support of political change and hope. Blair acknowledged: 'The skill set that brings you into power is then redundant'.[238] Echoing the former mayor of New York Mario Cuomo, Labour 'campaigned in poetry' but was compelled to 'govern in prose'. Labour gained two further substantive majorities, but the party never anticipated such a decisive mandate for reform. Blair and his followers saw the Kinnock period as integral to Labour's failed past, viewing the *Policy Review* with suspicion.[239] Having entered government, Blair's ministers struggled 'to find the space to really build strategically on the first term'.[240] The 1997 and 2001 manifestos were missed opportunities to define a bold agenda, given the palpable weaknesses of the Thatcher era. New Labour never faced up to the deep structural problems afflicting Britain, formulating a compelling rationale for activist government.[241] Labour's manifesto was derided for being light on detail, cautious ideologically, 'painfully short and insubstantial'.[242] Blair admitted the manifesto was 'written essentially to capture a mood. . . . Details were deliberately and necessarily limited'.[243] The 176 commitments were 'bomb-proofed' forensically to ensure no political hostages to fortune.[244] Every potential vulnerability was dealt with.

In sticking to the Major government's spending limits for the first two years of the Parliament, the prime minister and his chancellor emphasised their cautious instincts. As if to compensate for the absence of ideological conviction, the document was replete with grandiose rhetoric: 'Our case is simple', Blair announced:

> Britain can and must be better. The vision is one of national renewal. In each area of policy, a new and distinctive approach has been mapped out, one that differs from the old left and the Conservative right. This is why new Labour is new. What counts is what works. The objectives are radical. The means will be modern. This is our contract with the people.[245]

The manifesto was effective electoral politics, but Labour's idealism appeared to have dissipated.

New Labour as a party of opposition and power put 'safety first'.[246] Voters were asked to judge Blair's team of ministers on delivery of their promises. An annual report was published auditing the government's achievements. Yet as David Howell remarked: 'There is no sense within this administration of an agenda of economic and social reform which can be implemented to achieve a new and durable economic and social settlement'.[247] New Labour in 1997 had little desire to disturb the prevailing consensus in British society. The conclusive manner of its victory paradoxically encouraged Labour's hesitant and at times indecisive performance. Blair had the appearance of a leader who in Roy Jenkins's words was 'like a man carrying a priceless Ming vase across a highly polished floor'.

Conclusion

Under the leadership of Blair and Brown, Labour made peace with the acquisitive materialism of the 1980s. Yet critics asked: at what price? Blair's political success was a consequence of interpreting the party's 1992 defeat as favourable to the nascent modernising agenda. The victor rewrote the dominant account of Labour's post-war history as one of failure. As a consequence of this historical reinterpretation, 'complexities and ambiguities are lost', while alternative pathways are hidden.[248] The modernisation endeavour was less concerned with specific policies and reforms of the party's institutions. It related to Labour's identity, its character and its core doctrinal purpose. The aim was to rebuild the alliance between the professional classes and the working class which fragmented in the post-war decades by originating a new generation of political ideas. The coalition did not automatically arise but was 'brought into being and recreated by the construction and periodic reconstruction of a common political discourse'.[249] This fresh narrative centred on political ideas was constructed in the 1990s not least because, as leader, Blair fundamentally differed from his predecessors. He came from outside the traditional Labour culture and travelled lightly ideologically. Blair felt 'no debts to Labour's past'.[250]

Nonetheless, conflating the modernisation project with Blair exclusively, or with a narrow group of party reformers, is ultimately misleading. The adaptation of ideology and strategy was widely supported within the PLP and grassroots party membership, demoralised by recurrent defeats and the track record of political and intellectual underperformance. Labour's advance between 1979 and 1997 indicates that electoral defeat is a decisive catalyst of ideological transformation. Yet this chapter demonstrated the overwhelming importance of political ideas, as modernisation sought to resolve long-standing dilemmas within the socialist tradition while providing a coherent governing agenda. Defeat was a key motivation, but the task of rethinking that led to fundamental alterations in party doctrine was underway irrespective of these electoral setbacks. Rather than reflexively internalising Thatcherism, New Labour arose from recognition of Labourism's protracted demise in the aftermath of Wilson and Callaghan. The interrogation of the party's historic failings since the 1970s left a decisive imprint.

Even so, despite the reforms, ambiguities in Labour's ideology and strategy persisted under Blair. What did modernisation actually mean in practice? Few in the party were prepared for the all-out assault on Labour's identity that ensued. Moreover, despite fundamental changes in its power structure and concerted intellectual reappraisal, the party came to office in 1997 with no compelling ideological prospectus. Labour still lacked a governing theory, an overarching mission giving purpose to a centre-left administration in power. There was hardly a literary signpost for British social democracy that was comparable to Anthony Crosland's *Future of Socialism*. Gordon Brown sensed problems ahead, even in the propitious circumstances of the late 1990s. He told the Liberal Democrat leader Paddy Ashdown:

> There is no intellectual coherence about [New Labour's] position and so nothing to fall back on. You have accused us of being a bunch of control freaks. . . . That's what we have to be. There's no core idea to hold the party together in tough times.[251]

What did the absence of that substantive idea mean for Labour's impact in office, having secured three record-breaking parliamentary majorities? It is to that existential question the next chapters in the book will turn.

Notes

1 Ron Todd, General Secretary of the Transport and General Workers' Union, Cited in P. Kellner (ed.), *Thorns and Roses*, p. 130.
2 E. Heffer, *The Guardian*, 23rd June 1987.
3 Jack Dromey to Larry Whitty, September 1987, Churchill Archives Centre, The Papers of Neil Kinnock, KNNK 1/3/5.
4 J. Rentoul, *Tony Blair*, p. 79, London: Little Brown, 1995.
5 Cited in S. Fielding, *The Labour Party: Socialism and Society Since 1951*, p. 111, Manchester: Manchester University Press, 1997.
6 P. Seyd, *The Rise and Fall of the Labour Left*, Basingstoke: Palgrave Macmillan, 1987.
7 Cited in P. Tatchell, *The Battle for Bermondsey*, p. 16, London: Gay Men's Press, 1994.
8 S. Hannah, *A Party With Socialists In It: A History of the Labour Left*, pp. 169–170, London: Pluto Press, 2018.
9 Roy Jenkins's official biographer John Campbell speculates that Jenkins and his wife, Jennifer, probably voted Liberal in the 1979 general election.
10 W.T. Rodgers, 'What Happened to the SDP and What Could Still Happen', *The London Review of Books*, Volume 13 (3), 1991.
11 I. Aitken, 'Labour Rocked by Resignation of Roy Jenkins', *The Guardian*, 11th April 1972.
12 P. Clarke, *A Question of Leadership: From Gladstone to Thatcher*, p. 271.
13 R. Behrens, 'The Centre: Social Democracy and Liberalism', in L. Tivey & A. Wright (eds.), *Party Ideology in Britain*, p. 74, Basingstoke: Macmillan, 1989.
14 R. Behrens, 'The Centre: Social Democracy and Liberalism'.
15 R. Behrens, 'The Centre: Social Democracy and Liberalism'.

16 Cited in G. Stedman-Jones, *Languages of Class: Studies in English Working Class History 1832–1982*, p. 245.
17 Cited in P. Addison, *The Road to 1945: British Politics and the Second World War*, p. 46, London: Jonathan Cape, 1975.
18 W.T. Rodgers, 'What Happened to the SDP and What Could Still Happen'.
19 E. Dell, *A Strange, Eventful History: Democratic Socialism in Britain*, p. 480, London: Harper Collins, 2000.
20 W.T. Rodgers, 'Social Democratic Party', p. 215, in A. Adonis & K. Thomas (eds.), *Roy Jenkins: A Retrospective*, Oxford: Oxford University Press, 2004.
21 G. Stedman-Jones, *Languages of Class*, p. 246.
22 P. Jenkins, *Mrs Thatcher's Revolution: The Ending of the Socialist Era*, p. 367, London: Pan Books, 1989.
23 G. Stedman-Jones, *Languages of Class*, pp. 246–247.
24 G. Radice, *Diaries 1980–2001: From Political Disaster to Triumph*, p. 87, London: Weidenfeld & Nicolson, 2004.
25 F. Sutcliffe-Braithwaite, *Class, Politics and the Decline of Deference in England 1968–2000*.
26 'After the Landslide: The Labour Co-ordinating Committee', London: LCC, 1983.
27 D. Kavanagh, *The Reordering of British Politics: Politics After Thatcher*, Oxford: Oxford University Press, 1997.
28 http://banmarchive.org.uk/collections/mt/pdf/83_10_07.pdf. Accessed 18th November 2018.
29 M. Wickham-Jones, *Economic Strategy and the Labour Party*, p. 207, Basingstoke: Palgrave Macmillan, 1996.
30 'Report on the 1983 Election', Churchill Archives Centre, The Papers of Neil Kinnock, KNNK 1/3/5.
31 C. Leys, *Market-Driven Politics*, London: Verso, 2001.
32 N. Kinnock, John Macintosh Memorial Lecture, Edinburgh, 1983.
33 M. Westlake, *Kinnock: The Authorised Biography*, London: Little Brown, 2001.
34 Cited in Thomas-Symonds, *The Political Life of Nye Bevan*, London: IB Tauris, p. 5, 2014.
35 R. Heffernan & M. Marqusee, *Defeat from the Jaws of Victory*.
36 Letter from Neil Kinnock to Professor John Hatch, 10th November 1981, cited in M. Westlake, *Kinnock*, p. 166.
37 S. Bashevkin, 'From Tough Times to Better Times', pp. 410–411.
38 Quoted in *Life Magazine*, 'British Begin Election Battle', Volume 18 (26), 1945.
39 E. Shaw, *The Labour Party Since 1945: Old Labour, New Labour*, London: John Wiley, 1996; L. Minkin, *The Blair Supremacy: A Study in the Politics of Labour's Party Management*.
40 A. Offer, *The Challenge of Affluence*.
41 E. Shaw, *Losing Labour's Soul*, p. 153.
42 E. Shaw, 'The Wilderness Years, 1979–1994', in B. Brivati & R. Heffernan (eds.), *The Labour Party: A Centenary History*, Basingstoke: Palgrave Macmillan, p. 133, 2000.
43 S. Bashevkin, 'From Tough Times to Better Times', pp. 410–411.
44 M. Wickham-Jones, *Economic Strategy and the Labour Party*, p. 213, Basingstoke: Palgrave Macmillan, 1996.
45 M. Wickham-Jones, *Economic Strategy and the Labour Party*, p. 216.
46 M. Smith, 'Playing the Politics of "Catch-up"', pp. 558–559.
47 M. Wickham-Jones, *Economic Strategy and the Labour Party*, p. 214.
48 T. Blair, Correspondence, 25th March 1985, LP/Policy Committees and Study Groups of the NEC Research Department (PCSG)/69/11 (Labour Party archives).
49 J. Callaghan, 'Rise and Fall of the Alternative Economic Strategy', pp. 105–130.
50 M. Wickham-Jones, *Economic Strategy and the Labour Party*, p. 218.
51 P. Clarke, *A Question of Leadership: From Gladstone to Thatcher*, p. 392.
52 L. Whitty, 'National Executive Report', Labour Party Annual Conference, p. 37, 1987.
53 R. Heffernan & M. Marqusee, *Defeat from the Jaws of Victory*.

54 Philip Gould to Labour's Campaign Team, July 1987, Churchill Archives Centre, The Papers of Neil Kinnock, KNNK 1/3/5.
55 E. Hobsbawm, 'Out of the Wilderness', *Marxism Today*, October 1987.
56 Editorial, *The Guardian*, 25th June 1987; S. Fielding, *The Labour Party: Socialism and Society Since 1951*, p. 134.
57 A. Gamble, *The Free Economy and the Strong State*.
58 A. Thorpe, *A History of the Labour Party*, Basingstoke: Palgrave Macmillan, 2015.
59 'Mark Dowdney to Joe Haines', 5th August 1987, Churchill Archives Centre, The Papers of Neil Kinnock, KNNK 1/3/5.
60 'Analysis of Post-Election Verbatims – From NOP Poll: Reasons for Not Voting Labour', July 1987, Churchill Archives Centre, The Papers of Neil Kinnock, KNNK 1/3/5. The data in Figure 5.1 is from the British Election Study (1987).
61 L. Whitty, 'National Executive Report', Labour Party Annual Conference, p. 39, 1987.
62 G. Foote, *The Labour Party's Political Thought*, p. 329.
63 'Mark Dowdney to Joe Haines', 5th August 1987, Churchill Archives Centre, The Papers of Neil Kinnock, KNNK 1/3/5.
64 Philip Gould to Labour's Campaign Team, July 1987, Churchill Archives Centre, The Papers of Neil Kinnock, KNNK 1/3/5.
65 'Mark Dowdney to Joe Haines', 5th August 1987, Churchill Archives Centre, The Papers of Neil Kinnock, KNNK 1/3/5.
66 'Jack Dromey to Larry Whitty', September 1987, Churchill Archives Centre, The Papers of Neil Kinnock, KNNK 1/3/5.
67 E. Hobsbawm, 'Out of the Wilderness', *Marxism Today*, October 1987.
68 J. Goldthorpe, D. Lockwood, F. Bechhofer & J. Platt, *The Affluent Worker in the Class Structure*, Cambridge: Cambridge University Press, 1969.
69 Jack Dromey to Larry Whitty, September 1987, Churchill Archives Centre, The Papers of Neil Kinnock, KNNK 1/3/5.
70 Cited in J. Seabrook, *What Went Wrong? Working People and the Ideals of the Labour Movement*, p. 244.
71 A. Gamble, *The Free Economy and the Strong State*, p. 6.
72 A. Gamble, *The Free Economy and the Strong State*, p. 6.
73 A. Gamble, 'The Great Divide', p. 23.
74 R. Heffernan, *New Labour and Thatcherism: Political Change in Britain*, p. 17.
75 R. Heffernan & M. Marqusee, *Defeat from the Jaws of Victory*.
76 P. Burnham, 'New Labour and the Politics of Depoliticization', *British Journal of Politics and International Relations*, Volume 3 (2), pp. 127–149, 2002.
77 A. Gamble, *The Free Economy and the Strong State*, p. 15.
78 P. Hirst, *After Thatcher*.
79 G. Norris in O. Daddow, 'New Labour: A Witness History'.
80 Source: IFF Post-Election Survey, 19th November 1987, The Kinnock Archive, Churchill College, Cambridge.
81 E. Hobsbawm, 'Out of the Wilderness', *Marxism Today*, October 1987.
82 D. Edgerton, *The Rise and Fall of the British Nation: A Twentieth Century History*.
83 J. Tomlinson, *The Labour Governments 1964–70: Economic Policy*, p. 123.
84 S. Hall, *The Hard Road to Renewal*, p. 271, London: Verso, 1988.
85 J. Cronin, *Labour and Society in Britain 1917–89*.
86 R. Cook, 'A Hole in Labour's Heart', *Marxism Today*, p. 25, August 1987.
87 D. Blunkett, *The New Statesman*, 26th June 1992, in S. Fielding, *The Labour Party: Socialism and Society Since 1951*, p. 147.
88 E. Hobsbawm, 'Out of the Wilderness', p. 17, *Marxism Today*, October 1987.
89 C. Hughes & P. Wintour, *Labour Rebuilt*, p. 60.
90 Cited in E. Shaw, 'Retrieving or Re-Imagining the Past', p. 27.
91 C. Hughes & P. Wintour, *Labour Rebuilt: The New Model Party*, p. 61.
92 Source: 'Labour and Britain in the 1990s: IFF Survey', November 1987, LP/Policy Committees and Study Groups of the NEC Research Department (PCSG)/93/5 (Labour Party archives).

93 D. Mattinson, *Talking to a Brick Wall: How New Labour Stopped Listening to Voters*, London: Biteback, 2010.

94 'Labour and Britain in the 1990: IFF Survey', November 1987, LP/Policy Committees and Study Groups of the NEC Research Department (PCSG)/93/5 (Labour Party archives).

95 H. Frayman, 'Extremist Line Not Combated', *Labour Weekly*, p. 8, 19th June 1987.

96 E. Wood, 'So Far to Go for Labour', *Labour Weekly*, pp. 10–11, 3rd July 1987.

97 'Labour and Britain in the 1990: IFF Survey', November 1987, LP/Policy Committees and Study Groups of the NEC Research Department (PCSG)/93/5 (Labour Party archives).

98 B. Gould, 'How to Win!', *Labour Weekly*, p. 10, 10th July 1987.

99 Interview, Gavin Laird, *The New Statesman*, 10th July 1987, cited in S. Fielding, *The Labour Party: Socialism and Society Since 1951*, p. 134.

100 R. Heffernan & M. Marqusee, *Defeat from the Jaws of Victory*, p. 95.

101 R. Heffernan & M. Marqusee, *Defeat from the Jaws of Victory*, p. 156.

102 https://lrb.co.uk/v15/n03/ross-mckibbin/labour-blues. Accessed 4th September 2018.

103 A. Callinicos, 'Wither Marxism?', *Economic and Political Weekly*, Volume 31 (4), p. 9, 1996.

104 A. Gamble, *The Free Economy and the Strong State*.

105 A. Callinicos, 'Wither Marxism?', p. 9.

106 R. Barker, 'Political Ideas Since 1945, or How Long was the Twentieth Century?', *Contemporary British History*, Volume 10 (1), pp. 2–19, 1996.

107 The *Policy Review* comprised six thematic groups: A Productive and Competitive Economy, People at Work, Economic Equality, Consumers and the Community, Democracy for the Individual and the Community, Britain in the World and the Physical and Social Environment. The process drew on a variety of sources and inputs: the results of polling research, written evidence, meetings with interest groups and experts, specialist seminars and conferences as well as international comparisons. 'The Policy Review Groups: A note on their methods of working', November 1987, LP/Policy Committees and Study Groups of the NEC Research Department (PCSG)/93/4 (Labour Party archives).

108 'The PRG Reports: A Note on Themes and Structures', March 1988, LP/Policy Committees and Study Groups of the NEC Research Department (PCSG)/93/4 (Labour Party archives).

109 J. Eatwell, 'Policy Review Group: The Productive and Competitive Economy', December 1987, LP/Policy Committees and Study Groups of the NEC Research Department (PCSG)/72/10 (Labour Party archives).

110 'The PRG Reports: A Note on Themes and Structures', March 1988, LP/Policy Committees and Study Groups of the NEC Research Department (PCSG)/93/4 (Labour Party archives).

111 E. Shaw, 'Retrieving or Re-Imagining the Past?', p. 35.

112 P. Kellner (ed.), *Thorns and Roses*, p. 132.

113 'Common Themes in the Economics Policy Review Groups', December 1987, LP/Policy Committees and Study Groups of the NEC Research Department (PCSG)/72/10 (Labour Party archives).

114 'Common Themes in the Economics Policy Review Groups', December 1987, LP/Policy Committees and Study Groups of the NEC Research Department (PCSG)/72/10 (Labour Party archives).

115 'Productive and Competitive Economy Outline', March 1988, LP/Policy Committees and Study Groups of the NEC Research Department (PCSG)/93/4 (Labour Party archives).

116 P. Kellner (ed.), *Thorns and Roses*, p. 132.

117 The Labour Party, *Meet the Challenge, Make the Change: A New Agenda for Britain*, p. 8, London: The Labour Party, 1989.

118 Cited in https://washingtonpost.com/archive/politics/1988/10/07/british-labor-searches-for-winning-formula/2d790156-ee53-4848-8691-9de5ad42d41d/?noredirect=on&utm_term=.3329ce01b962. Accessed 4th October 2018.

119 Cited in E. Shaw, 'Retrieving or Re-Imagining the Past', p. 32.
120 C. Hughes & P. Wintour, *Labour Rebuilt: The New Model Party*, p. 15, London: Fourth Estate.
121 P. Hewitt, 'Brief for Shadow Communications Agency: Policy Review', 30th January 1989, LP/Policy Committees and Study Groups of the NEC Research Department (PCSG)/72/10 (Labour Party archives).
122 G. Radice, *Labour's Path to Power: The New Revisionism*, p. 124, London: Macmillan, 1989.
123 C. Hughes & P. Wintour, *Labour Rebuilt: The New Model Party*, p. 44.
124 Source: IFF Post-Election Survey, 19th November 1987, The Kinnock Archive, Churchill College, Cambridge.
125 A. Campsie, 'Socialism Will Never Be the Same Again: Reimagining British Left-Wing Ideas for the "New Times"', p. 177.
126 P. Seyd, 'Labour: The Great Transformation', in A. King (ed.), *Britain at the Polls*, London: Chatham House, 1993.
127 P. Hewitt, 'Brief for Shadow Communications Agency: Policy Review', 30th January 1989, LP/Policy Committees and Study Groups of the NEC Research Department (PCSG)/72/10 (Labour Party archives).
128 D. Butler & D. Kavanagh, *The British General Election of 1992*, London: Macmillan, 1992.
129 Cited in M. Smith, 'Playing the Politics of "Catch Up"', p. 558.
130 D. Wring, 'New Labour and the Media', in O. Daddow, 'New Labour: A Witness History', *Contemporary British History*, p. 119.
131 A. Campbell, 'Crying Out for Change: Labour Poll Points Way to the Future', *The Daily Mirror*, undated, LP/Policy Committees and Study Groups of the NEC Research Department (PCSG)/155/1 (Labour Party archives).
132 J. Eatwell, 'Policy Review Group: The Productive and Competitive Economy', December 1987, LP/Policy Committees and Study Groups of the NEC Research Department (PCSG)/72/10 (Labour Party archives).
133 P. Mandelson, 'Productive and Competitive Economy Policy Review Group', 6th April 1988, LP/Policy Committees and Study Groups of the NEC Research Department (PCSG)/93/4 (Labour Party archives).
134 Cited in C. Hughes & P. Wintour, *Labour Rebuilt: The New Model Party*, p. 206.
135 L. Whitty, 'untitled memorandum', 6th May 1988, LP/Policy Committees and Study Groups of the NEC Research Department (PCSG)/93/4 (Labour Party archives).
136 R. Desai, *Intellectuals and Socialism*.
137 D. Marquand, *The Unprincipled Society: New Demands and Old Politics*, London: Fontana, 1989.
138 K. Livingstone, 'Why the Policy Review's Proposed Economic Strategy Will Not Work', undated, LP/Policy Committees and Study Groups of the NEC Research Department (PCSG)/93/4 (Labour Party archives).
139 W. Hutton, *The State We're In*, London: Vintage, 1995.
140 D. Edgerton, *The Rise and Fall of the British Nation: A Twentieth Century History*.
141 B. Pimlott, *Frustrate their Knavish Tricks: Writing on Biography, History and Politics*, p. 354, London: Harper Collins, 1994.
142 Interview, Pat McFadden MP, former Minister of State, Department of Business, Innovation & Skills, October 2011.
143 B. Gould, *Goodbye to All That*.
144 B. Crick, 'The Labour Party: Our Values and Objectives', Letter to Geoff Bish, 17th February 1988, LP/Policy Committees and Study Groups of the NEC Research Department (PCSG)/150/1 (Labour Party archives).
145 P. Seyd & P. Whiteley, *Labour's Grassroots*, Oxford: Oxford University Press, 1985.
146 D. Butler & D. Kavanagh, *The 1987 General Election: Nuffield Election Study*, London: Macmillan, 1988.
147 M. Francis, 'Economics and Ethics: The Nature of Labour's Socialism 1945–51', *Twentieth Century British History*, Volume 6 (2), 1995.
148 R. Hill, *The Labour Party's Economic Strategy 1979–1997*, p. 39.

149 J. Eatwell, 'Responding to the Challenges of the 1990s', 1st April 1988, LP/Policy Committees and Study Groups of the NEC Research Department (PCSG)/93/4 (Labour Party archives).

150 D. Corry, 'Living with Capitalism: Macro-Economic Policy Alternatives', *Renewal*, Volume 2 (1), p. 52, 1994.

151 Cited in E. Jones, *Neil Kinnock*, p. 185, London: Robert Hale, 1989.

152 The Labour Party Manifesto, *It's Time to Get Britain Working Again*, London: The Labour Party, 1992.

153 H. Young, *The Hugo Young Papers*.

154 Cited in E. Jones, *Neil Kinnock*, p. 169.

155 J. Gray, *Beyond the New Right: Markets, Government and the Common Environment*, London: Routledge, 1994.

156 W. Hutton, *The State We're In*.

157 D. Sanders in A. King (ed.), *Britain at the Polls*.

158 'Campaign Priorities and Timing', General Election Planning Group, undated, LP/Policy Committees and Study Groups of the NEC Research Department (PCSG)/150/1 (Labour Party archives).

159 A. King, *Britain at the Polls*.

160 P. Ashdown, *The Ashdown Diaries*, p. 151.

161 The 1992 Labour Party Manifesto.

162 '1992 General Election Result: Reasons for Defeat', July 1992, Churchill Archives Centre, The Papers of Neil Kinnock, KNNK 3/4/5.

163 D. Sanders in A. King (ed.), *Britain at the Polls*.

164 D. Butler & D. Kavanagh, *The British General Election 1992*.

165 Interview, Rt. Hon. Charles Clarke, former Secretary of State for Education and Skills, November 2019.

166 'Campaign Priorities and Timing', General Election Planning Group, undated, LP/Policy Committees and Study Groups of the NEC Research Department (PCSG)/150/1 (Labour Party archives).

167 J. Eatwell, 'Policy Review Group: The Productive and Competitive Economy', December 1987, LP/Policy Committees and Study Groups of the NEC Research Department (PCSG)/72/10 (Labour Party archives).

168 'David Hare': Notes on the Fortunes of War', Undated, Churchill Archives Centre, The Papers of Neil Kinnock, KNNK 3/4/5.

169 G. Radice, *Southern Discomfort*, London: The Fabian Society, 1993.

170 R. Hill, *The Labour Party's Economic Strategy 1979–1997*, p. 41.

171 G. Radice, *Southern Discomfort*, p. 28.

172 T. Jowell, 'Viewpoint', Fabian Conference News, 28th September 1992, CLPD/25 Archive, Bishopsgate Institute.

173 Interview, Rt. Hon. Charles Clarke, former Secretary of State for Education and Skills, November 2019.

174 M. Stuart, *John Smith: A Life*, p. 209, London: Politico's Publishing, 2005.

175 Interview, Rt. Hon. Charles Clarke, former Secretary of State for Education and Skills, November 2019.

176 J. Rentoul, *Tony Blair*.

177 J. Rentoul, *Tony Blair*.

178 '1992 General Election Result: Reasons for Defeat', July 1992, Churchill Archives Centre, The Papers of Neil Kinnock, KNNK 3/4/5.

179 '1992 General Election Result: Reasons for Defeat', July 1992, Churchill Archives Centre, The Papers of Neil Kinnock, KNNK 3/4/5.

180 Cited in M. Westlake, *Kinnock: The Authorised Biography*, p. 573.

181 P. Whiteley, 'The Great Myth about Tax', *The Guardian*, 27th June 2003.

182 J. Curtice, A. Heath & R. Jowell, *The Rise of New Labour*.

183 J. Rentoul, *Tony Blair*, p. 252.

184 E. Hobsbawm, 'Interview with Neil Kinnock', *Marxism Today*, May 1985.

185 T. Blair, *A Journey*, p. 52.
186 H. Young, *The Hugo Young Papers*, p. 389.
187 D. Marquand, *The Progressive Dilemma*; A. Wright & B. Pimlott, *The Alternative*.
188 D. Miliband, 'Critique is Not Enough', Fabian Conference News, 30th September 1992, CLPD/25 Archive, Bishopsgate Institute.
189 P. Kellner (ed.), *Thorns and Roses*, p. 143.
190 D. Skinner, 'Labour Must Reject Maastricht', Socialist Campaign Group News, Labour Party Conference 1992, CLPD/25 Archive, Bishopsgate Institute.
191 Cited in P. Clarke, *A Question of Leadership: From Gladstone to Thatcher*, p. 326.
192 C. Byrne, 'Letter', *The Guardian*, 13th April 1992.
193 Cited in M. Stuart, *John Smith*, p. 307.
194 M. Wickham-Jones, *Economic Strategy and the Labour Party*, p. 213, Basingstoke: Palgrave Macmillan, 1996.
195 https://chroniclelive.co.uk/news/north-east-news/shamed-ex-newcastle-mp-piers-merchant-1460745. Accessed 14th December 2018.
196 Interview, Rt. Hon. Charles Clarke, former Secretary of State for Education and Skills, November 2019.
197 M. Stuart, *John Smith*, p. 346.
198 M. Stuart, *John Smith*, p. 291.
199 A. Heath, J. Curtice & R. Jowell, *The Rise of New Labour*.
200 H. Young, *A Political Journalist's Notebook*, p. 417.
201 Cited in M. Stuart, *John Smith*, p. 233.
202 Cited in J. Rentoul, *Tony Blair*, p. 4, London: Little Brown, 1995.
203 D. Miliband, Confidential Memorandum to the Prime Minister, 'Narrative: Modernization of Britain', March 2005.
204 P. Routledge, *Gordon Brown: The Biography*, p. 71, London: Simon & Schuster, 1998.
205 https://theguardian.com/politics/2003/jun/06/labour.uk. Accessed 14th March 2018. The memorandum was believed to have been written by Peter Mandelson in 1994 to heal the breach between the Blair and Brown camps.
206 Interview, R. Plant, House of Lords, 23rd February 2015.
207 Interview, Rt. Hon. Charles Clarke, former Secretary of State for Education and Skills, November 2019.
208 T. Blair, *Socialism*, p. 23, London: The Fabian Society, 1995.
209 P. Clarke, *A Question of Leadership: From Gladstone to Thatcher*, p. 341.
210 P. Clarke, *A Question of Leadership: From Gladstone to Thatcher*, p. 328.
211 *The Guardian*, Editorial, 18th November, 1994.
212 G. Foote, *The Labour Party's Political Thought: A History*, pp. 34–35.
213 T. Blair, *A Journey*, p. 77.
214 S. Bashevkin, 'From Tough Times to Better Times', p. 411.
215 S. Bashevkin 'From Tough Times to Better Times', p. 413.
216 P. Mandelson, IPPR Fringe, Labour Party Conference, Bournemouth, September 1999.
217 J. Cronin, *New Labour's Pasts: The Labour Party and Its Discontents*.
218 J. Tomlinson, *Managing the Economy, Managing the People*.
219 A. Offer, *The Challenge of Affluence: Self-Control and Well-Being in the United States and Britain Since 1950*, Oxford: Oxford University Press, 2008.
220 S. Brooke, 'Gender and Working-Class Identity in Britain During the 1950s', p. 789.
221 A. Black & S. Brooke, 'The Labour Party, Women, and the Problem of Gender, 1951–1966', *Journal of British Studies*, Volume 36, pp. 419–452, 1997.
222 A. Offer, *The Challenge of Affluence*.
223 B. Campbell, *The Iron Ladies*, p. 186, London: Virago.
224 The evidence that class no longer affects electoral behaviour is certainly not clear cut. In the 1990s, it was apparent that social class continued to shape the choices made by individual voters: R. Andersen, M. Yang & A.F. Heath, 'Class Politics and Political

Context in Britain, 1964–1997: Have Voters Become More Individualized?', *European Sociological Review*, Volume 22 (2), pp. 215–228, 2006.

225 F. Sutcliffe-Braithwaite, *Class, Politics and the Decline of Deference in England 1968–2000.*
226 T. Blair, *A Journey*, pp. 90–91.
227 T. Blair, Speech to the Labour Party Conference, London: The Labour Party, 1999.
228 P. Hyman, Confidential Memorandum to the Prime Minister, 'Note for Conference Speech: Renewing the Project', 20th September 2003.
229 L. Martell, 'New Ideas of Socialism', *Economy and Society*, Volume 21 (2). pp. 152–172, 1992.
230 L. Martell, 'New Ideas of Socialism', pp. 152–153.
231 S. Fielding, *The Labour Party: Continuity and Change in the Making of 'New' Labour.*
232 P. Mandelson & R. Liddle, 'Presentation to the Business Community', 1996.
233 Confidential Memorandum to the Leader of the Opposition: 'Developing Labour's Central Message', 1996.
234 A. Thorpe, *A History of the Labour Party.*
235 A. King, *New Labour Triumphs: Britain at the Polls*, London: CQ Press, 1998.
236 G. Evans & J. Tilley, *The New Politics of Class*, Oxford: Oxford University Press, 2015.
237 D. Marquand, 'Must Labour Win?' p. 9, London: The Fabian Society, 1998.
238 Interview, Rt. Hon. Tony Blair, former Prime Minister, June 2011.
239 Interview, Rt. Hon. Charles Clarke, former Secretary of State for Education and Skills, November 2019.
240 Interview, David Miliband, former Head of Policy, Number Ten Downing Street, September 2011.
241 Interview, David Miliband, former Head of Policy, Number Ten Downing Street, September 2011.
242 S. Beer, 'Britain After Blair', *The Political Quarterly*, Volume 68 (4), p. 318, 1997.
243 T. Blair, *A Journey*, p. 6.
244 Interview, David Miliband, former Head of Policy, Number Ten Downing Street, September 2011.
245 The Labour Party Manifesto, 'Britain Deserves Better', London: The Labour Party, 1997.
246 P. Anderson & N. Mann, *Safety First: The Making of New Labour.*
247 D. Howell, 'The Best and Worst of Times: The Rise of New Labour', *Economic and Political Weekly*, Volume 32 (28), p. 1704, 1997.
248 D. Howell, 'The Best and Worst of Times: The Rise of New Labour', p. 1697.
249 G. Stedman-Jones, *Languages of Class*, p. 253.
250 E. Dell, *A Strange, Eventful History*, p. 556.
251 P. Ashdown, cited in R. Toye, 'The Forgotten Revisionist: Douglas Jay and Britain's Transition to Affluence 1951–1964', in L. Black & H. Pemberton (eds.), *An Affluent Society? Britain's Post-War 'Golden Age' Revisited*, p. 16, London: Ashgate, 2004.

PART II

New Labour in power

6

INSTITUTIONAL LEGACIES

A radical party requires not merely high ideals and skilful leadership, but intellectual coherence and a willingness to jettison cherished assumptions in the face of changing realities.
David Marquand[1]

Introduction

Despite its cautious instincts, New Labour in power still desired to emulate the path-breaking reforms of the Attlee era. The following section of the book examines the impact of the Blair/Brown governments on Britain after 1997 while considering their cumulative effect on politics and policy. The key question posed throughout is this: what *difference* did New Labour make? What institutional legacies did it bestow? To what extent did the Blair administrations decisively alter the UK's economic and social trajectory? The overall verdict is that despite the Labour government's achievements, there was a pervasive breach between promise and performance. The party gained an enormous parliamentary majority, the largest in Labour's history. Ministers pledged to build a New Britain. The Blair's administrations inherited a robust economy characterised by the steady growth of per capita GDP. The Conservative Party was discredited and divided. Thatcherism was held in low esteem. The mood in the country was sympathetic to a shift in the dominant framework of policy and politics.

Yet despite unquestionable policy accomplishments, the expectations of New Labour were never fulfilled exacerbating voters' disillusionment with British democracy and the promise of the 'new' politics. Labour arguably missed its historic opportunity to transform the British polity and society. Unforeseen mistakes – most infamously, military intervention and the Iraq War alongside contentious policies, notably the perceived mistreatment of asylum seekers, incursions into civil liberties and the imposition of university tuition fees – angered longtime supporters. Money was poured into the health and education service. Yet the apparent rate of improvement was slow. It is a recurring theme that Labour governments promise much but then fail to deliver in office. Critics have complained that New Labour was still obsessed with electability. It had a project for the Labour Party, but no comparable agenda for revitalising Britain.

This chapter considers Labour's influence across the political and public policy landscape. Its major theme is how far New Labour succeeded in fashioning institutions that survived beyond the lifetime of the Blair/Brown governments. For social democratic parties, institutions are vital in effecting change. They remain the focal point of reform. The Fabian tradition contends that institutions lead to pronounced shifts in the economic and social order, transforming the values of citizens. The crucial test of New Labour's impact in breaking with the legacy of Thatcherism is how far institutions endured after ministers ceased to hold office. To what extent were Labour's reforms entrenched as the unquestioned framework for public policy in Britain, ensuring lasting and radical change?

Whether institutions survive the governing party's defeat is a vital indicator of political effectiveness. The Attlee governments were revered since the Conservative administrations that followed them preserved landmark reforms, particularly the welfare state and the NHS. Attlee's ministers laid the foundations of the post-war settlement. The Wilson and Callaghan administrations had less obvious impact on British society and politics. How well did New Labour perform in comparison?

In this section of the book, Chapter 7 then focuses on the government's capacity to reshape dominant trends in society from the level of inequality to the crime rate. If they created social democratic institutions, how far were the Blair and Brown administrations able to influence long-term developments through the policy-making and reform machinery of the state? Having addressed institutions and secular trends, Chapter 8 then considers the government's efficacy in remoulding the attitudes of the British people. How far were the preferences, beliefs and ethics of citizens altered as a consequence of Labour's long period in power? The dilemma for social democratic parties is that to win office, they must go with the grain of dominant values to secure electoral support. Yet to undertake progressive change, the centre-left has to redefine those prevailing norms, shifting the axis of politics Leftwards. Chapter 8 concludes by asking whether New Labour fashioned a lasting progressive settlement transforming the intellectual terms of trade? Any new orthodoxy is characterised by the shift in the dominant paradigm of policy and politics. In political terms, paradigms are 'frameworks of ideas and standards that specify not only the goals of policy and the kind of instruments that can be used to attain them, but also the very nature of the problems they are meant to be addressing'.[2] Radical transformation means redrawing the ascendent framework of ideas: converting opponents, winning public arguments, redefining popular common sense. Through post-war reconstruction, Attlee's ministers altered the prevailing agenda of government. Were New Labour's achievements to prove of comparable historical importance?

The chapters that follow do not provide an encyclopaedic overview of Labour's governing programme. Rather than undertaking a fine-grained audit of government policy, the purpose is to focus on key issues thematically. Before assessing the New Labour effect, this account begins by analysing the context in which Labour governed after 1997. The chapter addresses how the party's performance should be judged in comparison to previous left-of-centre administrations in Britain.

New Labour in the post–Cold War world

Understanding New Labour's impact and efficacy means addressing the political context confronting the party. What was extraordinary was the sheer *length* of time Labour was in power after 1997. Never before had the party won two, let alone three, consecutive parliamentary majorities. The New Times in which Blair and Brown governed were among the most perplexing in British post-war history.[3] The 1990s began propitiously marked by the end of the Cold War, accompanied by the long and sustained period of UK economic growth after the turmoil unleashed by crashing out of the Exchange Rate Mechanism (ERM).

For the first few years at least, Labour found governing apparently straightforward. In a memorandum to the prime minister, one of Blair's strategists concluded:

> Objectively we are in an incredibly strong position. We have a majority of 179. The Tory party have a weak and ineffectual leader. People credit us with economic success, constitutional reform, strength abroad. . . . This is a premiership whose best years lie ahead of it.[4]

Blair and Brown learnt keenly from Bill Clinton's initial mistakes. Clinton came to office as an inexperienced US president carrying a multitude of ambitious commitments from his election campaign which he was then forced to abandon. His administration erratically lurched from unforeseen incidents and international crises to personal scandals and damaging legislative defeats. New Labour, in sharp contrast, sought to control the political agenda from day one.

Yet the governing context was not as straightforward as it appeared initially. The Blair and Brown administrations were tested by a succession of global shocks and governing crises. Eric Hobsbawm argued presciently that 'the short twentieth century' ended with Communism's breakup in 1990–91.[5] The world that Blair and Brown confronted was fundamentally altered. There were five military conflicts in which British troops were deployed. Dark clouds were gathering on the horizon, particularly the spectre of ethnic cleansing in Sierra Leone and Kosovo, and the failure to integrate Russia into the liberal international order.[6] Terrorist attacks in New York and Washington on 11th September 2001 sent shockwaves through the Western world. The capitalist economies were being restructured by rapid technological change and financialisation. The shift from manufacturing to services was accelerating across the advanced economies.

Moreover, changing generational values were undermining existing social norms, encouraging far-reaching liberalisation. The transformation of gender roles continued, driven by women's ongoing demands for equality. Devolution redefined the nature of British governance, establishing power centres that threatened the UK's cohesion. English identity became more strident, animated by the growing sense of grievance. The consensus over post-war multiculturalism was disrupted by waves of immigration, alongside anxieties about the perceived failure of integration. Identity politics displaced class politics. Yet persistent inequalities in the economic and social structure belied the apparent decline of class conflict. The backdrop to the Labour governments was, in that sense, far from auspicious.

Governing in hard times

Despite the scale of Labour's victory, it was unclear whether 1997 represented the turning point equal to the radical 1906 and 1945 administrations or affirmed the settlement that endured since the Thatcher governments. The main theme of the Labour Party's 1997 manifesto was marrying a productive economy with social justice, reconciling the redistributive goals of social democracy with 'the efficiency-inducing properties of markets'.[7] The claim at the heart of Thatcherism was that economic success was only attainable by downgrading social cohesion. New Labour rejected this assumption. Before the election Blair spelt out his governing principles:

NEW LABOUR'S POLICY PLATFORM

- 'Partnership between a thriving private sector and public enterprise to prepare the country for economic change.
- Partnership at work and an end to the old conflicts between management and workforce.
- A revolution in our country's education and skills.
- The reform of welfare to make it, as it should be, a platform of opportunity not a recipe for dependency. Tackling the new challenges posed by the growing number of old people who will need both the security of a decent pension and affordable elderly care.
- Public services that are accountable and decentralised while rejecting two-tierism and division.
- A programme to fight crime that recognises both prevention and punishment – tough on crime and tough on the causes of crime.
- Democracy that is open, reformed and devolved.
- Engaging constructively with Europe so that we can shape it to meet Britain's needs'.[8]

Labour's programme espoused the high-minded ideals of national modernisation and reform forging 'a country with drive, purpose, and energy'. Blair wrote in the party's manifesto: 'New Labour is a party of ideas and ideals but not of outdated ideology'.[9] So what goals did Labour set itself in transforming Britain? A memorandum written for the prime minister in the first term stipulated eight objectives:

WHAT WE WANT TO ACHIEVE OVER 10 YEARS

- 'A period of unrivalled economic success spread across the country: **Labour the natural party of economic competence.**
- **A new constitutional and political settlement** (devolution, human rights, local government, mayors, House of Lords).
- **Britain cleverer and better educated – less elitism and snobbery in education.** 50 per cent going to university, the rest getting decent training and apprenticeships, lifelong learning embedded, schools unleashing opportunity.
- **Public service investment and reform** because without it the vast majority lose out on the opportunity to make the most of themselves.
- **Less poverty and social exclusion.** A new work ethic as part of a remodelled welfare state.
- **Respect and responsibility.** A society where there is less anti-social behaviour and crime.
- **Peace and prosperity in Northern Ireland.**
- **Strength in the world and leader in Europe.** With the best rapid reaction armed forces, a leader on the environment and the most effective aid programme'.[10]

For Blair and Brown, the Labour governments had three main purposes: to upgrade public services after the perceived neglect of the 1980s; to renew the social fabric and tackle poverty, refuting Thatcher's claim that 'there was no such thing as society'; and to create an inclusive knowledge economy that offered secure work and high wages to those willing to acquire human capital.[11] If they were not neoliberal, how recognisably social democratic were Labour's ambitions? Compared to the Attlee era, the Blair/Brown administrations are scorned as lacking political courage and principle. There were no promises to increase the share of the economy subject to government intervention and control. The language of class, redistribution and 'fair shares' was banished. Even the ideal of the universal welfare state epitomising social solidarity hardly featured in New Labour's rhetoric.

More than fifty years since the end of the Second World War, the priorities of social democracy had shifted inevitably. Novel aims emerged, not least the commitment to lifelong education, social inclusion, alongside constitutional reform. Yet the government retained the historic objective of reducing poverty alongside concerted action to tackle structural deprivation. Renewed importance was attached to the public realm. Echoing Attlee, New Labour's believed that 'Britain will only be truly successful when power, wealth, and opportunity are in the hands of the many not the privileged few'. Even in 1945, Labour's principal aim was to reduce insecurity by imposing a 'universal minimum' to tackle want.[12] Although they sought to equalise the income distribution in Dalton's 1946 budget, ministers' primary aim was to reduce poverty. Attlee's party presided over 'the establishment of a national minimum of subsistence, below which no one should fall'. As such, 'greater equality of outcome was not the initial objective of the welfare state'.[13] Attlee and New Labour were less far apart than critics claimed subsequently.

Like previous Labour parties, New Labour believed that government was a force for good in solving the economic and social problems of the nation. There was a conviction that 'no-one who does a hard days' work should end up in poverty' while 'investment in schools and hospitals should come before tax cuts'. It was said that 'Britain's future lies as a whole-hearted member of the European Union'.[14] In the age of insecurity inaugurated by Thatcherism, these were discernibly social democratic aims. The claim that Labour embraced the neo-liberal governing agenda is misleading.

That said, after 1997 political caution often prevailed. There are several pertinent examples worth recalling. New Labour disavowed 'tax and spend' politics, a reaction to the party's defeat five years previously. The manifesto claimed: 'The level of public spending is no longer the best measure of the effectiveness of government action'. Ministers promised to be 'wise spenders' rather than 'big spenders'.[15] There could be no return to the 'penal tax rates of the 1970s'. Raising the top rate of tax was a 'red line' the Labour government would never cross. For the first two years at least, Labour stuck to the Conservative chancellor's spending limits. Moreover, New Labour remained reticent about the state's role in the economy. Intervention meant strategic investment in 'skills, infrastructure and new technologies'.[16] It was no longer accepted that Keynesian policies of demand management could achieve full employment. New Labour did not regard economic policy as a major arena of partisan disagreement. Blair memorably told a gathering of French parliamentarians: 'There is no Left and Right in economic policy. Only right and wrong'. It was a far cry from the position of Dalton, Attlee and Cripps in the 1940s, forging a socialist planned economy that rejected market fundamentalism.

Another difficulty was the lack of governing experience that characterised Blair's team. Almost all the ministers appointed, including the prime minister, had never before held office. Blair's professional experience was his legal career. He had little practical knowledge of public service leadership and no track record of dealing with the civil service. At the outset, his view of policy-making and implementation rested on the naive view that, 'reform goes from being a campaign speech, to another speech, to a Green Paper, to a White Paper, with the Bill then being amended in the Commons, amended in the Lords, and then the implementation process'.[17] Of course there were efforts to mitigate New Labour's relative inexperience by appointing political advisers, while altering the operating structure and culture of government. Cabinet meetings were noticeably shorter. The system of committees deliberating on domestic policy became less important. Blair conducted meetings in shirtsleeves, often without a note-taker. Ministers and officials addressed the prime minister as Tony. Long-serving mandarins derided the Blair style as 'sofa government', alluding to the prime minister's fondness for informal meetings rather than traditional committees. One of Blair's own ministers, Donald Dewar, complained: 'Cabinet government is not really working. . . . The Blair government is mostly government by bilateral meeting'.[18] Jonathan Powell retorted such criticisms were trivial, revolving around a debate about the type of furniture in meetings.[19] Labour passed Freedom of Information legislation opening up British government to scrutiny, although Blair later regretted the move. Some ministers wanted to go further in reforming the Whitehall machinery. In a confidential note written in the summer of 1998, the minister without portfolio, Peter Mandelson, recommended the creation of a department of the prime minister to build 'strong strategic capacity at the centre of government . . . for systematic analysis of complex problems'.[20]

Patricia Hewitt, who led Labour's preparations for government from 1994, believed that most incoming ministers were ill equipped to manage Whitehall departments. Prospective ministers 'saw their role as taking policy decisions and leaving implementation to permanent secretaries'.[21] New Labour's mind-set was emblematic of early Fabianism where the state 'could push buttons and pull levers and change things throughout the country'.[22] Blair was oblivious to the force of inertia that exists in bureaucracies, and that 'it takes a long time and a lot of effort to really make things happen in government'.[23] Ministers became increasingly perplexed as they pulled bureaucratic levers in Whitehall that they discovered were connected to nothing much outside.

New Labour's statecraft: confronting the betrayal myth?

As Chapter 3 discussed, New Labour believed that the Old Labour governments, particularly the 1974 administration, were a miserable failure. Blair and Brown recoiled at the political disunity unleashed by the wholesale breakdown of party discipline. The unions accused ministers of betrayal. Activists attacked Labour's parliamentary leadership which they believed had 'repeatedly shown its inability to learn from its mistakes', imposing 'unjust wage norms, public spending cuts and high unemployment'.[24] There was little appreciation of the importance of competence and winning voters' trust. Labour politicians in the past too often had a deterministic view of electoral politics, believing the working class would support the party because it was created for the workers. Blair and Brown sought to be different. Among Labour's leaders, they uniquely understood the importance of statecraft, the art of governing in the British political system.[25] The leadership's aim was not just to govern for five years like Attlee or Wilson but to secure the full second term. Blair announced that he would tackle the 'culture of betrayal' that languished within the Labour movement. He was adamant New Labour must do only what was stated in its manifesto. There would be 'fairness, not favours' in dealing with the general secretaries of the trade unions. That meant no repeal of legislation introduced by the Thatcher governments to weaken the power of organised labour. The 1997 manifesto, *Britain Deserves Better,* was drafted carefully and costed meticulously, containing relatively few commitments.

Under New Labour, dissent was crushed. The media were encouraged to undermine Blair and Brown's opponents. Clare Short, a prominent member of the shadow cabinet and an important voice on the party's soft Left, complained of anonymous briefings by 'people who live in the dark'. New Labour was operating in a febrile environment shaped by media hostility, appealing to an electorate disengaged from the formal structures of politics. The leadership believed the ends of electoral success justified the means of centralised control and media management. New Labour was a 'cartel party'.[26] Political and organisational control was enforced ruthlessly by the disciplined professional elite at the centre.[27]

That skilled team focused on maintaining Labour's dominance, aware of constant threats to the party's standing with voters. Paranoia about their electoral prospects gripped Blair's followers leading some commentators to remark upon 'the strange insecurity of this mammothly powerful government'.[28] The year before winning the second-term landslide with a 167-seat majority in the aftermath of fuel blockades and petrol shortages, Philip Gould wrote in a secret note:

> Our current situation is serious. There is absolutely no room for complacency. There is now a chance that our majority will fall dramatically, following the pattern of 1945 and 1964. . . . The government has been drifting, growing almost monthly weaker and more diffuse. . . . We are outflanked on patriotism and crime; we are suffering from disconnection; we have been assailed for spin and broken promises; we are not believed to have delivered.[29]

In interpreting public opinion, Blair's instincts veered towards moral populism. Like Gladstone, Blair made a vital but ambiguous distinction between 'the people' and the political establishment.[30] In a note produced immediately before the 2001 election, the prime minister wrote that the popularity of his government was being undermined, 'by a sense that we aren't on people's side on issues like asylum, gay rights, Europe and now crime'. He complained British politics was now 'defined by disappointment at lack of delivery . . . in the absence of a clear sense of mission and purpose'.[31] A memorandum detailed the perceived threats facing New Labour towards the end of its first term:[32]

TABLE 6.1 New Labour's Vulnerabilities and Strengths

Strengths	Weaknesses
Political supremacy	Media hostility
Winning the battle of ideas	Perceptions of:
United Cabinet	Spin
Economy	Sleaze
Constitution	Cronyism
Standing abroad	Parliament
Northern Ireland	Slow delivery on public services
Primary schools	Caution/wasting the majority

Opportunities	Threats
Eight years of economic stability/ prosperity producing feel-good	Sleaze stories over several years
	Disunity
Six years of investment makes a difference	Soap opera out of control
	Money doesn't secure enough public service (health) change
Leadership in Europe	Backlash by public fuelled by unpredictable event – tax
Tory disarray	Becoming the boring establishment
	Euro

The list reveals New Labour's main political priorities. No surprisingly, the memorandum emphasises the importance attached to strong economic performance and rising prosperity, producing a 'feel-good factor' among voters. The book published in the mid-1990s by Clinton's political strategist, Dick Morris, titled *The New Machiavelli* fascinated Blair's advisers. Morris claimed that politics had shifted from representational democracy to direct democracy, 'where there is a need to win a daily mandate, in which strength comes from popularity, and in which the public is far more fickle and discerning'.[33] Labour's team were obsessive in winning the day-to-day media battle. They never acquired the confidence, the sense of legitimacy, to believe they could govern and take decisions for the long term.

Within Blair's circle, it was believed that by dominating the media the Conservatives could be permanently marginalised. For the first time in decades, it appeared Labour was winning the battle of ideas. Yet there is an acknowledgement that allegations of sleaze might hurt Labour in government. Failure to turn around public services was identified as a major vulnerability. Most striking is the recognition that Labour might be too cautious, at risk of squandering its majority, prone to become part of the British establishment – an insider rather than an insurgent force. This acknowledgement of New Labour's incipient conservatism and the danger of historic opportunities missed was to prove prescient.

Evaluating New Labour's impact: historical comparisons

The main theme of subsequent chapters is how the *impact* of the Labour governments on the society and politics of Britain should be judged. It is instructive to compare Blair and Brown with previous administrations. There are unquestionably affinities with the Liberal governments of 1906–12 and the Attlee ministries of 1945–51. Yet among historians, it is obvious both were path-breaking where the 1997 administrations were not. Lloyd George laid the foundations of the modern welfare state. Attlee's ministers inaugurated a new economic and political compromise that endured for three decades. In contrast, New Labour's footprint in history feels slight.

These are, of course, contentious judgements. The 1906 and 1945 administrations confronted very different political and economic circumstances. The context facing those governments is often poorly understood. The perceived radicalism of past administrations is then overstated, particularly the 1945 governments that operated in a historically exceptional and contingent post-war situation. It is vital to take account of the prevailing climate in the 1990s: the transformed political culture after eighteen years of Conservative rule, and the room for manoeuvre New Labour enjoyed during its years in power. Even so, Blair and Brown's party struggled to sustain its political cohesion and collective spirit of shared purpose. After 1997, damaging rifts soon appeared. The central bureaucracy of the party sought to impose favoured candidates in the London Mayoral, Welsh Assembly and Scottish parliamentary elections, stirring grassroots animosity. There was a backlash among activists against the reforms that gave the private sector its greater role in public services. The Iraq War brought internal tensions between ministers and the grassroots to breaking point. The trade unions felt excluded from Blair's inner circle, even sympathisers such as the TUC general secretary, John Monks. As Labour's popularity waned, 'chickens came home to roost'. The unions were not surprisingly reluctant to rally their members behind the government. Certainly, Blair and Brown's party lacked the sense of collective purpose that buoyed the Attlee governments through dark times in the 1940s.

Institutional legacies

So what was New Labour's institutional legacy after thirteen years in power? Since entering government, the party fashioned institutions to enact its economic and social agenda. In progressive circles, it was acknowledged that the Whitehall machinery ossified in the Thatcher years. Conservative administrations did not so much roll back the frontiers of the state as encourage benign neglect, depleting central government of its redistributive capabilities. Whitehall and Westminster were weak at co-ordination, struggling with 'joined-up' policy-making. Pressing social and economic problems were ignored. The centre of government in Britain had long been insubstantial: issues regularly slipped between the cracks. Departmentalism meant an inability to address overlaps between policies.[34] The efficient implementation of policy was a persistent problem throughout the post-war era. Ministers struggled to effectively carry out programmes.

In opposition, New Labour questioned the existing culture of Whitehall policy-making. There was growing scepticism that the state could act as the decisive agent of reform in a more diverse and complex society. Blair's team thought hard about how to improve policy-making and the efficacy of governing institutions. Ministers forged cross-departmental strategies to aid efficient implementation. Number Ten's Policy Unit dramatically expanded. The Cabinet Office Performance and Innovation Unit (PIU) was instructed to take a long-term view of policy, generating solutions to bypass the conservatism of departments. Hundreds of pilot trials of innovation were commissioned. Across the departmental landscape, pilots enabled ministers to test rival approaches. Pilots led to the reshaping of the policy-making process from the rational cause/effect approach towards experimentalism and the perpetual search for the holy grail of 'what works'.

The Blair administrations relied on a variety of 'policy styles' to build government's capacity rather than unilaterally shifting from the bureaucracy and hierarchy of the post-war era to neo-liberal networks and markets.[35] Where government depended on the private and voluntary sector, there was an emphasis on inclusive bottom-up practices. An official in the Department of Health reported:

> One of the things that is particularly different with this [New Labour] administration from the Conservatives . . . is that it tends to be fairly inclusive. If you went to any steering group, reference or taskforce group, external bodies would be in greater number than civil servants.[36]

Nonetheless, increasing public expenditure was matched by the centralised governance framework in the public sector focused on targets.[37] At the heart of Labour's agenda was the 'top-down directive tendency' concerned with pulling levers, issuing instructions to professionals.[38] Among the most infamous acts was Ed Balls' decision as secretary of state for children, schools and families to intervene in the 'Baby P' scandal in 2008, instructing Haringey Council to dismiss its head of children's services, Sharon Shoesmith. Balls was found by the high court to have acted unlawfully, superseding the secretary of state's competencies. Yet as a minister, Balls was all-too-typical in believing the gentleman in Whitehall knows best. Established in 2001, the Prime Minister's Delivery Unit tracked public sector performance. The goal, according to Blair, was to 'enforce that culture of New Labour throughout the system. . . . You've got to have an agenda driven from the top'.[39] The mind-set was imperious. There was a belief that economic and social reform meant overhauling institutions, pulling levers and marshalling expertise to reconfigure policy.[40]

Ultimately, counter to the neo-liberal narrative, Blair and Brown believed in advancing the scale and scope of national government, although New Labour remained cautious about extending its role in the economy. Blair's administrations adopted a unique approach to the public realm. Government's responsibilities grew significantly, not only spending as a share of GDP, but increasingly through intervening in the lives of families and communities. Central government acquired additional powers. Over 3,600 criminal offences were created.[41] There was recognition of 'the necessity of tough intervention . . . not allowing people to become detached from society'.[42] Ministers were accused of running a 'nanny state' that knew more about what citizens and civil society needed than they did themselves. In the enthusiasm to solve policy problems, Labour's strategy was some distance away from market fundamentalism.

Having increased resources, the Labour governments no longer viewed the public sector as the monopoly provider in public services, an integral assumption of the post-war settlement.[43] Even more controversially, provision was no longer unconditionally available as a matter of right, *only* if citizens fulfilled certain duties. The significance was hard to overstate. The post-1945 social contract guaranteed the welfare state as a categorical right of citizenship. In the Thatcher years the principle was eroded and then overturned with conviction by New Labour.

Unquestionably, Labour after 1997 constructed institutions that achieved political legitimacy, becoming sufficiently embedded to live on. The Low Pay Commission (LPC) and the national minimum wage (NMW) were likely to survive future governments. The LPC institutionalised co-ordination between government, employers and workers, providing a formal mechanism for consultative negotiation that did not previously exist. The LPC shifted the UK towards the collaborative corporatism of Northern Europe. In the NHS, the National Institute of Clinical Excellence (NICE) entrenched an 'evidence-led' approach to medical treatment. Having survived the transition to the Coalition, NICE is a permanent feature of the NHS landscape. Independent Foundation Hospitals (FH) are self-governing public interest bodies operating free of Whitehall interference. Foundation hospitals revived the model of operational autonomy jettisoned following the creation of the health service in 1948. Of 251 English NHS Trusts, 153 now have foundation status.

The devolved institutions similarly became a permanent feature of the constitutional landscape. The Northern Ireland peace settlement and the Good Friday Agreement (GFA) endured to end forty years of violence. The GFA was eventually agreed as Blair's team used the diplomacy of constructive ambiguity to transcend insurmountable differences. On becoming leader, Blair abandoned the long-established policy of Labour's Northern Ireland spokesman, Kevin McNamara, promising 'unity by consent'. He persuaded the unionist community that the GFA would normalise Northern Ireland's position within the UK. Moreover, the status of Belfast as part of Great Britain would be secured within the context of devolved government.[44] For nationalists, the principles of power-sharing and mutual consent reflected the fundamental recognition of shared identity within the pluralist, multi-ethnic state underpinned by respect for human rights and the rule of law. If social democracy had a less distinctive economic programme by the 1990s, the centre-left's governing strategy emphasised social and political inclusion, opening up fresh possibilities for peace in the aftermath of Ireland's long and bloody war. The approach built on the Major government's willingness to cast aside the legacy of colonialism. Yet it was the commitment to the institutional renovation of the British state that propelled Blair's efforts.

In contrast to the 1940s, institutional reform and constitutional renewal were considered essential to fulfil the social democratic agenda. Ministers saw no reason why devolution would impede efforts to tackle economic disadvantage. Expanding the judiciary's role need not undermine ministers' authority or prohibit the exercise of the national government's interventionist capacities. The post-1997 administrations replaced the unwritten constitution of A.V. Dicey, informed by precedents and tacit conventions, with a codified settlement devolving power and according protection to individual rights.[45] Labour effectively created 'a new constitution' in Great Britain.

The list of reforms was lengthy. Government was restored to London after the abolition of the Greater London Council (GLC) in the 1980s. Hereditary peers were almost entirely removed from the House of Lords. The European Convention on Human Rights (ECHR) was incorporated into UK law. The system of Law Lords residing in the House of Lords was replaced by the Supreme Court that formally separated the legislative and judicial branch. A commission was appointed to review the voting system for the House of Commons, chaired by the former home secretary, Roy Jenkins. Reform was intended to decentralise political power, creating a fairer 'partnership' between the nations of the UK while holding governments to account and re-establishing vibrant local democracies.[46] So how did Labour's institutional legacy appear across the diverse terrain of post-1997 public policy?

Rebuilding the public realm

Investment certainly allowed public institutions to be strengthened. New Labour rejected neo-liberal antipathy to the state. Ministers were prepared to use the Whitehall machinery in novel ways.[47] Iconic architecturally renowned school buildings, academies, Sure Start centres, hospitals and reinvigorated community spaces began to appear. As a result, there was evidence of improved performance across public services. In health, for example, average waits for inpatient care fell from 13.2 weeks to 4 weeks between 1997 and 2010.[48] At the end of Labour's period in power, 94.4 per cent of NHS patients saw a cancer specialist within two weeks of referral.

Nonetheless, problems with public-private partnerships (PPP) cast a pall over Labour's achievements. Moreover, there was concern that public expenditure was not always 'well spent'. Even Blair's advisers admitted that while 'ring-fenced funds achieved a lot and the capital spending programme should deliver very visible improvements to schools . . . in retrospect generous past settlements' did not always focus on the right priorities.[49] Blair's director of policy, Geoff Mulgan, noted: 'Much of the money committed in the last two Spending Reviews has gone into teachers' pay, which was not linked to performance'. Mulgan believed the priorities should be under-fives funding for early years centres alongside adult skills. John Birt, the former BBC director-general who was brought into Downing Street, complained Labour's plans were 'analytically weak in weighing the likely impact of different options for achieving better outcomes'. He believed school reforms 'lacked analytical rigour, are not backed by evidence, and are unconvincing'.[50] Evaluations revealed that classroom teaching assistants and police support officers (PSOs) had little impact on school attainment and crime rates.[51]

Meanwhile, the Private Finance Initiative (PFI) allowed the Treasury to meet its 'golden rule' of capital spending remaining below the 40 per cent limit. The initiative 'was a way of demonstrating [New Labour] could do business with the city'.[52] Yet PFI meant higher costs over the thirty-year lifetime of the asset than would have been entailed by standard procurement.[53] PFI enabled ministers to invest without raising taxes, but increased the fiscal burden on future generations of workers. To some, PFI was among New Labour's worst domestic failures. The private sector had long delivered public sector construction projects, but under PFI private companies built *and* maintained facilities. According to the King's Fund think-tank, of 68 new hospitals opened in England between 1997 and 2005, 64 were built using PFI financing. Experts concluded that as a result, 'the NHS capital building programme is larger than it has ever been. The physical condition of most NHS hospitals is now vastly better'. At the same time:

> Critics of PFI say that it has led to fewer beds, poor quality buildings, and that there have been extensive teething problems. . . . It also remains unclear whether PFI is cheaper than the traditional way of doing things. The cost of financing such schemes is higher than using public funding.[54]

Moreover, where it did occur, the increase in public resources was directed invariably towards hospitals and schools. These public services were 'consumed' by individual patients and parents. There was less emphasis on improving the common environment: parks, city gardens, public libraries, urban green spaces – attractive places that make life worthwhile and bring citizens together across social barriers. Still, the Blair government created the Social Exclusion Unit (SEU), tackling the interlocking problems of unemployment, poor housing, mental illness, family breakdown, poor physical health and rundown neighbour-hoods. Across Whitehall, the co-ordination of policy focused on deprivation had previously been inept. Moreover, Labour emphasised the importance of civil society where families, the voluntary sector and private business met shared goals.[55] The SEU challenged the assumption of post-war social democracy that Whitehall always knows best. At the same time, despite devolution the Labour administrations frequently resorted to centralisation and lever-pulling – a traditional view of the machinery of government. Not all of Labour's institutions in the public realm thrived and endured. There was still capacity at the centre to deal with problems of exclusion after 2010. The breakdown of communities and the growth of structural disadvantage were viewed as responsibilities of govern-ment long after Blair and Brown departed from office.[56] Yet the SEU (later the Social Exclusion Taskforce) was soon shut down, while the language of exclusion largely disappeared from government's rhetoric.

New Labour's new Keynesianism

In economic policy, ministers in no way blindly deferred to neo-liberal ortho-doxy. Brown and Blair's analysis incorporated the new Keynesianism seeking 'to reinterpret Keynes' insights in the modern world'.[57] While accepting neo-classical assumptions about the behaviour of individual economic agents includ-ing the persistence of 'sticky wages' in labour markets, New Labour acknowledged that market-clearing mechanisms could fail. Given recessions disrupt the normal functioning of markets, it was recognised national governments have to regulate capitalism to ensure efficiency and social justice. In a world of market uncertainty, the new social democracy believed state intervention would help to avoid problems such as unemployment remaining above equilibrium in the long run.[58]

In opposition in the 1990s, the party reaffirmed its support for 'the 1944 white paper commitment to achieve high and stable levels of employment'.[59] The new Keynesianism entailed public institutions performing functions not otherwise undertaken by markets. Furthermore, Labour sought to end the conflict between workers and capital that defined the twentieth-century political economy of Britain. New Keynesianism continued to emphasise the importance of the supply side alongside traditional macro-economic instruments, underlining the importance of investment in human capital over manufacturing industry. New Labour removed barriers to entry in the labour market by tackling skills shortages, promoting full employment. Learn Direct, a lifelong learning institution, was created to improve workplace skills, accompanied by Individual Learning Accounts (ILAs). There was investment in Further Education colleges (FE) and higher education institutions. As a consequence, public spending as a share of national income grew from 36 to 43 per cent.

Colin Hay and Matthew Watson wrote that, 'Labour had ceased effectively to be a social democratic party committed as it had then become to a pervasive neo-liberal economic orthodoxy'.[60] Yet such claims are misleading.[61] New Labour continuously emphasised the importance of government intervention rather than abandoning the economy to unfettered market forces. Competition policy was strengthened. The NMW and TUPE (Transfer of Undertakings Employment Protection legislation) enhanced labour market regulation. There was dialogue with trade unions, accompanied by investment in training and infrastructure.

Later on, the climate change levy was designed specifically to reduce carbon omissions. In order to ensure the UK could tackle climate change, the Stern Review was launched in 2005. The evidence of impending environmental catastrophe and the problem of energy security led to the abandonment of the pro-market framework, accompanied by new strategies of government intervention.[62] Regional development agencies (RDAs) sought to assist under-performing economic areas. Shareholders and employees were given greater voice through the review of company law. The 2010 Labour manifesto proposed additional rules on takeovers: two-thirds of shareholders would now have to support the takeover while there should be greater transparency in deal-making.[63]

As a consequence, the assertion that New Labour replicated neo-liberal policies is questionable. In any case, there was scarcely a coherent doctrine of Thatcherite political economy to emulate by the late 1980s. As prime minister, Thatcher used the state to intervene in markets.[64] The City of London's dominance was enabled by the Thatcher administrations, a post-industrial strategy centred on 'picking winners'. Nor did the Conservatives unequivocally impose a low-tax regime. Under Thatcher, the tax burden on citizens rose; although the basic and higher rates of income tax were cut, indirect taxes such as value added tax (VAT) increased. Expenditure on the welfare state continued to grow, despite the Conservatives' policy of reducing the generosity of pensions, linking their value to prices rather than earnings.

Deindustrialisation and the rise of long-term unemployment had undermined the neo-liberal aspiration of cutting back the welfare state.[65] The Conservative administrations devised measures that subsidised precarious employment, creating a range of social security benefits, principally Family Credit. The dramatic rise of worklessness then imposed pressures on the NHS and public services. Thatcher flirted with privatisation and vouchers for health, but her ministers were circumspect. The chancellor of the exchequer, Nigel Lawson, declared the NHS 'the closest thing the English people have to a religion'.[66] As a consequence, neo-liberalism was far from dominant in Britain. Hayek's belief that public policy and institutions should be subject to market forces certainly influenced many Conservative politicians. Hayek's thought had a decisive impact on the Thatcher governments. Yet in contrast, New Labour drew predominantly on the legacy of Keynes, rejecting the postulates of orthodox laissez-faire economics. The public institutions built after 1997 improved long-term economic performance while strengthening equity and fairness.

The transfer of power to independent institutions was the hallmark of Labour's legacy in economic policy, a shift known as constrained discretion. The Blair/ Brown administration reformed the structure of policy-making, handing powers to the Bank of England in setting interest rates while creating bodies at 'arm's-length' from ministers, even if Labour still believed there were limits to government's role in the economy. Brown's purpose was to create a 'macro-economic constitution' that specified fiscal and monetary rules by which New Labour could portray the economy as safe in its hands. The emphasis was on 'medium-term anti-inflationary strategy' alongside 'policies to strengthen the underlying capacity of the economy'.[67]

Furthermore, the impact of governments is determined as much by their 'non-decisions'. The most significant institutional choice Labour avoided after 1997 related to the European single currency. The difficulty was that in opposition, Blair was already committed to a referendum on the Euro. Brown then set five tests that would have to be met before Britain agreed to join. The first test concerned whether the UK and EU business cycles were aligned. Second, was there flexibility in the European monetary system to deal with unanticipated shocks? Third, would joining EMU encourage inward investment? Fourth, would EMU membership negatively impact financial services? Fifth, would entering the single currency promote growth, employment and economic stability?[68] The prime minister and his team had never fought a UK-wide referendum. At the beginning of the second term, according to polling, voters strongly opposed ditching the pound. In a secret memorandum, Blair wrote: 'I see two possible openings for the referendum: autumn 2002; or summer 2003'. Preconditions of entry were 'structural change at the European Central Bank' alongside progress on 'the economic reform agenda', achieved by 'building alliances necessary to establish a leading position for Britain in Europe'.[69]

Yet Blair faced innumerable difficulties over the politics of the Euro. Ministers spent the previous four years boasting Britain was the only European country where employment and growth were robust. If the European economy was under-performing, why would Britain want to integrate further? The EU suffered from high levels of structural unemployment; would British jobs not be imperilled if the UK joined? Brown believed the Treasury's financial policy was superior technically to the Eurozone.[70] What direction was Europe fundamentally taking, Brown queried, given the persistence of rhetoric about a 'united states of Europe?'[71] Was the goal of federalism compatible with British opinion about the European project? The UK diverged structurally since Britain's housing market was dependent on variable rate mortgages, while financial markets were more liberalised than in continental Europe.

Not surprisingly, there were disagreements about the campaign New Labour should fight. Brown believed there was less clarity about whether the Euro was fundamentally about identity or economics. Would the Euro allow Britain to fulfil its destiny as a European nation, or protect British prosperity? Had not the problems of 'boom and bust' in the British economy been resolved? Could the government insist the country would be no less 'British' having joined? To fight a credible campaign, the government must address these unresolved questions. It was little surprise the prime minister baulked at the referendum.

Even so, the contrast in political economy with the Thatcher governments was stark. During the 1980s, growth resulted from increased employment flexibility and the UK's incorporation into the EU single market, which was accompanied by rising wage inequality. The Conservative governments believed that the postwar compromise shifted the balance of power in favour of organised labour. They insisted that public institutions encouraged government interference, leading to sustained economic under-performance. Thatcherism was neo-liberal in disciplining labour, reversing the shift in the balance of power between employers and workers, while arresting decline by unleashing the dynamism of markets. In contrast, productivity growth under New Labour was driven by institutional intervention to enhance innovation and skills.[72] Reforms in competition policy, market regulation and investment in higher education alongside increasing immigration led to higher rates of growth. Public investment in education grew from 5 per cent of national income in 1997 to 5.4 per cent by 2007, higher than Germany (4.5 per cent) and the United States (5.3 per cent). There was a rise in the proportion of university-educated workers, although Britain's weakness in apprenticeships persisted.[73] Labour did not reverse all the legal restrictions on unions, nor did it end labour market flexibility. The party certainly feared being perceived as in the pocket of the trade unions. Yet curbs on the right to strike were removed. Workers acquired new rights. The government condemned companies that disrespected their workforce. Ministers used the 'bully pulpit' to encourage a culture of partnership. Labour's institution-building was further influenced by Europeanisation. The European social model was incorporated within UK employment legislation and welfare provision, reflecting Labour's willingness to learn from continental European and Nordic experience. There was a concerted effort to build an 'Anglo-Social' welfare state.

On the face of it, Labour's strategy represented a break with the Thatcher/ Major era. For the previous thirty years, performance 'was characterised by a lack of resilience to external shocks and a higher level of macro-economic instability than other G7 economies: unemployment, inflation and real interest rates were higher than comparable economies, while per capita incomes were markedly lower'.[74] After 1997, macro-economic policy was reformulated. The tax and benefits system narrowed the gap in household living standards. Unemployment was no longer believed to be a price worth paying for economic failure. The modification of employment regulation curtailed the 'hire and fire' culture. Policy-making authority was devolved in Scotland, Wales and Northern Ireland. At Brown's behest, the UK became much more active in international economic institutions.[75]

As chancellor, Brown created a viable domestic policy framework. Where necessary, he was ruthless in removing politics from decision-making. Not only did the Bank of England have operational independence; transparent fiscal rules were devised to oversee spending. Rule one was over the course of the cycle, borrowing should be used for capital investment rather than current expenditure. That rule was more flexible than the European Stability and Growth Pact (SGP) which imposed a ceiling of 3 per cent of GDP. The second fiscal rule was that public debt should be stable and prudent. Brown inherited a deficit of 3.5 per cent of GDP from the Major government following the 1990s recession. He believed a smaller deficit would lead to lower long-term interest rates.[76] New Labour insisted radicalism did not always entail higher spending. The government was judged by its effectiveness rather than the cumulative level of public expenditure.[77] Blair and Brown developed a new economic paradigm, despite their continuing reluctance to intervene in markets. Previous Labour governments ran into difficulties within weeks of gaining office. Post-1997 economic policy learned from experience. For the first time in the party's history, Labour turned the economy to its advantage, the bedrock of three consecutive election victories.[78]

The new welfare orthodoxy? Progressive universalism

Although Labour revisited the 1940s' Beveridge settlement, the government sought to entrench 'progressive universalism' as its institutional legacy in social policy. Labour's welfare strategy is depicted as merely resorting to targeting and means-testing. In practice, the Blair and Brown governments redesigned policy fundamentally.[79] Universal provision was extended over pensioner benefits: the winter fuel allowance, television licences (for over-75s) and bus travel were distributed to all citizens of pensionable age. Adair Turner's Pension Commission recommended increasing the state pension. Every three- and four-year-old had fifteen hours of free childcare. Universal child benefit was retained. Statutory parental leave provision was established: paid maternity leave increased to six months initially and then nine months; paid paternity leave of two weeks was introduced; carers were given the right to flexibly work.[80]

The UK increasingly resembled the 'family-friendly' welfare states of the Nordic countries. Not all of Labour's ideas were borrowed from across the Atlantic. The policies underpinning welfarism moved away from the male bread-winner model towards the social investment state centred on children, gender equality and family stability.[81] Tax credits increased the support available to low- and middle-income households: families with incomes up to £58,000 received help. The welfare expert, Howard Glennerster, has referred to Labour's 'selective universalism'.

Elsewhere, there was certainly greater targeting. Poorer pensioners received pension credit. Families on low incomes were entitled to tax credits. For both poorer pensioners and families with children, there was the minimum-income guarantee. Sure Start was targeted initially at children under four living in the poorest neighbourhoods. Young people from low-income households still at school at the age of sixteen received the education maintenance allowance (EMA). Moreover, despite the language of universalism, there was an erosion of the contributory principle through national insurance (NI). Employment benefits such as job seekers' allowance (JSA) became less generous.[82] In Blair's final year in office, the importance of tackling social exclusion among the bottom 2 per cent was reiterated, so-called 'problem families' who did not benefit from the NMW and tax credits. The focus was on the interlinked problems of drugs, alcohol and substance misuse, worklessness and financial insecurity.[83] The analysis of longi-tudinal data and the work of leading social scientists, particularly Professor Leon Feinstein, led to programmes such as family-nurse partnerships (FNPs) providing support to expectant and new mothers in vulnerable households.[84]

Yet the ambiguity of progressive universalism epitomised New Labour's fundamental disagreement over welfare policy. When Labour came to office, Frank Field, former director of the Child Poverty Action Group (CPAG), was appointed minister of state at the Department for Social Security (DSS). Having published innumerable studies on the British welfare state, Field was asked by the prime minister to 'think the unthinkable'. Despite Field's intellectual clarity and eloquence, the appointment proved misguided. Field was a strong opponent of means-testing which he claimed eroded personal responsibility. He believed that national insurance (NI) should fund the social security system. Field was a harsh critic of Richard Titmuss, rebuking 'the Fabian school of hand-out socialism'.[85] Field believed the contributory emphasis of welfare policy in Northern Europe was morally superior as well as more efficient economically.

As such, the minister for welfare reform faced insuperable constraints. Har-riet Harman, ally of Gordon Brown, was appointed secretary of state at the DSS. Harman believed Field's ideas were ill advised and would almost certainly harm women who made lower NI contributions.[86] As chancellor of the exchequer, Brown believed he alone controlled New Labour's social policy.[87] He attacked

Field's plans as incoherent and unaffordable. When Alistair Darling, Harman's successor as secretary of state asked to see Field's proposals, 'the civil servants said: "There is nothing written down, Minister". Frank is good at analysis, but hopeless at practical solutions'.[88]

Estimates by the Treasury indicated restoring the contributory principle to the welfare state would cost £3 billion a year. Brown believed that means-testing was inevitable, given the poverty Labour inherited from the Thatcher era. Resources should go to those in greatest need. Ann Bowtell, DSS permanent secretary, was dismayed by the constant bickering between ministers observing that the politicians were 'having an argument in government that they should have had in opposition'.[89] It proved impractical to reconcile Field's ideas about contributory welfare with the Treasury's commitment to abolish poverty. The clash over ideas was lethal politically. A year into the new government, Harman and Field resigned after a row about single-parent benefit cuts. Brown character-istically closed down the debate about the welfare state that experts felt merited closer examination.

The vision of progressive universalism typically sought to reconcile New Labour's contradictory aspirations. The major priority was tackling family and pensioner poverty. For twenty years, UK poverty had dramatically risen. As the Number Ten Policy Unit revealed, one in five of all families (4.5 million) by 1997 had to survive on less than half the average income (£129 a week after housing costs), compared to one in ten in 1979. In the late 1970s, 8 per cent of children lived in a household surviving on less than half the average income. By the late 1990s, the figure was 22 per cent. The income of the poorest 10 per cent of families fell from £80 to £70 a week in real terms. Income inequality grew exponentially. Among these families, 54 per cent had no adult in work. Lone parents and those with disabilities and long-term sickness were particularly vul-nerable. Structural disadvantage was increasingly concentrated in geographical areas, particularly the inner-cities and seaside towns.[90]

New Labour created distinctive institutions to tackle the growth of poverty and inter-generational disadvantage including the New Deal modelled on Swed-ish workfare to support the under 25s back into work paid for by the £5 bil-lion windfall tax on the privatised utilities; the NMW, tax credits and reform of personal tax allowances to ensure the unemployed were better off in work; increasing the long-term earning power of the workforce through public invest-ment in training and skills; and improving school standards dramatically in disadvantaged neighbourhoods. Yet the overall weakness of the government's strategy became increasingly evident. It was not clear whether sufficient well-paid jobs were being created in the UK economy. Welfare to work might depress the wages of the low skilled. The gains of the NMW would be offset by the introduction of tax credits. The government's strategy on skills had insufficient clarity and focus. Britain lacked the co-ordinating labour market institutions of Northern Europe that ensured long-term investment in workers. Moreover, the decision to implement cuts in lone-parent benefits undermined the credibility of the Blair government's anti-poverty agenda. The area-based initiatives such as health and education 'action zones' were weakly grounded in evidence. Even if New Labour's policies were successfully implemented, only some of the rise in workless households was likely to be reversed. The growth of poverty since the Thatcher era would not be eliminated.[91]

The purpose of progressive universalism was to retain middle-class support for public expenditure, ensuring families on relatively high incomes were beneficiaries of government largesse. Labour resisted the temptation to redistribute middle-class benefits, particularly child benefit. In the early years of the Blair and Brown governments, the strategy proved broadly successful. Ministers created institutions that improved the life chances of disadvantaged households without suffering adverse electoral consequences. Yet within five years, political tensions were emerging. Although Labour emphasised the merits of lower taxes, the burden of taxation began to rise for those on median incomes in Southern England. More fundamentally, progressive universalism compensated low-income households for systemic labour market failure instead of reforming employment markets to strengthen egalitarianism. Aside from the minimum wage, little was done to restructure the service economy away from its trajectory of low skills, low productivity and low wages.

Nonetheless, the claim that New Labour's welfare policy acquiesced to neo-liberalism is misleading. Neo-liberalism entailed a diminishing role for national government, the reassertion of market forces and a focus on unleashing 'possessive individualism'.[92] After 1997, there was a material shift in which the state was deliberately expanded to protect citizens from the negative consequences of unfettered markets. Even so, during this period private sector providers became much more involved in public service 'quasi-markets'. Ministers believed government must be the funder, not necessarily the provider of public services. The fundamental weakness of Labour's quasi-market strategy in public services is illustrated in distinctive areas, especially social housing and childcare provision.

Labour's record in housing is particularly striking. After 1997, there was a major increase in housing benefit payments so that citizens could live in private rented accommodation, reflecting the shortage of capacity in social housing following the selling-off of council houses at the behest of Thatcher's 'right to buy' programme. After initially falling, spending on housing benefit grew to deal with the systemic problems of the UK housing market as Figure 6.1 illustrates.

There was comparatively little investment to increase the supply of social housing, despite Labour's historic commitment to council homes. Council housing covered 30 per cent of dwellings at its peak. The Decent Homes Standard upgraded the quality of 1 million homes between 1997 and 2010, improving conditions for tenants at a cost of £22 billion.[93] Yet a strategy paper by the Prime Minister's Policy Unit warned the rate of new building was inadequate: 'Current plans for about 1.1 million homes over the next 12 years won't be enough (and are already failing behind)' while, 'investment in new social housing remains very low'.[94] The government was wary of reforming planning legislation. There

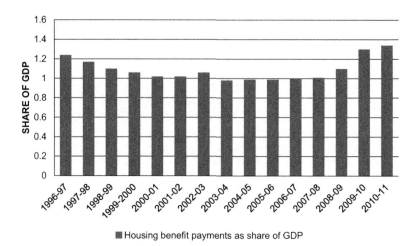

FIGURE 6.1 Housing benefit payments 1997–2010 as share of GDP

was no attempt to restore the ability of local authorities to borrow. Despite the rhetoric of localism, the Blair government's residual trust in local government was muted. New Labour was slow to recognise that since the early 1980s, housing costs made a greater contribution to UK inequality than disparities in labour market earnings. Poorer households had to pay a higher proportion of their disposable income towards housing than the richest, while living in less-attractive dwellings and neighbourhoods.[95] Meanwhile, rents in private accommodation continued to outstrip the growth of real incomes.[96] According to the Institute for Fiscal Studies (IFS), the fastest growth in costs occurred among low-income households with children as Figure 6.2 highlights.

The catastrophe of UK housing policy is not that the Labour governments pulled back and spending was slashed after 1997. As Andrew Hindmoor illustrates, fewer dwellings were built, yet the state actually spent *more* on subsidising housing for those on low incomes living in private rented accommodation. Local authorities lacked the capacity and resources to build homes for 'social rent'. The declining investment in social housing and the reliance on the private rental market appears to have exacerbated endemic problems, notably overcrowding and homelessness. Housing inequalities markedly increased in the 1980s. New Labour was unable to reverse them. The affluent continued to enjoy access to housing through private ownership, while the situation of the poorest failed to improve.[97] The consequence was that as households grew older, their chances of leaving private rented accommodation was falling across the generations (see Figure 6.3).

The IFS underlined that while expenditure on housing benefit more than doubled since the late 1990s, the effect was to merely push up rents, transferring wealth to private landlords. New Labour was slow to confront the depth

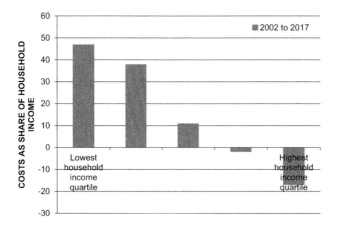

FIGURE 6.2 Growth in housing costs by household income quintile 2002–17

of the housing crisis and its contribution to a more unequal society. The refusal to intervene in housing supply was the consequence of unwarranted faith in public subsidy and quasi-markets. The undersupply of social housing and barriers to home ownership risked creating a lost generation reliant on the dysfunctional private sector market and long-term government support, as Figure 6.3 highlights. New Labour's strategy bequeathed a failed institutional legacy. The burdens are set to increase in the near future as younger generations reach pensionable age, creating a population more dependent on the state in the long-term for housing – a paradoxical consequence of embracing quasi-market solutions.

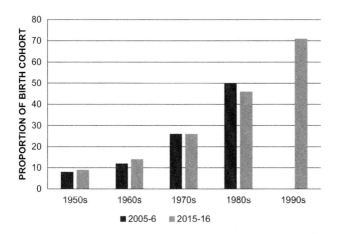

FIGURE 6.3 Households in private renting by birth decade in the UK 1950s–1990s

Labour ministers similarly intervened inadequately in childcare and the early years' sector. The New Labour governments sought to improve availability and affordability, particularly for lone parents and second earners. In fairness, the legacy inherited from previous governments was threadbare. The Conservative manifesto in 1997 hardly mentioned intervention in childhood or the role of government action to support families. In office, Labour's aim was to *reduce the financial pressures* on parents while *strengthening the capabilities of families*.[98] Once again, the Blair administrations embraced a quasi-market strategy where government did not invest in childcare supply directly but stimulated the market of private and voluntary providers through demand-side funding.[99] The approach was affirmed in the National Childcare Strategy (1998) and the Ten Year Strategy for Children (2004). The 2002 Childcare Review undertaken by the Prime Minister's Strategy Unit similarly concluded that subsidising the voluntary and private sector rather than expanding statutory provision was more economically efficient.[100]

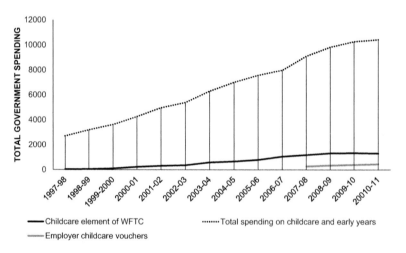

FIGURE 6.4 Spending on the childcare element of WFTC, employer childcare vouchers and total expenditure on childcare and early years in England 1997–2010, £m

As a consequence, the government focused on devising fiscal mechanisms, subsidising working parents through tax credits. Funding was available through the childcare element of the Working Families Tax Credit (WFTC) where low-income parents could claim up to 80 per cent of childcare costs, alongside vouchers for those on higher incomes, reducing tax by up to £1,100 a year.[101] The aim was to promote parental choice, giving flexibility to use either nurseries or childminders. The funding model illustrated in Figure 6.4 affirmed the Treasury's view that intervention was only justified to tackle market failure. The Treasury believed the primary goal was to encourage women to enter the labour market.[102] The 2006 Children's Act stipulated that local authorities should directly provide childcare only where the private or voluntary sector refused to do so.[103]

The result was that the increase in childcare supply after 1997 was modest. Sure Start and subsidies for neighbourhood nurseries were targeted at the most disadvantaged neighbourhoods where the majority of underprivileged children did not actually live. The most deprived households were least likely to access childcare, particularly beneficial for children under five.[104] Childcare was integrated poorly with schools and complex for parents to navigate. Many providers remained precarious financially and regularly went out of business.[105]

Overall, the verdict is that New Labour was reluctant for the state to assume responsibility for tackling inadequate supply and dysfunctional policies in housing and childcare.[106] Its institutional legacy was undermined as a consequence. The modernised social democratic agenda meant 'empowering' and subsidising citizens in markets through demand-led funding. The Blair administration's policies inverted the relationship between states and markets postulated by British post-war social democracy. Ministers were committed to the principle that government should not necessarily be the *sole* provider. Blair's programme acceded to path dependency in the welfare state, entrenching the culture of voluntary action and fiscal subsidy instead of forging a role for the British state comparable to Northern European countries. The initiatives neglected the supply-side of public policy, especially the quality, scope and availability of services. Moreover, too few tangible neighbourhood institutions were created that voters associated with the New Labour governments. The inherent difficulty with government action through the market is that citizens rarely link discernible benefits to the exercise of power by the state.[107] The only exception was Sure Start centres, cut dramatically during the Coalition's austerity programme after 2010. The Blair administration's determination to limit government's role as a provider was a matter of conviction, despite the prime minister's claim that in policy-making 'what matters is what works'.

Liberalisation and social norms: making Britain a more civilised society?

A further institutional legacy of New Labour was the liberalisation of British society. Of course, attitudes in Britain were already evolving in the 1980s and 1990s. Traditional moral conventions were eroding. Blair's governments then sought to bolster Britain's advance into a more civilised and tolerant country, echoing the rhetoric of Roy Jenkins in the 1960s. There was the equalisation of the age of consent for gay sex. Draconian legislation known as Section 28 preventing local authorities from 'promoting' homosexuality was scrapped. Gay citizens were allowed to openly serve in the armed forces. There was the concerted effort to tackle racial discrimination. Shortly after the 1997 election, the

Labour government established an official inquiry into the murder of the black teenager, Stephen Lawrence, on the streets of Eltham in South-East London. The report of the Macpherson Inquiry introduced the concept of institutional racism into UK law. For the first time in the modern state's history, institutions were held accountable for their actions in relation to race equality.

In 2000, the government established a new equality body, the Disability Rights Commission (DRC) to work alongside the Equal Opportunities Commission (EOC) and the Commission for Racial Equality (CRE). The Equality and Human Rights Commission (EHRC) was subsequently created in 2006 to advance equality and eradicate discrimination on grounds of gender, race, disability, sexuality, transgender status, religion/belief and age. Public sector agencies were subject to a 'positive duty' to end discrimination and the exclusion of protected groups while promoting equality.[108]

Controversially, the laws governing gambling and casinos were deregulated in the name of personal freedom and liberal modernisation. The 2005 Act encouraged gambling as a leisure activity, intending to promote the interests of the gambling industry as the driver of growth and urban regeneration.[109] The number of casinos across Britain grew by more than 40 per cent. Even drugs policy was liberalised. In the early 2000s, cannabis was reclassified from a class B to a class C drug with new guidance issued to police forces recommending only 'street warnings' for possession, despite the rhetoric of the war on drugs.[110] The licencing regime for selling alcohol in England enshrined in the 2003 Act was deregulated. The Blair government's infamous Millennium Dome in Greenwich, East London, was the symbol of New Labour's politics of pleasurable freedom – a spectacle it hoped would become 'the envy of the world'.[111]

The reforms chimed with the Blair government's emphasis on the liberalisation of society, stripping away red tape, advancing 'business-friendly' policies while promoting a 'vibrant' youth culture by permitting the expansion of the '24/7' society.[112] More edifying perhaps was the legislation passed in 2000 extending the 'right to roam' in the English countryside – a measure that alongside the ban on fox hunting encountered significant opposition from rural communities. All in all, Labour equated the rejuvenation of Britain with the deregulation of controls on lifestyles and moral norms. New Labour's policies meant Blair's interest in communitarian ideas emphasising civic duty and responsibility became noticeably less prominent.

Enhancing gender equality: the most feminist government in history?

The increasing presence of women in Parliament and the core executive meant gender issues were better represented on the agenda of policy and politics.[113] In 1997, 120 women were elected to the House of Commons of whom 101 were Labour, an all-time record. Feminist scholars claim despite some dubious initiatives, including the decision to impose punitive benefit sanctions on single mothers, Labour's policies institutionalised equality in British society.[114] After 1997, 'bodies and institutions devoted to women's concerns were more visible than ever before'.[115] When Patricia Hewitt announced the expansion of statutory maternity and paternity leave, 'for the first time, we had an avowed feminist cabinet minister pushing an explicitly feminist agenda and winning powerful allies to her cause'.[116] Labour Minister Tessa Jowell proclaimed the Blair governments to be the most feminist in history.

Women's rights were certainly strengthened by legislation to outlaw gender discrimination and expand publicly funded childcare while enhancing labour market protection. New Labour's budgets increased child benefit and the child-care element of the Working Families Tax Credit (WFTC). In 2004, the government announced 'wrap-around' childcare from 8am to 6pm for all children of primary-school age, elevated as the new frontier of the welfare state. Women were major beneficiaries of the NMW, union recognition legislation and provisions for paid parental leave.[117] The introduction of two weeks of paid paternity leave for men and the right to request flexible working made it clear that parental responsibility was not only women's concern. The Women and Work Commission was established to examine the structural causes of discrimination and the gender pay gap. Legislation was introduced to strengthen legal penalties against domestic violence, creating specialist domestic violence courts to increase the rate of prosecution.

Furthermore, Labour acknowledged families were changing structurally. Women should be independent earners. The Blair governments broke with the male breadwinner model at the heart of the Beveridge reforms, pursuing a 'dual earner' strategy that strengthened access to employment.[118] The measures advanced through the pragmatic partnership between modernisers alongside liberal and socialist feminists on the Left of British politics.[119] There was explicit recognition of public responsibility for the care of children which future governments struggled to reverse.

Nevertheless, the presence of women in political institutions does not inevitably lead to the implementation of equality policies.[120] The advance of gender equality was hindered by the decision not to appoint a paid minister for women of cabinet rank in 1997.[121] Labour's motives in advancing feminisation were largely instrumental, pursuing the electoral support of women in narrowing the voting gap. Conservative assumptions about gender still prevailed. New Labour's approach emphasised the importance of paid work, rather than acknowledging the centrality of unpaid household labour. The Blair administrations' stance on gender equality focused on employment participation at the expense of wider public policy concerns with the economy of care and domestic labour.[122]

Reordering the world? Foreign affairs and Iraq

New Labour's institution-building in foreign policy mirrored its activism in domestic policy. Blair's avowed purpose was to reconfigure the UK's foreign

affairs strategy and institutions. The prime minister believed Britain must identify a coherent geopolitical vocation in an era defined by the Cold War's end
and the 'brave new world' of globalisation. New Labour's view of Britain's role
was consistent intellectually, even if the Blair governments became profoundly
unpopular in the wake of the decision to take part in military action against
Iraq.[123] The wars in Afghanistan and Iraq are perceived as the most damaging
legacy of Blair's decade in power. The prime minister's policy inflicted massive
collateral damage on his administration, to say nothing of the 179 British service
personnel who died in combat, alongside hundreds of thousands of Iraqi civilians
killed in the conflict.

What was destructive for the Blair governments were the circumstances in
which Britain went to war. The absence of agreement in the international community about dealing with Iraq's malevolent dictator, Saddam Hussein, meant
there was no official United Nations (UN) authorisation for the American/UK
invasion. Iraq was a sovereign state. Legal experts contended the unilateral action
of Bush and Blair was illegal, an affront to international law. The president of
France, Jacques Chirac, and the German chancellor, Gerhard Schroder, became
vociferous opponents. Blair overestimated his capacity to persuade British voters
and the international community of the invasion's moral legitimacy. It remains
the case that Iraq was a US-driven undertaking that would have gone ahead with
or without British support. Yet Blair's fatal error was to commit the UK to participate in an American mission over which it had little direct control.

New Labour's foreign policy

After 1997, Blair sought to refashion Britain's global strategy, ending British
ambivalence about Europe while strengthening the Atlantic alliance. That drove
the prime minister to take bold, even reckless decisions. Blair's evangelical support for military intervention and the removal of Saddam was an audacious
stance for any Labour leader. It set Blair apart from all his predecessors, given the
fervour with which the government threw itself behind the American action.
Attlee and Bevin set a distinctly jingoistic tone in the 1940s. They remained
ardent Atlanticists, presiding over the development of the 'warfare state'. Yet
post-war leaders were pursuing Britain's national interest following the outbreak
of the Cold War, alongside the threat posed by Soviet Communism to Western
democracy. There were institutional linkages on security, foreign policy, defence
and trade which ensured post-war prime ministers maintained close ties with
Washington.[124]

New Labour and Blair were different. Having had no first-hand experience
of war, Blair had remarkable confidence in the effectiveness of military intervention following the engagement of UK armed forces in Sierra Leone and Kosovo.
The prime minister was a supporter of his generals, especially Sir Charles Guth-
rie and General Sir Mike Jackson. He felt the British military were able to get
things done, while Saddam posed an immediate threat to Western interests. Blair

recounted: 'Personally I have little doubt that at some point we would have to have dealt with him'.[125] It must be said Blair was 'hawkish' on Iraq before George Bush II became president of the United States. Iraq invaded Kuwait in 1990 and then continuously flouted the sanctions regime. The prime minister ominously warned in 1998: 'The failure or success of diplomacy [in Iraq] rests on Saddam'.

The doctrine of liberal internationalism

Blair's foreign policy was elaborated in the emerging doctrine of liberal internationalism, outlined in his infamous 1999 Chicago lecture. The prime minister insisted states had to uphold global ethics instead of defending sovereign territory and Westphalian self-interest. Globalisation broke down conventional borders, making national jurisdiction less important than 'shared values'. Blair proclaimed:

> We are all internationalists now, whether we like it or not. . . . We cannot refuse to participate in world markets if we want to prosper. We cannot ignore new political ideas in other countries if we wish to innovate. We cannot turn our backs on conflicts and the violation of human rights within other countries if we still want to be secure.[126]

There were striking similarities with the UN's 'Responsibility to Protect' doctrine. The prime minister's vision of the world was high minded, an echo of nineteenth-century Gladstonian liberalism extolling the Manichean view of good against evil. Blair was stirred by his own passionately held moral beliefs. The pivotal issue in foreign policy was 'to identify the circumstances in which we should get actively involved in the conflicts of others'. The Chicago speech set five tests of the 'just war':

> First, are we sure of our case . . . ? Second, have we exhausted all diplomatic options . . . ? Third, on the basis of a practical assessment of the situation, are there military operations we can sensibly and prudently undertake? Fourth, are we prepared for the long-term . . . ? And finally, do we have national interests involved?[127]

Behind the enlightened liberal rhetoric, the prime minister was accused of offering an apologia for the new imperialism. In the aftermath of the violence on 11th September 2001, Blair insisted:

> Out of the shadow of this evil, should emerge lasting good: destruction of the machinery of terrorism wherever it is found, hope amongst all nations of a new beginning where we seek to resolve differences in a calm and ordered way; greater understanding between nations and between faiths; and above all, justice and prosperity for the poor and the dispossessed.[128]

Although originating on the Left, Robin Cook who became foreign secretary in 1997 bolstered Blair's vision of the ethical dimension in foreign policy. Cook agreed Britain should eschew Palmerston's dictum of national interests, focusing instead on advancing 'British values' of justice and compassion abroad, a vision compatible with socialist internationalism. The beneficiaries of Blair's ethical policy should be 'the starving, the wretched, the dispossessed, the ignorant, those living in want and squalor from the deserts of North Africa to the slums of Gaza, to the mountain ranges of Afghanistan: they too are our cause'.[129] The incoming government established the Department for International Development (DFID) with an expanded budget, co-ordinating efforts to 'promote sustainable development and eradicate world poverty'.[130]

Yet Blair's priority was ultimately to legitimise military force. The prime minister believed if Western allies did not decisively act, they would be blamed for failing to rid the world of its most evil dictator. He averred:

> Saddam's regime is – now the Taliban have fallen – probably the most brutal, oppressive and dictatorial in the world, and its principal victims are the Iraqi people. . . . It would be odd for anyone on the Left to shed tears at his departure.[131]

The post-1997 governments 'pursued some traditional Labour aims, for example on aid and development, but have been prepared, as with Kosovo and Afghanistan to take military action to uphold our values'. Blair's thinking was shaped by foreign policy intellectuals, including Professor Lawrence Freedman of King's College, London, and the diplomat Robert Cooper. Freedman outlined an emerging doctrine of 'just wars', although both experts were circumspect about military intervention. Nonetheless, the vision of an ethical foreign policy was testimony to the seriousness with which New Labour approached ideas.

Blair was the first Labour prime minister elected after the end of the Cold War. The fall of the iron curtain compelled him to reassess the nature of the geopolitical threats confronting Britain. Blair believed the greatest risk to international security was the separation of the United States from its European allies, acting as world hegemon in the aftermath of the 9/11 attacks. The prime minister's goal was to 'prevent precipitate military action by the US, which he considered would undermine the success of the coalition which had been established for action against international terrorism'.[132] Blair's strategy was initially effective in persuading Bush to take the UN route. The negotiation of resolution 1441 in September 2002 gave Saddam's regime 'a final opportunity to comply with its disarmament obligations or face serious consequences'.[133] The prime minister had to deal with an inexperienced president under the influence of dogmatic neo-conservatives – notably Dick Cheney and Donald Rumsfeld. In the aftermath of 9/11, Bush naively spoke of an 'axis of evil' linking Iraq, North Korea and Iran, claiming these states posed a security threat to the West. For reasons never made explicit, Bush recommended military intervention only in Iraq.[134]

Many diplomats expected Clinton's vice president, Al Gore, to win the presidency in 2000. If Gore had won, it is likely that American foreign policy would have taken a different turn, even in the aftermath of 9/11. Whitehall was not well prepared for the Bush victory. Blair's team had to scramble to get to know their counterparts in Bush's team. The prime minister's chief of staff, Jonathan Powell, had contacts among the Republicans as the former political secretary in the British Embassy. Blair then assiduously worked to keep the Bush administration engaged with the international community, as Bush's predecessor, Bill Clinton, advised. The prime minister acknowledged even before 9/11: 'We now have a huge challenge in finding the common ground between the EU and the US'.[135] In acting as the bridge between Europe and America, Britain could preserve its influence in Washington while corralling its European allies towards a common position on international security.

The road to war in Iraq

In his momentous address to the House of Commons on 13th March 2003, Blair eloquently set out the arguments for military action. He claimed that as far back as April 1991, Saddam's regime had been given fifteen days to declare the existence of weapons of mass destruction to UN inspectors. Even then, the Iraqi government refused to comply, neglecting to disclose its capabilities. In August 1995, Saddam's brother-in-law, Hussein Kamal, defected to Jordan, telling the authorities Iraq was developing the WMD programme. Then, in 1996, Jordan intercepted components being transported into Iraq. In September 1997, UN weapons inspectors found a site in Iraq where VX nerve agent production equipment was stored. Blair claimed that once again, Saddam refused to admit the UN team of inspectors.

The prime minister believed materials never accounted for included 10,000 litres of anthrax, up to 6,500 chemical munitions, more than 80 tonnes of mustard gas, biological poisons including Sarin and botulinum toxin, as well as the remnants of the scud missile programme deployed against Israel in the first Gulf War.[136] On 7th March 2003, the UN weapons inspectors published a document that declared: 'Based on all the available evidence, the strong presumption is that about 10,000 litres of anthrax was not destroyed and may still exist'. In Parliament, Blair acknowledged the link between WMD in Iraq and international terrorism was at best 'loose'. In a note to President Bush, Blair stated: 'Any link to September 11th and AQ [Al Qaeda] is at best very tenuous'.[137] He also insisted the post-war reconstruction of Iraq ought to take place 'under full UN authorisation', a stance later undermined by the Bush administration.

The fundamental difficulty for Blair was that in the run up to war, the bridge between Europe and America collapsed. The argument for war stretched the prime minister's persuasive rhetorical powers to breaking point, his case never compelling enough to sustain a broad international alliance of European and American powers. Blair insisted only the threat of force would compel Iraq to follow the international authorities. Yet other countries, chiefly France, called on Saddam to disarm without military action. President Chirac declared France would veto *any* second UN resolution mandating military intervention. Even Clinton was sceptical about the rationale for any ground invasion, as he was over Kosovo. Clinton told the Labour Party conference in the autumn of 2002 that while Saddam's regime posed a threat to the Iraqi people, Middle East states and the entire world: 'Britain and the United States made real progress with our international allies through the UN with the inspection programme in the 1990s'.[138] Clinton stressed the importance of a UN resolution calling for the resumption of inspections, insisting military action should always be the last resort. He advocated regime change by non-military means. Other political allies of Blair, including Peter Mandelson, were circumspect about whether there was a compelling case for war.[139]

Bush and Blair felt the inspectors were given enough time. In any case, 'US willingness to act through the UN was limited'.[140] Saddam's regime was running out of excuses. Iraq was a test of whether the international community took seriously global threats. The risk was that the UN would become a 'talking shop', ridiculed by dictators and demagogues. The military planners in the Pentagon told the White House that a full-scale ground invasion should be underway by early spring. Otherwise conditions in the Iraqi desert would become impossible. The United States was now engaged in a rush to war, with or without UN support.

Initially, the advice provided by the British attorney general Peter Goldsmith was that explicit UN authorisation was necessary for war to be legal.[141] Realising the prime minister was with the US president in whatever circumstances, committing the government to military action, Goldsmith altered his legal submission.[142] Yet it was the absence of international support that encouraged Blair's government to make the case for war in a manner that exposed ministers to charges of duplicity. The prime minister neglected to present a balanced assessment of Iraq's capabilities. Military action was not 'a last resort', since diplomatic efforts were by no means exhausted.[143] The Chilcot report revealed three British combat brigades had been deployed in January 2003 yet 'there was no collective discussion of the decision by senior Ministers'.[144]

The case for war relied on intelligence material shown to be inaccurate. The Labour Party's historic relationship with the intelligence services was mutually suspicious. After all, Harold Wilson correctly believed that his telephone was bugged by MI5. Trade union leaders were placed under surveillance by the intelligence agencies in the 1960s and 1970s. Yet security threats meant MI5 had grown from 1,800 staff in 2001 to 4,000 by the time Blair left office, focused on countering Islamist extremism; John Scarlett and Richard Dearlove, key figures in the intelligence agencies, were among the prime minister's favourite officials.[145]

It soon became clear that Saddam's regime was incapable of using nuclear or chemical WMD in a first strike against Western targets, as the British government's dossier initially claimed. The weapons inspectors led by a Swede, Dr Hans Blitz, believed the strategy of containment was effective. At the Iraq Inquiry

PHOTO 6.1 British troops in Northern Kuwait, preparing for possible action against Iraq.

Source: Photo by Cpl Paul Jarvis/Mod/Getty Images.

hearings, Blair confirmed: 'Our intelligence was clear that Saddam had reconstituted his WMD programme'.[146] Yet no concrete evidence was revealed. The Baathist regime was crippled after years of sanctions. In his resignation statement as foreign secretary, Robin Cook concurred: 'Iraq probably has no weapons of mass destruction in the commonly understood sense of the term – namely a credible device capable of being delivered against a strategic city target'.[147] The intelligence failings were monumental. Nor did Saddam's refusal to follow Resolution 687 justify full-scale invasion. The view that the Iraqi government was the sponsor of terrorist organisations, notably Al Qaeda who carried out the 9/11 atrocities, was a fiction. Saddam's regime was Arab nationalist not Islamicist, carrying out purges against Shia Muslims. The Joint Intelligence Committee (JIC) reported in November 2001 that Saddam 'refused to permit any Al Qaeda presence in Iraq'.[148] There was 'no credible evidence of covert transfers of WMD-related technology and expertise to terrorist groups'.

Having gone to war on a pretext that many found illegitimate, his American allies' failure to plan for post-war reconstruction compounded Blair's political misjudgement. There were months of carnage and bloodshed in the provinces surrounding Baghdad and Basra. Civil war erupted between the Sunni and Shia spilling over into Syria, Iran and the Middle East. The State Department's knowledge of rebuilding war-torn states relied on its experience in Germany during the 1940s. As Foreign Office diplomats told Blair, Iraq was a combustible

combination of religious and ethnic rivalries.[149] It would take decades to construct a viable liberal democracy. The British government entered into military action without a plausible strategy for post-conflict peace-building and
reconstruction.

Why did Britain go to war: Blair as master of deception?

The question of why Britain and Blair went to war in the face of concerted
domestic and international opposition is certain to perplex historians for generations. The assertion that the British prime minister was Bush's 'poodle' scarcely
stands up to scrutiny. Blair owed little to the Bush presidency. Initially the president's entourage viewed him with suspicion, even disdain.[150] During the 2000
campaign, New Labour not surprisingly had given its covert support to the Democratic Party candidate, Al Gore. Blair was concerned his opposition counterpart,
the Conservative leader Iain Duncan-Smith, would forge ties with Bush's team.

Among the more persuasive explanations is that 'bad ideas caused Britain's
war in Iraq, ideas that were dogmatically held'.[151] This underlines the point that
New Labour continued to take ideas seriously. Blair's foreign policy focused on
how to achieve security in a more volatile and unstable world. They turned the
prime minister from being a calculating pragmatist into a high-minded moral-
ist and 'warlike idealist', willing to risk his premiership in ousting Saddam from
power. The international relations scholar, Patrick Porter, highlights the main
ideas at the core of Labour's security and foreign policy. The first was the necessity of 'regime change', the belief that countries posing a threat to the liberal
international order should be dismantled pre-emptively to uphold the rule of
law. The second idea concerned the need for action to contain 'rogue states',
countries ruled by despotic dictators regarded as unpredictable and aggressive.
The third 'warlike' idea was the so-called blood price fallacy, centred on the
claim Britain would become more influential in Washington if the UK was
willing to commit resources in conflict zones. According to Blair's bridge metaphor, the willingness to decisively act in international security would give the
UK geopolitical leverage *both* in the EU and the United States. As such, Porter
concluded, Blair's military intervention was 'an intellectual war'.[152]

The Labour government's stance in Iraq echoes Peter Clarke's distinction
between mechanical and moral reform. The prime minister had supreme confidence in his government's capacity to intervene alongside the United States to
remove Saddam and reorganise the society and polity of Iraq. This faith demonstrated Blair's adherence to the mechanical concept of top-down political and
social change. Yet Iraq also underlined Blair's credentials as a moral reformer, an
advocate of liberal internationalism seeking to instil 'moral change, a change of
heart, a new consciousness' in the global political community.[153] The difficulty
was that post-war reconstruction proved impossible since mechanical reform
could not override the resistance of large swathes of Iraqi society to occupation.
Saddam's Arab Socialist *Ba'ath party* was naively dismantled, driving thousands of

dissident military and civil service personnel underground to prolong the insurgency against coalition forces. In the meantime, his moral reform rhetoric meant Blair often sounded dogmatic and didactic.

The personal price Blair paid for his mistakes was incalculable. Although opinion shifted temporarily in favour of war as British troops entered battle, Blair's standing as prime minister dramatically declined after the summer of 2003, hardly recovering by the 2005 election. The belief that the prime minister would be celebrated as a war hero was mistaken.[154] A confidential memorandum by Blair's polling strategist, Mark Penn, revealed that in the aftermath of the invasion, Labour lost around a quarter of its voters. 'The main action in the electoral landscape' was 'leakage from Labour to the Liberal Democrats. . . . What is making this swing group question its allegiance to Labour is that they perceive Blair and Labour as not focused on the issues they care about – they view Iraq and Blair's foreign policy generally as distracting him from the real issues they elected him and Labour to focus on'.

Women voters believed 'that Iraq was wrong and that the case for it was at least faulty or disingenuous'.[155] Philip Gould's focus groups revealed a mood that was 'deeply, deeply negative. All respondents claimed, and most emphatically, that the country was going in the wrong direction. The hostility within the groups to the government was palpable. People veered between anger and despair throughout the evening's conversations'.[156] Blair was perceived as 'the master of deception. . . . Iraq has introduced a strong sense that TB has his own self-serving agenda at odds with ordinary British people; that he misled the nation and cannot be believed'. Labour then lost two by-elections at Brent East in September 2003 and Leicester South in July 2004 on swings of 30 per cent to the Liberal Democrats. The prime minister's ratings were in free fall. Iraq inflicted inestimable damage on Blair's standing and his party's reputation. Of greatest concern was the prime minister's dismissal of warnings from the JIC that the threat from Al Qaeda 'will be heightened by military action against Iraq'.[157]

In these circumstances, it proved almost impossible to move Britain closer to Europe. Shortly after becoming prime minister, Blair implored he sought to end Britain's role as a 'semi-detached member-state'. In 1998, he told European leaders in the German border town of Aachen: 'I want to end the uncertainty, the lack of confidence, the Europhobia'. Yet the prime minister's stance in Iraq made it less likely he would shape a 'new domestic consensus' on Europe.[158] Blair had even less political capital to make the pro-European case.[159] What is more, New Labour was haunted by fear of tabloid newspapers, particularly the *Sun*. Its proprietor, Rupert Murdoch, was an embittered opponent of the EU. In the 1997 election, Blair signed an article for the *Sun* titled 'Why I Love the Pound', in which he declared: 'Labour will have no truck with a European super-state. We will fight for British interests and to keep our independence every step of the way'. Labour's leader insisted: 'I am a British patriot'.

One of Blair's advisers concluded: 'Alastair Campbell is anti-British entry to the single currency because of his fear of *The Sun*. . . . Tony is too impressed by

Murdoch'.[160] Blair and his followers saw Britain as a world power rather than a medium-sized European country. The leadership ignored the argument that full EU engagement would aid the pursuit of domestic social democratic policies, taxing wealthy corporations and reforming the British model of capitalism. Murdoch's newspapers supported the government over Iraq, placing Blair in his political debt, making it harder to push the case for European co-operation. When the first draft of the EU constitutional treaty was published in 2003, ministers 'publicly rubbished the first Treaty articles in a way that delighted the Eurosceptic press'. Yet this approach, while encouraging favourable headlines, weakened the UK's long-term influence and negotiating position. The prime minister's European adviser, Sir Stephen Wall, feared that:

> The French will try very hard over the coming months to get those of our partners who have sided with us [over Iraq] back into their and the German camp on the basis that *they* represent good Europeans and that we are basically the same inter-governmentalist, free-trade-area-only Brits that they know and hate.[161]

Another of the prime minister's aides complained:

> We desperately need to find a means of changing the psychology of the European debate here [in the UK]. . . . Increasingly in the Party, Europe is seen as a problem and we are running scared of the Tories and the anti-European press. The pro-European cause is seen as in retreat before the forces of anti-Europeanism. Our posture has become wholly defensive.[162]

Blair was prepared to make the case persuasively for Europe while touring other capitals but less willing to do so among British voters. Over Iraq, he confirmed the worst fears of the French political class by siding with the United States against Western Europe. This was not forgotten easily in Paris and Berlin.

On becoming prime minister, Gordon Brown was even more ambivalent about Britain's EU vocation. In a climate shaped by anxieties about terrorism and the alleged refusal of Muslim communities to seamlessly integrate into national life, Brown obsessed over the debate about 'Britishness', the question of how 'national identity is defined by values we share in common'.[163] Brown spoke of Britain as a unique country that 'can lay claim to the idea of liberty'. The 'golden thread' running through British history Brown believed was freedom, 'a strong sense of duty and responsibility', kept alive by those who 'chose solidarity in preference to selfishness'. He told a previous party conference:

> I believe that Britain – this island of nations with a tradition of democracy deeper than any other, a history of scientific invention longer than any other, a foundation of hard work, enterprise, civic duty and fair play is stronger than any other.[164]

Britain served as a beacon to the world. Not surprisingly, Brown's speeches on Britishness hardly mentioned Europe.[165] He believed the UK remained 'an awkward partner'. Despite two-thirds of the electorate voting to join in 1975, voters were never committed to Europe emotionally. Brown's exceptionalism led him to claim Britain would 'lead the next stage of Europe's development', implying the UK was superior to other member-states. Outside the Euro, Britain was 'an increasingly successful leader of the global economy'. The UK would succeed in the future 'because of our inherently British values and qualities'.[166] Britain was no longer 'the sick man of Europe'. It was the European continent that risked economic stagnation. In 2007, Brown flew to Portugal to sign the Lisbon Treaty but deliberately arrived late to avoid attending the ceremony with other European leaders. Through his actions, Brown revived the mind-set and attitudes of incipient nationalism on the Left that prevailed in the 1940s.[167]

Conclusion: institutional legacies

This chapter demonstrated that the capacity to forge effective institutions is decisive for British progressive administrations. Institutions entrench the values of social democratic movements, as the NHS symbolised the reforming zeal of the Attlee era. Institutions ultimately effect change in the economy and society, reshaping prevailing norms and beliefs. Often dismissed as overly technocratic, social democrats emphasise constructing institutions that instil and embody the public good. Moreover, institutions enduring beyond the lifetime of governments radiate political power and influence. They entrench the reform of economic and social policy as Lloyd George achieved in 1906–12 and Attlee in 1945–51.

The Blair and Brown administrations adopted what political scientists term the 'new institutionalism'. They created plural networks of public and private sector organisations to deliver policies, a compelling alternative to the post-1945 hierarchical state and the neo-liberal reforms of the Thatcher era.[168] New Labour believed public choice reforms had created a fragmented arena of governance that depleted the capacity to enact policies. The post-1997 governments fashioned co-ordinating institutions in domestic and foreign affairs, underpinned by the animating idea of interdependence in economic and social policy: social justice requires a productive and efficient economy, while economic success is unobtainable without the commitment to social cohesion.

Yet New Labour's reticence about government's role following the ideological rout of the 1980s undermined its institution-building efforts, exposing the limitations of its radicalism. As one of the prime minister's advisers admitted, Blair and Brown lacked 'a clearly articulated philosophy of how government should work of the kind that the Conservatives successfully expounded' in the 1980s.[169] Labour believed governments could constructively intervene in social policy, but remained circumspect about the state's role in the economy. The Blair administration pursued unprecedented welfare activism, affirming the role of national government in tackling structural disadvantage. Even then, the public sector monopoly in the structure of provision was abandoned. As a consequence, problems in the delivery of public policies soon emerged.

The first difficulty was incoherence. Ministers confusingly veered between using incentives that encouraged the private and public sector to fulfil government's objectives, while imposing the top-down reforms of 'the all-knowing Fabian state'.[170] This perplexing strategy blunted New Labour's radicalism. Second, Labour's approach to institutions proved to be naive. In the first term, ministers indulged in an orgy of reform fetishism: institutions were reorganised constantly. Public bodies were created without dismantling the old ones. The NHS became a complex mosaic of arm's-length public agencies. It was impossible to know how they fitted together and who was in charge.[171] The 2013 inquiry into failings at the Mid–Staffordshire NHS Trust exposed the absence of effective regulation and oversight. The culture of blame avoidance was pervasive. Managers had an incentive to evade culpability. Depoliticisation, removing politics by ensuring decisions are taken at arm's-length from ministers, weakened accountability. Blair and his entourage welcomed reform of the public sector as disruptive. The coherence of the institutional landscape bequeathed by hyper-innovation did not greatly trouble them. The third problem was the Blair governments' relative neglect of civil society. There was insufficient emphasis on strengthening intermediate institutions between the state and individual – social enterprises, co-operatives, charities, trade unions, churches – vital for the achievement of social justice.[172] Since the early 1980s, unfettered market forces and the arbitrary growth of the welfare state had weakened community institutions. New Labour's continuing faith in central government blinded ministers to the rich potential of civil society.

As importantly, in a break with the 1940s and 1960s, the party no longer believed state intervention could protect failing industries and avert national economic decline. The instruments Labour governments wielded to restructure the British economy were dismantled after 1979. There was reluctance to intrude in markets extending the boundaries of the state in economic life, other than in egregious cases of regulatory failure. In rare instances where economic institutions were created such as regional development agencies (RDAs), they were quickly dismantled by the incoming Conservative government. The Low Pay Commission proved to be a striking exception. The lack of enthusiasm in reorganising the UK's political economy meant New Labour's effect on British economic performance was undeniably ambiguous.

Overall, the Blair governments' institutional legacy was compelling on constitutional reform while broadly positive in updating the welfare state. Yet its' inheritance was modest in economic and industrial policy, given the complacent assumption that the central question of economic growth in Britain had largely been solved. The repercussions of the Iraq War, and to a lesser extent missteps over Europe, then had serious implications. All in all, too few institutions emerged that were recognisable to citizens marking the inauguration of a distinctive social democratic paradigm. Blair and Brown were unable to translate the political advantages bequeathed by the 1997 victory into a lasting institutional settlement.

Notes

1 D. Marquand, *Ramsay MacDonald*, London: Jonathan Cape, 1977, p. 795.
2 P. Hall, 'Policy Paradigms, Social Learning, and the State', p. 279.
3 B. Brivati, 'The New Labour Government's Place in History', in P. Diamond & M. Kenny (eds.), *Reassessing New Labour: Market, State and Society Under Blair and Brown*, London: Wiley, 2011.
4 Confidential Memorandum to the Prime Minister, 'Half Way There: The Next Five Years in Blair's New Labour Project to Modernise Britain', 2001.
5 E. Hobsbawm, *The Age of Extremes, 1914–1991*.
6 A. Gamble, *Crisis Without End? The Unravelling of Western Prosperity*, Basingstoke: Palgrave Macmillan, 2014.
7 A. Vincent, 'New Ideologies for Old', p. 53.
8 As set out in T. Blair, 'Power for a Purpose', pp. 11–16.
9 'Britain Deserves Better: The 1997 Labour Party Manifesto, p. 3.
10 Confidential Memorandum to the Prime Minister, 'Half Way There: The Next Five Years in Blair's New Labour Project to Modernise Britain', 2001.
11 Confidential Memorandum to the Prime Minister, 'Strategy for the next 6 months', 19th December 2002.
12 J. Tomlinson, *Democratic Socialism and Economic Policy: The Attlee Years 1945–51*, p. 266, Cambridge: Cambridge University Press, 1997.
13 Cited in J. Tomlinson, *Democratic Socialism and Economic Policy: The Attlee Years 1945–51*, p. 267.
14 Confidential Memorandum to the Prime Minister, 'Half Way There: The Next Five Years in Blair's New Labour Project to Modernise Britain', 2001.
15 The Labour Party Manifesto, 1997.
16 The Labour Party Manifesto, 1997.
17 Interview, Rt. Hon. Charles Clarke, former Secretary of State for Education and Skills, September 2011.
18 G. Radice. *Diaries 1980–2001: From Political Disaster to Triumph*, p. 422.
19 J. Powell, *The New Machiavelli: How to Wield Power in the Modern World*, London: Vintage: 2011.
20 P. Mandelson, Confidential Paper to the Prime Minster, 'Organising the Centre', July 1998.
21 P. Riddell, *15 Minutes of Power: The Uncertain Life of British Ministers*, pp. 47–48, London: Profile Books, 2019.
22 Interview, Rt. Hon. Charles Clarke, former Secretary of State for Education and Skills, September 2011.
23 Interview, Lord Andrew Adonis, former Secretary of State for Transport and Minister of State in the Department for Education and Skills, May 2011.
24 'Campaign for Labour Party Democracy Newsletter', p. 1, June 1979 cited in S. Fielding, *The Labour Party: Socialism and Society Since 1951*.
25 J. Bulpitt, 'The Discipline of the New Democracy: Mrs Thatcher's Domestic Statecraft'.
26 P. Mair, *Ruling the Void: The Hollowing-Out of Western Democracy*, London: Virago, 2013.
27 L. Minkin, *The Blair Supremacy: A Study in the Politics of Labour's Party Management*.
28 https://www.theguardian.com/politics/1999/sep/05/politicalnews.observerpolitics
29 P. Gould, 'Memo to the Prime Minister', 11th May, 2000.
30 P. Clarke, *A Question of Leadership: From Gladstone to Thatcher*.
31 Prime Minister, Confidential Memorandum, 'Strategy, 27th April 2000.
32 Confidential Memorandum to the Prime Minister, 'Half Way There: The Next Five Years in Blair's New Labour Project to Modernise Britain', 2001.
33 P. Gould, 'Memo to the Prime Minister', 11th May, 2000; D. Morris, *The New Prince*, New York: Griffin Press, 2000.

34 Interview, Dr David Halpern, former official in the Social Exclusion Unit, October 2011.
35 R.A.W. Rhodes, *Transforming British Government*, London: Macmillan Press, 2000.
36 Cited in T. Larsen, P. Taylor-Gooby & J. Kanenen, 'New Labour's Policy Style: A Mix of Policy Approaches', *Journal of Social Policy*, Volume 35 (4), p. 633, 2006.
37 T. Larsen, P. Taylor-Gooby & J. Kanenen, 'New Labour's Policy Style: A Mix of Policy Approaches'.
38 Interview, Andy Burnham, former Secretary of State at the Department of Health, September 2011.
39 Interview with Rt. Hon. Tony Blair, former Prime Minister, June 2011.
40 M. Bevir & R.A.W. Rhodes, 'Interpretive Approaches to British Government and Politics', *British Politics*, Volume 1 (1), pp. 84–112, 2006.
41 https://telegraph.co.uk/news/uknews/2679148/Labour-has-created-3600-new-offences-since-1997.html. Accessed 10th December 2018.
42 Interview with Paul Corrigan, former Special Adviser, Department of Health and Number Ten Downing Street, June 2011.
43 H. Glennerster, *British Social Policy: 1945 to the Present*, Oxford: Wiley-Blackwell.
44 For these points, I am grateful to Dr Martyn Frampton, Reader in Modern History, Queen Mary, University of London.
45 V. Bogdanor, 'Constitutional Reform in Britain: The Quiet Revolution', *Annual Review of Political Science*, Volume 8 (1), p. 74, 2005.
46 The Prime Minister, 'Weekly Note', November 2000.
47 A. Gamble, 'New Labour and Political Change'.
48 The Kings Fund, 'How Much Have Waiting Times Reduced?', 2010. The figures quoted are England only.
49 G. Mulgan, Confidential Memorandum to the Prime Minister, '2004 policy – Directions and Decisions', 27th February, 2004.
50 J. Birt, Confidential Memorandum to the Prime Minister', 'Five year plans', 18th March 2004.
51 P. Farrell et al., 'The Impact of Teaching Assistants on Improving Pupils' Academic Attainment in Mainstream Schools: A Review of the Literature', *Educational Review*, Volume 62 (4), pp. 435–460, 2010; R. Rowland & T. Coupe, 'Patrol officers and Public Reassurance: A Comparative Evaluation of Police Officers, PCSOs, ACSOs and Private Security Guards', *Policing and Society*, Volume 24 (3), pp. 265–284, 2014.
52 W. Keegan, *Nine Crises: Fifty Years of Covering the British Economy from Devaluation to Brexit*, p. 269, London: Biteback.
53 R. Skidelsky, *Money and Government: A Challenge to Mainstream Economics*, p. 222.
54 https://kingsfund.org.uk/sites/default/files/field/field_publication_file/independent-audit-nhs-under-labour-1997–2005-sunday-times-march-2005.pdf. Accessed 16th December 2019.
55 A. Gamble, 'New Labour and Political Change'.
56 https://gov.uk/government/news/government-outlines-vision-to-empower-and-invest-in-society. Accessed 10th August 2018.
57 Cited in B. Clift & J. Tomlinson, 'Tale of a Death Exaggerated', p. 48.
58 R. Skidelsky, *Money and Government: A Challenge to Mainstream Economics*, p. 197.
59 The Labour Party, 'Conference 1995: A New Economic Future for Britain: Economic and Employment Opportunities for All', p. 15, London: The Labour Party, 1995.
60 C. Hay & M. Watson, 'Labour's Economic Policy: Studiously Courting Competence', p. 116.
61 Interview with Dan Corry, former Number Ten Special Adviser, February 2019.
62 Interview with Sam White, former Treasury Special Adviser, September 2011. Nonetheless, by 2007, only 2 per cent of UK energy was produced from renewable sources. The EU target was to achieve 20 per cent by 2020. The UK lagged significantly behind other EU member-states in recycling: 22 per cent of household waste was recycled compared to 68 per cent in Norway, 64 per cent in the Netherlands and 57 per cent in Germany. New Labour's target to reduce carbon monoxide emissions was missed:

M. Pugh, *State and Society: A Social and Political History of Britain Since 1870*, London: Bloomsbury, 2014.

63 The Labour Party Manifesto, *A Future Fair for All*, London: The Labour Party, 2010.

64 D. Edgerton, *The Rise and Fall of the British Nation: A Twentieth Century History*.

65 J. Tomlinson, *Managing the Economy, Managing the People*, pp. 114–116.

66 N. Lawson, *The View from Number 11: Memoirs of a Tory Radical*, London: Biteback, 2010.

67 The Labour Party, 'Conference 1995: A New Economic Future for Britain: Economic and Employment Opportunities for All', p. 15, London: The Labour Party, 1995.

68 G. Brown, 'Strategy Note on Europe', HMT, 2002.

69 Prime Minister, 'Personal Note', 23rd June 2001.

70 R. Skidelsky, *Britain Since 1918: A Success Story?*

71 D. Alexander, Confidential Note to the Prime Minister, 'Europe', 2nd November 2002.

72 D. Corry, A. Valero & J. Van Reenan, 'UK Economic Performance', London School of Economics Discussion Paper, March 2011.

73 D. Corry, A. Valero & J. Van Reenan, 'UK Economic Performance'. That said, an additional 750,000 apprenticeship places were created after 1997.

74 D. Cobham, C. Adam & K. Mayhew, 'The Economic Record of the 1997–2010 Labour Government: An Assessment', *Oxford Review of Economic Policy*, Volume 29 (1), p. 2, 2013.

75 D. Cobham, C. Adam & K. Mayhew, 'The Economic Record of the 1997–2010 Labour Government: An Assessment', *Oxford Review of Economic Policy*, p. 2.

76 B. Clift & J. Tomlinson, 'Tale of a Death Exaggerated: How Keynesian Policies Survived the 1970s'.

77 H. Young, *A Political Journalist's Notebook*, p. 715.

78 H. Thompson, 'The Economy', in M. Flinders et al. (eds.), *The Oxford Handbook of British Politics*, Oxford: Oxford University Press, 2011.

79 T. Horton, 'Solidarity Lost? Labour and the Politics of the Welfare State', *The Political Quarterly*, Volume 81 (1), pp. 35–42, 2011.

80 H. Glennerster, *British Social Policy: 1945 to the Present*.

81 P. Sabatier, An Advocacy Coalition Framework of Policy Change and the Role of Policy-Oriented Learning Therein', *Policy Sciences*, Volume 21 (2/3), pp. 122–168, 1998.

82 N. Timmins, *The Five Giants: A Biography of the Welfare State*, London: William Collins.

83 Interview with Anna Turley, former Cabinet Office Special Adviser, October 2011.

84 Interview with Dr David Halpern, former official in the Social Exclusion Unit, October 2011.

85 F. Field, cited in N. Timmins, *The Five Giants*, p. 564.

86 H. Harman, *A Woman's Work*, London: Allen Lane, 2017.

87 H. Glennerster, *British Social Policy: 1945 to the Present*.

88 G. Radice, *Diaries 1980–2001: From Political Disaster to Triumph*, p. 422.

89 Cited in N. Timmins, *The Five Giants*, p. 571.

90 Presentation by the Prime Minister's Policy Unit, 'Has New Labour Abandoned the Poor?', Summer 1999.

91 Presentation by the Prime Minister's Policy Unit, 'Has New Labour Abandoned the Poor?', Summer 1999.

92 S. Mudge, *Leftism Reinvented*.

93 https://nao.org.uk/wp-content/uploads/2010/01/0910212es.pdf. Accessed 14th May 2019. The data in Figures 6.1, 6.2 and 6.3 is provided by the Office for National Statistics (ONS).

94 G. Mulgan, Confidential Memorandum to the Prime Minister, '2004 Policy – Directions and Decisions Needed', 27th February 2004.

95 A. Hindmoor, *What's Left?*.

96 A. Heath, *Social Progress in Britain*, Oxford: Oxford University Press, 2018.

97 A. Heath, *Social Progress in Britain*, p. 112.

98 For more on this policy framework, see: N. Eisenstadt & C. Oppenheim, *Parents, Poverty and the State: 20 Years of Evolving Family Policy*, Bristol: Policy Press, 2019.

99 K. Stewart, 'Labour's Record on the Under Fives: Policy, Outcomes and Spending 1997–2010', Working Paper No. 4, London: LSE/CASE, 2013.

100 T. Larsen, P. Taylor-Gooby & J. Kanenen, 'New Labour's Policy Style: A Mix of Policy Approaches'.

101 K. Stewart, 'Labour's Record on the Under Fives: Policy, Outcomes and Spending 1997–2010'.

102 N. Eisenstadt & C. Oppenheim, *Parents, Poverty and the State: 20 Years of Evolving Family Policy*, Bristol: Policy Press, 2019.

103 K. Stewart, 'Labour's Record on the Under Fives: Policy, Outcomes and Spending 1997–2010'.

104 K. Stewart, 'Labour's Record on the Under Fives: Policy, Outcomes and Spending 1997–2010'.

105 J. Lewis, 'Developing Early Years Childcare in England, 1997–2002: The Choices for (Working) Mothers', *Social Policy and Administration*, Volume 37 (3), pp. 219–238, 2003.

106 The discussion in the chapter primarily relates to policies in England. Scotland, Wales and Northern Ireland diverged to some extent, particularly in the management of public services. The data in Figure 6.4 is provided by the Office for National Statistics (ONS).

107 S. Mettler, *The Submerged State: How Invisible Government Policies Undermine American Democracy*, Chicago: University of Chicago Press, 2011.

108 B. Hepple, 'The New Single Equality Act in Britain', *The Equal Rights Review*, Volume 5, pp. 11–24, 2011.

109 J. Orford, *An Unsafe Bet? The Dangerous Rise of Gambling and the Debate We Should Be Having*, Oxford: Wiley-Blackwell, 2011.

110 P. Hadfield, 'Party Invitations: New Labour and the (De)regulation of Pleasure', *Criminal Justice Matters*, Volume 67 (1), pp. 18–47, 2007.

111 T. Blair, cited in J. McGuigan, 'The Social Construction of a Cultural Disaster: New Labour's Millennium Experience', *Cultural Studies*, Volume 17 (5), p. 670, 2003.

112 J. Greenaway, 'How Policy Framing Is as Important as the Policy Content: The Story of the English and Welsh Licensing Act 2003', *British Politics*, Volume 6 (4), pp. 408–422, 2011.

113 C. Annesley & F. Gains, 'The Core Executive: Gender, Power and Change', *Political Studies*, Volume 58 (5), pp. 909–929, 2010.

114 J. Lewis & S. Giullari, 'The Adult Worker Model Family, Gender Equality and Care: The Search for New Policy Principles and the Possibilities and Problems of a Capabilities Approach', *Economy and Society*, Volume 34 (1), pp. 76–104, 2005.

115 C. Annesley, F. Gains & K. Rummery, *Women and New Labour: Engendering Politics and Policy*, pp. x, Bristol: Policy Press, 2007.

116 Cited in https://theguardian.com/society/2004/sep/27/children.gender. Accessed 14th July 2019.

117 S. Bashevkin, 'From Tough Times to Better Times'.

118 G. Pascall, 'Gender and New Labour: After the Male Breadwinner Model?', *Social Policy Review 20*, 2008.

119 H. Harman, *A Woman's Work*.

120 C. Annesley, F. Gains & K. Rummery, *Women and New Labour: Engendering politics and policy*.

121 S. Bashevkin, 'From Tough Times to Better Times'.

122 J. Lewis & M. Campbell, 'UK Work/Family Balance Policies and Gender Equality, 1997–2005', *Social Politics: International Studies in Gender, State & Society*, Volume 14 (1), pp. 4–30, 2007.

123 B. Brivati, 'The New Labour Government's Place in History'.

124 S.B. Dyson, 'What Difference Did He Make? Tony Blair and British Foreign Policy from 1997–2007', in T. Casey (ed.), *The Blair Legacy: Policy, Politics, Governance, Foreign Affairs*, Basingstoke: Palgrave Macmillan, 2009.

125 T. Blair, *A Journey*, p. 57.

126 Cited in D. Fisher, *Morality and War: Can War Be Justified in the Twenty First Century?* p. 157, Oxford: Oxford University Press, 2011.

127 The Chicago lecture is available here: https://webarchive.nationalarchives.gov.uk/+/ http://number10.gov.uk/Page1297. Accessed 14th Mary 2019. The speech is further discussed and summarised here: https://prospectmagazine.co.uk/magazine/tony-blair-second-thoughts-war-iraq-liberal-interventionism. Accessed 23rd July 2019.

128 T. Blair, 'Speech to the Labour Party Conference', London: The Labour Party, 2001.

129 T. Blair, 'Speech to the Labour Party Conference'.

130 https://gov.uk/government/organisations/department-for-international-development. Accessed 12th July 2019.

131 T. Blair, 'The Left Should Not Weep If Saddam Is Toppled'.

132 'The Report of the Iraq Inquiry: Report of a Committee of Privy Counsellors', p. 111.

133 'The Report of the Iraq Inquiry: Report of a Committee of Privy Counsellors', p. 5, London: House of Commons, 6th July, 2016.

134 Minute Straw to Prime Minister, 'Crawford/Iraq', 25th March 2002.

135 Prime Minister, 'Personal Note', 21st April 2001.

136 T. Blair, 'Parliamentary Debate in the House of Commons', 13th March 2003.

137 Paper [Blair to Bush], 'The War Against Terrorism: The Second Phase', 4th December 2001. https://webarchive.nationalarchives.gov.uk/20171123123022/http://iraqinquiry. org.uk/media/243731/2001-12-04-note-blair-to-bush-the-war-against-terrorism-the-second-phase.pdf

138 https://theguardian.com/politics/2002/oct/03/labourconference.labour1. Accessed 10th August 2018.

139 P. Mandelson, *The Third Man*, London: Random House, 2010.

140 'The Report of the Iraq Inquiry: Report of a Committee of Privy Counsellors', p. 5.

141 R. Skidelsky, *Britain Since 1900: A Success Story?*

142 In a note to President Bush, Prime Minister Blair now infamously wrote: 'I will be with you, whatever'. Note Blair [to Bush], 'Note on Iraq', 28th July 2002.

143 'The Report of the Iraq Inquiry: Report of a Committee of Privy Counsellors', p. 6.

144 'The Report of the Iraq Inquiry: Report of a Committee of Privy Counsellors', p. 22.

145 M. Phythian, 'Labour and the Intelligence Services', in O. Daddow, 'New Labour: A Witness History', *Contemporary British History*, pp. 128–129.

146 'The Report of the Iraq Inquiry: Report of a Committee of Privy Counsellors', p. 25.

147 House of Commons, Hansard, 17th March, 2003.

148 JIC Assessment, 'Iraq after September 11 – the Terrorist Threat', 28th November 2001.

149 V. Bogdanor, *The Coalition and the Constitution*, London: Hart Publishing, p. 10, 2010.

150 A. Rawnsley, 'His Greatest Gamble', *The Observer*, 4th November 2001.

151 P. Porter, *Blunder: Britain's War in Iraq*, p. 3, Oxford: Oxford University Press, 2018.

152 P. Porter, *Blunder: Britain's War in Iraq*, pp. 1–7.

153 P. Clarke, *Liberals and Social Democrats*, p. 5.

154 A. Campbell, 'Diaries'.

155 M. Penn, Confidential Memorandum to the Prime Minister, 'Targeting Memo', 14th September, 2004. The bursting of the Blair 'bubble' in public opinion began prior to the Iraq War, however. The decline of Blair's personal ratings began in 2000 symbolised by the prime minister being heckled by 10,000 delegates at a conference of the Women's Institute in London.

156 P. Gould, Confidential Memorandum to the Prime Minister, 'On your side', 9th December 2004.

157 JIC Assessment, 'International Terrorism: War with Iraq', 10th February 2003.

158 S. Bulmer, 'New Labour, New European Policy?', *Parliamentary Affairs*, Volume 61 (4), p. 600, 2008.

159 S. Bulmer, 'New Labour, New European Policy?, p. 603.

160 G. Radice. *Diaries 1980–2001: From Political Disaster to Triumph*, p. 400.

161 European Convention Memorandum to the Prime Minister, 'The Convention', 28th March 2003.

162 R. Liddle, Confidential Memorandum to the Prime Minister, 'Europe', 18th December 2003.

163 G. Brown, 'Speech to the Fabian New Year Conference', 2006.

164 G. Brown, Speech to the Labour Party Spring Conference, Manchester, 12th March 2004.

165 As David Edgerton points out in *The Rise and Fall of the British Nation: A Twentieth Century History*.

166 G. Brown, Confidential Memorandum, March 2000.

167 D. Edgerton, *The Rise and Fall of the British Nation: A Twentieth Century History*.

168 B. Guy-Peters, *Institutional Theory in Political Science: The New Institutionalism*, Cheltenham: Edward Elgar, 2019.

169 G. Mulgan, 'Renewal and Strategic Audit', Memorandum to the Prime Minister, 30th June 2003.

170 S. Griffiths, *Engaging Enemies: Hayek and the Left*, London: Rowman & Littlefield, 2014.

171 Interview, D. Blunkett, former Home Secretary, May 2011; Interview, Andy Burnham, former Secretary of State at the Department of Health, September 2011.

172 D. Marquand, *The Decline of the Public*.

7

SHAPING SECULAR TRENDS

The extent to which these physical divisions were compounded by so many other aspects of our daily lives was very evident. Separate educational arrangements, community and voluntary bodies, employment, places of worship, language, social and cultural networks, means that many communities operate on the basis of a series of parallel lives.

Ted Cantle[1]

We are intensely relaxed about people getting filthy rich . . . as long as they pay their taxes.

Peter Mandelson[2]

Introduction

Having examined the construction of social democratic institutions, the following chapter turns to New Labour's substantive impact on the structure of society and politics. How far did the Blair and Brown administrations influence secular trends in Britain, achieving decisive alterations in leading economic and social indicators? The chapter addresses New Labour's ability to reshape dominant trends in the economy and society from the level of inequality to the crime rate. If they created social democratic institutions, how far did the Blair and Brown administrations modify the social fabric of Britain through the policy-making and reform machinery of the state? The chapter examines economic growth, income inequality, educational participation, the rate of crime, the growth of migration and diversity and, finally, the Europeanisation of British national life.

The yardstick for governments' success in modifying prevailing economic and social developments is the Thatcher administrations. Ministers after 1979 apparently redefined the trajectory of British society and the economy. Thatcher's governments set the UK on course for decades of rising structural inequality, creating an economic growth model that encouraged sustained expansion in the financial and service sector accompanied by deindustrialisation and the contraction of manufacturing industry. Did New Labour's years in power after 1997 prove similarly pivotal?

Economic performance under Labour

At the outset, as the previous chapter demonstrated, New Labour's agenda was prudent and cautious. Before 1997, New Labour had downplayed expectations of what was achievable in managing the economy. Modernising social democrats believed there were inherent limits to the capacity of domestic policies to alter long-run economic performance. Moreover, they renounced measures such as raising direct taxation that might threaten the government's re-election. Prior to victory, the Shadow Treasury team refused to commit to full employment within a single parliament or to return industrial jobs to the UK. There should be no constraints on capital liberalisation or free trade. The 1997 manifesto stated: 'In economic management, we accept the global economy as a reality and reject the isolationism and 'go-it-alone' policies of the extremes of left or right'.[3] Labour's defensiveness underlined that in the previous twenty years, 'the left of centre vacated serious thinking about the economy'.[4] As a consequence, particular centre-left politicians and intellectuals came to believe there was little alternative to the doctrine of monetarism and neo-liberalism. Having studied post-war economic history, Blair and Brown were pessimistic about any social democratic government recasting the prevailing settlement. Wilson's abortive effort to modernise the British economy after 1964 exemplified the Left's inability to deliver, mismanaging expectations.

Yet by 2001, Brown's stance became less circumspect. New Labour was determined to take political credit for the UK economy's headline performance. The ministerial team in the Treasury debated how the government could maximise the electoral advantage of rising growth and living standards. Until the 2008 crisis, economic growth in Britain outstripped France and Germany, inflation averaged 1.5 per cent, the unemployment rate was half the Eurozone average, while the rise in per capita GDP meant Britain leapt from last to third place in the G7 countries.[5] Labour presided over the long decade of continuous expansion. Living standards grew across the income distribution particularly for low-income households. Income per head was now higher than most of Europe. Unemployment and inflation were low, a remarkable contrast to the 1970s. There were modest gains in labour productivity.[6] Ministers were assisted by the fall in the equilibrium rate of unemployment following the liberalisation of the UK labour market. Economic growth was achieved without triggering a balance-of-payments crisis (although the current account was in deficit permanently), while there was no inflationary wage spiral that characterised the 'stop-go' cycles of the 1960s.

The Labour governments oversaw the longest phase of continuous growth in British economic history. The UK was outperforming all its major competitors.[7]

Brown's decision to create an independent Monetary Policy Committee (MPC) whose goal was 'to maintain price stability' would ensure continuing economic success. Nor was growth unbalanced. The financial sector accounted for 0.4 per cent of the 2.8 per cent annual expansion in the British economy. Improvement in human capital supply and technological innovation led to rising productivity: 'The gains in productivity were real rather than a statistical artefact'.[8] In his 2006 budget, the chancellor boasted that when Labour came to office, Britain was seventh out of the G7 countries in national income per head. Now, the UK was second in the G7, beaten only by the United States.

Meanwhile, by the early 2000s, fiscal discipline meant UK public debt was lower than at any time since the seventeenth century. Prudence was the bedrock of Labour's strategy, the platform for its progressive ambitions. Brown and his adviser, Ed Balls, believed that fiscal rectitude would enable the long-term expansion of public spending. Drawing on modern macro-economic theory, Balls averred that capital markets would permit governments to determine 'the tax/spending share of GDP, the corporate tax rate, the level of the minimum wage, or the toughness of competition policy', provided there was confidence in projected inflation rates and fiscal deficits'.[9] Reforms of the labour market were then introduced, including the minimum wage with the reduced rate for workers under 25. Brown insisted full employment, the long-term ambition of socialist economic policy, was achievable if resources were shifted from 'paying the bills of social failure' to investing in human capital and infrastructure. Tax credits for those on low incomes with fewer marketable skills would 'make work pay'.[10] The numbers in work in Britain grew by 1.2 million; 53 per cent of new jobs were in the private sector.[11]

Martin Wolf wrote in the *Financial Times* that under Labour, Britain had an economic strategy 'that offered something new, at least for the UK'. The liberalisation of markets and an open economy were combined with the activist state, a formula that radically adjusted the terms of political trade. While entrepreneurial success was rewarded and private enterprise encouraged, governments pursued an ambitious redistributive agenda.[12] The proportion of national income devoted to health and education significantly increased. Inflation and public debt declined, creating space for expansionary fiscal policies. The poorest households gained from rising living standards.[13]

How far did the UK's performance reflect decisions taken by Labour ministers? New Labour's success certainly relied on benign conditions in the global economy. The growth of India and China flooded Britain with cheap imports. Inflation plummeted amid the availability of low cost capital. Consumers were encouraged to borrow. Property values increased rapidly. The EU, the UK's leading export market, enjoyed a return to impressive rates of growth, buoyed by the reunification of Germany. The Internet economy and the generation of US technology companies meant Western capitalism was experiencing a long boom. Structural changes improved the UK's relative economic position, irrespective of decisions taken by politicians.

Moreover, of growing concern was the reality that the headline data initially disguised soaring consumer debt and rising in-work poverty. Economic commentators worried that Britain resembled a 'fantasy island' that relied on consumption-fuelled expansion. The underlying weaknesses were then exposed by the 2008 financial crisis. Critics emphasised that since the 1990s, the economy was underpinned by rising household debt rather than productive investment. The UK economy was prone to asset bubbles. Housing was treated as an investment good. Productivity was weak compared to Britain's major industrial competitors. Despite the flurry of Treasury initiatives to strengthen research and skills, growth in output per worker continued to lag behind the United States.[14] Regional imbalances dramatically increased. As chancellor, Brown lambasted the 'old-style regional policy' of the 1960s, yet the regional development agencies (RDAs) he created had relatively little impact. The prime minister's Strategy Unit published a report that appeared to justify the government's complacency claiming that economic disparities *within* regions were more significant than differences *between* regions.

Despite a social democratic government being in power, the UK risked remaining imprisoned in the Anglo-Liberal growth model. The Anglo-Liberal model characterised by dependence on global trade, the pre-eminence of the financial sector, manufacturing decline, low investment in education and training, the dominance of shareholder value, alongside the reliance on consumer debt predated Thatcherism.[15] While the model is treated as synonymous with neo-liberalism, it goes further back to eighteenth- and nineteenth-century political economy. As a consequence, ministers were uncertain about how far they should break with the Anglo-Liberal regime. The City of London and financial services were still dominant. In the late 1990s, London became Europe's leading financial centre. Money poured into the capital. Under Labour, the City became an attractive safe haven for investors. Foreign direct investment (FDI) accounted for 45 per cent of UK fixed capital formation, compared to the EU average of 16 per cent.[16]

Meanwhile, financial services employed 1 million UK workers, more than those employed in the coal mines during the inter-war years. The value of sterling continued to rise. The pound-deutschmark exchange rate was 2:20 in 1995 but increased to 3:40 by 2000. As a consequence, after 1997 manufacturing continued to decline as a share of national income and employment. When Labour came to power, manufacturing as a share of GDP was 20 per cent but shrank to 11.3 per cent by 2007.[17] Manufacturing investment as a proportion of output fell from 13 per cent in 1997 to 9 per cent by 2004. The consequence was that by 2007, the UK balance-of-payments deficit on goods reached £7.2 billion. It was emblematic that when 1,150 manufacturing jobs were lost at the Jaguar car plant in Coventry in 2005, ministers expressed sympathy but refused to intervene.

After the Second World War, it has long been observed that Britain failed to cultivate the spirit of industriousness and entrepreneurial spirit that characterised Germany and Japan.[18] By the 1990s, the UK economy was increasingly dependent on growth from the deregulation of financial markets, coupled with rising consumer indebtedness.[19] The stock of household debt increased to over 150 per cent: households borrowed to purchase homes and acquire non-durable consumer goods, sustaining their living standards as real wages declined. Colin Crouch referred to the birth of 'privatised Keynesianism'.[20] Blair and Brown's long-term ambition was to combine the vigorous dynamism of American capitalism with the social cohesion of Western Europe. The goal was to fashion a novel economic dispensation simultaneously advancing national competitiveness and social justice. Yet the evidence indicated Labour was incapable of prising the UK economy onto a fundamentally different trajectory to that prevailing under post-war governments. As the previous chapter revealed, New Labour never constructed the institutions that were necessary to overhaul British political economy. The prevailing climate of economic ideas made radical new directions in policy-making hard to envisage.

Inequality after 1997: towards an inclusive society?

If Labour's performance on economic growth was less than convincing, how well did it handle the outstanding problem of the modern age in advanced democracies: sharply rising income and wealth inequality? New Labour's policies certainly slowed the growth of inequality, poverty and labour market disadvantage, the long-term legacy of the Thatcher era. There was progress in reducing inequalities at work relating to ethnicity and gender. Notable successes included rising real wages for the lowest paid, the growth of incomes for families with children, alongside the fall in the proportion of workless households.[21] The decrease in pensioner poverty was the sharpest decline in post-war history. Labour's programme balanced improving outcomes for the poorest with narrowing differences across society, as illustrated in Table 7.1:[22]

TABLE 7.1 Labour's goals in social policy

Policy area	*Policy goals*
Poverty and inequality	End child poverty by 2020, halving it by 2010. Eradicate pensioner poverty.
The under-fives	Ensure more equal 'starting points' for all children. The aim of the 1997 Labour manifesto was 'an inclusive society where everyone has an equal chance to achieve their full potential'.
Health	Improve the health and well-being of the UK population, while reducing health inequalities.
Education	Raise levels of educational equality, giving all pupils the opportunity to realise their potential while creating a strong economy and a fairer society.
Deprived neighbourhoods and spatial inequalities	By 2020, ensure that no one experiences serious disadvantage due to the neighbourhood or area they are living in.

After years of fatalism that little could be done to reverse inter-generational disadvantage, Labour restored confidence in the capacity of government to tackle long-term economic and social problems. Gordon Brown believed

New Labour was constructing the British model of the New Deal and the Great Society pioneered in the twentieth century by the US Democrats. Blair announced the ambitious target to halve, and then finally end, child poverty by 2020. Yet there was no automatic rise in welfare benefits after 1997: the relative value of Job Seekers Allowance (JSA) continued to decline, hitting working-age adults without children hard. New Labour believed social security meant spending on failure. The strategy for the unemployed entailed welfare-to-work combined with greater conditionality, including tough eligibility criteria for benefits. There were limits to redistribution. New Labour pledged not to raise the basic or higher rate of income tax. Inheritance and capital gains tax were largely untouched. As a consequence, there was a lack of concern about inequality fuelled by the 'filthy rich'.[23]

Labour ministers' success in arresting the growth of inequality must be understood in the light of the Thatcher legacy. By the late 1990s, the UK had among the worst poverty rates in the developed economies. Polarisation between households grew. The North/South divide was entrenched, while the real wages of the low skilled sharply declined after 1979.[24] The scale of poverty was unprecedented in post-war history: one in four children were affected compared to one in eight in the 1970s. Post-tax income inequality doubled. According to the Organisation for Economic Co-operation and Development (OECD), inequality among working-age households in the 1980s increased faster in Britain than in any other industrialised country. The incomes of the poorest were lower in real terms than when Margaret Thatcher entered Downing Street.[25]

Structural alterations in the labour market propelled inequality, not only the restructuring of the tax and benefits system. By the late 1990s, a fifth of working-age households had no one in work compared to 8 per cent in 1975, the result of deindustrialisation and the disappearance of manual jobs.[26] Inequality then increased due to disparities in wage growth: the economist Paul Gregg calculates that real median wages rose by 23 per cent between 1979 and 1995; in the highest percentile, salaries increased by more than 40 per cent. Declining public sector investment as a share of GDP from 5.9 per cent in the 1970s to 3.1 per cent by the mid-1990s had an impact.[27] Without concerted intervention the UK became more unequal. John Hills, the LSE social policy expert, insists Labour's policies from 1997 were broadly progressive in stark contrast to the Conservatives after 1979. The poorest tenth of households enjoyed a 12.8 per cent growth in incomes; the income of the richest tenth declined by 8.7 per cent.[28] Figure 7.1 illustrates the impact of tax and benefit changes from 1997.

Social policy concerns the distribution of income, services and public goods, addressing a pivotal question for politics in advanced capitalist countries: 'Who gets what, when, and how'? The prospects of low-income Britain improved significantly after 1997. The tax system was generally more progressive as Figure 7.2 indicates. New Labour's reforms ensured the wealthy in the main paid more tax. What is more, the distribution of public expenditure was then weighted towards the poorest households (Figure 7.3).

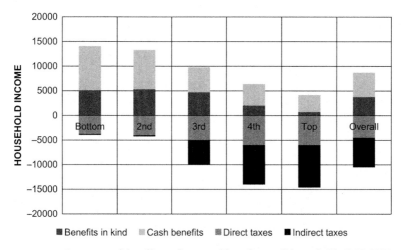

FIGURE 7.1 Summary of the effects of taxes and benefits on all households 1997–2007 by quintile

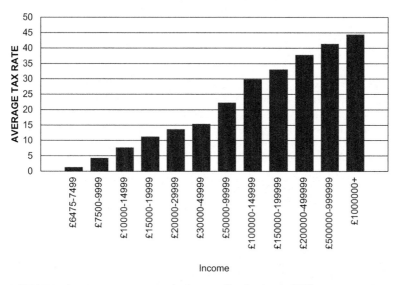

FIGURE 7.2 Average tax rate across the income distribution in 2010

In reflecting on New Labour's efforts, John Hills has concluded: 'It might be as good as it gets for some time to come'.[29] There was frustration that income inequality did not fall more dramatically: a large slice of the economy remained low waged and low skilled. There was little progress in narrowing the gender

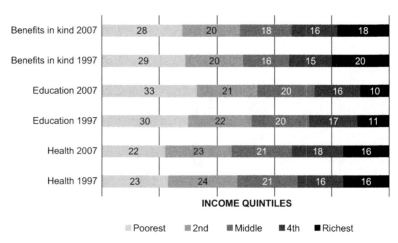

FIGURE 7.3 Share in public expenditure received by different income quintiles 1997–2007

and ethnic pay gap while class divisions hardened. The employment rate and the real wages of those with disabilities barely improved. By 2007, only 55 per cent of working-age adults in the ten most deprived neighbourhoods in England were in paid employment.[30] Meanwhile, the overall growth in real incomes varied over time. Between 1997 and 2002, average household incomes grew by more than 3 per cent and then slowed. After 2008, disposable incomes increased due to low inflation and low interest rates, alongside the VAT cut.[31] Wage inequalities continued to rise, although the pace was noticeably slower than the Thatcher/Major years.[32] As a consequence, health inequalities also increased. For instance, class inequalities in infant mortality have not fallen since 2000. Similarly, the gap in life expectancy has failed to close.[33]

As such, the post-1997 modifications in income inequality were relatively small. The Gini coefficient, which measures household income inequality on a scale from 0 to 100, increased in Labour's first term to 0.35 but fell again after 2001. The Gini rose during the financial crisis, leading to cumulative growth in inequality from 0.33 to 0.36 by 2010–11.[34] Yet in the government's final year, inequality declined substantially, 'the largest 1-year fall for at least 50 years'. The 50 per cent marginal tax rate and the impact of the crash on top incomes eventually restrained inequality.[35] Inequality did *not* decrease, although the Institute for Fiscal Studies (IFS) confirm that during the New Labour years income growth was highest in the second- and third-poorest income deciles. Yet the top 10 per cent still experienced the fastest rise in incomes.

Structural forces at the apex of the wage distribution made it hard for any government to reduce inequality. The growing share going to the top 1 per cent of earners, which increased from 7.1 per cent in 1970 to 14.3 per cent by the 2000s, fuelled the rise of inequality: prior to the crisis, 0.1 per cent of the population were earning 5 per cent of total pre-tax income.[36] The growth of inequality resulted from the highest paid increasing their working hours, the expansion of self-employment to one in seven of the workforce and more workers marrying within their 'earning class'.[37] Moreover, changes in the nature of global capitalism marked by the shift in production from tangible goods to intangible services widened the wage dispersion across advanced economies: new technologies and automation led to escalating wage differentials; deregulation in labour markets exacerbated wage inequalities; while trade integration deepened wage polarisation, encouraged by the growing supply of skilled workers in the global labour force.[38] The UK was increasingly exposed to international trade. The share of GDP from trade grew from 48 to 64 per cent since the 1980s.[39] Of course, political choices still made a substantial impact, as illustrated by the success of particular governments around the world in combating economic inequality in recent decades.

Moreover, although wealth inequality was often ignored while 'far more attention is paid to the flow of income to individuals and households than to their stock of assets',[40] wealth inequality soared during the New Labour years. By 2010, the top 10 per cent of households had net assets of more than £970,000, while the bottom 10 per cent owned less than £13,000.[41] As Gordon Brown departed office, the richest 1 per cent owned 20 per cent of all marketable wealth.[42] The net wealth of the top 10 per cent was 850 times greater than for the bottom. Younger generations were least likely to gain from rising property prices while they carried debts from higher education: 'In this way, inheritance tends to reinforce advantage and widen differences in wealth'.[43] The Labour government's strategy aimed to counter adverse trends following structural alterations since the 1970s.[44] Yet the incomes of working-age households without children decreased as benefits were frozen, while top incomes rose sharply. There was growing economic insecurity, reinforced by the dramatic decline in the generosity of company pensions. In the early 1980s, 97 per cent of members of an employers' scheme had a defined benefit (DB) pension. By 2015, it had fallen to 29 per cent.[45] The generosity of public sector pensions was eroded further.

The strategy prepared by Blair's team prior to the 2005 election warned that 'levels of social mobility are not increasing [in the UK], and many working people feel that even if they did get on the first rung of the ladder they are still insecure and badly off'. New Labour's third term agenda emphasised raising school standards, expanding higher education and improving vocational training; workers were to receive additional funding to acquire skills; housing supply for first-time buyers would increase; asset ownership for poorer households was encouraged through 'right to buy' and the Child Trust Fund (CTF).[46] Yet Labour struggled to identify workable policies that reversed economic inequality. Reports underlined the lack of progress in widening access to the 'elite' universities, notably Oxford and Cambridge, a totemic issue in British society. According to the review published by the prime minister's Strategy Unit in 2007, children from poor households were more likely to report problems with drugs and alcohol, and were less likely to go to university as Figure 7.4 indicates:[47]

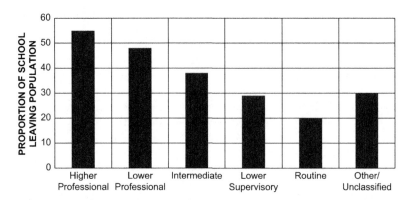

FIGURE 7.4 Percentage studying for a degree by parental class 2007

The fundamental problem was that in addressing inequality the Blair and Brown governments still relied on welfare and social policy to do the heavy lifting. Ministers were reluctant to tackle systemic weaknesses in the UK's political economy. The minimum wage was popular but assisted only a small percentage of the working-age population. New Labour's reluctance to reappraise the industrial relations reforms of the Thatcher era was a decisive factor in failing to reverse wage inequality. The 2004 Warwick Agreement with the TUC created new rights at work, preventing a 'two-tier' public sector workforce, while introducing safeguards for workers' pensions and protection for those on strike. Yet there was no renaissance in government/union relations. The Treasury believed the tightening labour market would compel employers to pay higher wages. Improving access to education ought to moderate the growth of wages at the very top. Yet these interventions did not have the radical impact initially hoped. It proved hard to reduce inequality in the British labour market without raising taxes on the rich.

Ministers and officials remained sceptical about the overall goal of narrowing inequality measured by the Gini coefficient. Since 1945, the objective rarely appeared in Labour Party manifestos. The priority was strengthening social cohesion, cutting poverty rates and promoting 'shared community experiences' while reducing educational exclusion and segregation.[48] Labour's record hardly amounted to collusion with neo-liberalism. Even so, painfully slow progress was the consequence of refusing to define a bold social democratic agenda.

Expanding education: did 'more mean worse'?

Blair's three priorities for government after 1997 were said to be 'education, education, education'. Whereas in 1945 the Left's overarching aim was bringing the commanding heights of industry into public ownership, fifty years later the party emphasised raising educational performance throughout the population as the central goal of the Left. During the New Labour period, Britain became better educated, measured by the proportion attaining school-leaving qualifications and a university degree. The Blair governments set the target of 50 per cent of eighteen- to thirty-year-olds entering higher education. As Figure 7.5 demonstrates, among leading industrial economies, the UK went from having the second-lowest to the highest tertiary participation rate. When Labour left office, 47 per cent of young people progressed to university, while the rate of participation continued to expand thereafter:[49]

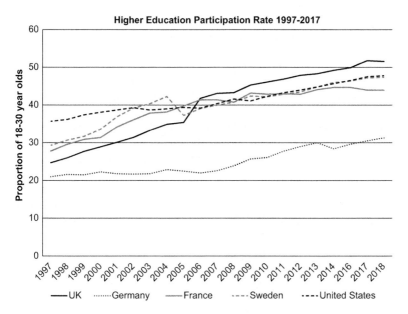

FIGURE 7.5 Tertiary education participation 1997–2017

Critics complained the HE participation target was misguided. The Blair governments adopted controversial financing reforms that shifted the burden of paying for university tuition onto the individual. Months into the new government, it was announced that students and their families would pay tuition fees of £1,000 a year. Maintenance grants would be abolished. The measures were a response to the Dearing Review, established to examine the future of UK higher education prior to the 1997 election.[50] The headline recommendation was that British university institutions required more funding, given the scale of the international competition, the ongoing concerns about quality and the need to lift the cap on undergraduate places to permit expansion. Dearing advised that students should be compelled to make financial contributions once they entered the labour market.

Although the Blair government agreed to Dearing's recommendations, Labour's policy was quickly judged to be inadequate. Flat-rate tuition fees were unpopular yet did little to solve the funding crisis.[51] New Labour failed to grasp the nettle. OECD data indicated that Britain was falling sharply down the global league table in the proportion of young people graduating from university. The quality of British higher education would continue to decline. The Labour governments struggled to resolve the funding shortfall in universities. Labour ruled out 'top-up' fees in its 2001 manifesto at the insistence of the education secretary, David Blunkett. Yet two years later, variable fees were recommended in the government's White Paper, *The Future of Higher Education*.[52] The government proposed to lift the cap to £3,000 allowing universities to set their own fees up to that limit. Students earning post-graduation incomes over £15,000 would repay the loans at a rate of 9 per cent per annum. The new secretary of state, Charles Clarke, insisted the policy had the advantages of a graduate tax which the Treasury favoured, without imposing an intolerable burden on the public sector balance sheet.

Nevertheless, Blair was an unpopular leader in the aftermath of the Iraq War and he struggled to get the measure through Parliament. Clarke and his minister of state, Alan Johnson, embarked on a desperate charm offensive in the Parliamentary Labour Party (PLP). As Johnson recalled: 'I was charming. Charles was offensive'. MPs believed the government's proposal to restore the maintenance grant for those in low-income households was insufficient. They disliked the creation of a university hierarchy that deterred poorer students from applying to 'top' institutions. Many MPs were themselves beneficiaries of free higher education in the post-war decades. The legislation squeaked through by a tiny majority. Blair's head of policy, Andrew Adonis, recalled meeting the National Youth Parliament to discuss university finance: 'As I replied to a rant about fees, the bit they latched on to was when I said they had a 'straight choice' – 'you can go with the Tories on this and abolish fees – but at the cost of slashing student numbers. So which of you want to be the ones who don't go to university so the Tories can make their sums stack up? Hands up. Silence. 'Come on, surely there's someone desperate to stack shelves at Tesco's for life for the greater good? Laughter all round. Alas, it won't be so easy with the PLP'.[53]

The goal of 50 per cent of school-leavers entering higher education was initially proposed in the confidential report for Number Ten authored by the LSE academic, Professor David Soskice.[54] Soskice believed the UK should emulate the American system of post-compulsory education. Like the United States, the British variety of capitalism was service orientated, dependent on human capital and a highly flexible labour market. Yet there was scepticism about expanding tertiary education. As HE participation rose, the economic and social returns to degrees might diminish. A large number of young people attending university could reduce quality dramatically. The *Daily Mail* echoed the novelist Kingsley Amis in believing that 'more really did mean worse' in the British education system.

Thoughtful critics worried Labour's policies neglected the proportion of the school-leaving population entering the world of work. Little progress was made in strengthening vocational qualifications, despite the launch of modern apprenticeships. A government report by the skills expert, Alison Wolf, noted that 'the staple offer for between a quarter and a third of the post-16 cohort is a diet of low-level vocational qualifications, most of which have little to no labour market value'.[55] The Tomlinson Review in 2004 advocated replacing A-levels with a version of the international baccalaureate. Yet the plans were shelved. After 1997, New Labour created a plethora of skills agencies. Departments were reorganised. The Treasury sought to take the lead. Dozens of skills ministers came and went. Yet no coherent vision of training for 'the other 50 per cent' emerged.

Nonetheless, the growth in the numbers participating in higher education was significant, a transformation since the 1970s. There was a marked rise in the proportion of young people from disadvantaged backgrounds going to university despite tuition fees, due to reforms designed to raise standards and equalise opportunities.[56] Critics alleged education became increasingly 'neo-liberal' in the Blair/Brown years. There was certainly increased focus on choice and competition. Students were encouraged to treat degrees as a private investment rather than a public good. Unquestionably, the Labour government absorbed an instrumentalist account of education, where priority was given to human capital and productivity over intellectual self-fulfilment and creativity.

Of undoubted political significance was the fact those attending higher education institutions were more likely to develop socially liberal attitudes as the consequence of socialisation.[57] Younger areas of urban Britain with concentrations of university graduates exhibited divergent voting patterns. The Blair administration's agenda of encouraging 50 per cent of school leavers into HE contributed towards further liberalisation. A leading social scientist wrote:

> There is plenty of evidence that people who have been through higher education not only have better chances in the labour market, but are also . . . more likely to engage in healthy lifestyles. They are more likely to believe that they have the skills to participate in politics. Increasing educational participation may have a wide variety of benefits for individuals and society.[58]

The expansion of post-compulsory education may have inadvertently stirred the polarisation of British society into liberal cosmopolitans and national communitarians. Yet there is less persuasive evidence that voters' identity became more divided during the Blair years on attitudes towards gender, homosexuality and racial prejudice as Chapter 8 will show.[59]

Tackling crime and its causes: law and order under New Labour

Another important secular trend after 1997 concerned the rate of crime in the UK. Despite its tough rhetoric on law and order, crime had risen dramatically under Conservative governments in the 1980s and 1990s. As shadow home secretary, Blair made political capital out of rising crime in the Thatcher/Major years. Fear of crime and disorder among the population exponentially rose. Blair's rhetoric about tackling 'crime and its causes' appealed to contrasting viewpoints in the contested law and order debate.

On the one hand, Labour's aim of reducing crime signalled it would restore the sense of moral responsibility with tough sanctions for those who broke the law. New Labour demonstrated it was willing to seize ideas once embraced by the Conservatives. The shift instigated by Blair signalled an appetite to reclaim political territory once dominated by the Right. Labour's incorporation of policy ideas from the United States, particularly 'zero tolerance' policing and longer prison sentences, bolstered its emphasis on social order. Commentators claimed because Labour 'increasingly disappointed much of its 'core' constituency on tax and income redistribution', the party developed an appeal to its traditional supporters 'with tough anti-crime initiatives and a burgeoning prison population'.[60]

At the same time, Labour exploited deftly the Left's intuition that crime had social causes. By the late 1990s, Britain was palpably a more unequal and divided society. Poorer places and rundown estates were allowed to badly deteriorate during the Thatcher decade. The fight against crime meant tackling the underlying causes of exclusion. There was an emphasis on regenerating deprived neighbourhoods with increasing opportunities for groups vulnerable to structural disadvantage and incivility.

How effective was New Labour in reducing crime? The crime rate fell significantly as Figure 7.6 demonstrates, although it had begun to fall during the Major governments. The previous home secretary, Michael Howard, adopted tough 'prison works' rhetoric and punitive sentencing policies. Under Labour, it was

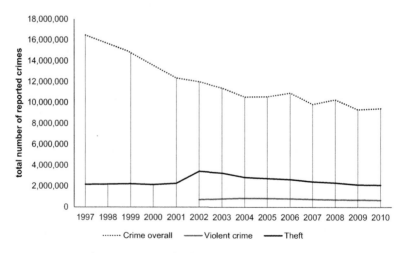

FIGURE 7.6 Trends in crime in England and Wales, Crime Survey data (BCS)

claimed, 'crime has fallen more in the last ten years than at any time in the past century'. In its 2005 manifesto, Labour stated that crime had doubled since the 1970s.
After the party came to power, crime fell 30 per cent, while violent crime decreased
by 26 per cent. Headline crime figures are, of course, notoriously unreliable. The
British Crime Survey (BCS) is regarded as more accurate than standard recording of
crime by the police. Under Labour, crime fell according to BCS data. Yet recorded
crime continued to rise.[61] Spending on policing and criminal justice increased significantly. The criminal justice system was continuously reformed, reducing the
time between arrest and sentencing of offenders. There was greater emphasis on
tackling domestic violence, racially motivated crime and sexual offences.

The paradox is that the fall in crime was matched by the growing prison population as Figure 7.7 indicates. The numbers in custody increased from 15,000
at the end of the Second World War to 85,000 by the time Blair left office.
The growth of the prison population had accelerated since the mid-1990s: more
offenders were sentenced to custody, judges handed down longer determinate
sentences, the average time spent in prison increased from 8.1 months in 1999 to
nearly 10 months by 2010, while the prison population increasingly comprised
serious offenders, mainly those convicted of drug offences and sexual crimes.[62]
Controversially, the 2003 Criminal Justice Act introduced indeterminate sentences for 'public protection' (IPP). In enacting such measures, ministers went
against the advice of officials in the home office and the prison service.[63] The
then home secretary, David Blunkett, estimated that around 900 prisoners convicted of serious violent and sexual offences would be eligible. Yet by 2010, the
number of prisoners subject to IPP reached 6,000, a population that had a self-
harm rate of 872 per 1,000 prisoners according to the Prison Reform Trust.

The growing shortage of prison places led ministers to give the private sector
an unprecedented role in procuring new prisons. Nevertheless, the performance

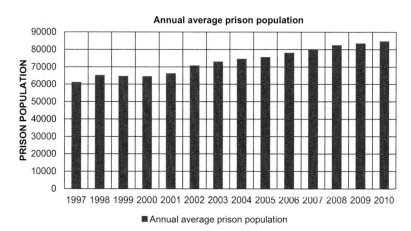

FIGURE 7.7   The prison population in England and Wales 1997–2010 (Home Office data)

of private prisons raised serious questions. More seriously, few would have expected the prison population to grow as rapidly under Labour home secretaries as under the punitive regime of Michael Howard. The condition of Young Offenders' Institutions (YOIs), revealed by Her Majesty's inspector of prisons to be cesspits of depravity and violence, was scandalous. New Labour continued to believe that the high rate of incarceration would lead to a long-term fall in crime. Yet the experience of the United States revealed the fallacy of that assumption. The cost of imprisonment dramatically increased with negative repercussions for the UK public finances.

It must be noted that elsewhere, criminal justice policy under Labour tilted towards more recognisably liberal approaches. Striking were the changes in youth justice, as well as efforts to create viable models of neighbourhood policing, curtailing punitive 'stop and search' practices that targeted ethnic minority communities. Nonetheless, the Blair/Brown governments made no decisive breakthrough in the politics of law and order. The declining crime rate was never harnessed to create political space for an alternative agenda. New Labour felt compelled to maintain its tough rhetoric and policies.

Identity in the era of migration and diversity: Britain 'sleep walking towards segregation'?

Under the Blair governments, the UK became more ethnically diverse. Labour oversaw rising levels of immigration, particularly from the EU under free movement after enlargement. 'The reasons they come reflect the core strengths of the UK', claimed an internal government review: 'A dynamic and open labour market; an outward-looking, trading nation with global networks; a generally liberal, tolerant society; and global language'.[64] Britain had a flexible labour market that was particularly attractive to migrants. Moreover, the UK was viewed as a 'safe haven' by asylum seekers fleeing persecution. The number of migrants entering Britain and staying at least one year increased from 326,100 in 1997 to 582,100 by 2007; 8.3 per cent of the UK population were now foreign-born.[65] The number of immigrants as a share of the working-age population grew from 8 per cent to 17 per cent, one-third of whom came from EU countries.[66] Two-thirds of the new migrants settled in London. Britain was becoming a 'migration state'. Labour did not arrive in power with a plan to alter the face of Britain by expanding migration.[67] Immigration was hardly an issue during the 1997 election campaign.[68] The Blair governments believed migration should be 'managed', so more immigrants could enter the UK to find work and study. Ministers insisted migration would generate substantive economic benefits. A report by the Cabinet Office Performance and Innovation Unit (PIU) calculated that foreign-born workers contributed 10 per cent more to public revenues than they received in support from the state.

Moreover, public services depended increasingly on migrant labour. Low-skilled service sector businesses from hospitality to hairdressing relied heavily on foreign workers. In a speech to the Institute for Public Policy Research (IPPR) in

2001, the home office minister, Barbara Roche, claimed migration would generate unprecedented material advantages for the UK in the globalising economy.[69] The liberalisation of immigration policy was driven by an economic rationale; consequently, ministers appeared insensitive to concerns about identity and belonging.[70] In relation to economic migration, the Labour government 'comprehensively changed policy and marked a decisive break with the previous policy model'.[71]

As a result, criteria for work permits were relaxed, low- and high-skilled migrant worker programmes were expanded, the number of international students more than doubled, while ministers enacted a permissive points-based immigration system.[72] The British government, a leading advocate of EU enlargement, then agreed in 2003 that citizens of the eight accession countries in Eastern Europe would enjoy free movement without any transition period. A study by University College, London, estimated that enlargement would increase the flow of migrants into the UK by 5,000–13,000 per annum.[73] Illegal immigration and the flow of 'bogus' asylum seekers would be stemmed through effective controls with new surveillance technologies and enforcement at borders. The liberalisation of economic migration was combined with a tough line on security.[74]

Yet New Labour's approach to asylum seekers, in particular, was incoherent. The former home office minister, Tony McNulty, acknowledged Labour's policy was flawed.[75] Under the Blair government's regime, asylum seekers were not permitted to accept paid work. They effectively became state dependents. The 1999 Immigration and Asylum Act placed those claiming asylum outside the social security system, allocating them a mixture of food vouchers and money that amounted to only 70 per cent of the standard level of income support.[76] The creation of a separate welfare infrastructure was ineffective and expensive, leading to innumerable layers of bureaucracy.[77] The consequence was growing destitution and hardship. Asylum seekers were dispersed into parts of the UK with a lower level of income per head, where pressures on public services were rising and social cohesion was weaker. They were more likely to be criminalised and detained: capacity in UK detention centres increased from 1,000 in 1998 to 4,000 by 2009.[78] New Labour continued to depict asylum seekers as a threat to social order. Labour's policies inadvertently weakened race relations, stirring the noxious politics of immigration.

There were subsequent efforts to strengthen integration strategies. Policy moved away from the post-war emphasis on multiculturalism, depicted by Roy Jenkins as 'not a flattening process of assimilation but equal opportunity accompanied by cultural diversity in an atmosphere of mutual tolerance'. Ministers were increasingly aware that the 'flood' of migrants was reshaping British politics, identity and culture. The government became concerned about the preservation of common values, alongside the perceived trade-off between diversity and solidarity.[79] The then chair of the Commission for Racial Equality (CRE), Trevor Philips, warned Britain was 'sleepwalking to segregation'. Serious disturbances in Bradford, Oldham and Burnley in the summer of 2001 led to growing disquiet about ethnic polarisation.

An influential report commissioned by the Home Office authored by the former chief executive of Nottingham City Council, Ted Cantle, struck a note of alarm: 'Whilst the physical segregation of housing estates and inner city areas came as no surprise, the team was particularly struck by the depth of polarisation of our towns and cities', the report concluded. Cantle continued:

> The extent to which these physical divisions were compounded by so many other aspects of our daily lives, was very evident. Separate educational arrangements, community and voluntary bodies, employment, places of worship, language . . . means that many communities operate on the basis of a series of parallel lives.[80]

David Bell, the chief inspector of schools, told a conference in 2005: 'I worry that many young people are being educated in faith-based schools with little appreciation of their wider responsibilities and obligations to British society'. In the light of the 9/11 attacks, there was heightened concern about prevailing attitudes within Muslim communities. Public policy had to address 'the moral oxygen for violence and confrontation' that existed within Western Islam.[81] Subsequent legislation meant immigrants were required to swear an oath of loyalty to the Queen, pass a citizenship test and display proficiency in the English language.[82]

New Labour's legacy was a relatively liberal immigration regime accompanied by a more diverse society. The UK was attractive as a destination, given its relative economic prosperity. Britain was an appealing place for asylum seekers who sought leave to remain, displaced by wars in which the UK was implicated, including Kosovo, Sierra Leone and Iraq. Still, the number of asylum seekers granted leave to remain fell from 32,500 in 1997 to 25,710 by 2005.[83] A subsequent Home Office report highlighted that new migrants to Britain had 'more diverse origins' since they came from a wider pool of source countries. Migration was becoming short term and 'opportunistic', driven by job openings and the desire to improve skills. New technologies and travel enabled migrants to remain in touch with their home country encouraging 'mixed loyalties and identities'. It was ever harder for national governments to control the movement of people.[84]

Labour's fundamental difficulty in handling the politics of migration lay in its detachment from the deindustrialising regions outside the South-East of England. The costs and benefits of economic migration were distributed unevenly. New Labour's identity rested on eschewing the party's roots in working-class industrialism, the culture of organised labour, the pride taken in manual work and the existence of vibrant centres of commerce in the towns of provincial England. Ministers had less appreciation of the tensions generated by immigration, alongside social and economic dislocation outside the metropolis. Technological changes meant the mature capitalist democracies experienced dramatic growth in the share of low-skilled, low-wage jobs, nowhere more so than Britain. The flexible labour market ensured wages rapidly decreased. Employment growth was strong in much of Britain, but there was continuing downward pressure on incomes.[85] New Labour embraced the premise of liberal political economy that citizens should be empowered as consumers, not producers in the workplace.[86]

As a consequence, risk was redistributed from employers to workers. The polarisation of employment coincided with the rapid growth of immigration. During the 2000s, the wage dispersion between the 10th and 90th percentiles grew by more than 50 per cent.[87] The expansion of the insecure low-wage economy had repercussions. There was the marked decline in the availability of high-status jobs, particularly for men with manual skills. A growing proportion of the workforce became dependent on benefits and tax credits to make work viable. For those without children, the value of benefits sharply declined. In regions that experienced deindustrialisation, the rate of economic inactivity continued to increase.[88] Particular areas experienced alarming pressures on public services. Immigrants entered a more polarised and unequal labour market. In 2006, John Denham, MP for Southampton Itchen, calculated that 14,000 migrants arrived in his city over a period of eighteen months following EU enlargement. The daily wage rate in the building trade consequently fell by 50 per cent. Not surprisingly, British citizens became less comfortable with migration.

Conflict over immigration led to growing divisions over national identity. In the early 2000s, the Home Office was able to claim: 'We have become part of an EU free movement zone that includes 350 million, soon to be half a million, without political controversy or social/economic upheaval'.[89] The government's aim was to 'create communities that thrive on diversity'. New Labour's liberal stance was encouraged by the belief that the Conservatives' efforts to exploit immigration cemented its reputation as 'the nasty party'. As Tory leader, Michael Howard fought the 2005 election on the infamous slogan 'Are you thinking what we're thinking'? In contrast, Labour emphasised it was committed to diversity and openness. Andrew Neather, a former Number Ten speechwriter, claimed that New Labour's intention was to 'rub the Right's nose in diversity and render their arguments out of date'.[90]

Yet it was social democracy that came under strain. While celebrating the economic benefits of the immigration boom:

> Ministers wouldn't talk about it. . . . They probably realised the conservatism of their core voters: while Ministers might have been passionately in favour of a more diverse society, it wasn't necessarily a debate they wanted to have in working men's clubs in Sheffield or Sunderland.[91]

Gordon Brown's claim that Britain was ideally placed to manage the inflow as a 'uniquely-rich, open and outward-looking culture' with 'a distinctive set of British values' appeared complacent.[92] Labour failed to foresee the emergence of the more aggrieved spirit of Englishness, with growing resentment towards migrants, asylum seekers, newcomers and the EU. External influences posed an imminent threat to the English people's identity and sovereignty. Underlying these sentiments were profound feelings of bewilderment and loss. At the same time, according to the sociologist Paul Gilroy, 'black Britons remained suspicious and distant from political institutions'.[93]

Across Europe, nationalist and 'anti-foreigner sentiment' was escalating according to Blair's polling strategist, Stan Greenberg. The hostility was hardly new. In 1992, the presidential candidate, Ross Perot, won almost 20 per cent of the popular vote in the United States. Perot's support came from younger working-class men who were 'anti-establishment, anti-immigrant, and anti-trade (NAFTA)'. Greenberg insisted the centre-left must act to ensure 'a sense of right and wrong . . . is brought to bear on the issue of immigration, asylum, borders and crime'. The Left would only address voters' disconnection by acknowledging, 'legitimate concerns. . . . Voters are not racist simply because they raise these issues. And if they do not get heard, the Right will reap the bounty'.[94] Greenberg's warning proved prophetic. In 2003, the prime minister warned, 'the Left has to be careful not to repeat the mistakes of the past by ignoring the electorate's genuine anxieties. . . . The Left has been behind the curve on the insecurity issues of asylum and crime'.[95] Yet Blair's awakening may have come too late.

No longer an 'awkward partner'? The Europeanisation of British politics

Under Labour, Britain's EU membership continued to influence the economy and political system fifty years after the end of the Second World War. The City of London became the centre of Eurozone activity, a global financial centre rivalling New York and Singapore. The EU reshaped leading UK manufacturing sectors from motor vehicles to pharmaceuticals. Opportunities for mobility and travel increased. A8 migration altered fundamentally the nature of the labour market. The links between British universities and continental Europe deepened. The Europeanisation of British society was a key development in the New Labour years.

As such, the UK's society and polity became more distinctly *European* under the Blair and Brown administrations. Although the government was reticent about making the constructive case for EU membership, structurally there is little doubt Britain was a more discernibly European country after 1997. The UK was closely aligned with EU member-states, which affected secular trends influencing economic and social policy. In relation to social investment and the welfare state, Britain conformed increasingly to European norms of protection and citizenship. There were efforts to fashion an 'Anglo-Social' welfare model. The structure of taxation and public expenditure moved in the direction of Northern European countries, particularly Sweden and the Netherlands. Moreover, Britain's civic culture centred on the formalised constitution, tolerance of minorities, pluralist institutions and respect for human rights reflected the normative European ideal of the liberal rules-based order, even if that inheritance was not sustained after the Brexit referendum in 2016. Despite its affinity with America, Labour still saw Europe as offering the most compelling vision for national modernisation and reform.

Conclusion: the New Labour effect

Did New Labour succeed in translating the 'poetry' of opposition politics into the 'prose' of deploying governmental power to transform existing society? This chapter posed a crucial question at the outset: what *difference* did Labour make in the major areas of policy and politics? How far did the Blair and Brown governments decisively alter Britain's society and economy? Unquestionably, the dominant trends were moving in a social democratic direction after thirteen years. The policies of the Blair and Brown governments sought to enhance economic growth and social cohesion, boosting the capacities of citizens to lead stable and fulfilling lives.

The accusation that New Labour 'normalised' neo-liberalism in Britain barely stands up to scrutiny.[96] Under Blair and Brown, growth disproportionately benefited low-income households. The rapid rise in income inequality diminished. The NMW transformed the politics of low pay. Participation in post-compulsory education grew dramatically. The crime rate fell, in part because attention was paid to underlying social pathologies. Above all, British society became more recognisably European, marked by the increasing commitment to solidarity rather than capital accumulation alone.

Nevertheless, the refusal to address Britain's deeply unequal political economy cast a long shadow, compounded by the 2008 financial crisis. The crash exposed the fragility of Blair and Brown's achievements. Some of the more distinctive New Labour policies and institutions survived post-2010 austerity. Yet the Labour governments' imprint in history became less perceptible. Insufficient attention was paid to fashioning agencies and policy programmes that captured citizens' loyalty and trust. New Labour lacked an organising concept for the state and public services. Moreover, alleged dishonesty over Iraq threatened the perceived legitimacy of British politics and representative democracy.

The financial crisis raised fundamental questions about the viability of British social democracy in the era of global capitalism. Blair and Brown's success was to prevent the economy prematurely destroying the Labour government as occurred in the 1940s and 1960s. Labour saw the prosperous and productive economy as critical to solving social ills. New Labour believed if the economy was performing well, the party would dominate electoral politics. Yet median wages sharply declined in the second term. Many voters were not much better off by the time Labour was defeated in 2010. What also became apparent was the growing disconnection between GDP growth and living standards. The Blair administration failed to anticipate the so-called Easterlin paradox: higher economic growth does not necessarily produce greater life satisfaction.[97] By the 2005 election, Labour was dependent on the administration's economic record to project its political message, despite the growing importance of post-materialist issues. Ethical socialists in the early twentieth century believed that society should not be exclusively concerned with material growth. At the turn of the twenty-first century, new themes arose concerning family stability, the quality of neighbourhoods, pressures to reconcile paid work with care, the threat posed to the planet by climate change to which New Labour often appeared oblivious.

Taken as a whole, the 2008 crash underlined the strategic dilemma for social democratic governments that rely on the stability of the global economy to achieve their objectives. The financial crisis proved to be a severe blow to Labour's hopes of fashioning the new progressive orthodoxy in British politics, as will become clear in the chapter that follows.

Notes

1 'Community Cohesion: A Report of the Independent Review Team Chaired by Ted Cantle', London: The Home Office, 2001.
2 P. Mandelson, 'Speech to Executives in Silicon Valley', California, October 1999.
3 The Labour Party Manifesto, 'Britain Deserves Better', p. 3, London: The Labour Party, 1997.
4 Interview, Geoffrey Norris, former No. 10 official, May 2011.
5 F. Faucher-King & P. Le Gales, *The New Labour Experiment*, Stanford: Stanford University Press, 2010.
6 K. Ussher, 'Labour's Record on the Economy', in P. Diamond & M. Kenny, *Reassessing New Labour*, p. 109, Oxford: Wiley, 2011.
7 D. Corry, 'Labour and the Economy 1997–2010: More Than a Faustian Pact', in P. Diamond & M. Kenny, *Reassessing New Labour: State, Society and Economy Under Blair and Brown*, London: The Political Quarterly, 2011.
8 D. Corry, A. Valero & J. Van Reenan, 'UK Economic Performance', p. 3, *LSE Discussion Paper*, March 2011.
9 E. Balls, 'Open Macroeconomics in an Open Economy', *Scottish Journal of Political Economy*, Volume 45 (2), pp. 113–132, 1998 cited in J. Tomlinson, 'It's The Economy, Stupid! Labour and the Economy', p. 100.
10 J. Tomlinson, 'It's The Economy, Stupid! Labour and the Economy', p. 435.
11 M. Wolf, 'How Labour Steered an Economy Going Global', *The Financial Times*, 16th September 2006.
12 M. Wolf, 'How Labour Steered an Economy Going Global'.
13 H. Glennerster, *British Social Policy: 1945 to the Present*.
14 M. Wolf, 'How Labour Steered an Economy Going Global'.
15 A. Gamble, *The Free Economy and the Strong State*.
16 H. Thompson, 'The Economy', p. 902.
17 G. Norris in O. Daddow, 'New Labour: A Witness History', *Contemporary British History*, p. 113.
18 A. Gamble, *The Free Economy and the Strong State*.
19 L. Elliot & D. Atkinson, *Fantasy Island*, London: Constable, 2000.
20 C. Crouch, *The Strange Non-Death of Neo-Liberalism*.
21 P. Gregg, 'Pre-Distribution as a New Set of Policy Tools', *Discussion Paper*, London: Policy Network, 2012.
22 Table 6.2 is based on R. Lupton, J. Hills, K. Stewart & P. Vizard, 'Labour's Social Policy Record: Policy, Spending and Outcomes 1997–2010', *Research Report 1*, Centre for the Analysis of Social Exclusion/LSE, June 2013.
23 J. Hills, *Towards a More Equal Society*, p. 134, Bristol: Policy Press, 2005.
24 J. Hills, *Inequality and the State*, Oxford: Oxford University Press, 2010.
25 P. Gregg, 'Pre-Distribution as a New Set of Policy Tools'.
26 P. Gregg, 'Pre-Distribution as a New Set of Policy Tools'.
27 K. Ussher, 'Labour's Economic Record'.
28 K. Ussher, 'Labour's Economic Record'. The data in Figure 7.1, 7.2 and 7.3 is provided by the Office for National Statistics (ONS).

29 Cited in N. Timmins, *The Five Giants: A Biography of the Welfare State*, p. 654, London: William Collins.
30 J. Hills, *Inequality and the State.*
31 R. Joyce & L. Sibieta, 'An Assessment of Labour's Record on Income Inequality and Poverty', *Oxford Review of Economic Policy*, Volume 29 (1), pp. 178–202, 2013.
32 J. Lindley & S. Machin, 'Wage Inequality in the Labour Years', *Oxford Review of Economic Policy*, pp. 165–177, Volume 29 (1), 2013.
33 A. Heath, *Social Progress in Britain*, pp. 58–59.
34 R. Joyce & L. Sibieta, 'An Assessment of Labour's Record on Income Inequality and Poverty', pp. 178–202.
35 R. Joyce & L. Sibieta, 'An Assessment of Labour's Record on Income Inequality and Poverty', p. 183.
36 OECD, 'Divided We Stand: Why Inequality Keeps Rising, Country Note – United Kingdom'.
37 OECD, 'Divided We Stand: Why Inequality Keeps Rising, Country Note – United Kingdom'.
38 OECD, 'Divided We Stand: Why Inequality Keeps Rising, Country Note – United Kingdom'.
39 M. Wolf, 'How Labour Steered an Economy Going Global', *The Financial Times*, 16th September 2006.
40 J. Hills et al., *Wealth in the United Kingdom*, Oxford: Oxford University Press, 2014.
41 J. Hills & H. Glennerster, 'Why the Left Need to Take Wealth Seriously Again', *Juncture*, Volume 20 (1), Summer 2013.
42 J. Hills et al., *Wealth in the United Kingdom.*
43 J. Hills & H. Glennerster, 'Why the Left Need to Take Wealth Seriously Again', p. 74.
44 P. Gregg, 'Pre-distribution as a New Set of Policy Tools'.
45 http://cep.lse.ac.uk/pubs/download/dp1536.pdf. Accessed 28th July 2018.
46 Confidential Memorandum to the Prime Minister, 'Towards an Election Strategy', 29th July 2004.
47 'Realising Britain's Potential: Future Strategic Challenges for Britain', The Prime Minister's Strategy Unit, London: The Cabinet Office, 2008. The report is the data source for Figure 7.4.
48 Private Note, 10 Downing Street, 'D. Miliband – Third Way Seminar', 22nd July 1999.
49 Source for Figure 7.5. https://gov.uk/government/statistics/participation-rates-in-higher-education-2006-to-2010. Accessed 10th December 2018.
50 'Higher Education in the Learning Society', London: HMG, January 1997.
51 H. Glennerster, *British Social Policy: 1945 to the Present.*
52 'The Future of Higher Education', London: HMG, January 2003.
53 A. Adonis, Confidential Memorandum to the Prime Minister, 'Tuition Fees', 25th July 2003.
54 Private Note, 10 Downing Street, 'D. Miliband – Third Way Seminar', 22nd July 1999.
55 A. Wolf, 'Review of Vocational Education: The Wolf Report': https://gov.uk/government/publications/review-of-vocational-education-the-wolf-report. Accessed 16th September 2019.
56 https://fullfact.org/education/young-peoples-participation-higher-education/. Accessed 14th June 2019.
57 P. Sturridge, 'Education and Social Liberalism: Pursuing the Link', *Oxford Review of Education*, Volume 42 (2), pp. 146–162, 2016.
58 A. Heath, *Social Progress in Britain*, p. 87.
59 B. Duffy et al., 'Divided Britain? Polarisation and Fragmentation Trends in the UK', London: The Policy Institute, King's College, 2019. Furlong (2019) draws our attention to the problems of such categories, which leads the predominantly white middle class to be lumped together with economically disadvantaged ethnic minorities as 'cosmopolitan' voters.
60 F. Klug, 'New Labour and the Distribution of Power: Constitutional Reform, Human Rights and Civil Liberties', in P. Diamond & M. Kenny (eds.), *Reassessing New Labour: Market, State and Society under Blair and Brown*, Oxford: Blackwell, 2011.

61 R. Reiner, 'Success or Statistics? New Labour and Crime Control', *Criminal Justice Matters*, Volume 67 (1), pp. 4–31, 2007.
62 https://assets.publishing.service.gov.uk/government/uploads/system/uploads/attachment_data/file/541667/prison-population-story-1993-2016.pdf. Accessed 15th December 2018.
63 https://theguardian.com/society/2019/jan/11/mental-anguish-and-wider-problems-with-ipp-sentences. Accessed 9th February 2019.
64 'The Future of Migration', Presentation to the Prime Minister's Policy Directorate by the Home Office Strategy Unit, 10 Downing Street, 19th December 2002, PD Personal Papers.
65 https://migrationpolicy.org/article/immigration-legacy-tony-blair. Accessed 12th October 2018.
66 http://cep.lse.ac.uk/pubs/download/EA019.pdf. Accessed 16th October 2018.
67 E. Consterdine, *Labour's Immigration Policy: The Making of the Migration State*, Basingstoke: Palgrave Macmillan, 2018.
68 Interview with Will Somerville, former Number Ten Strategy Unit Adviser, December 2019.
69 Interview with Tony McNulty, former Home Office Minister, September 2019.
70 Interview with Will Somerville, former Number Ten Strategy Unit Adviser, December 2019.
71 W. Somerville, *Immigration Under New Labour*, p. 79, Bristol: Policy Press, 2007.
72 E. Consterdine, *Labour's Immigration Policy: The Making of the Migration State*.
73 'The Future of Migration', Presentation to the Prime Minister's Policy Directorate by the Home Office Strategy Unit, 10 Downing Street, 19th December 2002, PD Personal Papers.
74 W. Somerville, *Immigration Under New Labour*.
75 Interview with Tony McNulty, former Home Office Minister, September 2019.
76 A. Bloc, 'A New Era or More of the Same? Asylum Policy in the UK', *Journal of Refugee Studies*, Volume 13 (1), 2000.
77 Interview with Will Somerville, former Number Ten Strategy Unit Adviser, December 2019.
78 G. Mulvey, 'When Policy Creates Politics: The Problematizing of Immigration and the Consequences for Refugee Integration in the UK', *Journal of Refugee Studies*, Volume 23 (4), pp. 437–462, 2010.
79 W. Somerville, *Immigration Under New Labour*, p. 51.
80 'Community Cohesion: A Report of the Independent Review Team Chaired by Ted Cantle', London: The Home Office, 2001.
81 Saggar, S. *Pariah Politics: Understanding Western Radical Islamism and What Should Be Done*, Oxford: Oxford University Press, 2008.
82 W. Somerville, *Immigration Under New Labour*, pp. 53–54.
83 W. Somerville, *Immigration Under New Labour*, p. 65.
84 'The Future of Migration', Presentation to the Prime Minister's Policy Directorate by the Home Office Strategy Unit, 10 Downing Street, 19th December 2002, PD Personal Papers.
85 J. Tomlinson, *Managing the Economy, Managing the People*, p. 89.
86 H. Thompson, 'The Economy'.
87 M. Goos & A. Manning, 'Lousy and Lovely Jobs: The Rising Polarization of Work in Britain', *The Review of Economics and Statistics*, Volume 89 (1), pp. 118–132, 2007; J. Tomlinson, *Managing the Economy, Managing the People*.
88 J. Tomlinson, *Managing the Economy, Managing the People*, pp. 93–94.
89 'The Future of Migration', Presentation to the Prime Minister's Policy Directorate by the Home Office Strategy Unit, 10 Downing Street, 19th December 2002, PD Personal Papers.
90 https://telegraph.co.uk/news/uknews/law-and-order/6418456/Labour-wanted-mass-immigration-to-make-UK-more-multicultural-says-former-adviser.html. Accessed 14 October 2019.
91 https://telegraph.co.uk/news/uknews/law-and-order/6418456/Labour-wanted-mass-immigration-to-make-UK-more-multicultural-says-former-adviser.html. Accessed 14 October 2019.

92 P. Snapper, 'The Elephant in the Room: Europe in the 2015 General Election', *French Journal of British Studies*, Volume 20 (3), 2015.
93 Cited in D. Swift, *A Left for Itself*, p. 55.
94 S. Greenberg, Confidential Memorandum to the Prime Minister, 'The Le Pen Problem', 2nd May 2002.
95 P. Wintour, 'Voters' Insecurities Must Not Be Neglected, Centre-Left Warned', *The Guardian*, 11th February 2003.
96 B. Jessop, 'New Labour and the Normalisation of Neo-Liberalism'.
97 R. Easterlin, 'Paradox Lost?', *Review of Behavioural Economics*, Volume 4 (4), pp. 311–339, 2017.

8

TOWARDS THE NEW PROGRESSIVE SETTLEMENT

The great weakness of British Labour . . . is its lack of a creed. The Labour party is hesitant in action because divided in mind. It does not achieve what it could because it does not know what it wants. It frets out of office and fumbles in it.

R. H. Tawney[1]

Introduction

The hallmark of radical administrations in twentieth century Britain is installing an enduring social and economic settlement that transforms domestic politics. This chapter's purpose is to examine how far New Labour succeeded in fashioning a new progressive dispensation, defining the agenda of government for a generation. To what extent did Labour permanently alter the terms of trade shifting British politics decisively towards the centre-left, away from Thatcherism and neo-liberalism? In the 1940s, Britain was shaped by the irrevocable turn towards collectivism. The embrace of market individualism dominated political life in the 1980s. Did the Blair and Brown administrations construct a new social democratic common sense, influencing how all future governments undertake politics and policy-making?

To be sure, the ability of ministers to entrench their governing legacy depends on the prevailing values and preferences of citizens, shaping the parameters of what is viable politically. Governments have the potential to remake popular values. Yet more often, they are compelled to go with the grain of the predominant mood. The chapter begins by examining Labour's influence on the attitudes of British voters. Labour did not inherit a blank canvas in public opinion. Some commentators believe voters were strongly influenced by the legacy of Thatcherism, transforming New Labour's inheritance while constraining the possibilities of social and economic reform.[2]

The chapter examines several related questions. How far did the Blair and Brown administrations transform attitudes and the 'mind-set' of the electorate, or did they merely accept the prevailing consensus? Why did attitudes towards welfare claimants become harsher during Labour's period in power despite the emphasis on reducing structural disadvantage? Why did support for higher taxes decline so sharply, given ministers' rhetoric about the pivotal importance of public services? Why did so many voters believe increasing spending on the NHS was wasted? Was the UK a more socially liberal society by 2010? And was there actually polarisation in Britain between 'anywheres' and 'somewheres'? How far did Labour's programme reconcile ostensibly contradictory values: an authoritarian populist view of social order, patriotism, national belonging and identity, against multiculturalism, social liberalisation and the enlightenment view of society? There are critical ambiguities in New Labour's politics and public opinion that merit further exploration throughout the chapter.

New Labour and British social attitudes

This chapter begins by considering whether public attitudes had become more social democratic in New Labour's wake. The benchmark for government's ability to alter the preferences of citizens were the 1945–51 Attlee administrations. There are historians who believe the post-war governments transformed Britain into a socialist society.[3] Meanwhile, Margaret Thatcher, it was argued, sought to reconstruct the political and moral character of the nation after 1979. Thatcher declared of her political mission: 'Economics are the method; the object is to change the soul'. Yet in post-war Britain, politicians more often accepted the constraints imposed by 'the existing patterns of values, beliefs and interests of the electorate'.[4] The evidence indicates attitudes barely shifted in a more social democratic direction under Blair and Brown.[5] Committed to 'big tent' politics, New Labour subtly constructed its extraordinary cross-class coalition. The party's identity meant representing all classes, refusing to take a side in the perennial struggle between labour and capital. It was accepted that Britain was a society marked by greater individualism, a situation Labour could not reverse easily. That meant a strategy of compromise with privileged interests.

The paradox of Labour's record is that on the main valence indicators of governing competence, the administrations performed well: as the previous chapter demonstrated, economic growth and stability were strong; the crime rate fell; major public services, particularly the NHS, improved. Yet voters became increasingly disenchanted. On departing office, Blair and Brown were perceived as mediocre, even incompetent prime ministers. There was loathing of Blair: the mood of sullen discontent went beyond Iraq. The quality of life apparently got no better. Public services, despite record spending, were not advancing quickly enough. Disadvantaged communities failed to prosper economically. There was disconnection between New Labour and voters.

This dismal situation was ironic since Labour's efforts to understand the attitudes of the electorate since the 1980s, pioneered by the polling strategist Philip Gould, bordered on the obsessive. Gould began his career in advertising. He came from an aspirational working-class family in Surrey, South-East England.[6] Gould started advising the Labour Party on political strategy in the mid-1980s, establishing the Shadow Communications Agency (SCA) at Peter Mandelson's behest. Labour's efforts to understand voters' attitudes had historically been ineffectual. Since the 1940s, the party was 'reluctant to focus much attention on understanding the views of the electorate, as opposed to developing policy positions and believing that the electorate could be persuaded to support those policies'.[7]

Throughout the post-war era, Labour stubbornly refused to commission opinion surveys. It believed the public would be persuaded to support its policies by the force of moral argument. Nye Bevan insisted that Labour 'having decided what our policy should be', must, 'put it as attractively as possible to the population; not to adjust our policy opportunely to the contemporary mood, but cling to our policy'.[8] Following the 1983 catastrophe, Labour gradually came to understand social change, drawing on polling *and* qualitative 'focus groups'. These moves proved to be controversial. Gould did not only reveal trends in public opinion. Through his work, he constructed a political 'image' of the electorate, centred on the idea of the 'aspirational' middle class as the critical electoral constituency. Mark Abrams gave similar advice to Hugh Gaitskell in the late 1950s. Yet Abrams relied on quantitative polling. Gould pioneered the use of qualitative research, using data to dictate the shape of Labour's policy agenda.

Critics lamented that Gould's research bolstered the innate conservatism of the New Labour leadership. Electoral politics meant primarily appealing to the self-interest and materialism of voters. Even in the aftermath of the financial crash, Blair insisted the party had to make a 'personal aspiration offer' focused on 'why [Labour] are good for you as an individual . . . showing we could make people make off'.[9] Tony Benn acidly remarked that the period after 1997 was the first time in history where British voters were recognisably to the Left of the government.[10]

Changes in attitudes: going against the grain of social democracy?

Political scientists have determined that between 1997 and 2010, the British electorate became more neo-liberal and Thatcherite.[11] Attitudes towards working-age benefit claimants and poorer households hardened considerably. Voters grew more ambivalent about the welfare state. They were markedly less sympathetic towards redistribution. Perceptions of the very poorest became more negative after several decades of targeting and means-testing. Thatcherism had an effect in shaping generational attitudes. Those aged eighteen to thirty-five were less sympathetic to welfarism. British Social Attitudes (BSA) survey data indicates that younger generations were more individualistic and self-reliant in tune with the ethics and ideology of Thatcherism. Ivor Crewe asked whether Britain had finally become a 'Thatcherite' nation: 'Thatcher's Children are indeed more right-wing and authoritarian than the generation preceding them'.[12] The proportion of voters who believed 'if welfare benefits weren't so generous, people would learn to stand on their own two feet', increased from 33 per cent in the mid-1980s to

55 per cent by 2010.[13] Moreover, 81 per cent in 2010 agreed, 'large numbers of people these days falsely claim benefits', rising from 67 per cent since 1987.

Yet the electorate undoubtedly became more concerned about inequality and the living standards of poorer pensioners and children. Support for spending on health and education increased. The proportion of voters who felt 'ordinary working people do not get their fair share of the nation's wealth', that there was 'one law for the rich and one for the poor', grew.[14] Three-quarters of voters believed the income gap in the UK was too large. Even so, voters were sceptical much could be done by governments.

How far were Blair and Brown's political generation responsible for reinforcing the change in social attitudes? The National Centre for Social Research (Nat Cen) concluded that the harsh rhetoric of Labour ministers in chastising the behaviour of welfare recipients had a marked effect. The prime minister's message about welfare support being a 'hand-up, not a hand-out' (rather than a 'lifestyle choice') undermined the welfare state's legitimacy. Labour's discourse reinforced popular sentiments about fairness and responsibility. Yet in using emotive and moralistic language, the Labour governments undermined their efforts to create an inclusive society.

As perplexing were Blair's attempts to legitimise the earnings of the wealthy. The prime minister claimed the gap between high and low earners was irrelevant to social justice. If government policies penalised the rich deliberately, the wealthy might take flight, moving capital to other jurisdictions. John Curtice believes that on inequality and redistribution, Labour shifted the electorate Rightwards. Curtice wrote in the aftermath of Brown's defeat: 'Britain is seemingly less concerned now about equality and fairness than it was during the last recession of the early 1990s. . . . The British public continue to adhere to a relatively inegalitarian mood'.[15] Attitudes were becoming less propitious for social democracy. Yet that cannot be blamed solely on the Labour governments. The thermostatic model used by political scientists indicates public opinion on taxation and public spending is inherently cyclical.[16] The appetite for policy reforms diminishes naturally as governments address voters' preferences in changing the tax and spending balance. After 1997, fiscal policy inevitably eroded long-term support for redistribution.

Public spending and tax rises: towards a new consensus?

Although commentators maintain Labour tilted the pendulum of public opinion towards the Right after 1997, the evidence is less clear cut. It is striking that support for spending on public services continued to rise. If Britain moved Rightwards, Blair and Brown still succeeded in entrenching the legitimacy of state-funded provision. The Thatcher and Major governments flirted with the privatisation of health and education.[17] Yet the electorate's appetite to dismantle taxpayer-funded services appeared limited. The post-war commitment to maintaining cradle-to-grave provision free at the point of use survived two decades of market liberalism. After 1997, New Labour bolstered the social democratic consensus. Although attitudes towards the poor became more negative, the majority believed that national governments still had major responsibilities to their citizens.

The BSA data in Figure 8.1 confirms that voters were still committed to the NHS and the state pension, even if support for social housing gradually eroded. Following the painful defeat in 1992, Labour strategists struggled to devise a strategy on taxation and public spending that appealed to the contradictory instincts of voters. British voters wanted public services typical of Scandinavia combined with the low rates of taxation usually found in the United States. Although the electorate's views on tax and redistribution became more ambiguous, Britain was now 'less socially divided over the classic political issue of redistribution'.[18] Under Labour, spending markedly rose. Figure 8.2 illustrates the scale of the increase as a share of national income. The cumulative growth in public expenditure was more dramatic in cash terms (Figure 8.3).

It is striking that under Labour, spending grew faster than in other industrialised countries. There was convergence among EU member-states well in advance of the 2008 financial crisis (Figure 8.4). Furthermore, the composition of public expenditure altered significantly. By the late 2000s, spending was focused increasingly on the NHS and social security, as well as education,

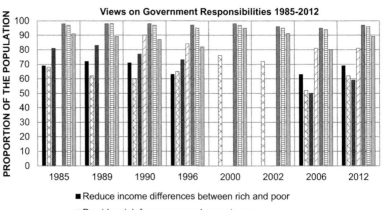

FIGURE 8.1 Views on government responsibilities 1985–2012 (British Social Attitudes Survey)

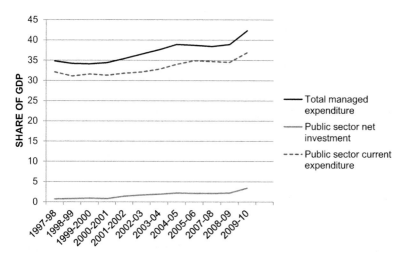

FIGURE 8.2 Growth of UK public spending as a share of GDP (Office for National Statistics)

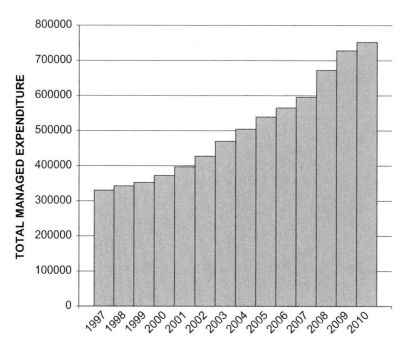

FIGURE 8.3 Growth of UK total managed expenditure in real terms 1997–2001 (Office for National Statistics)

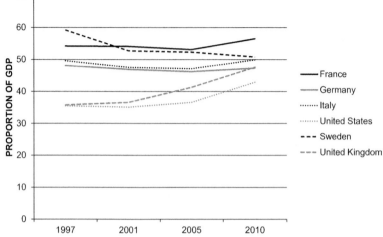

FIGURE 8.4 Government spending as a proportion of GDP among key OECD countries 1997–2010 (Organisation for Economic Co-operation and Development)

particularly schools and early years. The post-war priorities of nationalisation, defence and industrial subsidies dramatically declined, reflecting the shift in voters' preferences (Figure 8.5).

Figure 8.6 illustrates that tax revenues as a proportion of national income also rose in the UK relative to other countries, although Britain remained behind France, Germany and Sweden. Yet New Labour's approach of maintaining low taxes while spending increased entailed a precarious balancing act, particularly during an economic downturn when lower growth depleted government revenues. The British economy's erratic post-war performance had already undermined Croslandite optimism that high and stable growth meant extra resources for public spending. New Labour hoped that per capita GDP would increase in the late 1990s, yet the UK failed to achieve a level of growth that would permit a permanent shift in the size of the state. In its appeal to voters, Labour struggled to square the circle of restraining taxes and increasing spending. Not surprisingly, New Labour became increasingly defensive. Even after two decisive election victories, ministers were determined to appease high-income households. A confidential memorandum drafted by the prime minister's Policy Directorate concluded: 'The aggregate burden of taxation is reaching its economic limits. There is survey evidence of growing taxpayer resistance to increases in taxation', particularly among those caught by the 40p tax band.[19] The number of basic and higher rate taxpayers rose, as Figure 8.7 illustrates (see page 270).

Under the Blair administrations, adjustments in taxation noticeably benefited families with children: the average tax burden for a one-earner family fell from

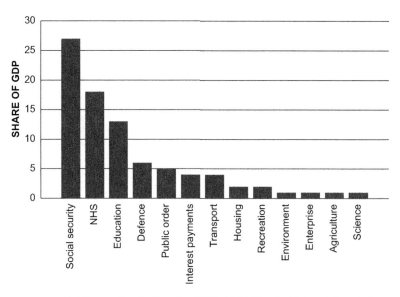

FIGURE 8.5 Public spending by function 2009–10 (Office for National Statistics)

25.8 per cent in 1997 to 12.9 per cent due to Working Families Tax Credit (WFTC). In contrast, single earners without children saw the tax burden rise from 17.8 to 24.7 per cent. The proportion of taxation as a share of national income averaged 35 per cent in the early 1990s, increasing to 38 per cent under New Labour, which put Britain among the average in the industrialised countries. Yet the Blair and Brown administrations refused to face up to voters about the level of taxation necessary to guarantee decent services in a cohesive society. Qualitative research conducted by the advertising executive Leslie Butterfield indicated divergence among the middle class. Some voters were prepared to pay more tax, particularly to address NHS underfunding. The support for public services was hardly surprising, given many were themselves public sector employees. Other voters believed personal responsibility and independence were preferable to collectivism. They greatly resented paying more tax.[20]

The perception that additional spending on health and education was poorly managed or even wasted deepened taxpayer resistance. Generally, voters believed that services were improving locally, but the NHS and schools were declining nationally. Blair and Brown lived in perpetual fear of the taxpayers' revolt. Before the 2005 election, tax cuts were openly discussed in 10 Downing Street. The Policy Unit submitted proposals to increase personal tax allowances, while introducing a 30-pence income tax band. Income tax reductions would be achieved without breaking Treasury fiscal rules by generating revenue through congestion charging, auctioning landing slots at airports and privatisation of the

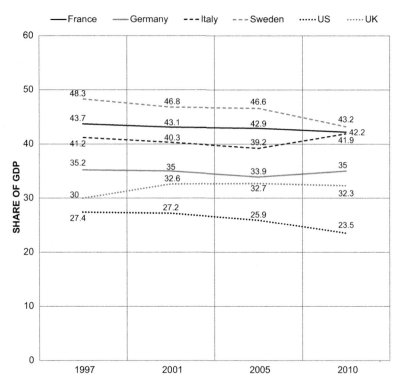

FIGURE 8.6 Tax revenue as a proportion of GDP in OECD countries (Organisation for Economic Co-operation and Development)

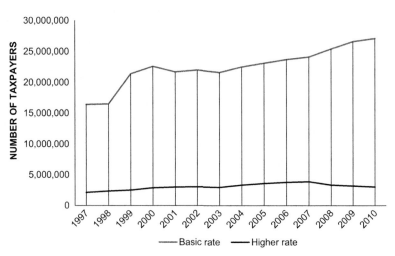

FIGURE 8.7 UK taxpayers paying basic and higher marginal income tax rate 1997–2010 (Office for National Statistics)

Royal Mail. There were efforts to reduce spending on welfare, particularly incapacity benefit. Number Ten's work on fiscal policy demonstrated Blair no longer trusted the Treasury's judgement, as the politics of tax and spend grew more toxic.

Was the money wasted?

The belief too much spending was wasted, aided by lurid media reporting of NHS bureaucracy and red tape, was the Achilles heel of Labour's effort to persuade the electorate of the virtue of public expenditure. The growth of public spending was significant, faster than under the Wilson and Callaghan administrations. Total public spending increased from 39.9 per cent of national income in 1996–97 to 48.1 per cent at the end of the Brown era, although that reflected the dramatic contraction of output and the bank bailouts after the financial collapse.[21] According to the IFS, the UK enjoyed the second-largest increase in spending among the industrialised nations. The perception of fiscal largesse led to several accusations. Firstly, extra spending was inefficiently allocated, inflating the number of public sector managers while encouraging profligate spending on infrastructure. The second claim was that Labour 'over-spent', failing to address the fundamental fiscal position, a view that became more credible in the aftermath of the 2008 crash.

The belief Labour governments habitually wasted taxpayers' money struck a chord. There were high-profile cases of NHS construction projects delivered incompetently. Public sector salaries increased sharply to stem the recruitment shortfall in teaching and nursing. Median weekly pay in the public sector rose significantly.[22] Yet the Institute for Fiscal Studies (IFS) found that productivity in health and education declined. The quality of public services certainly improved. Yet the increase in quality was less than would have been expected given the input of resources.[23] Despite structural reforms, the Labour governments had less effect than was anticipated. Attitudes towards public expenditure among voters became even more sceptical.

Yet there is precious little evidence that British voters were born-again neoliberals. Spending on working-age benefits was certainly resented. There was a growing perception that NHS investment was inefficient. Even so, the majority of voters valued the protective role of national government. Although support for raising income tax declined, by the end of Blair's tenure, support for the existing balance of taxation and spending at around 43 per cent of national income was stable, as Table 8.1 demonstrates. Few voters supported the minimal state with radically lower taxes and spending.

Despite that, progressive universalism came under strain. Support for redistribution began to wane. Labour's emphasis on conditionality in the welfare state – the principle that claimants had to show they were seeking work actively or retraining to receive benefits – made voters *more* sceptical of the welfare 'safety net'.[24] The proportion of voters who believed unemployment benefits were too low declined, especially among Labour voters as Table 8.2 highlights.

TABLE 8.1 Attitudes to taxation and spending[25]

	1997	2008
Increase taxes/spend more	62	39
Keep taxes/spend same	31	50
Reduce taxes/spend less	3	8

TABLE 8.2 Percentage of UK voters agreeing that unemployment benefits are too low[26]

	1986	1994	1998	2008
Conservative identifiers	24	34	15	12
Labour identifiers	63	67	37	28
Conservative-Labour gap	−39	−32	−23	−16

New Labour and social liberalism: a nation of tolerant authoritarians?

What of alterations in public attitudes beyond taxation and the size of government? After 1997, voters' identification with traditional norms and moral values in post-war Britain continued to decline. It is striking that the electorate were less committed to organised religion. Personal identities became more fluid. Attitudes towards sex and marriage had been transformed since the 1980s. The proportion of voters who believed there was 'nothing wrong' with sex outside marriage increased from 42 per cent in 1989 to 65 per cent by 2013.[27]

Gender roles were changing: fewer voters believed it was wrong for women to be in paid employment, although women continued to do the majority of household labour. The perception of men as 'breadwinners' and women as 'homemakers' sharply declined.[28] According to the BSA data, the number of voters who disagreed that men's role was to earn and women's role was to look after the family rose from 57 per cent in 1997 to 72 per cent by the 2010s. Older voters and those on low incomes espoused more traditional views of gender, but the gap was narrowing. The survey identified a sharp decline in the proportion of voters who believed women with pre-school children should remain in the home. It was striking that 57 per cent thought it is wrong for men to comment on women's appearance in the street. That said, the gender pay and employment gap remained stubbornly entrenched.

Attitudes towards same-sex relationships became more relaxed. By the 2010s, 68 per cent of voters thought sexual relations between two adults of the same sex were 'not wrong at all'. Moreover, 84 per cent claimed not to be prejudiced against transgender people.[29] Surveys indicated legislative changes under New Labour chimed with public views. Roy Jenkins remarked in the 1960s:

> We cannot, as we are often reminded, change men's minds and men's hearts by legislation, but at the same time, the correct legislative framework can

make it much more difficult for . . . men's hearts to move in the wrong direction.[30]

Research on the liberalisation of attitudes indicates British society was affected by the incipient rise of individualism. The implications of a more atomised society were examined in the American sociologist Robert Putnam's book *Bowling Alone*.[31] There was greater tolerance of minority lifestyles. While traditional solidarities centred on heavy industrial labour waned, not all moral norms dissipated. The Blair government's memorandum on 'the state of public attitudes' found there had been, 'a general fall in the proportion who think that people who want children ought to get married', while voters are 'more accepting of pre-marital sex'. At the same time: 'Large majorities would like to see greater punishment for convicted offenders, greater powers for police, parents held accountable for their children, and support for the right to smack their children'.[32] The British electorate were depicted plausibly as tolerant authoritarians.

It is striking that the individualisation of attitudes persisted under the post-1997 social democratic administration. Blair's ministers prioritised liberalising reforms in tune with the changes of recent decades. It proved harder to resurrect the ethic of collectivism, although class status still played a powerful role in shaping attitudes. To be sure, voters were concerned about inequality. But they had less confidence in the state's capacity to redistribute income. Social democracy in Britain celebrated the liberation of individual lifestyles, even as values of personal autonomy eroded support for the Left's historical mission of egalitarian redistribution alongside fair shares for all.

The new polarisation: 'somewheres' versus 'anywheres'?

As a consequence, during the New Labour decade British society allegedly became more divided between 'anywheres' (the liberal, cosmopolitan, urban-dwelling middle class) and 'somewheres' (the communitarian, nationalist working class inhabiting the suburbs, small towns and coastal regions outside the metropolis). Some commentators refer to the divide in Britain epitomised by the gulf in values between Clacton and Cambridge.[33] Education alongside age were the strongest predictors of attitudes, more so than income or occupation. The 'communitarian/cosmopolitan' divide echoed Seymour Lipset's claim in the 1970s that traditional materialist priorities were giving way to post-materialism. The cleavage of Left and Right was replaced by the new axis of liberal cosmopolitanism and authoritarian populism. The division long existed but was exposed graphically by the 2016 Brexit referendum.

The replacement of class with identity politics unleashed new tensions. For particular voters, the Blair governments cared more about tackling discrimination against ethnic minorities than restoring blue-collar industrial jobs to Britain. The traditional working class, it was claimed, felt disillusioned with mainstream politics, fuelling support for the UK Independence Party (UKIP).

There was the cultural backlash against New Labour's 'political correctness', a government dominated by university-educated politicians with allegedly little respect for the working class. These voters were not necessarily the most disadvantaged and insecure but felt they had lost out from several decades of economic restructuring.[34] The theory of relative deprivation captures the frustration that individuals subjectively experience when groups close to them undergo improvements in material prosperity.[35] Under New Labour, there is evidence blue-collar workers felt their relative status was declining amid fears their children would be worse off. Alienation was driven by feelings of being treated poorly by the established political and economic system, leading to disengagement and the long-term shift of allegiance.[36]

Further scholarship revealed the 'bifurcation' of 'two Englands'.[37] 'Somewhere' voters in 'backwater' towns that underperformed economically were more negative about Europe and immigration. It was felt the promotion of equal opportunities had gone too far. Labour struggled to bridge the gulf between globalisation's 'winners' and 'losers'. The impact of deindustrialisation was unmistakable. It proved difficult to reach across divides in the face of the declining industrial base. Blair and Brown's rhetoric of Global Britain led to the Panglossian narrative about the virtues of free trade and market openness. Some commentators highlighted that traditional working-class voters felt ignored.[38] No party appeared to speak for them. During the 1980s and 1990s, the Labour Party transformed its political identity amid the long-term crisis of Labourism as Chapter 2 explained. To create a viable governing party, the language and ethics of Old Labour were renounced. Labour consequently mislaid its attachment to the British working class. *Marxism Today's* analysis emphasised Labourism's political decomposition. The Blair and Brown administrations did bequeath tangible gains to lower- and middle-income households: the national minimum wage (NMW), tax credits, full employment, Sure Start, investment in urban regeneration, state-of-the-art schools and hospitals. Average working-class living standards in Britain markedly rose. There is evidence that the divergence between 'somewheres' and 'anywheres' was overstated, concealing the diversity of values and attitudes that shape life experiences across the class structure.[39] Some commentators insist that social fragmentation is nothing new but that the focus of conflict shifted from industrial relations – depicted in Samuel Beer's book *Britain Against Itself* (1982) – to the immigration system which is the new 'them and us' divide in British politics. The UK is no less cohesive than comparable countries.[40]

Labour certainly lost its emotional and aesthetic attachment to working-class communities. As real income growth dissipated, disenchantment with New Labour grew, aggravated by the backlash against immigration. By 2010, half of voters in working-class jobs with low levels of education did not vote.[41] Working-class people felt threatened. Most striking was cultural disconnection, the belief that Labour was no longer the party of traditional, socially authoritarian voters. Across Europe and the United States, the 'cultural backlash' drove working-class electors towards populist parties.[42] At the outset, New

Labour sought to address rifts in British society exposed in the Thatcher decade. Yet in key respects, the polarisation of identities between 'somewhere' and 'anywhere' Britain became more entrenched. A UK more bitterly divided was hardly anticipated when Blair stood on the Downing Street steps on a bright, sunny May morning in 1997.

Were attitudes becoming more social democratic?

Taken as a whole, what do shifts in voters' attitudes say about whether Britain became a more social democratic country in the wake of the Blair and Brown administrations? Did Labour encourage a decisive break with neo-liberalism in the minds of British voters? The question implies governing parties have the ability to alter a nation's character, reshaping underlying moral beliefs. New Labour certainly influenced voters' outlook. UK citizens' attachment to liberalism became more entrenched, as did support for spending on public services. Labour tapped into the shared moral sentiment that all children deserve a fair chance regardless of class background by virtue of being human. The public became more concerned about inequality.

Thatcherism meant the belief that the acquisition of wealth and money are what defines the good life. Yet *quality* of life was of increasing concern by the mid-1990s. One voter told a focus group convened by Philip Gould: 'Increasingly I feel it's not just about working hard and making money. Other things matter too – like my health, my family, my surroundings. My job is just one part of that bigger picture'.[43] Labour initially sought to understand the overall shape of Briton's lives, not only their jobs and living standards. Families were dealing with conflicting pressures. Happiness was at least as important as material prosperity. Business was not only about making money but *how* companies behaved given their social and environmental responsibilities. A politician close to Blair believed attention was shifting towards values: 'Income redistribution and cash transfers are no longer at the cutting edge of the political agenda'. He maintained a 10 per cent rise in take-home pay would not solve the problem of crime, pollution, health, family time, safer food, access to parks and recreation.[44]

At the same time, support for redistribution after 1997 hardly grew. There was the continuing decline in sympathy towards the poor of working age. The impact of ministers' punitive rhetoric was significant. Having decided not to raise income tax before the 1997 election, Labour ministers refused to prepare the ground for tax rises. Commentators despaired that the government's agenda often felt, 'like less than the sum of its parts because Ministers do not always feel confident enough to be explicit about the reasons for their actions. . . . It means voters are not being won to the cause of greater equality'. The prime minister failed to 'assert publicly that he backs the Left's traditional desire for a more equal society'.[45]

In mitigation, New Labour's agenda had to address the ambiguous preferences of voters.[46] Citizens wanted to be 'consumers' in public services yet disliked the implications of choice, particularly the impact of NHS 'postcode lotteries'. They sought an inclusive welfare state to support them in times of need but agreed targeting and means-testing were inevitable in a more heterogeneous society. Above all, voters embraced the freedom and prosperity of the global economy but demanded the protection of the activist state. Having lost four general elections, Labour felt compelled to go with the grain of incongruous public views instead of shifting opinion in a consistent direction. New Labour accepted that the population moved to the Right on taxation and welfare if not on public service provision.

Labour was unquestionably less successful in fashioning the 'common culture' that marked a decisive break with Thatcherism. At the centre of the social democratic tradition since the nineteenth century was the belief in equal citizenship, where citizens view one another as valued members of society regardless of wealth or status. R.H. Tawney, the great English ethical socialist, insisted democratic equality was 'the supreme political value'. Common citizenship was the major ideal of the Attlee governments and the New Liberalism of T.H. Green and L.T. Hobhouse. Constructive government intervention would erode barriers created by class differences, ensuring public goods and constraints on unfettered free markets enabled citizens to lead lives they had reason to value.

In this regard, New Labour's impact was less encouraging. After 1997, Britain became a more divided, fragmented, polarised country. Ipsos MORI report that pessimism about Britain's direction grew during Blair's decade in power, despite the UK's robust economic performance. Measures of well-being suggest voters were experiencing the rapid decline in life satisfaction. The level of psychosocial stress and depression was rising.[47] Structural alterations in the economy and society meant fashioning a common culture proved an unattainable aspiration for the Labour governments.

'No such thing as society'? New Labour after Thatcherism

Are these patterns in attitudes evidence of Labour's capitulation to Thatcherism and neo-liberalism? Such inferences are overly simplistic. It is true that from the late 1990s, Britain scarcely became an unequivocally social democratic nation. New Labour was unable to fundamentally transform prevailing beliefs, although it never set out to do so. No administration in post-war British history has altered single-handedly the norms and preferences of citizens. In the late 1970s, the Labour MP John Mackintosh chastised Left-Wing politicians for 'proposing to alter social attitudes by means of economic and institutional changes when it is by no means clear that the latter will bring about the former'.[48] Major structural events, including wars, economic depressions and pandemics, are more often necessary as the catalyst for the fundamental shift in the electorate's values.

By the time Labour came to office, the mood had already shifted in reaction to the Thatcher era. Voters were concerned about the state of Britain – in particular, the dire condition of public services and the NHS – epitomised by

Thatcher's proclamation that there was 'no such thing as society'. New Labour's victory was the consequence rather than the cause of the alteration in prevailing views of economic and social policy. The swing was subtle nevertheless. Voters believed governments had responsibility to protect citizens from insecurity and hardship. Yet the willingness to pay higher taxes or countenance welfare payments to the poorest remained narrow. These were the political and electoral constraints under which New Labour operated.

New Labour: towards the progressive settlement?

Previous chapters demonstrated that New Labour's long-term impact across the public policy landscape was considerable, even if the effect in reshaping the society and politics of Britain was less discernible. In redefining government's role, Labour sought to fashion the new Keynesianism through supply-side economics. The constitution and UK political system was transformed. In social policy, progressive universalism and the creation of landmark institutions proved effective in reducing poverty, maintaining support for the welfare state across the national community. Yet without question, opportunities to bequeath a lasting political inheritance were missed. New Labour was unremittingly cautious about extending the state's responsibilities in the economy, intervening and reshaping markets. In foreign policy, Blair sought to recast Britain's role in the world by engaging the UK in Europe. Nonetheless, misjudgements over Iraq fatally undermined Labour's legacy. Like Harold Wilson in the 1960s, the Blair governments believed they should modernise Britain through existing political institutions. Despite organisational innovation, the Labour administrations largely left the machinery of government untouched.

Developing these themes, the final section of the chapter turns to whether New Labour created a distinctive political settlement in the aftermath of Thatcherism. Did Blair and Brown succeed in forging a new progressive orthodoxy in British politics? Post-war governments are either 'consensus makers' or 'consensus takers'. The 1906 Liberal administration and the 1945 Attlee government established the new public policy framework. Attlee's ministry forged collectivist institutions in British politics and defined the terms of debate for a generation. The administration espoused radical humanitarian ideals. Likewise, the Thatcher regime shaped their own domestic consensus in battling to free the economy, dismantling capital controls and liberalising markets, unleashing the British entrepreneurial spirit. These governments were consensus-makers under the charismatic leadership of Thatcher. Political change meant converting opponents, winning the most significant public arguments, transforming the gut instincts of voters, putting iron in the soul of the British people.

Similarities between New Labour and the 1951–64 Conservative administrations are more striking.[49] The Churchill, Eden and Macmillan governments were compelled to accept the Attlee settlement. Electoral constraints, the scale of the 1945 defeat and the popularity of post-war reforms meant Churchill had little room for manoeuvre. Conservative governments then enabled Britain to adapt to alterations that shaped post-war decades: technological disruption that reconstructed the industrial economy, rising material affluence and shifts in popular culture, adjusting Britain's world role in the aftermath of Suez and managing the demise of British imperialism. The Conservative governments accepted the reforms instigated in the Attlee years. New Labour ostensibly followed a similar course in the aftermath of Thatcherism.

Yet is misleading to claim Labour remained trapped in the political and policy consensus of the Thatcher era. New Labour shared the egalitarian aspirations of post-war social democratic governments.[50] The administration sought to guarantee a minimum income for every 'deserving' citizen. The welfare state would still offer protection to those in need. The right to work was a key determinant of economic policy. Labour ministers made a concerted effort to strengthen the rights of employees, including the entitlement to paid holidays and parental leave. Cutting-edge public services enhanced equal opportunities, particularly through health and education. New Labour's focus on the NHS affirmed its commitment to a cohesive society. Like all post-war left-of-centre governments, Blair and Brown pursued social justice, equality of life chances, full employment, the social minimum.[51] The analysis prepared for the prime minister on 'the state of Britain' in 2001 underlined the strength of the Blair and Brown governments' commitment to egalitarian ideals:[52]

UK STRENGTHS

Economy: strong economic growth, high employment, low inflation and interest rates, low taxation and public spending.
Education: high literacy levels among children, high graduation rate.
Health: good value for money from low health spending.
Crime: low and stable homicide rate.
Transport: best road safety record in Europe, relatively cheap trains.
Values: relatively low suicide rate, high liberty rating, low corruption rating.
Technology: high levels of start-ups in high-growth sectors, relatively high level of innovation.
Environment: lower than average CO_2 emissions, high level of green tax.
Globalisation: relatively high level of Foreign Direct Investment, high level of involvement in international organisations.

UK WEAKNESSES

Economic: low GDP per head, poor productivity, low savings level, longer working hours and fewer holidays.
Education: low spending per pupil, high pupil/teacher ratios, poor participation in education at 17, low starting salaries for teachers.

Health: high rates of coronary heart disease, poor cancer survival rates, relatively small proportion of doctors in population, long waits.

Crime: high victimisation rates, high level of violent crime, large prison population.

Transport: high congestion level, lower than average rail use, investment and reliability.

Values: longer working hours, relatively high income inequality, low voter turnout.

Technology: below average number of Internet hosts per head of population.

Environment: low share for renewable energy.

The Blair administration's assessment of Britain is striking. Labour viewed low taxes as necessary electorally and expedient politically. The high rate of foreign direct investment (FDI), the measure of the economy's external exposure, was perceived as helpful to future competitiveness. There is no mention of the growing problems of declining real wages or the impact of financialisation on the UK housing market. There is little sense of striving to forge a deep-rooted political settlement. Yet concern is expressed about identifiably progressive aspirations: dealing with rising income inequality, regulating excessive working hours, addressing low levels of public spending, making progress in promoting renewable energy and dealing with the record prison population. What New Labour espoused was an unusual combination of conservative and radical ideals. There was the desire to make far-reaching alterations to the UK's polity and society. Yet the leadership was constrained by their instinctive caution over the politics of money, sovereignty, the constitution and Britain's role in Europe.

New Labour's New Keynesian political economy

The starting point for any substantive progressive settlement is reconstructing the political economy. As we have seen, New Labour inherited the model of the Anglo-Liberal free market, no longer tempered by the corporatist system that had disintegrated in the 1970s. Blair and Brown had few guiding orthodoxies from which to derive policy inspiration. Keynesianism was not dead, but its postulates needed to be re-imagined in the new economic order. Hayek's faith in the interplay of market forces had little appeal in the wake of Thatcherism. The early 1980s exposed the fatal flaws in the monetarist experiment. The Labour administrations sought to establish a credible set of 'norms' in economic policy, even if they were reluctant to entirely disavow neo-liberal assumptions.[53]

Indeed, the institutional architecture that gave Attlee and Wilson's ministers the instruments to intervene in the British economy was largely dismantled by 1997. The levers that the Labour government traditionally pulled to manage the economy, notably demand management through fiscal policy, were perceived to be obsolete. The ideological attachment to free markets had become firmly entrenched. Voters appeared reluctant to countenance increases in taxation and public spending. Blair claimed that in an international market for human capital, 'you have to be extremely careful [about tax], particularly with the very top earners'.[54] Any policy agenda that threatened the expansion of financial services risked compromising Labour's ability to attract electoral support in London and the South-East of England.

In contrast to twentieth-century socialist intellectuals, most notably R.H. Tawney and Anthony Crosland, New Labour accepted that higher income inequality was inevitable in a market economy. Even Blair appeared to believe that inequality was necessary to create and distribute wealth. The prime minister insisted that no one objected to the international footballer, David Beckham, earning millions if average incomes were rising. He told viewers of *BBC Newsnight*:

> The key thing is not the gap between the person who earns the most in the country and the person who earns the least. . . . It's not my burning ambition . . . to make sure that David Beckham earns less money.

As a consequence, there was little effort to curb the growth of Offshore Financial Centres (OFCs) that enabled asset holders to evade legal obligations to pay tax in national jurisdictions. The UK became one of the world's leading tax havens. Blair's views ignored the compelling evidence that income inequality is a major driver of instability in capitalist economies.

New Labour was certainly fearful of jettisoning the Thatcherite belief in extending prosperity to new occupational and class constituencies, particularly the skilled working class who purchased their own homes after 1980.[55] The relative decline of the industrial working class undermined the political community that was perceived to favour redistribution and active industrial intervention. Yet New Labour's stance on the political economy was shaped overwhelmingly by ideas rather than merely electoral strategy. Blair and Brown remained sceptical about state intervention in the UK economy. From the late 1980s, sympathetic intellectuals, particularly John Kay, Will Hutton, Paul Hirst and David Marquand, outlined the rationale for the developmental state, rebalancing the economy away from the City of London towards export-led manufacturing industry.[56] With the aspiration of a more egalitarian society, these ideas captivated the British progressive intelligentsia in the 1990s.

John Kay, an Oxford economics don, was the originator of 'stakeholding'. His book, *The Foundations of Corporate Success* (1993), insisted that firms must pay attention to the relationship with stakeholders, particularly their workforce, rather than focusing on profit maximisation alone.[57] The language of stakeholding was embraced warmly – particularly among trade unions, who gratefully seized on the rationale for social partnership in the cold industrial relations climate of the early 1990s. Stakeholder capitalism appealed to the historical aspirations of the social democratic Left, particularly the redistribution of wealth and worker participation through industrial democracy.[58] David Miliband, Blair's head of policy, alighted on stakeholding as offering the progressive thread for Blair's economic narrative that hitherto proved elusive.[59] Some commentators believed Hutton's book *The State We're In* provided the intellectual roadmap New Labour desperately needed.

Yet Blair, Brown and their advisers were ultimately sceptical of stakeholding. The experience of the 1960s and 1970s indicated that British governments had limited influence over economic performance and were unable to arrest relative decline.[60] Ministerial interference in industry, the practice of 'picking winners', became discredited and unfashionable politically. Thrown onto the intellectual defensive in the 1980s and 1990s, New Labour lacked confidence about intervening in markets.[61] Blair and Brown were petrified of being perceived as ideologues exploiting industrial policy to advance the trade union interest. The decomposition of corporatism and the Social Contract after the Winter of Discontent undermined faith in state intervention.[62] Centralised state planning was held in ill repute. The doctrine of monetarism and neo-classical economics further undermined intellectual support for government activism. The incoming Labour administration in 1997 was aghast at the low morale in the Department for Trade and Industry (DTI). Officials had been given 'an intellectual lobotomy' over the preceding eighteen years.[63] New Labour had no compelling prospectus to reverse the tide of ideas.

As Chapter 4 discussed, Labour's governing ideas were strongly influenced by the Clinton administration. The New Democrats eschewed the legacy of the New Deal and the Great Society predicated on federal government's expansion. Thatcher and Reagan claimed to have solved the economic management problems emerging in the era of managed corporatism, particularly chronic inflation. By the 1990s, Brown and his adviser, Ed Balls, produced a distinctive analysis of the economic situation confronting Britain that diverged markedly from Hutton and Kay. For the incoming chancellor, the major symptom of Britain's economic malaise was structural instability: a cycle of 'boom and bust' investment in the public sector, damaging currency fluctuations, the long-term vulnerability of the current account – each the inevitable consequence of weak industrial performance and plummeting productivity. Brown averred that stakeholder capitalism was a confused, even contradictory prospectus. The laudable aim of giving every working-age citizen an ownership stake in the economy was entirely separate from ensuring that workers had a meaningful voice in the management of their firm.[64] Brown believed there was little robust evidence that stakeholding improved national economic performance.

The divergence between stakeholding and New Labour's supply-side social democracy centred on important but nuanced intellectual disagreement between the so-called new Keynesians. This debate concerned how to apply the theoretical insights of John Maynard Keynes to the world of competitive global product markets and volatile capital flows. Hutton believed that government intervention and industrial policy were crucial to ensure Britain broke away from its post-war legacy of low skills, low productivity and low wages. After 1945, the UK lacked the dynamic industrial base necessary to sustain a recognisably Nordic-style welfare state. In 1997, Labour's incoming chancellor of the exchequer did not dispute the necessity of government activism in infrastructure and training. However, Brown believed it was a fundamental mistake to interfere in the legal structure of companies. In an era of capital mobility, ill-considered state inter-vention threatened to provoke investment flight while doing little to improve industrial efficiency. It was essential to preserve open capital markets that per-mitted a vigorous regime of mergers and acquisitions. The Treasury's view was that government's role must be to establish a long-term framework of growth and competitiveness centred on 'low taxes, a flexible labour market, and enough high skills and human capital . . . a market-driven approach'.[65]

Industrial policy was disparaged by ministers. Ed Balls told Peter Mandelson after the latter was appointed secretary of state at the Department of Business, Innovation and Skills (BIS): 'You know, the economy will work best if markets are free and competitive'.[66] In *The End of Laissez-Faire* (1926), Keynes stipulated: 'The important thing for government is not to do things which individuals are doing already, and to do them a little better or a little worse; but to do those things which at present are not done at all'.[67] New Labour accepted the necessity for government activism in tackling egregious market failure. Yet Will Hutton went further, advocating sectoral intervention and public investment in the pri-vate sector with government acting as the decisive agent of industrial modernisa-tion. This form of collective action and stakeholder economics would improve the functioning of capitalism. Yet Brown was convinced that public action was legitimate only where the state discharged functions that would otherwise not be undertaken by markets. Indeed, Keynes himself wrote that 'state action to regulate the value of money, or the course of investment . . . provokes passion-ate suspicions in many upright beasts'.[68] Those suspicions were shared by Blair and Brown: New Labour's stance was hardly the impetus for a new progressive orthodoxy in British political economy.

Even so, neither Brown nor Hutton anticipated the catastrophic financial col-lapse that afflicted the world economy in 2007–8. The crisis raised fundamen-tal questions about the cumulative impact of New Labour's conservatism and intellectual defensiveness. After a decade of apparently robust economic per-formance, the crash undermined Brown's hard-won credibility. The crises of 1931, 1949, 1967, 1976 and 2008 all resulted in the downfall of Labour govern-ments. Not surprisingly, the meltdown in the financial system more often ben-efits the Right creating a propitious climate for the politics of fiscal conservatism and retrenchment. While economic calamities create an opportunity to attack entrenched intellectual orthodoxies, crises more often strengthen the yearning for stability. The Nobel prize–winning economist, Joseph Stiglitz, insisted the collapse of Lehman Brothers in 2008 was as disastrous for global capitalism as the fall of the Berlin wall for Soviet Communism. A decade later, how far had monetary and regulatory policy actually changed? The 2008 crash reopened the controversy of whether Blair and Brown were correct to embrace liberal market doctrines. After 1997, the financial sector was deregulated and liberalised. The public expenditure underpinning British social democracy depended on a model of growth acutely vulnerable to global shocks. In James Graham's play, *Labour of Love*, the MP's parliamentary assistant poignantly chastises the superficial nature of investment in the New Labour years. While, 'it looks all shiny on the outside . . . ', there was a reluctance to address the roots causes of systemic under-investment.

Nonetheless, the 2008 collapse was not the product of virulent Anglo-American capitalism alone. The origins of the crisis lie in the United States where irresponsible lending practices in the housing market led to the unsustainable boom in sub-prime mortgages that ended when the bubble inevitably burst.[69] All American governments were committed to increasing the rate of home ownership to strengthen their electoral popularity. Yet in this context, the Federal Reserve's monetary policy proved reckless. Despite strong evidence of an alarming asset price bubble in the early 2000s, the Fed cut interest rates to prevent any housing market slowdown. Low interest rates then continued as the result of high global liquidity, matched by the Chinese current account surplus.[70] As long-term interest rates remained low, banks and financial institutions sought alternative investment vehicles to generate returns, purchasing bundles of sub-prime mortgages known as 'Mortgage-Backed Securities' that were given triple A status by the ratings agencies.[71] In London during 2007, for instance, trading in derivatives averaged $2.105 trillion a day. In New York, the figure reached $959 billion.[72] The assets purchased by banks and building societies subsequently proved of 'dubious credit quality'. The IMF estimated US-originated toxic assets were worth $3.1 trillion before the crisis.

Fearing an uncontrolled asset price crash, the Fed then raised interest rates, leading to the huge default in sub-prime mortgages. Financial institutions were subsequently exposed to enormous losses. The 'global inverted pyramid' of household and financial sector debt collapsed with calamitous consequences in the world financial markets.[73] American institutions immediately ceased lending to consumers and businesses, creating an unprecedented 'credit crunch'. The downturn was sharper than in the aftermath of the 1929 Wall Street crash. The contagion then rapidly spread to Britain. The City of London was among the world's leading financial centres. Under New Labour, nine specialist regulators were brought together into a single agency, the Financial Services Authority (FSA), ensuring 'light but limited regulation'.[74] Yet the regulatory system palpably failed. The government spent £850 billion rescuing the banks including Lloyds, the Royal Bank of Scotland (RBS), and HBOS. Brown and his chancellor, Alistair Darling, refused to depict the takeover of the Northern Rock building society as nationalisation, fearing their action would be misrepresented as taking Britain back to the 1970s. Still, the British government was left holding £41 billion in mortgages that no one else wanted to touch.[75] By the final quarter of

2009, 6 per cent of GDP was lost. The UK proved more exposed to the financial contagion than any other advanced economy, apart from Japan and Italy.[76]

It was not unreasonable to depict the disastrous events of 2008 as fomented in the neo-liberal heartland of Anglo-America. Brown was the personal friend of the chairman of the US Federal Reserve, Alan Greenspan, inviting him to Kirk-caldy, Brown's Scottish constituency, to give a lecture about Adam Smith's leg-acy and the virtues of free markets. Greenspan, Brown implored, was 'a towering figure in the international financial community'.[77] Peer Steinbruck, Germany's finance minister, blamed the financial crisis on rapacious Anglo-Liberal capital-ism. Steinbruck insisted that the insatiable 'lust' for higher profits and bonuses in New York and London propelled the financial system towards chaos.[78] The UK banking system prioritised consumer lending over productive investment, mak-ing the economy dangerously unbalanced.

Yet dozens of financial institutions across Europe were affected by the finan-cial meltdown not least in Italy, Spain and Germany. The Belgian/Dutch/Luxembourg Bank, Fortis, was on the verge of bankruptcy. The French mort-gage lender, Dexia, had to be rescued.[79] In the meantime, the European Central Bank (ECB) made the calamitous decision to tighten monetary policy, raising interest rates following the sharp rise in the global oil price. This policy deci-sion had a devastating impact on growth in the Eurozone area, particularly in the southern periphery.[80] Ironically, US policy after the crash proved to be more Keynesian than in continental Europe. Neither did the governments of France and Germany support the huge global stimulus that Gordon Brown proposed.[81] Angela Merkel believed the priority was to reform British and American banks, while she reinforced Germany's reputation as the fiscal hawk of Europe.

In Britain, these events were a devastating blow to Labour's reputation for economic competence. In the months afterwards, Brown was lauded as the 'saviour' of the world economy for the decisiveness of the UK government's response. For Brown, the crisis was an intellectual liberation, allowing him to express his long-standing commitment to active government: 'If he believes in anything', said an ally, 'it is the transformative power of the state'.[82] In macro-economic policy, Alastair Darling adopted expansionary fiscal measures: Value Added Tax (VAT) was reduced; the Bank of England cut interest rates and began printing money to stimulate demand.[83] Darling warned in a *Guardian* interview that the British economy was 'at a sixty year low', sparking a furious reaction from Brown's spin doctors. The chancellor recalled it was 'like the 'forces of hell' being unleashed on me. . . . I was reminded of the words Henry II uttered about Thomas Beckett: will no one rid me of this turbulent priest?'[84]

Nonetheless, the Labour government immediately announced a £2 bil-lion rescue package to support homeowners struggling to pay their mortgages; there was greater assistance for jobseekers; businesses were given flexibility to spread payments to HM Revenue and Customs.[85] By 2010, as the former trea-sury minister Kitty Ussher recounts, the UK unemployment rate was 1 mil-lion less than forecast. There was a lower rate of repossession and small business insolvency than feared initially. Moreover, Brown's government acknowledged the significance of international co-operation, seeking to replicate Keynes's ground-breaking efforts at Bretton-Woods in 1944 which stabilised the post-war economy. The prime minister had the ear of senior figures in the incoming Obama administration, including his chief economic adviser, Larry Summers, and the treasury secretary, Tim Geithner. Global leadership gatherings enthused over the British government's Keynesian activism. Brown labelled the crash perceptively as the first great crisis of globalisation; he warned of the urgency of co-ordinated action through multilateral institutions.[86] Both Brown and Obama believed that only active government domestically and internationally could shelter citizens from the gathering storm.

Even so in domestic policy, the crash badly undermined confidence in New Labour. Brown initially sought to leverage the crisis to bring about a 'social democratic moment', tilting the axis of British politics to the Left. Yet the prime minister had spent the previous decade taking the politics out of economic policy decision-making. Brown made economic management 'less politically problematic' than any Labour chancellor since the First World War.[87] Yet there was a cost: the government's tone became managerial and technocratic. Even in the aftermath of the crisis, Brown and Darling refused to adopt the rhetoric of class war, fair shares and ardent redistribution. There was no equal of Dalton's pledge during post-war austerity to tax the rich 'until the pips squeak'. In the eye of the storm, Labour was reluctant to criticise the financial sector and the bankers whose appetite for risk-taking and profit imperilled the world economy. The Brown administration's reticence epitomised social democracy's intellectual and political paralysis.

In the early 1930s, the Left advanced an intellectually plausible analysis of the great depression focused on the evils of under-consumption and depressed real wages. Politicians made the persuasive case for public ownership and national economic planning. Yet in the wake of the 2008 crisis, no compelling ideological position was forthcoming from the British centre-left. The language of market liberalism had permeated public life, from the corridors of power in Whitehall to the ivory tower of academic institutions. Economics undergraduates in British universities were taught the narrow curriculum of mathematical econometrics and one-size-fits-all theory, leavened with a dose of doctrinal monetarism. Few on the Left dared to contest the efficient markets hypothesis, which dismissed the possibility of financial system dislocation. There were few alternative political economy paradigms with practical policy insights that were available to Brown and Darling, forging a new path in the wake of the crash. Darling reflected subsequently that 'we did deal with the crisis and guided the economy through the storm, but we failed to navigate a political course for the future that would convince the public'.[88]

The Labour administration's fundamental difficulties actually began in 2007, not because Brown refused to call a general election, but following the decision to match the shadow chancellor George Osborne's commitment to cut inheritance tax. Osborne announced that under a future Conservative administration, the threshold for paying inheritance tax on estates would rise to £1 million. The Labour government responded by pledging to cut inheritance tax in the 2008 budget. In doing so, Brown and Darling conceded significant ideological territory to the Right. The decision helped revive the Conservatives as a political force, until that point an opposition in the doldrums compelled to accept Labour's spending plans. The cuts in inheritance tax subsequently weakened the UK tax base at a time of mounting fiscal pressures. Darling's decision was a political misjudgement that epitomised the absence of ideological self-confidence on the British Left.

Brown's claim to have abolished the 'boom and bust' cycle that afflicted the British economy in the post-war decades underlined his failure to manage voters' expectations. The years of relative stability and prosperity following Britain's exit from the Exchange Rate Mechanism (ERM) in 1992 could not last forever. There were problems too with the government's management of public spending. Osborne's claim that Labour 'over-spent' bordered on reckless economic illiteracy. After all, the post-1997 governments spent less as a share of national income than other major industrialised countries. As the economic historian Robert Skidelsky highlighted, the government bailouts of financial institutions in 2008–9 transformed private debt into public debt. It was nonsensical to claim the crisis was created by accumulating public sector debt through overspending. Moreover, unlike other Eurozone states, Britain had retained its monetary and fiscal autonomy. After the crash, sterling was devalued by over 25 per cent.[89] The British government faced fewer constraints in using monetary and fiscal policy to allow the economy to adjust.

Nonetheless, it remains the case that as chancellor, Brown relied on distinctly optimistic Treasury forecasts to justify increases in public spending with no rise in income tax.[90] Officials were encouraged to redefine when economic cycles started and ended, balancing early surpluses against later deficits.[91] Brown's judicious fiscal rules were re-interpreted to justify politically motivated budget decisions, undermining the credibility of the government's self-proclaimed fiscal discipline. Ministers came to believe their own rhetoric that boom and bust was eradicated. When the Labour government unveiled its major programme of public sector investment, it was assumed, 'the present benign constellation of economic indicators' would continue and that growth 'is the natural condition of things'.[92] Brown failed to recognise that since the late 1990s, the UK was witnessing an extraordinary phase in the global economy where emerging markets, the Internet, cheap credit and the plentiful supply of low-cost labour promised limitless growth accompanied by endless tax revenues. The good times inevitably came to a juddering halt. The financial crisis naturally led to fiscal crisis and rapid deterioration of the public finances. The day after the governor of the Bank of England, Mervyn King, told the European Parliament that governments 'had to be cautious about going further in using discretionary measures to expand the size of . . . deficits', the cover ratio for the sale of UK Treasury thirty-year bonds fell to its lowest level ever.[93] The markets were rattled by King's pronouncement, which then imposed limits on government action.

These events meant that a major political and economic question resurfaced. If public spending was now to be cut in relative terms, what was social democracy in Britain for? After a decade in the wilderness, Conservative politicians vilified Brown for fiscal profligacy. Echoing the politics of the 1930s, Osborne claimed the UK was vulnerable to a confidence crisis that would lead to speculative attacks on sterling and capital flight, as foreign investors withdrew their money to safer havens. The deficit was a 'cruise missile' heading straight for the British economy, which meant 'higher interest rates, more business failures, sharper rises in unemployment, and even a catastrophic loss of confidence'.[94] The UK had the second-highest structural deficit among the advanced economies, Osborne warned. The Tories claimed Labour's promise of reconciling economic efficiency with social justice through higher public expenditure was reckless and irresponsible. David Cameron claimed that 'Gordon Brown's debt, waste and taxes have wrecked the economy and threatened to kill the recovery'.[95] Cutting government debt and the deficit to return the finances to balance entailed drastic cutbacks in the public sector. Certainly, it appears Osborne was prosecuting a bogus argument. The 2008 crisis was unprecedented: the government would have had to run surpluses for decades beforehand to avoid debts incurred by bailing out the banking sector. The Conservative Party's claims were potent nonetheless.

Darling countered that UK debt following the financial crisis were comparable to other Western economies. In spring 2009, the government outlined plans to bring down debt through prudent and sensible fiscal decisions. The Treasury would use supportive fiscal policy for as long as necessary but would then pursue deficit reduction at an appropriate pace.[96] In the Budget, the chancellor introduced a marginal tax rate of 50p on incomes over £150,000. Any bankers' bonus of more than £25,000 would be subject to a levy. The crash made New Labour, in the words of the distinguished commentator William Keegan, 'accidental Keynesians'. Indeed, one government adviser reiterated there was nothing wrong with running a fiscal deficit during a recession:

> We are doing more to increase the deficit in order to counter the recession through a pro-active stimulus rather than simply allowing the automatic stabilisers to work. We start with an underlying structural deficit which reflects what was a necessary catch-up in public spending from the Tory years on both physical infrastructure and growth-enhancing current expenditure.[97]

The Conservatives insisted they would reduce the deficit faster, cutting public spending instead of raising taxes. Labour's difficulty was that disquiet was rising among the middle class prior to the crisis due to the impact of 'stealth taxes'. Taxing middle-income earners in London and the South-East, caught by the 40p marginal rate in unprecedented numbers, funded the series of initiatives to support poorer families and pensioners. Indeed, the fiscal position improved between 2005 and 2008 due to tax rises and the comparatively lower rate of public spending. On the eve of the crisis, UK debt stood at 2.4 per cent of GDP, while Brown's 'golden rule' was upheld on current spending.[98]

Yet the government failed to produce a convincing economic and political strategy for navigating beyond the financial crash. At the outset, Brown was convinced the crisis would be short-lived rather like the Asian turmoil at the beginning of the 2000s.[99] Unfortunately, the relationship between the prime minister and his chancellor then broke down, as occurred in the past during periods of economic adversity. Darling believed Brown's spokesman, Damian MacBride, was instructed to attack him in the press.[100] Allegedly a heavy drinker, MacBride gave vitriolic briefings against cabinet ministers who fell out with Number Ten. The atmosphere inside the administration became poisonous. After Brown decided not to call an election in October 2007, 'everything seemed to go wrong. He appeared accident prone, not in control, the government and Cabinet became increasingly restless and rebellious'.[101] The prime minister had already dismantled the structure of decision-making in Number Ten inherited from the Blair era. As a consequence, he struggled to get anything done in Whitehall. Peter Mandelson, Brown's longtime political enemy, was even brought back from the European Commission, a last ditch effort to stabilise the dysfunctional government.

The prime minister's 'paranoid style' and ministerial infighting bred confusion about the government's overarching purpose at a time of national crisis. On spending, Brown refused to accept that cuts were necessary, fearing he would be portrayed as another treacherous and expedient politician like the hapless duo of Ramsay MacDonald and Philip Snowdon in the 1930s. The prime minister insisted the 'dividing-line' between Labour and the Conservatives was still that of 'investment versus cuts'. Darling and Mandelson wanted to be upfront about the necessity of reduced spending, preparing the ground for fiscal consolidation.[102] Neither was the Labour government prepared to make the positive case for economic rebalancing in the aftermath of the crash. Mandelson expounded the virtues of sectoral 'government activism', including bailouts for the motor industry and support for research, investing in 'catapult centres' that mirrored the German Fraunhofer Institute. Mandelson claimed there could be no return to 'business as usual' after the financial crash. Yet even he feared that the language of state industrial policy implied a nostalgic return to the 1970s.

New Labour's paranoia about intervening in markets, even after the crisis, was notorious.[103] Mandelson advocated 'market-driven' industrial activism that rejected 1970s'-style 'statist' solutions. In a memorandum written by his closest advisers, the secretary of state was told to demonstrate 'pro-business intentions', acknowledging 'the essential role that competition plays in the dynamics of innovation and growth. Economic growth depends on keeping markets open'.[104] Even in the midst of the 2008 firestorm, New Labour exhibited the hallmarks of uncritical pro-market thinking. Brown and his Downing Street team were even less convinced about the merits of government intervention, as sceptical as when they confronted Hutton's concept of stakeholding in the early 1990s. They believed national economies with smaller financial centres had not experienced a less severe recession after 2008, as Table 8.3 illustrates. Nor was the UK's financial sector demonstrably too large: as a share of GDP, British manufacturing was still ahead of financial services. Moreover, the financial sector had been an important source of employment growth and tax revenues since the 1980s. Thousands of banking jobs were created in London and the South East of England, as well as the conurbations surrounding Manchester, Leeds, Bradford and Newcastle (as Table 8.4 indicates).

The claim that UK growth in per capita GDP was driven entirely by over-dependence on the financial sector is misleading. This argument ignores British success in seizing advantage of the globalisation of production: the growth of niche manufacturing industries; the emergence of innovative industrial clusters;

TABLE 8.3 Change in real GDP during the 2008–9 recession and financial services share of GDP in seven countries (percentages)[105]

Country/region	Change in real GDP in 2008–9 recession	Financial services share of GDP
Canada	3.1	–
France	3.2	4.6
Germany	6.3	3.8
Italy	6.5	–
Japan	8.0	6.7
United Kingdom	5.9	8.3
United States	3.5	7.5

TABLE 8.4 Financial and related professional services sector employment in the UK[106]

Region	Total employment in financial and related professional services in the UK (2010)
Scotland	150,400
Northern Ireland	31,100
North West	227,300
Wales	59,900
West Midlands	133,200
South West	150,200
South East	251,000
London	692,500
East	149,700
East Midlands	82,600
Yorkshire and The Humber	128,900
North-East	45,200
Total employment	2,102,200

Britain's strength in sectors from aerospace to defence; the contribution of higher education in generating overseas earnings; the expansion of the creative industries and design, broadcasting, culture and sport; the impact of devolution in creating vibrant capitals and core cities – notably Edinburgh, Belfast, Cardiff, Manchester, Birmingham, Bristol, Sheffield, Newcastle and Leeds.[107] The financialisation narrative that insisted GDP growth relied exclusively on the financial sector is much overplayed.

During its final twelve months in office, the Labour government nevertheless became bitterly divided over its core purpose. Ministers appeared paralysed by indecision. They feared pushing a bolder policy response where voters seemingly demanded reassurance and decisiveness. Labour might have gained from attacking 'greedy bankers' and 'locusts' who sought to profit from financial sector instability. Yet Brown's priority remained restoring normality to the capitalist order. His administration focused on market stabilisation rather than tackling the excess and irresponsibility that led to the crash. As prime minister, Labour's most successful chancellor of the exchequer since the Second World War had become the quintessential economic technocrat.

It is simplistic to assume the Labour governments merely picked up where Thatcher left off in the 1980s. Even so, Blair and Brown lacked an alternative framework to create a more productive economy. Their approach dealt with the long-run structural problems of chronic inflation and unemployment, but they were unable to decisively alter the underlying dynamic of growth to increase living standards and widen prosperity across the UK population. The long-term legacy of deindustrialisation in Northern England, South Wales and the central belt of Scotland was never dealt with effectively. The British Left in the early-twentieth century rose to prominence as a consequence of its critique of the productive efficiency of capitalism. The party's wholesale rejection of nationalisation and planning after 1983 left a major gap in the Left's armoury. New Labour understood capitalism as a well-oiled machine that generated the goods for redistribution, a world-view shattered in the wake of the 2008 crash. Not surprisingly, too few radical, path-breaking policy ideas emerged subsequently. Despite the Blair and Brown government's constructive track record in welfare and social policy, no distinctive progressive orthodoxy emerged in political economy.

New Labour's 'new' constitution

Equally, for all the well-developed plans and the phase of legislative hyper-activity after 1997, the Blair governments were unable to build an enduring constitutional settlement in Britain. New Labour's political reforms remained incomplete and have struggled to stand the test of time. Having won power, the party unquestionably had radical intentions. The government's draft programme was the most far-reaching since 1832. Baroness Helena Kennedy, a prominent human rights lawyer, observed: 'That first term of Labour in office produced more far-reaching reforms than anything seen since the Great Reform Act'.[108] Yet unintended consequences have meant that constitutional changes are imperilling the UK's long-term future, undermining political institutions and weakening affiliation with British national identity. Instead of cohering into a progressive settlement, New Labour's reforms led to instability and confusion.[109]

The first reason related to the use of referenda to provide legitimacy for constitutional change. Clement Attlee denounced referendums in the 1940s as 'alien to all our traditions'. Yet New Labour used referendums in an ad hoc manner to endorse devolution in Wales, Scotland and Northern Ireland, while deciding whether the North-East of England should have an elected regional assembly. Blair conceded there ought to be a referendum to ratify the European constitutional treaty in 2003, then rejected by French and Dutch voters. Despite resorting to referendums, the Labour governments never articulated the role that referenda should play in a representative democracy. Ministers refused to clarify the logic of embracing direct democracy.

The second explanation for confusion and instability was the sheer diversity of electoral systems introduced for the European Parliament, the Scottish Parliament, Scottish local government, the Welsh Assembly, the Northern Ireland Assembly, the Greater London Authority (GLA) and the directly elected mayor for London. More proportional voting systems led inevitably to electoral fragmentation, enabling fringe parties, notably the UK Independence Party (UKIP), to gain a foothold in political institutions. Over time, greater pluralism in electoral competition led to the fracturing of the two-party system, culminating in the 2010 Coalition government. Yet New Labour appeared determined to preserve the two-party duopoly by rejecting the politics of co-operation.

Another source of constitutional misunderstanding was the emergence of constraints on executive power: vetoes on decision-making were imposed through the European Union (EU), reforms of the judiciary, devolved institutions and the House of Lords alongside the introduction of referenda.[110] The UK no longer resembled the 'elective dictatorship' foreseen by Lord Hailsham in the 1970s. There was an increasingly effective separation of constitutional powers. Yet New Labour had never intended to limit executive authority and undermine the Westminster model. Blair and Brown did not wish to give up the unfettered powers of the centralised British state in the 'winner takes all' political system. Although they paid lip-service to the rhetoric of decentralisation and localism, the rationale for the constitutional reforms remained ambiguous. The rules of the game underpinning the functioning of the British constitution became less coherent over time.

The paradox was that the social democratic governments of Blair and Brown conspired in 'cutting up' political power. The government was no longer able to guarantee equality of treatment across the territorial jurisdiction of the UK given the devolution of powers to elected bodies.[111] Devolution led to divergence in the management of the NHS, the funding of higher education and provision of adult social care across England, Scotland and Wales. In England, care was provided through a system of direct payments. In Scotland, social care was 'free' at the point of delivery. The Welsh government tenaciously clung to the collectivism of the post-war settlement. The *British* welfare state, originally sculpted by Beveridge and Bevan in the 1940s, was a thing of the past.

Another difficulty was that the Labour governments left political institutions at Westminster unreformed. Most hereditary peers in the House of Lords were removed. Yet ministers failed to devise a distinctive legislative function for the second chamber. Blair opposed any legislative modernisation and mechanism of election that undermined the primacy of the House of Commons.[112] The Number Ten Policy Unit recommended 'a proper codification of powers between the Commons and the Lords', combined with other reforms, notably limiting the number of terms a peer could serve to two, so that 50 per cent of the chamber was replaced at regular intervals. Yet there was little substantive progress. Blair's advisers admitted: 'The biggest criticism at the moment on constitutional reform is that we do not know what we are doing, and this is damaging us in dealing with our legislative programme in the Lords'.[113]

Furthermore, the Blair government evaded the challenge of reforming the voting system for the House of Commons. The Jenkins Commission, established by the Labour government in December 1997, proposed to replace First-Past-the-Post with the 'Alternative Vote-Plus' where candidates are ranked in order of preference. MPs are elected for constituencies or via a 'top-up' regional list. The cabinet were bitterly divided over the reforms. John Prescott and Jack Straw opposed changes that prevented Labour from securing decisive majorities. Blair told a private meeting: 'The main reason for opposition to the Jenkins proposals is dislike of the Liberals'.[114] The rotten nature of the unreformed Westminster institutions was exposed graphically by the expenses scandal that erupted in May 2009 with the publication of revelations in the *Daily Telegraph*, alleging MPs' Jacuzzis were installed and duck ponds cleaned on the public purse.

In this climate, Blair's promise of the new politics appeared threadbare. Errant MPs and peers who stole from taxpayers proved difficult to remove, particularly MPs representing so-called safe constituencies, defended loyally by the party establishment. The *Daily Telegraph* exposures provoked outrage. Labour MPs were enjoying lifestyles far removed from their constituents, prompting debate about the unrepresentative nature of the political class.[115] The proportion of Labour parliamentarians who had working-class jobs before entering Parliament fell from around 40 per cent in 1959 to less than 10 per cent.[116] Reforms intended to create transparency such as Freedom of Information (FOI) actually fomented distrust. It was hardly surprising that in 2010 voters elected a government, albeit without a decisive majority, that promised to end public sector largesse and 'clean up' the system.

At the same time, New Labour was ultimately reluctant to prepare the ground for major constitutional changes, including the Human Rights Act (HRA). There was the growing backlash against 'liberal Britain' and its promotion of civil liberties. In voters' eyes, court judgements often favoured convicted criminals and unpopular minorities such as 'bogus' asylum seekers with connections to terrorism. Yet despite its liberal credentials, the Labour government proposed legislation subsequently that allowed the police to hold terrorist suspects up to 90 days without trial alongside the introduction of compulsory identity cards, measures eventually defeated in the House of Commons.[117] While the HRA did not give the courts powers to overturn the decisions of ministers or strike down primary legislation, it was easy for the Murdoch press to portray human rights as contrary to the 'common sense will' of the majority.

Even more problematic was the uneven and asymmetrical nature of devolution. Wales, Scotland and Northern Ireland had greater say over their affairs as a result of the constitutional reforms. Yet remarkably, Labour had little to say about English governance. In autumn 2004, a referendum was held on whether to introduce an elected assembly in the North-East of England. The proposal was defeated by 696,519 (78 per cent) to 197,310 votes (22 per cent), the 'No' campaign co-ordinated skilfully by the Machiavellian anti-European political strategist Dominic Cummings. Meanwhile, outside London and the prosperous South-East grievances festered among the English, particularly those in more remote towns, rural communities and coastal areas. The Barnett formula meant public spending per head of population was higher in Scotland than in deprived regions of Northern England. The formula was outdated since no 'needs assessment' was carried out since the 1970s. Yet Barnett was 'a can of worms' no minister in the Blair/Brown governments was willing to reopen.

There was also the belief that London was simply too powerful relative to parochial communities and provincial towns on the English periphery. The government dismissed plans for 'English votes for English laws' as unworkable since that meant 'different classes of MPs, shifting majorities on different issues and endless arguments about whether a Bill applied to England only or not'.[118] Yet there is little doubt that following devolution, the English felt poorly represented. The so-called West Lothian question meant Scottish MPs voted on health and education policies in England, while English MPs were prevented from having a say in Scottish matters. Scotland, Wales and Northern Ireland were believed to have been advantaged unfairly by the devolved institutions. English identity was now politicised, a climate exploited deftly by Nigel Farage's insurgent UKIP. Blair sought to reshape the devolution settlement through directly elected mayors for 'city-regions' in England. Yet of thirty-seven referendums held, only twelve had endorsed a mayor.

Many commentators insisted that as prime minister, Blair never understood devolution. In his diaries, the former leader of the Liberal Democrats, Paddy Ashdown, recounts a discussion with the prime minister following the 1999 Scottish parliamentary elections. In coalition talks, the Liberal Democrats demanded the abolition of tuition fees. Blair admonished Ashdown: 'You can't have Scotland doing something different from the rest of Britain', he exclaimed. The Liberal leader retorted:

Then you shouldn't have given the Scots devolution . . . specifically, the power to be different on this issue. You put yourself in a ridiculous position if, having produced the legislation to give power to the Scottish Parliament, you then say it is a matter of principle they can't use it.

The prime minister remarked jocularly: 'Yes, that is a problem. I am beginning to see the defects in all this devolution stuff!'[119] The former Scottish secretary Donald Dewar concluded: 'Tony is not really in favour of devolution'.[120] Another former minister, John Denham, believes devolution was seen as 'a politically calculated necessity' by the party, which retained its fundamental commitment to the centralised 'unitary Imperial state'.[121]

    Despite Blair's pledge of the new localism, the language of rate-capping and earned autonomy in local government inherited from the Thatcher years persisted. Ministers believed there was little appetite for localism among an electorate that rejected 'postcode lotteries'. If they gave away control to local councils, ministers would get the blame when things went wrong. The legacy of the 1980s and so-called loony Left councils meant instinctive mistrust of local government. Ministers felt local authorities had little to contribute in constructively addressing economic and social problems. In service delivery, targets were imposed while revenue was raised centrally, allocated through Whitehall departments. After the debacle of the poll tax, there was less enthusiasm to revisit the structure of local taxation. NHS foundation trusts were created to involve local communities, yet councils were kept deliberately at arm's-length. The city academies programme centralised power, weakening the role of local education authorities (LEAs). Academies were a 'cultural revolution', as management fell outside the control of LEAs.[122] Moreover, Treasury rules were retained that restricted the ability of local authorities to borrow for capital investment. In 2001, Ken Livingstone, the mayor of London, was told London Underground modernisation must be undertaken through a public-private partnership (PPP). Livingstone maintained PPP was less efficient, imposing long-term costs on the taxpayer. Treasury controls on borrowing made it more difficult to replenish social housing, reducing affordable supply while forcing up prices in urban areas. The housing crisis was the direct consequence of the over-centralisation of English governance.

    Ministers never fully understood the repercussions of devolving power within the centralised political system of the UK. Rhodri Morgan's selection as Labour candidate for first minister in Wales was blocked to impose a Whitehall insider, Alun Michael. The Blair and Brown administrations never acknowledged that an inevitable consequence of devolution is that politicians will emerge whose popularity relies on their willingness to dissent from the policies of central government. Indeed, there is political and electoral advantage to be gained in confronting the expressed will of Whitehall and Westminster. The reality of political life following the reforms compelled the centre to frame a post-devolution strategy for UK governance. Yet London-centric New Labour never identified a plausible approach. Despite this, it was ironically local government where New Labour most clearly bequeathed a legacy, electing a succession of modernising leaders who pragmatically governed communities in the image of Blair and Brown.

Meanwhile, constitutional reforms altered the political landscape but failed to make citizens feel more 'empowered'.[123] The Thatcher reforms after 1979 encouraged the popular consumer revolution in Britain through privatisation, share ownership, alongside 'choice' in public services. Yet citizens' voice was still limited politically, other than voting roughly once a year in local and national elections. The better educated, less deferential citizenry wanted to make its voice heard, exercising greater popular control over public bureaucracies and political institutions.[124] Yet New Labour ministers demonstrated limited understanding of the agenda of redistributing power. The constitutional reforms proved something of a damp squib. No compelling progressive settlement emerged.

Transforming public services: Labour's 'garbage can' reforms?

Among New Labour's more pronounced successes was forging the renewed political consensus for investment in education and health, rebuilding confidence in the public realm. So how far did the Blair and Brown governments create a lasting settlement? Even in public services, Labour's record was perceived as a relative disappointment. The party was crippled at the outset, since it came to power without a coherent agenda. Indeed, Labour may have been *too* effective during the opposition years. As Shadow Health Secretary, Robin Cook castigated the NHS internal market which fragmented service delivery. Alan Milburn disparagingly referred to the 'men in grey suits', the managers paid grossly inflated salaries who now ran the health service under the Conservatives.[125] Having turned the NHS to its political advantage before 1997 by launching devastating attacks on the Tories, Labour was reluctant to announce its own strategy. The NHS was a religion both for British voters and Labour Party members, many of whom were content to preserve the post-1945 system in aspic. As a consequence, Labour arrived in government with an almost empty policy cupboard. According to the Number Ten adviser, Matthew Taylor: 'Labour quickly fell into the trap of believing that the Tories introduced the internal market because they were nasty ideologues. . . . [As a result] Labour had no coherent approach'.[126] Commentators compared Labour's strategy after 1997 to a 'garbage can' where solutions emerged erratically and often lacked an underlying logic. Despite the flurry of initiatives, it was often unclear what problems the policies were designed to solve.[127]

In the post-war era, British governments typically went through several stages in renovating public services. At the outset, they naively believed improvement would be achieved by putting the right managers in charge and more money in place. Then, panic would set in as there was little evidence of substantive progress. In the next phase, governments resorted to top-down delivery using centralisation and targets to improve standards and productivity across the service: 'The Government does not trust the professionals but it tells people what to do, it sets targets and performance manages – known as 'targets and terror' in the jargon'.[128] That approach achieves results but runs out of steam quickly. In the final stage, the system departs from the monolithic top–down framework, using a combination of incentives: contestability, competition, alongside bottom–up pressures, including citizen 'choice and voice'. The insight from economic theory was that choice for public service users means 'if somebody is getting a poor service, they go elsewhere'.[129] It took Labour six or seven years to get to the third phase, recognising that money and new faces at the top was not enough.[130]

Labour's pledge card reforms

Insofar as it had any policies, Labour came to power in 1997 brandishing its eye-catching, voter-friendly pledges to reduce NHS waiting times, increase the number of trained doctors and nurses, and end large class sizes in primary schools. The 1988 Education Act had introduced national tests for all seven-, eleven- and fourteen-year-olds, complemented by the imposition of the literacy and numeracy hour in primary schools. New Labour had no intention of dismantling the policy framework.[131] The government abolished GP fundholding but retained the NHS purchaser/provider split in the delivery of clinical and elective care. The five commitments on Labour's pledge card were sharp retail politics, unquestionably fruitful in appealing to middle-class families in English marginal constituencies.

LABOUR'S 1997 ELECTION PLEDGES[132]

- Cut class sizes to thirty or under for five-, six- and seven-year-olds by using money from the assisted places scheme.
- Fast-track punishment for persistent young offenders by halving the time from arrest to sentencing.
- Cut NHS waiting lists by treating an extra 100,000 patients as a first step by releasing £100 million saved from NHS red tape.
- Get 250,000 under-twenty-five-year-olds off benefit and into work by using money from a windfall levy on the privatised utilities.
- No rise in income tax rates, cut VAT on heating to 5 per cent and inflation and interest rates as low as possible.

Yet New Labour's commitments hardly amounted to a compelling long-term strategy for improvement. In fact, the party did little original thinking on public services after losing the 1987 and 1992 elections. The IPPR's Social Justice Commission, chaired by Sir Gordon Borrie, outlined its vision of the mixed economy in public services bringing together the state, private and not-for-profit sectors. There was a willingness to think radically, concluding that the public sector need not have a monopoly in the provision of services. Yet the implication of the Social Justice

Commission's findings were uncomfortable for a centre-left party that was instinctively conservative. As a consequence, Borrie's ideas were never developed fully. It was far easier to castigate the decade of Tory marketisation. Labour promised to end the NHS internal market. GP fundholding was scrapped. Grant-maintained schools that opted-out of local authority control would be eliminated.[133]

Nonetheless, the shortfall in the government's stance after 1997 soon became apparent. New Labour's formula of discarding internal markets while injecting additional resources into the system proved inadequate. The NHS crisis continued. During the 2001 election campaign, Blair was confronted outside the Queen Elizabeth Hospital in Edgbaston, Birmingham, by Sharon Storer, the partner of a cancer patient who received inadequate treatment, having waited months for an operation.[134] Damaging stories circulated in the press of patients experiencing deficient care. Another problem was that the Labour government lacked an organising concept for public services that offered an alternative to the internal market. Ministers initially resorted to exhortation from Whitehall combined with central planning, neither of which led to sustained improvement. There was a mistaken belief that announcing a target was the same as a policy. The ten-year *NHS Plan* published in 2000 was a traditional social democratic programme containing over 300 targets, envisaging twelve separate inspectorates to oversee the health service.[135] Staff now operated in a climate characterised by a perplexing and confusing mix of 'targets and terror'.[136]

By 2001, Blair and Brown boasted of major spending on health and education after early prudence. Yet voters became cynical, as expectations were raised by promised improvements that never seemed to materialise. The chancellor of the exchequer was notorious for adding together spending increases over the three years of the spending review cycle to create an exaggerated impression of money flowing into the NHS. Meanwhile, Blair too became frustrated. The prime minister told the *Observer* newspaper:

> It is far harder to change the way a public service works because it doesn't have the great engine that the market is always creating for change in the private sector. You don't want the health service to be turned into a marketplace, but you've got to look at ways of pioneering change.[137]

The third difficulty was that Labour could not resolve easily the problems of historic under-funding. The party promised in 1997 and 2001 that there would be no rise in the basic or higher rate of income tax. Blair and Brown gave middle-class voters the impression it was somehow feasible to combine Scandinavian-quality public services with American levels of taxation. The prime minister, in particular, feared he was confronting a middle-class electorate where 'the culture of contentment' diminished the willingness of citizens to pay more tax.[138] To fund the increase in NHS spending, lower-paid workers started to pay more tax, while households without children received much less generous support. These voters became noticeably more disillusioned with the government by the mid-2000s.

The fourth impediment to Labour's policies on public services was the fact that public sector workers still dominated the party. Labour continued to perceive itself as *the* party of public services. As a consequence, Labour struggled to confront long-standing ideological shibboleths about the public sector. Blair agonised over the 'scars on his back' inflicted by opponents of what he believed were only modest reforms. Labour never developed the necessary leadership style combining respect for professionalism with appropriate challenge. Meanwhile, efforts to devise cogent policies were undermined amid ministerial infighting. The prime minister believed the NHS was an antiquated system rooted in post-war paternalism, dismissive of its legacy of queuing, rationing and centralisation. Frank Dobson, the gruff, no-nonsense politician who was appointed secretary of state, remained a vocal opponent of the internal market and the private sector.[139] In the first term, Robert Hill, health adviser in the Number Ten Policy Unit, advocated the centrally planned NHS where variations in performance were tackled by telling staff what to do, issuing edicts and directives and sending inspectors into failing hospitals. Yet performance against the prescribed NHS targets still plummeted. In fact, Dobson 'spent lots of time dismantling the health service only for Alan Milburn to come along and rebuild it later'.[140] According to Julian Le Grand, subsequently Blair's health adviser in Downing Street, Dobson and Hill made the classic mistake of believing 'the real problem with health or education or any public service is there are not enough resources. You pump a bit of money in . . . and trust the professionals to deliver'. Within a year, 'waiting times increased. . . . Frank Dobson had to go on television to apologise'.[141]

Flirting with the private sector?

Four years on with dissatisfaction rising, Labour battled to get its public service reforms back on track. Yet even the 2001 manifesto failed to clarify its direction. The Blair administration's plans were simply not plausible intellectually. The only pre-existing blueprint for Labour's strategy was a thin report by the IPPR titled *Building Better Partnerships*.[142] The IPPR's starting-point drawing on the Borrie Commission was that stimulating private sector involvement was a legitimate centre-left strategy, as long as services remained universal and free at the point of use. Across Northern Europe, social democratic governments accepted the role of non-state providers in public service delivery, from trade union mutuals and religious foundations to private companies. The year before the 2001 election, the IPPR team had gone to brief Robert Hill in Number Ten. They informed Hill their forthcoming report would recommend that there was no practical or ideological reason why the private sector should not provide clinical services in the NHS. During the meeting, Hill reportedly went 'crazy', exclaiming talk of collusion with the private sector was 'really dangerous'.[143] The IPPR's report was launched during the 2001 election campaign. It was seized on by Alastair Campbell as outlining Labour's 'real second term agenda', given the relative lack of substance in the party's own manifesto. Yet the report elicited a furious reaction from the trade unions, Brown's Treasury team and even members of Blair's own staff in Number Ten.

Nevertheless, it was apparent that the intellectual consensus was shifting. Simon Stevens, then Dobson's special adviser in the Department of Health (DoH) who later joined the Number Ten Policy Unit, became less averse to the internal market, recognising the value of the purchaser/provider split in improving NHS efficiency. For Stevens, there was no coherent rationale for the central state having an operational monopoly over the provision of care, even if Whitehall still controlled the funding. Stevens acknowledged the limits of governance by command and control in the NHS.

Aside from the internal disagreement over structural reform of the health service, public spending increased dramatically in the case of the NHS. Figure 8.8 indicates the general trends in public expenditure since the late 1980s:

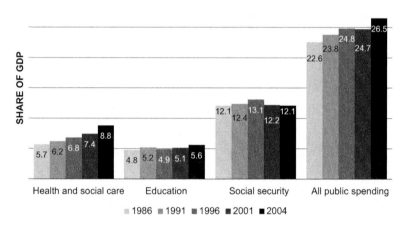

FIGURE 8.8 UK public spending 1986–2005 (Office for National Statistics)

Since Blair and Brown believed that additional spending must be justified prudently to win voters' consent, public investment was accompanied by the litany of reforms intended to improve efficiency, responsiveness and choice. In the 2001–5 parliament, there were notable successes, including improved school test results and reductions in NHS waiting times, leading to the dramatic fall in deaths from heart disease and cancer. The Blair government's ambition was not only improved service delivery but greater choice and diversity of provision for patients and parents.

The scale of expanded capacity in education alone was striking: after 2001 there were 820 children's centres alongside 650,000 additional childcare places; 15,000 extra places in oversubscribed primary schools; 2,000 specialist secondary schools offering an innovative curriculum and 200 city academies focused on disadvantaged communities across England; there were more faith schools and voluntary-aided schools alongside takeovers of weak and failing schools where performance was persistently below the national average.[144] Empirical research measuring the impact of competition and 'quasi-markets' in English primary schools indicated an initial widening of class segregation in urban areas. Yet there was evidence that poorer families were able to take advantage over time.[145] For all the talk of parental choice, however, New Labour's approach continued to mandate outcomes defined by the centre:[146]

Policy area	How we want to be judged
Education:	
Secondary schools	• Fourteen-year-old tests plus GCSEs
	• Number of city academies and specialist schools
Health:	
Hospital waiting	• Meeting six-month waits plus A&E waiting
Cancer and heart disease	times down
	• Two week wait for cancer treatment
	• Short waits for heart treatment
Transport:	
Railways	• More than nine out of ten trains on time
Home Office:	
Crime	• Overall crime down, violent crime down
Asylum	• Applications down plus removals
All: staff	• 20,000 nurses; 10,000 doctors
Staff recruitment	• 10,000 teachers; 6,000 police plus better morale/motivation as measured in surveys and polling.

Under Labour, the dominant culture in public services was being altered. An NHS manager enthused: 'We are being asked to think what patients might want. . . . We have never done that before'.[147] The prime minister believed that choice for 'citizen-consumers' was a progressive and redistributive goal. Firstly, universal choice 'gives poorer people the same choices available only to the middle-class', tackling the inequality that only the better-off can make an escape from failing provision. Moreover, choice entrenches solidarity, ensuring wealthy citizens continue to use public services – 'a prerequisite for continuing public support for the tax increases required for funding equitable public services'. Finally, choice where money follows patients and parents compels providers to raise standards through competitive pressure.[148] An internal government memorandum noted that, 'In the four months after the heart treatment choice scheme was launched [in 2002], half of all eligible patients chose to switch provider'. Moreover, one in ten parents appealed against the allocation of secondary school by their local authority.[149] Andrew Adonis concluded: 'People want choice. Where they are offered it, they seize it in very large numbers, revealing . . . huge pent up discontent with the previous service. Greater choice is exposing weak provision ruthlessly'.[150] Yet extending choice in public services is a limited ambition for any government. What was New Labour's policy and delivery impact? Did the Blair governments entrench the new settlement, affirming the critical importance of the public realm in British society? Labour ministers certainly brought to an end the feeling since the 1980s that the NHS and state schools were in perpetual decline. Beyond that, the Blair/Brown administrations' legacy is more contingent.

Labour's NHS reforms: the gentleman in Whitehall no longer knows best?

In its second term, the Labour government was compelled to embark on more intricate and contested reforms of the public sector. New Labour's strategy sought to break away from centralisation in the NHS, widening the scope for competition, private sector involvement and greater operational autonomy. Following the politically embarrassing winter crisis in the NHS two years into the Blair government, performance improvement had been driven aggressively from Whitehall. Yet by 2001, the reforms were no longer succeeding according to the DoH's internal data.[151] As a consequence, policy-makers began to formulate the new approach focused on creating hospitals independent of Whitehall control, a competitive system where money followed patients.[152] The secretary of state, Alan Milburn, and his adviser Simon Stevens became convinced that top-down targets in the health service were no longer effective, despite extra spending. They were particularly alarmed that hospital activity rates appeared to be stagnating.

Milburn made a series of politically provocative speeches criticising the command and control mind-set that tacitly underpinned the NHS since the 1940s. Milburn was a pugnacious character. Born in 1958, he grew up in the North-East of England in the County Durham mining community of Tow Law, then an inner-city estate in Benwell, West Newcastle. His grandfather was a labourer, while his mother, a single parent, became a secretary. The first in his family to go to university, Milburn's background gave him street-fighting qualities that proved beneficial in his battles with the Treasury throughout the next Parliament. Milburn's vision was of a universal health service responsive to patients with autonomously managed hospitals and booked appointments so patients could see their GP when they chose, augmented by large-scale treatment centres carrying out elective procedures.[153] This diversity of provision was combined with measures to promote public health and reduce health inequalities, notably the ban on smoking in public places introduced in 2006.[154] Even so, Milburn's ideas were heresy for much of the traditional Left. The ideological shibboleth that NHS care must be provided exclusively through state monopoly was rejected. Milburn believed the health service must be funded through general taxation, but *who* provided clinical treatment should be decided pragmatically. Milburn believed there was no compelling reason not to operate NHS services through the private sector.

By 2001, improved economic performance and dissatisfaction with the state of public services meant spending was dramatically increased. Panicked by reports of decrepit hospitals and rising waiting times, Blair appeared on the BBC *Frost Programme* to announce without any prior cabinet consultation that health spending would rise to the European average, around 6 per cent of national income.

As usual, the chancellor was furious roaring at Blair: 'You've stolen my fuck-ing Budget!' That weekend, Blair's aides arranged conference calls to work out the spending figures with the Department of Health's chief economist, Michael Smee. Labour's improvements would be funded by the one-off rise in national insurance while freezing tax allowances. The resulting budget was celebrated as 'the boldest and clearest reassertion of social democracy to be heard since the 1970s'. For commentators, it was 'a distinctively Labour Budget' affirming the rise in spending as Table 8.5 confirms:[155]

TABLE 8.5 UK public spending 2001–5[158]

	2001–2	*2002–3*	*2003–4*
Real increases			
Education	5.5 (3.1)	5.4 (4.9)	5.5 (5.2)
NHS	6.1 (5.6)	5.2 (5.0)	5.5 (5.3)
Home Office	6.3	2.6	1.4
Transport	9.1	6.8	7.6

Through its reforms, the Labour government was confronting the central assumption of the welfare state under post-war social democracy that there should be a government monopoly in the delivery of public services. 'After a number of false starts', Blair's administration came to believe that 'the existing structure of largely monopoly provision would not raise standards sufficiently'.[156] The private sector's efficiency and dynamism would be harnessed to 'modernise' the public sector. This strategy inverted Labour's approach in the decades after 1945 where state intervention was used to inject innovation and enhanced productivity into private enterprise. Now, it was the private sector that was used to strengthen public services. Blair sought to portray this shift as an expression of technocratic realism: the belief that in the public sector, 'what matters is what works'.

The Left, it should be remembered, had begun to reassess its position on competi-tion and markets in the 1980s. The emerging philosophy was labelled 'market social-ism'. The influential book *The Alternative: Politics for a Change* (1989) recommended the old-style Beveridge state should be broken up. Governments must provide citi-zens with 'wider choice wherever possible', experimenting with quasi-markets in health and education.[157] This approach implied continuity between the Thatcher/Major governments and their Labour successors. After initial hesitation and confu-sion, Blair and Brown 'picked up the threads' of quasi-market reforms, particularly GP fundholding as well as grant-maintained schools and City Technology Colleges (CTCs). The Labour governments combined structural reform of institutions with unprecedented increases in funding. The cumulative growth of the public sector after 1997 makes it difficult to plausibly claim that Labour pursued neo-liberalism with a human face. The Blair governments continued to emphasise their commit-ment to the social democratic tradition. In an *Observer* interview, the prime minister was adamant: 'You don't want the health service turned into a market place'.

Nonetheless, the fundamental difficulty Blair faced was that the public sector was still the lynchpin of the party's identity. In the 1990s, the Labour membership hesitantly embraced the redrafting of Clause Four, a decision that acknowledged tacitly the primacy of the market economy. At that time, despite embracing market forces, New Labour accepted there should not be any weakening in the traditional role of the state in public services – the last guarantee a socialist society could somehow be constructed in Britain. By imperilling this assumption, the post-1997 reforms not surprisingly provoked rancorous cabinet and internal party division. The prime minister believed the difference between the public and private sectors related to whether the service was funded through taxation rather than by individual consumers.[159] Brown, influenced by the philosopher Michael Sandel's writings on the public square, believed there were ethical limits to markets. The private sector centred on profit-making and market exchange was counter-posed to the public sector focused on care, duty and equal treatment regardless of wealth. Brown believed that citizens could not be consumers in public services since they lacked the information to efficiently respond to price signals. Private providers were inclined to 'cream-skim', taking on the patients or pupils who were easiest to teach or treat.[160] Moreover, privatisation of public assets had 'damaging effects'.[161] Brown's ally Ed Balls remarked that the provision of health and education 'depend upon an ethic of public service and a commitment to the services; if you go down that marketizing route, you run grave risks with that ethic of public service'.[162]

Meanwhile, professionals in the NHS and schools had been demoralised by the litany of bureaucratic edicts since 1997. Diversity of provision with organisations chasing their own performance targets meant co-ordination and 'joining-up' services became nearly impossible. One senior Whitehall official concluded: 'I don't think we can say at the end of the period the government was any more joined up on difficult issues that cross departmental boundaries than it was in 1997'.[163] A letter to the *Guardian* newspaper signed by health experts warned:

> Government reforms threaten both the ethos of the NHS, and the planned and equitable way in which it delivers care to patients. At the heart of the changes is the creation of a market that welcomes profit-driven international corporations and will compel hospitals and health professionals to compete with each other.[164]

New Labour strategists countered that the private sector had always played a role in public service delivery. Where to draw the line between public and private was a pragmatic judgement, not a matter of fundamental ideological conviction. Blair insisted Labour's reforms, combined with the injection of public investment, had a very different purpose to their Conservative predecessors. There was nothing particularly novel or dangerous about PPP. For decades, private contractors had fulfilled NHS contracts and maintained infrastructure. Treasury officials insisted that PPP created robust incentives for improvement, injecting scarce private sector skills and resources into the public sector.[165] Moreover, extra capacity improved the quality of treatment for those who could never afford to opt out and go private, an affirmation of Labour's egalitarian ideals.

New Labour's education policy: terminating the 'bog standard' comprehensive

The similar process of rethinking was underway in English schools policy. The Number Ten Policy Unit examined how to improve the quality of state education in the wake of the 2001 victory. It was felt that Labour's 2001 manifesto had been insufficiently radical. The instinct of Andrew Adonis, Blair's head of policy, was to re-establish the city technology colleges (CTCs) created in the early 1990s. Adonis believed the top-down 'naming and shaming' approach David Blunkett championed in the first term was not working. An exemplar of Labour's centralising approach was the ministerial edict which dictated that all primary-school pupils must do at least ten minutes of homework a night.[166] The improvement strategy relied on a tiny cohort of 'super-heads' to turn around failing schools. The belief among ministers was that 'the way to quick improvement was to tell people what to do', centred on the imposition of, 'imperious evaluation and auditing'. That almost inevitably led to the haemorrhaging of teaching staff.[167]

Education policy was still dominated by the 'central government knows best' mentality. Yet Labour's stance was fundamentally altered as ideas forged in 10 Downing Street after the 2001 election had a decisive impact, emphasising 'much more autonomous schools, better led, reducing LEA influence'. This approach inverted New Labour's pre-1997 mantra of 'standards not structures'.[168] The aim was to rely less on initiatives from the centre after the phase of hypercentralisation during Labour's first term. Blair acknowledged school reforms where central government 'sends down guidance and issues instructions and even monitors them' had limited impact. Rather than recreating LEAs, institutional reforms meant 'new disruptive providers that were going to do things differently and . . . create a dynamic for change'.[169]

The new generation of schools were a break with past practice in post-war Britain, where Labour left secondary education largely in the hands of LEAs. The schools created by New Labour were 'largely free to structure their governing bodies as they wish'. They were autonomous of LEAs with 'a strong mission and ethos'. The purpose was removing the 'shackles' of local bureaucratic control.[170] Targeted at deprived areas, academies were accountable to parents.[171] According to Adonis:

> What commends the concept is the compelling evidence from CTCs, specialist schools, ex-GM schools, and other schools with strong independent ethos and governance, that such independence tends to produce better schools than does a culture of local authority mediocrity, uniformity and weaker school-level governance and accountability.[172]

He believed there was an 'independence premium': 86 per cent of pupils attending CTCs got five good GCSEs compared to 47 per cent in non-specialist comprehensive schools. In its 2005 manifesto, Labour committed to an additional 200 academies by the end of the next Parliament.

New Labour's mission was 'to extend academy attributes across the entire system', refocusing capital investment for schools and identifying philanthropic and private sector sponsors, while reforming governing bodies.[173] The aim was to retain middle class parents within public services rather than incentivising opting out as successive Tory governments had done after 1979. Another aspiration was 'to break down the divide between the state and private sector', encouraging charitable foundations that ran independent schools to manage academy chains.[174] Although Labour became ardent advocates of comprehensive education in the 1960s and 1970s, Blair's team questioned that legacy. Number Ten advisers claimed the Left failed to advance a vision of post-selective education that suited the abilities of every pupil. Robert Skidelsky, Keynes's biographer and a leading economic historian, believed hostility to grammar schools was self-defeating, leading to the tolerance of mediocrity which further entrenched elitism by increasing the popularity of public schools.[175] The head of Harold Wilson's Policy Unit, Bernard Donoughue, agreed that Labour's post-war education policies were flawed:

> You needed to be clearer what you put in [grammar schools'] place. Vast factory comprehensives were not necessarily better. I didn't think it was necessary to abolish grammar schools. You could have a more pluralistic system. There was something Stalinist about comprehensives. . . . Too many people in the Labour party weren't interested in quality, [they were] interested in ideology.[176]

Despite the comprehensive revolution inaugurated by Anthony Crosland in 1965, education policies in the subsequent decades proved inadequate. Labour had too little to say about the curriculum, standards and teaching – issues addressed by Jim Callaghan in his 1976 Ruskin speech.[177]

The criticisms of Labour's post-war legacy in education policy had a decisive impact within Blair's inner circle. Alastair Campbell castigated 'bog standard' comprehensives. Adonis claimed that in the hands of incompetent LEAs, comprehensives became a byword for mediocrity. Adonis believed there was 'an almost unanswerable argument, in principle, for defining minimum standards of schooling which a parent has a right to expect in their locality'. Academies did not amount to privatisation given they were independent state schools where government regulated their admissions, curriculum, governance and financing.[178] There was even discussion in Labour circles of a 'failure voucher', where if parents' only local option was a 'sink school', they could use the entitlement to go into the private sector if they wished (although there was an acceptance that such innovations did not appear to have worked in the United States).[179] Adonis drove through legislation that enabled the Department for Education (DfE) to order competitions for new schools.[180] Blair's advisers claimed their reforms were inspired by other social democratic governments, especially in Sweden and the Netherlands.[181]

The educational establishment was not surprisingly enraged by Number Ten's ideas. Ted Wragg, the *Times Educational Supplement* (TES) columnist and former professor of education at Exeter University gave Adonis the nickname 'Tony Zoffis'. Commenting on a leaked draft of the 2005 Schools White Paper, Wragg acerbically quipped:

> To call these proposals 'a dog's breakfast' would be to insult Britain's pet owners, who take care to feed Bowser a balanced diet. They are the ultimate disaster from the No 10 wheeze factory. Leave Tony Zoffis free all summer . . . and this is what ensues.[182]

Even the secretary of state for education, Estelle Morris, was noticeably unimpressed by Number Ten's ideas. Morris insisted the major problem for schools was not control and interference by LEAs but 'bad teaching, bad leadership, difficult intake, lousy buildings, rotten curriculum'.[183] In Morris's view, Downing Street's policies were the result of narrow consultation with an elite cadre of headteachers – 'the thrusting, ambitious, motivated, successful, risk-takers, go-getters' – who were in the minority. Moreover, academic research demonstrated that comprehensives still outperformed selective grammar schools.[184] Adonis and the prime minister were obsessive about institutional change, but there was too little emphasis on curriculum reform and improving teacher quality.

John Dunford, general secretary of the Secondary Heads' Association (SHA), believed that Number Ten's policies were motivated by electoral politics rather than the best interests of the education service: 'They were still fearful of headlines in *The Daily Mail* that they were going soft on standards'.[185] As a consequence, 'Blair made the job of one of his major public service delivery departments very difficult'. Even John Birt, by now an adviser in 10 Downing Street, complained that Adonis's approach was not sufficiently strategic: 'We needed much bigger and more radical reforms'.[186] Blair and Adonis had a conservative view of the curriculum, treating A-levels as the untouchable gold standard. The *Times* columnist Jenny Russell worried that Labour's policies 'delivered impressive statistics rather than students with impressive educations'. The education system in England 'drilled children through their school lives, at the expense of teaching them how to learn, think and create'.[187]

The prime minister insisted that centre-left governing parties had to energetically pursue reforms responding to the rising expectations of pupils and parents. His approach now recognised that 'flog the system' targets were unlikely to bring about improvements. The emphasis should shift towards opening up the marketplace of provision.[188] Blair's ideas echoed the influence of *Marxism Today* in the 1980s reviewed in Chapter 2. *Marxism Today's* analysis provided the Left with a lens to observe the process of social change in Britain that social democracy hitherto lacked. In the management of public services, Blair and his follow-ers claimed Labour had to come to terms with modernity and the values of the consumer-orientated society. Yet efforts to roll out initiatives to drive up school standards produced less than spectacular results, at least when measured by inter-national benchmarking surveys such as the OECD's Programme for International Student Assessment (PISA).[189]

Of Knights and Knaves, Queens and Pawns: competition and markets

Even so, New Labour's strategy in public services amounted to an intellectual revolution. Among its most persuasive advocates was the LSE's Richard Titmuss professor of social policy, Julian Le Grand, subsequently appointed to the Down-ing Street Policy Unit. In his seminal work, *Motivation, Agency, and Policy: Of Knights and Knaves, Queens and Pawns*, Le Grand disputed the claim that public service organisations and professionals were inherently altruistic.[190] He pointed out that public service staff were likely to pursue their own material and status interests. Moreover, Le Grand insisted the post-1945 welfare state in Britain worked better for the affluent middle class. Paradoxically, those living in poverty and low-income households were less likely to be beneficiaries. The middle class had taken possession of the public sector.

In making this argument, Le Grand confronted the sacred cows of post-war social democracy, disputing the assumption that the public realm was naturally egalitarian. In fact, Le Grand's ideas had a long lineage on the British Left. They can be traced to the revisionist writers of the 1940s – most importantly, the social-ist intellectual and post-war Labour minister, Evan Durbin. Durbin identified two fundamental problems with the existing structure of state provision. The first related to public sector monopolies. Because these monopolies were not exposed to competition or the threat of exit, Durbin feared they might exploit citizens by providing a poor service. The second problem concerned the psychological incen-tives facing those employed in public services. Like Durbin, Le Grand feared that professionals were inclined to protect their interests. It was naive to assume they should be subservient to the ethic of public duty.[191] Le Grand's ideas appealed to the prime minister and his team of advisers in 10 Downing Street. Adonis set out to liberalise the internal market in education, allowing successful schools to expand, enabling money to follow the pupil and giving successful schools the incentives to recruit additional pupils, while promoting local management along-side changing admissions criteria for schools.[192] Market forces and competition were harnessed in education to fulfil the public good.

Scars on his back? Opposition to reform

Nonetheless, despite the intellectual clarity of the reforms, by the 2005 elec-tion dissatisfaction among backbench Labour MPs was rising. There were fears of 'backdoor selection' alongside demands for greater democratic control of admissions policy in schools.[193] MPs became more rebellious over New Labour's reforms. Yet Treasury officials also raised objections to the policies, notably the proposal for NHS foundation hospitals. If hospitals took out commercial loans and then went bankrupt, who would deal with their liabilities? The Treasury were adamant that hospitals were not like housing associations or universities. They had no guaranteed stream of income. If a local hospital became financially unsustainable, the impact on the local population would be devastating.[194] More-over, if hospital trusts raised the cap on the number of procedures that could be undertaken by hospital consultants working privately, the NHS risked becoming a two-tier system. Opposition to the reforms was co-ordinated by two of the most prominent figures in the cabinet: Gordon Brown and John Prescott, the deputy prime minister.[195]

New Labour's settlement in public services was undermined initially by intellectual confusion among ministers and then by growing ideological dis-agreement. Politicians acknowledged they had to govern in the era of devolu-tion and active democracy, in which a more engaged citizenry had less patience with traditional bureaucratic obstinance. Yet it proved difficult for ministers to discard the fundamental instinct of command and control from the centre, rig-orously monitoring performance in the name of national modernisation. New Labour never escaped from the ambiguity implied by the distinction between the top-down directive tendency and the desire to break with centralism in pursuit of choice and competition. The then principal private secretary to the prime minister, Jeremy Heywood, admitted that departments were perplexed by the Blair government's apparently muddled strategy.[196] When ministers after the 2001 election realised that more should be done to stimulate innovation, they discovered that skilled professionals had become wedded to the compli-ance culture enforced by audit, performance measurement and continuous inspection. Not surprisingly, there was now a fear of taking risks or adapting procedures in public services, undermining the Labour government's effort to transform standards and quality.

The new British progressive settlement?

Despite the setbacks, by the time of the 2005 election the optimists in Blair's entourage believed the Labour governments were on the cusp of forging 'a last-ing New Labour settlement . . . as profound for this century as the Attlee Gov-ernment's reforms were for the last'.[197] Those who defended Blair's premiership insisted Labour had historic achievements to its credit: new progressive institu-tions had been built, social attitudes were transformed, while Britain was now a more tolerant and open society. The British political class had been compelled to come to terms with the loss of empire, accepting the UK's future role in Europe.[198] There was a major shift in the dominant agenda of British politics. According to this account, 1997 joined 1906 and 1945 as 'the third great progressive electoral landslide'. Whereas the Thatcher governments had obsessed about reducing the size of the state to liberalise the British economy, New Labour was motivated by reviving public services and building an active welfare state, using the discretionary power of government to solve economic and social problems.

Far from being fixated by electoral politics, the post-1997 administrations displayed 'high intellectual capacity'. Their initiatives were underpinned by rigorous analysis of policy-related evidence.[199] As the political scientist David Coates recalls: 'The New Labour government has been, to an unprecedented degree in modern UK politics, intellectually informed and academically sustained'.[200] The ideas informing the Labour government's policy-making had invariably been tested rigorously. It was recognised that the needs and aspirations of citizens were changing rapidly, as UK households were better educated and increasingly affluent. The governance of the domestic economy necessitated novel reforms of macro-economic policy. Public services had to be modernised to preserve the social democratic ethic of universality and equal access. At the frontline of policy implementation, the evidence of progressive change became more tangible. Sure Start had transformed the lives of poorer children. Deprived places were less vulnerable to crime as the result of more police officers and neighbourhood policing initiatives. Full employment, the age-old aspiration of Labour governments and socialist economic policy, was finally achieved. The sociologist Anthony Giddens wrote: 'It is difficult to think of a single area of government intervention since 1997 which has not been related to questions of poverty and inequality'. The 'veritable maze' of programmes included the child tax credit, working tax credit, pension credit, the minimum wage, New Deal, the child trust fund, child benefit increases, Sure Start, the childcare tax credit, education action zones, alongside large-scale public investment in schools and hospitals.[201]

Elsewhere, the Macpherson Inquiry following the murder of Stephen Lawrence established by the Labour home secretary, Jack Straw, in 1997 codified the existence of institutional racism. It was not only a few 'bad apples' that perpetrated racial discrimination, but the everyday culture and practices of public institutions. The recognition of institutional racism was the bedrock of a more inclusive society. Civil liberties and the rights of vulnerable minorities received the protection of the Human Rights Act (HRA) in 1998.[202] Although Labour was attacked over its legal reforms by the judicial establishment, the abolition of the convention of double jeopardy by another home secretary, David Blunkett, led to the eventual conviction of Jamie Acourt and David Norris for Stephen Lawrence's murder. In Northern Ireland, by implementing the Good Friday Agreement, the Blair and Brown governments brought to an end the horror of thirty years of bloody conflict and violence.

Yet to critics, New Labour's 'progressive' settlement had made innumerable concessions to Thatcherism and neo-liberalism. The individual consumer in public services was privileged over society and the public good. There was a continuing shift from collective risk-sharing in the welfare state, emphasising the financial and moral liberty of citizens. The rational choice approach to reform perpetuated the obsession with financial levers and incentives in public policy. In the Blair era, the purpose of government action was reduced to helping more households 'earn and own'. Labour's reforms relied on narrow managerialism, while the emphasis on 'consumer choice' reduced public provision to the calculus of maximising individual utility. As such, the priority accorded to choice and competition in public services bred an ethos of acquisitive individualism at odds with the tradition of ethical socialism.[203] It was believed that ministers were too willing to accommodate the commercial interests of the private sector. For essential public health interventions – notably banning junk food advertising and tackling alcohol addiction – voluntary regulation was prioritised despite the advice of the medical profession and health experts, leading almost inevitably to escalating pressures on the NHS. All in all, Labour remained reticent about expanding government's role in the economy, even in the aftermath of the 2008 crash. If agendas in British politics comprise 'ideas and standards that specify not only the goals of policy and the kind of instruments that can be used to attain them, but the very nature of the problems they are meant to be addressing', it is implausible to claim that any major shift in UK public policy orthodoxy occurred after 1997.[204]

To be sure, external forces that emerged in the aftermath of Thatcherism constrained Labour's ability to reshape the domestic political consensus. Blair's project sought to combine a productive and efficient economy with social inclusion by modernising domestic policy-making. Yet Britain continued to suffer the long-term structural consequences of deindustrialisation, leading to weak productivity and regional polarisation. UK inequality was driven less by Anglo-American capitalism than the transition to the service-orientated economy and the post-industrial labour market characterised by the dramatic growth in earnings disparities.[205] Whoever was to blame for the scale of deindustrialisation, marginalised communities, 'those on the wrong side of social change . . . [who] feel increasingly threatened by the way their communities and country are changing', perceived themselves to be under threat and 'left behind'.[206] Moreover, Labour ministers were clearly running out of steam by the end of the second term. Landmark constitutional reforms had been enacted, as had the national minimum wage. After being in office for nearly ten years, Labour lost the ability to think imaginatively, striving to overcome the long-term problems bedevilling Britain's economy and society. In his final year in office, the prime minister gave insightful speeches about the future policy agenda.[207] Blair's ideas focused on personalising public services while updating the post-1945 settlement. But clearly time was running out. He was destined to remain the 'unfulfilled' prime minister.[208]

Meanwhile, the warring factions of 'Blairites' and 'Brownites' undermined Labour's ability to forge fresh policies, cultivating the new generation of progressive thought and ideas. The government was divided between 'consolidators' who prioritised Treasury-driven tax-and-spend social democracy and 'reformers' whose fundamental aim was to recast the British state transferring power to citizens while breaking up centralised bureaucracies. Labour was now divided bitterly over the reforms. Blair was emphasising pluralism and alternative mechanisms of service delivery. Brown wanted ever tighter control of public spending.[209] Despite agreeing with the Chancellor, John Prescott valiantly tried to broker peace between No.10 and No.11 Downing Street to little effect. On two occasions, Blair came close to removing Brown from the Treasury. The 2001 election campaign was particularly fraught. Blair wrote that the campaign convinced him 'the TB/GB story was unlikely to have a happy ending'.[210] The morning after the election, Blair toyed with despatching Brown to the Foreign Office, but he relented acknowledging the strength of Brown's reputation for prudent economic management. Prior to the 2005 election, John Birt, David Halpern and Gareth Davies from Number Ten's Strategy Unit were asked to produce plans to break up the Treasury, separating the macro-economic policy-making function from taxation and public spending.[211] A separate department for industrial strategy was to be established, echoing Wilson's plans for the Department of Economic Affairs (DEA) in the 1960s. Yet by this stage of the political cycle, Blair who was weakened by the fallout from the Iraq invasion could no longer countenance all out war with his chancellor. He feared dismantling Brown's Treasury Empire would 'bring the entire building tumbling down'.[212]

The psychodrama of Blair and Brown's turbulent political relationship gripped the Labour Party for more than a decade. The political theatrics were choreographed by the apparently irreconcilable personalities of these extremely talented and intensely ambitious politicians. Popular television productions such as *The Deal* (2003) presented Blair as a slippery and mendacious figure, able to willingly manipulate his more ponderous, emotionally unavailable rival at the infamous *Granita* dinner where Brown agreed to stand aside for the leadership. In *The Deal*, Brown is depicted as the product of the honourable tradition of the Labour movement, deeply loyal to John Smith, while Blair is a trendy, shallow and ambitious public schoolboy.[213] Yet at heart, the enmity between Blair and Brown flowed from divergent ideas about the party's modernisation. Brown believed the party's policy prospectus now veered too far from Labour's historic mission of economic and social justice.

In 2007, Brown intended to revitalise the party's agenda after becoming leader, but instead a comprehensive debate about Labour's future was avoided. The Brown administration then seemed to fall apart, unable to withstand the pressure of innumerable Whitehall plots and ministerial resignations. Ministers appeared exhausted after thirteen years in office, rather like the Attlee government in 1950–51. The party lost power in 2010 not only due to its loss of economic credibility. It appeared that Labour had no compelling prospectus to put before the country. The government failed to develop a persuasive vision of Britain's future, posing very different questions to those addressed in 1997. Blair believed the only ideas required were those he personally came up with.[214] Brown traded on his reputation as a big thinker, but he had lost his intellectual spark. He admitted the country was bored at the 'fag end' of New Labour. Yet he remained confused until the 2010 defeat about whether to repudiate or consolidate Blair's governing project.[215]

The liberal progressive intelligentsia who in the past supplied the party with ideas and programmes were still disillusioned in the aftermath of the Iraq War. Strategists acknowledged that voters now lacked 'a sense of Labour's mission'. It was hard to know 'who Labour was fighting for'.[216] The party failed to create the new domestic political orthodoxy. As a consequence, the historical footprint of the Blair and Brown governments was now difficult to discern. Labour was unable to use ideas and the affirmative power of democratic government to entrench political support, the bedrock of any viable social democratic politics in Britain.

Conclusion

In many ways, it is hardly surprising that no path-breaking progressive consensus emerged in Britain after 1997. The New Labour governments remained largely wedded to the existing political and social order. They had no intention of fundamentally altering the power structure of the UK's iniquitous institutions. The independent schools and elite universities still dominated public life. Ministers often felt like 'outsiders in the corridors of power'.[217] The targets of intrusive government intervention were invariably benefit claimants, asylum seekers, drug addicts, teenage mothers and the socially excluded. There was little desire to disturb the structural advantages of the economically privileged. What is more, the British public were viewed as instinctively Eurosceptic. As a consequence, New Labour tiptoed cautiously around the issue of Europe.

Throughout its period of office, the importance of ideas in moulding New Labour's politics and policy was self-evident. The Blair and Brown governments were constrained by inherited traditions and intellectual assumptions that served to undermine their achievements in office. What became the conventional wisdom for New Labour, the ideological scaffolding that upheld the party's policies, emerged after successive defeats in the 1980s and 1990s: the commitment to the Westminster tradition of parliamentary sovereignty; trepidation over the electorate's attitudes towards taxation and public spending; paranoia about the media's antipathy to Europe; and the 'tabloid friendly' disdain towards benefit claimants and asylum seekers.

This section of the book examined the nature of New Labour's impact on the British polity and economy. The discussion considered how far the Blair/Brown governments transformed the attitudes, beliefs and preferences of British citizens. A fundamental question was addressed throughout: did New Labour succeeded in forging a new governing orthodoxy in British politics akin to Attlee and Thatcher? The verdict was that no new social democratic settlement emerged after 1997.

In political economy, Britain under Blair and Brown struggled to break free of the Anglo-Liberal legacy that predated Thatcherism. After the defeats of the 1980s, the centre-left across the industrialised world 'moved to a more realistic analysis of the economic context and of the art of the possible'. Yet by the time New Labour came to power, there were still 'major holes' in the Left's armoury. Indeed, there was:

> Little clear account of the economy, where it can and should evolve, how much it can be shaped. There [was] inadequate analysis of the room for manoeuvre of national states, and a mismatch between a rhetoric of much diminished capacity and the reality.[218]

The prevailing debate about economic policy within the Labour government was almost non-existent. There was certainly nothing to equal the compelling cabinet arguments of the 1960s and 1970s. Any move to force the private sector to adopt prescriptive regulations and pay additional corporate taxation was considered anathema. The climate of deregulation and labour market flexibility continued. Regional imbalances grew. Tackling inequality was equated with Old Labour, 'levelling-down' and the politics of envy. New Labour accepted a limited role for the state in governing the economy.

That said, dismissing New Labour as unequivocally 'neo-liberal' is ultimately misleading. The Blair/Brown administrations still affirmed the positive purpose of government as a force for good in the economy and society. In public services, the New Labour governments initially refused to adopt the policy inheritance of their predecessors, reflecting ministers' anxieties about 'two-tier' services and the growth of inequity. The Labour administrations moved to address historical under-funding in health and education. Yet the reforms often appeared muddled and incoherent. The evolution from the command and control structure of the first term to adopting decentralised 'quasi-markets' instilled much confusion in Whitehall. Not surprisingly, professionals at the frontline became demoralised. In overhauling the current governing orthodoxy, New Labour made most progress in relation to constitutional reform. But even here, having implemented its first term agenda, ministers had little invigorating to say about political revitalisation despite the pervasive crisis of trust in representative democracy.[219]

For all the criticisms, the post-1997 governments were scarcely barren of social democratic achievement. Many opponents on Left and Right have scorned the Blair era indiscriminately, ignoring its obvious accomplishments. Nonetheless, a conspicuous gap emerged between promised achievement and governing performance. New Labour's 1997 victory initially engendered great hope in progressive Britain. The party had an unprecedented parliamentary majority. The Conservatives had been routed, and then shifted dramatically to the Right. The prevailing mood favoured a new settlement, a break with market fundamentalism. Yet political expectations were never fulfilled, fuelling voters' disenchantment with British democracy. The period after 1997 will be viewed inevitably as a missed opportunity to frame a lasting social democratic consensus in Britain. If the Labour Party's impact on politics and society during its period of office was ambiguous, to what extent did the Blair/Brown governments influence the agenda of Left and Right that came after defeat? It is to that question the penultimate chapter will turn.

Notes

1 R.H. Tawney, 'The Choice Before the Labour Party', *The Political Quarterly*, Volume 3 (3), p. 336, 1932.
2 I. Crewe, cited in S. Hall, 'A Long Hall', p. 6.
3 P. Addison, *The Road to 1945: British Politics and the Second World War*, London: Jonathan Cape, 1975; S. Fielding, *The Labour Party*; N. Tiratsoo (ed.), *The Attlee Years*, New York: University of Columbia Press.
4 A. Gamble, 'New Labour and Political Change', p. 645.
5 P. Toynbee & D. Walker, *The Verdict: Did New Labour Change Britain?*, London: Granta, 2011; A. Heath, J. Curtice & R. Jowell, *The Rise of New Labour*.
6 P. Gould, *The Unfinished Revolution*.
7 J. Tomlinson, 'It's the Economy, Stupid! Labour and the Economy, *circa* 1964', p. 339.
8 Cited in J. Tomlinson, 'It's the Economy, Stupid! Labour and the Economy, *circa* 1964', p. 339.
9 Cited in A. Campbell, *From Crash to Defeat: Diaries – Volume 7, 2007–2010*, p. 678, London: Biteback, 2018.
10 https://theguardian.com/politics/blog/2014/mar/14/tony-benn-has-died-reaction-and-tributes. Accessed 26th July 2018.
11 M. Grasso et al., 'Thatcher's Children, Blair's Babies, Political Socialization and Trickle-Down Value Change: An Age, Period and Cohort Analysis', *British Journal of Political Science*, Volume 49 (1), pp. 17–36, 2017.
12 M. Grasso et al., 'Thatcher's Children, Blair's Babies, Political Socialization and Trickle-Down Value Change'.
13 http://bsa.natcen.ac.uk/media/38723/bsa30_full_report_final.pdf. Accessed 12th January 2019.
14 http://bsa.natcen.ac.uk/media/38723/bsa30_full_report_final.pdf. Accessed 16th February 2019.
15 J. Curtice, 'The Uphill Battle for "Responsible Capitalism"', *Public Policy Research*, Volume 19 (2), pp. 129–130, 2012.
16 S. Soroka & C. Wlezien, 'Political Institutions and the Opinion-Policy Link', Paper presented at the European Consortium for Political Research Joint Sessions of Workshops, St. Gallen, Switzerland, 12th–17th April 2011.
17 R. Vinen, *Thatcher's Britain: The Political and Social Upheaval of the 1980s*, London: Simon & Schuster.
18 A. Heath, *Social Progress in Britain*, p. 196.
19 Prime Minister's Policy Directorate, 'Medium Term Strategy for Taxation and Public Spending', 12th November 2004.
20 L. Butterfield, 'What Do the Middle-Classes Want?', Private Presentation, 2nd July 2004.
21 https://ifs.org.uk/bns/bn92.pdf. Accessed 16th October 2018.
22 file:///C:/Users/User/Downloads/CBP-8037.pdf. Accessed 15th January 2019.
23 The IFS accept in their report that it is harder to raise the level of productivity in labour-intensive sectors such as health, education and social care.
24 T. Horton, 'Solidarity Lost'.
25 Data source: A. Heath, *Social Progress in Britain*.
26 Data source: Nat Cen British Social Attitudes Survey, London: National Centre for Social Research, 2010.
27 http://bsa.natcen.ac.uk/media/38723/bsa30_full_report_final.pdf. Accessed 17th October 2018.
28 http://bsa.natcen.ac.uk/media/39248/bsa35_gender.pdf. Accessed 5th April 2019.

29 https://assets.publishing.service.gov.uk/government/uploads/system/uploads/
    attachment_data/file/775589/Attitudes-equality-social-attitudes-survey-2017a.pdf.
    Accessed 23rd January 2019.
30 R. Jenkins, 'Speech to the Annual Conference of the London Labour Party', *Jenkins
    Papers 291*, 13th May 1967.
31 R. Putnam, *Bowling Alone: The Collapse and Revival of American Community*, New York:
    Simon & Schuster, 2000.
32 Confidential Memorandum to the Prime Minister, 'Half Way There: The Next Five
    Years in Blair's New Labour Project to Modernise Britain', 2001.
33 D. Goodhart, *The Road to Somewhere: The Populist Revolt and the Future of Politics*,
    London: C Hurst & Co, 2017; M. Goodwin & R. Eatwell, *National Populism: The
    Revolt Against Liberal Democracy*, London: Penguin, 2018.
34 J. Furlong, 'The Changing Electoral Geography of England and Wales: Varieties of
    "Left-Behindness"', *Political Geography*, Volume 75, pp. 1–12, 2019.
35 W.G. Runciman, *Relative Deprivation and Social Justice: A Study of Attitudes to Social
    Inequality in Twentieth Century England*, London: Routledge & Kegan Paul, 1966.
36 J. Furlong, 'The Changing Electoral Geography of England and Wales: Varieties of
    "Left-Behindness"'.
37 https://thebritishacademy.ac.uk/two-englands-and-divided-world. Accessed 17th Octo-
    ber 2018.
38 G. Evans & J. Tilley, *The New Politics of Class.*
39 J. Lawrence, *Me, Me, Me: The Search for Community in Post-War England*, p. 37.
40 A. Heath, *Social Progress in Britain*, p. 196.
41 G. Evans & J. Tilley, *The New Politics of Class.*
42 R. Inglehart & P. Norris, *Cultural Backlash: Trump, Brexit and the Rise of Authoritarian
    Populism*, Cambridge: Cambridge University Press, 2018.
43 Cited in L. Butterfield, 'What Do the Middle-Classes Want?', Confidential Memoran-
    dum, 2nd July 2004.
44 P. Mandelson, IPPR Fringe, Labour Party conference, Bournemouth, September 1999.
45 S. Buckby & N. Lawson, 'Third Way? No Way, Tony', *The New Statesman*, 13th March
    1998.
46 https://ipsos.com/sites/default/files/201704/sri_blairs_britain_the_social_and_
    cultural_legacy_2008.pdf. Accessed 15th October 2018.
47 https://ipsos.com/sites/default/files/201704/sri_blairs_britain_the_social_and_
    cultural_legacy_2008.pdf. Accessed 15th October 2018.
48 J.P. Mackintosh, 'Has Social Democracy Failed in Britain?', *The Political Quarterly*,
    Volume 49 (3), August–October, 1978.
49 B. Brivati, 'The New Labour Government's Place in History'.
50 E. Shaw, *Losing Labour's Soul?*, p. 6.
51 E. Shaw, *Losing Labour's Soul?*.
52 Confidential Memorandum to the Prime Minister, 'Half Way There: The Next Five
    Years in Blair's New Labour Project to Modernise Britain', 2001.
53 M. Matthijs, *Ideas and Economic Crises in Britain from Attlee to Blair*, London: Routledge, 2011.
54 Cited in M. Wickham-Jones, 'From Reformism to Resignation and Remedialism?
    Labour's Trajectory through British Politics', in E.C. Hargrove (ed.), *The Future of the Dem-
    ocratic Left in Industrial Societies*, Pennsylvania, PA: Penn State University Press, p. 37, 2003.
55 H. Thompson, 'The Economy'.
56 W. Hutton, *The State We're In*; J. Kay, *The Foundations of Corporate Success*; P. Hirst, *After
    Thatcher*; D. Marquand, *The Unprincipled Society*.
57 J. Kay, *The Foundations of Corporate Success: How Business Strategies Add Value*, Oxford:
    Oxford University Press, 1993.
58 A. Gamble & G. Kelly, 'Stakeholder Capitalism and One Nation Socialism', *Renewal*,
    Volume 4 (1), pp. 23–32, 1995.
59 K. Pike & A. Hindmoor, 'Do As I Did Not As I Say: Blair, New Labour and Party
    Traditions', *The Political Quarterly*, forthcoming.

60 E. Dell, *A Strange, Eventful History*; G. Mulgan & C. Leadbeater, *Misstakeholding*, London: Demos, 1996.
61 Interview, Pat McFadden MP, former Minister of State, Department of Business, Innovation & Skills, October 2011.
62 Interview, Roger Liddle, former Number Ten Special Adviser, April 2011.
63 Interview with Geoffrey Norris, former Special Adviser, 10 Downing Street, May 2011.
64 A. Gamble & G. Kelly, 'Stakeholder Capitalism and One Nation Socialism'.
65 Interview, Sam White, former Treasury Special Adviser, September 2011.
66 Interview, Rt. Hon. Peter Mandelson, former Secretary of State, Department of Business, Innovation and Skills, October 2011.
67 J.M. Keynes, *The End of Laissez-Faire/The Economic Consequences of the Peace*, Great Minds Series, London: Penguin, 2004.
68 J.M. Keynes, *The End of Laissez-Faire/The Economic Consequences of the Peace*.
69 A. Gamble, 'New Labour and Political Change'; H. Thompson, 'The Economy'; M. Matthijs, *Ideas and Economic Crises in Britain from Attlee to Blair*, pp. 191–192.
70 M. Matthijs, *Ideas and Economic Crises in Britain from Attlee to Blair*, pp. 191–192.
71 R.B. Barrell & P. Davis, 'The Evolution of the Financial Crisis of 2007–08', *National Institute Economic Review*, Volume 206 (1), pp. 5–14, 2008.
72 S. Newton, *The Reinvention of Britain 1960–2016: A Political and Economic History*, London: Routledge, 2017.
73 M. Matthijs, *Ideas and Economic Crises in Britain from Attlee to Blair*, p. 190; A. Tooze, *Crashed: How a Decade of Financial Crises Changed the World*, London: Allen Lane, 2018.
74 A. Tooze, *Crashed: How a Decade of Financial Crises Changed the World*, p. 81.
75 A. Tooze, *Crashed: How a Decade of Financial Crises Changed the World*, p. 184.
76 M. Matthijs, *Ideas and Economic Crises in Britain from Attlee to Blair*.
77 https://uk.reuters.com/article/brown-greenspan/brown-welcomes-greenspan-and-his-book-idUKNOA14192320071001. Accessed 10th August 2018.
78 https://telegraph.co.uk/finance/financialcrisis/3081909/Financial-Crisis-US-will-lose-superpower-status-claims-German-minister.html. Accessed 8th August 2018.
79 A. Tooze, *Crashed: How a Decade of Financial Crises Changed the World*, p. 184.
80 H. Thompson, 'Post-Crisis, Post-Devolution Politics and the Mansion Tax'.
81 A. Tooze, *Crashed: How a Decade of Financial Crises Changed the World*, p. 266.
82 P. Stephens, 'Politics Cannot Escape the Muddled Centre', *The Financial Times*, p. 11, 11th January 2009.
83 S. Newton, *The Reinvention of Britain 1960–2016*.
84 A. Darling, *Back from the Brink*, p. 146.
85 Cited in K. Ussher, 'Labour's Economic Record', p. 111.
86 G. Brown, *Beyond the Crash*.
87 H. Thompson, 'The Economy', p. 906.
88 A. Darling, *Back from the Brink: A Thousand Days at Number 11*, p. 4, London: Biteback, 2011.
89 A. Gamble, 'The Economy'.
90 J. Tomlinson, *Managing the Economy, Managing the People*.
91 R. Skidelsky, *Money and Government: A Challenge to Mainstream Economics*, p. 222.
92 P. Stephens, 'A Chancellor Writing a Cheque for Change', *The Financial Times*, p. 23, 19th July 2000.
93 Cited in A. Tooze, *Crashed: How a Decade of Financial Crises Changed the World*, p. 275.
94 Cited in R. Skidelsky, *Money and Government: A Challenge to Mainstream Economics*, p. 227.
95 The Conservative Party Manifesto, 'Invitation to Join the Government of Britain', p. 3, London: The Conservative Party, 2010.
96 J. Tomlinson, *Managing the Economy, Managing the People*, p. 116.
97 R. Liddle, Confidential Memorandum to the Secretary of State for Business, Innovation and Science, 'New Labour and the Economic Crisis', 2009.

98 K. Ussher, 'Labour's Economic Record'.
99 Interview, Roger Liddle, former Number Ten Special Adviser, April 2011.
100 A. Darling, *Back from the Brink: A Thousand Days at Number 11*, London: Biteback, 2011.
101 Interview, Rt. Hon. Peter Mandelson, former Secretary of State, Department of Business, Innovation and Skills, October 2011.
102 A. Darling, *Back from the Brink*; P. Mandelson, *The Third Man*.
103 Interview, Roger Liddle, former Number Ten Special Adviser, April 2011.
104 R. Liddle, Confidential Memorandum to the Secretary of State for Business, Innovation and Science, 'Industrial Activism', 30th March 2009.
105 Cited in K. Ussher, 'Labour's Economic Record', p. 119.
106 Source: City UK https://thecityuk.com/news/financial-and-related-professional-services-fuelling-uk-growth-and-productivity/. Accessed 16th May 2019.
107 R. Liddle, Confidential Memorandum to the Secretary of State for Business, Innovation and Science, 'Industrial Activism', 30th March 2009.
108 H. Kennedy, 'Power to the People', in P. Facey, B. Rigby & A. Runwick (eds.), *Unlocking Democracy: Twenty Years of Charter 88*, p. 43, London: Methuen Politicos.
109 V. Bogdanor, 'Constitutional Reform in Britain: The Quiet Revolution'.
110 V. Bogdanor, 'Constitutional Reform in Britain: The Quiet Revolution'.
111 V. Bogdanor, 'Constitutional Reform in Britain: The Quiet Revolution'.
112 M. Russell, *The Contemporary House of Lords: Westminster Bicameralism Revived*, Oxford: Oxford University Press, 2013.
113 C. Sumner & M. Taylor, Confidential Memorandum to the Prime Minister, 'House of Lords Reform: Third Stage', 11th March 2004.
114 G. Radice, *Diaries 1980–2001: From Political Disaster to Triumph*, p. 437.
115 P. Allen, *The Political Class: Why It Matters Who Our Politicians Are*, Oxford: Oxford University Press, 2018.
116 G. Evans & J. Tilley, *The New Politics of Class*.
117 MPs agreed that the police could hold suspects for up to 28 days. The decision was viewed as a major defeat for the Blair government.
118 A. McGowan, Confidential Memorandum, 'Devolution – Next 18 Months', 16th December 2003.
119 This exchange is cited in V. Bogdanor, 'Constitutional Reform in Britain: The Quiet Revolution', p. 53.
120 G. Radice, *Diaries 1980–2001: From Political Disaster to Triumph*, p. 422.
121 J. Denham, 'Labour and England, 1997–2010', in M. Kenny, I. McLean & A. Paun (eds.), *Governing England: English Identity and Institutions in a Changing UK*, Oxford: Oxford University Press, 2018.
122 Interview, Lord Andrew Adonis, former Secretary of State for Transport and Minister of State in the Department for Education and Skills, May 2011.
123 V. Bogdanor, 'Constitutional Reform in Britain: The Quiet Revolution'.
124 V. Bogdanor, 'Constitutional Reform in Britain: The Quiet Revolution'.
125 N. Timmins, *The Five Giants: A Biography of the Welfare State*, London: William Collins, 2015.
126 Interview, Matthew Taylor, former Number Ten Special Adviser, September 2011.
127 C. Paton, 'Blair and the NHS: Resistible Force Meets Moveable Object', in T. Casey (ed.), *The Blair Legacy: Politics, Policy, Governance and Foreign Affairs*, Basingstoke: Palgrave Macmillan, 2009.
128 Interview, Professor Julian Le Grand, former Number Ten Special Adviser, October 2011.
129 Interview, Professor Julian Le Grand, former Number Ten Special Adviser, October 2011.
130 Interview, Matthew Taylor, former Number Ten Special Adviser, September 2011.
131 The commitment to the literacy and numeracy strategy was affirmed in the government's White Paper, 'Excellence in Schools', London: HMG, September 1997.

132 http://labour-party.org.uk/manifestos/1997/1997-labour-manifesto.shtml. Accessed 12th February 2019.
133 S. Driver & L. Martell, *New Labour*.
134 A. Campbell, *The Blair Years: Extracts from the Alastair Campbell Diaries*, p. 538, London: Arrow Books, 2012.
135 'The NHS Plan: A Plan for Investment, a Plan for Reform', London: HMG, July 2000.
136 G. Bevan & C. Hood, 'What's Measured Is What Matters: Targets and Gaming in the English Public Healthcare System', *Public Administration*, Volume 84 (3), pp. 517–538, 2006.
137 https://www.theguardian.com/politics/1999/sep/05/politicalnews.observerpolitics
138 J.K. Galbraith, *The Culture of Contentment*, Princeton: Princeton University Press, 2017.
139 N. Timmins, *The Five Giants: A Biography of the Welfare State*.
140 Interview, Matthew Taylor, former Number Ten Special Adviser, September 2011.
141 Interview, Professor Julian Le Grand, former Number Ten Special Adviser, October 2011.
142 G. Kelly & M. Taylor, *Building Better Partnerships*, London: Institute for Public Policy Research, 2001.
143 Interview, Matthew Taylor, former Number Ten Special Adviser, September 2011.
144 Confidential Memorandum to the Prime Minister, 'Education Reform: Choice and Contestability', 18th December 2002.
145 S. Gorard & J. Fitz, 'Markets and Stratification: A View from England and Wales', *Educational Policy*, Volume 14 (3), pp. 405–424, 1998; S. Gerwitz, S.J. Ball & R. Bowe, 'Parents, Privilege and the Education Market-Place', *Research Papers in Education*, Volume 9 (1), pp. 3–29, 1994.
146 Confidential Memorandum to the Prime Minister, 'Half Way There: The Next Five Years in Blair's New Labour Project to Modernise Britain', 2001.
147 Cited in R. Skidelsky, *Britain Since 1918: A Success Story?* p. 381.
148 Speech by the Prime Minister, 'Progress and Justice in the 21st Century', Fabian Society Lecture at the Old Vic Theatre, 17th June 2003.
149 A. Adonis, Confidential Memorandum to the Prime Minister, 'Choice and Contestability – Next Reform Steps', 19th December 2002, PD Personal Papers.
150 A. Adonis, Confidential Memorandum to the Prime Minister, 'Choice and Contestability – Next Reform Steps', 19th December 2002, PD Personal Papers.
151 Interview, Roger Liddle, former Number Ten Special Adviser, April 2011.
152 H. Glennerster, *British Social Policy: 1945 to the Present*.
153 N. Timmins, *The Five Giants: A Biography of the Welfare State*; plans for diversity in NHS provision were enacted in *The Health and Social Care Act*, November 2003 and 'Commissioning a Patient-Led NHS', London: HMG, July 2005.
154 'Public Health White Paper: Choosing Health', London: HMG, November 2004.
155 P. Riddell, *The Unfulfilled Prime Minister*, p. 322.
156 P. Riddell, *The Unfulfilled Prime Minister*, p. 321.
157 B. Pimlott, A. Wright & T. Flower (eds.), *The Alternative: Politics for a Change*, p. 121.
158 Treasury data: https://assets.publishing.service.gov.uk/government/uploads/system/uploads/attachment_data/file/630896/Public_Spending_Statistics_July_2017.pdf. Accessed 15th May 2019; figures in brackets are current spending.
159 R. Skidelsky, *Britain: A Success Story?*.
160 R. Skidelsky, *Britain: A Success Story?*; G. Brown, *My Life, Our Times*, London: Bodley Head, 2017.
161 D. Marquand, *Decline of the Public: The Hollowing-Out of Citizenship*, p. 2, Cambridge: Polity Press, 2004.
162 Cited in D. Coates, *Prolonged Labour*, p. 194.
163 Interview, Jeremy Heywood, Cabinet Secretary, September 2011.
164 https://theguardian.com/society/2005/sep/24/health.politics. Accessed 16th December 2018.

165 M. Taylor & G. Kelly, 'Quality not Quantity', London: Policy Network, June 2001.

166 Interview, Estelle Morris, former Secretary of State for Education and Skills, September 2011; 'Homework Guidelines', London: Department for Education and Skills, March 1998.

167 Interview, Anastasia De Waal, Deputy Director, *Civitas*, May 2011.

168 Interview, Sir David Normington, former Permanent Secretary, Department for Education and Skills, May 2011.

169 Interview, Rt. Hon. Tony Blair, former Prime Minister, June 2011.

170 Interview, Rt. Hon. Charles Clarke, former Secretary of State for Education and Skills, September 2011.

171 Proposals to radically extend specialist schools were outlined in the government's White Paper 'Schools Achieving Success', London: HMG, September 2001.

172 A. Adonis, Confidential Memorandum to the Prime Minister, 'The Independent State School', 5th March 2004.

173 A. Adonis, Confidential Memorandum to the Prime Minister, 'The Independent State School', 5th March 2004.

174 Interview, Lord Andrew Adonis, former Secretary of State for Transport and Minister of State in the Department for Education and Skills, May 2011.

175 R. Skidelsky, *Britain Since 1900: A Success Story?*

176 Interview, B. Donoughue, 26th February 2015.

177 K. Morgan, *Ages of Reform: Dawns and Downfalls of the British Left*, p. 136.

178 Interview, Lord Andrew Adonis, former Secretary of State for Transport and Minister of State in the Department for Education and Skills, May 2011. Labour's plans for a 'quasi-market' in secondary education were outlined in the White Paper, 'Higher Standards, Better Schools for All', London: HMG, October 2005.

179 A. Adonis, Confidential Memorandum to the Prime Minister, 'Public Service Guarantees', 14th April 2004.

180 A. Adonis, Confidential Memorandum to the Prime Minister, 'Choice and Contestability – Next Reform Steps', 19th December 2002, PD Personal Papers.

181 A. Adonis, Confidential Memorandum to Alan Milburn, 'Education Pledges – 'Universal Tutoring' and Wider Schools Strategy', 29th November 2004.

182 https://theguardian.com/education/2005/nov/10/schools.uk. Accessed 15th December 2018.

183 Interview, Estelle Morris, former Secretary of State for Education, June 2011.

184 V. Boliver & A. Swift, 'Do Comprehensive Schools Reduce Social Mobility?', *The British Journal of Sociology*, Volume 61 (1), pp. 89–110, 2011.

185 Interview, John Dunford, former General Secretary, Secondary Heads' Association, June 2011.

186 Interview, Lord John Birt, former Strategy Adviser, Number Ten Downing Street, October 2011.

187 J. Russell, 'Drilled, Not Educated', *The Guardian*, 20th August 2004, Cited in D. Coates, *Prolonged Labour*, p. 245.

188 Interview, Jeremy Heywood, Cabinet Secretary, September 2011.

189 A. Heath, *Social Progress in Britain*.

190 J. Le Grand, *Motivation, Agency, and Policy: Of Knights and Knaves, Queens and Pawns*, Oxford: Oxford University Press, 2003.

191 H. Glennerster, *British Social Policy: 1945 to the Present*; E. Durbin, *The Politics of Democratic Socialism*, London: W. Pickering, 1940.

192 Interview, Lord Andrew Adonis, former Secretary of State for Transport and Minister of State in the Department for Education and Skills, May 2011.

193 H. Glennerster, *British Social Policy: 1945 to the Present*.

194 N. Timmins, *The Five Giants: A Biography of the Welfare State*.

195 Interview, Rt. Hon. Charles Clarke, former Secretary of State for Education and Skills, September 2011.

196 Interview, Sir Jeremy Heywood, former Principal Private Secretary to the Prime Minister, October 2011.
197 A. Milburn, p. 20, *The Guardian*, 15th January 2005.
198 T. Blair, *A Journey*; P. Mandelson, *The Third man*.
199 D. Coates, *Prolonged Labour: The Slow Birth of New Labour Britain*, p. 186.
200 D. Coates, *Prolonged Labour: The Slow Birth of New Labour Britain*, p. 186.
201 A. Giddens, 'Did They Foul Up My Third Way?', *The New Statesman*, 24th September 2004.
202 A. Thorpe, *A History of the Labour Party*.
203 D. Marquand, *The Decline of the Public*.
204 P. Hall, 'Policy Paradigms, Social Learning, and the State', p. 279.
205 J. Tomlinson, *Managing the Economy, Managing the People*; A. Manning & M. Goos, 'Lovely and Lousy Jobs'.
206 R. Ford & M. Goodwin, *Revolt on the Right*, p. 46, London: Routledge, 2014.
207 R. Skidelsky, *Britain Since 1900: A Success Story?*
208 P. Riddell, *The Unfulfilled Prime Minister*.
209 A. Gamble, 'New Labour and Political Change'.
210 T. Blair, *A Journey*, p. 313.
211 https://theguardian.com/politics/2007/may/09/uk.topstories3. Accessed 12th February 2019.
212 T. Blair, *A Journey*, p. 494.
213 S. Fielding, 'New Labour, 'Sleaze' and Television Drama', *The British Journal of Politics and International Relations*, Volume 16 (2), pp. 326–348, 2014.
214 Interview with Rt. Hon. Charles Clarke, former Secretary of State for Education and Skills, November 2019.
215 Interview with Lord Stewart Wood, former Special Adviser to Gordon Brown and Ed Miliband, February 2020.
216 Memorandum to the Prime Minister by Philip Gould, Douglas Alexander & Stan Greenberg, 20th April 2000, PD Personal Papers.
217 R. Skidelsky, *Britain Since 1918: A Success Story?*, p. 394.
218 G. Mulgan, Confidential Memorandum to the Prime Minister, 'The Progressive Project – Notes on the Discussion at Bellagio', 5th May 2002.
219 B. Brivati, 'The New Labour Government's Place in History'.

PART III

New Labour's legacies in British politics

9

NEW LABOUR'S BROKEN INHERITANCE

In every generation, there comes a moment when the existing way of doing things is challenged. It happened in 1945. It happened in 1979 and again in 1997. This is another of those moments.

Ed Miliband[1]

Rise, like lions after slumber In unvanquishable number! Shake your chains to earth like dew Which in sleep had fallen on you: Ye are many – they are few!

Percy Shelley[2]

Introduction

The historical purpose of New Labour was to reshape the party after Labourism's degeneration and decline, drawing a line under the past following the traumatic political events of the 1970s and 1980s. Even so, the process of ideological reformulation and the recasting of party institutions unleashed a ferocious political backlash as Tony Blair and Gordon Brown's electoral dominance receded. Their leadership successors, Ed Miliband and Jeremy Corbyn, believed that at heart New Labour was a neo-liberal enterprise that must be renounced if the party was to find a productive future role in British politics. The altered distribution of power within the party consigned Blair's modernising project to the fringes of British politics. The Labour Party has since undergone sweeping transformation, even if fundamental questions of ideology and strategy remain unresolved.

The final section of the book turns to the question of what the Blair/Brown governments have bequeathed to modern Britain as a political legacy. Having addressed the impact of the Labour administrations on the economy and polity since 1997, this chapter considers their long-term effect on the terrain of British representative democracy. From the outset, New Labour was a controversial endeavour to recast the party's identity provoking discord and conflict. When the Labour government was defeated in 2010, a strong counter-reaction from within the party was widely anticipated. The chapter considers not only Blair and Brown's long-term ideological influence on the Left, but their wider impact on the British centre-right and the Conservative Party. The chapter begins by considering New Labour's imprint on the British constitution and political institutions, amid the increasingly vocal chorus of dissatisfaction with British democracy.

New Labour's influence on British politics

Some of the most vociferous critics believe the truly damaging legacy of New Labour was less the continuation of neo-liberalism than the poisoning of Britain's *body politic*. During their years in power, Blair and Brown allegedly imported the culture of 'spin' into British government, degrading political debate, politicising the permanent bureaucracy and undermining rational policy-making. New Labour relied on the adept packaging and presentation of its policies, courting the Right-Wing tabloid press. Prioritising communications in the run up to the 1997 election was understandable even if it was undesirable, but the approach ought to have been abandoned during the first term.[3] Instead, Blair's spin machine was expanded after the 2001 election, symbolised by the promotion of Alastair Campbell to the post of director of strategy in 10 Downing Street.

Under New Labour, British politics in the words of the political theorist, Colin Leys, became relentlessly 'market-driven'.[4] The corporate interests of Bernie Eccelstone and Rupert Murdoch were enabled to ply their wares freely in government. New Labour's desire to placate the media had a significant impact on its policy-making agenda. The Iraq War led to the huge decline of trust, a reaction against the insidious use of the government's spin machine. Election turnout among the young and those on low incomes precipitously declined by 2005. A year later, Blair was accused of conferring peerages in return for undeclared loans that financed Labour's election campaign, the first prime minister questioned under police oath since Lloyd George. The parliamentary expenses scandal exacerbated the crisis of faith in Britain's representative democracy. Revelations that peers in the House of Lords were selling influence to foreign businessmen depleted the public esteem in which parliamentary institutions were held.

Not surprisingly, the perceived efficacy of representative democratic institutions plummeted. The alterations to the constitution after 1997, particularly the growth of devolution, created power centres beyond Whitehall and Westminster. Yet the new institutions did little to fundamentally redefine the relationship between citizen and state. Across the UK, particularly in England where devolution was treated as an afterthought, voters appeared no more engaged by the conduct of democracy. Labour's reforms felt like shuffling the constitutional deckchairs rather than pursuing a vigorous, popular revolution in democratic life. Scholars of political science published books with ominous titles – notably *Why People Hate Politics* (2007), *Why Politics Matters* (2006) and *In Defence of*

Politics (2012) – echoing the troubling mood of disillusionment.[5] Several arguments were put forward to explain why voters appeared to be losing faith in liberal democracy. The first argument was that during the New Labour era, too many decisions were taken out of the hands of politicians and passed to technocratic 'arm's-length' bodies that denuded politics of ideological conviction to strengthen managerial competence. The second contention was that convergence between the major parties in politics and policy since the 1990s left voters without an effective choice at election time. A further argument was that political representatives were out of touch with the electorate due to the decline of working-class involvement in democratic institutions.[6] These claims certainly had currency among disillusioned and disengaged voters.

The growth of cynicism led to the disturbing rise of anti-politics manifested in support for the UK Independence Party (UKIP), accompanied by overt hostility to British membership of the European Union (EU). According to the Fabian Society, by 2015 there were 'a large set of seats where UKIP's insurgency is most likely to hurt Labour. . . . These include many safe Labour seats with large concentrations of the 'left behind' electoral groups most attracted to UKIP'.[7] A confidential Number Ten report had already acknowledged the need 'to deal directly with disengagement and have an active target for turnout at the next election'.[8] In the 2001 election, turnout plummeted to 59.4 per cent. In the safe Labour seat of Liverpool Riverside, participation fell to 34.1 per cent, the lowest in Great Britain:

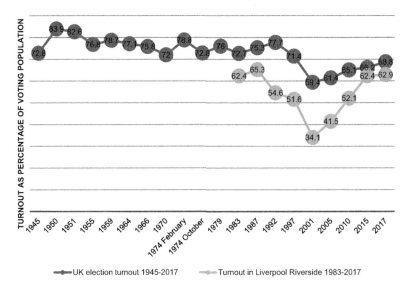

FIGURE 9.1   General election turnouts in Britain 1945–2010 and turnout in Liverpool Riverside 1983–2017 (British Election Study)

The collapse in turnout at the 2001 general election was blamed on New Labour's 'increasing shift to the centre', its failure in government to pursue the traditional Left-Wing agenda favoured by working-class voters.[9] The difference in reported turnout between middle-class and working-class voters was 19 per cent in 2010 compared to 5 per cent in 1964.[10] Yet turnout was already falling dramatically just a year into the Blair government. In the 1998 local elections, for example, turnout collapsed while in the 1999 European elections, it fell to 23 per cent. Despite this, during the 1997–2001 parliament the Blair government had record public approval ratings, an almost continuous poll lead, and did not lose a single by-election, indicating that the disposition in Labour's heartlands was not unequivocally one of revolt. It was likely that long-term sociological changes were undermining established habits of voting.[11]

New Labour's strategy to tackle democratic disengagement prescribed by Philip Gould was to 'under-state, under-claim, under-promise'. Yet the mood of anti-politics was growing exponentially in the former industrial towns and suburbs of the major cities, where there was a sense of alienation from the liberal metropolis. A report titled 'Anger not Apathy' drawing on qualitative polling in the constituency of Barking found working-class voters incensed by Labour's inability to improve the physical conditions of their neighbourhoods – in particular, the quality of social housing.[12] As the Labour minister Margaret Hodge told the *Guardian*: 'This wasn't apathy. . . . The non-voters expressed anger. They just felt that nobody with power listened to them'.[13] The Liverpool Walton MP Peter Kilfoyle believed Labour was fast losing its heartland supporters.[14] Party membership fell from a peak of 420,000 in 1997 to 215,000 by 2004.

The Blair government's effort to tackle the causes of political disaffection, such as removing the influence of corporate money from politics through state funding, came to little. Proposals were tabled to allocate public funding to parties on the basis of registered support, while focusing subsidies on legitimate activities such as policy development. Individual and corporate donations would be capped, while the Electoral Commission would be given powers to enforce the law.[15] Yet the trade unions, the Labour Party's main funder throughout the twentieth century, were reluctant to endorse wholesale reform. State funding would diminish their power base and policy influence. Blair's hope of creating a new politics, recalling the SDP's aspiration to 'break the mould' of British politics, was confounded. New Labour lacked a cogent conception of democratic citizenship. Attlee's governments had a vision of social citizenship that built upon civil and political rights to ensure democratic inclusion, famously elaborated by the LSE social policy academic, T.H. Marshall. Yet New Labour never had a big democratic idea, and by the time it left office, trust in representative institutions had deteriorated further.

The resurgence of Celtic and English nationalism

What of New Labour's effect elsewhere? Did the Labour government's agenda contribute to the rise of Celtic and English nationalism after 2010? An unintended consequence of the Blair and Brown era was the growing influence of nationalist parties across England, Wales, Scotland and Northern Ireland. Surprising to many was the emergence of a virulent strain of national identity that demanded political rights for the English. Blair's devolution reforms were designed to quell nationalist discontent, shoring up support for the union. Yet the changes to the UK polity appeared to have the opposite effect. Why did the UK seem ever more prone to constitutional fragmentation in the aftermath of the post-1997 governments?

It was striking that the devolved institutions in Cardiff, Edinburgh and Belfast not only oversaw decentralised policy-making but created opportunities for insurgent political parties to build electoral support, running against the London establishment. New Labour failed to acknowledge that devolution almost inevitably leads to institutions being captured by politicians who thwart central government's authority, mobilising against the imperial British state.[16] Nicola Sturgeon and her predecessor as SNP leader, Alex Salmond, were skilful in exploiting discontent with Westminster politics. New Labour's strategy assumed that devolution could function by stuffing the mouths of the Scottish, Welsh and Northern Irish governments with gold. Yet in the climate of austerity after 2010, nationalist parties were able to capitalise on disillusionment with central political institutions. Nationalist sentiments were stoked by the perception that governments in London were remote, disinterested in the grievances experienced by vocal minorities in Scotland and Northern Ireland.[17]

Another driver of fragmentation in the aftermath of New Labour was the UK's asymmetrical devolution framework. The vision for English governance had amounted to elected mayors in city-regions, augmented by unaccountable regional development agencies (RDAs). Ministers spoke of giving powers and 'earned autonomy' to local councils, but progress was frustratingly slow. Meanwhile, the growing sense of unfairness led to the politicisation of English identity, expressed in rising support for UKIP. After a controversial speech in which Jack Straw claimed that 'the British people are potentially very aggressive, very violent', the headline in *The Daily Mail* read: 'Why does New Labour hate the English'?[18] Yet Figure 9.2 indicates just how proud older voters in particular were to identify themselves as English. These voters were much more likely to support UKIP, although attitudinal surveys demonstrated there was nothing conservative or inherently reactionary about English identity.

It is also striking that the nationalist parties were updating their political rhetoric and appeal. Since the beginning of the Northern Ireland peace process, Sinn Fein had gradually been transformed into the party of constitutional nationalism, marginalising the Social Democratic and Labour Party (SDLP). Their embrace of democratic institutions and commitment to the welfare state made Sinn Fein more acceptable to the wider electorate. In Wales and Scotland, Plaid Cymru and the Scottish National Party (SNP) developed a distinctive social democratic message. Gone was the language of exclusive nationhood, replaced by the inclusive politics of defending the economic and social rights of all citizens. The 'progressive' nationalist vision was attractive to disillusioned Welsh and Scottish voters. Economic polarisation meant that many were locked outside the prosperity

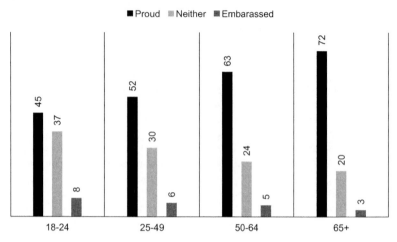

FIGURE 9.2   How proud or embarrassed are you about identifying as English? (You Gov survey, 2018)

that characterised the South-East of England since the 1980s. Meanwhile, New Labour had allegedly abandoned the traditional aspirations of social democracy – full employment, redistribution and the welfare state – to placate Middle England. Welfare and the public sector were defended more robustly by Plaid Cymru and the SNP than politicians in London willing to accede to Conservative austerity. Labour activists north of the border were quickly labelled 'Tartan Tories' in the aftermath of the 2014 independence referendum, leading to the disastrous general election result in 2015 when Labour lost all but one of its seats in Scotland.

Devolution and reform of the electoral system outside Westminster meant the UK experienced political disintegration. In 2015, a different political party won most votes in each of the UK's four constituent nations: the Conservatives in England, Labour in Wales, the SNP in Scotland and the Democratic Unionist Party (DUP) in Northern Ireland. A similar pattern was repeated in 2017, although the major parties were able to reassert their dominance. In 1997, New Labour came to office determined to shore up support for the union and its cohesion. The strategy was to concede limited powers to devolved institutions, while sustaining the 'new localism' narrative. Blair believed that as a consequence of devolving power, 'the union will be strengthened and the threat of separation removed'. George Robertson, a Scottish MP and minister, declared that devolution would 'kill nationalism stone dead'.[19]

As a consequence, the policy always appeared expedient. English identity was largely ignored. There was too little understanding of how devolution might help to ensure better governance and increased political legitimacy throughout Britain.[20] The UK drifted further towards breakup. Devolution had proved to be a 'slippery slope' towards independence, as the closely fought 2014 referendum underlined.[21] Labour's difficulty was that the essential idea of the *British* Labour movement as a collective force for social justice among the working class throughout the British Isles appeared less credible given the changing nature of the UK, accompanied by the rise of English, Welsh and Scottish nationalism.[22] As a consequence, the British state was more imperilled than at any point since the 1707 Act of Union. The Left believed the situation arose because of neo-liberal policies pursued by the New Labour governments at Westminster. Yet the focus on economic and fiscal policy, while important, ignores the possibility that under the leadership of Brown and Miliband, the party proved itself profoundly incapable of speaking for England.

Remaking the centre-right: 'the heir to Blair'?

If New Labour failed to create a new politics in Britain, did Blair and Brown's party compel the Conservatives to alter their strategy and ideological posture? The claim of continuity between Thatcher and Blair is bolstered by the contention that David Cameron was the ideological 'heir to Blair'. The perspective is ultimately misleading as Cameron's modernisation of the Conservatives had less in common with Labour's evolution in the 1990s than is commonly thought. To be sure, Cameron claimed to be Blair's 'heir' on taking over as leader. The Conservatives undertook the process of rethinking, influenced unquestionably by Blair's political style. They accepted planks of New Labour's inheritance, particularly its embrace of social liberalism. In the aftermath of the 1997 defeat, the Conservative Party was in profound difficulty. It went through four leaders in eight years: Hague, Duncan-Smith, Howard and then Cameron. Until 2010, the party's share of the vote barely recovered from the catastrophe of 1997. The Conservatives had not won a national election since 1992. Blair was willing to co-opt traditional Tory agendas and narratives, throwing the party into confusion, leading them to shift even further to the Right.[23] The Conservatives were unable to grasp why they lost elections repeatedly.

Leading Tory modernisers read Philip Gould's book *The Unfinished Revolution* (1998), charting New Labour's protracted emergence in the 1980s and 1990s.[24] Blair's ally, Peter Mandelson, insisted Cameron's political positioning when he became leader affirmed New Labour's long-term influence. To get a hearing with voters, Cameron was forced to acknowledge that the Conservatives were perceived to be 'nasty', lacking compassion while believing 'there was no such thing as society'. Cameron sought to tackle these preconceptions, insisting public spending was not an inherent obstacle to economic efficiency as the New Right asserted in the 1980s. As the father of a severely disabled child, he appeared genuinely committed to the NHS.[25] Cameron was determined the Conservatives should tackle their reputation for selfishness and acquisitive individualism.

Under previous leaders, the party moved sharply to the Right and repeatedly lost elections. All three leaders before Cameron sought to exploit disquiet over immigration. The Tories were viewed as a nostalgic party, hankering after an

Imperial vision of Britain that was no longer relevant while opposed to social lib-eralisation. Cameron, in contrast, self-consciously sought to emulate Blair's lead-ership style. Cameron recast the identity of his party as liberal, compassionate, optimistic, and open to the future. He fought to drag the Tories back towards the centre-ground of British politics. Cameron made the case for a diverse society. He expressed concern about poverty at home and abroad. Cameron demon-strated compassion for young men on rundown housing estates wearing 'hood-ies'. And he apologised for the vile attacks by Young Conservatives on Nelson Mandela in the 1980s.[26] Like New Labour, the rhetoric of Cameron's party in opposition stressed the imperative of transcending the traditional dividing line between Left and Right.[27] Prior to the 2008 crash, the Conservatives accepted Labour's spending priorities while Cameron emphasised his commitment to the NHS. He battled to transform the Conservatives into the party of social con-science as well as economic success. Oliver Letwin, the intellectual architect of Cameron's party, believed modern Conservatism must be rooted in social and economic liberalism, 'aiming to achieve two significant paradigm shifts'.[28] The first shift was moving from an 'econocentric paradigm' to a 'sociocentric' paradigm, recognising there was more to life than wealth. The second shift was recasting the role of the state from a 'provision-based' paradigm where gov-ernment funds and provides services to a 'framework-based' paradigm where a variety of organisations serve the common good by advancing 'the big society'. According to Letwin, the Tory party 'understand society as existing and flour-ishing on a human scale – in hugely varied people-sized institutions that are connected by a complex web of mutuality'.[29]

Although the Conservatives altered their strategy following the financial crash by making the case for fiscal austerity, Cameron succeeded in partially 'detoxify-ing' the party's image. While the 2010 election was a blow since they failed to win a majority despite Brown's unpopularity, Cameron was decisive, broker-ing the Coalition agreement with Nick Clegg's Liberal Democrats. Cameron pursued audaciously the realignment of British politics from the centre-right, espousing the creed of liberal Conservatism.[30] Nonetheless, it is questionable whether the remaking of the Conservatives under Cameron indicates ideologi-cal convergence with New Labour, illustrating the pervasive grip of neo-liberal ideas. Cameron never undertook the fundamental reappraisal of his party's doc-trine and ideology that the Left initiated in the 1980s and 1990s. The big society was fundamentally different from Labour's approach. The big society envisaged replacing the public sector with private and voluntary sector bodies. Under Blair and Brown, the size of government grew considerably. Cameron's belief in social justice was balanced by underlying antipathy to the state.[31] Blair picked fights with vested interests in his party, telling traditionalists they must accept a shift of ideological direction while claiming no veto over policy. In contrast, Cameron was more than willing to placate Tory activists, particularly over the issue of Europe. Had the PLP not suffered a nervous breakdown during Brown's premiership, it appears unlikely the Tories would have been the largest party in 2010. Cameron's party were a long way from establishing renewed political dominance.

New Labour and the British Left

It was under Ed Miliband's leadership that the 'New Labour as neo-liberalism' narrative gripped the party. Rather than promoting a wide-ranging and candid debate about why Labour had been defeated in 2010, Miliband found a simplistic target in the accusation that New Labour was the inheritor of Thatcherism, brokering a Faustian pact with markets. His own leadership echoed the claim that the party under Blair and Brown was the ideological bedfellow of neo-liberalism. In the aftermath of his leadership victory, Miliband insisted: 'A new generation has taken over the Labour party', separating himself in ideological terms from the Blair era.

The paradox that arises is that New Labour's main legacy was shifting the party sharply to the Left, more than at any previous moment in its history. The alteration occurred during Miliband's leadership, then even more strongly under Jeremy Corbyn. In the aftermath of the 1970 and 1979 defeats, Labour reacted similarly, not by moving to the centre but shifting substantially leftwards. There was evidence of a visceral desire to repudiate what New Labour and Blair bequeathed. Few agreed with the former prime minister's claim that 'Labour won when it was New Labour. It lost [in 2010] because it stopped being New Labour'.[32] There was the venomous reaction against Blair's project that led to the immoral war in Iraq, while failing to counter rising inequality. The financial crisis demonstrated New Labour was merely another party of capital. The Blair governments advanced the interests of globalisation's 'winners': entrepreneurs, the City, service industries, the professional middle class in the South East of England. The 'losers' – industrial workers, precarious low-paid service workers, the regions in the Northern and Celtic periphery – felt increasingly marginalised, *politically* and economically. Blair insisted there was 'a new divide' in British politics transcending Left and Right; the divide was 'open versus closed', whether you are for or against globalisation.[33] Many believed that the Labour Party under his leadership renounced its historical vocation of assisting the underdog, the downtrodden and the dispossessed. If Labour stood for an open society, it could no longer protect globalisation's victims. The price of electoral success was the loss of Labour's soul.[34]

The internal reaction within the Labour Party was shaped not only by objection to the Blair governments but fundamental disagreement over New Labour's strategy to remake the party's identity. Social democratic parties across Europe experienced defeats since the 1980s and were compelled to adapt their approach. New Labour sought to revitalise the party by jettisoning traditional symbols and rhetoric, insisting on wholesale reinvention.[35] The leadership's methods were often brutal, adopting the practice of centralised manipulative managerialism to control the party. Inevitably, a backlash quickly ensued. Modernisation provoked an unstoppable counter-reaction as the electoral and intellectual dominance of the Blair/Brown governments receded. New Labour's top-down, elitist style stored up grassroots hostility. Generational change meant that by 1997, traditional forms of political activism had begun to atrophy while 'protest politics' movements linked to environmentalism, community organising and anti-globalisation grew in prominence. As a party of liberal democracy immersed in the Westminster establishment, Labour struggled to connect with the new social and political forces. Politicians such as the former home secretary, David Blunkett, expressed interest in advancing participatory democracy, but were more often thwarted by the leadership's adherence to established institutions.

Blunkett was certainly a remarkable politician. He served as the leader of Sheffield City Council during the 1980s. Blunkett believed Labour must give citizens a proper voice in the governance of local communities and public services. Yet Blair and Brown's party believed voters ultimately desired strong government, representative in so far as there were intermittent elections to parliamentary institutions.[36] The understanding of the growing appetite for deliberative participation in decision-making was poor. The reform of membership structures that occurred at the behest of the Collins Review then brought new activists into the party, propelling the Corbyn surge during the 2015 leadership election. Corbyn's ascendency emphasised the negation of New Labour's ideological inheritance, underlining the Left's domination of the party.

Politics for a new generation? Miliband's party

The Labour government's demise in 2010 raised a fundamental question for the British Left. What did the Labour Party now stand for after fifteen years of Tony Blair and Gordon Brown at the helm? What were the party's ideals in a society where inequalities appeared rampant, where nation-states struggled to control capital, where traditional ideological certainties had been lost? Moreover, was it even possible to create a viable social democratic society in a world shaped by the New Times of globalisation, security threats and the spectre of environmental catastrophe? In the aftermath of the leadership election, Miliband spoke of his desire to 'turn the page' and move beyond the Blair/Brown era, fulfilling the aim of being a 'one term' opposition leader. He believed New Labour was now an electoral millstone around the party's neck. Since the 2008 crash, Labour's programme no longer addressed the insistent egalitarian preoccupations of the age.

What Miliband actually meant by leaving behind New Labour was ambiguous. Labour's 2015 manifesto hardly marked a fundamental departure from the 2010 government's policies.[37] There was little sustained effort to understand why Labour had lost under Brown. What Miliband did was to provide legitimacy for critics to attack the Blair/Brown legacy indiscriminately, defining the political territory of Corbynism. Miliband resorted to populist tropes subsequently deployed to lethal effect in the Corbyn era: the idea that politics is the virtuous battle of good versus evil; that the economy is controlled by sinister and predatory forces; that society has declined from the post-war golden age of social democracy to atomised individualism and selfishness under Thatcher and Blair.[38] Miliband's victory in September 2010 was certainly unexpected. He defeated his brother David, Ed Balls, Andy Burnham and Diane Abbot – triumphing in the final round by 50.65 to 49.35 per cent.[39] The battle between David and Ed is among the most peculiar in British political history. At the outset, Ed never told his brother he intended to run in the contest. There is speculation that David agreed not to challenge Brown in the summer of 2009 after James Purnell's resignation from the cabinet, on the basis an understanding was reached that Ed would give David a free run after the election defeat.[40]

The NEC's decision to go ahead with the four-month leadership contest in 2010 rewarded Ed with copious opportunities to target trade union levy-payers, aided by heavyweight support from their general secretaries. At every turn, Ed sought to distance himself from New Labour's inheritance despite the fact that all the candidates – other than Diane Abbot – were ministers and special advisers in the post-1997 administrations. Miliband attacked Blair's actions in Iraq, insisting too little was done to tackle pervasive inequalities during Labour's decade in power. Ed concluded that New Labour had run out of steam, consequently failing to capitalise on the 'social democratic moment' inaugurated by the 2008 financial crash that severely discredited global capitalism. A novel ideological project was required for the party and the country.[41]

Ed was helped by the fact David Miliband lost support in the PLP by behaving in an apparently aloof and arrogant manner. Ed's campaign team invented the slogan 'Ed speaks human' to emphasise David's tendency to talk down to his audience using impenetrable jargon. David Miliband's campaign was generously resourced, but lacked any compelling and persuasive message. His candidacy was easily portrayed as 'continuity' New Labour. At a leadership hustings organised by the *New Statesman*, David was dragged into defending the Iraq War while Ed confidently attacked the Labour government's record. Despite being an influential adviser in the Treasury, Ed was content to harvest misinformation about Labour's policies. Among the most damaging was the accusation that the party did little to address wealth inequality, despite taxing pension funds, increasing stamp duty on property and imposing the windfall tax on privatised utilities. Yet the counter-attack on Ed by Blair and Peter Mandelson – that he was leading the party towards 'an electoral cul-de-sac' – underlined Miliband's credentials as the candidate of change.[42]

Ed Miliband was born on Christmas Eve 1969, the son of Jewish immigrants forced to flee the terror of Nazism in Europe: the political theorist, Ralph Miliband, and his wife, Marion Kozak. Miliband attended state schools in Leeds and North London, graduating in Politics, Philosophy and Economics (PPE) from Corpus Christi College, Oxford. He began his ascent through Labour's ranks soon after Oxford, working as a television producer and then as policy adviser to Harriet Harman. At the Treasury after 1997, Ed pioneered the implementation of tax credits to tackle child and pensioner poverty. He played a role in the transition from Blair to Brown, attempting to negotiate Blair's amicable departure in 2004. Miliband was elected to the House of Commons in 2005 as MP for Doncaster North, serving as minister in the Cabinet Office and then secretary of state at the Department for Energy and Climate Change (DECC). Miliband's governmental experience enabled him to make a credible pitch for the leadership after the Brown government's ignominious defeat.

Having been triumphantly elected at the 2010 party conference, Ed's first act was to unveil his policy review, *New Politics, Fresh Ideas*, led by the former chief secretary to the Treasury, Liam Byrne. The mission was to reinvigorate Labour's economic and social policies, providing an alternative to the political economy of austerity. Ed believed the crisis of 2008 exposed endemic flaws in the institutions of Anglo-American capitalism. Left politics for the next generation would rebuild support for government intervention as a counterweight to market forces. Miliband told *The Observer*: 'In every generation, there comes a moment when the existing way of doing things is challenged. It happened in 1945. It happened in 1979 and again in 1997. This is another of those moments'.[43]

There were intriguing parallels between Miliband and Wilson's strategy in the 1960s. Miliband's agenda was to overhaul the British economy, redefining the politics of production. He and his entourage believed the financial crisis revealed inherent weaknesses in British capitalism. These themes had been rehearsed by the Left since the publication of Andrew Shonfield's book *Modern Capitalism* in the mid-1960s. The UK economy was prone to short-termism, dominated by finance and the City. British productivity was anaemic due to the inadequacy of post-compulsory education, a hangover of the 1944 Butler Act which prioritised academic training. There was the absence of effective partnership between employers and workers. Like Wilson, Miliband denounced 'gentlemanly' capitalism's inefficiencies. The analysis chimed with Blue Labour thinking advanced by the London Metropolitan University academic, Maurice Glasman, who insisted that New Labour's embrace of global finance left communities vulnerable to insecurity and inequality.[44] The leadership emphasised the moral separation of 'producer' capitalists who invested for the long-term in science and skills from 'predatory' capitalists who exploited consumers and asset-stripped British companies.[45] Miliband read the biography of the former US president, Theodore Roosevelt, avidly. Roosevelt railed against endemic 'crony capitalism' which encouraged tax avoidance, price-fixing and monopoly in early-twentieth-century America. Roosevelt used the government's power to create the 'square deal' for American working people.

Miliband's advisers told the *Financial Times* that Theodore Roosevelt and Harold Wilson inspired his 'One Nation' political appeal: industrial activism would again propel 'the white heat of scientific revolution' to create a square deal for the working-class.[46] The incoming Labour government's purpose was to create a high-wage, high-skill economy, fashioning a new 'supply-side politics of the Left'. In fact, Miliband largely returned the party to where it fought the 1992 election under Kinnock in which the state performs an 'enabling' role in the economy. In the 2015 manifesto, *Britain Can Be Better*, Labour outlined measures that included a technical baccalaureate, providing a high-esteem 'non-university' route through post-compulsory education; private sector companies awarded government contracts would be required to offer apprenticeships; there would be a public investment bank lending to small- and medium-sized businesses akin to the regional *Sparkassen* in Germany. The industrial strategy would back sectors 'where the UK has a competitive edge'. Moreover, competition in utilities markets, particularly energy, would be strengthened to protect consumers, if necessary instructing the government regulator to impose a statutory price cap. The minimum wage would rise to £8 per hour by 2020, while public sector employers would pay a 'living wage'. 'Exploitative' zero hours contracts would be prohibited. There was an impressive effort to stimulate new public policy thinking in advancing the concept of 'predistribution', addressing rising inequality in a climate shaped by globalisation and technological disruption. Predistribution, the inelegant phrase coined by the US academic, Jacob Hacker, focused particularly on the structure of the labour market.[47] Miliband was astute in recognising that wages now lagged behind GDP and productivity growth, a key source of rising political discontent.

There is some evidence that Miliband was initially successful in reframing the political argument. His concern with 'predatory' capitalism and irresponsible businesses resonated across the ideological spectrum. Thoughtful Conservative politicians questioned whether they could afford to be positioned as 'pro-business' in the aftermath of the 2008 financial collapse. Ministers in the Coalition government denounced Miliband's signature policies, particularly the energy price cap and living wage to tackle poverty pay, but then adopted identical measures. Ed could claim to be a transformative figure in British politics.[48]

Miliband's revisionism related to the politics of identity, not merely economics. The leadership began to redefine Labour's stance on immigration. New Labour extolled the virtues of open borders. Under Miliband, the party shifted its ground, symbolised by the 2015 campaign mug with the slogan 'Controls on immigration' emblazoned on its side. The leader insisted: 'It's not prejudiced when people worry about immigration'. Miliband's position was intended to correct the terrible error of the 2010 election campaign in which Gordon Brown had berated a pensioner, Gillian Duffy, who complained about the impact of migration on former Lancashire mill towns (Photo 9.1). Miliband stated that Labour would tackle the exploitation of low-skilled migrants while reducing net migration. The repositioning on immigration responded to disquiet in 'heartland' seats where loyal Labour voters were defecting to UKIP. The Fabian Society report, *Revolt on the Left* (2014), indicated that blue-collar working-class voters in the North and Midlands were disillusioned by the refusal to acknowledge that Eastern European migration meant fewer jobs and

PHOTO 9.1 Prime Minister Gordon Brown talks with resident Gillian Duffy on 28th April 2010 in Rochdale, England.

Source: Photo by Jeff J Mitchell/Getty Images.

declining wages. In the by-election at Heywood and Middleton in 2014, UKIP came within 400 votes of defeating the Labour candidate. The party performed unimpressively in the local and European elections, prompting Yvette Cooper (the Shadow Home Secretary) and John Prescott to demand support for restrictions on EU migration.

The British Labour Party was increasingly debilitated by the so-called meritocratic divide, much like social democratic parties across Europe. The party was led by the university-educated, professional classes. Yet its voters may have had no formal educational qualifications and refused to adhere slavishly to liberal norms. Key figures around Miliband worried that the outlook of the working class was becoming harder to reconcile with the libertarian post-materialism of the middle class.[49] Social scientists pointed out there was little robust evidence that voters were becoming more polarised around social issues – attitudes to gender, homosexuality and racial prejudice.[50] If anything, there was greater convergence across classes since the 1980s.

Miliband's response was to overhaul the party's doctrine and strategy – 'turning the page' on New Labour. Yet on fiscal policy, caution prevailed while the leadership were slow to confront the Coalition's austerity. Ed Balls claimed during the leadership election that Cameron's ministers were 'growth deniers' who relied on flawed conventional wisdom about macro-economic policy. Balls insisted the threat of 'unending austerity' undermined economic confidence; cuts should be imposed when growth was firmly re-established.[51] Yet by 2012

Miliband and Balls were forced to acknowledge they had lost the argument. The shadow chancellor admitted that under a future Labour government, budgets would be squeezed 'across the piece' to enable deficit reduction.[52] Balls refused to promise the reversal of the Coalition's public sector pay freeze. Labour flirted with proposals for a mansion tax while pledging to reintroduce the 50p tax band on income over £150,000. Yet the difficulty for Balls was that he was quickly labelled 'Gordon Brown's consigliere and chosen heir . . . laden with the political and economic baggage of the last government'.[53]

Miliband's caution, encouraged by his career as a treasury adviser, made the claim of substantively breaking with New Labour appear delusional, despite employing the rhetoric of transformational socialism. While Miliband dis-avowed neo-liberalism, Labour's safety-first mind-set still prevailed. The Labour peer David Lipsey observed that 'Labour today remains tentative and nervous about measures to tackle the sumptuary wealth of the successful'.[54] An academic commentator noted that:

> Miliband's political language is the discourse of crisis and the desperate need for structural reform of the economy to reduce inequality. . . . Yet there is nothing in the policies he has thus far offered, from the mansion tax to freezing energy prices that would remotely amount to a radical economic programme aimed at addressing what is purportedly so badly wrong.[55]

The MP, Jon Cruddas, dismissed Labour's 'minimalist, safety-first offer . . . a Bal-kanised strategy that sliced and diced the electorate', a composite of disconnected policies tested relentlessly in focus groups.[56] The dilemma for the party was that its reputation for economic competence was lost in 2008–9. There was funda-mental confusion over whether to contest the Conservative narrative of austerity or concede the argument and move on. The party did neither. Miliband's team appeared indecisive. The leadership was like a rabbit caught in the headlights.

Why did Miliband's leadership fail to generate political momentum? Ed had certainly not expected to win in 2010. Miliband's team lacked political matu-rity and experience. He spoke an arid technocratic language honed in central London think-tanks. Ed struggled to connect with voters outside the Westmin-ster bubble. Miliband clearly lacked street-fighting political skills. He was a cau-tious operator in managing his party, refusing to take political risks. In 2014, for example, the IPPR think-tank published a significant report, *The Condition of Britain*, which defined a bold departure for post-war social democracy. The report recommended radical changes to the social security system while switch-ing funding from housing benefit to capital investment in the housing stock.[57] The leader's office were unnerved given the proposals were depicted as an attack on welfare claimants, anathema to the traditional Left. Miliband launched the report but stopped short of endorsing specific IPPR plans.

Moreover, the leadership had no counter-narrative to the Tory charge that reforming predatory capitalism was anti-business, harming workers by provoking capital flight and job losses. Even experts who championed the 'varieties of capitalism' scholarship were critical of Miliband's sudden love affair with Germany. David Soskice, professor of political economy at the London School of Economics (LSE), recognised that 'the German system is different to ours'. Labour should go with the grain of the US model, which was compatible with British capitalism. Soskice believed German economic performance had been unimpressive over the previous twenty years. In this climate, Miliband was unable either to win over elite opinion or articulate a mission resonating with voters at the sharp end of the 'hour-glass' economy.

Miliband had even less idea how to deal with the structural aftershocks of the 2014 Scottish independence referendum, notably growing anxieties about English identity. The SNP attacked Labour for collaborating with the Conservative government at Westminster during the 2014 campaign. David Cameron proposed a formula of 'English votes for English laws' that threw the Labour Party into disarray. In reality, the party had done little serious thinking about the so-called English question. In 2015, Labour's vote in Scotland promptly collapsed, while in the South of England, the Tories hammered Miliband for being the 'puppet' of the SNP leader, Nicola Sturgeon. Meanwhile, Labour was coming under pressure from UKIP in its heartland constituencies in Northern England.

In 2011, a referendum was held on whether Britain should introduce the Alternative Vote (AV) for Westminster elections. Labour supported the AV referendum in its 2010 manifesto. Yet Miliband refused to enthusiastically campaign for reform. In circumstances such as these, the leadership was perceived to lack political imagination, refusing to acknowledge AV's potential to transform the strategic landscape of British politics, inculcating a more pluralist style. On Europe, Miliband was paranoid and defensive like his predecessors. To critics, Miliband was manifestly in the mould of Brown and Blair, having matured in the elite culture of the Westminster village. He had little connection with provincial England. Miliband lacked empathy and was incredulous that any 'ordinary' person would ever vote Conservative. The town of Doncaster that Miliband represented was a hive of political corruption and scandal. There was widespread disillusionment with the Labour establishment. Miliband rarely visited his constituency, epitomising the feeling of detachment.[58] Ed was the quintessential Westminster insider.

For all the professed opposition to neo-liberalism, Miliband was easily caricatured as a typical career politician. He was accused of flagrant opportunism after withdrawing support for military intervention against the Assad regime – which had used chemical weapons against its own citizens in 2013 – to inflict a defeat on the Cameron government.[59] Miliband was understandably anxious not to repeat the errors of Iraq. Yet Labour MPs were uncomfortable their leader was prevaricating on whether to remove Assad. He surrounded himself with advisers who gave contradictory advice. His former treasury colleague, Stewart Wood, counselled Ed to run on a 'bold' Left platform while Spencer Livermore, once Gordon Brown's Director of Strategy who Miliband appointed campaign director, told the leader to adopt the safety-first strategy that achieved election victories in 1997 and 2001.[60]

Labour's defeat in 2015 was hardly surprising but a serious setback nonetheless. The Coalition government became unpopular. The treasury was compelled to moderate austerity as the threat of the 'double-dip' recession loomed. The cuts in health and social care led to a marked rise in the UK mortality rate. The Conservative Party remained divided over Europe and badly split on social reform, including legislative proposals for equal marriage. It was believed the electoral system would work to Labour's advantage, as UKIP split the Conservative vote. The Liberal Democrats haemorrhaged support during the Coalition era after breaking their headline commitment to abolish university tuition fees. Labour seemed poised to perform well in English marginals.[61]

The 2015 election defeat

Yet ultimately, the Labour Party's share of the vote increased only modestly to 30.4 per cent, less than was achieved in 1987. Labour won 232 seats by consolidating its position in Northern England. Forty seats were lost to the SNP in Scotland, while eight English seats went to the Conservatives. Labour gained ten seats from the Conservatives and twelve from the Liberal Democrats. Overall, the party appeared to be going backwards. Ipsos MORI estimate that Labour held on to only 72 per cent of its 2010 vote, losing support among the over sixty-fives, that demographic most likely to vote in British general elections. The vote held up where it had been strong since the Second World War: among eighteen- to thirty-year-olds, welfare claimants, public sector workers, those renting in the private sector, as well as ethnic minority voters. Among skilled workers (C1 and C2s), the key 'swing' constituency, the Conservatives advanced by exploiting Labour's loss of economic credibility. For all his calm insouciance, Miliband had no compelling formula to rebuild the party's fractured electoral coalition.

In the wake of defeat, the acting leader, Harriet Harman, commissioned Margaret Beckett, the former deputy leader and foreign secretary, to author a report examining why the party had lost. Beckett cited five main factors.[62] The first was that the Coalition government proved to be a formidable opponent. The Conservatives and the Liberal Democrats put up a unified front, attacking Labour's fiscal irresponsibility. As a consequence, Miliband lost the main economic argument. The second factor was Labour's refusal to offer a robust defence of its pre-2010 economic record. By turning the page on the Blair/Brown era, Miliband left his party defenceless in the face of Tory attacks. The weakness of Labour's campaign was the inability to foresee shifting sentiment among voters. By spring 2015, food and energy prices were falling, while interest rates and mortgage rates were at record lows. The Tories were able to warn that voting Labour would risk the fragile recovery in personal prosperity. *The Economist* concluded Labour's message that 'the recovery is failing to lift living standards' ran out of road.[63]

Furthermore, Beckett noted that across Europe, the climate was becoming more hostile for social democrats. Inward migration and globalisation increased voters' insecurity. Labour's manifesto contained an impressive array of initiatives but lacked an overarching political theme. The party opted for 'a narrow strategy to win power by appealing to Labour's core voters'.[64] Ed later admitted he was pursuing a core vote strategy.[65] The party's message was 'negative and gloomy'.[66] Finally, Labour's electoral organisation on the ground was ineffectual. Not enough resources were devoted to defending the party's position in Scotland. Labour's method of identifying target voters was outdated.

Miliband was always unlikely to become the transformational figure that he once believed was his political destiny. His support base was shallow. More MPs and members supported his brother, David. The breakdown in David and Ed's relationship – the two hardly spoke after the 2010 leadership election, and David's wife, Louise, believed Ed's ruthless ambition betrayed his brother's trust – had a catastrophic impact on voters' perceptions.[67] Miliband's weakness led to relentless speculation about a divided party throughout the Parliament.[68] Former ministers complained Ed wasn't a leader; he was 'a therapist' who wanted to make the party feel better about itself.[69] Nor did Miliband seize the political opportunities available. In the wake of the post-2008 recession that exacerbated the regional economic divide, Labour might have positioned itself as the party of English decentralisation. Yet the Labour Party remained wedded to the centralising orthodoxies of the post-1945 settlement. Underlying conservatism meant Miliband's party was unable to exploit new debates in British politics. Instead, Labour's leader presided over 'a perceptible drift back into the party's comfort zones'. The Labour Party lacked 'a model for modern social democracy that fits its aspirations to the new economic realities'.[70] Miliband's ambition to regulate energy markets while tackling poverty pay proved popular. Yet he remained out of step with the public on economic competence, attitudes to welfare claimants, alongside immigration policy. Above all, there was little confidence Miliband had the hallmarks of an effective prime minister.[71]

Jeremy Corbyn and after

Ed Miliband resigned immediately after Labour's devastating 2015 defeat. Jeremy Corbyn was elected leader, beating his opponents, Andy Burnham, Yvette Cooper and Liz Kendall convincingly. Corbyn was the first leader in his party's history to be a self-proclaimed Marxist. Unlike his predecessors, Corbyn sought to transform the economic system into socialism, not to improve the existing structure of capitalism and liberal democracy.[72] His hostility towards America and overt scepticism towards the EU were unusual for a post-war Labour leader. In fact, Corbyn had few 'conventional qualifications' for the job.[73] He had little experience of handling the media and had never run a large organisation. Corbyn was an unlikely leadership figure, yet he inspired messianic fervour among his followers. With his white beard and loose cotton shirts, Corbyn appeared almost saintly, a secular Jesus Christ able to inspire the faithful towards the promised land. Above all Corbyn inspired hope in an anti-political age.

Corbyn's 2015 triumph

Corbyn's victory in the wake of Miliband's leadership was depicted as vindication of Ed's strategy, moving Labour sharply to the Left. Miliband spoke regularly to his successor, hinting he was anxious to serve in Corbyn's shadow cabinet.[74] Others believe Corbyn's triumph was a reaction against Ed's reputation as the establishment insider.[75] The centrepiece of Corbyn's leadership was his claim that New Labour, neo-liberalism and austerity were inseparable. Corbyn agreed that since the early 1990s New Labour had been 'playing the politics of catch up', embracing Thatcherite initiatives.[76] He promised to end the remorseless drift towards neo-liberalism.

Jeremy Corbyn was born on 26th May 1949, raised in Wiltshire and Shropshire by middle-class parents who were veteran peace campaigners. He attended a private preparatory school and then a selective grammar. Corbyn travelled extensively in South America, studied at North London Polytechnic and then worked as a trade union organiser for the National Union of Public Employees (NUPE) and the Amalgamated Engineering and Electrical Union (AEEU). He was elected to Haringey Borough Council in 1974. By the early 1980s, local authorities were in the frontline of the ideological struggle between the Thatcher governments and the new municipal Left, particularly in London. This new 'urban Left' had 'a common concern for the socialist potential of local government arising often from a belief in the inadequacy of traditional models of socialist politics'.[77]

Having cultivated his power base in local government as an influential ally of Tony Benn, Corbyn was selected as parliamentary candidate for Islington North in 1983. He was actively involved in Left newspapers including the Trotskyite *London Labour Briefing*. Corbyn's interests epitomised the fashionable views of the London Left of the 1970s, dominated by the cabal of so-called 'Polytechnic Trots'. He supported a united Ireland, forming links to the leaders of Sinn Fein, Gerry Adams and Martin McGuiness, at a time when the Provisional IRA was prosecuting a live bombing campaign on the British mainland. Corbyn's views on foreign policy were shaped by virulent anti-Americanism and anti-Imperialism. He identified with the Palestinian struggle for statehood against Israel (later prompting accusations of anti-Semitism), the fight against Apartheid in South Africa and with Castro's leadership of Cuba against the United States. He was no supporter of Europe, writing in the early 1990s that 'the Maastricht Treaty seeks to create a new capitalist trade block to compete with the USA/ North America. . . . Maastricht restricts public spending and public ownership and rules out the kind of industrial intervention needed to build full employment'.[78] Corbyn then became a key player in the 'Stop the War' coalition prior to the outbreak of the Iraq War.

Politically, Corbyn was somewhat typical of the post-1968 generation. In the late 1960s, a succession of European cities were brought to a standstill by violent protests involving students and workers organised by Leftist organisations. Rather than building their uprising around traditional pillars of the class struggle, the 1968 demonstrations were centred on post-materialist movements embracing feminism, unilateral nuclear disarmament, civil rights and environmentalism. Epitomising the tradition of British romantic protest, 1968 was a reaction against the emergence of the post-war consumption economy, emphasising the importance of nature, non-violence, anti-materialism and the agency of the individual: the protestors' 'critique of modern society was essentially a faith commitment'.[79] Not surprisingly, given its association with acquisitive capitalism, these views coincided with moral contempt for the United States. The Left was offering a variety of 'liberation politics' that had a decisive impact on Corbyn and the evolution of his political ideas. Yet the politics of the 1968 generation espoused the deep undercurrents of radical individualism. It was to prove more difficult to reconcile the burgeoning politics of personal autonomy with the Left's traditional emphasis on solidarity and communitarianism.

After a long career in Parliament, Corbyn was an unlikely political hero. In the aftermath of Miliband's resignation, the Left debated whether they should even run a candidate. John McDonnell, Corbyn's longtime ally, was unable to gather enough signatures to run against Gordon Brown in 2007. In 2010, Diane Abbot required David Miliband's supporters to get on the ballot paper. In the summer of 2015, a survey of 1,200 members revealed only two believed Jeremy Corbyn could become leader.[80] Since Benn's defeat in the deputy leadership election in 1981, the organised Left had been on the defensive. Peter Mandelson joked that the Left-Wing Campaign Group were placed in a 'sealed tomb'. Corbyn admitted in an interview that he only stood because no one else would; as he put it, 'unfortunately, it's my hat in the ring'.[81]

Yet in September 2015, Corbyn won 59.5 per cent of first preference votes in the Electoral College, without question a decisive victory.[82] He almost secured a simple majority across all three sections of the College: 84 per cent of registered supporters, 57.6 per cent of affiliated trade unionists and 49.7 per cent of the membership.[83] By now, Labour had over 565,000 members. The party's composition was transformed. Only fifteen out of 232 Labour MPs had voted for Corbyn. Yet he benefited from the overhaul of the Electoral College that followed the allegedly corrupt parliamentary selection process in the Scottish constituency of Falkirk. Officials from the trade union, Unite, had exerted inappropriate influence in the selection to favour their own national officer, Karie Murphy, later appointed Corbyn's political secretary. At the time, Murphy was working for Tom Watson MP, who later resigned from the shadow cabinet over the affair. An internal review led by the former general secretary of the Labour Party, Ray Collins, recommended one member, one vote (OMOV) for the future selection of all candidates and the party leadership. Even Tony

Blair welcomed the reforms as completing the modernisation effort begun in the 1980s. Centre-left parties across Europe were experimenting with internal party democratisation.[84]

Nevertheless, while Corbyn benefited from the reformed Electoral College, he was propelled to victory by younger 'millennial' activists whose lives since the great recession had been precarious economically – the price exacted by austerity as well as the rising cost of university tuition and housing. New Labour's inheritance was inseparable from Britain's political economy more than a decade after the 2008 crash, the most serious recession to afflict the UK since the great depression in the 1930s. After 1997, Britain enjoyed unprecedented stability and prosperity. Over the ten years since the crisis, the climate had rarely been more turbulent. To avoid an even steeper depression, governments adopted extraordinary measures. The policies of low interest rates and cheap money had a devastating impact on inter-generational inequality, boosting asset prices, preventing young people on stagnant incomes from accessing home ownership and stoking the buy-to-let housing market: average house prices rose by 37 per cent from 2009 to 2017; in London, the figure was 89 per cent.[85] The real wages of young people stagnated. Although the young benefited from the expansion of public services in the late 1990s, austerity swept many of the gains away.

It was easy to blame inter-generational disadvantage on austerity during the Coalition years. Yet policy problems could be traced back to the New Labour era, particularly the dysfunctional housing market and Britain's low-wage, low-skill economy, damaging for those leaving school without qualifications. It was difficult to dispute that the inter-generational divide was in part New Labour's legacy. As a consequence, politicised young people flocked to Corbyn. In the United States, it was reported that 51 per cent of eighteen- to thirty-year-olds had 'a positive view of socialism', while more young voters supported Bernie Sanders in the 2016 primary than Donald Trump and Hilary Clinton combined.[86] Corbyn's party performed relatively well in 2017 because 'just as [the] older, white, working-classes are moving towards the Conservatives, younger, precariously employed-workers are aligning to Labour'.[87]

Despite the youth surge, Corbyn's position was further strengthened by the radicalised cohort of 'baby-boomers' who grew disillusioned with New Labour in the wake of the Iraq invasion, alongside public sector white-collar workers whose wages and pensions were squeezed following cuts in spending after 2010.[88] By 2015, two-thirds of Labour members were university graduates, while 44 per cent were public sector employees.[89] Corbyn's coalition was framed by a 'post-bourgeois' politics where the desire to dismantle capitalism was augmented by concerns about the environment, civil liberties, social equality and democratic participation. Left politics in Britain was becoming a 'consumption activity . . . better understood as less of a political movement and more as a form of identity or enjoyable pastime'.[90] Corbyn's victory was possible since he demonstrated the willingness to move beyond New Labour decisively, as Miliband ultimately failed to do. No one looked less like an establishment politician than Corbyn. One of his supporters, Clive Lewis, insisted he was an authentic 'anti-hero' rather than a 'rock-star politician'. Corbyn was perceived to be 'principled, modest and human'.[91] Like George Lansbury in the 1930s, he was regarded as a 'prophet' and a 'poet' who would cleanse Labour of the squalid compromises of power.[92]

Indeed, the parallels between Corbyn and Lansbury are striking. Both became leader in the wake of a major economic crisis that destroyed the credibility of social democratic governments. Both of their predecessors, MacDonald and Blair, were apparently traitors.[93] Neither Lansbury nor Corbyn ever held ministerial office. Both promised to give the party back its soul and pursue an ethical programme. If Labour's ideas are defined by compromise between ethics and economic efficiency, Corbynism represented the unambiguous assertion of the ethical tradition. The focus on markets and macro-economic policy was subordinated to moral concerns about the legitimacy of economic outcomes and material growth. Corbyn lived his life by values. His demeanour was humble. He travelled by bicycle and public transport, rarely using a chauffeured car. Corbyn was a vegetarian who tended his own allotment in North London. He even made his own damson jam. By 2015 Corbyn's socialism could be presented as fresh, dynamic, vibrant, energising. Memories of the Winter of Discontent were banished. Few voters remembered the nationalisation of the 1940s and 1950s. Trade union power in Britain precipitously declined. Socialism was no longer portrayed as a threat against which voters should be mobilised in defending free markets and private property rights.

The Labour Party under Corbyn

Yet the long-term impact of Corbyn's leadership proved far from straightforward. In fairness, he inherited an already fractious and discordant party. On becoming leader, Corbyn had to address three fundamental issues. Firstly, could he define a new ideological agenda in the wake of New Labour that unified the party, ensuring Labour remained a viable governing force? Secondly, in electoral terms did Labour have a strategy to defeat the Conservatives in England, while seeing off the nationalist threat posed by UKIP and the SNP? Finally, could the party be rebuilt as a serious vehicle for change, re-unifying its industrial and political wings?

Sooner than expected, Corbyn faced a bruising election campaign. Yet Labour's unexpected success in 2017 epitomised the new political landscape. The party polled over 40 per cent of the popular vote, depriving the prime minister, Theresa May, of a working majority. Labour achieved the largest increase in its vote between two general elections than at any time since 1945. It gained thirty-six seats across the country, including Conservative heartlands in Southern England. Canterbury and Stroud fell to Labour, as did the relatively affluent London constituency of Kensington.[94] The party's communications were effective, particularly in mobilising voters through social media.[95] Corbyn recruited the wily *Guardian* journalist Seumus Milne as director of communications. Milne was reviled in the PLP given his support for Putin's Russia and refusal to countenance robust action against anti-Semitism. Yet he proved an effective operator, trusted by the parliamentary lobby, able to secure compelling coverage during the campaign.

Labour's Manifesto, *For the Many, Not the Few*, was praised for its expansive agenda. The document was Labour's most 'left-wing' since 1992.[96] Utilities were to be brought back into public ownership, particularly rail and water, when existing franchises expired. Energy would be supplied through a network of companies that were publicly owned.[97] Public sector austerity would end by raising taxes on those earning more than £80,000 a year – the top 5 per cent – while clamping down on tax avoidance. Tuition fees would be scrapped immediately. On Brexit, Labour tried to appeal to both Leave and Remain Britain. Its manifesto pledged the party would work towards 'a close new relationship with the EU', pursuing a 'jobs-first' Brexit; retaining the advantages of the single market and customs union; guaranteeing settlement rights for EU nationals; while preventing a hard border between Northern Ireland and the Republic.[98] Yet the party's manifesto stipulated that the UK's EU departure meant an end to free movement alongside restrictions on migration. Corbyn welcomed the fact that state aid rules would no longer apply, enabling a Labour government to bring industries into public ownership. 'Constructive ambiguity' over Europe proved persuasive electorally.

Of course, Labour did not actually win the 2017 election. The party lost seats in so-called heartland places, not least the iconic constituency of Mansfield. It suffered a sharp reversal in former mining constituencies such as Ashfield in Nottinghamshire. Turnout among eighteen- to twenty-four-year-olds in social class DE was 35 per cent, indicating lack of enthusiasm among young working-class voters.[99] The party's proclaimed forward march was scarcely convincing. In marginal seats Labour expected to win, including Stevenage and the Norfolk seaside constituency of Waveney, the swing to Labour was unimpressive. The Tories ultimately emerged with more seats since they led on the core indicators of economic competence and leadership. May was a poor campaigner, robotic and uncharismatic, lacking a persuasive vision. 'Maybot's' repetitive mantra of 'strong and stable leadership' was met with audible groans by the end of the campaign. The Tory manifesto contained damaging promises, particularly the 'dementia tax' which cost May's party support. Terrorist attacks at the Manchester Arena and Borough Market in London heightened public anxieties about police budget cuts. Yet the Conservative Party still won the largest number of seats. The BBC's former political analyst, David Cowling, calculates that the national swing to Labour was only 2 per cent. Theresa May secured the second-largest rise in her party's vote share since 1931.[100] In 2017, Labour benefited from the large swing in London (6.3 per cent). But in the North, there was a swing away towards the Conservatives. Corbyn's team felt they won a moral victory, yet Labour was still 63 seats short of a parliamentary majority.

The election was fought in highly unusual circumstances. The aftershocks of major referendums reshaped the political landscape: the 2014 Scottish referendum and the 2016 plebiscite on the European Union (EU). The referendums accelerated the breakdown of traditional class allegiances, fomenting cleavages that undermined the conventional hold of Left and Right. In 2017, Labour secured more support among voters in higher occupational grades. While Labour's vote increased among the traditional working class, Conservative support grew even more rapidly.[101] In Scotland, voters backed candidates according to their stance on the union, leading to the unanticipated recovery of Labour and the Conservatives. The SNP lost twenty seats, including the former leader Alex Salmond's constituency of Gordon in North-East Scotland. In England, Labour was the natural home for 'Remain' voters, leading the Conservatives by 47 to 33 per cent. The Tories won the election among 'Leave' supporters by 46 to 39 per cent.[102] The divide in British politics reflected attitudes to EU membership and national identity. Voters appeared more polarised between support for the open, liberal, cosmopolitan conception of Britishness and those harbouring a more closed, authoritarian, inward-looking world-view.

As a consequence, Labour still had a mountain to climb to win the next election. The party required a swing of 4.9 per cent to gain a majority, a surge of support it achieved only in 1945 and 1997.[103] It lacked a strategy to win over communitarian working-class voters in industrial towns, alongside affluent voters in southern marginals. Labour was losing elections in the aftermath of the worst economic crisis to afflict Western capitalism since the great depression in the 1930s. Loss of trust and perceived mismanagement of immigration and welfare before 2010 cost the party long-term support.[104] It may have staved off disaster in 2017, but Corbyn's party was still staring into the electoral abyss.

The Corbyn project

How will 'Corbynism' as a political project be judged ultimately? Although portrayed as inhabiting separate moral universes, the similarities between Blair's New Labour Party and Corbynism are intriguing. Both leaders emphasised the importance of political style alongside ideas. In 1997, Blair invited the *Oasis* guitarist Noel Gallagher and *Simply Red's* Mick Hucknell to a reception in Downing Street. New Labour sought to present Britain as a young country. Corbyn spoke at the Glastonbury festival. The 2017 and 2019 campaigns were aided by endorsements from musicians and grime artists. Corbyn and Blair tried to connect younger voters with their political agenda. Both espoused cultish hero worship of the leader. Blair believed he uniquely personified New Labour's political beliefs, his face emblazoned on the front cover of the 1997 manifesto. Corbyn was viewed as a messianic figure. True believers called him 'Jeremy'. Corbyn t-shirts and coffee mugs circulated among party activists. Corbyn's beard even invited comparisons with Jesus.

The third similarity was that Corbyn and Blair were wedded to centralised control of the party machine. The Blair era was notorious for centralised interference in internal party selection contests, as Rhodri Morgan and Ken Livingstone attest.[105] Yet despite preaching the virtues of democratisation, Corbyn's operation proved willing to sully its hands. In the Lewisham East by-election, for example, the general secretary, Jenny Formby, intervened ruling out one of the Left's candidates, preventing the vote being split for Corbyn's favoured choice. For four years, conference resolutions were fixed to prevent destructive debates over Brexit and Europe. Fourth, both Blair and Corbyn acknowledged the centrality of identity politics. Under Blair, the relative status of women in the party began to be addressed. Corbyn recognised the importance of social liberal movements on the Left, even if tensions erupted over anti-Semitism and relations with the British Jewish community. Both leaders were metropolitan, with links to the urban progressive Left that had weak roots outside the liberal cities. Blair lived in the Islington borough of London, the area represented by Corbyn in parliament. The final similarity is that both politicians have been depicted as disconnected from the traditional working class. Blair's rhetoric and style embodied the aspirations of the professional middle class in Southern England. Corbyn espoused the virtues of the university-educated, public sector salariat that grew in influence from the late 1960s. New Labour and Corbynism were undeniably middle class movements.

Of course, the differences in doctrine and strategy between the two camps were still vast. Corbyn believed that the British political system was more polarised ideologically than at any time since the 1980s. Labour's shift to the Left addressed the demand for 'clear red water', a fundamental break with New Labour. Yet commentators questioned whether that was actually the electorate's mood. In 2017, the Conservatives ran on a manifesto akin to the 1950s. Labour's programme echoed the 1970s. Both had remarkably little to say about the country's future after Brexit.

The alternative economic strategy?

For all the divisions over Europe, Labour's political vulnerability centred historically on economic policy. The party's 2017 manifesto was heralded as a vote winner, the most radical since 1945. One commentator concluded that the programme was 'reminiscent of Wilsonian era Labour advocating a technocratic vision of improving technology to develop the economy'.[106] In the *Financial Times*, its leading columnist Martin Wolf wrote that Labour was confronting 'outworn shibboleths' by positing an 'entrepreneurial state' to drive economic growth.[107] With long-term interest rates at zero, the party advocated a major increase in public investment. It was necessary to reform taxation, especially inheritance tax, long evaded by the wealthy. Wolf agreed that the Bank of England's policy mandate ought to be updated, adopting the target focused on nominal GDP rather than inflation. The Labour leadership assembled a remarkable 'brains trust' of economists that included Joseph Stiglitz, Thomas Piketty, Simon Wren-Lewis, Marianna Mazzucato and David Blanchflower.[108] Corbyn's radicalism no longer appeared so incredible. After all, the financial and political elite itself was discredited in the aftermath of the 2008 crisis.[109]

Even so, Corbyn and his shadow chancellor, John McDonnell, struggled to identify a coherent economic strategy. McDonnell was among the most serious political operators on the Left of the Labour Party. Having trained as a Catholic priest, McDonnell began his career as a local government and trade union official. In 1981, he was elected to the Greater London Council (GLC), becoming deputy leader to Ken Livingstone. The GLC was attacked for promoting 'loony Left' policies but the institution pioneered a series of initiatives including public investment in the arts, subsidised fares on London transport, alongside efforts to extend equal opportunities to women and BME communities. According to the gay rights campaigner, Peter Tatchell: 'For the first time in Britain, politicians in power sought to engage seriously with women's issues and the concerns of marginalised minorities'.[110] McDonnell was elected as MP for Hayes and Harlington in 1997 becoming a leading member of the Socialist Campaign Group. He was opposed to the privatisation of public services and led resistance in the PLP to the Iraq War. In the 2015 leadership race, McDonnell served as Corbyn's campaign manager. He was rewarded with the position of shadow chancellor. McDonnell immediately set out to reinvigorate Labour's thinking, appointing James Meadway from the New Economics Foundation (NEF) as his adviser. The first major idea McDonnell proposed was 'People's Quantitative Easing'. Rather than propping up the ailing banking system, people's QE focused on public investment in infrastructure and services. The purpose of government was to 'democratise and redistribute wealth', creating new models of ownership, including worker's co-operatives.[111]

McDonnell claimed his views of capitalism were influenced by Marx and Lenin.[112] Yet he was a curious blend of ideologue and pragmatist who hired the former cabinet secretary, Bob Kerslake, to advise on reforming the Whitehall machinery. McDonnell proclaimed he would be 'the first socialist Labour Chancellor'. Yet since 2015, he emphasised the commitment to fiscal responsibility, pledging Labour would 'eliminate the government's deficit on day to day spending within five years'.[113] A future Labour administration was determined 'to live within our means'. McDonnell's claim that governments must not borrow for day-to-day spending, only long-term investment echoed Brown's fiscal rules in the 1990s. The industrial strategy was a recognisable centre-left cocktail of initiatives on skills, procurement, infrastructure, research and development, supply chains and the launch of the national investment bank.

Moreover, Labour remained cautious about levying taxes on those other than the 'super-rich'. The party scrapped proposals for a 'mansion tax' on homes worth more than £2 million. The Shadow Treasury team refused to confront the disproportionate tax advantages enjoyed by wealthy pensioners. McDonnell organised regular meetings with senior figures in the City, insisting they had nothing to fear from a Labour government. His rhetoric was remarkably conciliatory. On the EU, the shadow chancellor was closer to the business community than the government, signalling support for a customs union and continuing membership of the single market. He was conscious that to protect the economy, Labour must not trigger a collapse of private sector confidence. If the party entered government, it seems McDonnell would have been more Bevanite than Trotskyite.[114]

In the 2017 campaign, there was little detailed scrutiny of Labour's programme. Wealthy individuals and corporations would be required to pay more tax, but it was recognised the effort was unlikely to produce quick results. McDonnell believed the long-term costs of the manifesto would be met through his new growth model, enlarging the UK's fiscal base. Yet the Left historically had been over-optimistic about the potential for growth. The International Monetary Fund (IMF) forecast a negative long-term impact on GDP in the wake of Brexit. Despite its claim to fiscal responsibility, an incoming Labour government may well have faced a collapse of confidence in its ability to borrow. The Corbyn administration was likely to confront similar difficulties to all Labour governments since the First World War. The government would seek to adjust British capitalism, altering the behaviour of producers to fulfil its egalitarian ideals. Yet the state was still dependent on private sector growth and profitability. Moreover, the UK had ceased to be a recognisably national economy.[115] All British governments assumed the economy was open and global, centred increasingly on finance and services rather than production and industry. How in these circumstances would the underlying problems of the UK economy, its weak productivity, regional economic imbalances and spiralling inequality actually be reversed? Could any peacetime administration have realistically altered such pervasive forces? Labour's economic strategy remained oddly circumspect and opaque given the professed radicalism of the leadership.

Labour's identity crisis

More broadly, Corbyn's project as leader explicitly contested New Labour's reinvention of the party. Yet 'Corbynism' was riddled with its own ambiguities and contradictions. One paradox related to the party's identity. Labour was believed to have reclaimed its heritage in 2015, symbolised by the leader's attendance at the Durham Miner's Gala alongside the festival in Dorset to commemorate the Tolpuddle Martyrs. Corbyn told an interviewer that Labour was now 'a class-based socialist party'. He assured supporters that under a future government, coal mines would be reopened.[116] A year later, Corbyn announced to a trade union conference: 'Labour is back as the political voice of the working-class'. Throughout history, Labour had retreated to the comforting illusion of its 'homogenous proletarian base' in Britain.[117] Yet in so doing, Corbynism never addressed the fundamental question of what were the party's roots in a world transformed by the demise of class politics and the halting of Labour's forward march? Confusingly, the more Labour sought to emphasise its credentials as a working-class party, the more alienated working-class voters became.

There were pervasive contradictions of strategy and ideology in Corbyn's party. Had Labour reverted to becoming a traditional party of Labourism, or did it now represent a new 'social movement'? The leader's team operated by controlling the national executive and trade unions, imposing discipline through oligarchy and centralised control. Yet Corbyn's grassroots organisation, *Momentum*, espoused the virtues of collective participation and internal democracy in the Labour Party. The Left instinctively opposed the presidential style that encouraged blind loyalty and deference to the leader. If the leadership had too much power, it risked being caught in an 'aristocratic embrace' that would lead to betrayal – a repeat of the Ramsay MacDonald debacle.[118] The NEC, the trade unions and the annual conference were necessary to constrain the leadership's authority. Yet Corbyn's rise to power and his ability to defend his leadership from PLP opposition centred precisely on his messianic quasi-presidential appeal. Was the leader a disciplinarian asserting the Left's dominance through central control of party institutions; or a pluralist committed to post-1968-style liberation politics? The search was underway for Corbyn's soul.

Other paradoxes of Corbynism soon emerged. The first concerned the ongoing tension in Corbyn's party between 'Labourism' and 'socialism'. The trade unions had regained their ascendency by 2015. The Labourist wing historically believed the party must focus on ameliorative reforms that improved the living standards of working people. The philosophy was 'bread today, not jam tomorrow'. Improving working-class prosperity and welfare must take precedence over ideological victory. Labourism was committed to the existing Westminster institutions, parliamentary government, collective wage bargaining and moderate class politics. It aimed to advance 'a mild form of social democracy'.[119] Yet throughout his career, Corbyn's politics strenuously emphasised the limits of Labourism. Intellectuals who influenced the Left most – notably, Ralph Miliband, Leo Panitch, Colin Leys, Perry Anderson and David Coates – focused on the constraints imposed by the conservative and anti-intellectual predisposition of the Labour tradition.[120] They emphasised the backwardness of British socialism, its inability to act as an agent of modernisation within the economy and polity.[121] Through the Labour Party's formation, 'the now enclosed and defensive world of working-class culture had in effect achieved its apotheosis'.[122] Marx deplored Labourism as striving to modify capitalism rather than transforming the economic system. Ralph Miliband referred to the 'bankruptcy of Labourism'.[123] He insisted socialism must be a transformational creed, inculcating revolutionary political consciousness among the working class.[124] Throughout his career, Corbyn paid lip service to Labourism while decrying its limitations.[125]

The second paradox of Corbynism related to the politics of personal autonomy and collectivism. Not surprisingly, Corbynism was soon labelled 'populism for the middle-classes, serving the material and psychological needs of the relatively affluent and well-heeled'.[126] The electoral strategy of Corbyn's party centred on embracing the educated and prosperous middle class. The central plank of the 2017 manifesto focused on the abolition of university tuition fees combined with no tax rises on incomes below £80,000. Labour's programme reflecting changes underway across the industrialised countries, where social democratic parties relied increasingly on educated voters.[127] As a consequence, the centre-left became less focused on class and redistribution.

Under Corbyn, the party's agenda emphasised individualism, personal autonomy and the politics of identity to an unprecedented degree. Corbyn's twenty-
first-century socialism celebrated the individualism of the Left, exemplified by
the party's embrace of Universal Basic Income (UBI) alongside the four-day
working week in the public sector. A report on the four-day week by Lord
Robert Skidelsky for the Shadow Treasury team claimed in libertarian terms:
'Having to work less at what one needs to do, and more at what one wants to do,
is good for material and spiritual well-being'.[128] The historian Thomas Franks
believed that the growth of identity politics encouraged an emphasis on 'demographic self-recognition and self-expression . . . the bread and butter not of leftist
ideology but consumerism'.[129] The thirst for self-actualisation was the underlying orientation of Corbynism. Neither in 2017 nor 2019 did Labour insist that
taxes should rise for middle- and high-income earners to improve public services. The party's prospectus sought to ease the burden on the middle class rather
than tackling endemic disadvantage in the structure of the economy and society.

As a consequence, Corbyn never confidently embraced the traditional politics
that had dominated the party since the Second World War. Under his leadership, Labour was a long way from being a movement 'of the trade unions and
working-class, pursuing socialist reforms of capitalism using the state'.[130] Corbyn
was determined to appear at the Durham Miner's Gala (Photo 9.2) marching
behind the banner of the National Union of Mineworkers (NUM). Yet this act
evoked nostalgic memories of working-class politics that had long passed into
abeyance. The 2017 manifesto contained doses of Labourism, underlining the
dominance of the trade unions (not least as the major source of campaign funding), but their influence was actually to nudge the party to the Right. Labour
committed to retaining the Trident nuclear submarine against the leader's wishes.
Foreign affairs were downplayed following attacks on Corbyn's links to terrorist
organisations. After the Manchester arena bombing, Corbyn denied he blamed
terrorism on the conduct of British foreign policy.

Nevertheless, elsewhere the Labour Party advanced the undiluted statism that
was historically anathema to moderate Labourism. The manifesto committed
to 'bring key utilities back into public ownership to deliver lower prices, more
accountability and a more sustainable economy', including the railways, water,
gas, electricity and the Royal Mail.[131] The emphasis was on the top-down restructuring of the British economy. Yet it was not clear that the party's industrial
policy would produce more well-paid jobs, benefiting working-class voters.
The proposal for a 'Citizen's Wealth Fund' (CWF) and the broader 'institutional
turn' in economic policy was certainly imaginative.[132] Yet practical questions
remained. Would the CWF be overseen by civil service technocrats, creating
a new bureaucratic elite; or elected politicians?[133] There was little evidence of
any concerted thinking about involving citizens in the design of public policy.
Labour's 2017 manifesto felt as if it was forty years behind the times. Many figures on the Left grew frustrated at the perceived poverty of ambition in Corbyn's
project. They envisaged a radical social movement overcoming obstacles to the
reform of capitalism imposed by the economic and political elite.[134] There was

PHOTO 9.2   Jeremy Corbyn attends the Annual Durham Miner's Gala, July 2017.

Source: Photo by Ian Forsyth/Getty Images.

the emphasis on democratic ownership by workers and citizens in contrast to the centralised corporatism of the Attlee years. Furthermore, it was feared that automation was likely to shift power towards capital, requiring countervailing measures. For radical thinkers and activists, Corbynomics had to extend democracy from politics to the economy, echoing the twentieth-century syndicalism of G.D.H. Cole that favoured self-government and workplace democracy rather than suffocating managerial control.[135] There were demands for the rebalancing of power: reforming the institutions of the British economy, extending workers' co-operatives and instilling a 'right to own' where employees were given the right to purchase a company collectively. McDonnell's adviser, James Meadway, insisted that in economic policy, 'Keynesianism is not enough'. The strategy must democratise the economy, redistributing income, wealth and power.[136]

The leadership henceforth adopted the language of transformational socialism. A party document acknowledged: 'State ownership has historically tended to be too centralised, with power in the hands of a private and corporate elite'.[137] Yet the party's programme hardly matched the ambition of the Alternative Economic Strategy (AES) in the 1970s. Meanwhile, the Institute for Fiscal Studies (IFS) calculated that the Liberal Democrat manifesto in 2017 was more redistributive and fiscally progressive than Labour's. Scrapping £9,250 tuition fees took priority over reversing welfare cuts. Labour professed to be a party on the side of the dispossessed. Yet it was wedded constitutionally to the sectionalism of the public sector unions and the vocal grievances of the public service middle class. Its commitment to the disadvantaged in British society appeared shallow.

As a consequence, 'contradictions [were] opening up within [Corbyn's] own support base'. In particular, 'concerns over the softening of the position on immigration and Brexit left supporters feeling uneasy'.[138] Many of those supporting him reacted against New Labour's illiberalism. They sought to advance civil liberties and human rights. They wanted to scrap the independent nuclear deterrent. They welcomed EU free movement, emphasising the right of migrants and asylum seekers to settle in Britain. They continued to view Brexit as repugnant nativism, evoking a past of imperialism, colonialism and empire. The former Greek finance minister, Yanis Varoufakis, eventually persuaded Corbyn to oppose Brexit in the 2016 referendum.[139] Corbyn's most committed supporters advocated a second referendum on EU membership, or even parliamentary revocation of Article 50. Eighty per cent of the Labour Party membership by 2019 supported a second referendum. Yet since 2016, the leadership were drawn back repeatedly to accepting the Leave position. Corbyn's contribution to the Remain campaign in 2016 was, at the very least, half-hearted. The day after the referendum, he called for Article 50 to be triggered immediately. Corbyn rejected European Economic Area (EEA) membership, a form of 'soft' Brexit, as it entailed free movement. He expressed sympathy with so-called white working-class voters in Leave areas. While 65 per cent of Labour voters supported Remain, 70 per cent of Labour-held constituencies voted Leave. In these seats, MPs feared the party's instinct in supporting freedom of movement would be electorally damaging.[140]

Labour's 'core' voters, many of whom drifted to UKIP by 2015, were perceived to be the 'losers' of globalisation, opposed bitterly to cultural openness. In 2017, the party performed worst in former industrial seats dominated by Leave supporters.[141] The seeds of Labour's catastrophic defeat in 2019 were sowed two years previously. One commentator noted: 'Many Labour MPs remain frightened of losing the white working-class vote in old mining and metal working constituencies in the Midlands and the North. In poor, post-industrial areas there are not yet many votes in being pro-European'.[142] The decisive influence on Corbyn's views of European integration was Tony Benn, who in the 1970s viewed the EEC as undermining British national sovereignty while blocking the passage of the radical socialist agenda. Benn declared: 'I loathe the Common Market. It's bureaucratic and centralised, there's no political discussion, officials control Ministers, and it just has a horrible flavour about it'.[143] Corbyn believed the EU:

> Knowingly, deliberately maintains a number of tax havens and tax-evasion posts around the Continent – Luxembourg, Monaco and a number of others. I think we should be making demands: universal workers' rights, universal environmental protection, end the race to the bottom on corporate taxation, end the race to the bottom in working age protection.[144]

Yet after 2016, Corbyn's dilemma was that even he acknowledged the class grouping of Leave voters could not propel the onward march that Labour required to win power. His political identity rested on opposition to the economic system,

Britain's 'dominant ideology', which had little appeal to these voters.[145] As a consequence, Corbyn manifestly lacked a coherent long-term political programme underpinned by a cohesive cross-class electoral coalition. On Europe and migration, the choices that Corbyn confronted were unenviable. Labour shifted tentatively, eventually becoming the second referendum party. Yet over Brexit, Corbyn's Labour appeared as divided as the Conservatives, some achievement given the divisions threatening to tear the Tories apart.

Ultimately, the Corbyn agenda embodied the contradictions that afflicted Labourism and the Left for the last century. The party was anxious 'to speak for the people' yet at the same time was determined 'to change them'.[146] Corbyn sought to give voice to popular anxieties while developing his participative style of democratic politics. At the same time, the party's programme of transformational socialism was achievable only if citizens became less materially acquisitive, more altruistic and motivated by the common good. Not surprisingly, Labour politicians struggled not to sound self-righteous and condescending. They seemed out of tune with popular sentiment. Corbyn's politics were easily ridiculed as bureaucratic, interfering, bossy and overbearing. The party's outlook recalled George Orwell's observation in the 1930s:

> To many people calling themselves Socialists, revolution does not mean a movement of the masses with which they hope to associate themselves; it means a set of reforms which 'we', the clever ones, are going to impose upon 'them', the Lower Orders.[147]

An incoming Labour government under Corbyn and McDonnell would compel companies in the UK to offer ownership stakes to employees. The party advocated the compulsory purchase of privatised utilities without compensation. Labour was convinced it could increase private sector investment while imposing austere physical controls on the British economy.[148] Following a period of prolonged crisis for British capitalism, Labour insisted the power of government would restructure the economy. Corbynomics took inspiration from Thatcherism's relentless pursuit of neo-liberal policies, without acknowledging the anti-democratic nature of the Thatcher government's 'elective dictatorship'.[149]

Moreover, for all the damage inflicted by post-2010 austerity, Britain was not a country that voters felt had gone to the dogs. There were innumerable problems in the nation's public sphere, from rising youth violence and knife crime to endemic discrimination against minorities; the health service was visibly failing. Still, longitudinal research did not indicate that Britons were less contented than in the past or in comparison to other countries.[150] The belief that Britain became more individualistic and atomised in the aftermath of Thatcherism is questionable. Those who enjoyed unprecedented personal autonomy often found new means of negotiating the subtle relationship between self and society.[151] They did not give up on community life or civic association, even if the balance tilted towards individualism and private consumption. There was still the desire for social connection, evidenced by the continuation of volunteer-run cafes, parks, recreational facilities and community spaces in the face of austerity. In reality, economic and social change since the 1970s advanced and hindered the Left's project in equal measure.[152]

The problem was that the image of Britain on which the contemporary Left relied was partial and inaccurate. Corbyn's socialism was torn between the deeply contradictory instincts of trusting citizens and re-educating them. His project went against the grain of the 'individualist popular culture' that had been reshaping Britain since the end of the Second World War.[153] Corbyn's leadership pitch in 2015 repudiated the Blair era and adopted the rhetoric of transformational socialism. Yet what had replaced the New Labour project still remained nebulous and imprecise four years after Corbyn had taken the helm.

Revitalising socialism in the 'new hard times': the 2019 defeat

Having defied expectations in 2017, Labour went into the election two years later declaring 'It's Time for Real Change'. The party's manifesto deployed populist tropes, identifying ideological enemies and attacking the immoral spectre of global capitalism. In his foreword to the manifesto, Corbyn proclaimed 2019 was the year of the 'change election'. The political and economic system was failing: 'The last decade has seen a wealth grab by the privileged few . . . big polluters, financial speculators, and corporate tax dodgers'. Despite Corbyn's flirtation with populism, Martin Wolf agreed. What had emerged in Britain was 'rentier capitalism . . . an economy in which market and political power allows privileged individuals and businesses to extract a great deal of rent from everybody else'.[154] The UK financial sector was 'detrimental' to productivity growth, diverting resources into unproductive activities. The Bank of England's chief economist, Andy Haldane, believed shareholder capitalism was in danger of 'eating itself'. In this climate of systemic failure, Labour's most radical manifesto ever would 'rewrite the rules of the economy'.[155] Although critics disparaged his programme as returning Britain to the 1970s, Corbyn proclaimed the manifesto was inspired by Attlee's victory in 1945. Then, as now, free market capitalism was failing demonstrably. The transformational agenda of socialism was required.[156]

THE LABOUR PARTY MANIFESTO 2019: 'IT'S TIME FOR REAL CHANGE'[157]

A Green Industrial Revolution

- The Green New Deal with substantially reduced UK emissions by 2030.
- A £250 billion Green Transformation Fund to promote renewable and low carbon energy.
- A National Investment Bank with a network of regional banks.

- Delisting companies on the London Stock Exchange that fail to address the climate crisis.
- Introducing a public interest test for hostile takeovers.
- A third of directors on company boards to be elected by workers.
- Three per cent of UK GDP to be spent on Research and Development by the end of the Parliament.
- A Ministry of Employment Rights to oversee sectoral collective bargaining.
- £10 per hour minimum wage for all workers and banning zero-hours contracts.
- A 32 hour maximum working week for the public sector with no reduction in pay.
- 'Inclusive Ownership' compelling firms to place ten per cent of their shares over ten years in collectively owned funds paying dividends to staff.
- Within five years, 150,000 council and social rented homes to be built a year (over a million homes in a decade).
- Private renters given the right to open-ended tenancies.
- The rail network across the UK renationalised, along with Royal Mail.
- Local authorities given powers to control bus services. HS2 will go ahead as will the upgrading of Northern rail routes.

Rebuild our public services

- Increase NHS spending by 4.3 per cent per annum.
- Free dental health check-ups on the NHS.
- End the process of privatisation in NHS services.
- A national care service with a lifetime cap of £100,000 on personal care costs.
- Introduce a levy on sugary drinks, ban fast food outlets near schools, and restrict junk food advertising.
- Scrap university tuition fees and bring back maintenance grants.
- Return academy and free schools to local authority control while abolishing OFSTED.
- Remove the tax loopholes that currently benefit independent schools.
- Thirty hours of free nursery care for 2–4 year olds.
- An additional 2,000 extra police officers recruited while the disproportionate impact of 'stop and search' policies on ethnic minority communities will be addressed.

Tackling poverty and inequality

- The main plank of Labour's social security reforms is to scrap universal credit.
- The child benefit cap and two-child limit will be removed. 'Dehumanising' work assessments will end.

- The retirement age will remain at 66 while universal pensioner benefits (free TV licenses, bus passes, the winter fuel allowance) will be protected.
- A windfall tax on oil and gas companies to raise £11 billion, increase corporation tax from 19 to 26 per cent, and raise income tax for those earning over £80,000 a year. No increase in VAT.
- Align capital gains and dividend tax with income tax. Reverse the inheritance tax cut introduced by the 2010 Coalition Government.
- An immediate 5 per cent pay rise for all public sector workers.
- If the UK votes to stay in the EU, free movement will continue. Net migration targets will be abolished.
- There will be a Constitutional Convention and Citizen's Assembly to address the distribution of power across the UK.
- The remaining hereditary peers will be removed from the House of Lords. A Labour Government will, 'work to abolish the House of Lords in favour of . . . an elected senate of the Nations and Regions'.
- Directly elected mayors will be made more accountable to local councillors and elected representatives.

The final say on Brexit

- Within three months, negotiate a new Brexit deal with the EU that ensures 'close alignment' with the single market and protects workers' rights and the environment.
- After six months, 'put that deal to a public vote alongside the option to remain'.

A new internationalism

- The 'bomb first, talk later' approach to national security will end.
- A Labour government would spend at least two per cent of GDP on defence, and spend 0.7 per cent of national income on international development.
- The recommendations of the Chilcott Report into the Iraq War will be implemented in full while a 'War Powers' Act' will prevent the Prime Minister from bypassing parliament.
- There will be an inquiry into the UK's historic involvement in torture and rendition.

The litany of 2019 manifesto commitments was undeniably ambitious. But was there an underpinning political idea decisively moving the party beyond the apparently insipid social democracy of the Blair/Brown era? Corbyn's agenda espoused support for the 'red-green egalitarianism' that became fashionable among German Social Democrats in the 1970s. Confronting the climate crisis and tackling pervasive economic inequalities were depicted as two sides of the same coin.

Beyond red-green egalitarianism, Labour's manifesto advocated less reliance on fiscal redistribution through the welfare state, instead seeking to restructure Britain's inegalitarian political economy. Throughout the twentieth century, Britain had been prone to low productivity, low growth and depressed real wages. Earnings in 2019 were no higher than eleven years previously, the worst performance since the Napoleonic wars.[158] For Corbyn's Labour, the answer was to rewire the economy through structural reform and a major programme of public investment. While interest rates remained at record lows and capital was abundant, the state had the unique opportunity to invest in the UK's productive (R&D, science, innovation, transport) and social (care services, health) potential. Labour's agenda would break the long-term stranglehold of the financial sector and the City of London.

Inequality would be tackled by democratising wealth, notably through inclusive ownership funds. Around the world, governments were launching sovereign wealth funds that captured the gains of productivity-enhancing technologies and intangible commodities, purchasing stakes directly in companies.[159] Labour's purpose was to identify policies, 'to deal with broad economic dislocation and insecurity caused by technological change, especially automation and Artificial Intelligence'.[160] Workers' rights would be protected through domestic legislation to strengthen sectoral wage bargaining and trade unions, outlawing 'the race to the bottom'. The aim was to 'hardwire' a more egalitarian economy.

The second key idea in the manifesto was forging a 'civic capitalism' in which economic success was judged not only by indicators of national income and growth but well-being and life satisfaction – emphasising the moral over the material economy.[161] Conventional macro-economic policies focused on promoting the UK's ability to gain from expanding global markets; as important, according to Labour, was the household economy, the green economy and the public service economy that enhanced the well-being of citizens and the capacity for long-term wealth creation. Local economic policies such as the 'Preston model' were intended to keep money circulating within communities rather than being extracted by global corporations. The proposal for a four-day working week underlined the commitment to tackling the long-hours culture that undermined human contentment in the developed economies. Corbyn's manifesto epitomised a socialist humanism that stressed the importance of satisfying and fair work.

The third major idea was to strengthen the Beveridge welfare state and public services by reversing the austerity decade. Universalism would be restored in social security (although much of the benefit freeze would not be reversed). The universal credit reforms were to be scrapped. The public sector privatisation programme originating in the 1980s' new public management reforms, particularly in the NHS, would be dismantled. Public services would be governed by enlightened local bureaucracies. Academies and free schools would be returned to local authority control. Over the parliament, public spending would increase to 45 per cent of GDP placing the UK in a similar position to Germany.

Moreover, Labour insisted the UK tax base could be strengthened following similar recommendations to the Mirrlees Commission which argued that taxes should be levied at a similar rate for capital gains, inheritance, land and dividends, alongside income.[162] The focus on universal basic services would provide 'the essentials of modern life' – food, shelter, education, healthcare, transport, broadband (delivered by bringing British Telecom back into public ownership) – to every citizen from the cradle to the grave. Traditional community amenities such as parks, libraries, youth centres and play spaces would be protected against the cold winds of austerity. Corbyn's programme thus channelled the spirit of Keynes:

> Assuredly we can afford this and much more. Anything we can actually do we can afford. Once done, it is there. Nothing can take it from us. We are immeasurably richer than our predecessors. It is not evident that some sophistry, some fallacy, governs our collective action if we are forced to be so much meaner than they in the embellishments of life?[163]

Yet critics inevitably questioned whether Labour's plans were achievable. Was the ideological mood in Britain in 2019 remotely sympathetic to Corbyn's agenda? In 1945, Labour's manifesto chimed with the intellectual and political climate framed by the spirit of collectivism. Faith in central state planning was at an all-time high. Government intervention played a decisive role in the Allied victory. In the wartime coalition years, Labour demonstrated it was able to govern, as ministers notably Hugh Dalton, Ernest Bevin and Herbert Morrison distinguished themselves in overseeing domestic policy. Seventy-five years later, the political circumstances in Britain were markedly different. Despite the financial crash of 2008, support for the significant extension of the powers of national government was less obvious. Nowhere in the advanced capitalist countries was there a persuasive prototype of the planned economy that might give legitimacy and credibility to Corbyn's programme. Socialism's purpose was in danger of being reduced to how much the state owned and spent, instead of focusing on how to transform the fabric of economic and social life – a concern elaborated by the ethical socialism of R.H. Tawney and William Morris.

Another issue concerned fiscal practicality. The IFS think-tank estimated that Labour's plans would increase day-to-day spending by £80 billion per annum and capital expenditure by £55 billion. On tax, the IFS claimed that Labour's plans would not raise the sums projected. Moreover, the UK would have the highest corporation tax in the G7. Combined with the windfall tax on oil and gas companies, there would be a serious risk of investment flight. The UK's weak productivity was the consequence of the low rate of business investment, which Labour's taxation plans might exacerbate. Britain already had the lowest rate of private sector investment among the industrialised countries, other than Greece. The burden of tax rises would be felt beyond the wealthy.

On public investment, sceptics questioned whether there were sufficient 'shovel ready' projects to drive the capital investment programme. Local authorities were expected to lead the construction of new homes for social rent. Yet most local councils lacked the capacity and expertise. The public sector had been 'hollowed out' over the previous thirty years. The commitment to ditch universal credit would impose huge administrative costs, requiring years of bureaucratic reform to be unwound. Elsewhere, Labour gave the impression of instigating an uncontrolled spending spree. Keeping the pension age at 66 had a price tag of £24 billion a year according to the IFS, with the burden falling on the working-age population. Expanding childcare to thirty hours free for all two- to four-year-olds would require 150,000 additional qualified staff, an ambitious commitment given Britain's imminent EU departure and the loss of migrant labour. Scrapping tuition fees and restoring maintenance grants would increase the government subsidy to higher education by £7 billion, assuming static student numbers at today's prices.[164] The list of expenditure and investment commitments was interminable. It appeared that British socialism no longer spoke the language of priorities.[165]

Another concern was whether Labour's agenda acknowledged the relationship between economic revitalisation and democratic accountability. Since the 1990s, power in the UK was 'cut up' across four nations.[166] Yet the party's 2019 prospectus invested overriding faith in central government's capability and legitimacy. Although there would be a constitutional convention under a Corbyn government, Labour made little effort to outline its vision of a federal polity where political power was redistributed across Great Britain. There was no concerted plan to pluralise the structures of political and economic control, embracing instruments such as citizen's juries in the policy-making process. Labour would 'make directly elected mayors more accountable to local councillors and elected representatives', yet there was no mention of accountability to citizens. The city-region agenda was barely mentioned in the manifesto.[167] There was remarkable confidence that majority-party rule at Westminster would solve Britain's long-standing economic and social problems. Neither did Labour's manifesto address national identity. The underlying tone of Corbynism was that nationalism and patriotism represented a form of false consciousness. 'The web of trust-based reciprocal obligations' and the sentiments associated with belonging – to a nation, a political union, a community – were apparently irrelevant to socialism.[168] The resentment of non-metropolitan English communities, the threat of Scottish independence and the potential instability of the UK in the wake of Brexit were largely ignored by Corbyn's new model Labour Party.

As a consequence, in 2019 Labour suffered its fourth consecutive defeat. Fifteen years had passed since it last won a national election. The party secured 32 per cent of the vote and 203 parliamentary seats, its worst result since 1935. Constituencies were lost in Northern England that had been in Labour hands since the end of the First World War. While Labour's programme was the most radical economically since 1983, its support declined perilously in working-class constituencies.[169] The Conservatives achieved the largest swing by an incumbent administration since 1945.[170] And they won their biggest parliamentary majority since 1987, the heyday of Thatcherism. It was astonishing for the opposition to have lost almost sixty seats to the governing party. Yet by the time of the election, it appeared as if Labour had saddled itself with the most unpopular leader of a major political party since opinion poll records began.

Electoral politics also played a critical role. Since 1979, there has been a long-term transformation in the structure of the Labour vote. Whereas the traditional heartlands were once found in the Lancashire, Yorkshire and Durham coalfields, the South Wales valleys and the West of Scotland, the party's 'new heartlands' were located in London, the big cities and the English university towns. Cities that once had significant Conservative representation in the mid-twentieth century – Liverpool, Manchester, Birmingham, Nottingham, Cardiff, Bristol, Newcastle, Leicester, Leeds – now had almost none as Tory middle-class home-owners fled the metropolis replaced by voters from BME backgrounds and the educated public sector middle-class.[171] In 2019, 33 per cent of middle-class voters supported Labour, compared to just 18 per cent in 1987.

Meanwhile, in the former Labour strongholds, cultural resistance to voting Conservative was breaking down. In the seat of North-West Durham, for example, the Tory vote rose from 6,463 in 2005 to 19,990 by 2019. The 1980s' battle-cry of resistance to Thatcherism in the face of pit closures and rapid deindustrialisation fell on deaf ears. Dramatic alterations in Britain's social structure were underway. In fact, many of the so-called Red Wall seats had more homeowners than the national average. There were fewer trade union members, particularly among those employed in the private sector; industrial workers and self-defined members of the working class were in sharp decline.[172] Labour's existential difficulty was that its core electorate focused on the public sector middle-class, ethnic minority voters and the younger precariat was now too small and concentrated in particular localities to win a parliamentary majority. The membership base of the party was culturally liberal and cosmopolitan.[173]

Yet structural forces did not in themselves determine the collapse of Labour's vote. The party's disastrous performance was the consequence of ideas, chiefly the ideological shift to the Left which meant Labour was less able to respond adroitly to the decomposition of traditional class identities in its former strongholds. After abandoning working-class voters in the Welsh, Scottish and Northern English industrial heartlands for middle-class millennials in Cambridge and Canterbury, it seemed there was to be no revival of Labour's forward march.

Conclusion

Jeremy Corbyn's ascent to the Labour leadership was among the most extraordinary events in post-war British politics, highlighting the Blair/Brown governments' enduring impact on the trajectory of the British Left. Yet Corbynism was bedevilled by paradoxes and inconsistencies that undermined its onward march to power. The Left had no convincing strategy to bring about transformational change in a society that remained suspicious of profound upheaval in the existing economic and social order. The Attlee governments came closest to upending dominant institutions in the extraordinary circumstances of winning a major world war. Yet such conditions hardly existed in British society in 2019, despite the impending threat of Brexit and the legacy of austerity. Meanwhile, the electoral alliance underpinning Corbynism remained deeply unstable. Since the early-twentieth century, the party struggled to unify its proletarian heartlands with the property-owning middle-class, forging a permanent majority in a First-Past-the-Post electoral system. Under Corbyn, Labour regressed to the belief that there was still a 'homogenous proletarian base' in Britain. Yet it reconfigured the party's programme to appeal directly to the public sector middle-class.

The Labour Party moved towards the perceived stronghold of electoral support, reshaping its dominant ideas. Yet across the industrialised world, social democratic parties were reeling after a decade of disastrous election results. Not only were they losing at the ballot-box. Social democracy appeared intellectually bereft. In France and Germany, socialist parties stood on the edge of oblivion. Their long-term weakness had less to do with inept leadership and the out of touch political class. The crisis was the result of alterations in capitalism, class and representative democracy that inflicted inestimable damage on left-of-centre parties. The apparent success of Corbynism in the general election of 2017 merely served to conceal the long-term problems afflicting the Left. Many in the party feared that inexorable decline was now the settled fate of British social democracy.

Notes

1 https://theguardian.com/commentisfree/2011/nov/05/ed-miliband-business-finance-politics. Accessed 14th August 2018.

2 P. Shelley, 'The Masque of Anarchy', cited in S. Hannah, *A Party With Socialists in It: A History of the Labour Left*, p. 239.

3 Interview, Rt. Hon. Charles Clarke, former Secretary of State for Education and Skills, November 2019.

4 C. Leys, *Market-Driven Politics*.

5 C. Hay, *Why People Hate Politics*; G. Stoker, *Why Politics Matters*; M. Flinders, *In Defence of Politics*.

6 P. Allen, *The Political Class: Why It Matters Who Our Politicians Are*; A. Hindmoor, *Twelve Days That Made Modern Britain*, Oxford: Oxford University Press, 2019.

7 M. Roberts, 'Revolt on the Left: Labour's UKIP Problem and How It Can Be Overcome', p. 33, London: The Fabian Society.

8 Peter Hyman, Confidential Memorandum to the Prime Minister, 'Half Way There: The Next Five Years in Blair's New Labour Project to Modernise Britain', 2001.

9 G. Evans & J. Tilley, *The New Politics of Class*, p. 193, Oxford: Oxford University Press, 2015.

10 O. Heath, 'Political Alienation, Social Alienation, and Working-Class Abstentionism in Britain, 1964–2010', *British Journal of Political Science*, Volume 48 (4), pp. 1053–1073, 2018.

11 I am grateful to Greg Cook, the Labour Party's former head of research and polling, for data and insights here.

12 D. Mattinson, *Talking to a Brick Wall*.
13 Cited in D. Coates, *Prolonged Labour*, p. 244.
14 P. Kilfoyle, *Left Behind: Lessons from Labour's Heartland*, London: Methuen Politico's, 2000.
15 Andrew Adonis, Confidential Memorandum to the Prime Minister, 'Party Funding', 5th June 2002.
16 M. Kenny & D. Gover, 'Answering the West Lothian Question? A Critical Assessment of English Votes for English Laws in the UK Parliament', *Parliamentary Affairs*, Volume 71 (4), pp. 760–782, 2017.
17 A. Heath, *Social Progress in Britain*, p. 116.
18 Cited in R. Weight, *Patriots: National Identity in Britain 1940–2000*, p. 721.
19 Cited in R. Weight, *Patriots: National Identity in Britain 1940–2000*, p. 697.
20 M. Kenny, I. McLean & A. Paun (eds.), *Governing England: English Identity and Institutions in a Changing UK*.
21 V. Bogdanor, 'Constitutional Reform in Britain: The Quiet Revolution'.
22 G. Hassan & E. Shaw, *The Strange Death of Labour Scotland*, Edinburgh: Edinburgh University Press, 2012.
23 A. Gamble, 'New Labour and Political Change'.
24 T. Bale, *The Conservative Party: From Thatcher to Cameron*, Cambridge: Polity Press, 2008.
25 P. Mandelson, *The Third Man*.
26 Interview, Rt. Hon. Charles Clarke, former Secretary of State for Education and Skills, November 2019. https://newstatesman.com/uk-politics/2009/02/clarke-interview-labour. Accessed 5th November 2019.
27 S. McAnulla, 'Heirs to Blair's Third Way? David Cameron's Triangulating Conservatism', *British Politics*, Volume 5 (3), pp. 234–254, 2010.
28 O. Letwin, *Hearts and Minds: The Battle for the Conservative Party from Thatcher to the Present*, London: Biteback, 2018.
29 O. Letwin, 'Sustainability and Society', *A Speech to the Adam Smith Institute*, July 2002.
30 A. Gamble, 'New Labour and Political Change'.
31 S. McAnulla, 'Heirs to Blair's Third Way? David Cameron's Triangulating Conservatism', *British Politics*, Volume 5 (3), pp. 234–254, 2010.
32 T. Blair, *A Journey*, p. 679.
33 T. Blair, *A Journey*, p. 685.
34 E. Shaw, *Losing Labour's Soul*, 2008.
35 J. Cronin, *New Labour's Pasts: The Labour Party and Its Discontents*.
36 A.H. Birch, *Representative and Responsible Government*, London: Allen & Unwin, 1964.
37 N. Allen & J. Bara, 'Marching to the Left? Programmatic Competition and the 2017 Party Manifestos', *The Political Quarterly*, Volume 90 (1), pp. 124–133, 2019.
38 C. Clarke, *Warring Fictions*, London: Rowman and Littlefield, 2019.
39 T. Bale, *Five Year Mission: The Labour Party Under Ed Miliband*, Oxford: Oxford University Press.
40 Interview with James MacIntyre, Ed Miliband's biographer, April 2019.
41 Interview with Lord Stewart Wood, former Special Adviser to Gordon Brown and Ed Miliband, February 2020.
42 T. Bale, *Five Year Mission*, p. 19.
43 https://theguardian.com/commentisfree/2011/nov/05/ed-miliband-business-finance-politics. Accessed 14th August 2018.
44 E. Goes, *The Labour Party Under Ed Miliband*, Manchester: Manchester University Press, 2015.
45 B. Pimlott, *Harold Wilson*.
46 https://ft.com/content/f8bacb60-d640-11e4-b3c7-00144feab7de. Accessed 28th July 2018.
47 J. Hacker, *The Institutional Foundations of Middle-Class Democracy*, London: Policy Network, 2011.
48 E. Goes, *The Labour Party Under Ed Miliband*.
49 J. Cronin, G. Ross & J. Schoch, *What's Left of the Left?*

50 B. Duffy et al., 'Divided Britain? Polarisation and fragmentation trends in the UK', London: The Policy Institute, King's College, 2019.
51 M. Wolf, 'Why the Balls Critique Is Correct', *The Financial Times*, 3rd September 2010.
52 https://theguardian.com/politics/2012/jan/13/ed-balls-labour-party-economic-redibility. Accessed 19th July 2018.
53 P. Stephens, 'I Told You So' Will Not Be Enough for Mr Miliband', *The Financial Times*, p. 13, 27th September 2011.
54 D. Lipsey, 'The Meritocracy Myth – What Ever Happened to the Old Dream of a Classless Society?', *The New Statesman*, 26th February 2015.
55 H. Thompson, 'Post-Crisis, Post-Devolution Politics and the Mansion Tax'.
56 https://theguardian.com/politics/2015/may/16/labour-great-crisis-ever. Accessed 14th June 2019.
57 https://ippr.org/files/publications/pdf/the-condition-of-britain_June2014.pdf. Accessed 14th January 2019.
58 https://theguardian.com/politics/2010/sep/26/ed-miliband-doncaster-north-reaction. Accessed 14th August 2018.
59 https://chathamhouse.org/sites/default/files/field/field_document/INTA91_5_11_Strong_0.pdf. Accessed 14th March 2019.
60 Interview, James MacIntyre, Ed Miliband's biographer, April 2019.
61 P. Cowley & D. Kavanagh, *The British General Election of 2010*, Basingstoke: Palgrave Macmillan, 2011.
62 M. Beckett, 'The Beckett Report: Why Labour Lost the 2015 Election', London: The Labour Party, 2016.
63 'Running Out of Road: Labour Is an Increasingly Unpopular Party with Lots of Popular Policies', *The Economist*, 24th May 2014.
64 'Miliband's Myopic Vision for the State', *The Financial Times*, p. 12, 2014.
65 Interview, James MacIntyre, Ed Miliband's biographer, April 2019.
66 'Running Out of Road: Labour Is an Increasingly Unpopular Party with Lots of Popular Policies', *The Economist*.
67 Interview, James MacIntyre, Ed Miliband's biographer, April 2019.
68 E. Goes, *The Labour Party Under Ed Miliband*.
69 Cited in T. Bale, *Five Year Mission*, p. 10.
70 P. Stephens, 'I Told You So' Will Not be Enough for Mr Miliband', *The Financial Times*, p. 13, 27th September 2011.
71 E. Shaw, 'The Wall Was Too High: The Four Predicaments of Mr Miliband', *French Journal of British Studies*, Volume 20 (3), 2015.
72 P. Seyd, *The Rise and Fall of the Labour Left*, p. 2.
73 R. McKibbin, 'The Anti-Candidate', *The London Review of Books*, Volume 37 (19), p. 26, 2015.
74 https://theguardian.com/politics/2016/may/29/jeremy-corbyn-hints-ed-miliband-labour-shadow-cabinet-job. Accessed 2nd May 2019.
75 Interview, James MacIntyre, Ed Miliband's biographer, April 2019.
76 R. Heffernan, *New Labour and Thatcherism: Political Change in Britain*, p. 129.
77 J. Gyford, *The Politics of Local Socialism*, p. 18, London: Allen & Unwin, 1985.
78 J. Corbyn, 'No to Maastricht', Labour Party Socialists Bulletin for Labour Party Conference 1992', CLPD/25 Archive, Bishopsgate Institute.
79 M. Veldman, *Fantasy, the Bomb and the Greening of Britain*, pp. 254–256.
80 T. Bale & J. Watts, 'Populism as an Intra-party Phenomenon: The British Labour Party under Jeremy Corbyn', *British Journal of Politics and International Relations*, Volume 21 (2), pp. 99–115, 2017.
81 https://theguardian.com/politics/2015/jun/17/jeremy-corbyn-labour-leadership-dont-do-personal. Accessed 4th July 2018.
82 Nevertheless, Corbyn only gained a place on the ballot paper because twenty-two Labour MPs who had no intention of actually voting for him in the leadership contest

were willing to sign his nomination papers, ensuring the Left had a stake in the debate about the party's future.

83 A. Gamble, 'The Economy'.
84 F. Faucher-King, 'New Forms of Political Participation: Changing Demands or Changing Opportunities to Participate in Parties?', *Comparative European Politics*, Volume 13 (4), pp. 405–429, 2015.
85 H. Thompson, 'Post-Crisis, Post-Devolution Politics and the Mansion Tax', p. 392.
86 Cited in 'Millennial Socialism', p. 9, *The Economist*, 16th February 2019.
87 J. Furlong, 'The Changing Electoral Geography of England and Wales: Varieties of "Left-Behindness"', p. 2.
88 J. Rutherford, 'Labour Must Choose Between Two Fundamentally Different Understandings of the Human Condition', *The New Statesman*, 26th September 2017.
89 T. Bale & J. Watts, 'Populism as an Intra-Party Phenomenon: The British Labour Party under Jeremy Corbyn'.
90 D. Swift, *A Left for Itself: Left Wing Hobbyists and Performative Radicalism*, p. 8, London: John Hunt Publishing, 2019.
91 S. Hannah, *A Party With Socialists In It: A History of the Labour Left*, p. 225.
92 A. Reid & H. Pelling, *A Short History of the Labour Party*, Basingstoke: Palgrave Macmillan, 2005.
93 S. Fielding, 'Hell, no! Labour's Campaign: The Correct Diagnosis but the Wrong Doctor', in A. Geddes & J. Tonge (eds.), *Britain Votes 2015*, Oxford: Oxford University Press/Hansard Society, 2015'.
94 The rise in Labour support in the 2017 election was chiefly due to voters in the thirty-five to fifty-four age category, who switched heavily towards the party. Ipsos Mori estimate that the turnout among eighteen- to twenty-four-year-olds grew from 43 to 54 per cent, but among twenty-five- to thirty-four-year-olds, it increased by only 1 per cent.
95 S. Howell, *Game-Changer: Eight Weeks that Transformed British Politics*, London: Accent Press, 2018.
96 N. Allen & J. Bara, 'Marching to the Left? Programmatic Competition and the 2017 Party Manifestos'.
97 The Labour Party Manifesto, *For the Many, Not the Few*, London: The Labour Party, 2015.
98 The Labour Party Manifesto, p. 25, *For the Many, Not the Few*.
99 C. Berry, 'Labour's Lost Tribe: Winning Back the Working-Class', *Policy Network*, September 2018.
100 D. Cowling, 'The 2017 Contest', *The Independent*, 18th November 2019.
101 Ipsos MORI: https://ipsos.com/sites/default/files/2017-06/how-britain-voted-in-the-2017-election_1.pdf. Accessed 12th March 2019.
102 Ipsos MORI: https://ipsos.com/sites/default/files/2017-06/how-britain-voted-in-the-2017-election_1.pdf. Accessed 12th March 2019.
103 J. Curtice, 'General Election 2017: A New Two Party Politics?', *Political Insight*, Volume 8 (2), pp. 4–8, 2017.
104 H. Clarke, D. Sanders, J. Stewart & P. Whiteley, *Affluence, Austerity and Electoral Change in Britain*, Cambridge: Cambridge University Press, 2015; G. Evans & K. Chzhen, 'Explaining Voters' Defection from Labour over the 2005–10 Electoral Cycle: Leadership, Economics and the Rising Importance of Immigration', *Political Studies*, Volume 61 (1), pp. 138–157, 2013.
105 L. Minkin, *The Blair Supremacy: A Study in the Politics of Labour's Party Management*.
106 S. Hannah, *A Party With Socialists In It: A History of the Labour Left*, p. 235.
107 https://ft.com/content/d0f0e212-6773-11e5-a57f-21b88f7d973f. Accessed 4th June 2018.
108 https://ft.com/content/d0f0e212-6773-11e5-a57f-21b88f7d973f. Accessed 4th June 2018.
109 A. Gamble, 'The Corbyn Insurgency', *British Politics Review*, Volume 13 (4), pp. 3–5, 2019.

110 P. Tatchell in J. Davis & R. McWilliam (eds.), *Labour and the Left in the 1980s*, p. xi, Manchester: Manchester University Press, 2018.
111 https://labour.org.uk/wp-content/uploads/2017/10/Alternative-Models-of-Ownership.pdf. Accessed 17th October 2018.
112 https://newstatesman.com/politics/economy/2018/09/who-real-john-mcdonnell. Accessed 15th October 2018.
113 The Labour Party Manifesto, *For the Many, Not the Few*, London: The Labour Party, 2017.
114 https://newstatesman.com/politics/economy/2018/09/who-real-john-mcdonnell. Accessed 15th October 2018.
115 J. Tomlinson, *Managing the Economy, Managing the People*; D. Edgerton, *The Rise and Fall of the British Nation: A Twentieth Century History*.
116 Cited in https://theguardian.com/politics/2015/sep/29/marxism-today-forgotten-visionaries-whose-ideas-could-save-labour. Accessed 16th December 2018.
117 G. Stedman-Jones, *Languages of Class*, p. 256.
118 J. Cronin, *New Labour's Pasts: The Labour Party and Its Discontents*.
119 F. Beckett & M. Seddon, *Jeremy Corbyn and the Strange Rebirth of Labour England*, p. 320, London: Biteback, 2018.
120 R. Miliband, *Parliamentary Socialism*; L. Panitch & C. Leys, *The End of Parliamentary Socialism*; D. Coates, 'Labour Governments: Old Constraints, New Parameters'.
121 P. Anderson, 'The Figures of Descent', *New Left Review*, Volume 161 (1), pp. 20–77, 1987; T. Nairn, *The Break-Up of Britain*, London: Verso, 1981; A. Gamble, *The Free Economy and the Strong State*.
122 G. Stedman Jones, *Languages of Class: Studies in English Working-Class History 1832–1982*, p. 238.
123 R. Miliband, 'Review: The Forward March of Labour Halted', p. 39, *Marxism Today*, April 1982; G. Foote, *Labour's Political Thought*, p. 25.
124 R. Miliband, *Parliamentary Socialism*.
125 P. Clarke, 'The Social Democratic Theory of the Class Struggle', in J. Winter (ed.), *The Working-Class in Modern British History: Essays in Honour of Henry Pelling*, pp. 3–18, 1983.
126 J. Gray, 'Labour's Populism for the Middle-Classes', *The New Statesman*, p. 6, 10th June 2017.
127 T. Picketty, 'Brahmin Left versus Merchant Right: Rising Inequality and the Changing Structure of Political Conflict', *World Inequality Lab*, March 2018.
128 See the report by Lord Skidelsky: https://progressiveeconomyforum.com/wp-content/uploads/2019/08/PEF_Skidelsky_How_to_achieve_shorter_working_hours.pdf. Accessed 14th September 2019.
129 Cited in D. Swift, *A Left for Itself*, p. 57.
130 L. Martell, 'New Labour and the Social Democratic Alternative', *British Politics Review*, Volume 13 (4), pp. 14–15, 2019.
131 The Labour Party Manifesto, 'For the Many, Not the Few', London: The Labour Party, 2017.
132 Interview with Dr Martin O'Neill, University of York, February 2020.
133 C. Berry, 'Labour's Lost Tribe: Winning Back the Working-Class', *Policy Network*, September 2018.
134 C. Berry & J. Guinan, *People Get Ready!: Preparing for a Corbyn Government*; R. Seymour, *Corbyn: The Strange Rebirth of Radical Politics*, London: Verso, 2016; A. Bastani, *Fully Automated Luxury Communism*, London: Verso Books, 2019.
135 G.D.H. Cole, *Self-Government in Industry*, London: G. Bell & Sons, 1917; G.D.H. Cole, *Guild Socialism Restated*, London: Leonard Parsons, 1920.
136 Cited in 'Life, Liberty and the Pursuit of Property', p. 19, *The Economist*, 16th February 2019.
137 The Labour Party, 'Alternative Models of Ownership', London: The Labour Party, 2017.

138 S. Hannah, *A Party With Socialists In It: A History of the Labour Left*, p. 231.

139 T. Shipman, *All Out War: The Full Story of How Brexit Sank Britain's Political Class*.

140 G. O'Hara, 'Don't be Fooled: Labour Are Still Divided', *British Politics Review*, Volume 13 (4), pp. 6–7, 2019.

141 H. Clarke, M. Goodwin & P. Whiteley, *Brexit: Why Britain Voted to Leave the European Union*, Cambridge: Cambridge University Press, 2017.

142 Cited in J. Blitz, 'Jeremy Corbyn is a Brexit Bystander', pp. 8–9, *The Financial Times*, 29th June 2017.

143 T. Benn, *Conflicts of Interest: Diaries: 1977–80*, p. 439, London: Arrow Books, 1991.

144 Cited in T. Shipman, *All Out War: The Full Story of How Brexit Sank Britain's Political Class*, p. 183, London: William Collins, 2016.

145 R. McKibbin, 'The Anti-Candidate', p. 26.

146 J. Lawrence, 'Labour – The Myths It Has Lived By', in P. Thane, N. Tiratsoo & D. Tanner (eds.), *Labour's First Century*, p. 349, Cambridge: Cambridge University Press, 2000; J. Nuttell & H. Schettle, *Making Social Democrats*.

147 G. Orwell, *The Road to Wigan Pier*, London: Penguin, 1937.

148 'The Economy in 2020', London: The Jeremy Corbyn Leadership Campaign, 2015.

149 C. Berry & J. Guinan, *People Get Ready!: Preparing for a Corbyn Government*.

150 http://oecdbetterlifeindex.org/countries/united-kingdom/. Accessed 24 March 2019. It is striking that Britain performs least well on measures relating to housing and work/life balance.

151 J. Lawrence, *Me, Me, Me: The Search for Community in Post-War England*.

152 C. Clarke, *Warring Fictions*; https://theguardian.com/commentisfree/2020/feb/08/happiness-wellbeing-political-agenda-tories-optimism-labour. Accessed 10th February 2020.

153 J. Lawrence, *Me, Me, Me: The Search for Community in Post-War England*, p. 235.

154 M. Wolf, 'Why Rigged Capitalism Is Damaging Liberal Democracy', *The Financial Times*, 19th September 2019.

155 The Labour Party Manifesto, 'It's Time for Real Change', pp. 2–3, London: The Labour Party, 2019.

156 L. Elliot, 'Radical, Populist and Worthy of Attlee', *The Guardian*, 22nd November, 2019.

157 The Labour Party Manifesto, 'It's Time for Real Change'; 'The Manifesto: Repairing the NHS – and a Green New Deal', pp. 6–7, *The Guardian*, 22nd November 2019.

158 M. Wolf, 'Why Rigged Capitalism Is Damaging Liberal Democracy', *The Financial Times*, 19th September 2019.

159 https://ft.com/content/04830250-eb45-11e9-a240-3b065ef5fc55. Accessed 20th October 2019.

160 E.O. Wright, *How to Be an Anti-Capitalist in the 21st Century*, p. 106, London: Verso, 2019.

161 C. Hay & T. Payne (eds.), *Civic Capitalism*, Cambridge: Polity Press, 2015; A. Gamble, *Open Left: The Future of Progressive Politics*, London: Rowman & Littlefield, 2018; also see the reports by the Centre for Research on Socio-Cultural Change (CRESC) regarding the foundational economy: https://cresc.ac.uk/research/remaking-capitalism/; J. Tomaney et al., 'Building Foundational Britain: From Paradigm Shift to New Political Practice', *Renewal*, Volume 27 (2), pp. 5–12, 2019.

162 P. Collier, *The Future of Capitalism: Facing the New Anxieties*, London: Allen Lane, 2018.

163 J.M. Keynes, BBC Lecture 1942 Cited in J. Butler, 'We Can Afford This', *London Review of Books*, 18th November 2019.

164 'Labour Manifesto: An Initial Reaction from IFS Researchers', London: Institute for Fiscal Studies, 21st November 2019.

165 'Doubling Down on a Big State: Assessing Labour's 2019 Manifesto', London: The Resolution Foundation, 22nd November, 2019.

166 V. Bogdanor, 'Social Democracy'.

167 The Labour Party Manifesto, 'It's Time for Real Change', p. 68.

168 P. Collier, *The Future of Capitalism: Facing the New Anxieties*, p. 214.

169 J. Furlong, 'The Changing Electoral Geography of England and Wales: Varieties of "left-behindness"', p. 10. The 2019 election result undermines the argument of Evans and Tilley (2015) that working-class voting declined in the 1990s because Labour adopted an ideologically moderate platform. As Furlong emphasises, the relative decline of working-class support for the Labour Party appears to have accelerated under Corbyn who adopted a more traditional Left-Wing programme. Labour now faces an unpropitious electoral landscape: to gain a parliamentary majority at the next election requires a uniform swing to the party of 9.6 per cent.

170 Polling conducted on the eve of the election by Ipsos MORI indicated that when asked which party looked after the interests of working people, 35 per cent of the skilled working class favoured the Conservatives against 32 per cent for Labour. Analysis by the Resolution Foundation think-tank found that Labour did best in seats in the youngest areas of the UK, reinforcing the growing importance of age in determining voting patterns.

171 For these points, I am grateful to Greg Cook, the Labour Party's former head of research and polling. Cook points out that after 2019, the Labour vote is more concentrated than ever before. In 1983, Labour won just one seat with more than 70 per cent of the vote. In 2019, there were 22 seats including Liverpool Walton (84.7 per cent), Birmingham Ladywood (79.2 per cent), Manchester Gorton (77.6 per cent), East Ham (76.3 per cent) and Bradford West (76.2 per cent).

172 Across Britain, the proportion of the electorate in blue-collar/skilled/semi-skilled/unskilled manual work (C2DE) declined from 62 per cent in 1987 to 43 per cent in 2019. Meanwhile, the share in white-collar/professional/managerial work (ABC1) increased from 38 per cent to 57 per cent. Trade union membership in the private sector fell from 21 per cent in 1995 to 13 per cent in 2018.

173 As elaborated by Professor Rob Ford: https://theguardian.com/politics/2019/nov/09/election-2019-big-squeeze-conservative-labour-rebels-switchers?utm_source=dlvr.it&utm_medium=twitter. Accessed 12th January 2020. The ESRC Party Members Project in January 2019 found that 72 per cent of Labour Party members supported a second referendum on Britain leaving the EU, while 88 per cent would have voted to remain.

10

CONCLUSION

The strange death of Labour England?

On August 2nd 2003 we will have been in power for longer than the Attlee government. A settled view will soon emerge – that we have used our huge majorities to the full or wasted them.

Peter Hyman[1]

The party has always been disposed to work through existing institutions, trusting in the rationality and acceptance of consensual values of those with whom it had to bargain. Integrationism was a meaningful strategy for politicians who accepted the fundamental values enmeshed within a culture shared with their opponents, seeing differences as negotiable and honouring the rules of the game. The strategy implied that Labour sought to improve the existing social order, not to change it.

David Howell[2]

Labour England . . . has got its party back.

Francis Beckett & Mark Seddon[3]

Introduction

The Labour Party's ideological transformation over the last forty years is little short of remarkable. The structure of Labour's political support has been irrevocably altered, reflected in its shifting doctrine and strategy. The preceding pages of the book examined the party's long years in opposition and power after 1979. The development of the party and New Labour's emergence are addressed in the context of debate about political ideas responding to major changes in the sociological landscape of post-war Britain. Drawing on a multitude of written and oral sources, this account examines how the party overcame successive defeats in 1979, 1983, 1987 and 1992 to mount an astonishing recovery, undertaking the long march back to power. The historical perspective traces New Labour's origins to the breakdown and failure of twentieth-century British Labourism alongside the consequent evolution of the Left's political thought.

As such, the historiographical analysis critically appraises orthodox conceptions of New Labour. The contention that Blair and Brown were merely concerned with winning political power by co-opting Thatcherite policies and accommodating Middle England swing voters is disputed. It is quite misleading to claim that New Labour's ideas were the product of tactical accommodation with neo-liberalism. The party's political agenda came from *within* the ecosystem of the British Left with fluid and wide-ranging intellectual antecedents. Moreover, there were striking political and intellectual continuities between New Labour and parties of the past.

The book then proceeded to survey New Labour's achievements in office. Instead of reaching a one-dimensional and unsophisticated binary verdict of success or failure, various yardsticks were used to assess the Blair and Brown administrations' impact.[4] How far did ministers fashion economic and social institutions that outlived them? To what extent was Labour successful in reshaping secular trends from economic growth to inequality? How far did the Blair governments alter the beliefs and values of citizens? And most fundamentally of all, did New Labour succeed in establishing a permanent progressive settlement, shifting the axis of British politics to the Left while moulding a new political landscape?

Forward march halted? Labourism's crisis and the birth of New Labour

For the Labour Party, the last forty years were a turbulent and unstable period. By 1979, the triumphant march of Labour since World War Two was abruptly halted. Labourism was in terminal decay, symbolised by the traumatic disintegration of the Wilson/Callaghan governments. Then Labour spent a decade embroiled in sectarian introspection and factional discord, exacerbating its doctrinal sterility. The party was shipwrecked, broken on the rocks of Thatcherism's dominance of British politics. Yet despite the unpropitious climate and mounting fatalism that the party might ever win office again, the crisis of Labourism stimulated a fertile and productive debate about the future of the Left. The inquiry stimulated by Labourism's demise concerned political ideas rather than electoral strategy and was shaped by several interwoven themes.

The first related to *socialist ideology*. After the demise of the post-war social democratic settlement, the party's doctrine was no longer straightforward. What were Labour's principal political ideas? Was it any longer a socialist or a social democratic party? Was Clause Four of Labour's constitution still relevant in the post-Thatcher age? Did social democracy have a viable future anywhere in the world? What precisely was the social democratic governing prospectus after the breakdown of Keynesian orthodoxy and corporate socialism? If Labour owed more to Methodism than to Marx, how could the party's ideological identity advance in a more secular society? Should Labour even continue to view itself as an ideological movement? Ought it instead to pursue pragmatism and technocracy? The Left was confronted by innumerable awkward questions. Even in the early 1990s, it had few persuasive answers.

The second dimension of the breakdown of Labourism focused on *structural change*, alongside the politics of sectional interests. The party no longer represented the proletarian underdog of the industrial era. So what or who was Labour now for? Could Labour any longer be considered a party of the working class? In any case, *who* were the working class? The growing heterogeneity of class undermined the party's identity, exacerbated by Labour's inability after the Second World War to alter the electoral dynamics of British politics. In the mid-1950s, it was acknowledged the party increasingly alienated millions of voters, particularly women, hostile to its prevailing proletarian culture. By the twenty-first century, Labour was manifestly the party of urban 'Waitrose liberals'. When asked what image characterised the party under Corbyn, a focus group of Essex residents replied the traditional pint of beer had been replaced by the wholegrain food, quinoa. The working-class pastimes of bingo and dog racing were supplanted by student protests and anti-austerity demonstrations in the Left's iconography alongside music festivals and Glastonbury.[5] The moral commitment Labour owed to the 'exploited poor' and the industrial working class appeared to have withered away.[6]

The third aspect of the crisis addressed Labour's status as a viable *contender for power* in British politics. The party lost four consecutive elections after 1979. Labour's voter base was perilously fluid. Historical loyalties were withering in the face of class dealignment. Like centre-left parties across the Western world, Labour was experiencing a protracted period of electoral marginalisation. Throughout the twentieth century, Labour politicians grew disappointed by the fickle British electorate that eschewed tribal loyalties. Many on the Labour Right now instinctively distrusted voters, believing 'the gentleman in Whitehall' and the municipal bureaucrats knew best. On the Labour Left, there was bewilderment and frustration that the working class were so easily impressed by affluence, preferring the hedonistic pleasures of the consumer society to perusing learned socialist newspapers.

The crisis of Labourism related to the party's *political organisation*. Labour's membership base was dramatically declining. Since 1945, Labour had lost an average of 11,000 members a year. Union membership fell throughout the 1980s in the face of rapid deindustrialisation and the privatisation of public utilities. The industrial working class, the critical agent of British Labourism since the late-nineteenth century, was dwindling. The Labour movement's political self-confidence was understandably evaporating, hastened by traumatic events, notably the defeat of the National Union of Mineworkers (NUM) in the 1984–85 strike.

The fifth aspect of the crisis involved the perceived *decline of institutions* affiliated with the Left. An obvious response to resolving Labour's strategic difficulties was aligning the party with popular post-war institutions, particularly the welfare state and the NHS that began to humanise British capitalism after 1945. However, Labour's difficulty was that the British welfare state had been modified drastically since the Second World War. Resource pressures and rising popular expectations led to the shift in policy, an acknowledgement that access to public provision would have to be managed prudently, even rationed through charges.[7] The welfare state was forged in an era of post-war collectivism but compelled to adapt to the age of incipient individualism. Should Labour governments defend the traditional welfare institutions or seek to reform them? It was far from clear how the party should respond.

The final feature of the crisis concerned Labour's comparative historical *failure as a governing party*. Labour administrations invariably inflated expectations. They were destined to disappoint their activists and natural supporters. The thread linking these administrations since 1918 was the determination to govern through the established institutions of the British state, alongside their abiding faith in mechanical over moral reform as the framework for public policy. As one scholar observed, Labour upheld 'a centralist tradition in which strong executive government was viewed to be the key instrument of statecraft for achieving and promoting greater social equality'.[8]

With the passage of time, the protracted inquiry into the failings of British Labourism forced the Left to confront unpalatable truths. In the early 1980s, Tony Blair observed the decay of social democratic parties across Europe, emphasising the importance of persuasive ideas while drawing inspiration from eclectic traditions. The sectarianism that long characterised the Labour movement was an obstacle to innovation and creativity in the battle of ideas. Gordon Brown's *Red Paper on Scotland* illuminated the systemic weakness of state socialism in an age where national identity was gaining purchase. Blair and Brown highlighted the discrediting of post-war Labourism attached to its obsolete view of how to govern the economy: ownership centred on the commanding heights of the state, giving primacy to the interests of producers, neglecting the democratisation of institutions, concerned with class at the expense of personal and collective identities centred on nationhood and the self.

The party's modernisation sprang from acknowledging the decline of Labourism alongside post-war corporatist social democracy. The wholesale revaluation of the Left's political position did not occur only in the UK but across the leading industrialised nations. Throughout the West, socialism and social democracy were decaying. Left parties in Europe and the United States were degenerating – their membership falling, the forces of organised labour in humiliating retreat. Even where socialist parties such as Mitterrand's *Parti Socialiste* reached the corridors of power, they were compelled to abandon their programmes in the hostile climate created by global capitalism.

An eclectic grouping of modernisers came to believe the ideas and identity around which the British Labour Party was constructed were anachronistic. They argued new alliances must be created, fashioning ideas, a rhetoric and political style to overcome the debilitating Left/Right divide in British politics.

It was unrealistic to reverse the long-term tide of industrial decline. Nostalgia was the enemy and Britain could become a young country again. The Left had to jettison the discourse and imagery of Labourism. In the past, the Labour Party was said to represent 'the archetypal mining/industrial town in the North'.[9] Blair's party embraced modernity: the global economy; international trade; technological innovation; the primacy of knowledge-based production; multicultural identities; and the post-industrial society. The Left should no longer base its appeal on a bygone era of heavy industrial organisation and muscular trade unionism. To its detractors, New Labour unsentimentally renounced the past. Yet it was primarily motivated by intellectual imperatives rather than electoral expediency, intended to tackle the glaring deficiencies in political thought and practice on the British Left.

New Labour in power: 1997–2010

Having triumphed at the ballot box in 1997, Labour's record in power appears ambiguous. To some commentators, the Blair/Brown governments were little short of disastrous. To others, they were the greatest peacetime administrations of the last century. Dismissing them as barren of social democratic achievement is misguided. Rather than being the heir of Thatcherism, the Labour administrations advanced the cause of constitutional innovation, liberal internationalism and social justice. Following the government's ignominious demise in the wake of the financial crisis, it was easy to forget that New Labour was once an intellectually vigorous project, determined to break free of post-war social democracy's self-evident limitations. Labour embraced cross-currents of ideas, making its political mission ideologically dynamic. Corporate socialism that dominated Labour's political thought from the 1930s to the 1980s was held to be redundant.

It is difficult to overstate the novelty of Blair and Brown's ideas, from giving national government an unprecedented role in tackling inequality in the early years of childhood, to promoting humanitarian justice through the Northern Ireland peace process and preventing ethnic cleansing in Kosovo. Under New Labour, the UK acquired a new constitution. The party assembled a plethora of ideas for rejuvenating the economy and politics fifty years after the end of the Second World War. There were continuities with the radical Liberal and Labour governments of 1906–12 and 1945–51. In retrospect, Labour's record will be judged as substantively social democratic. Its defenders argue the party's achievements in power were very considerable. Optimists insist Blair and Brown were successful in reversing Labour's recurrent tendency to defeat, establishing its reputation as an effective governing party. This strong electoral platform led to intellectual revitalisation. When Blair became leader, Labour lacked the governing agenda to supplant the intellectual marriage of Beveridge and Keynes that disintegrated in the 1970s. The leadership confronted the party's ideological sterility, attacking traditional shibboleths to fashion new programmes and ideas. Blair and Brown were progressive political reformers *par excellence*.

After four years in power, Blair wrote: 'It is time to end the confusion as to whether we are a Government that has mitigated the worst aspects of Thatcherism – but basically represent a compromise with it'. He acknowledged: 'The Thatcher agenda achieved certain things important to the country's future . . . but what was achieved was overshadowed by serious failures: economic instability; under-investment in public services; social division; and isolationism abroad'.[10] Blair's self-declared mission was to 'consign Thatcherism to its time, in the same way old-style socialism was'. New Labour's ambition remained 'to give the liberal and social democratic tradition a renewed purpose for today's world. That purpose is the liberation of human potential, economically and as citizens'.

In office, New Labour fulfilled its role 'as the party of economic competence; [as] reformers of public services, not just investors'. The Labour governments developed 'a robust policy stance on crime and welfare', outlining 'a coherent view of Britain's place in the world'.[11] The party fashioned social and welfare institutions permitting the advance towards a more equal society. There was the reversal of decades of rising child and pensioner poverty. The fundamental principles of the British welfare state were strengthened: there should be universal provision for all from cradle to grave with funding provided through partnership between the individual and the state. The party then altered the terms of trade in British politics, jettisoning the orthodoxies of Thatcherism. The academic Howard Glennerster concludes: 'Every other Labour government has begun with ambitious social goals then either retrenched or sometimes abandoned them. This is the first to have begun with modest ambitions and steadily enlarged them, building on economic success'.[12]

Like the Attlee governments, New Labour sought to advance 'equality and working-class interests, redistributing wealth and income where disparities grew too wide and using capitalism's wealth to help the poor'.[13] The Blair/Brown administrations may well be seen as the last triumph of social democracy, given their dedication to tackling unjustified disparities in life chances.[14] It will prove difficult to instil a more equal society in the future as growth stagnates while the political consensus for redistribution remains fragile. Environmental sustainability imposes resource limits, while technological change and automation heighten middle-class insecurity. The expansion of Britain's economy is undermined by economic power shifting eastwards. The years ahead may prove to be a cold climate for social democracy.

After the Second World War, voters clearly trusted Labour on social justice, notably its determination to build the NHS. The party was thwarted by its perceived weakness in managing the British economy. New Labour was determined to prove that a centre-left government would not only distribute wealth but generate it in the first place. The historian Anthony Seldon's view that 'almost everything Blair has done personally . . . has been an extension of Conservative policy between 1979 and 1997' is a mischaracterisation.[15] The charge that Labour made a Faustian pact with neo-liberalism is an over-simplification.[16] More than a decade since the party left office, more nuanced analytical perspectives are surely required.

New Labour in power: a critique

Given the party's success in establishing a more democratic and socially just Britain in the aftermath of Thatcherism, it is striking how quickly supporters became disillusioned in light of the perceived breach between promise and governing achievement. New Labour was accused of transforming the party but having no distinct project for the country. Blair had won power but was unable to win the contest of ideas converting electoral success into governing orthodoxy. New Labour had vivid media-friendly rhetoric but no big idea or 'bold, unifying theme' to transform the political agenda.[17] The government's mind-set was distrusting of those not under its direct control. Voters the party once represented felt increasingly betrayed. The Blair and Brown governments ameliorated economic disadvantage but were at risk of squandering the unique opportunity to transform British society and politics. They judged that the UK was a conservative country in Thatcherism's wake. Scarred by successive defeats, particular assumptions were held to be sacrosanct. The ideological scaffolding that reinforced New Labour's caution and conservatism was erected during the long years of opposition. The former cabinet secretary Sir Richard Wilson believed: 'It is not possible to understand the workings of the Blair government without understanding what happened before they came to power'.[18] New Labour lacked the intellectual self-confidence that characterised previous centre-left administrations.

Despite their overwhelming victories, the Blair/Brown governments (in which the author served as a special adviser in Number Ten) were unable to forge a political settlement leading, in the words of the cultural critic Raymond Williams, to 'the steady, irreversible expansion of democratic voice and power through building [and] reforming institutions of society, market and state'.[19] As a consequence, a pall of disappointment hangs over the New Labour era. Like the Wilson years, the party failed to create a recognisably social democratic polity and society. The Blair/Brown administrations' footprint in history is difficult to discern after ten years of Conservative-led austerity. There are legitimate criticisms that have been made of New Labour's governing performance.

Markets and social democracy

By the mid-1990s, Labour had become increasingly enthusiastic about the prospect of reconciling markets with social democracy. New Labour's policies were intended to correct historical failings in economic performance, particularly stubbornly weak productivity and the inadequate level of training in the UK. Yet there was a renewed confidence on the centre-left that flexibly regulated markets were more efficient. As Gordon Brown proclaimed, 'Instead of being suspicious of competition we should embrace it. . . . Instead of being suspicious of enterprise and entrepreneurs, we should celebrate an entrepreneurial culture'.[20] However, Labour's conception of financial markets in particular proved to be spectacularly misguided. The logic of the market failure hypothesis was that government action was justified only where markets broke down. This intellectual rationale proved counter-productive when it was applied to emblematic policies, notably social housing and childcare. Moreover, the party entered government without an alternative growth strategy. Economic policy had been formulated defensively in the 1990s. Global capitalism was viewed as an efficient machine that produced the goods for material redistribution rather than an inherently dysfunctional system prone to instability and disorder. Blair and Brown had no persuasive view of the moral economy, even though ethics are inseparable from the functioning of the economic system and its purpose of advancing the well-being of citizens.

Meanwhile, the language of partnership between firms and employees obscured fundamental power imbalances between workers and capital, exacerbated by the forces of technological disruption and the integration of the global labour market. Tellingly, Keynes warned in the 1920s that inept public policies dictated by financial markets fuelled ideological polarisation, promoting the growth of political populism. His prophecies proved to be prescient. Unquestionably, governing the economy was the weak spot in New Labour's armoury. The unwillingness to address how the UK's economic model might be reconfigured led to glaring contradictions.[21] On the one hand, Labour presided over the emergence of a 'work-intensive' economy driven by increasing pressures on the public sector workforce. Over 4 million employees in Britain did more than 48 hours of work a week, exceeding the limit proposed by the European Working Time Directive which Blair's government refused to implement. Yet in the same breath, ministers acknowledged the growing importance of work/life balance. Since being exposed to communitarian ideas in the 1970s and 1980s, Blair grew understandably concerned about the quality of family life in Britain. The host of issues from the fragmentation of families to rising levels of crime and anti-social behaviour were related to how parents raised their children. Yet parenting was inescapably influenced by working hours and the stress experienced by employees.[22] New Labour's commitment to labour market flexibility sat uneasily with its legitimate aspirations for stronger families and communities.

Moreover, the belief in the supremacy of markets made New Labour fearful of increasing the burden of personal and corporate taxation. Blair and Brown simply did not believe the evidence which indicated that voters were prepared to pay more tax to fund improvements in health and education. Although it instigated a one-off rise in national insurance in 2002, New Labour sought to resolve the long-standing dilemma by squeezing more from existing resources through the use of targets and quasi-markets. Yet the growth of performance measurement and bureaucratic oversight in public services had unintended consequences. The intrusive performance management of English schools and the NHS led to staff becoming demoralised, while managers and practitioners were distracted from focusing on their priority – the quality of treatment for patients and pupils in hospitals, GP surgeries and schools.

The Iraq legacy and UK foreign policy

It was evident that the Labour governments also made a catastrophic error in foreign and security policy: taking Britain to war in Iraq. As the playwright David Hare remarked, 'Blair was much the best Prime Minister of the last fifty years', but 'big figures make big mistakes and Blair has made the greatest mistake in British foreign policy since Suez'.[23] By joining the American mission for regime change in the Middle East, Blair squandered the government's political and moral authority. The legal case for war was tenuous without formal UN authorisation.

The absence of agreement in the international community encouraged the prime minister to justify military invasion on questionable grounds. That led to rapid loss of trust, not least among those whose loved ones were injured or killed in battle. Blair was compromised by allegations that British forces were under-resourced, lacking essential equipment in the theatre of war. Opposition to the Iraq war united the entire progressive intelligentsia in Britain. The road to war and Blair's conduct as prime minister were endlessly debated. The Chilcot inquiry cleared his administration of the egregious charge of duplicity and lying. Yet the war ultimately destroyed Labour's alignment with the progressive left of centre tradition in British politics. It left the UK without a viable security strategy in the world of escalating threats. Meanwhile, hundreds of thousands of innocent Iraqi lives were lost.

Drift and indecision over Europe

Another of New Labour's failings was drift and indecision on the issue of Europe. Blair sought to end post-war British ambivalence and was determined the UK should play a leading role in the EU. But when major decisions arose such as joining the single currency, caution overwhelmingly prevailed. Blair and Brown remained ambivalent about the European economic model's virtues. Under the influence of the treasury, Brown never failed to point out that Britain was outperforming the Eurozone, disparaging Europe's statism. The Labour governments opted out of key European competencies in labour market regulation and migration. Ministers did try to develop a positive vision of Britain's long-term role in Europe. Blair saw himself as the most pro-European British politician since Roy Jenkins, making eloquent speeches, sometimes in fluent French, arguing for closer engagement. In reality, the prime minister was reluctant to tackle the underlying causes of anti-Europeanism. After 1997, European integration as a salient issue declined in UK politics. Yet there was no coherent effort to make the positive case for EU membership. Blair was terrified of the Murdoch press. The prime minister's strategy to make EU membership acceptable to UK voters was that the EU should become more like America. The Anglophone critique that the continent was overwhelmed by 'Euro sclerosis' – rising unemployment, swollen welfare states, high taxes, and bloated bureaucracies – was endorsed by New Labour.[24] As proselytisers of Anglo-American economic policies, Blair and Brown were reluctant to accept that Britain should be integrated with European varieties of the social market economy. New Labour failed to demonstrate effective political and intellectual leadership over Europe.

The progressive alliance thwarted

The final shortcoming of New Labour was political: its refusal to countenance reform of the British constitution to promote the long-term realignment of UK party politics. Before 1997, Labour spoke inventively about forging the progressive alliance, confronting the historical forces of conservatism in British society. Blair insisted the Conservative Party's electoral dominance was a consequence of the painful breach between liberalism and social democracy in the early-twentieth century. New Labour would heal this divide, reconstituting the political landscape. Although there was a historic moment in 1997 to reconfigure the British polity wielding Labour's massive parliamentary majority, the opportunity was never seized. Of course, there were significant reforms of Britain's constitutional arrangements. Yet Labour ministers could not countenance dismantling the majoritarian Westminster system that bequeathed unique and unfettered powers to the executive.

New Labour and the role of ideas

Why were the Labour governments unable to realise expectations given the weakness of the opposition Conservative Party, and why did they fail to win the contest of ideas in British politics? An explanation emphasised throughout the book is that the Blair/Brown administrations were constrained by the influence of political ideas in the minds of leading politicians. The pivotal importance of ideas was captured in the once famous aphorism of Keynes:

> The ideas of economists and political philosophers . . . are more powerful than is commonly understood. Madmen in authority, who hear voices in the air, are distilling their frenzy from some academic scribbler from a few years back. I am sure that the power of vested interests is vastly exaggerated compared with the gradual encroachment of ideas.[25]

Similarly, the German political theorist Max Weber observed, 'Very frequently the "world images" that have been created by ideas have, like switchmen, determined the tracks along which action has been pushed'.[26]

Any judicious interpretation of the Labour Party's development since 1979 will appreciate the decisive role of ideas. Ideas have been hammered out among politicians and intellectuals searching for 'rhetorical tools to promote one grand idea against the other' – promoting rival visions of social democracy.[27] Since the beginning of the twentieth century, the party's vision and programme was shaped by disagreement over ideas – rival conceptions of capitalism, the economy, the state, sovereignty and the nation – which defined Labour's political trajectory from protest to power. Labour was 'the thinking man's party', the party of the Workers' Educational Association (WEA), trade union summer schools, the Fabian Society, learned newspapers and public intellectuals alongside scholars in the universities. We can make little sense of Labour's politics without understanding the elemental role of ideas.

As such, Left intellectual traditions, the institutions of British politics and the historical thought and practice of the British Labour movement have continued to shape New Labour since the 1990s.[28] Despite bitter ideological discord, there have been important continuities across time in the party's principal ideas. Like its predecessors, New Labour remained committed to the *centralised British state*. Throughout the twentieth century, the party was wedded to the concept of the *British model of capitalism*. These postulates have imposed innumerable constraints on Labour's policies and programmes, and what was considered viable for the party to achieve in office.

The British central state: moral and mechanical reform

Labour's view of government's role reflected the antagonism between moral and mechanical reform. This clash created persistent confusion in Labour's strategy and doctrine. As R.H. Tawney wrote: 'The Labour party is hesitant in action because divided in mind'.[29] Moral versus mechanical reform has been the fault line running through the twentieth-century British social democratic tradition.[30] *Mechanical reformers* are 'wirepullers' who believe that political change is achieved through the 'desiccated calculating machines' of public bureaucracy: technocratic institutions, an enlightened civil service, knowledge supplied by social science. *Moral reformers*, on the other hand, have faith in democratic deliberation and self-government. Moral reformers are sceptical of central government action, emphasising decentralisation to localities and communities. Social reform is achieved by nurturing citizens' capacities rather than imposing legislation on a recalcitrant society.

Some believe New Labour after 1997 embraced the moral reform ethic. Ministers acknowledged the limits of central authority. Constitutional modernisation, devolution, localism and community participation became more entrenched. Human rights and civil liberties were enshrined in the new constitutional settlement. The Left's prospects appeared bleak in the 1970s and early 1980s as the Labour Party was associated indelibly with bureaucratic management and centralisation. Fresh thinking emerged as the Left drew on diverse traditions, responding to the dilemmas of electoral defeat, permanent opposition and intellectual impotence.[31] The party espoused a commitment to reform, decentralisation and participatory governance. The ideas associated with moral reform acquired greater vitality on the Left.

In practice, however, it was mechanical reform that decisively shaped New Labour's approach to the governance of Britain. Social reform meant the pursuit of top-down policies, central oversight, bureaucratic edict, rampant managerialism and prescribed targets. Since the First World War, Labour believed it should govern through the existing machinery of Whitehall. It proved impossible to reconcile the vision of socialist democracy with the dominant Westminster tradition. The Labour Party's adherence to constitutional orthodoxy undermined the emergence of creative thinking about reforming Britain's governing institutions. Labour's conservatism stemmed from the nature of its political ideas, notably its normative attachment to liberal democracy through unitary political authority. Throughout the twentieth century, radicals on the Left in Britain 'exhibited a cautious conservatism in their dealings with the state, rarely confronting it and seeking incremental reform of its institutions'.[32]

As New Labour entered government in 1997, the mood among ministers was indefatigably pragmatic. Despite the rethinking initiated by modernisation, the party's mind-set was still that of establishment civil service Keynesianism. The Labour government introduced devolution to Wales, Scotland and Northern Ireland as a matter of political expediency rather than intellectual conviction. During the twentieth century, moral reform and participatory democracy never became entrenched within the Labour tradition. The ideas proved inimical to Labour's prevailing mind-set determined by mechanical reform and elitist Fabian collectivism. In the Labour Party, ideas of moral reform were alien antigens entering a host body that rejected them. From the 1920s, the Labour movement was captivated by the prospect of ruling through the prestigious institutions of Whitehall and Westminster. After all, government interventionism provided ready-made solutions to the terrible depression in the inter-war years, an antidote to the economics of laissez-faire. The state machinery then won the war in the 1940s. In the second half of the twentieth century, even Labour revisionists believed that national government was the critical agent of the egalitarian society. Despite revising the major tenets of post-war social democracy, New Labour barely questioned the Left's abiding faith in the Rolls-Royce Whitehall apparatus.

In demonstrating their fitness to govern, Blair and Brown were determined to show they could manage the Whitehall machinery as efficiently as their opponents. Labour's modernisation effort focused on reviving the national economy and polity, breathing life into the ancién regime of the British constitution. The party's remarkable admiration for the British state was epitomised by Peter Mandelson's remark: 'I've always had an abiding view that change is brought about by government actions and parliamentary legislation'.[33] Revealing too was Blair's declaration that the decision he regretted most as prime minister was enacting Freedom of Information legislation: 'There is really no description of stupidity, no matter how vivid, that is adequate. I quake at the imbecility of it'.[34] The deputy prime minister, John Prescott, reflected: 'We are a naturally centralised party; we believe in capturing power. . . . Most of our people were centralisers when we came in'.[35]

In a mirror-image of the 1960s, policy-making institutions and public bodies ill suited to the task of social democratic renovation were relied upon to enact New Labour's programme. The Westminster tradition was inadequate as the seedbed for a new politics entailing devolved decision-making, deliberative governance and civic participation. This conception of British governance failed to encourage constructive co-operation between producers, both capital and labour, nor did it provide the state with popular legitimacy to intervene in national economic and social life.[36] The Whitehall bureaucracy was ill equipped to put in place evidence-led reforms across the landscape of social policy. The reliance on purely technocratic expertise meant endemic problems were ignored. Until the 2008 crash, intervention in the industrial base was strongly discouraged. The First-Past-the-Post election system reinforced Labour's cautious safety-first instincts. The reform of the constitution lost momentum, bequeathing unresolved difficulties to future UK governments. An effusive embrace of the British state is the central thread that defined the Labour tradition since the party's creation at the dawn of the twentieth century. In the Blair/Brown era, statism bolstered New Labour's enduring conservatism and its abiding attachment to orthodoxy.

The British model of capitalism

Despite its radical rhetoric, the Labour Party was similarly wedded throughout its history to the *British model of capitalism*. The continuities in Labour's economic strategy have been woefully under-appreciated: 'For the historian, claims of novelty always arouse suspicion and certainly, in the economic field, New Labour appears less of a departure [from previous Labour governments] than its rhetoric suggests'.[37] In the course of the twentieth century, the image of the economy that dominated the political thought of the Labour Party undoubtedly evolved. In 1945, Labour understood the British economy to be predominantly *national*, industrial, large scale, amenable to macro-economic fine-tuning through discretionary state intervention. Fifty years later, the economy was perceived to be predominantly *international*, post industrial, focused on finance and services, manageable primarily through the monetary policy of the central bank and supply-side reform. Although New Labour was adamant that state interference in the economy should be circumscribed, even in the Attlee era ministers were reluctant to intervene in the private sector. While Labour's leadership embraced globalisation by 1997, rejecting protectionism and capital controls, they still believed in the virtues of the *British* economic model. Gordon Brown remained wary of EU integration and the European varieties of capitalism. There was little interest in redistributing power to regions outside London or to workers. Syndicalism had long since lost its purchase in socialist political thought.

Many on the Left wondered why the ideas of stakeholder capitalism advanced by John Kay and Will Hutton in the 1990s were never fully embraced. The ethos of stakeholding was premised on the Northern European view of the market economy in which institutions in the public and private sector work co-operatively to achieve growth and social cohesion. The stakeholder economy caught the intellectual tide at a moment when the ideology of Thatcherism was receding. It seemed to be a logical end point for Kinnock's *Policy Review* launched in the late 1980s. Yet Hutton's ideas were ultimately rejected by the leadership. Despite its social democratic ideology, the Labour Party continued to perceive British capitalism as an engine from which the surplus for material redistribution should be extracted. The party's leaders looked across the Atlantic for inspiration far more than the English Channel.[38] For decades Labour's political economy was framed by the existential choice between the state and the market, an intel-lectual debate that had long prevailed in the United States. Largely ignored was the vital question of European political economy: how to enable stakeholders across society to contribute to raising economic performance.[39] Blair and Brown celebrated the virtues of Anglo-American capitalism, which appeared to be out-competing other Western economies by the late 1990s. Their rhetoric reflected the zeal of the converted. New Labour was reluctant to overturn the established institutional structures of liberal capitalism. Since the 'prawn cocktail offensive' was launched by John Smith in the late 1980s, the leadership ceased to attack the City for under-investment. They displayed almost limitless admiration for the British entrepreneurial class. The evidence that large swathes of UK indus-try had been under-investing and poorly performing for decades was down-played.[40] By the mid-1990s, the British economy had returned to growth but still lagged behind the United States on productivity and the European continent on equity.[41] Executives continued to reward themselves pay rises incommensurate with company performance. The reluctance to pursue radical reform persisted under New Labour, despite the daunting legacy imposed by financial capitalism.

The Labour leadership convinced themselves that abandoning the dominant model of shareholder capitalism was likely to be politically protracted and elec-torally painful. Viewed in historical terms, what was surprising was not that the stakeholder economy was never seized on by the party. It was quite remark-able that the vision of stakeholder capitalism ever seriously influenced New Labour's thinking, given the party's intellectual defensiveness and conservativ-ism throughout the twentieth century, as it remained in thrall to economically orthodox precepts. Keynes was correct that in the British Labour Party, 'the difficulty lies, not in the new ideas, but in escaping from the old ones'.[42]

Political ideas and power

The question posed throughout the book is why ideas to overhaul British gov-ernment and capitalism have barely prospered, given Labour's pretensions to be a radical, progressive party of social democratic reform. The answer lies squarely in the nature of the Labour tradition. Despite the agonised debate of the 1980s and 1990s, residues of British Labourism have remained central to the party's identity and habits of mind.[43] Labourism treats ideas as illegitimate if they threaten to weaken the party's prospects of holding power or concede political advantage to its opponents.[44] This mind-set was reinforced by the uneasy, distrusting relationship between the party and the radical intelligentsia in Britain. For generations, thinkers on the Left were suspicious of the Labour Party's seemingly entrenched conservatism. As a consequence, the transmission of innovative thinking into the party was often negated.

Although acquiring the mandate in 1997 to pursue radical change, New Labour was conservative by temperament. As a result, no compelling governing prospectus emerged throughout its years in office. The party's defensiveness and passivity having won power from the discredited Major administration was extraordinary. The political landscape was still viewed as unalterable. Labour politicians failed to appreciate that the Conservative Party's historical victories were founded not on accommodation, but on transforming the political climate to further the chances of both electoral success and ideological ascendency.[45] During the 1980s, the Thatcher governments introduced successive initiatives – notably right to buy, share-ownership schemes, mortgage and pension tax relief, tax cuts and incentives to purchase health insurance that strengthened Conservative support among the 'aspirational' working class. Thatcherism began erratically and uncertainly after 1979, yet developed its governing project with a confidence and élan that ultimately eluded New Labour.

The Labour Party in the decades after 1945 never created comparable social democratic institutions, reallocating property rights while redistributing capital, wealth and assets on a scale matching the privatised industries, council house ownership and the saving schemes championed by Conservative governments. Only at rare moments did New Labour fuse together the politics of ideas with the politics of administrative power. The radicalism engendered by the debate about Labourism's decay in the aftermath of four humiliating defeats certainly revived discarded traditions of thought. Yet the new thinking was rarely advanced, as New Labour stood on the brink of power in 1997. The Blair/Brown era exhibited debilitating timidity that refused to confront the existing structure of power and privilege in Britain, an insuperable obstacle to rebuilding economic competitiveness and social cohesion through national modernisation.

In his second term, Blair spoke of formulating 'a very clearly articulated vision of the post-Thatcherite agenda'. Yet New Labour found it more congenial to accede to the prevailing framework of public policy.[46] As a Number Ten adviser reflected, Labour's task was to, 'break out of the straightjacket imposed by a 1980s view of the world – above all the collapse of centre-left alternatives, whether economic or social, to Thatcherism that infected domestic policy'.[47] It is hard to disagree with him that 'New Labour in government too often continued to seek public definition by contrasting itself with traditional Labour instincts, closing down progressive space ahead of government'.[48] In an echo of Wilson's tenure in the 1960s, ministers often acted like technocratic *problem solvers* instead of *crusaders* for progressive values. By 2001, Blair could list more than twenty-five priorities for his government, but he failed to maintain focus in vital areas, particularly education. On Number Ten's instructions, ministers in Whitehall departments were cautious, refusing to put, 'key achievements and policies – on poverty, work, low pay, the constitution, social exclusion – in our shop window'. New Labour appeared to be a 'clique' operating through technocratic managerialism rather than a bottom-up political movement. The Blair/Brown administrations never developed into a cultural force capable of winning major debates about Europe, public investment and migration. The government's agenda in public services was overwhelmingly focused on targets and bureaucratic edicts rather than improving the lives of citizens and communities.[49]

New Labour and after: the strange death of Labour England?

After 1979, Labour's politics were overwhelmingly shaped by the contested nature of political ideas. At stake was how a centre-left party should relate to a transformed economy and society, and how in due course its ideas could frame the party's agenda in government.

The battle of ideas in the Labour Party proved to be fraught. In the late 1990s, optimistic progressive intellectuals hoped that Labour would create a European-style social democracy in Britain combining the stakeholder economy, a reformed and pluralistic polity, constitutional modernisation, alongside integrated communities and a post-imperial global strategy. Yet there was never a cogent strategy in place to fundamentally alter the political landscape. The Blair and Brown governments failed to establish a durable legacy. Like social democratic parties across Europe, Labour neglected to identify a plausible ideological purpose in the aftermath of the great financial collapse. Under Miliband and Corbyn, the compromises of power struck by New Labour were torn up. What has replaced them?

In 2010, New Labour was defeated after an unprecedented thirteen years in office. It was easy to blame the fall from grace on the psychodrama and twists and turns of the Blair/Brown relationship together with their alleged adherence to 'neo-liberalism'. Ed Miliband quickly turned the page on New Labour's achievements. As a consequence, the Labour governments' record was never properly examined and debated. The question of why the Labour Party was unable to effect a fundamental transformation in the politics of Britain after 1997, despite the Conservative Party's evident vulnerability, was barely discussed. It was an uncomfortable truth that Labour and other progressive parties failed to create a new style of politics embracing co-operation, reform of the British constitution, decentralisation, participatory governance and the wide-ranging overhaul of the British state. The refusal to countenance working constructively with political forces that existed outside the narrow confines of the Labour Party was much lamented, but sprang from the deep impulses of British Labourism's sectarian traditions that even New Labour could not shed.

As a consequence, the Labour governments were unable to capitalise on Conservative disarray in creating a brand-new political dispensation for the UK. Fundamental errors over the role of private sector markets, the war in Iraq, Europe and electoral realignment severely undermined the policies of the Labour governments. Deeply entrenched assumptions about the nature of British capitalism and the role of the state compromised ministers' reforming direction and purpose. In failing to restore the vitality of the social democratic tradition in a post-devolution UK, the loss of office in 2010 permitted the aggressive Conservative counter-reaction. That was symbolised by the decision – predominantly of English voters – to leave the EU in 2016. In the aftermath of the referendum on Brexit and Scottish independence, Labour was a long way from forging the progressive century Blair and his allies visualised in the early 1990s. The reassertion of the Conservative Party's electoral dominance was accompanied by fiscal austerity, the determination to repeat the 1980s' free market experiment, the chaotic departure from the EU, and potentially the end of 'Great Britain' as it has been known since the Act of Union.

By 2015, Corbyn's Labour Party was recruiting thousands of new members and activists, but it was unable to address the defects of strategy and doctrine that now imperilled the party. The 2019 general election then brought defeat on a mortifying scale, the worst result since 1935. Having collapsed in Scotland, was Britain now witnessing the 'strange death' of Labour in its Northern English heartlands? The fundamental problem was that migration, the Scottish independence plebiscite and the EU referendum had redefined prevailing political identities. Over the last forty years, the 'dominant categories' of British identity – class, gender, ethnicity, nationality, sexuality – had undergone significant alteration.[50] Traditional identities were dissipating in the face of epoch-defining shifts in the economic and social structure. Politics appeared less concerned with *interests*, where pragmatic bargains could be struck between workers and capital as was the case after 1945, and increasingly focused on *identities*. Labour politicians appeared bewildered as they observed a febrile and dangerously polarised political climate, the party itself haunted by horrific allegations of anti-Semitism and institutional racism. The Left's political ideas had less purchase than ever in national life.

As was the case in the 1970s, the party had visibly degenerated. British politics became ever more volatile. The stench of decay overwhelming Labour was suffocating. To many observers, Labour was an atrophying party, disoriented and confused about its fundamental direction – 'a tired old political machine' with no persuasive purpose.[51] Yet in truth, the halting of the party's forward march did not begin with the political insurgency of Corbynism. Throughout the 2010s, Labour had remarkably little innovative thinking to contribute to the debate about economic and social policy in Britain. During the 1930s in the wake of the great depression, a party devastated by defeat hammered out a practical governing programme. Eighty years later, it seemed shorn of intellectual vitality and direction. Despite talk of an intellectual revolution on the Left, there was little evidence of substantive ideas to reconfigure the polity and society of the UK. Labour was unable to delineate a convincing formula that demonstrated governing competence while overhauling the British economy, as Hugh Dalton, Evan Durbin, Hugh Gaitskell and G.D.H. Cole had achieved in the 1930s and 1940s. Ever since the 2008 financial crisis, the party was plagued by the pervasive tension resurfacing throughout the party's history between managing liberal capitalism and creating an alternative system known as socialism. The post-2015 leadership resorted to statist remedies tested to destruction in the 1970s. For all the rhetoric of socialist transformation, the party's role was again to defend the terms of the post-1945 settlement which had long since passed into abeyance. A compelling strategy to reconstruct the economy and politics of Britain was to prove elusive. In the Corbyn era, it seemed that all Labour could do was celebrate a better yesterday.

The historian Kenneth Morgan highlighted Labour's propensity to become a 'nostalgic' party with an appeal to the past, 'the world of Tonypandy and the Jarrow March, of Clem and Nye and the legend of 1945'. Morgan wrote that in the absence of any compelling ideological prospectus, 'a movement committed to future change and a socialist transformation looks to the ages in heroic contemplation of past leaders and age-old triumphs, while the radicalism comes from . . . the enemy'.[52] In the absence of any cogent ideology or doctrine, Labour in 2019 was a less capable political force than at any point since the Second World War. The party was gripped by bitter internal conflict. Labour's status as the dominant centre-left force in British politics was more endangered than at any moment since the eclipse of the Liberals after 1918. Brexit and the threat of Scottish independence had unleashed successive political shocks that reinforced the party's electoral vulnerability. Labour's 'strange death' across much of former industrial England could not be discounted. If Scotland left the union in the foreseeable future, an event that informed commentators believed may 'only be a matter of time', the party's identity would have to be entirely re-imagined if it was to have any hope of remaining a credible contender for power.[53]

Of course, Labour was not alone in the scale of the existential crisis confronting it, as social democratic parties in Germany and France were perched on the precipice of electoral oblivion. Still, the British Labour Party had proved itself an unreliable political force throughout the last century. It was rarely in office, too often uninspiring when in government, and experienced decades of wearisome defeats. The image of the forward march as the inevitable triumph of Labourism was exposed as illusory. Marx wrote that history repeats itself 'first as tragedy, then as farce'. The Labour Party has again found itself caught in the long downward spiral of opposition as it was after 1979. The Left has been paralysed as its politics are increasingly shaped by identity rather than policy and ideas.[54] Even if the party survived the disorder wrought by the COVID-19 pandemic and Brexit to emerge as a viable governing force under Sir Keir Starmer's leadership, its advance from opposition to government appeared certain to be gruelling and laborious.

Notes

1 Confidential Memorandum to the Prime Minister, 'Strategy for the Next 6 Months', 19th December 2002.
2 D. Howell, *British Social Democracy*, p. 118.
3 F. Beckett & M. Seddon, *Jeremy Corbyn and the Strange Rebirth of Labour England*, p. 322, London: Biteback, 2018.
4 Of course, the scholarship of other authors has undoubtedly contributed towards the development of a more balanced verdict on New Labour, notably the work of Mark Bevir, John Callaghan, David Coates, Jim Cronin, Steven Fielding, Andrew Gamble, Eric Shaw, Florence Sutcliffe-Braithwaite and Andrew Thorpe.
5 https://theguardian.com/politics/2018/sep/10/swing-voters-say-labour-is-the-party-of-quinoa. Accessed 9th October 2018.
6 F. Williams, *Fifty Years March: The Rise of the Labour Party*.
7 T. Bale, *Of Sacred Cows and Common Sense*.
8 M. Evans, 'New Labour and the Rise of the New Constitutionalism', in M. Beech & S. Lee, *Ten Years of New Labour*, p. 66, Basingstoke: Palgrave Macmillan.
9 T. Blair, 'Lecture in Perth, Western Australia', August 1982.
10 Prime Minister, Confidential Note, 21st April 2001.
11 Prime Minister's Policy Unit, 'Second Phase New Labour: Pulling Together the Threads', June 2000.
12 H. Glennerster, 'Blair's Surprise Successes: Review of Toynbee and Walker, *Better or Worse? Has Labour Delivered?*', *The Guardian*, 12th March 2005, cited in P. Riddell, *The Unfulfilled Prime Minister*, p. 200.
13 S. Driver & L. Martell, *New Labour: Politics After Thatcherism*, p. 46.
14 A. Gamble, 'New Labour and Political Change'.
15 A. Seldon, *The Blair Effect II: The Blair Government 1997–2001*, p. 174, London: Little Brown.
16 Interview, Dan Corry, former Special Adviser, Department of Business, Innovation and Skills, February 2019.
17 J. Cronin, *New Labour's Pasts: The Labour Party and Its Discontents*, p. 397.
18 R. Wilson, 'Review of Peter Riddell's *Hug Them Close*', *The Times Literary Supplement*, p. 13, October 2003.
19 R. Williams, *The Long Revolution*.
20 Cited in N. Thompson, *Political Economy and the Labour Party*, p. 279.
21 D. Coates, *Prolonged Labour*.
22 M. Bunting, *Willing Slaves: How the Overwork Culture Is Ruling Our Lives*, London: Harper, 2005.
23 'David Hare: Interview with Rachel Sylvester', *The Daily Telegraph*, 15th November 2003.
24 J. Callaghan, 'Rise and Fall of the Alternative Economic Strategy', p. 127.
25 J.M. Keynes, *The General Theory of Employment, Interest and Money*, p. 383.
26 Cited in A. Finlayson, *Making Sense of New Labour*, p. 11.
27 D. Kennedy, *A World of Struggle: How Power, Law, and Expertise Shape Global Political Economy*, p. 25.
28 A. Finlayson, *Making Sense of New Labour*, p. 10.
29 R.H. Tawney, 'The Choice Before the Labour Party', p. 336.
30 P. Clarke, *Liberals and Social Democrats*.
31 M. Bevir, The Making of British Socialism.
32 B. Jones & M. Keating, *The Labour Party and the British State*, p. 10, Oxford: Oxford University Press, 1985.
33 B. Campbell, 'Interview with Peter Mandelson', *Marxism Today*, July 1989.
34 T. Blair, *A Journey*, p. 516.
35 Cited in J. Denham, 'Labour and England, 1997–2010', in M. Kenny, I. McLean & A. Paun (eds.), *Governing England: English Identity and Institutions in a Changing UK*.

36 D. Marquand, *The Unprincipled Society.*
37 Cited in G. O'Hara & H. Parr, 'Conclusions: Harold Wilson's 1964–70 Governments and the Heritage of "New" Labour', p. 486.
38 G. Brown, Confidential Memorandum, Strategy Document, March 2000.
39 Interview with Lord Stewart Wood, former Special Adviser to Gordon Brown and Ed Miliband, February 2020.
40 D. Coates, *Prolonged Labour: The Slow Birth of New Labour Britain.*
41 D. Coates, *Prolonged Labour: The Slow Birth of New Labour Britain.*
42 J.M. Keynes, *The General Theory of Employment, Interest and Money*, p. 383.
43 H. Drucker, *Doctrine and Ethos in the Labour Party.*
44 G. Foote, *The Labour Party's Political Thought*; D. Coates, 'Labour Governments: Old Constraints, New Parameters'.
45 J. Turner, 'A Land Fit for Tories to Live In'.
46 The Prime Minister, 'Personal Note', 21st April 2001.
47 Prime Minister's Policy Unit, 'Second Phase New Labour: Pulling Together the Threads', June 2000.
48 S. Katwala, 'Ideology in Politics: Reflections on Lady Thatcher's Legacy', p. 75.
49 P. Hyman, Confidential Memorandum to the Prime Minister, 'Note for Conference Speech: Renewing the Project', 20th September 2003.
50 C. Ellis, 'The Younger Generation: The Labour Party and the 1959 Youth Commission', *Journal of British Studies*, Volume 41 (3), pp. 199–231, 2002.
51 G. Hassan & E. Shaw, *The Strange Death of Labour Scotland*, Edinburgh: Edinburgh University Press, 2012.
52 K. Morgan, *Labour in Power*, p. 10.
53 https://independent.co.uk/voices/boris-johnson-brexit-indyref2-sturgeon-scotland-independence-union-a9039986.html. Accessed 17th September 2019.
54 K. Marx, *The Eighteenth Brumaire of Louis Bonaparte.*

BIBLIOGRAPHY

Archives

Public Records Office, Kew
CAB 128 Cabinet Conclusions
Churchill College, Cambridge Archives Centre
The Papers of Lord Kinnock, KNNK
Labour Party Archives, Manchester
Policy committees and study groups of the National Executive Committee Research
    Department
University College, London, Special Collection
Papers of Rt. Hon. Hugh Gaitskell, C192
The London School of Economics, LSE Library Archives and Special Collections
Rt. Hon. Anthony Crosland, GB 97 Crosland
Rt. Hon. Hugh Dalton, GB 97 Dalton
Fabian society tracts

Labour periodicals and journals

Chartist
Labour Left Briefing
Labour Weekly
Marxism Today
New Left Review
New Socialist
New Statesman and Society
Tribune

Government reports and white papers

'Excellence in Schools', London: HMG, September 1997.
'Higher Education in a Learning Society', London: HMG, January 1997.

'National Childcare Strategy', London: HMG, July 1998.
'The NHS Plan: a plan for investment, a plan for reform', London: HMG, July 2000.
'Schools Achieving Success', London: HMG, September 2001.
'The Future of Higher Education', London: HMG, January 2003.
'The Public Health White Paper: Choosing Health', London: HMG, November 2004.
'The Ten Year Strategy for Children', London: HMG, April 2004.
'Commissioning a Patient-led NHS', London: HMG, July 2005.
'Higher standards, better schools for all', London: HMG, October 2005.

Biographies, memoirs and diaries

Ashdown, P. *The Ashdown Diaries 1988–1997*, London: Penguin, 2001.
Benn, T. *Years of Hope: Diaries, Papers and Letters*, London: Hutchinson, 1994.
Bew, J. *Citizen Clem: A Biography of Attlee*, London: Riverun, 2016.
Blair, T. *A Journey*, London: Random House, 2010.
Brivati, B. *Hugh Gaitskell*, London: Politicos Publishing, 2006.
Brown, G. *My Life, Our Times*, London: Bodley Head, 2017.
Campbell, A. *From Crash to Defeat: Diaries – Volume 7, 2007–2010*, London: Biteback, 2018.
Dalton, H. *The Political Diary 1918–40*, London: Jonathan Cape, 1987.
Darling, A. *Back from the Brink: A Thousand Days at Number 11*, London: Biteback, 2011.
Donoughue, B. *Downing Street Diary*, London: Politicos, 2006.
Harris, J. *William Beveridge: A Biography*, Oxford: Oxford University Press, 1977.
Hattersley, R. *Who Goes Home? Scenes from a Political Life*, London: Little Brown, 1995.
Jones, E. *Neil Kinnock*, London: Robert Hale, 1989.
Marquand, D. *Ramsay MacDonald*, London: Jonathan Cape, 1977.
Morgan, K.O. *My Histories*, University of Wales Press, 2015.
Rentoul, J. *Tony Blair*, London: Little Brown, 1995.
Rodgers, W.T. *Hugh Gaitskell 1906–1963*, London: Thames & Hudson, 1964.
Routledge, P. *Gordon Brown: The Biography*, London: Simon & Schuster, 1998.
Shinwell, E. *I've Lived Through it All*, London: Gollancz, 1971.
Skidelsky, R. *John Maynard Keynes: Economist, Philosopher, Statesman*, London: Penguin, 2003.
Stuart, M. *John Smith: A Life*, London: Politico's Publishing, 2005.
Tatchell, P. *The Battle for Bermondsey*, London: Gay Men's Press, 1994.
Thomas-Symonds, N. *Nye: The Political Life of Aneurin Bevan*, London: IB Tauris, 2014.
Thorpe, R.A. *Super-Mac: The Life of Harold Macmillan*, London: Pimlico Press, 2011.
Williams, P. *Hugh Gaitskell: A Political Biography*, London: Jonathan Cape, 1979.
Young, H. *The Hugo Young Papers: A Journalist's Notes from the Heart of Politics*, London: Penguin, 2009.

Secondary sources

Abrams, P., Rose, R. & Hinden, R. *Must Labour Lose?* London: Harmondsworth, 1960.
Addison, P. *No Turning Back: The Peacetime Revolutions of Post-War Britain*, Oxford: Oxford University Press, 2010.
Addison, P. *The Road to 1945: British Politics and the Second World War*, London: Jonathan Cape, 1975.
Akala, *Natives: Race and Class in the Ruins of Empire*, London: Two Roads, 2019.

Allen, N. & Bara, J. 'Marching to the Left? Programmatic Competition and the 2017 Party Manifestos', *The Political Quarterly*, Volume 90 (1), pp. 124–133, 2019.

Allen, P. *The Political Class: Why it Matters Who Our Politicians Are*, Oxford: Oxford University Press, 2018.

Allender, P. 'What's New About New Labour', *Politics*, Volume 21 (1), pp. 56–62, 2000.

Andersen, R., Yang, M. & Heath, A.F. 'Class Politics and Political Context in Britain, 1964–1997: Have Voters Become More Individualized?', *European Sociological Review*, Volume 22 (2), pp. 215–228, 2006.

Anderson, P. 'Components of the National Culture', *New Left Review*, Volume 50 (1), 1968.

Anderson, P. *English Questions*, London: Verso, 1992.

Anderson, P. 'The Figures of Descent', *New Left Review*, Volume 161 (1), pp. 20–77, 1987.

Anderson, P. 'Introduction', in P. Anderson & P. Camiller (eds.), *Mapping the West European Left*, London: Verso, 1994.

Anderson, P. 'An Invertebrate Left', *The London Review of Books*, Volume 31 (5), 12th March 2009.

Anderson, P. 'The Left in the Fifties', *New Left Review*, Volume 29 (1), January–February 1965.

Anderson, P. 'Sweden: Study in Social Democracy', *New Left Review*, Volume I/9, May–June 1961.

Andersson, J. *The Library and the Workshop: Social Democracy and Capitalism in the Age of Knowledge*, Stanford: Stanford University Press, 2009.

Andrews, G. 'Shifting to the Bright – In Search of the Intellectual Left', in A. Coddington & M. Perryman (eds.), *The Moderniser's Dilemma: Radical Politics in the Age of Blair*, London: Lawrence & Wishart, 1998.

Annesley, C. & Gains, F. 'The Core Executive: Gender, Power and Change', *Political Studies*, Volume 58 (5), pp. 909–929, 2010.

Annesley, C., Gains, F. & Rummery, K. *Women and New Labour: Engendering Politics and Policy*, Bristol: Policy Press, 2007.

Arthur Lewis, W. 'Recent Controversies over Economic Policy in the British Labour Party', *World Politics*, Volume 10 (2), pp. 171–181, 1958.

Ayer, A.J. *Language, Truth and Logic*, London: Dover Publications, 1952.

Baer, K. *Reinventing Democrats: The Politics of Liberalism from Reagan to Liberalism*, Lawrence: University of Kansas Press, 2000.

Bale, T. *The Conservative Party: From Thatcher to Cameron*, Cambridge: Polity Press, 2008.

Bale, T. 'The Conservatives: Trounced, Transfixed – and Transformed?', in T. Casey (ed.), *The Blair Legacy: Politics, Policy, Governance and Foreign Affairs*, Basingstoke: Palgrave Macmillan, 2009.

Bale, T. 'Dynamics of a Non-Decision: The "Failure" to Devalue the Pound, 1964–67', *Contemporary British History*, Volume 10 (2), 1999.

Bale, T. *Five Year Mission: The Labour Party Under Ed Miliband*, Oxford: Oxford University Press, 2015.

Bale, T. *Sacred Cows and Common Sense: The Symbolic Statecraft and Political Culture of the British Labour Party*, London: Ashgate, 1999.

Bale, T. & Watts, J. 'Populism as an Intra-Party Phenomenon: The British Labour Party under Jeremy Corbyn', *British Journal of Politics and International Relations*, Volume 21 (2), pp. 99–115, 2017.

Barker, R. 'Political Ideas Since 1945, or How Long was the Twentieth Century?', *Contemporary British History*, Volume 10 (1), pp. 2–19, 1996.

Bartlett, B. 'Keynes and Keynesianism', *The New York Times*, 14th May 2013.

Bashevkin, B. 'From Tough Times to Better Times: Feminism, Public Policy, and New Labour Politics in Britain', *International Political Science Review*, Volume 21 (4), pp. 407–421, 2000.

Bastani, A. *Fully Automated Luxury Communism*, London: Verso Books, 2019.

Beckett, F. & Seddon, M. *Jeremy Corbyn and the Strange Rebirth of Labour England*, London: Biteback, 2018.

Beckett, M. 'The Beckett Report: Why Labour Lost the 2015 Election', London: The Labour Party, 2016.

Beech, M. *The Political Philosophy of New Labour*, London: IB Tauris, 2006.

Beer, S. 'Britain After Blair', *The Political Quarterly*, Volume 68 (4), 1997.

Beer, S. *British Politics in the Collectivist Age*, New York: Knopf, 1965.

Behrens, R. 'The Centre: Social Democracy and Liberalism', in L. Tivey & A. Wright (eds.), *Party Ideology in Britain*, Basingstoke: Macmillan, 1989.

Bell, D. 'Welcome to the Post-Industrial Society', *Physics Today*, Volume 29 (2), pp. 48–49, 1976.

Benn, T. *Conflicts of Interest: Diaries: 1977–80*, London: Arrow Books, 1991.

Benn, T. *The End of an Era: Diaries: 1980–90*, London: Hutchinson, 1992.

Bentham, J. 'The IPPR and Demos: Think-Tanks of the New Social Democracy', *The Political Quarterly*, Volume 77 (2), pp. 166–187, 2006.

Berman, S. *The Primacy of Politics: Social Democracy and the Making of Europe's Twentieth Century*, Cambridge: Cambridge University Press, 2006.

Berry, C. & Guinan, J. *People Get Ready!: Preparing for a Corbyn Government*, London: Or Books, 2019.

Bevan, G. & Hood, C. 'What's Measured Is What Matters: Targets and Gaming in the English Public Healthcare System', *Public Administration*, Volume 84 (3), pp. 517–538, 2006.

Beveridge, W. Cmd 6404, 'Social Insurance and the Allied Services', London: HMSO, 1942.

Bevir, M. *The Logic of the History of Ideas*, Cambridge: Cambridge University Press, 1999.

Bevir, M. *The Making of British Socialism*, Princeton: Princeton University Press, 2011.

Bevir, M. *New Labour: A Critique*, London: Routledge, 2005.

Bevir, M. & Rhodes, R.A.W. 'Interpretive Approaches to British Government and Politics', *British Politics*, Volume 1 (1), pp. 84–112, 2006.

Birch, A.H. *Responsible and Representative Government*, London: Allen & Unwin, 1964.

Black, A. & Brooke, S. 'The Labour Party, Women, and the Problem of Gender, 1951–1966', *Journal of British Studies*, Volume 36 (4), pp. 419–452, 1997.

Black, L. 'Coming to Terms with Affluence: Socialism and Social Change in 1950s Britain', Conference on 'Consensus or Coercion? The State, the People and Social Cohesion in Post-War Britain', London: UCL, 13th March 1999.

Black, L. *The Political Culture of the Left in Affluent Britain 1951–64*, Basingstoke: Palgrave Macmillan, 2002.

Black, L. *Redefining British Politics: Culture, Consumerism and Participation 1954–70*, Basingstoke, Palgrave Macmillan, 2010.

Black, L. 'What Kind of People Are You?' Labour, the People and the New Political History', in J. Callaghan, S. Fielding & S. Ludlum (eds.), *Interpreting the Labour Party*, Manchester: Manchester University Press, 2003.

Black, L., Pemberton, H. & Thane, P. *Britain in the 1970s*, Manchester: Manchester University Press, 2014.

Blair, T. 'Diary', *The London Review of Books*, Volume 9 (19), 29th October 1987.

Blair, T. 'Forging a New Agenda', *Marxism Today*, 1991.

Blair, T. 'The Left Should Not Weep if Saddam is Toppled', *The Guardian*, p. 18, 10th February 2003.

Blair, T. 'Let Us Face the Future: 1945 Anniversary Lecture', *The Fabian Society*, 1995.

Blair, T. *My Vision of a Young Country*, London: Fourth Estate, 1996.

Blair, T. 'Power for a Purpose', *Renewal*, Volume 3 (4), 1995.

Blair, T. 'Social-ism', Fabian Tract 565, London: The Fabian Society, 1995.

Blair, T. *The Third Way*, London: The Fabian Society, 1998.

Bloc, A. 'A New Era or More of the Same? Asylum Policy in the UK', *Journal of Refugee Studies*, Volume 13 (1), 2000.

Bloodworth, J. *The Decline of American Liberalism 1968–1992*, Lexington: University of Kentucky Press, 2015.

Bogdanor, V. 'Constitutional Reform in Britain: The Quiet Revolution', *Annual Review of Political Science*, Volume 8 (1), pp. 74, 2005.

Bogdanor, V. 'The General Election 1959', Gresham College Lecture, 11th November 2014.

Bogdanor, V. 'Labour in Opposition 1951–64', in V. Bogdanor & R. Skidelsky (eds.), *The Age of Affluence*, London: Penguin, 1970.

Bogdanor, V. 'Social Democracy', in A. Seldon (ed.), *Blair's Britain*, Cambridge: Cambridge University Press, 2007.

British Social Attitudes 31, London: National Centre for Social Research, 2014.

Brivati, B. *The End of Decline: Blair and Brown in Power*, London: Politicos, 2007.

Brivati, B. 'The New Labour Government's Place in History', in P. Diamond & M. Kenny *Reassessing New Labour: Market, State and Society Under Blair and Brown*, London: Wiley, 2011.

Brivati, B. & Bale, T. (eds.), *New Labour in Power*, London: Routledge, 1997.

Brivati, B. & Wincott, D. 'The Evolution of Social Democracy in Britain', *Contemporary Record*, Volume 7 (2), pp. 360–362, 1993.

Brooke, S. 'Gender and Working-Class Identity in Britain During the 1950s', *Journal of Social History*, Volume 34 (4), pp. 773, 2001.

Brooke, S. 'The Party and the 1945 Election', *Contemporary Record*, Volume 9 (1), 1995.

Brown, G. *Constitutional Change and the Future of Britain*, London: Charter 88 Trust, 1992.

Brown, G. 'Debate: Smaller Worlds', *Marxism Today*, November 1989.

Brown, G. (ed.), 'Introduction: The Socialist Challenge', in G. Brown (ed.), *The Red Paper on Scotland*, Edinburgh: EUSPB, 1975.

Brown, G. 'A Modern Agenda for Prosperity and Social Reform', London: Social Market Foundation, 3rd February 2003.

Brown, G. 'The Politics of Potential', in D. Miliband (ed.), *Reinventing the Left*, Cambridge: Polity Press, 1994.

Brown, G. *Where There Is Greed*, Edinburgh: Mainstream Press, 1989.

Brown, G. & Wright, T. *Values, Visions and Voices: An Anthology of Socialism*, Edinburgh: Mainstream Press, 1995.

Brown, W. 'Industrial Relations in Britain under New Labour, 1997–2010: A Post-Mortem', *Journal of Industrial Relations*, 2011.

Bulmer, S. 'New Labour, New European Policy?', *Parliamentary Affairs*, Volume 61 (4), pp. 597–620, 2008.

Bulpitt, J. 'The Discipline of the New Democracy: Mrs Thatcher's Domestic Statecraft', *Political Studies*, Volume 34 (1), pp. 19–39, 1986.

Bunting, M. *Willing Slaves: How the Overwork Culture Is Ruling Our Lives*, London: Harper, 2005.

Burnham, P. 'New Labour and the Politics of Depoliticization', *British Journal of Politics and International Relations*, Volume 3 (2), pp. 127–149, 2002.

Butler, D. & Kavanagh, D. *The 1987 General Election: Nuffield Election Study*, London: Macmillan, 1988.

Cairncross, A. *The British Economy Since 1945*, Oxford: Blackwells, 1992.

Callaghan, J. 'Rise and Fall of the Alternative Economic Strategy: From Internationalization of Capital to "Globalization"', *Contemporary British History*, Volume 14 (3), pp. 120–134, 2000.

Callaghan, J. 'Social Democracy and Globalisation: The Limits of Social Democracy in Historical Perspective', *British Journal of Politics and International Relations*, Volume 4 (3), pp. 421–450, 2009.

Callaghan, J., Fielding, S. & Ludlum, S. (eds.), *Interpreting the Labour Party*, Manchester: Manchester University Press, 2004.

Callinicos, A. 'Wither Marxism?', *Economic and Political Weekly*, Volume 31 (4), 1996.

Campbell, B. *The Iron Ladies*, London: Virago.

Campbell, J. *Roy Jenkins: A Well-Rounded Life*, London: Jonathan Cape, 2014.

Campsie, A. 'Socialism Will Never Be the Same Again: Reimagining British Left-Wing Ideas for the "New Times"', Volume 31 (2), pp. 166–188, 2017.

Clarke, C. *Warring Fictions*, London: Rowman and Littlefield, 2019.

Clarke, H., Goodwin, M. & Whiteley, P. *Brexit: Why Britain Voted to Leave the European Union*, Cambridge: Cambridge University Press, 2017.

Clarke, H., Sanders, D, Stewart, J. & Whiteley, P. *Affluence, Austerity and Electoral Change in Britain*, Cambridge: Cambridge University Press, 2015.

Clarke, P. *Keynes: The Twentieth Century's Most Influential Economist*, London: Bloomsbury, 2009.

Clarke, P. *Liberals and Social Democrats*, Cambridge: Cambridge University Press, 1978.

Clarke, P. 'The Progressive Movement in England', *Transactions of the Royal Historical Society*, Volume 24, 1974.

Clarke, P. *A Question of Leadership: From Gladstone to Thatcher*, London: Penguin, 1991.

Clift, B. *French Socialism in a Global Era: The Political Economy of the New Social Democracy in France*, London: Continuum, 2005.

Clift, B. & Tomlinson, J. 'Tale of a Death Exaggerated: How Keynesian Policies Survived the 1970s', *Contemporary British History*, Volume 21 (4), pp. 429–443, 2007.

Coates, D. 'Labour Governments: Old Constraints, New Parameters', *New Left Review*, Volume 1/219, September–October, 1996.

Coates, D. *Models of Capitalism*, Cambridge: Polity Press, 2000.

Coates, D. *Prolonged Labour: The Slow Birth of New Labour Britain*, Basingstoke: Palgrave Macmillan, 2005.

Cobham, D., Adam, C. & Mayhew, K. 'The Economic Record of the 1997–2010 Labour Government: An Assessment', *Oxford Review of Economic Policy*, Volume 29 (1), 2013.

Cole, G.D.H. *Guild Socialism Restated*, London: Leonard Parsons, 1920.

Cole, G.D.H. *Self-Government in Industry*, London: G. Bell & Sons, 1917.

Collier, P. *The Future of Capitalism: Facing the New Anxieties*, London: Allen Lane, 2018.

Collini, S. *Liberalism and Sociology: L.T. Hobhouse and Political Argument in England 1880–1914*, Cambridge: Cambridge University Press, 1979.

Consterdine, E. *Labour's Immigration Policy: The Making of the Migration State*, Basingstoke: Palgrave Macmillan, 2018.

Cook, R. 'A Hole in Labour's Heart', *Marxism Today*, August 1987.

Cooke, G. et al., 'The Condition of Britain: Strategies for Social Renewal', London: Institute for Public Policy Research, 2014.

Corry, D. 'Labour and the Economy 1997–2010: More than a Faustian Pact', in P. Diamond & M. Kenny (eds.), *Reassessing New Labour: State, Society and Economy Under Blair and Brown*, London: The Political Quarterly, 2011.

Corry, D. 'Living with Capitalism: Macro-Economic Policy Alternatives', *Renewal*, Volume 2 (1), pp. 41–60, 1994.

Corry, D., Valero, A. & Van Reenan, J. 'UK Economic Performance', London School of Economics Discussion Paper, March 2011.

Cottam, H. *Radical Help: How We Can Remake the Relationships between Us and Revolutionise the Welfare State*, London: Little Brown, 2018.

Coutts, K. & Gudgin, G. 'The Macroeconomic Impact of Liberal Economic Policies in the UK', Centre for Business Research, Judge Business School: University of Cambridge, April 2015.

Cowley, P. & Kavanagh, D. *The British General Election of 2010*, Basingstoke: Palgrave Macmillan, 2011.

Cronin, J. *Labour and Society in Britain 1917–89*, London: Harper Collins, 1984.

Cronin, J. *New Labour's Pasts: The Labour Party and Its Discontents*, Harlow: Pearson Education, 2004.

Cronin, J., Ross, G. & Schoch, J. (eds.), *What's Left of the Left*, Durham: Duke Press, 2010.

Crosland, A. 'Can Labour Win?' London: The Fabian Society, 1960.

Crosland, A. 'Social Democracy in Europe', Fabian Tract 438, London: Fabian Society, 1975.

Crosland, A. *The Conservative Enemy*, London: Jonathan Cape, 1962.

Crosland, A. 'The Future of the Left', *Encounter*, March 1960.

Crosland, A. *The Future of Socialism*, London: Jonathan Cape, 1956.

Crossman, R.H.S. *The Diaries of a Cabinet Minister Volume I*, London: Mandarin, 1991.

Crossman, R.H.S. 'The Lessons of 1945', in P. Anderson & R. Blackburn (eds.), *Towards Socialism*, p. 153, London: Verso, 1965.

Crossman, R.H.S. 'Socialism and the New Despotism', Fabian Tract 298, London: The Fabian Society, 1956.

Crotty, J. *Keynes Against Capitalism: His Economic Case for Liberal Socialism*, London: Routledge, 2019.

Crouch, C. *The Strange Non-Death of Neo-Liberalism*, Cambridge: Polity Press, 2011.

Curtice, J. 'A Defeat to Reckon With: On Scotland, Economic Competence, and the Complexity of Labour's Losses', *Juncture*, 17th June 2015.

Curtice, J. 'General Election 2017: A New Two Party Politics?', *Political Insight*, Volume 8 (2), pp. 4–8, 2017.

Curtice, J. 'The Uphill Battle for "Responsible Capitalism"', *Public Policy Research*, Volume 19 (2), pp. 129–130, 2012.

Curtice, J., Jowell, R. & Heath, A. *Labour's Last Chance: The 1992 Election and Beyond*, London: Dartmouth, 1992.

Daddow, O. 'New Labour: A Witness History', *Contemporary British History*, Volume 29 (1), 2014.

Dahrendorf, R. *Report on Wealth Creation and Social Cohesion in a Free Society*, 1996.

Dalton, H. *Practical Socialism for Britain*, London: George Routledge & Sons, 1935.

Davies, A., Freeman, J. & Pemberton, H. '"Everyman a Capitalist?" or "Free to Choose?" Exploring the Tensions within Thatcherite Individualism', *Historical Journal*, Volume 61 (2), pp. 477–501, 2018.

Davies, W. *The Limits of Neo-Liberalism*, London: Verso, 2014.

Davis, J.B. *The State of Interpretation of Keynes*, New York: Springer Science, 1994.

Dell, E. *A Strange Eventful History: Democratic Socialism in Britain*, London: Harper Collins, 2000.

Desai, R. *Intellectuals and Socialism*, London: Lawrence & Wishart, 1991.

Dionne, E.J. *They Only Look Dead: Why Progressives Will Dominate the Next Political Era*, New York: Simon & Schuster, 1996.

Dionne, E.J. *Why Americans Hate Politics*, New York: Simon & Schuster, 1996.

Donoughue, B. *Prime Minister: The Conduct of Policy under Harold Wilson & James Callaghan*, London: Jonathan Cape, 1987.

Dow, J.C.R. & Saville, I.D. *A Critique of Monetary Policy: Theory and British Experience*, Oxford: Oxford University Press, 1990.

Driver, S. & Martell, L. 'From Old Labour to New Labour: A Comment on Rubenstein', *Politics*, Volume 21 (1), 2001.

Driver, S. & Martell, L. *New Labour*, Cambridge: Polity Press, 2005.

Driver, S. & Martell, L. 'New Labour's Communitarianisms', *Critical Social Policy*, Volume 17 (52), pp. 26–42, 1997.

Drucker, H. *Doctrine and Ethos in the Labour Party*, London: Harper Collins, 1979.

Dunn, J. *Western Political Theory in the Face of the Future*, Cambridge: Cambridge University Press, 1993.

Durbin, E. *New Jerusalem: The Labour Party and the Economics of Democratic Socialism*, London: Routledge & Keegan Paul, 1985.

Durbin, E. *The Politics of Democratic Socialism*, London: Labour Book Service, 1940.

Dyson, S.B. 'What Difference Did He Make? Tony Blair and British Foreign Policy from 1997–2007', in T. Casey (ed.), *The Blair Legacy: Policy, Politics, Governance, Foreign Affairs*, Basingstoke: Palgrave Macmillan, 2009.

Easterlin, R. 'Paradox Lost?', *Review of Behavioural Economics*, Volume 4 (4), pp. 311–339, 2017.

Edgerton, D. *The Rise and Fall of the British Nation: A Twentieth Century History*, London: Allen Lane, 2018.

Eisenstadt, N. & Oppenheim, C. *Parents, Poverty and the State: 20 Years of Evolving Family Policy*, Bristol: Policy Press, 2019.

Elliot, L. & Atkinson, D. *Fantasy Island*, London: Constable, 2000.

Ellis, C. 'The Younger Generation: The Labour Party and the 1959 Youth Commission', *Journal of British Studies*, Volume 41 (3), pp. 199–231, 2002.

Esping-Anderson, G. 'Equality and Work in the Post-Industrial Life-Cycle', in D. Miliband (ed.), *Reinventing the Left*, Cambridge: Polity Press, 1994.

Esping-Anderson, G. *The Incomplete Revolution*, Cambridge: Polity Press, 2002.

Esping-Andersen, G. *The Three Worlds of Welfare Capitalism*, Cambridge: Polity Press, 1999.

Etzioni, A. 'The Road to the Good Society', *The New Statesman*, 15th May 2000.

Evans, G. & Chzhen, K. 'Explaining Voters' Defection from Labour over the 2005–10 Electoral Cycle: Leadership, Economics and the Rising Importance of Immigration', *Political Studies*, Volume 61 (1), pp. 138–157, 2013.

Evans, G. & Mellon, J. 'Working Class Votes and Conservative Losses: Solving the UKIP Puzzle', *Parliamentary Affairs*, pp. 1–16, Advanced Access, April 2015.

Evans, G. & Tilley, J. *The New Politics of Class*, Oxford: Oxford University Press, 2015.

Evans, M. 'New Labour and the Rise of the New Constitutionalism', in M. Beech & S. Lee (eds.), *Ten Years of New Labour*, pp. 60–82, Basingstoke: Palgrave Macmillan.

Evans, R.J. *Eric Hobsbawm: A Life in History*, London: Little Brown, 2019.

Farrell, P. et al., 'The Impact of Teaching Assistants on Improving Pupils' Academic Attainment in Mainstream Schools: A Review of the Literature', *Educational Review*, Volume 62 (4), pp. 435–460, 2010.

Faucher-King, F. 'New Forms of Political Participation: Changing Demands or Changing Opportunities to Participate in Parties?', *Comparative European Politics*, Volume 13 (4), pp. 405–429, 2015.

Faucher-King, F. 'The Party is Over: The Modernisation of the British Labour Party', in T. Casey (ed.), *The Blair Legacy: Politics, Policy, Governance and Foreign Affairs*, Basingstoke: Palgrave Macmillan, 2009.

Faucher-King, F. & Le Gales, P. *The New Labour Experiment*, Stanford: Stanford University Press, 2010.

Fielding, S. 'Activists against "Affluence": Labour Party Culture during the "Golden Age", circa 1950–70', *Journal of British Studies*, Volume 40, pp. 258, April 2001.

Fielding, S. 'Hell, no! Labour's Campaign: The Correct Diagnosis but the Wrong Doctor', in A. Geddes & J. Tonge (eds.), *Britain Votes 2015*, Oxford: Oxford University Press/Hansard Society, 2015.

Fielding, S. *The Labour Governments 1964–70: Labour and Cultural Change*, Manchester: Manchester University Press, 2003.

Fielding, S. *The Labour Party: Socialism and Society Since 1951*, Manchester: Manchester University Press, 1997.

Fielding, S. 'New Labour, "Sleaze" and Television Drama', *The British Journal of Politics and International Relations*, Volume 16 (2), pp. 326–348, 2014.

Figgis, J.N. *Studies of Political Thought from Gerson to Grotius*, Cambridge: Cambridge University Press, 1916.

The Financial Times, 'Labour Needs an Honest Debate about Tony Blair', 10th June 2015.

Finlayson, A. *Making Sense of New Labour*, London: Lawrence & Wishart, 2003.

Foley, M. *The British Presidency*, Manchester: Manchester University Press, 1998.

Foote, G. *The Labour Party's Political Thought*, Basingstoke: Macmillan, 1985.

Ford, R. & Goodwin, M. *Revolt on the Right: Explaining Support for the Radical Right in Britain*, London: Routledge, 2014.

Ford, R. & Goodwin, M. 'Understanding UKIP: Identity, Social Change and the Left Behind', *The Political Quarterly*, Volume 85 (3), 2014.

Fox, P. & Scott-Gordon, H. 'The Early Fabians: Economists and Reformers', *The Canadian Journal of Economics and Political Science*, Volume 17 (3), 1951.

Francis, M. 'Economics and Ethics: The Nature of Labour's Socialism 1945–51', *Twentieth Century British History*, Volume 6 (2), 1995.

Francis, M. 'The Labour Party: Modernisation and the Politics of Restraint', in B. Conekin, F. Mort & C. Waters (eds.), *Moments of Modernity: Reconstructing Britain 1945–64*, pp. 154–155, London: Verso, 1997.

Francis, M. *Ideas and Policies Under Labour 1945–1951: Building a New Britain*, Manchester: Manchester University Press, 1997.

Frazer, E. *The Problems of Communitarian Politics: Unity and Conflict*, London: Routledge, 1999.

Freeden, M. 'The Ideology of New Labour', *The Political Quarterly*, Volume 70 (1), pp. 42–51, 1999.

Freeden, M. *The New Liberalism: An Ideology of Social Reform*, Oxford: Clarendon Press, 1978.

From, A. *The New Democrats and the Return to Power*, Basingstoke: Palgrave Macmillan, 2013.

Fukuyama, F. *Trust: The Social Virtues and the Creation of Prosperity*, New York: The Free Press, 1996.

Furlong, J. 'The Changing Electoral Geography of England and Wales: Varieties of "Left-Behindness"', *Political Geography*, Volume 75, pp. 1–12, 2019.

Galbraith, J.K. *The Culture of Contentment*, Princeton: Princeton University Press, 2017.

Galston, B. & Kamarck, E. *The Politics of Evasion*, Washington, DC: Progressive Policy Institute, 1989.

Gamble, A. 'After the Watershed: The Conservative Eclipse', in A. Codington & M. Perryman (eds.), *The Moderniser's Dilemma*, pp. 27–28, London: Lawrence & Wishart, 1998.

Gamble, A. *Between Europe and America: The Future of British Politics*, Basingstoke: Palgrave Macmillan, 2003.

Gamble, A. *Britain in Decline*, Basingstoke: Macmillan, 1983.

Gamble, A. *The Conservative Nation*, London: Routledge, 1975.

Gamble, A. 'The Corbyn Insurgency', *British Politics Review*, Volume 13 (4), pp. 3–5, 2019.

Gamble, A. *Crisis Without End? The Unravelling of Western Prosperity*, Basingstoke: Palgrave Macmillan, 2014.

Gamble, A. 'The Economy', in A. Geddes & J. Tonge (eds.), *Britain Votes 2015*, Oxford: Oxford University Press/Hansard Society, 2015.

Gamble, A. *The Free Economy and the Strong State*, Basingstoke: Palgrave Macmillan, 1994.

Gamble, A. 'The Great Divide', *Marxism Today*, 1981.

Gamble, A. 'Neo-Liberalism', *Capital & Class*, Volume 25, 2001.

Gamble, A. 'New Labour and Political Change', *Parliamentary Affairs*, Volume 63 (4), pp. 639–651, 2010.

Gamble, A. *Open Left: The Future of Progressive Politics*, London: Rowman & Littlefield, 2018.

Gamble, A. 'The Progressive Dilemma Revisited', *The Political Quarterly*, Volume 88 (1), pp. 3–21, 2016.

Gamble, A. 'Progressive Politics: A New Beginning', *Policy Network*, 23rd September 2015.

Gamble, A. *The Spectre at the Feast*, Basingstoke: Palgrave Macmillan, 2009.

Gamble, A. & Kelly, G. 'The British Labour Party and Monetary Union', *Western European Politics*, Volume 23 (1), pp. 1–25, 2000.

Gamble, A. & Kelly, G. 'Stakeholder Capitalism and One Nation Socialism', *Renewal*, Volume 4 (1), pp. 23–32, 1995.

Gamble, A. & Prabhakar, R. 'The New Assets Agenda', in G. Dench (ed.), *The Rise and Rise of Meritocracy*, Oxford: Political Quarterly/Blackwell Publishing, 2006.

Gamble, A. & Wright, A. 'The New Social Democracy', *Political Quarterly*, London, 2004.

Gerwitz, S., Ball, S.J. & Bowe, R. 'Parents, Privilege and the Education Market-Place', *Research Papers in Education*, Volume 9 (1), pp. 3–29, 1994.

Giddens, A. *The Third Way and Its Critics*, Cambridge: Polity, 2000.

Giddens, A. *The Third Way: The Renewal of Social Democracy*, Cambridge: Polity Press, 1998.

Giddens, A. *The Transformation of Intimacy*, Cambridge: Polity Press, 1992.

Glennerster, H. *British Social Policy: 1945 to the Present*, Oxford: Wiley-Blackwell.

Glyn, A. *The British Economic Disaster*, London: Pluto, 1980.

Goldman, L. *The Life of R.H. Tawney: Socialism and History*, London: Bloomsbury, 2013.

Goldthorpe, J., Lockwood, D., Bechhofer, F. & Platt, J. *The Affluent Worker in the Class Structure*, Cambridge: Cambridge University Press, 1969.

Goodhart, D. *The Road to Somewhere: The Populist Revolt and the Future of Politics*, London: C Hurst & Co, 2017.

Goodwin, M. & Eatwell, R. *National Populism: The Revolt Against Liberal Democracy*, London: Penguin, 2018.

Goos, M. & Manning, A. 'Lousy and Lovely Jobs: The Rising Polarization of Work in Britain', *The Review of Economics and Statistics*, Volume 89 (1), pp. 118–132, 2007.

Gorard, S. & Fitz, J. 'Markets and Stratification: A View from England and Wales', *Educational Policy*, Volume 14 (3), pp. 405–424, 1998.

Gorz, A. *Farewell to the Working-Class: An Essay on Post-Industrial Socialism*, London: Pluto, 1982.

Gould, B. *A Future for Socialism*, London: Jonathan Cape, 1989.

Gould, B. *Goodbye to All That*, Basingstoke: Macmillan, 1995.

Gould, P. *The Unfinished Revolution: How the Modernisers Saved the Labour Party*, London: Abacus, 2011.

Gramsci, A. *Prison Notebooks*, London: Lawrence & Wishart, 1971.

Grasso, M. et al., 'Thatcher's Children, Blair's Babies, Political Socialization and Trickle-down Value Change: An Age, Period and Cohort Analysis', *British Journal of Political Science*, Volume 49 (1), pp. 17–36, 2017.

Gray, J. *Beyond the New Right: Markets, Government and the Common Environment*, London: Routledge, 1994.

Greenaway, J. 'How Policy Framing is as Important as the Policy Content: The Story of the English and Welsh Licensing Act 2003', *British Politics*, Volume 6 (4), pp. 408–422, 2011.

Greenberg, S. *Dispatches from the War Room: In the Trenches with Five Extraordinary Leaders*, New York: Thomas Dunne Books, 2009.

Greenleaf, W.H. *The British Political Tradition: The Rise of Collectivism Volume I*, London: Routledge, 1983.

Griffiths, S. *Engaging Enemies: Hayek and the Left*, London: Rowman & Littlefield, 2014.

Grimes, A. 'Introduction', in L.T. Hobhouse (ed.), *Liberalism*, Oxford/New York: Oxford University Press, 1964.

Guy-Peters, B. *Institutional Theory in Political Science: The New Institutionalism*, Cheltenham: Edward Elgar, 2019.

Gyford, J. & Haseler, S. 'The Labour Party: Beyond Revisionism', Fabian Tract 302, London: The Fabian Society, 1971.

Gyford, J. *The Politics of Local Socialism*, London: Allen & Unwin, 1985.

Haddon, C. 'The Commission on Social Justice 1992–92', London: Institute of Government, July 2014.

Hadfield, P. 'Party Invitations: New Labour and the (De)regulation of Pleasure', *Criminal Justice Matters*, Volume 67 (1), pp. 18–47, 2007.

Hajer, M. 'Policy Without Polity? Policy Analysis and the Institutional Void', *Policy Sciences*, Volume 36 (1), pp. 175–195, 2003.

Hale, S. 'The Communitarian Philosophy of New Labour', in S. Hale, W. Leggett & L. Martell (eds.), *The Third Way and Beyond: Criticisms, Alternatives, Futures*, Manchester: Manchester University Press, 1998.

Hall, P. 'Policy Paradigms, Social Learning and the State: The Case of Economic Policy-Making in Britain', *Comparative Politics*, Volume 25 (3), pp. 275–298, 1993.

Hall, S. *The Hard Road to Renewal*, London: Verso, 1988.

Hall, S. 'The Neo-Liberal Revolution', *Cultural Studies*, Volume 25 (6), pp. 705–726, 2011.

Hall, S. *Selected Political Writings*, Durham: Duke University Press, 2017.

Hannah, S. *A Party With Socialists In It: A History of the Labour Left*, London: Pluto Press, 2018.

Harman, H. *A Woman's Work*, London: Allen Lane, 2017.

Harris, J. 'Labour's Political and Social Thought', in P. Thane, N. Tiratsoo & D. Tanner (eds.), *Labour's First Century*, Cambridge: Cambridge University Press, 2000.

Harris, J. 'Social Policy, Saving, and Sound Money', in P. Clarke & C. Trebilcock (eds.), *Understanding Decline: Perceptions and Realities of British Economic Performance*, Cambridge: Cambridge University Press, 1997.

Harris, K. *Attlee*, London: Wiedenfeld & Nicholson, 1982.

Harrison, B. *Seeking a Role: The United Kingdom 1951–70*, Oxford: Oxford University Press, 2009.

Harvey, D. *A Brief History of Neo-Liberalism*, Oxford: Oxford University Press, 2005.

Hassan, G. & Shaw, E. *The Strange Death of Labour Scotland*, Edinburgh: Edinburgh University Press, 2012.

Hattersley, R. *Choose Freedom*, London: Michael Joseph, 1987.

Hattersley, R. *Who Goes Home? Scenes from a Political Life*, London: Little Brown, 1995.

Hay, C. 'Labour's Thatcherite Revisionism: Playing the "Politics of Catch-up"', *Political Studies*, Volume XLII, pp. 700–707, 1994.

Hay, C. & Payne, T. (eds.), *Civic Capitalism*, Cambridge: Polity Press, 2015.

Hay, C. & Watson, M. 'Labour's Economic Policy: Studiously Courting Competence', in G. Taylor (ed.), *The Impact of New Labour*, p. 116, Basingstoke: Macmillan, 1999.

Hayter, D. *Fightback! Labour's Traditional Right in the 1970s and 1980s*, Manchester: Manchester University Press, 2005.

Healey, D. 'Power Politics and the Labour Party', in R.H.S. Crossman (ed.), *New Fabian Essays*, London: Turnstile, 1952.

Healey, D. *The Time of My Life*, London: Methuen, 2015.

Heath, A. *The Rise of New Labour: Party Policies and Voter Choices*, Oxford: Oxford University Press, 2001.

Heath, A. *Social Progress in Britain*, Oxford: Oxford University Press, 2018.

Heath, O. 'Political Alienation, Social Alienation, and Working-Class Abstentionism in Britain, 1964–2010', *British Journal of Political Science*, Volume 48 (4), pp. 1053–1073, 2018.

Heffernan, R. *New Labour and Thatcherism: Political Change in Britain*, Basingstoke: Palgrave Macmillan, 1999.

Heffernan, R. & Marqusee, M. *Defeat from the Jaws of Victory*, London: Verso, 1993.

Hennessy, P. *Establishment and Meritocracy*, London: Haus Publishing, 2015.

Hennessy, P. *Having it So Good: Britain in the Fifties*, London: Penguin, 2007.

Hepple, B. 'The New Single Equality Act in Britain', *The Equal Rights Review*, Volume 5, pp. 11–24, 2011.

Hickson, K. *The IMF Crisis of 1976 and British Politics*, London: IB Tauris, 2005.

Hickson, K. & Griffiths, S. *British Party Politics and Ideology after New Labour*, Basingstoke: Palgrave Macmillan, 2014.

Hill, R. *The Labour Party's Economic Strategy 1979–1997*, p. 39, Basingstoke: Palgrave MacMillan, 2001.

Hills, J. *Good Times, Bad Times: The Welfare Myth of Them and Us*, Bristol: Policy Press, 2014.

Hills, J. *Towards a More Equal Society*, Bristol: Policy Press, 2005.

Hills, J. & Glennerster, H. 'Why the Left Need to Take Wealth Seriously Again', *Juncture*, Volume 20 (1), Summer 2013.

Hills, J. et al., *Wealth in the United Kingdom*, Oxford: Oxford University Press, 2014.

Hindmoor, A. *Constructing Political Space: New Labour at the Centre*, Oxford: Oxford University Press, 2005.

Hindmoor, A. *Twelve Days that Made Modern Britain*, Oxford: Oxford University Press, 2019.

Hindmoor, A. *What's Left?*, Oxford: Oxford University Press, 2018.

Hirsch, A. *Brit-ish: Race, Identity and Belonging*, London: Vintage, 2018.

Hirst, P. *After Thatcher*, London: Harper Collins, 1989.

Hobhouse, L.T. *Liberalism*, Oxford/New York: Oxford University Press, 1964.

Hobsbawm, E. 'The Forward March of Labour Halted?', *Marxism Today*, September 1978.

Hobsbawm, E. 'Past Imperfect, Future Tense', *Marxism Today*, p. 15, October 1986.

Hobson, J. *The Crisis of Liberalism: New Issues of Democracy*, London: P.S. King, 1920.

Hodgson, G. *Labour at the Crossroads*, Oxford: Martin Robertson, 1981.

Holland, S. *The Socialist Challenge*, London: Quartet Books, 1975.

Holmes, A. *The Third Way: Globalisation's Legacy*, Leicester: Matador, 2009.

Howell, D. 'The Best and Worst of Times: The Rise of New Labour', *Economic and Political Weekly*, Volume 32 (28), pp. 1672–1698, 1997.

Howell, D. *British Social Democracy: A Study in Development and Decay*, London: Croom Helm, 1976.

Howell, S. *Game-Changer: Eight Weeks that Transformed British Politics*, London: Accent Press, 2018.

Hughes, C. & Wintour, P. *Labour Rebuilt: The New Model Party*, London: Fourth Estate, 1990.

Hutton, W. *The State We're In*, London: Vintage, 1995.

Hyman, P. *One Out of Ten: From Downing Street Vision to Classroom Reality*, London: Vintage, 2005.

Inglehart, R. 'The Silent Revolution in Europe: Intergenerational Change in Post-Industrial Societies', *American Political Science Review*, Volume 65 (4), pp. 991–1017, 1971.

Inglehart, R. & Norris, P. *Cultural Backlash: Trump, Brexit and the Rise of Authoritarian Populism*, Cambridge: Cambridge University Press, 2018.

Jackson, B. *Equality and the British Left*, Manchester: Manchester University Press, 2006.

Jackson, B. 'Currents of Neo-Liberalism: British Political Ideologies and the New Right, 1955–79', *The English Historical Review*, Volume 131 (1), pp. 823–850, 2016.

Jackson, B. 'Review: Citizen and Subject: Clement Attlee's Socialism', *History Workshop Journal*, Volume 86 (1), pp. 291–298, 2018.

Jackson, B. 'Revisionism Reconsidered: "Property-Owning Democracy" and Egalitarian Strategy in Post-War Britain', *Twentieth Century British History*, Volume 16 (4), 2005.

Jacques, M. & Hall, S. *The Changing Face of Politics: New Times*, London: Lawrence & Wishart, 1989.

Jeffreys, K. *Anthony Crosland: A New Biography*, London: John Blake, 1999.

Jeffreys, K. 'The Old Right', in R. Plant, M. Beech & K. Hickson (eds.), *The Struggle for Labour's Soul: Understanding Labour's Political Thought Since 1945*, London: Routledge, 2004.

Jenkins, P. *Mrs Thatcher's Revolution: The Ending of the Socialist Era*, London: Pan Books, 1989.

Jessop, B. 'New Labour or The Normalisation of Neo-Liberalism', *British Politics*, Volume 2 (2), pp. 278–292, 2007.

Johnson, C. & Tonkiss, F. 'The Third Influence: The Blair Government and Australian Labour', *Policy and Politics*, Volume 30 (1), pp. 5–18, 2011.

Jones, B. & Keating, M. *The Labour Party and the British State*, Oxford: Oxford University Press, 1985.

Jones, E. *Neil Kinnock*, London: Robert Hale, 1989.

Jones, P. *America and the British Labour Party: The Special Relationship at Work*, London: IB Tauris, 1997.

Jones, T. *Remaking the Labour Party: From Gaitskell to Blair*, London: Routledge, 1996.

Jospin, L. *Modern Socialism*, London: The Fabian Society, 1999.

Joyce, J. *Ulysses*, London: Wordsworth Classics, 2010.

Joyce, R. & Sibieta, L. 'An Assessment of Labour's Record on Income Inequality and Poverty', *Oxford Review of Economic Policy*, Volume 29 (1), pp. 178–202, 2013.

Katwala, S. 'After New Labour', *Renewal*, Volume 3 (4), pp. 23–32, 2008.

Kavanagh, D. *The Politics of the Labour Party*, London: Routledge, 1982.

Kavanagh, D. *The Reordering of British Politics: Politics After Thatcher*, Oxford: Oxford University Press, 1997.

Kay, J. *The Foundations of Corporate Success: How Business Strategies Add Value*, Oxford: Oxford University Press, 1993.

Keating, M. *Rescaling the State: The Making of Territory and the Rise of the Meso*, Oxford: Oxford University Press, 2014.

Keegan, W. *Nine Crises: Fifty Years of Covering the British Economy from Devaluation to Brexit*, London: Biteback.

Kellner, P. (ed.), *Thorns and Roses: The Speeches of Neil Kinnock 1983–91*, London: Radius, 1990.

Kennedy, D. *A World of Struggle: How Power, Law, and Expertise Shape Global Political Economy*, Princeton: Princeton University Press, 2016.

Kennedy, H. 'Power to the People', in P. Facey, B. Rigby & A. Runwick (eds.), *Unlocking Democracy: Twenty Years of Charter 88*, p. 43, London: Methuen Politicos, 2008.

Kenny, M. 'After the Deluge: Politics and Civil Society in the Wake of the New Right', *Soundings*, Issue 4, pp. 13–26, 1996.

Kenny, M. *The First New Left British Intellectuals After Stalin*, London: Lawrence and Wishart, 1995.

Kenny, M. 'Habits of the Mind: *Marxism Today* and Today's Left', *Juncture*, Volume 18 (3), pp. 30–35, 2011.

Kenny, M. & Gover, D. 'Answering the West Lothian Question? A Critical Assessment of English Votes for English Laws in the UK Parliament', *Parliamentary Affairs*, Volume 71 (4), pp. 760–782, 2017.

Kenny, M., McLean, I. & Paun, A. (eds.), *Governing England: English Identity and Institutions in a Changing UK*, Oxford: Oxford University Press, 2018.

Keynes, J.M. *Am I a Liberal?*, London: Royal Economic Society, 1925.

Keynes, J.M. 'The Dilemma of Modern Socialism', *The Political Quarterly*, Volume 3 (3), July–September 1932.

Keynes, J.M. 'The Economic Possibilities for Our Grandchildren', in L. Pecchi & G. Piga (eds.), *Revisiting Keynes*, Cambridge, MA: MIT Press, 2010.

Keynes, J.M. *The End of Laissez-Faire/The Economic Consequences of the Peace*, Great Minds Series, London: Penguin, 2004.

Keynes, J.M. *The General Theory of Employment, Interest and Money*, London: Macmillan, 1936.

Keynes, J.M. 'Liberalism and Labour', *The New Republic*, 3 March 1926.

Kilfoyle, P. *Left Behind: Lessons from Labour's Heartland*, London: Methuen Politico's, 2000.

King, A. *New Labour Triumphs: Britain at the Polls*, London: CQ Press, 1998.

King, D. & Wood, S. 'The Political Economy of Neo-Liberalism: Britain and the United States in the 1980s', in H. Kitschelt et al. (eds.), *Continuity and Change in Contemporary Capitalism*, pp. 371–397, Cambridge: Cambridge University Press, 1999.

Kingdon, K. *Agendas, Alternatives and Public Policies*, Boston: Longman Press, 1984.

Kitschelt, H. *The Transformation of European Social Democracy*, Cambridge: Cambridge University Press, 1994.

Klug, F. 'New Labour and the Distribution of Power: Constitutional Reform, Human Rights and Civil Liberties', in P. Diamond & M. Kenny (eds.), *Reassessing New Labour: Market, State and Society under Blair and Brown*, Oxford: Blackwell, 2011.

Kotz, D.M. *The Rise and Fall of Neo-Liberal Capitalism*, Cambridge, MA: Harvard University Press, 2015.

Kymlicka, W. 'Liberalism and Communitarianism', *Canadian Journal of Philosophy*, Volume 18 (2), pp. 181–203, 1988.

Labour Market Trends, 'Percentage of the Labourforce Who Were Trade Union Members', 2000.

The Labour Party, *Meet the Challenge, Make the Change: A New Agenda for Britain*, London: The Labour Party, 1989.

The Labour Party Manifesto, 'Let's Go with Labour for the New Britain', London: The Labour Party, 1964.

The Labour Party Manifesto, 'Let Us Face the Future', London: The Labour Party, 1945.

The Labour Party Manifesto, 'Let Us Work Together – Labour's Way Out of the Crisis', London: The Labour Party, 1974.

Larsen, T., Taylor-Gooby, P. & Kanenen, J. 'New Labour's Policy Style: A Mix of Policy Approaches', *Journal of Social Policy*, Volume 35 (4), 2006.

Lawrence, J. 'Labour – The Myths It Has Lived By', in P. Thane, N. Tiratsoo & D. Tanner (eds.), *Labour's First Century*, p. 349, Cambridge: Cambridge University Press, 2000.

Lawrence, J. *Me, Me, Me: The Search for Community in Post-War England*, Oxford: Oxford University Press, 2019.

Lawson, N. *The View from Number 11: Memoirs of a Tory Radical*, London: Biteback, 2010.

Lawton, D. *Education and Labour Party Ideologies 1900–2001*, London: Routledge, 2005.

Layton-Henry, Z. *The Politics of Immigration*, Oxford: Blackwells, 1992.

Leadbeater, C. 'The State of the Movement', *Marxism Today*, September 1986.

Le Grand, J. *The Strategy of Equality: Redistribution and the Social Services*, London: Allen & Unwin, 1982.

Leonard, D. (ed.), *Crosland and New Labour*, Basingstoke: Macmillan, 1996.

Letwin, O. *Hearts and Minds: The Battle for the Conservative Party from Thatcher to the Present*, London: Biteback, 2018.

Lewis, J. 'Developing Early Years Childcare in England, 1997–2002: The Choices for (Working) Mothers', *Social Policy and Administration*, Volume 37 (3), pp. 219–238, 2003.

Lewis, J. & Campbell, M. 'UK Work/Family Balance Policies and Gender Equality, 1997–2005', *Social Politics: International Studies in Gender, State & Society*, Volume 14 (1), pp. 4–30, 2007.

Lewis, J. & Giullari, S. 'The Adult Worker Model Family, Gender Equality and Care: The Search for New Policy Principles and the Possibilities and Problems of a Capabilities Approach', *Economy and Society*, Volume 34 (1), pp. 76–104, 2005.

Leys, C. *Market-Driven Politics*, London: Verso, 2001.

Lindley, J. & Machin, S. 'Wage Inequality in the Labour Years', *Oxford Review of Economic Policy*, pp. 165–177, Volume 29 (1), 2013.

Lipsey, D. 'The Meritocracy Myth – Whatever Happened to the Old Dream of a Classless Society?', *The New Statesman*, 26th February 2015.

Loewenberg, G. 'The Transformation of British Labour Party Policy Since 1945', *Journal of Politics*, Volume 21, pp. 234–254, 1965.

Lukes, S. 'The Future of British Socialism', in B. Pimlott (ed.), *Fabian Essays in Socialist Thought*, London: Heinemann, 1984.

Lupton, R., Hills, J., Stewart, K. & Vizard, P. 'Labour's Social Policy Record: Policy, Spending and Outcomes 1997–2010', Research Report 1, Centre for the Analysis of Social Exclusion/LSE, June 2013.

Mackintosh, J.P. 'Has Social Democracy Failed in Britain?', *The Political Quarterly*, Volume 49 (3), August–October, 1978.

Mair, P. *Ruling the Void*, London: Verso Books, 2013.

Marquand, D. *Britain Since 1918: The Strange Career of British Democracy*, London: Weidenfeld & Nicolson, 2009.

Marquand, D. *Decline of the Public: The Hollowing-Out of Citizenship*, Cambridge: Polity Press, 2004.

Marquand, D. 'How Liberalism Lost Its Way', *The New Statesman*, 12–18th September 2014.

Marquand, D. 'Inquest on a Movement: Labour's Defeat and its Consequences', *Encounter*, p. 10, July 1979.

Marquand, D. 'Moralists and Hedonists', in A. Seldon & D. Marquand (eds.), *The Ideas That Shaped Post-War Britain*, London: Fontana, 1996.

Marquand, D. 'Must Labour Win?', London: The Fabian Society, 1998.

Marquand, D. *The Progressive Dilemma: From Lloyd George to Kinnock*, London: Heinemann, 1991.

Marquand, D. *The Unprincipled Society: New Demands and Old Politics*, London: Jonathan Cape, 1988.

Marquand, D., Mackintosh, J. & Owen, D. 'Change Gear! Towards a Socialist Strategy', *Socialist Commentary*, 1967.

Marshall, T.H. *Social Citizenship*, Cambridge: Cambridge University Press, 1950.

Martell, L. 'New Ideas of Socialism', *Economy and Society*, Volume 21 (2), pp. 152–172, 1992.

Martell, L. 'New Labour and the Social Democratic Alternative', *British Politics Review*, Volume 13 (4), pp. 14–15, 2019.

Marx, K. *The Eighteenth Brumaire of Louis Bonaparte*, London: International Publishers, 1852.

Marx, K. & Engels, F. *Collected Works Volume 6 1845–48*, London: Harmondsworth, 1970.

Matthijs, M. *Ideas and Economic Crises in Britain from Attlee to Blair*, London: Routledge, 2011.

Mattinson, D. *Talking to a Brick Wall: How New Labour Stopped Listening to Voters*, London: Biteback, 2010.

Mazzucato, M. *The Entrepreneurial State: Debunking Public versus Private Sector Myths*, London: Anthem Press, 2013.

McAnulla, S. 'Heirs to Blair's Third Way? David Cameron's Triangulating Conservatism', *British Politics*, Volume 5 (3), pp. 234–254, 2010.

McGuigan, J. 'The Social Construction of a Cultural Disaster: New Labour's Millennium Experience', *Cultural Studies*, Volume 17 (5), pp. 669–690, 2003.

McKibbin, R. 'The Anti-Candidate', *The London Review of Books*, 24th April 2015.

McKibbin, R. *The Ideologies of Class*, Oxford: Clarendon Press, 1990.

McKibbin, R. 'The Luck of the Tories: The Debt to Kinnock', *The London Review of Books*, 7th March 2002.

McKibbin, R. *Parties and People 1914–1951*, Oxford: Oxford University Press, 2008.

McKibbin, R. 'With or Without the Workers', *The London Review of Books*, 25th April 1991.

McRobbie, A. 'Review: New Times: the Changing Face of Politics in the 1990s by S. Hall & M. Jacques', *Feminist Review*, Volume 36, Autumn 1990.

Meredith, S. 'Labour Party Revisionism and Public Expenditure: Divisions of Social Democratic Political Economy in the 1970s', *Labour History Review*, Volume 70 (3), pp. 253–273, 2005.

Mettler, S. *The Submerged State: How Invisible Government Policies Undermine American Democracy*, Chicago: University of Chicago Press, 2011.

Middleton, S. 'Affluence and the Left in Britain', *The English Historical Review*, Volume 129 (396), pp. 101–127, 2014.

Miliband, D. (ed.), 'Introduction', in *Reinventing the Left*, Cambridge: Polity Press, 1994.

Miliband, R. *Parliamentary Socialism: A Study in the Politics of Labour*, London: Merlin Press, 1969.

Miliband, D. 'Political Quarterly Annual Lecture', London School of Economics, 2012.

Miliband, R. 'Socialist Advance in Britain', in R. Miliband & J. Saville (eds.), *The Socialist Register 1983*, London: Merlin Press, 1983.

Miller, D. *Citizenship and National Identity*, Cambridge: Polity Press, 2000.

Milward, A. *The European Rescue of the Nation State*, London: Routledge, 1999.

Milward, A. *The United Kingdom and the European Community, Volume I: The Rise and Fall of a National Strategy, 1945–1963*, London: Frank Cass, 2003.

Minkin, L. *The Blair Supremacy: A Study in the Politics of Labour's Party Management*, Manchester: Manchester University Press, 2014.

Mirowski, P. *Never Let a Serious Crisis Go to Waste: How Neo-Liberalism Survived the Financial Meltdown*, London: Verso, 2013.

Moran, M. *The Regulatory State*, Oxford: Oxford University Press, 2003.

Morgan, K.O. *Ages of Reform: Dawns and Downfalls of the British Left*, London: IB Tauris, 2008.

Morgan, K.O. 'Britain in the Seventies – Our Unfinest Hour?', *Revue Francaise de Civilisation Britannique*, 2017.

Morgan, K.O. *Labour in Power 1945–51*, Oxford: Clarendon Press, 1984.

Morris, D. *The New Prince*, New York: Griffin Press, 2000.

Morton, A.R. 'After Socialism? The Future of Radical Christianity', *University of Edinburgh Centre for Theology and Public Issues*, Occasional Paper 32, Edinburgh: University of Edinburgh, 1994.

Mulgan, G. 'Labour Britain', *Fabian Review*, London: The Fabian Society, Summer 2005.

Mulgan, G. 'Lessons of Power', *Prospect*, August 2005.

Mulgan, G. 'Special Issue: Wrong', *Marxism Today*, 1998.

Mullard, M. & Swaray, R. 'New Labour Legacy: Comparing the Labour Governments of Blair and Brown to Labour Governments since 1945', *The Political Quarterly*, Volume 81 (4), 2010.

Mulvey, G. 'When Policy Creates Politics: The Problematizing of Immigration and the Consequences for Refugee Integration in the UK', *Journal of Refugee Studies*, Volume 23 (4), pp. 437–462, 2010.

Murray, R. 'Benetton Britain: The New Economic Order', *Marxism Today*, November 1985.

Musgrave, R. 'The Voluntary Exchange Theory of Public Economy', *Quarterly Journal of Economics*, Volume 53, pp. 213–238, 1939.

Nairn, T. *The Break-Up of Britain*, London: Verso, 1981.

Newman, J. *Modernising Governance: New Labour, Policy and Society*, London: Sage.

The New Statesman, 'Clement Attlee: Editorial', London: The New Statesman, 1954.

Newton, S. 'The Sterling Devaluation of 1967, the International Economy and Post-War Social Democracy', *English Historical Review*, Volume 125 (2), pp. 912–945, 2010.

Nuttall, J. 'Tony Crosland and the Many Falls and Rises of British Social Democracy', *Contemporary British History*, Volume 18 (4), pp. 52–79, 2004.

Nuttall, J. & Schattle, H. *Making Social Democrats: Citizens, Mindsets, Realities – Essays for David Marquand*, Manchester: Manchester University Press, 2018.

O'Hara, G. 'Don't be Fooled: Labour Are Still Divided', *British Politics Review*, Volume 13 (4), pp. 6–7, 2019.

O'Hara, G. *Governing Post-War Britain: The Paradoxes of Progress 1951–73*, Basingstoke: Palgrave Macmillan, 2012.

O'Hara, G. & Parr, H. 'Conclusions: Harold Wilson's 1964–70 Governments and the Heritage of "New" Labour', *Contemporary British History*, Volume 20 (3), pp. 477–489, 2006.

Oakeshott, M. *Rationalism in Politics and Other Essays*, New York: Liberty Fund, 2010.

Offer, A. *The Challenge of Affluence: Self-Control and Well-Being in the United States and Britain Since 1950*, Oxford: Oxford University Press, 2006.

Offer, A. 'The Market Turn: From Social Democracy to Market Liberalism', *University of Oxford Discussion Papers in Economic and Social History*, No. 149, December 2016.

Office for National Statistics (ONS), 'The Effects of Taxes and Benefits on Household Income 2012–13', Statistical Bulletin, 26th June 2014.

Office for National Statistics (ONS), 'UK Earnings Mobility', 23rd September 2014.

Orford, J. *An Unsafe Bet? The Dangerous Rise of Gambling and the Debate We Should Be Having*, Oxford: Wiley-Blackwell, 2011.

Organisation for Economic Co-operation and Development (OECD), 'Divided We Stand: Why Inequality Keeps Rising, Country Note – United Kingdom', 5th December 2011.

Orwell, G. *The Road to Wigan Pier*, London: Penguin, 1937.

Ostry, J, Berg, A. & Tsangarides, C. 'Redistribution, Inequality and Growth', Washington: International Monetary Fund, April 2014.

Paine, T. *The Rights of Man*, London: Wordsworth Publishing, 1996.

Panitch, L. and Leys, C. *The End of Parliamentary Socialism: From New Left to New Labour*, London: Verso, 1997.

Parr, H. *Britain's Policy towards the European Community: Harold Wilson and Britain's World Role 1964–67*, London: Routledge, 2006.

Parr, H. 'European Integration', in M. Beech, K. Hickson & R. Plant (eds.), *The Struggle for Labour's Soul: Understanding Labour's Political Thought Since 1945*, London: Routledge, 2018.

Pascall, G. 'Gender and New Labour: After the Male Breadwinner Model?', *Social Policy Review*, Volume 20, 2008.

Paton, C. 'Blair and the NHS: Resistible Force Meets Moveable Object', in T. Casey (ed.), *The Blair Legacy: Politics, Policy, Governance and Foreign Affairs*, Basingstoke: Palgrave Macmillan, 2009.

Pelling, H. *America and the British Left: From Bright to Bevan*, London: Adam and Charles Black, 1956.

Pelling, H. *A Short History of the Labour Party*, London: Macmillan, 1961.

Pemberton, H. 'Relative Decline and British Economic Policy in the 1960s', *The Historical Journal*, Volume 47 (4), 2004.

Pemberton, H. 'Strange Days Indeed: British Politics in the 1970s', *Contemporary British History*, Volume 23 (4), 2009.

Pemberton, H., Black, L. & Thane, P. (eds.), *Reassessing 1970s Britain*, Manchester: Manchester University Press, 2013.

Piachaud, D. 'Revitalising Social Policy', *The Political Quarterly*, Volume 62 (2), 1991.

Picketty, T. *Capital in the Twenty-First Century*, Harvard: Harvard University Press, 2014.

Pierson, C. 'Globalisation and the End of Social Democracy', *Australian Journal of Politics and History*, Volume 47 (4), pp. 459–474, 2001.

Pimlott, B. 'Hugh Was That? Review of Hugh Gaitskell', *The Independent on Sunday*, 29th September 1996.

Pimlott, B. 'Uber-Tony', *London Review of Books*, 3 September 1998.

Pimlott, B. *Frustrate their Knavish Tricks: Writing on Biography, History and Politics*, London: Harper Collins, 1994.

Pimlott, B. *Harold Wilson*, London: William Collins, 1993.

Pimlott, B. *Labour and the Left in the 1930s*, Cambridge: Cambridge University Press, 1978.

Pimlott, B., Wright, A. & Flower, T. (eds.), *The Alternative: Politics for a Change*, London: W.H. Allen, 1990.

Plant, R. 'Democratic Socialism and Equality', in D. Leonard & D. Lipsey (eds.), *The Socialist Agenda: Crosland's Legacy*, London: Jonathan Cape, 1981.

Pollard, S. *Britain's Pride and Britain's Decline: The British Economy 1870–1914*, London: Edward Arnold, 1989.

Porter, P. *Blunder: Britain's War in Iraq*, Oxford: Oxford University Press, 2018.

Powell, J. *The New Machiavelli: How to Wield Power in the Modern World*, London: Vintage: 2011.

Pugh, M. *Speak for Britain: A New History of the Labour Party*, London: Vintage, 2011.

Pugh, M. *State and Society: A Social and Political History of Britain Since 1870*, London: Bloomsbury, 2014.

Putnam, R. *Bowling Alone: The Collapse and Revival of American Community*, New York: Simon & Schuster, 2000.

Radice, G. *Diaries 1980–2001: From Political Disaster to Triumph*, London: Weidenfeld & Nicolson, 2004.

Radice, G. *Friends and Rivals: Crosland, Jenkins and Healey*, London: Abacus, 2003.

Radice, G. *Labour's Path to Power: The New Revisionism*, London: Macmillan, 1989.

Radice, G. *Southern Discomfort*, London: The Fabian Society, 1993.

Radice, G. *The Tortoise and the Hares: Attlee, Bevin, Cripps, Dalton, Morrison*, London: I.B. Tauris, 2008.

Radice, H. 'The National Economy: A Keynesian Myth?', *Capital & Class*, Volume 8 (1), pp. 111–140, 1984.

Randall, N. 'Understanding Labour's Ideological Trajectory', in J. Callaghan, S. Fielding & S. Ludlum (eds.), *Interpreting the Labour Party*, Manchester: Manchester University Press, 2003.

Reich, R. *Locked in the Cabinet*, New York: Knopf, 1995.

Reid, A.J. & Pelling, H. *A Short History of the Labour Party*, Basingstoke: Palgrave Macmillan, 2005.

Reiner, R. 'Success or Statistics? New Labour and Crime Control', *Criminal Justice Matters*, Volume 67 (1), pp. 4–31, 2007.

Rhodes, R.A.W. *Transforming British Government*, London: Macmillan Press, 2000.

Riddell, P. *15 Minutes of Power: The Uncertain Life of British Ministers*, London: Profile Books, 2019.

Riddell, P. *The Thatcher Government*, London: Martin Robertson and Co, 1985.

Riddell, P. *The Thatcher Legacy*, Oxford: Basil Blackwell, 1989.

Riddell, P. *The Unfulfilled Prime Minister: Tony Blair's Quest for a Legacy*, London: Methuen Politico's, 2005.

Riesman, D. *Anthony Crosland: The Mixed Economy*, Basingstoke: Macmillan, 1997.

Roberts, R. *When Britain Went Bust*, London: OMFIF Press, 2017.

Rodgers, W.T. 'Social Democratic Party', in A. Adonis & K. Thomas (eds.), *Roy Jenkins: A Retrospective*, Oxford: Oxford University Press, 2004.

Rodgers, W.T. 'What Happened to the SDP and What Could Still Happen', *The London Review of Books*, Volume 13 (3), 1991.

Rowland, R. & Coupe, T. 'Patrol Officers and Public Reassurance: A Comparative Evaluation of Police Officers, PCSOs, ACSOs and Private Security Guards', *Policing and Society*, Volume 24 (3), pp. 265–284, 2014.

Rowthorn, B. *Capitalism, Conflict and Inflation*, London: Lawrence & Wishart, 1981.

Runciman, W.G. *Relative Deprivation and Social Justice: A Study of Attitudes to Social Inequality in Twentieth Century England*, London: Routledge & Kegan Paul, 1966.

Russell, M. *The Contemporary House of Lords: Westminster Bicameralism Revived*, Oxford: Oxford University Press, 2013.

Rutherford, J. 'Labour Must Choose between Two Fundamentally Different Under-standings of the Human Condition', *The New Statesman*, 26th September 2017.

Ryner, M. 'An Obituary for the Third way: The Financial Crisis and Social Democracy in Europe', *The Political Quarterly*, Volume 81 (4), pp. 554–563, 2010.

Sabatier, P. 'An Advocacy Coalition Framework of Policy Change and the Role of Policy-Oriented Learning Therein', *Policy Sciences*, Volume 21 (2/3), pp. 122–168, 1998.

Saggar, S. *Pariah Politics: Understanding Western Radical Islamism and What Should be Done*, Oxford: Oxford University Press, 2008.

Sassoon, D. *One Hundred Years of Socialism*, New York: The New Press, 1996.

Sassoon, D. 'Reflections on the Labour Party's Programme for the 1990s', *The Political Quarterly*, Volume 62 (2), 1991.

Saville, J. 'Labourism and the Labour Government', *The Socialist Register*, 1967.

Seabrook, J. *What Went Wrong? Working People and the Ideals of the Labour Movement*, London: Victor Gollancz, 1978.

Seldon, A. *The Blair Effect II: The Blair Government 1997–2001*, London: Little Brown.

Seyd, P. 'Labour: The Great Transformation', in A. King (ed.), *Britain at the Polls*, London: Chatham House, 1993.

Seyd, P. *The Rise and Fall of the Labour Left*, Basingstoke: Palgrave Macmillan, 1987.

Seyd, P. & Whiteley, P. *Labour's Grassroots*, Oxford: Oxford University Press, 1985.

Seymour, R. *Corbyn: The Strange Rebirth of Radical Politics*, London: Verso, 2016.

Shaw, E. *The Labour Party since 1945: Old Labour, New Labour*, London: John Wiley, 1996.

Shaw, E. *The Labour Party since 1979: Crisis and Transformation*, London: Routledge, 1996.

Shaw, E. *Losing Labour's Soul?* London: Routledge, 2008.

Shaw, E. 'Retrieving or Re-imagining the Past', in J. Davis & R. McWilliam (eds.), *Labour and the Left in the 1980s*, Manchester: Manchester University Press, 2018.

Shaw, E. 'The Wall Was Too High: The Four Predicaments of Mr Miliband', *French Journal of British Studies*, Volume 20 (3), 2015.

Shaw, E. 'The Wilderness Years, 1979–1994', in B. Brivati & R. Heffernan (eds.), *The Labour Party: A Centenary History*, Basingstoke: Palgrave Macmillan, 2000.

Shepherd, J. *Crisis? What Crisis? The Callaghan Government and the British 'Winter of Discontent'*, p. 162, Manchester: Manchester University Press, 2015.

Shipman, T. *All Out War: The Full Story of How Brexit Sank Britain's Political Class*, London: William Collins, 2016.

Skidelsky, R. *Britain since 1900: A Success Story?* London: Vintage Books, 2014.

Skidelsky, R. *Money and Government: A Challenge to Mainstream Economics*, London: Allen Lane, 2018.

Skidelsky, R. *Politicians and the Slump: The Labour Government 1929–31*, London: Penguin, 1970.

Sloman, P. 'Partners in Progress? British Liberals and the Labour Party Since 1918', *Political Studies Review*, Volume 12 (1), p. 43, 2014.

Smith, M. 'Understanding the "Politics of Catch Up": The Modernisation of the Labour Party', *Political Studies*, Volume XLII, pp. 708–715, 1994.

Snapper, P. 'The Elephant in the Room: Europe in the 2015 General Election', *French Journal of British Studies*, Volume 20 (3), pp. 225–244, 2015.

Somerville, W. *Immigration Under New Labour*, Bristol: Policy Press, 2007.

Soroka, S. & Wlezien, C. 'On the Limits to Inequality in Representation', *Political Science and Politics*, Volume 41 (2), pp. 319–327, 2008.

Soroka, S. & Wlezien, C. 'Political Institutions and the Opinion-Policy Link', Paper presented at the European Consortium for Political Research Joint Sessions of Workshops, St. Gallen, Switzerland, April 12th–17th, 2011.

Stedman-Jones, G. *Languages of Class: Studies in English Working-Class History 1832–1982*, Cambridge: Cambridge University Press, 1984.

Steinmo, S. 'Historical Institutionalism', in D. Della Porta & M. Keating (eds.), *Approaches and Methodologies in the Social Sciences: A Pluralist Perspective*, Cambridge: Cambridge University Press, 2008.

Steinmo, S. 'The Political Economy of Swedish Success', in W. Schafer & W. Streek (eds.), *Politics in the Age of Austerity*, Cambridge: Polity Press, 2013.

Stewart, K. 'Labour's Record on the Under Fives: Policy, Outcomes and Spending 1997–2010', Working Paper No. 4, London: LSE/CASE, 2013.

Stoker, G. *Why Politics Matters: Making Democracy Work*, Basingstoke, Palgrave Macmillan, 2006.

Stratchey, J. *Contemporary Capitalism*, London: Jonathan Cape, 1956.

Sturridge, P. 'Education and Social Liberalism: Pursuing the Link', *Oxford Review of Education*, Volume 42 (2), pp. 146–162, 2016.

Sutcliffe-Braithwaite, F. *Class, Politics and the Decline of Deference in England 1968–2000*, Oxford: Oxford University Press, 2013.

Swift, D. *A Left for Itself: Left Wing Hobbyists and Performative Radicalism*, London: John Hunt Publishing, 2019.

Tawney, R.H. 'The Choice Before the Labour Party', *The Political Quarterly*, Volume 3 (3), pp. 323–345, 1932.

Tawney, R.H. *Equality*, London: Allen & Unwin, 1928.

Thompson, E.P. *The Making of the English Working-Class*, London: Penguin Classics, 2013.

Thompson, H. *The British Conservative Government and the European Exchange Rate Mechanism 1979–1994*, London: Routledge, 1996.

Thompson, H. 'The Economy', in M. Flinders et al. (eds.), *The Oxford Handbook of British Politics*, Oxford: Oxford University Press, 2011.

Thompson, H. 'Post-Crisis, Post-Devolution Politics and the Mansion Tax', *The Political Quarterly*, Volume 86 (1), January–March 2015.

Thompson, N. *Political Economy and the Labour Party: The Economics of Democratic Socialism 1884–2005*, London: Routledge, 1996.

Timmins, N. *The Five Giants: A Biography of the Welfare State*, London: William Collins.

Tiratsoo, N. (ed.), *The Attlee Years*, New York: University of Columbia Press.

Tiratsoo, N. 'Popular Politics, Affluence and the Labour Party in the 1950s', in A. Gorst, L. Johnman & W. Scott Lucas (eds.), *Contemporary British History 1931–61: Politics and the Limits of Policy*, London/New York: Pinter Press, 1991.

Tiratsoo, N. 'Reconstruction, Affluence and Labour Politics', in N. Tiratsoo (ed.), *The Attlee Years*, New York: University of Columbia Press.

Tomaney, J. et al. 'Building Foundational Britain: From Paradigm Shift to New Political Practice', *Renewal*, Volume 27 (2), pp. 5–12, 2019.

Tomlinson, J. 'Can Governments Manage the Economy?', Fabian Tract 524, London: Fabian Society, 1988.

Tomlinson, J. 'The Decline of the Empire and the Economic "Decline" of Britain', *Twentieth Century British History*, Volume 14 (3), 2003.

Tomlinson, J. *Democratic Socialism and Economic Policy: The Attlee Years 1945–51*, pp. 295–319, Cambridge: Cambridge University Press, 1997.

Tomlinson, J. 'It's the Economy, Stupid! Labour and the Economy, circa 1964', *Contemporary British History*, Volume 21 (3), 2007.

Tomlinson, J. *The Labour Governments 1964–70: Economic Policy*, Manchester: Manchester University Press, 2004.

Tomlinson, J. 'The Limits of Tawney's Ethical Socialism: A Historical Perspective on the Labour Party and the Market', *Contemporary British History*, Volume 16 (4), pp. 1–16, 2002.

Tomlinson, J. *Managing the Economy, Managing the People*, Oxford: Oxford University Press, 2015.

Tooze, A. *Crashed: How a Decade of Financial Crises Changed the World*, London: Allen Lane, 2018.

Toye, R. 'The Forgotten Revisionist: Douglas Jay and Britain's Transition to Affluence 1951–1964', in L. Black & H. Pemberton (eds.), *An Affluent Society? Britain's Post-War 'Golden age' Revisited*, London: Ashgate, 2004.

Tudor, H. *The Preconditions of Socialism*, Cambridge: Cambridge University Press, 1993.

Turner, J. 'A Land Fit for Tories to Live In: The Political Ecology of the British Conservative Party, 1944–94', *Contemporary European History*, Volume 4 (2), pp. 189–208, 1995.

Unger, R. *The Critical Legal Studies Movement*, Cambridge, MA: Harvard University Press, 1986.

Ussher, K. 'Labour's Record on the Economy', in P. Diamond & M. Kenny (eds.), *Reassessing New Labour*, Oxford: Wiley, 2011.

Veldman, M. *Fantasy, the Bomb and the Greening of Britain: Romantic Protest 1945–1980*, Cambridge: Cambridge University Press, 1994.

Vincent, A. 'New Ideologies for Old', *The Political Quarterly*, Volume 70 (2), pp. 175–184, 1998.

Wainwright, H. *Labour: A Tale of Two Parties*, London: Hogarth Press, 1987.

Wall, S. *The Official History of Britain and the European Community Volume II: From Rejection to Referendum 1963–75*, London: Routledge, 2013.

Wapshott, N. *Keynes/Hayek: The Clash That Defined Modern Economics*, New York: W.W. Norton, 2012.

Ware, A. *Inequality in Britain*, London: Routledge, 2019.

Webb, S. & Webb, B. *Industrial Democracy*, London: Longmans Green, 1893.

Weber, M. 'Politics as a Vocation', in M. Weber (ed.), *The Vocation Lectures: Science as a Vocation, Politics as a Vocation*, Indianapolis/Cambridge: Hackett Publishing, 2004.

Weight, R. *Patriots: National Identity in Britain 1940–2000*, Basingstoke: Macmillan, 2002.

Weir, M. 'The Collapse of Bill Clinton's Third Way', in S. White (ed.), *New Labour: The Progressive Future*, Basingstoke: Palgrave Macmillan, 1999.

Westlake, M. *Kinnock: The Authorised Biography*, London: Little Brown, 2001.

White, S. (ed.), *New Labour: The Progressive Future*, Basingstoke: Palgrave Macmillan, 1999.

Wickham-Jones, M. *Economic Strategy and the Labour Party*, Basingstoke: Palgrave Macmillan, 1996.

Wickham-Jones, M. 'From Reformism to Resignation and Remedialism? Labour's Trajectory through British Politics', in E.C. Hargrove (ed.), *The Future of the Democratic Left in Industrial Societies*, Pennsylvania, PA: Penn State University Press, 2003.

Wiener, M. *English Culture and the Decline of the Industrial Spirit 1850–1980*, Cambridge: Cambridge University Press, 1985.

Williams, F. *Fifty Years' March: The Rise of the Labour Party*, London: Odhams Press, 1950.

Wilson, H. *The Labour Government 1964–70: A Personal Record*, London: Harmondsworth, 1974.

Wootton, B. *Plan or No Plan*, London: Gollancz, 1934.

Wright, A. *British Politics: A Very Short Introduction*, Oxford: Oxford University Press, 2013.

Wring, D. "'New Labour and the Media", in O. Daddow, "New Labour: A Witness History"', *Contemporary British History*, Volume 29 (1), 2014.

Young, M. *The Rise of the Meritocracy*, London: Penguin, 1958.

Ziegler, P. *Wilson: The Authorised Life*, London: Weidenfeld & Nicolson, 1993.

Zweig, F. *The Worker in an Affluent Society*, London: The Free Press, 1961.

Zweiniger-Barcielowska, I. 'Rationing, Austerity and the Conservative Party Recovery after 1945', *The Historical Journal*, Volume 37 (1), 1994.

INDEX

Printed in Great Britain
by Amazon